THE NORTON BOOK OF
SPORTS

THE NORTON BOOK OF
SPORTS

 Edited by GEORGE PLIMPTON

W · W · NORTON & COMPANY · NEW YORK · LONDON

The text of this book is composed in Avanta (electra)
with the display set in Bernhard Modern
Composition and Manufacturing by The Haddon Craftsmen, Inc.
Book design by Antonina Krass.

ISBN 0-393-03040-7
W.W. Norton & Company, Inc., 500 Fifth Avenue, New York, N.Y. 10110
W.W. Norton & Company Ltd., 10 Coptic Street, London WC1A 1PU
1 2 3 4 5 6 7 8 9 0

For Sidney James, Andre LaGuerre, Gil Rogin, Mark Mulvoy, Whitney Tower, and my friends at *Sports Illustrated.*

In compiling this anthology I am greatly indebted to Edwin Barber, Rowan Gaither, Debra Makay, Robin Mendelson, and Antonio Weiss.

CONTENTS

Summer · 117

AUTUMN · 257

WINTER · 397

INTRODUCTION

Some years ago I was asked to write an assessment of quality sports literature. In the course of doing this, I evolved what I called the "Small Ball Theory." This stated that there seemed to be a correlation between the standard of writing about a particular sport and the ball it utilizes—that the smaller the ball, the more formidable the literature. There are superb books about golf, very good books about baseball, not many good books about football, or soccer, very few good books about basketball, and no good books at all about beach balls. I capped off the Small Ball Theory by citing Mark Twain's "The Celebrated Jumping Frog of Calaveras County," perhaps the most universally known of sports stories, in which bird shot (very small balls indeed!) is an important element in the plot.

In compiling this anthology (which predictably starts off with the Twain yarn) I have found little to suggest that the Theory does not hold. The golf material—by Bernard Darwin, Herbert Warren Wind, Dan Jenkins, Don Marquis, John Updike, and P. G. Wodehouse, among others (some of them represented here)—suggests that something about the vagaries of the game truly seems to suit the writer, especially the humorist. I once had suggested to me that the reason for the permanence of much of golf literature was due to the game itself—in which the bad shot so surely in the future was conducive to the state of contained melancholy that so often produces first-rate writing—Dostoevsky's, for instance. Conrad's. Hardy. Even the professional *golfers* seem to write decently about what they do. Robert Tyre Jones's *Golf Is My Game*, which he wrote himself (a rarity indeed for a sports figure), is done with a skill comparable to his abilities with a golf stick.

Baseball—next up on the scale in size—has, of course, a monumental shelf, only limited compared to golf because the game doesn't have as much international appeal. Still, the sport has an even richer shelf than I am able to suggest in this collection, among those who have contributed marvelously to it: Roger Angell, T. Coraghessan Boyle, Jim Brosnan, Robert Creamer, David Halberstam, Mark Harris, Pat Jordan, Roger Kahn, Ring Lardner, Bernard Malamud, Philip Roth, Lawrence Ritter, Wilfrid Sheed, and George Will. Once again, something about the nature of the game applies. Bart Giamatti, the late commissioner of baseball, once touched on this in a speech: "Baseball fits America so well because it embodies the interplay of individual and group that we so love, and because it expresses our longing for the rule of law while licensing our resentment of law givers."

Admittedly, the Small Ball Theory is on shaky ground with tennis. The ball is about the same size as baseball's, though lighter obviously, fuzzy, without much density, and perhaps the same can be said of its literature. However, always one should mention John McPhee's *Levels of the Game*, which is about the thought processes of two players, Arthur Ashe and Clark Graebner, as they play a match at Forest Hills as well as his essay on Wimbledon which is included here. I might add that one of the more unique instructional books in sports is Timothy Gallwey's *The Inner Game of Tennis* in which the author urges players to focus their attention by *listening* to the ball as it approaches, thus tuning up their sensitivities to the level of bats in a room full of wires!

Football has relatively slim pickings, perhaps because the ball is not only large but misshaped! Here, the novel seems to serve the game better than nonfiction: Peter Gent's *North Dallas Forty*, Don DeLillo's *End Zone*, Dan Jenkins's *Semi-Tough*. As for nonfiction, perhaps as a matter of self-preservation I should mention my own *Paper Lion*, along with Jerry Kramer's *Instant Replay*. Not much else. The inestimable *Reader's Catalogue* (which calls itself "the essential source for book buyers") is reduced to listing such as-told-to books as *Cruisin' with the Tooz* and *Kill, Bubba, Kill!*

The slim basketball shelf is enhanced by John McPhee's *A Sense of Where You Are* (a portrait of Bill Bradley when he was a star at Princeton), David Halberstam's *The Breaks of the Game*, and Peter Axthelm's *The City Game*. The best as-told-to books by those in the game are Bill Russell's *Second Wind*, Red Auerbach's books on the Boston Celtics, and Kareem Abdul-Jabbar's *Kareem*. But that's about all. The startling success of *A Season on the Brink*, which to the surprise of everyone, including the publishers, settled onto the best-seller lists for months, was due more to the irascible nature of its subject, Bobby Knight—the brilliant coach of the Indiana basketball team—and the public's curiosity about him than to the manner of the book's presentation.

Soccer has no important literature at all that I can find, though it is such a universal activity that surely I am at fault here—I must have missed a South American novel, or a Yugoslav's essay on the bicycle kick, or an appreciation by a Frenchman on the existential qualities of the game. Albert Camus once played goal for the Oran Football Club of Algiers but did not seem moved to write about it. The best I've come across is Pelé's *My Life and the Great Game.* The evident lack may have something to do with the practitioners of the game, who tend to be more agile with their feet than with articulation. A well-known definition is that soccer is a gentleman's game played by thugs, whereas rugby is a thug's game played by gentlemen. This might hold, but in fact I don't know that rugby has produced much of a literature either!

Hockey has an oddly limited shelf—odd because its world (at least as I experienced it as an ersatz goaltender with the Boston Bruins) was rife with storytellers and legend-keepers and has a long and absorbing history. Could it be that a hockey puck is not a proper spheroid, squashed to its familiar shape as if by a steamroller? An exception is the work of the Canadiens' long-time goaltender Ken Dryden, whose book *The Game* is by far the most notable, indeed a classic. So is "The Hockey Sweater," a curiosity really, a short unpretentious boy's tale about the influence of the Montreal Canadiens hockey team in Quebec. Both are represented in this anthology.

The problem with the Small Ball Theory, of course, is that it does not take a considerable number of sports into consideration that do not utilize a ball or a projectile of some sort—skiing, wrestling, the 100-yard dash, boxing, auto racing, and so on. Indeed, some authorities think these are the purer sports and actually decry the use of a ball. None other than Garp, John Irving's alter ego in his best-seller *The World According to Garp,* is one of these. He is a wrestler. "I do not care for balls," he says. "The ball stands between the athlete and his exercise. So do hockey pucks and badminton birdies and skates, like skis, intrude between the body and the ground. And when one further removes one's body from the contest by an extension device—such as a racket, a bat, or a stick—all of the purity of movement, strength, and focus is shot."

Whatever one's opinion about the use or non-use of balls, it would seem, though, that another Theory can be proposed. That is that the literary quality of works about sports without balls seems connected with the degree of danger involved—the higher the risk, the more memorable the literature. There are very good books about automobile racing (Stirling Moss, Ken W. Purdy, Jackie Stewart), mountain climbing (William O. Douglas, Maurice Herzog, Peter Matthiessen), the more dangerous kinds of big-game hunting (Ernest Hemingway), and boxing (John Lardner, A. J. Liebling, W. C. Heinz, Budd Shulberg, Norman Mailer), and less good books about the 100-yard dash, swimming, canoeing, the tug-of-war, and so on in which danger does not figure. Most of the great accounts have someone teetering on the edge, if not to the point of tragedy itself. Do I dare refer to this as the "Look Out!" or "Uh-Oh" Theory?

But enough of theory! On with more practical matters about this collection. Readers will note that the selections have been organized into four parts representing the seasons—a somewhat arbitrary device since some sports lap over from one season to the next, often into a third. Baseball starts spring training in February and concludes with the World Series, often referred to as the Fall Classic. Nonetheless, lumping all the baseball material under one heading, say, or presenting the contents alphabetically, or chronologically, seems to smack too much of the catalogue. On occasion I have written some introductory matter to the selections when it seemed appropriate to do so. Also, from time to time I have tossed in a surprise, what the French call an *amuse*—a column or a feature hardly classifiable as high-quality sports lit., but which seemed irresistible nonetheless. In these matters of anthologizing one is allowed a small self-indulgence.

All the literary forms are represented here—fiction, nonfiction, poetry. It has always puzzled me why poets have not devoted more of their skills to sports subjects: so many of the ingredients seem involved—triumph, despair, prowess, beauty, the oft-quoted idea that sport is a microcosm of life itself. Yet an anthology of great poetry, a thousand pages long, will include A. E. Houseman's "To an Athlete Dying Young," and little else.

I once asked Donald Hall about this. One of America's leading poets, he did a participatory stint with the Pittsburgh Pirates (wearing a heavy beard which made him look like a member of the famous House of David baseball team) and wrote about it in a lovely book entitled *Fathers Playing Catch with Sons.* After its publication he told me, "Half my poet friends think I am insane to waste my time writing about sports and to loiter in the company of professional athletes. The other half would murder to be in my place."

He agreed with me that though hundreds of poems have been written about sports almost invariably all are second rate. He said, "One of the problems, of course, is that poems should never be *about* anything."

"Oh."

I mentioned that Robert Frost had once remarked that he always wished to be mistaken for an old-time baseball player. If he felt *that* strongly, why hadn't anything about baseball turned up in his verse?

"Well, there's that line from 'Birches,' " Hall reminded me. *"A boy too far from town to play baseball."* He went on: "T. S. Eliot read a mystery novel every night to help get himself to sleep. But there's no evidence the influence ever turned up in his poems. I don't take sport seriously," he concluded. "That's what's so wonderful about it."

Robert Bly, a poet and contemporary of Hall's (and whose work also appears in this volume), had two additional notions of interest. He suggested that in ancient times poets (he mentioned Pindar) composed odes celebrating the winners of the Games. But then with the advent of Christianity—the religion (as Nietzsche described it) of pity and weakness—the poets' attention shifted to losers, love unrequited, victims of society, the struggles of the meek, "people who get beaten up a lot."

"And the second?" I asked.

This was that most of his contemporaries were in the academic community, which looked down on the institutions' athletic programs, especially the mammoth machinery of football, as alien, unimportant, beneath consideration.

"Frivolous."

"Exactly," Bly said.

This question of "seriousness" has been a long-time issue among sportswriters themselves—many with a very low esteem for what they do, as if they felt they should abide by a caste system which held that they were at the bottom of the heap, the Untouchables, residents of what Stanley Woodward, the editor of the New York *Herald-Tribune*, once christened the "Toy Department." This feeling was far more prevalent years ago than it is now. Paul Gallico, the highest-paid sportswriter of the twenties and thirties, described his peers as being "one grade above the office cat." He himself left sportswriting for the higher planes of fiction writing; in his novels he never used sports as a background.

Red Smith of the New York *Herald-Tribune*, the most widely respected of Gallico's successors on the sports page, once commented that sportswriting was the most pleasant way of making a living yet devised by man, but he also had reservations. He wrote: "I've tried not to exaggerate the glory of the athletes. I'd rather if I could preserve a sense of proportion, to write about them as excellent ball-players, first-rate players." Then he adds somewhat mournfully: "But I'm sure I have contributed to false values—as Stanley Woodward said, 'Godding up those ballplayers' . . . I've always tried to remember—and this is an old line—that sports isn't Armageddon. These are just little games that little boys can play, and it isn't important to the future of civilization whether the Athletics or the Browns win. If you accept it as entertainment, then that's what spectator sports are meant to be."

It always struck me that Red Smith never identified himself in his columns with the personal pronoun "I"—as if he wished to remove himself as far as possible from his subject. He invariably disguised his presence with various pseudonyms—"a friend" or "a passerby" or "a guy," as in "a guy wondered if Stan Musial . . ."

This attitude of disassociation has by no means completely disappeared. Frank Deford, one of *Sports Illustrated*'s finest contributors and editor-in-chief of the late lamented sports daily *The National,* has referred to his fellow journalists as "the world's tallest midgets" and indeed used the catchy phrase as the title of a book of his collected essays.

Because of this pervasive sense of self-deprecation, it is not surprising that so little serious writing has come out of sports. Mark Harris, the author of four fine books whose narrator, Henry W. Wiggen, is a big-league pitcher *(The Southpaw, Bang the Drum Slowly, A Ticket for a Seamstitch,* and *It Looked Like for Ever),* spoke to this point in a speech he gave at the New York Public Library in 1987—why it had taken so long for a "serious" baseball novel to evolve. He suggested that up until 1950 no baseball novel could be thought of as art or literature with the exception of Ring Lardner's *You Know Me, Al,* published in 1914. Baseball novels, really little more than juveniles, utilized either the Horatio Alger hero, the individual who succeeds in overcoming great odds through his own grit, or, somewhat later, the individual who learns through experience to subjugate his ego for the good of the team, a favorite theme of John R. Tunis in his teenager novels.

Ring Lardner himself (in a preface to a reprinting of *You Know Me, Al* in 1925) dismissed his book as literature. Irreverently, he tells us that his protagonist, Jack Keefe, the busher writing home, is actually one "Jane Addams of Hull House, a former Follies girl." He concludes his preface as follows: "The writer wishes to acknowledge his indebtedness to the Mayo brothers, Ringling brothers, Smith brothers, Rath brothers, the Dolly sisters, and former President Buchanan for their aid in instructing him in the technical terms of baseball, such as 'bat,' 'ball,' 'pitcher,' 'foul,' 'sleeping car,' and 'sore arm.' "

At the end of his talk Harris suggested that this attitude has finally begun to change. He quoted Philip Roth, who had long delayed writing a baseball novel because although he loved the game, he wasn't able to convince himself for a long time that the sport offered the "seriousness and profundity" he believed the subject of a novel should have.

What is my own attitude here? I grew up in a family which felt that sports were to be played not watched, or even read about unless the material was instructional—such as the Spaulding pamphlets on "How to Pitch." At the breakfast table my father, though a fine athlete, never read the sports pages, referring to them as a "waste of time," a far more savage indictment, even, than "frivolous" or "unimportant." Though he watched his college (Amherst) play Williams in their traditional football game in the fall, I only remember him at one professional game—one he took me to between the Yankees and the Giants in the World Series. So I meandered into sportswriting feeling slightly guilty. I was relieved to read Bernard Darwin and discover that my situation was not especially unique. He once described writing about sports as a job "into which men drift, since no properly constituted parent would agree to his son starting his career that way. Having tried something else which bores them they take to this thing which is lightly esteemed by the outside world but which satisfies in them some possibly childish but romantic feeling."

More recently, I have been comforted by an associate at *Sports Illustrated,* Robert W. Creamer (author of a highly praised biography of Babe Ruth), who described a conversation with a fellow sportswriter, Hal Leibowitz from the Cleveland *Plain Dealer.* Leibowitz was bemoaning what they both did for a profession—treating kids' games as if what they were covering were the Nuremburg trials. Creamer rose to the defense of sportswriters. He had found a nice word to describe them: *troubadours.* I checked the word and was pleased to read that the troubadours of the Middle Ages were often of knightly rank—many rungs up from Paul Gallico's office cat! True, what the troubadours usually offered from their repertoires had a strong amatory strain. But then again, that is the relationship that Americans have with sports—a love affair.

Still, the transition has been uneasy. There was a time in the early sixties when the young New York sportswriters—of whom I was one— were referred to by their elders as "chipmunks." I don't know for sure why we were called this; it may be that representatives of that school were prone to squirrel away facts that seemed unimportant to the more traditional sportswriters who tended to stick to impersonal, objective journalism. Al Silverman, the editor of the magazine *Sport,* once offered a perfect example of chipmunkery. The magazine's custom was to give a car to the Most Valuable Player of the World Series. In 1962 Ralph Terry, the Yankee pitcher, won the award. During the awards ceremony in the locker room Terry was signaled to the telephone. His wife had called to congratulate him about the award and tell him their newly born baby was doing just fine. Off the telephone, when he was asked what his wife had been doing, Terry replied, "Feeding the baby."

A chipmunk waved his pad. "Breast or bottle?" he asked, his pencil poised.

A further word about the selections. Readers will note that few of the contents are about specific events. No recounting of Don Larsen's perfect game in the World Series, or Henry Aaron's 715th home run, or the American hockey team's victory over the Russians at Lake Placid. The most memorable sports events by no means elicit the best writing— invariably because deadlines are in effect and William Wordsworth's suggestion of "recollection in tranquility" cannot be applied. Besides, including an account of a specific game means that supporters of the losing team, distressed when it happened, will hardly be pleased to read about it once again in an anthology. I have broken this rule only once. I have included Red Smith's account of Bobby Thomson's home run against the Brooklyn Dodgers, the so-called shot heard 'round the world that won the National League Pennant for the Giants in 1951. Dodger fans will hurriedly skip by this selection, which is included not only for its literary distinction but because I am a Giant fan. I heard that momentous home run described over the Armed Services Network when I was at Cambridge University; seated at a bridge table, I fell back in my excitement and caught the table with a foot, sending the cards flying— thereafter to be known in the college as the "American eccentric."

Many will be saddened by what has been left out—which is also, of course, the anthologist's despair. The great sports novels, such as W. C. Heinz's *The Professional,* the Mark Harris quartet, Robert Coover's *The Universal Baseball Association, Inc.,* and Bernard Malamud's *The Natural,* are extremely difficult to excerpt without seeming to be offering simply samples of the author's work. The same can be said of important nonfiction classics—David Halberstam's *Summer of '49,* Michael Novak's *The Joy of Sport,* and Robert Lipsyte's *Sportsworld,* among others. Nor is it easy to find material from the daily columnists—especially the old-timers, Jimmy Cannon, Arthur Daley, and Westbrook Pegler, among others—since the columns are so often about specific topics long outdated.

It should be mentioned that sports literature has been limited to a certain extent because the great modern games (with the exception of golf) were developed in fairly recent times—baseball and hockey in the mid-1800s, football (the American variety) in the 1870s, lawn tennis about the same time, and basketball, the youngest of the majors, in 1891 when Dr. James Naismith nailed up the peach basket in Springfield, Massachusetts. No doubt to the dismay of many, I have left out almost all the classics which preceded the modern era, even A. E. Houseman's "To an Athlete Dying Young." Absent are Pindar's Odes, Homer's description of the funeral games of Patroclus in the *Iliad,* the great racing story of Atlanta and Hippomenes in Ovid's *Metamorphoses,* Xenophon, R. J. Surtees, Nimrod, Siegfried Sassoon, Pierce Egan, and even Izaak Walton who wrote the first classic book on sport in the English language, *The Compleat Angler,* published in 1653. I have included William Hazlitt's "The Fight," but not his famous essay on Cavanagh.

Still, there should be enough in what follows. After all, former Giants baseball fans can always refresh themselves with Red Smith's account of Bobby Thomson's historic home run. As far as I'm concerned, that can be referred to three or four times a month.

—G.A.P.

 SPRING

MARK TWAIN

"The Celebrated Jumping Frog of Calaveras County"

"The Celebrated Jumping Frog of Calaveras County" was Mark Twain's first published short story. A yarn he enjoyed telling friends, Artemus Ward persuaded him to put it to paper. Originally entitled "Jim Smiley and His Jumping Frog," the story was eventually published in the New York Saturday Press. It caught the public's fancy and was reprinted in a number of newspaper supplements. Indeed James Russell Lowell described it as the "finest piece of humorous fiction yet produced in America." Twain himself was somewhat rueful about the story's popularity. In his autobiography he complains, "I was aware that it was only the frog that was celebrated. It wasn't I. I was still an obscurity."

For a number of years the yarn has been commemorated by a frog-jumping contest in Angel's Camp, California, which is known as the "Calaveras County Frog Jump Jubilee." In the spring of 1990 there was considerable consternation when an animal importer named Andy Koffman entered two giant African frogs from Cameroon which were rumored to routinely leap up to 40 feet! In truth, the best jump the Africans could produce was one of 7 feet 10 inches. The winner was a homegrown frog from Concord, California, named Help Mr. Wizard. He jumped 19 feet 3 inches. Koffman excused his entries' performance on the weather, insisting that his big frogs, accustomed to the equatorial tropics, had "got cold feet"—an excuse that Twain surely would have appreciated.

In compliance with the request of a friend of mine, who wrote me from the East, I called on good-natured, garrulous old Simon Wheeler, and inquired after my friend's friend, Leonidas W. Smiley, as requested to do, and I hereunto append the result. I have a lurking suspicion that *Leonidas W.* Smiley is a myth; and that my friend never knew such a personage; and that he only conjectured that if I asked old Wheeler about him, it would remind him of his infamous *Jim* Smiley, and he would go to work and bore me to death with some exasperating reminiscence of him as long and as tedious as it should be useless to me. If that was the design, it succeeded.

I found Simon Wheeler dozing comfortably by the bar-room stove of the dilapidated tavern in the decayed mining camp of Angel's, and I noticed that he was fat and bald-headed, and had an expression of winning gentleness and simplicity upon his tranquil countenance. He roused up, and gave me good-day. I told him a friend had commissioned me to make some inquiries about a cherished companion of his boyhood named *Leonidas W.* Smiley—*Rev. Leonidas W.* Smiley, a young minister of the Gospel, who he had heard was at one time a resident of Angel's Camp. I added that if Mr. Wheeler could tell me anything about this Rev. Leonidas W. Smiley, I would feel under many obligations to him.

Simon Wheeler backed me into a corner and blockaded me there with his chair, and then sat down and reeled off the monotonous narrative which follows this paragraph. He never smiled, he never frowned, he never changed his voice from the gentle-flowing key to which he tuned his initial sentence, he never betrayed the slightest suspicion of enthusiasm; but all through the interminable narrative there ran a vein of impressive earnestness and sincerity, which showed me plainly that, so far from his imagining that there was anything ridiculous or funny about his story, he regarded it as a really important matter, and admired its two heroes as men of transcendent genius in *finesse*. I let him go on in his own way, and never interrupted him once:

Rev. Leonidas W. H'm, Reverend Le—well, there was a feller here once by the name of Jim Smiley, in the winter of '49—or maybe it was the spring of '50—I don't recollect exactly, somehow, though what makes me think it was one or the other is because I remember the big flume warn't finished when he first came to the camp; but any way, he was the curiousest man about always betting on anything that turned up you ever see, if he could get anybody to bet on the other side; and if he couldn't he'd change sides. Any way that suited the other man would suit *him*— any way just so's he got a bet, *he* was satisfied. But still he was lucky, uncommon lucky; he most always come out winner. He was always ready and laying for a chance; there couldn't be no solit'ry thing mentioned but that feller'd offer to bet on it, and take any side you please, as I was just telling you. If there was a horserace, you'd find him flush or you'd find him busted at the end of it; if there was a dog-fight, he'd bet on it; if there was a cat-fight, he'd bet on it; if there was a chicken-fight, he'd bet on it; why, if there was two birds setting on a fence, he would bet you which one would fly first; or if there was a camp-meeting, he would be there reg'lar to bet on Parson Walker, which he judged to be the best exhorter about here, and he was, too, and a good man. If he even see a straddle-bug start to go anywheres, he would bet you how long it would take him to get to—to wherever he was going to, and if you took him up, he would foller that straddle-bug to Mexico but what he would find out where he was bound for and how long he was on the road. Lots of the boys here has seen that Smiley and can tell you about him. Why, it never made no difference to *him*—he'd bet on *any* thing—the dangest feller. Parson Walker's wife laid very sick once, for a good while, and it seemed as if they warn't going to save her; but one morning he come in, and Smiley up and asked him how she was, and he said she was considerable better—thank the Lord for his inf'nit' mercy—and coming on so smart that with the blessing of Prov'dence she'd get well yet; and Smiley, before he thought, says, "Well, I'll risk two-and-a-half she don't anyway."

Thish-yer Smiley had a mare—the boys called her the fifteen-minute nag, but that was only in fun, you know, because, of course, she was faster than that—and he used to win money on that horse, for all she was so slow and always had the asthma, or the distemper, or the consumption, or something of that kind. They used to give her two or three hundred yards start, and then pass her under way; but always at the fag-end of the race she'd get excited and desperate-like, and come cavorting and straddling up, and scattering her legs around limber, sometimes in the air, and sometimes out to one side amongst the fences, and kicking up m-o-r-e dust and raising m-o-r-e racket with her coughing and sneezing and blowing her nose—and *always* fetch up at the stand just about a neck ahead, as near as you could cipher it down.

And he had a little small bull-pup, that to look at him you'd think he warn't worth a cent but to set around and look ornery and lay for a chance to steal something. But as soon as money was upon him he was a different dog; his under-jaw'd begin to stick out like the fo'-castle of a steamboat, and his teeth would uncover and shine like the furnaces. And a dog might tackle him and bully-rag him, and bite him, and throw him over his shoulder two or three times, and Andrew Jackson—which was the name of the pup—Andrew Jackson would never let on but what he was satisfied, and hadn't expected nothing else—and the bets being doubled and doubled on the other side all the time, till the money was all up; and then all of a sudden he would grab that other dog jest by the j'int of his hind leg and freeze to it—not chaw, you understand, but only just grip and hang on till they throwed up the sponge, if it was a year. Smiley always come out winner on that pup, till he harnessed a dog once that didn't have no hind legs, because they'd been sawed off in a circular saw, and when the thing had gone along far enough, and the money was all up, and he come to make a snatch for his pet holt, he see in a minute how he'd been imposed on, and how the other dog had him in the door, so to speak, and he 'peared surprised, and then he looked sorter discouraged-like, and didn't try no more to win the fight and so he got shucked out bad. He gave Smiley a look, as much as to say his heart was broke, and it was *his* fault, for putting up a dog that hadn't no hind legs for him to take holt of, which was his main dependence in a fight, and then he limped off a piece and laid down and died. It was a good pup, was that Andrew Jackson, and would have made a name for hisself if he'd lived, for the stuff was in him and he had genius—I know it, because he hadn't no opportunities to speak of, and it don't stand to reason that a dog could make such a fight as he could under them circumstances if he hadn't no talent. It always makes me feel sorry when I think of that last fight of his'n, and the way it turned out.

Well, thish-yer Smiley had rat-tarriers, and chicken cocks, and tom-cats and all of them kind of things, till you couldn't rest, and you couldn't fetch nothing for him to bet on but he'd match you. He ketched a frog one day, and took him home, and said he cal'lated to educate him; and so he never done nothing for three months but set in his back yard and learn that frog to jump. And you bet you he *did* learn him, too. He'd give him a little punch behind, and the next minute you'd see that frog whirling in the air like a doughnut—see him turn one summerset, or maybe a couple, if he got a good start, and come down flat-footed and all right, like a cat. He got him up so in the matter of ketching flies, and kep' him in practice so constant, that he'd nail a fly every time as fur as he could see him. Smiley said all a frog wanted was education, and he could do 'most anything—and I believe him. Why, I've seen him set Dan'l Webster down here on this floor—Dan'l Webster was the name of the frog—and sing out, "Flies, Dan'l, flies!" and quicker'n you could wink he'd spring straight up and snake a fly off'n the counter there, an' flop down on the floor ag'in as solid as a gob of mud, and fall to scratching the side of his head with his hind foot as indifferent as if he hadn't no idea he'd been doin' any more'n any frog might do. You never see a frog so modest and straightfor'ard as he was, for all he was so gifted. And when it come to fair and square jumping on a dead level, he could get over more ground at one straddle than any animal of his breed you ever see. Jumping on a dead level was his strong suit, you understand; and when it come to that, Smiley would ante up money on him as long as he had a red. Smiley was monstrous proud of his frog, and well he might be, for fellers that had travelled and been everywheres, all said he laid over any frog that ever *they* see.

Well, Smiley kep' the beast in a little lattice box, and he used to fetch him downtown sometimes and lay for a bet. One day a feller—a stranger in the camp, he was—come acrost him with his box, and says:

"What might be that you've got in the box?"

And Smiley says, sorter indifferent-like, "It might be a parrot, or it might be a canary, maybe, but it ain't—it's only just a frog."

And the feller took it, and looked at it careful, and turned it round this way and that, and says, "H'm—so 'tis. Well, what's *he* good for?"

"Well," Smiley says, easy and careless, "he's good enough for *one* thing, I should judge—he can outjump any frog in Calaveras County."

The feller took the box again, and took another long, particular look, and give it back to Smiley, and says, very deliberate, "Well," he says, "I don't see no p'ints about that frog that's any better'n any other frog."

"Maybe you don't," Smiley says. "Maybe you understand frogs and maybe you don't understand 'em; maybe you've had experience, and maybe you ain't only a amature, as it were. Anyways, I've got *my* opinion and I'll risk forty dollars that he can outjump any frog in Calaveras County."

And the feller studied a minute, and then says, kinder sad like, "Well, I'm only a stranger here, and I ain't got no frog; but if I had a frog, I'd bet you."

And then Smiley says, "That's all right—that's all right—if you'll hold my box a minute, I'll go and get you a frog." And so the feller took the box, and put up his forty dollars along with Smiley's and set down to wait.

So he set there a good while thinking and thinking to hisself, and then he got the frog out and prized his mouth open and took a teaspoon and filled him full of quail shot—filled him pretty near up to his chin—and set him on the floor. Smiley he went to the swamp and slopped around in the mud for a long time, and finally he ketched a frog, and fetched him in, and give him to this feller, and says:

"Now, if you're ready, set him alongside of Dan'l, with his forepaws just even with Dan'l's, and I'll give the word." Then he says, "One— two—three—*git!*" and him and the feller touched up the frogs from behind, and the new frog hopped off lively, but Dan'l give a heave, and hysted up his shoulders—so—like a Frenchman, but it warn't no use— he couldn't budge; he was planted as solid as a church, and he couldn't no more stir than if he was anchored out. Smiley was a good deal surprised, and he was disgusted too, but he didn't have no idea what the matter was, of course.

The feller took the money and started away; and when he was going out at the door, he sorter jerked his thumb over his shoulder—so—at

Dan'l, and says again, very deliberate, "Well," he says, "*I* don't see no p'ints about that frog that's any better'n any other frog."

Smiley he stood scratching his head and looking down at Dan'l a long time, and at last says, "I do wonder what in the nation that frog throwed off for—I wonder if there ain't something the matter with 'im—he 'pears to look mighty baggy, somehow." And he ketched Dan'l up by the nap of the neck, and hefted him, and says, "Why blame my cats if he don't weigh five pounds!" and turned him upside down and he belched out a double handful of shot. And then he see how it was, and he was the maddest man—he set the frog down and took out after that feller, but he never ketched him. And—

(Here Simon Wheeler heard his name called from the front yard, and got up to see what was wanted.) And turning to me as he moved away, he said: "Jest set where you are, stranger, and rest easy—I ain't going to be gone a second."

But, by your leave, I did not think that a continuation of the history of the enterprising vagabond *Jim* Smiley would be likely to afford me much information concerning the Rev. *Leonidas W.* Smiley, and so I started away.

At the door I met the sociable Wheeler returning, and he button-holed me and recommenced:

"Well, thish-yer Smiley had a yaller, one-eyed cow that didn't have no tail, only jest a short stump like a bannanner, and—"

However, lacking both time and inclination, I did not wait to hear about the afflicted cow, but took my leave.

BABETTE DEUTSCH

"Morning Workout"

The sky unfolding its blankets to free
The morning.
Chill on the air. Clean odor of stables.
The grandstand green as the turf,
The pavilion flaunting its brilliance

For no one.
Beyond hurdles and hedges, swans, circling, cast
A contemplative radiance over the willow's shadows.
Day pales the toteboard lights,
Gilds the balls, heightens the stripes of the poles.
Dirt shines. White glisten of rails.
The track is bright as brine.
Their motion a flowing,
From prick of the ear to thick tail's shimmering drift,
The horses file forth.
Pink nostrils quiver, as who know they are showing their colors.
Ankles lift, as who hear without listening.
The bay, the brown, the chestnut, the roan have loaned
Their grace to the riders who rise in the stirrups, or hunch
Over the withers, gentling with mumbled song.
A mare ambles past, liquid eye askance.
Three, then four, canter by: voluptuous power
Pours through their muscles,
Dancing in pulse and nerve.
They glide in the stretch as on skis.
Two
Are put to a drive:
Centaur energy bounding as the dirt shudders, flies
Under the wuthering pace,
Hushes the hooves' thunders,
The body's unsyllabled eloquence rapidly
Dying away.
Dark-skinned stable-boys, as proud as kin
Of their display of vivacity, elegance,
Walk the racers back.
Foam laces the girths, sweaty haunches glow.
Slowly returning from the track, the horse is
Animal paradigm of innocence, discipline, force.
Blanketed, they go in.
Odor of earth
Enriches azuring air.

THOMAS McGUANE

"The Longest Silence"

To represent the enormous literature of the outdoors, I have picked a fishing story. I treasured books about fishing during my own upbringing—perhaps because as a boy, barefooted on a country road, heading for a pond with a bamboo pole, I could experience in some small degree the excitement recorded in my reading: the trout fishermen in their waders, or on a flat-bottomed skiff poled across the saltwater flats, or on the Gulf Stream after marlin, wherever. It occurs to me now that fishermen's lives are indeed bracketed by bamboo . . . that they start with a bamboo pole with a string tied to one end, the whole outfit costing a couple of dollars at most, and move on—if totally possessed—to handcrafted bamboo fishing rods that can cost $2,000. I never reached, much less could afford, that state, but no matter: the literature suffices. What a list! Frank Forester, John Mcdonald, Norman Maclean, Thaddeus Norris, Ernest Hemingway ("The Big Two-Hearted River"), Theodore Gordon, Philip Wylie, Sparse Grey Hackle ("If fishing interferes with your business, give up your business"), Lee Wulff, and Zane Grey, the first man to catch a fish weighing over a thousand pounds—a Pacific blue marlin, 1,040 pounds minus an estimated 200 pounds removed by sharks before the fish was boated. Grey was so enthusiastic about deep-sea fishing that at his home in Altadena, California, he rigged up a sport-fishing chair on the porch, the line attached to a distant and spirited cow. Indeed, this simulation, far inland, proved too strenuous and is supposed to have caused his death on October 23, 1939.

One of Grey's great friends was Van Campen Heilner, the author of Salt Water Fishing. *Grey wrote the foreword to the classic, in which Heilner popularized bonefishing ("the sportiest things with fins," he called them)—this in the late twenties before light-tackle reels had braking mechanisms and the drag was provided by pressing a gloved thumb down on the spool. In those same salt flats are the subjects of Tom McGuane's essay—permits, surprisingly a fish not mentioned in the Heilner classic, despite credentials that make them seem even more ghostly and wily than the bonefish.*

What is emphatic in angling is made so by the long silences—the unproductive periods. For the ardent fisherman, progress is toward the kinds of fishing that are never productive in the sense of the blood riots of the hunting-and-fishing periodicals. Their illusions of continuous action evoke for him, finally, a condition of utter, mortuary boredom. Such an angler will always be inclined to find the gunnysack artists of the heavy kill rather cretinoid, their stringerloads of gaping fish appalling.

No form of fishing offers such elaborate silences as fly fishing for permit. The most successful permit fly fisherman in the world has four catches to describe to you. The world record (twenty-three pounds) is a three-way tie. There probably have been fewer than fifty caught on a fly since fishing for them began. No permit fisherman seems discouraged by these rarefied odds; there is considerable agreement that taking a permit on a fly is the extreme experience of the sport. Even the guides allow enthusiasm to shine through their cool, professional personas. I once asked one who specialized in permit if he liked fishing for them. "Yes, I do," he said reservedly, "but about the third time the customer asks, 'Is they good to eat?' I begin losing interest."

The recognition factor is low when you catch a permit. If you wake up your neighbor in the middle of the night to tell him of your success, shaking him by the lapels of his Doctor Dentons and shouting to be heard over his million-BTU air conditioner, he may well ask you what a permit is, and you will tell him it is like a pompano and, rolling over, he will tell you he cherishes pompano like he had it at Joe's Stone Crab in Miami Beach, with Key lime pie afterward. If you have one mounted, you'll always be explaining what it is to people who thought you were talking about your fishing license in the first place. In the end you take the fish off the conspicuous wall and put it upstairs where you can see it when Mom sends you to your room. It's private.

I came to it through bonefishing. The two fish share the same marine habitat, the negotiation of which in a skiff can be somewhat hazardous. It takes getting used to, to run wide open at thirty knots over a close bottom, with sponges, sea fans, crawfish traps, conchs, and starfish racing under the hull with awful clarity. The backcountry of the Florida Keys is full of hummocks, narrow, winding waterways and channels that open with complete arbitrariness to basins and, on every side, the flats that preoccupy the fisherman. The process of learning to fish this region is one of learning the particularities of each of these flats. The narrow channel flats with crunchy staghorn coral bottoms, the bare sand flats, and the turtle-grass flats are all of varying utility to the fisherman, and, depending upon tide, these values are in a constant condition of change. The principal boat wreckers are the yellow cap-rock flats and the more mysterious coral heads. I was personally plagued by a picture of one of these enormities coming through the hull of my skiff and catching me on the point of the jaw. I had the usual Coast Guard safety equipment, not excluding floating cushions emblazoned FROST-FREE KEY WEST and a futile plastic whistle. I added a Navy flare gun. As I learned the country, guides would run by me in their big skiffs and 100-horse engines. I knew they never hit coral heads and had, besides, CB radios with which they might call for help. I dwelled on that and sent for radio catalogs.

One day when I was running to Content Pass on the edge of the Gulf of Mexico, I ran aground wide open in the backcountry. Unable for the moment to examine the lower unit of my engine, I got out of the boat, waiting for the tide to float it, and strolled around in four inches of water. It was an absolutely windless day. The mangrove islands stood elliptically in their perfect reflections. The birds were everywhere— terns, gulls, wintering ducks, skimmers, all the wading birds, and, crying down from their tall shafts of air, more ospreys than I had ever seen. The gloomy bonanza of the Overseas Highway with its idiot billboard mont- ages seemed very far away.

On the western edge of that flat I saw my permit, tailing in two feet of water. I had heard all about permit but had been convinced I'd never see one. So, looking at what was plainly a permit, I did not know what it was. That evening, talking to my friend Woody Sexton, a permit expert, I reconstructed the fish and had it identified for me. I grew retroactively excited, and Woody apprised me of some of the difficulties associated with catching one of them on a fly. A prompt immobilizing humility came over me forthwith.

After that, over a long period of time, I saw a good number of them. Always, full of hope, I would cast. The fly was anathema to them. One look and they were gone. I cast to a few hundred. It seemed futile, all wrong, like trying to bait a tiger with watermelons. The fish would see the fly, light out or ignore it, but never, never touch it.

During the next few months, I became an active fantasizer.

The engine hadn't been running right for a week, and I was afraid of getting stranded or having to sleep out on some buggy flat or, worse, being swept to Galveston on an offshore wind. I tore the engine down and found the main bearing seal shot and in need of replacement. I drove to Big Pine to get parts and arrived about the time the guides, who center there, were coming in for the day. I walked to the dock, where the big skiffs with their excessive engines were nosed to the breakwater. Guides mopped decks and needled each other. Customers, happy and not, debarked with armloads of tackle, sun hats, oil, Thermoses, and picnic baskets. A few of these sporty dogs were plastered. One fragile lady, owlish with sunburn, tottered from the casting deck of a guide's skiff and drew herself up on the dock. "Do you know what the whole trouble was?" she dramatically inquired of her husband, a man very much younger than herself.

"No, what?" he said. She smiled and pitied him.

"Well, *think* about it." The two put their belongings into the trunk of some kind of minicar and drove off too fast down the Overseas Highway. Four hours would put them in Miami.

It seemed to have been a good day. A number of men went up the dock with fish to be mounted. One man went by with a bonefish that might have gone ten pounds. Woody Sexton was on the dock. I wanted to ask how he had done, but knew that ground rules forbid the asking of this question around the boats. It embarrasses guides who have had bad days, on the one hand, and on the other it risks passing good fishing information promiscuously. Meanwhile, as we talked, the mopping and needling continued along the dock. The larger hostilities are reserved for the fishing grounds themselves, where various complex snubbings may be performed from the semianonymity of the powerful skiffs. The air can be electric with accounts of who cut off whom, and so on. The antagonism among the skiff guides, the offshore guides, the pompano fishermen, the crawfishermen, the shrimpers, produces tales of shootings, of disputes settled with gaffs, of barbed wire strung in guts and channels to wreck props and drive shafts. Some of the tales are true. Woody and I made a plan to fish when he got a day off. I found my engine parts and went home.

One day I went out and staked the boat during the middle-incoming water of another set of new moon tides. I caught one bonefish early in the tide, a lively fish that went 100 yards on his first run and doggedly resisted me for a length of time that was all out of proportion to his weight. I released him after giving him a short revival session and then just sat and looked at the water. I could see Woody fishing with a customer, working the outside of the bank for tarpon.

It was a queer day to begin with. The vital light flashed on and off around the scudding clouds, and there were slight foam lines on the water from the wind. The basin that shelved off from my bank was active with diving birds, particularly great brown pelicans whose wings sounded like luffing sails and who ate with submerged heads while blackheaded gulls tried to rob them. The birds were drawn to the basin by a school of mullet that was making an immense mud slick hundreds of yards across. In the sun the slick glowed a quarter of a mile to the south of me. I didn't pay it much attention until it began by collective will or chemical sensors to move onto my bank. Inexorably, the huge disturbance progressed and

flowed toward me. In the thinner water the mullet school was compressed, and the individual fish became easier targets for predators. Big
oceanic barracuda were with them and began slashing and streaking
through the school like bolts of lightning. Simultaneously, silver sheets
of mullet, sometimes an acre in extent, burst out of the water and rained
down again. In time my skiff was in the middle of it.

Some moments later not far astern of me, perhaps seventy feet, a large
blacktip shark swam up onto the bank and began moving with grave
sweeps of its tail through the fish, not as yet making a move for them.
Mullet and smaller fish nevertheless showered out in front of the shark as
it coursed through. Behind the shark I could see another fish flashing
unclearly. I supposed it was a jack crevalle, a pelagic fish, strong for its
size, that often follows sharks. I decided to cast. The distance was all I
could manage. I got off one of my better shots, which nevertheless fell
slightly behind target. I was surprised to see the fish drop back to the fly,
turn and elevate high in the water, then take. It was a permit.

I set the hook sharply, and the fish started down the flat. I kept the
loose, racing line well away from the reel handle for the instant the fish
took to consume it. Then the fish was on the reel. I lowered the rod tip
and cinched the hook and the fish began to accelerate, staying on top of
the flat so that I could see its wildly extending wake. Everything was
holding together: the hookup was good, the knots were good. At 150
yards the fish stopped, and I got back line. I kept at it and got the fish
within 80 yards of the boat. Then suddenly it made a wild, undirected
run, not permitlike at all, and I could see that the blacktip shark was
chasing it. The blacktip struck and missed the permit three or four
times, making explosions in the water that sickened me. I released the
drag, untied the boat, and started the engine. Woody was poling toward
me at the sound of my engine. His mystified client dragged a line astern.

There was hardly enough water to move in. The prop was half buried,
and at full throttle I could not get up on plane. The explosions continued, and I could only guess whether or not I was still connected to the
fish. I ran toward the fish, a vast loop of line trailing, saw the shark once
and ran over him. I threw the engine into neutral and waited to see what
had happened and tried to regain line. Once more I was tight to the
permit. Then the shark reappeared. He hit the permit once, killed it, and
ate the fish, worrying it like a dog and bloodying the muddy water.

Then an instant later I had the shark on my line and running. I fought
him with irrational care: I now planned to gaff the blacktip and retrieve
my permit piece by piece. When the inevitable cutoff came I dropped
the rod in the boat and, empty-handed, wondered what I had done to
deserve this.

I heard Woody's skiff and looked around. He swung about and coasted alongside. I told him it was a permit, as he had guessed from my starting up on the flat. Woody started to say something when, at that not unceremonial moment, his client broke in to say that it was hooking them that was the main thing. We stared at him as if he were a simple, unutterable bug, until he added, "Or is it?"

Often afterward we went over the affair and talked about what might have been done differently. One friend carries a carbine on clips under the gunwale to take care of sharks. But I felt that with a gun in the skiff during the excitement of a running fish, I would plug myself or deep-six the boat. Woody knew better than to assure me there would be other chances. Knowing that there might very well not be one was one of our conversational assumptions.

One morning we went to look for tarpon. Woody had had a bad night of it. He had awakened in the darkness of his room about three in the morning and watched the shadowy figure of a huge land crab walk across his chest. Endlessly it crept to the wall and then up it. Carefully silhouetting the monster, Woody blasted it with a karate chop. At breakfast he was nursing a bruise on the side of his hand.

We laid out the rods in the skiff. The wind was coming out of the east, that is, over one's casting hand from the point we planned to fish, and it was blowing fairly stiff. But the light was good, and that was more important. We headed out of Big Pine, getting into the calm water along Ramrod Key. We ran in behind Pye Key, through the hole behind Little Money and out to Southeast Point. The sun was already huge, out of hand, like Shakespeare's "glistering Phaeton." I had whitened my nose and mouth with zinc oxide and felt, handling the mysterious rods and flies, like the tropical edition of your standard shaman. I still had to rig the leader of my own rod; and as Woody jockeyed the skiff with the pole, I put my leader together. I retained enough of my trout-fishing sensibilities to continue to be intrigued by tarpon leaders with their array of arcane knots: the butt of the leader is nail-knotted to the line, blood-knotted to monofilament of lighter test; the shock tippet that protects the leader from the rough jaws of tarpon is tied to the leader with a combination Albright Special and Bimini Bend; the shock tippet is attached to the fly either by a perfection loop, a clinch, or a Homer Rhodes loop; and to choose one is to make a moral choice. You are made to understand that it would not be impossible to fight about it or, at the very least, quibble darkly.

We set up on a tarpon pass point. We had sand spots around us that would help us pick out the dark shapes of traveling tarpon. And we expected tarpon on the falling water, from left to right. I got up on the bow with fifty feet of line coiled on the deck. I was barefoot so I could feel if I stepped on a loop. I made a couple of practice casts—harsh, indecorous, tarpon-style, the opposite of the otherwise appealing dry fly caper—and scanned for fish.

The first we saw were, from my point of view, spotted from too great a distance. That is, there was a long period of time before they actually broke the circle of my casting range, during which time I could go, quite secretly but completely, to pieces. The sensation, for me, in the face of these advancing forms, was as of a gradual ossification of the joints. Moviegoers will recall the early appearances of Frankenstein's monster, his ambulatory motions accompanied by great rigidity of the limbs, almost as though he could stand a good oiling. I was hard put to see how I would manage anything beyond a perfunctory flapping of the rod. I once laughed at Woody's stories of customers who sat down and held their feet slightly aloft, treading the air or wobbling their hands from the wrists. I giggled at the story of a Boston chiropractor who fell over on his back and barked like a seal.

"Let them come in now," Woody said.

"I want to nail one of these dudes, Woody."

"You will. Let them come."

The fish, six of them, were surging toward us in a wedge. They ran from 80 to 110 pounds. "All right, the lead fish, get on him," Woody said. I managed the throw. The fly fell on a line with the fish. I let them overtake before starting my retrieve. The lead fish, big, pulled up behind the fly, trailed, and then made the shoveling, open-jawed uplift of a strike that is not forgotten. When he turned down I set the hook, and he started his run. The critical stage, that of getting rid of loose lines piled around one's feet, ensued. You imagine that if you are standing on a coil, you will go to the moon when that coil must follow its predecessors out of the rod. This one went off without a hitch, and it was only my certainty that someone had done it before that kept me from deciding that we had made a big mistake.

The sudden pressure of the line and the direction of its resistance apparently confused the tarpon, and it raced in close-coupled arcs around the boat. Then, when it had seen the boat, felt the line, and isolated a single point of resistance, it cleared out at a perfectly insane rate of acceleration that made water run three feet up my line as it sliced the water. The jumps—wild, greyhounding, end over end, rattling— were all crazily blurred as they happened, while I imagined my reel exploding like a racing clutch and filling me with shrapnel.

This fish, the first of six that day, broke off. So did the others, destroying various aspects of my tackle. Of the performances, it is not simple to generalize. The closest thing to a tarpon in the material world is the Steinway piano. The tarpon, of course, is a game fish that runs to extreme sizes, while the Steinway piano is merely an enormous musical instrument, largely wooden and manipulated by a series of keys. However, the tarpon when hooked and running reminds the angler of a piano sliding down a precipitous incline and while jumping makes cavities and explosions in the water not unlike a series of pianos falling from a great height. If the reader, then, can speculate in terms of pianos that herd and pursue mullet and are themselves shaped like exaggerated herrings, he will be a very long way toward seeing what kind of thing a tarpon is. Those who appreciate nature as we find her may rest in the knowledge that no amount of modification can substitute the manmade piano for the real thing—the tarpon. Where was I?

As the sun moved through the day the blind side continually changed, forcing us to adjust position until, by afternoon, we were watching to the north. Somehow, looking up light, Woody saw four permit coming right in toward us, head on. I cast my tarpon fly at them, out of my accustomed long-shot routine, and was surprised when one fish moved forward of the pack and followed up the fly rather aggressively. About then they all sensed the skiff and swerved to cross the bow about thirty feet out. They were down close to the bottom now, slightly spooked. I picked up, changed direction, and cast a fairly long interception. When the fly lit, well out ahead, two fish elevated from the group, sprinted forward, and the inside fish took the fly in plain view.

The certainty, the positiveness of the take, in the face of an ungodly number of refusals and the long, unproductive time put in, produced immediate tension and pessimism. I waited for something to go haywire.

I hooked the fish quickly and threw slack. It was only slightly startled and returned to the pack, which by this time had veered away from the shallow flat edge and swung back toward deep water. The critical time of loose line passed slowly. Woody unstaked the skiff and was poised to see which way the runs would take us. When the permit was tight to the reel I cinched him once, and he began running. The deep water kept the fish from making the long, sustained sprints permit make on the flats. This fight was a series of assured jabs at various clean angles from the skiff. We followed, alternately gaining and losing line. Then, in some way, at the end of this blurred episode, the permit was flashing beside the boat, looking nearly circular, and the only visual contradiction to his perfect poise was the intersecting line of leader seemingly inscribed from the tip of my arcing rod to the precise corner of his jaw.

Then we learned that there was no net in the boat. The fish would have to be tailed. I forgave Woody in advance for the permit's escape. Woody was kneeling in the skiff, my line disappearing over his shoulder, the permit no longer in my sight, Woody leaning deep from the gunwale. Then, unbelievably, his arm was up, the black symmetry of tail above his fist, the permit perpendicular to the earth, then horizontal on the floorboards. A pile of loose fly line was strewn in curves that wandered around the bottom of the boat to a gray-and-orange fly that was secured in the permit's mouth. I sat down numb and soaring.

I don't know what this kind of thing indicates beyond the necessary, ecstatic resignation to the moment. With the beginning over and, possibly nothing learned, I was persuaded that once was not enough.

DONALD HALL

"Old Timers' Day"

When the tall puffy
figure wearing number
nine starts
late for the fly ball,
laboring forward
like a lame truckhorse
startled by a gartersnake,
—this old fellow
whose body we remember
as sleek and nervous
as a filly's—

and barely catches it
in his glove's
tip, we rise
and applaud weeping:
On a green field
we observe the ruin
of even the bravest
body, as Odysseus

wept to glimpse
among shades the shadow
of Achilles.

PAUL GALLICO

"THE FEEL"

Paul Gallico was sports editor and columnist of the New York Daily News *for a dozen years during the so-called Golden Age of Sport—the era of Jack Dempsey, Bobby Jones, Bill Tilden, Babe Ruth, Red Grange, and company. Writing a thousand-word column, seven days a week, Gallico was the highest-paid sportswriter in the country; a skilled pilot, he often moved from one event to another in an amphibian named Daisy-the-Duck. In 1936, when he was thirty-nine, he left his job and gave up sportswriting to concentrate on fiction:* The Snow Goose, *the famous parable about World War II; the* Mrs. 'Arris *stories; the* Posiedon Adventure *perhaps the most familiar. He also wrote a recollection of his* Daily News *days, a book entitled* Farewell to Sport. *Dedicated to a number of his fellow sportswriters, it was among the most popular of his books, going through six printings. A chapter from it, "The Feel," appears here—of special meaning to me since it inspired my career in participatory journalism.*

A child wandering through a department store with its mother, is admonished over and over again not to touch things. Mother is convinced that the child only does it to annoy or because it is a child, and usually hasn't the vaguest inkling of the fact that Junior is "touching" because he is a little blotter soaking up information and knowledge, and "feel" is an important adjunct to seeing. Adults are exactly the same, in a measure, as you may ascertain when some new gadget or article is produced for inspection. The average person says: "Here, let me see that," and holds out his hand. He doesn't mean "see," because he is already seeing it. What he means is that he wants to get it into his hands and feel it so as to become better acquainted. . . .

I do not insist that a curiosity and capacity for feeling sports is necessary to be a successful writer, but it is fairly obvious that a man who has been tapped on the chin with five fingers wrapped up in a leather boxing glove and propelled by the arm of an expert knows more about that particular sensation than one who has not, always provided he has the gift of expressing himself. I once inquired of a heavyweight prizefighter by the name of King Levinsky, in a radio interview, what it felt like to be hit on the chin by Joe Louis, the King having just acquired that experience with rather disastrous results. Levinsky considered the matter for a moment and then reported: "It don't feel like nuttin'," but added that for a long while afterwards he felt as though he were "in a transom."

I was always a child who touched things and I have always had a tremendous curiosity with regard to sensation. If I knew what playing a game felt like, particularly against or in the company of experts, I was better equipped to write about the playing of it and the problems of the men and women who took part in it. And so, at one time or another, I have tried them all, football, baseball, boxing, riding, shooting, swimming, squash, handball, fencing, driving, flying, both land and sea planes, rowing, canoeing, skiing, riding a bicycle, ice-skating, roller-skating, tennis, golf, archery, basketball, running, both the hundred-yard dash and the mile, the high jump and shot put, badminton, angling, deep-sea, stream-, and surf-casting, billiards and bowling, motorboating and wrestling, besides riding as a passenger with the fastest men on land and water and in the air, to see what it felt like. Most of them I dabbled in as a youngster going through school and college, and others, like piloting a plane, squash, fencing, and skiing, I took up after I was old enough to know better, purely to get the feeling of what they were like.

None of these things can I do well, but I never cared about becoming an expert, and besides, there wasn't time. But there is only one way to find out accurately about human sensations in a ship two or three thousand feet up when the motor quits, and that is actually to experience that gone feeling at the pit of the stomach and the sharp tingling of the skin from head to foot, followed by a sudden amazing sharpness of vision, clear-sightedness, and coolness that you never knew you possessed as you find the question of life or death completely in your own hands. It is not the "you" that you know, but somebody else, a stranger, who noses the ship down, circles, fastens upon the one best spot to sit down, pushes or pulls buttons to try to get her started again, and finally drops her in, safe and sound. And it is only by such experience that you learn likewise of the sudden weakness that hits you right at the back of the knees after you have climbed out and started to walk around her and that comes close to knocking you flat as for the first time since the engine quit its soothing drone you think of destruction and sudden death.

Often my courage has failed me and I have funked completely, such as the time I went up to the top of the thirty-foot Olympic diving-tower at Jones Beach, Long Island, during the competitions, to see what it was like to dive from that height, and wound up crawling away from the edge on hands and knees, dizzy, scared, and a little sick, but with a wholesome respect for the boys and girls who hurled themselves through the air and down through the tough skin of the water from that awful height. At other times sheer ignorance of what I was getting into has led me into tight spots such as the time I came down the Olympic ski run from the top of the Kreuzeck, six thousand feet above Garmisch-Partenkirchen, after having been on skis but once before in snow and for the rest had no more than a dozen lessons on an indoor artificial slide in a New York department store. At one point my legs, untrained, got so tired that I couldn't stem (brake) any more, and I lost control and went full tilt and all out, down a three-foot twisting path cut out of the side of the mountain, with a two-thousand-foot abyss on the left and the mountain itself on the right. That was probably the most scared I have ever been, and I scare fast and often. I remember giving myself up for lost and wondering how long it would take them to retrieve my body and whether I should be still alive. In the meantime the speed of the descent was increasing. Somehow I was keeping my feet and negotiating turns, how I will never know, until suddenly the narrow patch opened out into a wide, steep stretch of slope with a rise at the other end, and *that* part of the journey was over.

By some miracle I got to the bottom of the run uninjured, having made most of the trip down the icy, perpendicular slopes on the flat of my back. It was the thrill and scare of a lifetime, and to date no one has been able to persuade me to try a jump. I know when to stop. After all, I am entitled to rely upon my imagination for something. But when it was all over and I found myself still whole, it was also distinctly worth while to have learned what is required of a ski runner in the breakneck *Abfahrt* or downhill race, or the difficult *slalom*. Five days later, when I climbed laboriously (still on skis) halfway up that Alp and watched the Olympic downhill racers hurtling down the perilous, ice-covered, and nearly perpendicular *Steilhang*, I knew that I was looking at a great group of athletes who, for one thing, did not know the meaning of the word "fear." The slope was studded with small pine trees and rocks, but half of the field gained precious seconds by hitting that slope all out, with complete contempt for disaster rushing up at them at a speed often better than sixty miles an hour. And when an unfortunate Czech skidded off the course at the bottom of the slope and into a pile of rope and got himself snarled up as helpless as a fly in a spider's web, it was a story that I could write from the heart. I had spent ten minutes getting myself untangled after a fall, *without* any rope to add to the difficulties. It seems that I couldn't find where my left leg ended and one more ski than I had originally donned seemed to be involved somehow. Only a person who has been on those fiendish runners knows the sensation.

It all began back in 1922 when I was a cub sports-writer and consumed with more curiosity than was good for my health. I had seen my first professional prizefights and wondered at the curious behavior of men under the stress of blows, the sudden checking and the beginning of a little fall forward after a hard punch, the glazing of the eyes and the loss of locomotor control, the strange actions of men on the canvas after a knock-down as they struggled to regain their senses and arise on legs that seemed to have turned into rubber. I had never been in any bad fist fights as a youngster, though I had taken a little physical punishment in football, but it was not enough to complete the picture. Could one think under those conditions?

I had been assigned to my first training-camp coverage, Dempsey's at Saratoga Springs, where he was preparing for his famous fight with Luis Firpo. For days I watched him sag a spar boy with what seemed to be no more than a light cuff on the neck, or pat his face with what looked like no more than a caressing stroke of his arm, and the fellow would come all apart at the seams and collapse in a useless heap, grinning vacuously or twitching strangely. My burning curiosity got the better of prudence and a certain reluctance to expose myself to physical pain. I asked Dempsey to permit me to box a round with him. I had never boxed before, but I was in good physical shape, having just completed a four-year stretch as a galley slave in the Columbia eight-oared shell.

When it was over and I escaped through the ropes, shaking, bleeding a little from the mouth, with rosin dust on my pants and a vicious throbbing in my head, I knew all that there was to know about being hit in the prize-ring. It seems that I had gone to an expert for tuition. I knew the sensation of being stalked and pursued by a relentless, truculent professional destroyer whose trade and business it was to injure men. I saw the quick flash of the brown forearm that precedes the stunning shock as a bony, leather-bound fist lands on cheek or mouth. I learned more (partly from photographs of the lesson, viewed afterwards, one of which shows me ducked under a vicious left hook, an act of which I never had the slightest recollection) about instinctive ducking and blocking than I could have in ten years of looking at prizefights, and I learned, too, that as the soldier never hears the bullet that kills him, so does the fighter rarely, if ever, see the punch that tumbles blackness over him like a mantle, with a tearing rip as though the roof of his skull were exploding, and robs him of his senses.

There was just that—a ripping in my head and then sudden blackness, and the next thing I knew, I was sitting on the canvas covering of the ring floor with my legs collapsed under me, grinning idiotically. How often since have I seen that same silly, goofy look on the faces of dropped fighters—and understood it. I held on to the floor with both hands, because the ring and the audience outside were making a complete clockwise revolution, came to a stop, and then went back again counterclockwise. When I struggled to my feet, Jack Kearns, Dempsey's manager, was counting over me, but I neither saw nor heard him and was only conscious that I was in a ridiculous position and that the thing to do was to get up and try to fight back. The floor swayed and rocked beneath me like a fishing dory in an off-shore swell, and it was a welcome respite when Dempsey rushed into a clinch, held me up, and whispered into my ear: "Wrestle around a bit, son, until your head clears." And then it was that I learned what those little love-taps to the back of the neck and the short digs to the ribs can mean to the groggy pugilist more than half knocked out. It is a murderous game, and the fighter who can escape after having been felled by a lethal blow has my admiration. And there, too, I learned that there can be no sweeter sound than the bell that calls a halt to hostilities.

From that afternoon on, also, dated my antipathy for the spectator at prizefights who yells: "Come on, you bum, get up and fight! Oh, you big quitter! Yah yellow, yah yellow!" Yellow, eh? It is all a man can do to get up after being stunned by a blow, much less fight back. But they do it. And how a man is able to muster any further interest in a combat after being floored with a blow to the pit of the stomach will always remain to me a miracle of what the human animal is capable of under stress.

Further experiments were less painful, but equally illuminating. A couple of sets of tennis with Vinnie Richards taught me more about what is required of a top-flight tournament tennis-player than I could have got out of a dozen books or years of reporting tennis matches. It is one thing to sit in a press box and write caustically that Brown played uninspired tennis, or Black's court covering was faulty and that his frequent errors cost him the set. It is quite another to stand across the net at the back of a service court and try to get your racket on a service that is so fast that the ear can hardly detect the interval between the sound of the server's bat hitting the ball and the ball striking the court. Tournament tennis is a different game from week-end tennis. For one thing, in average tennis, after the first hard service has gone into the net or out, you breathe a sigh of relief, move up closer, and wait for the cripple to come floating over. In big-time tennis second service is practically as hard as the first, with an additional twist on the ball.

It is impossible to judge or know anything about the speed of a forehand drive hit by a champion until you have had one fired at you, or, rather, away from you, and you have made an attempt to return it. It is then that you first realize that tennis is played more with the head than with the arms and the legs. The fastest player in the world cannot get to a drive to return it if he hasn't thought correctly, guessed its direction, and anticipated it by a fraction of a second.

There was golf with Bob Jones and Gene Sarazen and Tommy Armour, little Cruickshank and Johnny Farrell, and Diegel and other professionals; and experiments at trying to keep up in the water with Johnny Weissmuller, Helene Madison, and Eleanor Holm, attempts to catch football passes thrown by Benny Friedman. Nobody actually plays golf until he has acquired the technical perfection to be able to hit the ball accurately, high, low, hooked or faded and placed. And nobody knows what real golf is like until he has played around with a professional and seen him play, not the ball, but the course, the roll of the land, the hazards, the wind, and the texture of the greens and the fairways. It looks like showmanship when a top-flight golfer plucks a handful of grass and lets it flutter in the air, or abandons his drive to march two hundred yards down to the green and look over the situation. It isn't. It's golf. The average player never knows or cares whether he is putting with or across the grain of a green. The professional *always* knows. The same average player standing on the tee is concentrated on getting the ball somewhere on the fairway, two hundred yards out. The professional when preparing to drive is actually to all intents and purposes playing his *second* shot. He means to place his drive so as to open up the green for his approach. But you don't find that out until you have played around with them when they are relaxed and not competing, and listen to them talk and plan attacks on holes.

Major-league baseball is one of the most difficult and precise of all games, but you would never know it unless you went down on the field and got close to it and tried it yourself. For instance, the distance between pitcher and catcher is a matter of twenty paces, but it doesn't seem like enough when you don a catcher's mitt and try to hold a pitcher with the speed of Dizzy Dean or Dazzy Vance. Not even the sponge that catchers wear in the palm of the hand when working with fast-ball pitchers and the bulky mitt are sufficient to rob the ball of shock and sting that lames your hand unless you know how to ride with the throw and kill some of its speed. The pitcher, standing on his little elevated mound, looms up enormously over you at that short distance, and when he ties himself into a coiled spring preparatory to letting fly, it requires all your self-control not to break and run for safety. And as for the things they can do with a baseball, those major-league pitchers . . . ! One way of finding out is to wander down on the field an hour or so before game-time when there is no pressure on them, pull on the catcher's glove, and try to hold them.

I still remember my complete surprise the first time I tried catching for a real curve-ball pitcher. He was a slim, spidery left-hander of the New York Yankees, many years ago, by the name of Herb Pennock. He called that he was going to throw a fast breaking curve and warned me to expect the ball at least two feet outside the plate. Then he wound up and let it go, and that ball came whistling right down the groove for the center of the plate. A novice, I chose to believe what I saw and not what I heard, and prepared to catch it where it was headed for, a spot which of course it never reached, because just in front of the rubber, it swerved sharply to the right and passed nearly a yard from my glove. I never had a chance to catch it. That way, you learn about the mysterious drop, the ball that sails down the alley chest high but which you must be prepared to catch around your ankles because of the sudden dip it takes at the end of its passage as though someone were pulling it down with a string. Also you find out about the queer fade-away, the slow curve, the fast in- and out-shoots that seem to be timed almost as delicately as shrapnel, to burst, or rather break, just when they will do the most harm—namely, at the moment when the batter is swinging.

Facing a big-league pitcher with a bat on your shoulder and trying to hit his delivery is another vital experience in gaining an understanding of the game about which you are trying to write vividly. It is one thing to sit in the stands and scream at a batsman: "Oh, you bum!" for striking out in a pinch, and another to stand twenty yards from that big pitcher and try to make up your mind in a hundredth of a second whether to hit at the offering or not, where to swing and when, not to mention worrying about protecting yourself from the consequences of being struck by the ball that seems to be heading straight for your skull at an appalling rate of speed. Because, if you are a big-league player, you cannot very well afford to be gun-shy and duck away in panic from a ball that swerves in the last moment and breaks perfectly over the plate, while the umpire calls: "Strike!" and the fans jeer. Nor can you afford to take a crack on the temple from the ball. Men have died from that. It calls for un-dreamed-of niceties of nerve and judgment, but you don't find that out until you have stepped to the plate cold a few times during batting practice or in training quarters, with nothing at stake but the acquisition

of experience, and see what a fine case of the jumping jitters you get.
Later on, when you are writing your story, your imagination, backed by
the experience, will be able to supply a picture of what the batter is going
through as he stands at the plate in the closing innings of an important
game, with two or three men on base, two out, and his team behind in
the scoring, and fifty thousand people screaming at him.

The catching and holding of a forward pass for a winning touchdown
on a cold, wet day always make a good yarn, but you might get an even
better one out of it if you happen to know from experience about the
elusive qualities of a hard, soggy, mud-slimed football rifled through the
air, as well as something about the exquisite timing, speed, and courage
it takes to catch it on a dead run, with two or three 190-pound men
reaching for it at the same time or waiting to crash you as soon as your
fingers touch it.

Any football coach during a light practice will let you go down the
field and try to catch punts, the long, fifty-yard spirals and the tricky,
tumbling end-over-enders. Unless you have had some previous experience, you won't hang on to one out of ten, besides knocking your fingers
out of joint. But if you have any imagination, thereafter you will know
that it calls for more than negligible nerve to judge and hold that ball
and even plan to run with it, when there are two husky ends bearing
down at full speed, preparing for a head-on tackle.

In 1932 I covered my first set of National Air Races, in Cleveland, and
immediately decided that I had to learn how to fly to find out what that
felt like. Riding as a passenger isn't flying. Being up there all alone at the
controls of a ship is. And at the same time began a series of investigations
into the "feel" of the mechanized sports to see what they were all about
and the qualities of mentality, nerve, and physique they called for from
their participants. These included a ride with Gar Wood in his latest and
fastest speedboat, *Miss America X,* in which for the first time he pulled
the throttle wide open on the Detroit River straightaway; a trip with the
Indianapolis Speedway driver Cliff Bergere, around the famous brick
raceway; and a flip with Lieutenant Al Williams, one time U. S.
Schneider Cup race pilot.

I was scared with Wood, who drove me at 127 miles an hour, jounced,
shaken, vibrated, choked with fumes from the exhausts, behind which I
sat hanging on desperately to the throttle bar, which after a while got too
hot to hold. I was on a plank between Wood and his mechanic, Johnson,
and thought that my last moment had come. I was still more scared
when Cliff Bergere hit 126 on the Indianapolis straightaways in the tiny
racing car in which I was hopelessly wedged, and after the first couple of
rounds quite resigned to die and convinced that I should. But I think the
most scared I have ever been while moving fast was during a ride I took

in the cab of a locomotive on the straight, level stretch between Fort Wayne, Indiana, and Chicago, where for a time we hit 90 miles per hour, which of course is no speed at all. But nobody who rides in the comfortable Pullman coaches has any idea of the didoes cut up by a locomotive in a hurry, or the thrill of pelting through a small town, all out and wide open, including the crossing of some thirty or forty frogs and switches, all of which must be set right. But that wasn't sport. That was just plain excitement.

I have never regretted these researches. Now that they are over, there isn't enough money to make me do them again. But they paid me dividends, I figured. During the great Thompson Speed Trophy race for land planes at Cleveland in 1935, Captain Roscoe Turner was some eight or nine miles in the lead in his big golden, low-wing, speed monoplane. Suddenly, coming into the straightaway in front of the grandstands, buzzing along at 280 miles an hour like an angry hornet, a streamer of thick, black smoke burst from the engine cowling and trailed back behind the ship. Turner pulled up immediately, using his forward speed to gain all the altitude possible, turned and got back to the edge of the field, still pouring out that evil black smoke. Then he cut his switch, dipped her nose down, landed with a bounce and a bump, and rolled up to the line in a perfect stop. The crowd gave him a great cheer as he climbed out of the oil-spattered machine, but it was a cheer of sympathy because he had lost the race after having been so far in the lead that had he continued he could not possibly have been overtaken.

There was that story, but there was a better one too. Only the pilots on the field, all of them white around the lips and wiping from their faces a sweat not due to the oppressive summer heat, knew that they were looking at a man who from that time on, to use their own expression, was living on borrowed time. It isn't often when a Thompson Trophy racer with a landing speed of around eighty to ninety miles an hour goes haywire in the air, that the pilot is able to climb out of the cockpit and walk away from his machine. From the time of that first burst of smoke until the wheels touched the ground and stayed there, he was a hundred-to-one shot to live. To the initiated, those dreadful moments were laden with suspense and horror. Inside that contraption was a human being who any moment might be burned to a horrible, twisted cinder, or smashed into the ground beyond all recognition, a human being who was cool, gallant, and fighting desperately. Every man and woman on the field who had ever been in trouble in the air was living those awful seconds with him in terror and suspense. I, too, was able to experience it. That is what makes getting the "feel" of things distinctly worth while.

JACKIE STEWART

FROM *FASTER*, WITH PETER MANSO

It's the rare athlete who can describe in intricate detail the mental state involved in competition in terms other than the most prosaic. One exception is Jackie Stewart, the former champion race-car driver, who is capable of offering an absorbing and near-elegiac portrait-in-words of what it is like to sit in a high-powered racing machine. It has been my luck to know Jackie Stewart, having worked with him on two television documentaries. In one of them as a lark he and I happened to compete in a number of sports events. Early in the morning we started with skeet shooting. Jackie is a crack shot. In fact, he told me that he would have traded his world championships in racing to have made the British Olympic skeet-shooting team, which he missed joining by a single clay pigeon. Naturally he won our competition with ease; I don't remember that he missed a shot. The skeet-shooting range was on the grounds of the marine base at Camp Pendleton north of San Diego. After the match I asked the public-relations officer if the marines had tanks on the base. I explained that at one point in my army career I had been a tank driver. Perhaps he could arrange a tank race against Jackie so I could avenge myself for the loss at skeet shooting. The public-relations officer looked a little startled—it was not an everyday request—but then he said that the base had a lot of tanks, the Abrams M1, always in need of exercise, and he saw no reason why an ex–tank driver and Stewart, who obviously knew his way around machines, shouldn't use a couple of them.

We had the race a couple of hours later—a mile in length on the proving grounds. The word got around. The course was lined with marines, many of them betting on Stewart, the odds-on favorite. I thought I had a good chance. The tank I had driven in the army was a Sherman, which functioned by a complicated gear system—three forward speeds and two reverse, as I recall—and it required a certain amount of man-handling and double-clutching to keep the big machine moving. To my surprise, when I settled into the seat of the M1 I discovered an automatic transmission system—no wrestling with gears at all! I expected to find the long brake handles to steer the tank, locking the right treads to turn right, and so on. Instead, quite a change from the Sherman, I discovered a tiny steering wheel, about the size one finds on a kiddie-car. I looked over and saw Jackie, his head visible, talking to his tank commander on an intercom. He got off to a great start and won handily. It turned out he knew quite a lot about tanks—having test-driven Peugot tanks in France. So that was all right. But then that afternoon we played tennis. Jackie's partner was Pancho Segura. Jackie scampered around the court, very quick, and although he hasn't played much tennis, jockeyed about by Pancho he made a noticeable contribution. Their team won. We shook hands at the net. "Hey!" I said. And that evening, darned if he didn't win quite a lot of money at backgammon. So in one day he beat me at skeet shooting, backgammon, tennis, and tanks!

The humiliation of all this was, of course, mitigated by the pleasure of his company. One can get a sense of this by what follows: an excerpt from his book Faster, *which was fashioned from a series of talks with Stewart's editor, Peter Manso.*

March 8, 1970

Speed: really the whole business is the reverse of speed, how to eliminate it.

In a racing car, speed doesn't exist for me except when I'm driving poorly. Then things seem to be coming at me quickly instead of passing in slow motion. It's the surest sign that I'm off form, the kind of thing that happens whenever I go too fast too early on a strange circuit. For the first lap or two, everything seems too fast. Then once I've learned the course, I see things a long way off, in fine detail. A corner will come toward me very slowly, not unexpectedly. There's plenty of time as I'm closing in on it, plenty of time to brake and balance the car, to turn in, hit the apex, go through and hit the exit, and even look down at the rev counter to see how quickly I've gone around. On the other hand, when I'm driving poorly I'll go into the corner at the same speed, but everything is a great rush. Things are coming at me rather than passing me, and I'm all ruffled. None of it's of a piece, my movements are not coordinated; and it's like first learning how to drive.

Speed is therefore what I compete *against*. It's the thing that stops me from conquering a corner because I'm the master of the car and the car is coming along with me, and speed—what I'm calling speed—exists only when the car takes over, when something goes wrong or I'm really not getting down to it.

When some people speak of speed in conjunction with racing, they really don't know what they're talking about. Two hundred or 180 miles an hour in a Formula I car, if you're plugged in, is literally like eighty or sixty on the highway. The car is made to go that fast. It's stable and very easy to drive in a straight line, and once you're used to it, things don't rush past in an enormous flurry or blur. They're actually very clear. I remember once going down the Masta straight at Spa and there was a marshal sitting in a wheelchair with his leg in a cast, and as I went past him at about 190 I was thinking, "What an idiot! What happens if there's an accident, what good will he be?" I'll also usually recognize photographers there, even at those speeds, recognize their faces and clothing, and I'll have time to look over to my right to see who's going up the hill on the other side of the track, which is all of a mile away. I'll be able to spot particular cars. Everything is clear, neither hurried nor distorted, a tableau spread out in front of you, things going past, a new field coming into view, all of it in sequence, like a slowed-down movie film.

Through the turns, though, is where the true character of the car shows itself. A Formula I car is really an animal; a machine, yes, of course, but beyond that an animal because it responds to different kinds of treatment. A highly bred race horse, a thoroughbred in its sensitivity and nervousness. To get the best out of it you must coax it, treat it gently and sympathetically. In a corner it's right on its tiptoes, finely balanced, on the very edge of adhesion, just fingertips on the road, and if you dominate it or try to push it around, it will go straight on or slide off or do any number of things that leave you without control. So you coax it— gently, very gently—to get it to do what you want. You point it and coax it into the apex, and even after you've pointed it and it's all set up, committed to the corner which might still be fifty or a hundred feet away, you must be tender with it, holding it in nicely, because it's got an angle on it, an angle of roll, and it's building to its climax of hitting that apex. You've set a rhythm and now you must keep it. And as it hits the apex, you take it out nicely; you don't say, "You've got your apex, now I'll put my boot in it and drive however I want." No, your exit speed is very important, so you've got to maintain that balance or rhythm which you've been building all along. You've got to follow through, let the car fulfill itself.

Obviously, all this suggests that a car is very much like a woman, and however banal it sounds, the analogy holds. I know of no better. Cornering is like bringing a woman to a climax. The two of you, both you and the car, must work together. You start to enter the area of excitement of that corner, you set up a pace which is right for the car, and after you've told it that it's coming along with you, you guide it through at a rhythm which has by now become natural. Only after you've cleared that corner can you both take pleasure in knowing that it's gone well. If you do otherwise, alter the car's line, sometimes by no more than three or four inches, scrape a curbing, give it too much throttle or fail to feed it in gently, you'll spoil it. You'll ruin it. Through your own impatience you'll have taken away all the pleasure. It'll be finished, yet there will be something still to come.

March 9, 1970

Yesterday's thoughts continued.

This business of being sensitive to the car, very true, especially with today's Formula I car. Any ripple in the road, any small change in the surface, any oil or water or rubber that's been laid down radically affects the car's performance, more than most people would believe. And yet here again the car resembles a woman, if only because it's so unpredictable. You'll be driving well and all of a sudden the car may turn around and do something completely unexpected, shift its mood entirely. It turns on you viciously, abruptly, taking you by surprise, and when this happens it snaps away from you, immediately, spontaneously, and at that moment you've got to work very hard and very fast to bring it back because what's happening is happening so quickly that you don't know where you are. You've stopped thinking about coaxing it through and you're deep into a big recovery job, and now speed is showing itself quite vividly. You've got to stop what's happening and then start all over again, almost from scratch, really, because the car has chosen to protest your relationship.

March 12, 1970

It occurs to me that I ought to tell what I do with myself before a race, since I might overlook this as the season progresses. Because it's now ritual, a veritable countdown, I can talk about it in the abstract.

The process is akin to a deflating ball. The point of it is to shape my mood, really to expel mood, all mood. Beginning the night before, I start to pace myself into an emotional neutrality, a flatness or isolation that is imperative for a good start. By the time I go to bed, I will have obliterated all contact with people around me, Helen included. Usually I'll be reading, lying there beyond anybody's reach, trying to cleanse my mind, empty it of all extraneous thoughts, all impingements, anything that might encroach. Around eleven or twelve, perhaps, I'll go off to sleep. I'll awaken at half past six or seven, stay in bed, pick up my reading, then probably doze off to reawaken around nine. Breakfast in my room, always in my room, and usually alone, and perhaps, too, I'll have a massage, if one's available. Then back to sleep, up at noon, dress, and leave for the track.

By now I'm fairly bouncy. After the calm of being alone, the ball has started to inflate again. I'll have thoughts of what I'm going to do on the first lap, where I'm going to pass if someone gets off ahead of me, but immediately I'll then become aware of having to change my mood, of the need to put aside all these thoughts lest I lock myself into a plan that might interfere with my driving. More than anything, I know I need to stay loose, so I force myself to deflate, consciously, concentrating on it. I don't want Helen around me, I don't want to be bugged by reporters or film people or magazine photographers, by people wanting my autograph or by anyone. I'm into it, I need to be alone.

By race time I should have no emotions inside me at all—no excitement or fear or nervousness, not even an awareness of the fatigue that's been brought on by pacing myself. I'm absolutely cold, ice-cold, totally within my shell. I'm drained of feeling, utterly calm even though I'm aware of the many things going on around me, the mechanics, people running about, the journalists and officials and everything else.

Ten minutes or so from the start, I'll walk out to the car. My mechanics will belt me in, do up my seat belts, and I'll just sit there waiting. If there is a warm-up lap, I'll leave from the pits rather than the grid, go out and bed the brakes, get the temperatures up, using the brakes heavily all the way around, even riding my left foot on the pedal, and I'll also do a few corners very fast to warm up the tires.

Back on the dummy grid, I'll get out of the car and move around a bit, then with four or five minutes to go I'll get back in, again get belted up, and the mechanics will wait there with me, kneeling down beside the car or sitting on one of the tires, not talking. At the two-minute signal I'll start the engine, they'll have to leave, and I'll hold it revving fairly high, somewhere between 5,000 and 7,000, with occasional blips up to about 9,000. A minute to go, they'll move us up to the grid proper and I'll keep the clutch out until the very last before sticking it in gear.

The engines are revving all around you, and you hear them even with your earplugs and helmet, but I'm still in my shell, concentrating on what I'm going to have to do in the next minute. I may be looking around, or down at the instruments, but I'm still concentrating, the ball totally deflated. Thirty seconds left, I'll put it in gear. Twenty seconds, or maybe when the starter begins thinking about lifting the flag, I'll take the revs up to about 8,500 and hold it there, and that's when I take my foot off the clutch.

A. J. LIEBLING

"Boxing with the Naked Eye"

A. J. Liebling's book The Sweet Science *remains the standard by which boxing literature must be judged. After a short career in journalism Liebling started writing for the* New Yorker *in 1935. At that most genteel of periodicals his beat was what his editor, Harold Ross, referred to as "low-life"—the boxing fraternity in particular. Despite his subject his accounts were graceful and literate, almost invariably set amidst historical references to fights described by Pierce Egan, author of the nineteenth-century classic* Boxiana.

I never met Liebling, though I spoke once to him over the phone. He called me at Sports Illustrated *the day after I had, as a participatory journalist, "fought" Archie Moore, then the light-heavyweight champion of the world, suffering a severe nosebleed as a result. Liebling wanted to hear about the fight firsthand. He also wanted to welcome me to the brotherhood of people who had been bopped on the nose. He himself, an enthusiastic amateur, had been bopped on the nose by "Philadelphia" Jack O'Brien, who had been hit by Bob Fitzsimmons, who had been hit by "Gentleman Jim" Corbett, Corbett by John L. Sullivan, he by Paddy Ryan, all the way back to Jem Mace. As he writes in* The Sweet Science: *"It is a great thrill to feel that all that separates you from the early Victorians is a series of punches on the nose . . . the Sweet Science is joined onto the past like a man's arm to his shoulder."*

Watching a fight on television has always seemed to me a poor substitute for being there. For one thing, you can't tell the fighters what to do. When I watch a fight, I like to study one boxer's problem, solve it, and then communicate my solution vocally. On occasion my advice is disregarded, as when I tell a man to stay away from the other fellow's left and he doesn't, but in such cases I assume that he hasn't heard my counsel, or that his opponent has, and has acted on it. Some fighters hear better and are more suggestible than others—for example, the pre-television Joe Louis. "Let him have it, Joe!" I would yell whenever I saw him fight, and sooner or later he would let the other fellow have it. Another fighter like that was the late Marcel Cerdan, whom I would coach in his own language, to prevent opposition seconds from picking up our signals. *"Vas-y, Marcel!"* I used to shout, and Marcel always *y allait.* I get a feeling of participation that way that I don't in front of a television screen. I could yell, of course, but I would know that if my suggestion was adopted, it would be by the merest coincidence.

Besides, when you go to a fight, the boxers aren't the only ones you want to be heard by. You are surrounded by people whose ignorance of the ring is exceeded only by their unwillingness to face facts—the sharpness of your boxer's punching, for instance. Such people may take it upon themselves to disparage the principal you are advising. This disparagement is less generally addressed to the man himself (as "Gavilan, you're a bum!") than to his opponent, whom they have wrong-headedly picked to win ("He's a cream puff, Miceli!" they may typically cry. "He can't hurt you. He can't hurt nobody. Look—slaps! Ha, ha!"). They thus get at your man—and, by indirection, at you. To put them in their place, you address neither them nor their man but your man. ("Get the other eye, Gavilan!" you cry.) This throws them off balance, because they haven't noticed anything the matter with either eye. Then, before they can think of anything to say, you thunder, "Look at that eye!" It doesn't much matter whether or not the man has been hit in the eye; he will be. Addressing yourself to the fighter when you want somebody else to hear you is a parliamentary device, like "Mr. Chairman . . ." Before television, a prize fight was to a New Yorker the nearest equivalent to the New England town meeting. It taught a man to think on his seat.

Less malignant than rooters for the wrong man, but almost as disquieting, are those who are on the right side but tactically unsound. At a moment when you have steered your boxer to a safe lead on points but can see the other fellow is still dangerous, one of these maniacs will encourage recklessness. "Finish the jerk, Harry!" he will sing out. "Stop holding him up! Don't lose him!" But you, knowing the enemy is a puncher, protect your client's interests. "Move to your left, Harry!" you call. "Keep moving! Keep moving! Don't let him set!" I sometimes finish a fight like that in a cold sweat.

If you go to a fight with a friend, you can keep up unilateral conversations on two vocal levels—one at the top of your voice, directed at your fighter, and the other a running *expertise* nominally aimed at your companion but loud enough to reach a modest fifteen feet in each direction. "Reminds me of Panama Al Brown," you may say as a new fighter enters the ring. "He was five feet eleven and weighed a hundred and eighteen pounds. This fellow may be about forty pounds heavier and a couple of inches shorter, but he's got the same kind of neck. I saw Brown box a fellow named Mascart in Paris in 1927. Guy stood up in the top gallery and threw an apple and hit Brown right on the top of the head. The whole house started yelling, 'Finish him, Mascart! He's groggy!' " Then, as the bout begins, "Boxes like Al, too, except this fellow's a southpaw." If he wins, you say, "I told you he reminded me of Al Brown," and if he loses, "Well, well, I guess he's no Al Brown. They don't make fighters like Al any more." This identifies you as a man who (a) has been in Paris, (b) has been going to fights for a long time, and (c) therefore enjoys what the fellows who write for quarterlies call a frame of reference.

It may be argued that this doesn't get you anywhere, but it at least constitutes what a man I once met named Thomas S. Matthews called communication. Mr. Matthews, who was the editor of *Time,* said that the most important thing in journalism is not reporting but communication. "What are you going to communicate?" I asked him. "The most important thing," he said, "is the man on one end of the circuit saying 'My God, I'm alive! You're alive!' and the fellow on the other end, receiving his message, saying 'My God, you're right! We're both alive!' "

I still think it is a hell of a way to run a news magazine, but it is a good reason for going to fights in person. Television, if unchecked, may carry us back to a pre-tribal state of social development, when the family was the largest conversational unit.

Fights are also a great place for adding to your repertory of witty sayings. I shall not forget my adolescent delight when I first heard a fight fan yell, "I hope youse bot' gets knocked out!" I thought he had made it up, although I found out later it was a cliché. It is a formula adaptable to an endless variety of situations outside the ring. The only trouble with it is it never works out. The place where I first heard the line was Bill Brown's, a fight club in a big shed behind a trolley station in Far Rockaway.

On another night there, the time for the main bout arrived and one of the principals hadn't. The other fighter sat in the ring, a bantamweight with a face like a well-worn coin, and the fans stamped in cadence and whistled and yelled for their money back. It was thirty years before television, but there were only a couple of hundred men on hand. The preliminary fights had been terrible. The little fighter kept looking at his hands, which were resting on his knees in cracked boxing gloves, and every now and then he would spit on the mat and rub the spittle into the canvas with one of his scuffed ring shoes. The longer he waited, the more frequently he spat, and I presumed he was worrying about the money he was supposed to get; it wouldn't be more than fifty dollars with a house that size, even if the other man turned up. He had come there from some remote place like West or East New York, and he may have been thinking about the last train home on the Long Island Railroad, too. Finally, the other bantamweight got there, looking out of breath and flustered. He had lost his way on the railroad—changed to the wrong train at Jamaica and had to go back there and start over. The crowd booed so loud that he looked embarrassed. When the fight began, the fellow who had been waiting walked right into the new boy and knocked him down. He acted impatient. The tardy fellow got up and fought back gamely, but the one who had been waiting nailed him again, and the latecomer just about pulled up to one knee at the count of seven. He had been hit pretty hard, and you could see from his face that he was wondering whether to chuck it. Somebody in the crowd yelled out, "Hey, Hickey! You kept us all waiting! Why don't you stay around awhile?" So the fellow got up and caught for ten rounds and probably made the one who had come early miss his train. It's another formula with multiple applications, and I think the man who said it that night in Far Rockaway did make it up.

Because of the way I feel about watching fights on television, I was highly pleased when I read, back in June, 1951, that the fifteen-round match between Joe Louis and Lee Savold, scheduled for June thirteenth at the Polo Grounds, was to be neither televised, except to eight theater audiences in places like Pittsburgh and Albany, nor broadcast over the radio. I hadn't seen Louis with the naked eye since we shook hands in a pub in London in 1944. He had fought often since then, and I had seen his two bouts with Jersey Joe Walcott on television, but there hadn't been any fun in it. Those had been held in public places, naturally, and I could have gone, but television gives you so plausible an adumbration of a fight, for nothing, that you feel it would be extravagant to pay your way in. It is like the potato, which is only a succedaneum for something decent to eat but which, once introduced into Ireland, proved so cheap that the peasants gave up their grain-and-meat diet in favor of it. After that, the landlords let them keep just enough money to buy potatoes. William Cobbett, a great Englishman, said that he would sack any workmen of his he caught eating one of the cursed things, because as soon as potatoes appeared anywhere they brought down the standard of eating. I sometimes think of Cobbett on my way home from the races, looking at the television aerials on all the little houses between here and Belmont Park. As soon as I heard that the fight wouldn't be on the air, I determined to buy a ticket.

On the night of the thirteenth, a Wednesday, it rained, and on the

next night it rained again, so on the evening of June fifteenth the promoters, the International Boxing Club, confronted by a night game at
the Polo Grounds, transferred the fight to Madison Square Garden. The
postponements upset a plan I had had to go to the fight with a friend,
who had another date for the third night. But alone is a good way to go
to a fight or the races, because you have more time to look around you,
and you always get all the conversation you can use anyway. I went to the
Garden box office early Friday afternoon and bought a ten-dollar seat in
the side arena—the first tiers rising in back of the boxes, midway between Eighth and Ninth Avenues on the 49th Street side of the house.
There was only a scattering of ticket buyers in the lobby, and the man at
the ticket window was polite—a bad omen for the gate. After buying the
ticket, I got into a cab in front of the Garden, and the driver naturally
asked me if I was going to see the fight. I said I was, and he said, "He's all
through."

I knew he meant Louis, and I said, "I know, and that's why it may be
a good fight. If he weren't through, he might kill this guy."

The driver said, "Savold is a hooker. He breaks noses."

I said, "He couldn't break his own nose, even," and then began to
wonder how a man would go about trying to do that. "It's a shame he's
so hard up he had to fight at all at his age," I said, knowing the driver
would understand I meant Louis. I was surprised that the driver was
against Louis, and I was appealing to his better feelings.

"He must have plenty socked away," said the driver. "Playing golf for
a hundred dollars a hole."

"Maybe that helped him go broke," I said. "And anyway, what does
that prove? There's many a man with a small salary who bets more than
he can afford." I had seen a scratch sheet on the seat next to the hackie.
I was glad I was riding only as far as Brentano's with him.

The driver I had on the long ride home was a better type. As soon as I
told him I was going to the fight, which was at about the same time that
he dropped the flag, he said, "I guess the old guy can still sock."

I said, "I saw him murder Max Baer sixteen years ago. He was a sweet
fighter then."

The driver said, "Sixteen years is a long time for a fighter. I don't
remember anybody lasted sixteen years in the big money. Still, Savold is
almost as old as he is. When you're a bum, nobody notices how old you
get."

We had a pleasant time on the West Side Highway, talking about
how Harry Greb had gone on fighting when he was blind in one eye, only
nobody knew it but his manager, and how Pete Herman had been the
best in-fighter in the world, because he had been practically blind in

both eyes, so he couldn't afford to fool around outside. "What Herman did, you couldn't learn a boy now," the driver said. "They got no patience."

The fellow who drove me from my house to the Garden after dinner was also a man of good will, but rather different. He knew I was going to the fight as soon as I told him my destination, and once we had got under way, he said, "It is a pity that a man like Louis should be exploited to such a degree that he has to fight again." It was only nine-fifteen, and he agreed with me that I had plenty of time to get to the Garden for the main bout, which was scheduled to begin at ten, but when we got caught in unexpectedly heavy traffic on Eleventh Avenue he grew impatient. "Come on, Jersey!" he said, giving a station wagon in front of us the horn. "In the last analysis, we have got to get to the Garden sometime." But it didn't help much, because most of the other cars were heading for the Garden, too. The traffic was so slow going toward Eighth Avenue on Fiftieth Street that I asked him to let me out near the Garden corner, and joined the people hurrying from the Independent Subway exit toward the Garden marquee. A high percentage of them were from Harlem, and they were dressed as if for a levee, the men in shimmering gabardines and felt hats the color of freshly unwrapped chewing gum, the women in spring suits and fur pieces—it was a cool night—and what seemed to me the prettiest hats of the season. They seemed to me the prettiest lot of women I had seen in a long time, too, and I reflected that if the fight had been televised, I would have missed them. "Step out," I heard one beau say as his group swept past me, "or we won't maybe get in. It's just like I told you—he's still one hell of a draw." As I made my way through the now crowded lobby, I could hear the special cop next to the ticket window chanting, "Six-, eight-, ten-, and fifteen-dollar tickets only," which meant that the two-and-a-half-dollar general-admission and the twenty-dollar ringside seats were sold out. It made me feel good, because it showed there were still some gregarious people left in the world.

Inside the Garden there was the same old happy drone of voices as when Jimmy McLarnin was fighting and Jimmy Walker was at the ringside. There was only one small patch of bare seats, in a particularly bad part of the ringside section. I wondered what sort of occupant I would find in my seat; I knew from experience that there would be somebody in it. It turned out to be a small, frail colored man in wine-red livery. He sat up straight and pressed his shoulder blades against the back of the chair, so I couldn't see the number. When I showed him my ticket, he said, "I don't know nothing about that. You better see the usher." He was offering this token resistance, I knew, only to protect his self-esteem—to maintain the shadowy fiction that he was in the seat by error. When an usher wandered within hailing distance of us, I called him, and the little man left, to drift to some other part of the Garden, where he had no reputation as a ten-dollar-seat holder to lose, and there to squat contentedly on a step.

My seat was midway between the east and west ends of the ring, and about fifteen feet above it. Two not very skillful colored boys were finishing a four-rounder that the man in the next seat told me was an emergency bout, put on because there had been several knockouts in the earlier preliminaries. It gave me a chance to settle down and look around. It was ten o'clock by the time the colored boys finished and the man with the microphone announced the decision, but there was no sign of Louis or Savold. The fight wasn't on the air, so there was no need of the punctuality required by the radio business. (Later I read in the newspapers that the bout had been delayed in deference to the hundreds of people who were still in line to buy tickets and who wanted to be sure of seeing the whole fight.) Nobody made any spiel about beer, as on the home screen, although a good volume of it was being drunk all around. Miss Gladys Gooding, an organist, played the national anthem and a tenor sang it, and we all applauded. After that, the announcer introduced a number of less than illustrious prizefighters from the ring, but nobody whistled or acted restless. It was a good-natured crowd.

Then Louis and his seconds—what the author of *Boxiana* would have called his faction—appeared from a runway under the north stands and headed toward the ring. The first thing I noticed, from where I sat, was that the top of Louis's head was bald. He looked taller than I had remembered him, although surely he couldn't have grown after the age of thirty, and his face was puffy and impassive. It has always been so. In the days of his greatness, the press read menace in it. He walked stiff-legged, as was natural for a heavy man of thirty-seven, but when his seconds pulled off his dressing robe, his body looked all right. He had never been a lean man; his muscles had always been well buried beneath his smooth beige skin. I recalled the first time I had seen him fight—against Baer. That was at the Yankee Stadium, in September, 1935, and not only the great ball park but the roofs of all the apartment houses around were crowded with spectators, and hundreds of people were getting out of trains at the elevated I.R.T. station, which overlooks the field, and trying to loiter long enough to catch a few moments of action. Louis had come East that summer, after a single year as a professional, and had knocked out Primo Carnera in a few rounds. Carnera had been the heavyweight champion of the world in 1934, when Baer knocked him out. Baer, when he fought Louis, was the most powerful and gifted heavyweight of the day, although he had already fumbled away his title. But this mature Baer, who had fought everybody, was frightened stiff by the twenty-one-year-old mulatto boy. Louis outclassed him. The whole thing went only four rounds. There hadn't been anybody remotely like Louis since Dempsey in the early twenties.

The week of the Louis-Baer fight, a man I know wrote in a magazine: "With half an eye, one can observe that the town is more full of stir than it has been in many moons. It is hard to find a place to park, hard to get a table in a restaurant, hard to answer all the phone calls. . . . Economic seers can explain it, if you care to listen. We prefer to remember that a sudden inflation of the town's spirit can be just as much psychological or accidental as economic." I figured it was Louis.

Savold had now come up into the other corner, a jutty-jawed man with a fair skin but a red back, probably sunburned at his training camp. He was twenty pounds lighter than Louis, but that isn't considered a crushing handicap among heavyweights; Ezzard Charles, who beat Louis the previous year, was ten pounds lighter than Savold. Savold was thirty-five, and there didn't seem to be much bounce in him. I had seen him fight twice in the winter of 1946, and I knew he wasn't much. Both bouts had been against a young Negro heavyweight named Al Hoosman, a tall, skinny fellow just out of the Army. Hoosman had started well the first time, but Savold had hurt him with body punches and won the decision. The second time, Hoosman had stayed away and jabbed him silly. An old third-rater like Savold, I knew, doesn't improve with five more years on him. But an old third-rater doesn't rattle easily, either, and I was sure he'd do his best. It made me more apprehensive, in one way, than if he'd been any good. I wouldn't have liked to see Louis beaten by a good young fighter, but it would be awful to see him beaten by a clown. Not that I have anything against Savold; I just think it's immoral for a fellow without talent to get too far. A lot of others in the crowd must have felt the same way, because the house was quiet when the fight started—as if the Louis rooters didn't want to ask too much of Joe. There weren't any audible rooters for Savold, though, of course, there would have been if he had landed one good punch.

I remembered reading in a newspaper that Savold had said he would walk right out and bang Louis in the temple with a right, which would scramble his thinking. But all he did was come forward as he had against Hoosman, with his left low. A fellow like that never changes. Louis walked out straight and stiff-legged, and jabbed his left into Savold's face. He did it again and again, and Savold didn't seem to know what to do about it. And Louis jabs a lot harder than a fellow like Hoosman.

Louis didn't have to chase Savold, and he had no reason to run away from him, either, so the stiff legs were all right. When the two men came close together, Louis jarred Savold with short punches, and Savold couldn't push him around, so that was all right, too. After the first round, the crowd knew Louis would win if his legs would hold him.

In the second round Louis began hitting Savold with combinations— quick sequences of punches, like a right under the heart and a left hook to the right side of the head. A sports writer I know had told me that Louis hadn't been putting combinations together for several fights back. Combinations demand a superior kind of coordination, but a fighter who has once had that can partly regain it by hard work. A couple of times it looked as if Louis was trying for a knockout, but when Savold didn't come apart, Louis returned to jabbing. A man somewhere behind me kept saying to a companion, "I read Savold was a tricky fighter. He's got to do something!" But Savold didn't, until late in the fifth round, by which time his head must have felt like a sick music box. Then he threw a right to Louis's head and it landed. I thought I could see Louis shrink, as if he feared trouble. His response ten years ago would have been to tear right back into the man. Savold threw another right, exactly the same kind, and that hit Louis, too. No good fighter should have been hit twice in succession with that kind of foolish punch. But the punches weren't hard enough to slow Louis down, and that was the end of that. In the third minute of the sixth round, he hit Savold with a couple of combinations no harder than those that had gone before, but Savold was weak now. His legs were going limp, and Louis was pursuing him as he backed toward my side of the ring. Then Louis swung like an axman with his right (he wasn't snapping it as he used to), and his left dropped over Savold's guard and against his jaw, and the fellow was rolling over and over on the mat, rolling the way football players do when they fall on a fumbled ball. The referee was counting and Savold was rolling, and he got up on either nine or ten, I couldn't tell which (later, I read that it was ten, so he was out officially), but you could see he was knocked silly, and the referee had his arms around him, and it was over.

The newspapermen, acres of them near the ring, were banging out the leads for the running stories they had already telegraphed, and I felt sorry for them, because they never have time to enjoy boxing matches. Since the fight was not broadcast, there was no oily-voiced chap to drag Louis over to a microphone and ask him stupid questions. He shook hands with Savold twice, once right after the knockout and again a few minutes later, when Savold was ready to leave the ring, as if he feared Savold wouldn't remember the first handshake.

I drifted toward the lobby with the crowd. The chic Harlem people were saying to one another, "It was terrific, darling! It was terrific!" I could see that an element of continuity had been restored to their world. But there wasn't any of the wild exultation that had followed those first Louis victories in 1935. These people had celebrated so many times— except, of course, the younger ones, who were small children when Louis knocked out Baer. I recognized one of the Garden promoters, usually a sour fellow, looking happy. The bout had brought in receipts of $94,684, including my ten dollars, but, what was more important to the Garden, Louis was sure to draw a lot more the next time, and at a higher scale of prices.

I walked downtown on Eighth Avenue to a point where the crowd began to thin out, and climbed into a taxi that had been stopped by the light on a cross street. This one had a Negro driver.

"The old fellow looked pretty good tonight," I said. "Had those combinations going."

"Fight over?" the driver asked. If there had been television, or even radio, he would have known about everything, and I wouldn't have had the fun of telling him.

"Sure," I said. "He knocked the guy out in the sixth."

"I was afraid he wouldn't," said the driver. "You know, it's a funny thing," he said, after we had gone on a way, "but I been twenty-five years in New York now and never seen Joe Louis in the flesh."

"You've seen him on television, haven't you?"

"Yeah," he said. "But that don't count." After a while he said, "I remember when he fought Carnera. The celebration in Harlem. They poisoned his mind before that fight, his managers and Jack Blackburn did. They told him Carnera was Mussolini's man and Mussolini started the Ethiopian War. He cut that man down like he was a tree."

WOODY ALLEN

"A Fan's Notes on Earl Monroe"

Toward the end of the 1976–77 basketball season, the editors of this magazine [*Sport*], aware of my interest in the game, called me and asked how I'd feel about covering the NBA playoffs for them. At first the idea seemed provocative, but then the thought of traveling around, and the time required to do a good job, not to mention the disappointment of the Knicks not making the playoffs, rendered the whole notion unappealing. But I said I wouldn't mind writing something about Earl Monroe, who had given me a great deal of pleasure watching him play over the years. I didn't really know Monroe, although we had exchanged several sentences on the Madison Square Garden floor two years ago. I was filming a comic sequence for my movie, *Annie Hall,* in which certain actors, including myself, played basketball against the Knicks. The sequence was later cut from the film because it didn't come off funny enough, but I did get to meet Monroe, who said hello and mentioned that he had received a fan letter I once sent him. He said it had meant something to him and that he had carried it around and showed it to friends. I didn't believe him because, exposed as I am to gratuitous pleasantries all the time in my profession, I am not a trusting person.

That was two years ago and it was the first and last time I met or spoke with Earl Monroe for any reason. When I suggested writing about him, *Sport*'s editors suggested I spend lots of time with him, at practice, in the Knick locker room, even travel with the team for an away game.

All these things seemed superfluous to me. My ideas on Monroe had nothing to do with getting the feel of the locker room, experiencing the smell of sweat, hearing the players curse, and all that rigmarole.

The truth was, I immediately saw myself cast in the role of the bespectacled, white, pseudo-intellectual trying to form a "heavy" thesis about a gift of grace and magical flair the black athlete possesses that can never be reduced to anything but poetry. I have always envied this gift and have often said that if I could live life over as someone else it would be wonderful to be Sugar Ray Robinson or Willie Mays. With my luck, however, I would undoubtedly wind up John Maynard Keynes.

Assured finally that Monroe was thrilled about the cover story and even invited by the great man to his house in eager anticipation of a long chat, I agreed to meet him for a few hours on the weekend. Of course, I knew there was also the outside chance that when I met the magician Earl Monroe he would be disappointing. This has happened to me before when I've met famous people whose work I've loved. Not every time. Not with Groucho Marx, for instance, but with certain other comedians and film directors who shall remain nameless. I did meet another magician who did not disappoint me. It was Stan Musial and he is indeed an amateur magician. For hours, in the bedroom at a party in Washington, D.C., he delighted me with astounding card tricks. It was quite thrilling to see the menacing left-handed slugger who had made my Brooklyn childhood miserable by lining one shot after another off of and over the rightfield wall at Ebbets Field, produce from his wallet the restored ace of spades that I had moments before torn up.

I didn't follow basketball until 1967. Baseball, boxing, and the theater provided most of my entertainment. The theater has since become boring and there are no plays approaching the pleasure given by a good sporting event. Even a game against a last-place team holds the possibility of thrills, whereas in the theater all seems relatively predictable. Baseball remains a joy for me, but basketball has emerged as the most beautiful of sports. In basketball, more than in virtually any other sport, personal style shines brightest. It allows for eccentric, individual play.

Give the basketball to such diverse talents as Julius Erving, Kareem Abdul-Jabbar, Walt Frazier, Rick Barry, George McGinnis, Dave Bing, or Bob McAdoo, to name a tiny fraction, and you get dramatically distinctive styles of dribbling, passing, shooting, and defensive play. There is great room in basketball for demonstrable physical artistry that often can be compared to serious dance.

So there I was in 1967 leafing through the sports section of a newspaper one day (I still read that section first) when I came across the name Earl Monroe. I had never heard of Monroe, knew nothing of his daily rookie brilliance, nor ever heard of his astounding feats at Winston-Salem. I just liked the name, free-floating, three syllables, and euphonious to me. Earl Monroe. The name worked. (Years later, when I did a film called *Sleeper,* I named myself Miles Monroe. On me it was kind of a funny name.) I came across Monroe's name again every few days as I glanced over the basketball box scores in a casual, disinterested way and noticed that he invariably led the scoring column.

Monroe 34, Monroe 36, Monroe 24, Monroe 28, Monroe 40! I was impressed by the consistent high numbers and repeated his name every now and then like it was a mantra. It still sounded musical. Earl Monroe. I think I even recall seeing a picture of him on the cover of *Sports Illustrated* that year and thinking he was very interesting looking. I was, and I don't know why, aware of Monroe in some special way. Although I didn't follow his sport much then, if someone had awakened me in the middle of the night and said, "Quick, name your favorite basketball player," I'd have snapped back: "Earl Monroe." This was probably his first working of magic on me, though I had no real idea of what Baltimore Bullet fans were witnessing and feeling each night when they saw him play and referred to him as the Pearl or Black Jesus.

The first time I saw Monroe, an actor friend said, "Come with me to the Garden tonight. I want you to see this guy. You'll like his style. It's real herky-jerky." That was in 1968. By then I was more interested in basketball and had begun following the Knicks a little. They had made the play-offs and had captured the imagination of New York. I went and saw Monroe score 32 points against Walt Frazier. This is Walt Frazier, mind you, who played the guard position as perfectly as it has ever been played and who was to be voted on the all-defensive team seven years running. Thirty-two points and Frazier said, "I had my hand in his face all night. He shoots without looking."

I went the next night too and while the Knicks double-teamed Monroe at every turn, he tore the place up with a buzzer beater that he flipped in as he ran across the midcourt line at halftime, and he kept running right into the locker room.

My impressions of Monroe then? I immediately ranked him with Willie Mays and Sugar Ray Robinson as athletes who went beyond the level of sports as sport to the realm of sports as art. Seemingly awkward and yet breathtakingly graceful, with an unimpressive physique, knobby knees, and the tiny ankles of a thoroughbred racehorse, Monroe in seasons to come would put on exhibition after exhibition of simply magical shot-making. One sportswriter wrote that his misses are more exciting than most guys' baskets. It's pointless to describe Monroe on the court. It's been done a thousand times by good writers who try vainly to communicate in print the excitement with which he plays. They refer to his head fakes, shoulder fakes, spins, double pumps, stutter steps, hip shots, arms and legs flying in different directions at once, but these things in themselves do not sum up the ferocious rush he gives the audience. After all, there are players like Nate Archibald, Dave Bing, Walt Frazier, Julius Erving, Connie Hawkins, who have unusual grace, beauty, and excitement, and who also dip and twist and toss their bodies one way while their arms move another way as they hang in space.

What makes Monroe different is the indescribable heat of genius that burns deep inside him. Some kind of diabolical intensity comes across his face when he has the ball. One is suddenly transported to a more primitive place. It's roots time. The eyes are big and white, the teeth flash, the nostrils flare. He dribbles the ball too high, but with a controlled violence. The audience gets high with anticipation of some new type of thrill about to occur. Seconds later he is moving in aggressively, one on one, against a defender and you sense the man is in trouble. Monroe is suddenly double-teamed and now there are two men hanging all over him. Then it happens. A quick twist, a sudden move, and he's by both men. Either that or a series of flashing arm moves cease with a lightning pass to a teammate he has never even bothered to look at.

It's amazing, because the audience's "high" originates inside Monroe and seems to emerge over his exterior. He creates a sense of danger in the arena and yet has enough wit in his style to bring off funny ideas when he wants to. He has, as an athlete-performer, what few actors possess. Marlon Brando is one such actor. The audience never knows what will happen next and the potential for a sudden great thrill is always present. If we think of an actor like George C. Scott, for instance, we feel he is consistently first rate, but he cannot move a crowd the way Brando does. There is something indescribable in Brando that pins an audience on the edge of its seats at all times. Perhaps because we sense a possible peak experience at any given moment, and when it occurs, the performance transcends mere acting and soars into the sublime. On a basketball court, Monroe does this to spectators.

I began watching the Baltimore Bullets, and while still a Knicks fan, always rooted for Monroe when Baltimore played New York. "We had no set offense," one Bullet player once said. "We gave the ball to Earl. He *was* our offense." The Bullets did very well with Monroe (not to mention such other great stars as Wes Unseld and Gus Johnson) and I followed his career like any dedicated fan. I was sorry I had missed his rookie year and his college games and I tried to imagine what he must have been like at that age, before the problems with his arthritic knees set in. Monroe is not overly fast these days, though he once was, but like the magician he is, he creates the *illusion* of speed. When he takes off with the ball and races the length of the court, he resembles an animated cartoon character whose feet never touch the floor. I recall a newspaper interview with Monroe after he had scored clusters of points against the Knicks in a playoff game, and he confessed to the desire to be a comedian. I thought, *A comedian? But why? Why would anyone want to be a comedian when he can do what* he *does?*

Then in 1971 he got traded to the Knicks. Naturally, I was happy to be able to watch him more often, but there were two uneasy questions. Could he play alongside Walt Frazier? Frazier was then the premier all-around guard in basketball and had set standards so high that years later when he might be off his game a fraction and could no longer single-handedly win games, the fans could not deal with it and turned on him. I found this unforgivable and it certainly says something about the myth of the New York sports fan.

In those days, however, Walt Frazier played with a serene brilliance that made it seem that he could steal the ball *whenever he wanted to,* dribble it behind his back, and score at will. He was wonderful to look at (great posture, perpetual "cool"), dressed flashy off the court, drove a Rolls, and got an awful lot of rebounds for a guard.

Monroe, who when he joined the Knicks reportedly said, "Man, I got two Rolls," was also used to being the cynosure of his team. He had never had to be overly concerned with defense and never had to share the limelight with anyone approaching Frazier's greatness. This didn't worry me, because I felt the two guards would be simply breathtaking together, which they indeed were. They played brilliantly in tandem. Frazier was the steadier of the two. He did everything perfectly. Monroe was, as always, the more dramatic and explosive one. Consequently, when Frazier dribbled up the middle you could count on your two points because of his smooth-as-satin style. When Monroe drove, his lust for danger took him in directions where he might get the ball slapped away or might miss a shot because of spectacular gyrations. Again, like Brando, Monroe takes risks, and while some fail, enough come off to make him an artist.

The second and more irritating question to me was, can Monroe fit into the flow of team play? Can he become part of that superb combination of Bill Bradley, Walt Frazier, Willis Reed, Dave DeBusschere, etc., that hits the open man, retains poise, and sooner or later grinds up opponents like a well-oiled machine? Some said Monroe would not be able to adjust. Others felt Monroe could learn to give off the ball, to play defense, to sublimate his brilliant one-on-one skills and contribute to this championship club. But I asked, why would anyone want that of him? After all, here is the single most exciting player in basketball, a solo performer. Do we really want him to abandon his individuality and become a cog in a machine? Would we ask Heifetz to become a sublimated member of the string section? Great Knick fan that I was, I would rather have seen the team set up Monroe for his dazzling solo feats than the other way around. Is winning so important that we can afford to sacrifice Monroe's essential gift to the game of basketball?

Now there were those who argued with me and said they derived more aesthetic satisfaction out of watching a five-man unit execute with the precision of the Knicks at their height. Nothing was more beautiful, they said, than the ball going from Frazier to Bradley, to DeBusschere, back to Frazier, to Reed for a basket. Well, what can I say? I don't agree. Perhaps because I'm a performer. Artistry like Monroe's does not come along often and I for one feel sacrifices must be made for art. It's great if the team wins (Baltimore did quite well with a Monroe-oriented offense), but if the price included the conformity of Earl Monroe to a patterned offense, I didn't like it.

The outcome we now know. Monroe learned defense. He modified his style in favor of team play. He scored fewer points. At other times, his irrepressible genius on the court asserted itself. The Knicks won with him until Reed and DeBusschere retired. Then Frazier and Monroe carried the offense. The team acquired other stars in Spencer Haywood and Bob McAdoo, but the Knicks have yet to jell. Monroe at 32 years old has emerged as the toast of New York's basketball fans because with the team's demise as a power, more and more they turned to his older one-on-one skills to get them out of jams.

While Knickerbocker problems seem to run deep, Monroe again burns brightly and enjoyed a great season in 1976–77. He has grown in all his skills and has returned to much of his own style of play. The difference now is that, if a given night demands it, he can play defense, hand off, steal, and quarterback the team. He is now the Knick captain. He is also still the magician. He might play a game as he did on January 1 and take ten shots and not miss one. Or he might win the game with a clutch basket in the last three seconds or, in the final ten minutes, score 16 of the Knicks' last 18 points. These are just a few feats he performed last year. When the fans see him pulling off his warmup jacket they get ready for the closest thing to a magical experience. They sense nature will be defied in some way.

At precisely two P.M., the appointed hour, I ring the bell of a fine old townhouse on New York's upper West Side. The name on the bell reads: Monroe. I am buzzed in and stand at the bottom of a staircase like a supplicant before Dr. No or the head of SMERSH. Suddenly an unbelievably beautiful woman descends the staircase and says with confidence unseen since the days of Mae West, "Hi—I'm Earl's lady." I smile, cough, look at my shoe tops, and mutter something that sounds like, "Aha-un-eh." As usual, I'm right on top of things. "Earl's not back yet. Would you care to wait?"

"Wait? Yes. Sure." The music from the rock station on the radio is flowing through the house at a level that would drown out the takeoff of an SST. I follow this utterly devastating woman up the stairs. The juxtaposition of our bodies causes me to think, my God, she's packed into those jeans with an ice cream scoop. We sit opposite one another and I manage to achieve maximum awkwardness in 30 seconds. To call "Earl's lady" beautiful is an understatement. I writhe, shuffle. She tells me her name is Tina and assures me Earl had some errands but was looking forward to our meeting. The house is simply furnished and here and there are mementoes of the great man's career. Plaques, photos, a game ball under glass, certificates of athletic achievement that bear the name Vernon Earl Monroe. (Vernon?) I learn through conversation with Tina that the photos of beautiful kids on the wall are Monroe's children from previous love affairs in other cities. "He's a good father," she tells me. "He loves his kids."

A half hour goes by as I chat with Tina. I learn how they met: at a disco-dance. I am told that Earl adores watching television. "There's a set in every room in the house and they're on all day and night." Tina tells me Earl eats lightly. Fish mostly. She says Earl took up tennis as a hobby a year or so ago and swiftly achieved tournament level ability. I learn that Knick players don't fraternize with one another that much, although they are friendly. An hour is gone. Still no Earl. Tina says that Earl has two cars and, unlike Clyde, no chauffeur because, "He's such a fantastic driver he could never have anyone else drive him." She says Dr. J has acknowledged Earl as an inspiration and model. Now and then the two phones ring and since they are identical but with different numbers, Tina must hold her hand on each instrument and feel it in order to tell which one is ringing.

"Earl's not here," she would tell various callers in her Mae West style, "he's been de-tained." I learn Earl and Tina stay in a lot, play board games, now and then dine late, sometimes around midnight, though then they might hit a dance hall and stay out late. They generally keep to themselves. I ask about a story on Earl wherein he quoted Descartes and Tina tells me, "He likes reading sports magazines mostly."

Hours have now gone by and we are out of conversation. Finally I must leave for another appointment. "Earl will be so disappointed he missed you," Tina says.

I back out the door, fumbling and apologizing, for what, I don't know. Then, walking home this sunny, Saturday afternoon, I think to myself, how wonderful. This great athlete is so unconcerned about the usual nonsense of social protocol. Unimpressed by me, a cover interview, and all the attendant fuss and adulation that so many people strive for, he simply fails to show up. Probably off playing tennis or fooling with his new Mercedes.

Whatever he was doing, I admired him for his total unconcern. Tina said he would be very upset that he had missed me, but I knew it was not the kind of thing Earl Monroe would dwell on with the anguish of a Raskolnikov.

That night Earl scored 28 points and had eight misses against Washington; the next day he tossed in 31 points against the same team.

I thought about how *Sport*'s editors had relayed Monroe's enthusiasm about the prospect of our interview. I thought, too, that if I had missed an interview I'd be consumed with guilt. But that's me and I'm not a guy who can ask for the ball with the team down by a point, two seconds left on the clock, and, with two players hacking at my body and shielding my vision, score from the corner. If I miss that basket and lose the game for my team, I commit suicide. For Monroe, well, he's as nonchalant about that tension-strung situation as he is about keeping appointments. That's why I'd tense up and blow clutch shots, while Monroe's seem to drop through the hoop like magic.

FREDERICK C. KLEIN

"Sports Talk with a Non-Fan"

I never have trouble making conversation with people I meet on airplanes. All I have to do is tell them that I write about sports and they open right up. Sports are a great bond among men (and some women, too), and even the dumbest guys have something to say on the subject.

Thus, I was taken aback some weeks ago when, on a Miami-to-Chicago flight, I found myself sitting next to someone who merely grimaced when I revealed my occupation. "It has always been my bad luck to be thrown in with sports fans," he said. "I can say without hesitation that I am not one."

The gentleman introduced himself as Robert Anderson, an agronomist on the faculty of the University of Minnesota. A few minutes of general chitchat revealed him to be an intelligent fellow, and a good-humored one to boot. After we got to know one another a bit, I expressed surprise that he, a middle-aged American, could expect to avoid sports. He conceded he had had some contact with them over the years.

"I've gone to two baseball games in my life—my first and my last," he quipped. "It was at Wrigley Field in Chicago, and I remember that the weather was chilly. Someone sang the national anthem nicely, but it was downhill from there. If it had been up to me, I'd have left after the third inning.

"I went to one football game in Minneapolis. Minnesota played the University of Nebraska, where I went to school. The only thing that kept it from being a total loss for me was that a dog got loose and ran around on the field.

"I took a group of Cub Scouts to see a hockey game once, but I didn't see much of it, because the kids kept racing off for hot dogs or to go to the washroom. I spent the whole evening worrying that the game would end and I'd have fewer kids than I brought."

Mr. Anderson said that he had made several stabs at informing himself about sports by reading newspaper sports pages, but the experiences left him feeling like a man from Mars. "Sports pages are written for the cognoscenti," he said. "You can read whole, long stories that never mention what sport they're about." (I've checked this out, and he's right!)

He said that he's not totally oblivious, and as a resident of Minneapolis knows who the Twins and Vikings are, but other sports-page terms still throw him. "What is the Stanley Cup?" he asked. "What is the USFL?" (What, indeed?)

"It's not because of lack of exposure that I'm not a fan; goodness knows, I've had my chances," he said. "As a scientist, I can only conclude that my aversion to sports is congenital. There must be something in me that doesn't allow them to 'take.'"

(I have long suspected the same thing. My 12-year old daughter, Jessie, has grown up in a household of avid fans, and has been dragged to numerous athletic contests. Yet every time the rest of us settle in for an evening of ballgame-watching on television, she wails "Sports again?!" and stomps away. I guess I'm going to have to get her a set of her own one of these days.)

Nonetheless, my flying companion noted that being a non-fan hasn't spared him the company of sports nuts. To the contrary, "at meetings and such, they seem to sense my presence and seek me out," he said. "For a long time I was faced with the choice of being rude and telling them to buzz off, or standing there and being bored."

Then, he went on, he discovered how to avoid both of those unpleasant alternatives. "I found out that if I could throw out one little line about sports—anything at all—they'd grab it and jabber on, ad infinitum. I could think my own thoughts while they were talking, and slip away gracefully after they were done."

Mr. Anderson's line was "the Twins haven't been the same since they traded Vic Power." He said it worked great for quite a while, but recently it has been getting him some funny looks. I said that was no wonder, because the Twins traded Power in 1964, and the memory of him might have dimmed for some.

He said he didn't realize that, and asked me if I could suggest another one. I told him I thought "Cal Griffith should sell the team" might do. He thought that seemed too obvious ("you have to show *some* sophistication"), but he said he'd think it over.

I've thought it over, too, and I've decided that a sports column ought to be of use to everyone once in a while. So here are a few getaway lines for you non-fans out there:

"The Phillies blew the pennant when they traded away Reed and Hernandez."

"Bob Horner would be a heckuva lot better hitter if he'd lose 20 pounds."

"If the refs called all the fouls they should on Moses Malone, he'd never finish a game."

"Joe Namath was a better quarterback than any of those guys who are around now."

"The Vikings will never be the same without Bud Grant."

Oh yes. The sports involved in the above statements are baseball, basketball, football, and football. And the Twins are a baseball team.

JAMES LIPTON

FROM *An Exaltation of Larks*

James Lipton's Exaltation of Larks *is the definitive book on group terms, collectives—his own as well as traditional—from five hundred years ago (a murder of crows, a pride of lions, a parliament of owls) to the contemporary (a slouch of models, a wince of dentists, an om of Buddhists). Here are a few of Lipton's inspired inventions from the world of sports.*

FOOTBALL

A cuss of coaches
A pocket of quarterbacks
A sack of linebackers
A run of backs
A pit of linemen
A frenzy of cheerleaders

BASEBALL

A crouch of catchers
A mound of pitchers
A deck of batters
A spit of benchwarmers
A myopia of umpires

HOCKEY

A faceoff of centers
A score of forwards
A slash of defensemen
A sprawl of goalies

BASKETBALL

A dribble of guards
A liftoff of forwards
A block of centers
An oops of turnovers
A conniption of coaches
An outrage of basketball fans

THE BEST OF THE REST

A tumble of gymnasts
A perch of jockeys
A parlay of horseplayers
A pitch of soccer players
A roquet of croquet players
A massé of pool players
A draft of race drivers
A volley of tennis players
A raft of swimmers
A tube of surfers
An uprising of mountaineers
A lie of golfers
A skitter of golf carts
A wheeze of joggers
A bowl of keglers (or vice versa)
A buzz of flyweights
A quarrel of commissioners
A slam of wrestlers
A grand slam of tag team wrestlers
A mountain of sumo wrestlers

SIR EDMUND HILLARY

"ADVENTURE'S END"

*Climbers have written wondrously about the mountains (see my intro-
duction and the "Uh-Oh Theory"). Perhaps the most admired of their
work is Maurice Herzog's* Annapurna, *an account of scaling that Hima-
layan peak in 1952. It proved to be a terrifying ordeal: frostbite damaged
Herzog's limbs, particularly his feet, most of which had to be carved
away. After being carried off the mountain on a stretcher, in an ironic
twist Herzog received the highest Gurkha award for valor—the Gurkha
Right Hand! The sacrifice was apparently worth it as the last paragraph
of his book suggests. "For us the mountains had been a natural field of
activity where, playing in the frontiers of life and death, we had found
the freedom for which we were blindly groping and which was as necessary to us as bread. The mountains had bestowed on us their beauties,
and we adored them with a child's simplicity and revered them with a
monk's veneration of the divine. Annapurna, to which we had gone
empty-handed, was a treasure on which we should live the rest of our
days. With this realization we turn the page: a new life begins.*

"There are other Annapurnas in the lives of men."

I was tempted to pick a section from Annapurna *but chose instead a
section of* High Adventure, *Sir Edmund Hillary's account of his successful ascent of Mount Everest. It is as dramatically described, and of
course the mountain, at 29,028 feet, is the highest in the world. I was in
London at the time to watch Queen Elizabeth's coronation. The timing
was perfect. The news about the successful climb came in the evening
before. "A gift for Her Majesty!" the newsboys shouted in the streets.*

*Many years after his ascent, I had the privilege of interviewing Sir
Hillary. As one might expect of the "gentle beekeeper" (in fact, he told
me he had not looked into a beehive for twenty-odd years), he was
quietly self-deprecatory about what he had done. His account was full of
practical, understated comments: "Everest is not a particularly beautiful
mountain," he said, "but when you look at it, you have the feeling it's
going to take a lot of work to get to the top." When I asked about his
feelings at the summit (which he described as a rounded knoll of snow
and ice on which six to eight people could have stood, though not espe-*

cially comfortably since the east face drops off abruptly thousands of feet
to the glacier below), he said that after a moment of "quiet satisfaction,
no ecstasy," he began worrying about how to get down.

This account starts with the final assault from the ninth camp, only
1,100 feet below the summit. The first assault pair, Bourdillon and
Evans, had failed because of bad weather. That left the opportunity to
the second team—Hillary and the Sherpa, Tenzing.

At 6:30 A.M. we crawled slowly out of the tent and stood on our little
ledge. Already the upper part of the mountain was bathed in sunlight. It
looked warm and inviting, but our ledge was dark and cold. We lifted
our oxygen on to our backs and slowly connected up the tubes to our
face-masks. My 30-pound load seemed to crush me downward and stifled
all enthusiasm, but when I turned on the oxygen and breathed it deeply,
the burden seemed to lighten and the old urge to get to grips with the
mountain came back. We strapped on our crampons and tied on our
nylon rope; grasped our ice-axes and were ready to go.

I looked at the way ahead. From our tent very steep slopes covered
with deep powder snow led up to a prominent snow shoulder on the
Southeast ridge about a hundred feet above our heads. The slopes were
in the shade and breaking trail was going to be cold work. Still a little
worried about my boots, I asked Tenzing to lead off. Always willing to do
his share, and more than his share if necessary, Tenzing scrambled past
me and tackled the slope. With powerful thrusts of his legs he forced his
way up in knee-deep snow. I gathered in the rope and followed along
behind him.

We were climbing out over the tremendous South face of the mountain, and below us snow chutes and rock ribs plummeted thousands of
feet down to the Western Cwm. Starting in the morning straight on to
exposed climbing is always trying for the nerves, and this was no exception. In imagination I could feel my heavy load dragging me backward
down the great slopes below; I seemed clumsy and unstable and my
breath was hurried and uneven. But Tenzing was pursuing an irresistible
course up the slope, and I didn't have time to think too much. My
muscles soon warmed up to their work, my nerves relaxed, and I dropped
into the old climbing rhythm and followed steadily up his tracks. As we
gained a little height we moved into the rays of the sun, and although we
could feel no appreciable warmth, we were greatly encouraged by its
presence. Taking no rests, Tenzing ploughed his way up through the
deep snow and led out onto the snow shoulder. We were now at a height

of 28,000 feet. Towering directly above our heads was the South Summit—steep and formidable. And to the right were the enormous cornices of the summit ridge. We still had a long way to go.

Ahead of us the ridge was sharp and narrow, but rose at an easy angle. I felt warm and strong now, so took over the lead. First I investigated the ridge with my ice-axe. On the sharp crest of the ridge and on the right-hand side loose powder snow was lying dangerously over hard ice. Any attempt to climb on this would only produce an unpleasant slide down toward the Kangshung glacier. But the left-hand slope was better—it was still rather steep, but it had a firm surface of wind-blown powder snow into which our crampons would bite readily.

Taking every care, I moved along onto the left-hand side of the ridge. Everything seemed perfectly safe. With increased confidence, I took another step. Next moment I was almost thrown off balance as the wind-crust suddenly gave way and I sank through it up to my knee. It took me a little while to regain my breath. Then I gradually pulled my leg out of the hole. I was almost upright again when the wind-crust under the other foot gave way and I sank back with both legs enveloped in soft, loose snow to the knees. It was the mountaineer's curse—breakable crust. I forced my way along. Sometimes for a few careful steps I was on the surface, but usually the crust would break at the critical moment and I'd be up to my knees again. Though it was tiring and exasperating work, I felt I had plenty of strength in reserve. For half an hour I continued on in this uncomfortable fashion, with the violent balancing movements I was having to make completely destroying rhythm and breath. It was a great relief when the snow conditions improved and I was able to stay on the surface. I still kept down on the steep slopes on the left of the ridge, but plunged ahead and climbed steadily upward. I came over a small crest and saw in front of me a tiny hollow on the ridge. And in this hollow lay two oxygen bottles almost completely covered with snow. It was Evans' and Bourdillon's dump.

I rushed forward into the hollow and knelt beside them. Wrenching one of the bottles out of its frozen bed I wiped the snow off its dial—it showed a thousand-pounds pressure—it was nearly a third full of oxygen. I checked the other—it was the same. This was great news. It meant that the oxygen we were carrying on our backs only had to get us back to these bottles instead of right down to the South Col. It gave us more than another hour of endurance. I explained this to Tenzing through my oxygen mask. I don't think he understood, but he realized I was pleased about something and nodded enthusiastically.

I led off again. I knew there was plenty of hard work ahead and Tenzing could save his energies for that. The ridge climbed on upward rather more steeply now, and then broadened out and shot up at a sharp angle to the foot of the enormous slope running up to the South Summit. I crossed over onto the right-hand side of the ridge and found the snow was firm there. I started chipping a long line of steps up to the foot of the great slope. Here we stamped out a platform for ourselves and I checked our oxygen. Everything seemed to be going well. I had a little more oxygen left than Tenzing, which meant I was obtaining a slightly lower flow rate from my set, but it wasn't enough to matter and there was nothing I could do about it, anyway.

Ahead of us was a really formidable problem, and I stood in my steps and looked at it. Rising from our feet was an enormous slope slanting steeply down onto the precipitous East face of Everest and climbing up with appalling steepness to the South Summit of the mountain 400 feet above us. The left-hand side of the slope was a most unsavory mixture of steep loose rock and snow, which my New Zealand training immediately regarded with grave suspicion, but which in actual fact the rock-climbing Britons, Evans and Bourdillon, had ascended in much trepidation when on the first assault. The only other route was up the snow itself and still faintly discernible here and there were traces of the track made by the first assault party, who had come down it in preference to their line of ascent up the rocks. The snow route it was for us! There looked to be some tough work ahead, and as Tenzing had been taking it easy for a while I hard-heartedly waved him through. With his first six steps I realized that the work was going to be much harder than I had thought. His first two steps were on top of the snow, the third was up to his ankles, and by the sixth he was up to his hips. But almost lying against the steep slope, he drove himself onward, ploughing a track directly upward. Even following in his steps was hard work, for the loose snow refused to pack into safe steps. After a long and valiant spell he was plainly in need of a rest, so I took over.

Immediately I realized that we were on dangerous ground. On this very steep slope the snow was soft and deep with little coherence. My ice-axe shaft sank into it without any support and we had no sort of a belay. The only factor that made it at all possible to progress was a thin crust of frozen snow which tied the whole slope together. But this crust was a poor support. I was forcing my way upward, plunging deep steps through it, when suddenly with a dull breaking noise an area of crust all around me about six feet in diameter broke off into large sections and slid with me back through three or four steps. And then I stopped; but the crust, gathering speed, slithered on out of sight. It was a nasty shock. My whole training told me that the slope was exceedingly dangerous, but at the same time I was saying to myself: "Ed, my boy, this is Ever-

est—you've got to push it a bit harder!" My solar plexus was tight with
fear as I ploughed on. Halfway up I stopped, exhausted. I could look
down 10,000 feet between my legs, and I have never felt more insecure.
Anxiously I waved Tenzing up to me.

"What do you think of it, Tenzing?" And the immediate response,
"Very bad, very dangerous!" "Do you think we should go on?" and there
came the familiar reply that never helped you much but never let you
down: "Just as you wish!" I waved him on to take a turn at leading.
Changing the lead much more frequently now, we made our unhappy
way upward, sometimes sliding back and wiping out half a dozen steps,
and never feeling confident that at any moment the whole slope might
not avalanche. In the hope of some sort of a belay we traversed a little
toward the rocks, but found no help in their smooth, holdless surfaces.
We plunged on upward. And then I noticed that, a little above us, the
left-hand rock ridge turned into snow and the snow looked firm and safe.
Laboriously and carefully we climbed across some steep rock, and I sank
my ice-axe shaft into the snow of the ridge. It went in firm and hard. The
pleasure of this safe belay after all the uncertainty below was like a
reprieve to a condemned man. Strength flowed into my limbs, and I
could feel my tense nerves and muscles relaxing. I swung my ice-axe at
the slope and started chipping a line of steps upward—it was very steep,
but seemed so gloriously safe. Tenzing, an inexpert but enthusiastic step
cutter, took a turn and chopped a haphazard line of steps up another
pitch. We were making fast time now and the slope was starting to ease
off. Tenzing gallantly waved me through, and with a growing feeling of
excitement I cramponed up some firm slopes to the rounded top of the
South Summit. It was only 9 A.M.

With intense interest I looked at the vital ridge leading to the summit—the ridge about which Evans and Bourdillon had made such
gloomy forecasts. At first glance it was an exceedingly impressive and
indeed a frightening sight. In the narrow crest of this ridge, the basic
rock of the mountain had a thin capping of snow and ice—ice that
reached out over the East face in enormous cornices, overhanging and
treacherous, and only waiting for the careless foot of the mountaineer to
break off and crash 10,000 feet to the Kangshung glacier. And from the
cornices the snow dropped steeply to the left to merge with the enormous rock bluffs which towered 8,000 feet above the Western Cwm. It
was impressive all right! But as I looked my fears started to lift a little.
Surely I could see a route there? For this snow slope on the left, although
very steep and exposed, was practically continuous for the first half of the
ridge, although in places the great cornices reached hungrily across. If
we could make a route along that snow slope, we could go quite a distance at least.

With a feeling almost of relief, I set to work with my ice-axe and cut a platform for myself just down off the top of the South Summit. Tenzing did the same, and then we removed our oxygen sets and sat down. The day was still remarkably fine, and we felt no discomfort through our thick layers of clothing from either wind or cold. We had a drink out of Tenzing's water-bottle and then I checked our oxygen supplies. Tenzing's bottle was practically exhausted, but mine still had a little in it. As well as this, we each had a full bottle. I decided that the difficulties ahead would demand as light a weight on our backs as possible so determined to use only the full bottles. I removed Tenzing's empty bottle and my nearly empty one and laid them in the snow. With particular care I connected up our last bottles and tested to see that they were working efficiently. The needles on the dials were steady on 3,300 pounds per square inch pressure—they were very full bottles holding just over 800 liters of oxygen each. At three liters a minute we consumed 180 liters an hour, and this meant a total endurance of nearly four and a half hours. This didn't seem much for the problems ahead, but I was determined if necessary to cut down to two liters a minute for the homeward trip.

I was greatly encouraged to find how, even at 28,700 feet and with no oxygen, I could work out slowly but clearly the problems of mental arithmetic that the oxygen supply demanded. A correct answer was imperative—any mistake could well mean a trip with no return. But we had no time to waste. I stood up and took a series of photographs in every direction, then thrust my camera back to its warm home inside my clothing. I heaved my now pleasantly light oxygen load onto my back and connected up my tubes. I did the same for Tenzing, and we were ready to go. I asked Tenzing to belay me and then, with a growing air of excitement, I cut a broad and safe line of steps down to the snow saddle below the South Summit. I wanted an easy route when we came back up here weak and tired. Tenzing came down the steps and joined me, and then belayed once again.

I moved along onto the steep snow slope on the left side of the ridge. With the first blow of my ice-axe my excitement increased. The snow— to my astonishment—was crystalline and hard. A couple of rhythmical blows of the ice-axe produced a step that was big enough even for our oversize high-altitude boots. But best of all the steps were strong and safe. A little conscious of the great drops beneath me, I chipped a line of steps for the full length of the rope—forty feet—and then forced the shaft of my ice-axe firmly into the snow. It made a fine belay and I looped the rope around it. I waved to Tenzing to join me, and as he moved slowly and carefully along the steps I took in the rope. When he reached me, he thrust his ice-axe into the snow and protected me with a good tight rope as I went on cutting steps. It was exhilarating work—the summit ridge of Everest, the crisp snow, and the smooth easy blows of the ice-axe all combined to make me feel a greater sense of power than I had ever felt at great altitudes before. I went on cutting for rope length after rope length.

We were now approaching a point where one of the great cornices was encroaching onto our slope. We'd have to go down to the rocks to avoid it. I cut a line of steps steeply down the slope to a small ledge on top of the rocks. There wasn't much room, but it made a reasonably safe stance. I waved to Tenzing to join me. As he came down to me I realized there was something wrong with him. I had been so absorbed in the technical problems of the ridge that I hadn't thought much about Tenzing, except for a vague feeling that he seemed to move along the steps with unnecessary slowness. But now it was quite obvious that he was not only moving extremely slowly, but he was breathing quickly and with difficulty and was in considerable distress. I immediately suspected his oxygen set and helped him down onto the ledge so that I could examine it. The first thing I noticed was that from the outlet of his face-mask there were hanging some long icicles. I looked at it more closely and found that the outlet tube—about two inches in diameter—was almost completely blocked up with ice. This was preventing Tenzing from exhaling freely and must have made it extremely unpleasant for him. Fortunately the outlet tube was made of rubber and by manipulating this with my hand I was able to release all the ice and let it fall out. The valves started operating and Tenzing was given immediate relief. Just as a check I examined my own set and found that it, too, had partly frozen up in the outlet tube, but not sufficiently to have affected me a great deal. I removed the ice out of it without a great deal of trouble. Automatically I looked at our pressure gauges—just over 2,900 pounds (2,900 pounds was just over 700 liters; 180 into 700 was about 4)—we had nearly four hours' endurance left. That meant we weren't going badly.

I looked at the route ahead. This next piece wasn't going to be easy. Our rock ledge was perched right on top of the enormous bluff running down into the Western Cwm. In fact, almost under my feet, I could see the dirty patch on the floor of the Cwm which I knew was Camp IV. In a sudden urge to escape our isolation I waved and shouted, and then as suddenly stopped as I realized my foolishness. Against the vast expanse of Everest, 8,000 feet above them, we'd be quite invisible to the best binoculars. I turned back to the problem ahead. The rock was far too steep to attempt to drop down and go around this pitch. The only thing to do was to try to shuffle along the ledge and cut handholds in the bulging ice that was trying to push me off it. Held on a tight rope by Tenzing, I cut a few handholds and then thrust my ice-axe as hard as I could into the solid snow and ice. Using this to take my weight I moved quickly along the ledge. It proved easier than I had anticipated. A few more handholds, another quick swing across them, and I was able to cut a line of steps up onto a safe slope and chop out a roomy terrace from which to belay Tenzing as he climbed up to me.

We were now fast approaching the most formidable obstacle on the ridge—a great rock step. This step had always been visible in aerial photographs, and in 1951 on the Everest Reconnaissance we had seen it quite clearly with glasses from Thyangboche. We had always thought of it as the obstacle on the ridge which could well spell defeat. I cut a line of steps across the last snow slope, and then commenced traversing over a steep rock slab that led to the foot of the great step. The holds were small and hard to see, and I brushed my snow-glasses away from my eyes. Immediately I was blinded by a bitter wind sweeping across the ridge and laden with particles of ice. I hastily replaced my glasses and blinked away the ice and tears until I could see again. But it made me realize how efficient was our clothing in protecting us from the rigors of even a fine day at 29,000 feet. Still half blinded, I climbed across the slab, and then dropped down into a tiny snow hollow at the foot of the step. And here Tenzing joined me.

I looked anxiously up at the rocks. Planted squarely across the ridge in a vertical bluff, they looked extremely difficult, and I knew that our strength and ability to climb steep rock at this altitude would be severely limited. I examined the route out to the left. By dropping fifty or a hundred feet over steep slabs, we might be able to get around the bottom of the bluff, but there was no indication that we'd be able to climb back onto the ridge again. And to lose any height now might be fatal. Search as I could, I was unable to see an easy route up to the step or, in fact, any route at all. Finally, in desperation I examined the right-hand end of the bluff. Attached to this and overhanging the precipitous East face was a large cornice. This cornice, in preparation for its inevitable crash down the mountainside, had started to lose its grip on the rock and a long narrow vertical crack had been formed between the rock and the ice. The crack was large enough to take the human frame, and though it offered little security, it was at least a route. I quickly made up my mind—Tenzing had an excellent belay and we must be near the top—it was worth a try.

Before attempting the pitch, I produced my camera once again. I had no confidence that I would be able to climb this crack, and with a surge of competitive pride which unfortunately afflicts even mountaineers, I determined to have proof that at least we had reached a good deal higher than the South Summit. I took a few photographs and then made another rapid check of the oxygen—2,550 pounds pressure. (Two thousand five hundred and fifty from 3,300 leaves 750; 750 over 3,300 is about two-ninths; two-ninths off 800 liters leaves about 600 liters; 600 divided by 180 is nearly 3½.) Three and a half hours to go. I examined Tenzing's belay to make sure it was a good one and then slowly crawled inside the crack.

In front of me was the rock wall, vertical but with a few promising holds. Behind me was the ice-wall of the cornice, glittering and hard but cracked here and there. I took a hold on the rock in front and then jammed one of my crampons hard into the ice behind. Leaning back with my oxygen set on the ice, I slowly levered myself upward. Searching feverishly with my spare boot, I found a tiny ledge on the rock and took some of the weight off my other leg. Leaning back on the cornice, I fought to regain my breath. Constantly at the back of my mind was the fear that the cornice might break off, and my nerves were taut with suspense. But slowly I forced my way up—wriggling and jambing and using every little hold. In one place I managed to force my ice-axe into a crack in the ice, and this gave me the necessary purchase to get over a holdless stretch. And then I found a solid foothold in a hollow in the ice, and next moment I was reaching over the top of the rock and pulling myself to safety. The rope came tight—its forty feet had been barely enough.

I lay on the little rock ledge panting furiously. Gradually it dawned on me that I was up the step, and I felt a glow of pride and determination that completely subdued my temporary feelings of weakness. For the first time on the whole expedition I really knew I was going to get to the top. "It will have to be pretty tough to stop us now" was my thought. But I couldn't entirely ignore the feeling of astonishment and wonder that I'd been able to get up such a difficulty at 29,000 feet even with oxygen.

When I was breathing more evenly I stood up and, leaning over the edge, waved to Tenzing to come up. He moved into the crack and I gathered in the rope and took some of his weight. Then he, in turn, commenced to struggle and jam and force his way up until I was able to pull him to safety—gasping for breath. We rested for a moment. Above us the ridge continued on as before—enormous overhanging cornices on the right and steep snow slopes on the left running down to the rock bluffs. But the angle of the snow slopes was easing off. I went on chipping a line of steps, but thought it safe enough for us to move together in order to save time. The ridge rose up in a great series of snakelike undulations which bore away to the right, each one concealing the next. I had no idea where the top was. I'd cut a line of steps around the side of one undulation and another would come into view. We were getting desperately tired now and Tenzing was going very slowly. I'd been cutting steps for almost two hours, and my back and arms were starting to tire. I tried cramponing along the slope without cutting steps, but my feet slipped uncomfortably down the slope. I went on cutting. We seemed to have been going for a very long time and my confidence was fast evaporating. Bump followed bump with maddening regularity. A patch of shingle barred our way, and I climbed dully up it and started cutting steps around another bump. And then I realized that this was the last bump, for ahead of me the ridge dropped steeply away in a great corniced curve, and out in the distance I could see the pastel shades and fleecy clouds of the highlands of Tibet.

To my right a slender snow ridge climbed up to a snowy dome about forty feet above our heads. But all the way along the ridge the thought had haunted me that the summit might be the crest of a cornice. It was too late to take risks now. I asked Tenzing to belay me strongly, and I started cutting a cautious line of steps up the ridge. Peering from side to side and thrusting with my ice-axe, I tried to discover a possible cornice, but everything seemed solid and firm. I waved Tenzing up to me. A few more whacks of the ice-axe, a few very weary steps, and we were on the summit of Everest.

It was 11:30 A.M. My first sensation was one of relief—relief that the long grind was over; that the summit had been reached before our oxygen supplies had dropped to a critical level; and relief that in the end the mountain had been kind to us in having a pleasantly rounded cone for its summit instead of a fearsome and unapproachable cornice. But mixed with the relief was a vague sense of astonishment that I should have been the lucky one to attain the ambition of so many brave and determined climbers. It seemed difficult at first to grasp that we'd got there. I was too tired and too conscious of the long way down to safety really to feel any great elation. But as the fact of our success thrust itself more clearly into my mind, I felt a quiet glow of satisfaction spread through my body—a satisfaction less vociferous but more powerful than I had ever felt on a mountain top before. I turned and looked at Tenzing. Even beneath his oxygen mask and the icicles hanging from his hair, I could see his infectious grin of sheer delight. I held out my hand, and in silence we shook in good Anglo-Saxon fashion. But this was not enough for Tenzing, and impulsively he threw his arm around my shoulders and we thumped each other on the back in mutual congratulations.

But we had no time to waste! First I must take some photographs and then we'd hurry down. I turned off my oxygen and took the set off my back. I remembered all the warnings I'd had of the possible fatal consequences of this, but for some reason felt quite confident that nothing serious would result. I took my camera out of the pocket of my windproof and clumsily opened it with my thickly gloved hands. I clipped on the lenshood and ultraviolet filter and then shuffled down the ridge a little so that I could get the summit into my viewfinder. Tenzing had been waiting patiently, but now, at my request, he unfurled the flags wrapped around his ice-axe and standing on the summit held them above his head. Clad in all his bulky equipment and with the flags flapping furiously in the wind, he made a dramatic picture, and the thought drifted through my mind that this photograph should be a good one if it came out at all. I didn't worry about getting Tenzing to take a photograph of me—as far as I knew, he had never taken a photograph before and the summit of Everest was hardly the place to show him how.

I climbed up to the top again and started taking a photographic record in every direction. The weather was still extraordinarily fine. High above us were long streaks of cirrus wind cloud and down below fluffy cumulus hid the valley floors from view. But wherever we looked, icy peaks and somber gorges lay beneath us like a relief map. Perhaps the view was most spectacular to the east, for here the giants Makalu and Kanchenjunga dominated the horizon and gave some idea of the vast scale of the Himalayas. Makalu in particular, with its soaring rock ridges, was a remarkable sight; it was only a few miles away from us. From our exalted viewpoint I could see all the northern slopes of the mountain and was immediately struck by the possibility of a feasible route to its summit. With a growing feeling of excitement, I took another photograph to study at leisure on returning to civilization. The view to the north was a complete contrast—hundreds of miles of the arid high Tibetan plateau, softened now by a veil of fleecy clouds into a scene of delicate beauty. To the west the Himalayas stretched hundreds of miles in a tangled mass of peaks, glaciers, and valleys.

But one scene was of particular interest. Almost under our feet, it seemed, was the famous North Col and the East Rongbuk glacier, where so many epic feats of courage and endurance were performed by the earlier British Everest Expeditions. Part of the ridge up which they had established their high camps was visible, but the last thousand feet, which had proved such a formidable barrier, was concealed from our view as its rock slopes dropped away with frightening abruptness from the summit snow pyramid. It was a sobering thought to remember how often these men had reached 28,000 feet without the benefits of our modern equipment and reasonably efficient oxygen sets. Inevitably my thoughts turned to Mallory and Irvine, who had lost their lives on the mountain thirty years before. With little hope I looked around for some sign that they had reached the summit, but could see nothing.

Meanwhile Tenzing had also been busy. On the summit he'd scratched out a little hole in the snow, and in this he placed some small offerings of food—some biscuits, a piece of chocolate, and a few sweets—a small gift to the Gods of Chomolungma which all devout Buddhists (as Tenzing is) believe to inhabit the summit of this mountain. Besides the food, I placed the little cross that John Hunt had given me on the South Col. Strange companions, no doubt, but symbolical at least of the spiritual strength and peace that all peoples have gained from the mountains.

P. G. WODEHOUSE

"The Heart of a Goof"

P. G. Wodehouse wrote about golf in several dozen short stories. A collection was entitled Divots. *Most of the tales used the device (as this one does) of an exchange on the clubhouse porch between the "Oldest Member," wise in years, and a young golfer inevitably in despair about either his golfing game or his love life, often both, and who is put right by the Oldest Member, almost always by a parable involving golf.*

It was a morning when all nature shouted "Fore!" The breeze, as it blew gently up from the valley, seemed to bring a message of hope and cheer, whispering of chip-shots holed and brassies landing squarely on the meat. The fairway, as yet unscarred by the irons of a hundred dubs, smiled greenly up at the azure sky; and the sun, peeping above the trees, looked like a giant golfball perfectly lofted by the mashie of some unseen god and about to drop dead by the pin of the eighteenth. It was the day of the opening of the course after the long winter, and a crowd of considerable dimensions had collected at the first tee. Plus fours gleamed in the sunshine, and the air was charged with happy anticipation.

In all that gay throng there was but one sad face. It belonged to the man who was waggling his driver over the new ball perched on its little hill of sand. This man seemed careworn, hopeless. He gazed down the fairway, shifted his feet, waggled, gazed down the fairway again, shifted the dogs once more, and waggled afresh. He waggled as Hamlet might have waggled, moodily, irresolutely. Then, at last, he swung, and, taking from his caddie the niblick which the intelligent lad had been holding in readiness from the moment when he had walked on to the tee, trudged wearily off to play his second.

The Oldest Member, who had been observing the scene with a benevolent eye from his favourite chair on the terrace, sighed.

"Poor Jenkinson," he said, "does not improve."

"No," agreed his companion, a young man with open features and a handicap of six. "And yet I happen to know that he has been taking lessons all the winter at one of those indoor places."

"Futile, quite futile," said the Sage with a shake of his snowy head. "There is no wizard living who could make that man go round in an average of sevens. I keep advising him to give up the game."

"You!" cried the young man, raising a shocked and startled face from the driver with which he was toying. "*You* told him to give up golf! Why I thought—"

"I understand and approve of your horror," said the Oldest Member, gently. "But you must bear in mind that Jenkinson's is not an ordinary case. You know and I know scores of men who have never broken a hundred and twenty in their lives, and yet contrive to be happy, useful members of society. However badly they may play, they are able to forget. But with Jenkinson it is different. He is not one of those who can take it or leave it alone. His only chance of happiness lies in complete abstinence. Jenkinson is a goof."

"A what?"

"A goof," repeated the Sage. "One of those unfortunate beings who have allowed this noblest of sports to get too great a grip upon them, who have permitted it to eat into their souls, like some malignant growth. The goof, you must understand, is not like you and me. He broods. He becomes morbid. His goofery unfits him for the battles of life. Jenkinson, for example, was once a man with a glowing future in the hay, corn, and feed business, but a constant stream of hooks, tops, and slices gradually made him so diffident and mistrustful of himself, that he let opportunity after opportunity slip, with the result that other, sterner, hay, corn, and feed merchants passed him in the race. Every time he had the chance to carry through some big deal in hay, or to execute some flashing *coup* in corn and feed, the fatal diffidence generated by a hundred rotten rounds would undo him. I understand his bankruptcy may be expected at any moment."

"My golly!" said the young man, deeply impressed. "I hope I never become a goof. Do you mean to say there is really no cure except giving up the game?"

The Oldest Member was silent for a while.

"It is curious that you should have asked that question," he said at last, "for only this morning I was thinking of the one case in my experience where a goof was enabled to overcome his deplorable malady. It was owing to a girl, of course. The longer I live, the more I come to see that most things are. But you will, no doubt, wish to hear the story from the beginning."

The young man rose with the startled haste of some wild creature, which, wandering through the undergrowth, perceives the trap in his path.

"I should love to," he mumbled, "only I shall be losing my place at the tee."

"The goof in question," said the Sage, attaching himself with quiet firmness to the youth's coat-button, "was a man of about your age, by name Ferdinand Dibble. I knew him well. In fact, it was to me—"

"Some other time, eh?"

"It was to me," proceeded the Sage, placidly, "that he came for sympathy in the great crisis of his life, and I am not ashamed to say that when he had finished laying bare his soul to me there were tears in my eyes. My heart bled for the boy."

"I bet it did. But—"

The Oldest Member pushed him gently back into his seat.

"Golf," he said, "is the Great Mystery. Like some capricious goddess—"

The young man, who had been exhibiting symptoms of feverishness, appeared to become resigned. He sighed softly.

"Did you ever read 'The Ancient Mariner'?" he said.

"Many years ago," said the Oldest Member. "Why do you ask?"

"Oh, I don't know," said the young man. "It just occurred to me."

Golf (resumed the Oldest Member) is the Great Mystery. Like some capricious goddess, it bestows its favours with what would appear an almost fat-headed lack of method and discrimination. On every side we see big two-fisted he-men floundering round in three figures, stopping every few minutes to let through little shrimps with knock knees and hollow cheeks, who are tearing off snappy seventy-fours. Giants of finance have to accept a stroke per from their junior clerks. Men capable of governing empires fail to control a small, white ball, which presents no difficulties whatever to others with one ounce more brain than a cuckoo-clock. Mysterious, but there it is. There was no apparent reason why Ferdinand Dibble should not have been a competent golfer. He had strong wrists and a good eye. Nevertheless, the fact remains that he was a dub. And on a certain evening in June I realised that he was also a goof. I found it out quite suddenly as the result of a conversation which we had on this very terrace.

I was sitting here that evening thinking of this and that, when by the corner of the clubhouse I observed young Dibble in conversation with a girl in white. I could not see who she was, for her back was turned. Presently they parted and Ferdinand came slowly across to where I sat. His air was dejected. He had had the boots licked off him earlier in the afternoon by Jimmy Fothergill, and it was to this that I attributed his gloom. I was to find out in a few moments that I was partly but not entirely correct in this surmise. He took the next chair to mine, and for several minutes sat staring moodily down into the valley.

"I've just been talking to Barbara Medway," he said, suddenly breaking the silence.

"Indeed?" I said. "A delightful girl."

"She's going away for the summer to Marvis Bay."

"She will take the sunshine with her."

"You bet she will!" said Ferdinand Dibble, with extraordinary warmth, and there was another long silence.

Presently Ferdinand uttered a hollow groan.

"I love her, dammit!" he muttered brokenly. "Oh, golly, how I love her!"

I was not surprised at his making me the recipient of his confidences like this. Most of the young folk in the place brought their troubles to me sooner or later.

"And does she return your love?"

"I don't know. I haven't asked her."

"Why not? I should have thought the point not without its interest for you."

Ferdinand gnawed the handle of his putter distractedly.

"I haven't the nerve," he burst out at length. "I simply can't summon up the cold gall to ask a girl, least of all an angel like her, to marry me. You see, it's like this. Every time I work myself up to the point of having a dash at it, I go out and get trimmed by some one giving me a stroke a hole. Every time I feel I've mustered up enough pep to propose, I take ten on a bogey three. Every time I think I'm in good mid-season form for putting my fate to the test, to win or lose it all, something goes all blooey with my swing, and I slice into the rough at every tee. And then my self-confidence leaves me. I become nervous, tongue-tied, diffident. I wish to goodness I knew the man who invented this infernal game. I'd strangle him. But I suppose he's been dead for ages. Still, I could go and jump on his grave."

It was at this point that I understood all, and the heart within me sank like lead. The truth was out. Ferdinand Dibble was a goof.

"Come, come, my boy," I said, though feeling the uselessness of any words. "Master this weakness."

"I can't."

"Try!"

"I have tried."

He gnawed his putter again.

"She was asking me just now if I couldn't manage to come to Marvis Bay, too," he said.

"That surely is encouraging? It suggests that she is not entirely indifferent to your society."

"Yes, but what's the use? Do you know," a gleam coming into his eyes for a moment, "I have a feeling that if I could ever beat some really fairly good player—just once—I could bring the thing off." The gleam faded. "But what chance is there of that?"

It was a question which I did not care to answer. I merely patted his shoulder sympathetically, and after a little while he left me and walked away. I was still sitting there, thinking over his hard case, when Barbara Medway came out of the clubhouse.

She, too, seemed grave and pre-occupied, as if there was something on her mind. She took the chair which Ferdinand had vacated, and sighed wearily.

"Have you ever felt," she asked, "that you would like to bang a man on the head with something hard and heavy? With knobs on?"

I said I had sometimes experienced such a desire, and asked if she had any particular man in mind. She seemed to hesitate for a moment before replying, then, apparently, made up her mind to confide in me. My advanced years carry with them certain pleasant compensations, one of which is that nice girls often confide in me. I frequently find myself enrolled as a father-confessor on the most intimate matters by beautiful creatures from whom many a younger man would give his eye-teeth to get a friendly word. Besides, I had known Barbara since she was a child. Frequently—though not recently—I had given her her evening bath. These things form a bond.

"Why are men such chumps?" she exclaimed.

"You still have not told me who it is that has caused these harsh words. Do I know him?"

"Of course you do. You've just been talking to him."

"Ferdinand Dibble? But why should you wish to bang Ferdinand Dibble on the head with something hard and heavy with knobs on?"

"Because he's such a goop."

"You mean a goof?" I queried, wondering how she could have penetrated the unhappy man's secret.

"No, a goop. A goop is a man who's in love with a girl and won't tell her so. I am as certain as I am of anything that Ferdinand is fond of me."

"Your instinct is unerring. He has just been confiding in me on that very point."

"Well, why doesn't he confide in *me*, the poor fish?" cried the high-spirited girl, petulantly flicking a pebble at a passing grasshopper. "I can't be expected to fling myself into his arms unless he gives some sort of a hint that he's ready to catch me."

"Would it help if I were to repeat to him the substance of this conversation of ours?"

"If you breathe a word of it, I'll never speak to you again," she cried. "I'd rather die an awful death than have any man think I wanted him so badly that I had to send relays of messengers begging him to marry me."

I saw her point.

"Then I fear," I said, gravely, "that there is nothing to be done. One can only wait and hope. It may be that in the years to come Ferdinand Dibble will acquire a nice lissom, wristy swing, with the head kept rigid and the right leg firmly braced and—"

"What are you talking about?"

"I was toying with the hope that some sunny day Ferdinand Dibble would cease to be a goof."

"You mean a goop?"

"No, a goof. A goof is a man who—" And I went on to explain the peculiar psychological difficulties which lay in the way of any declaration of affection on Ferdinand's part.

"But I never heard of anything so ridiculous in my life," she ejaculated. "Do you mean to say that he is waiting till he is good at golf before he asks me to marry him?"

"It is not quite so simple as that," I said sadly. "Many bad golfers marry, feeling that a wife's loving solicitude may improve their game. But they are rugged, thick-skinned men, not sensitive and introspective, like Ferdinand. Ferdinand has allowed himself to become morbid. It is one of the chief merits of golf that non-success at the game induces a certain amount of decent humility, which keeps a man from pluming himself too much on any petty triumphs he may achieve in other walks of life; but in all things there is a happy mean, and with Ferdinand this humility has gone too far. It has taken all the spirit out of him. He feels crushed and worthless. He is grateful to caddies when they accept a tip instead of drawing themselves up to their full height and flinging the money in his face."

"Then do you mean that things have got to go on like this for ever?"

I thought for a moment.

"It is a pity," I said, "that you could not have induced Ferdinand to go to Marvis Bay for a month or two."

"Why?"

"Because it seems to me, thinking the thing over, that it is just possible that Marvis Bay might cure him. At the hotel there he would find collected a mob of golfers—I used the term in its broadest sense, to embrace the paralytics and the men who play left-handed—whom even he would be able to beat. When I was last at Marvis Bay, the hotel links were a sort of Sargasso Sea into which had drifted all the pitiful flotsam and jetsam of golf. I have seen things done on that course at which I shuddered and averted my eyes—and I am not a weak man. If Ferdinand can polish up his game so as to go round in a fairly steady hundred and five, I fancy there is hope. But I understand he is not going to Marvis Bay."

"Oh yes, he is," said the girl.

"Indeed! He did not tell me that when we were talking just now."

"He didn't know it then. He will when I have had a few words with him."

And she walked with firm steps back into the clubhouse.

It has been well said that there are many kinds of golf, beginning at the top with the golf of professionals and the best amateurs and working down through the golf of ossified men to that of Scotch University professors. Until recently this last was looked upon as the lowest possible depth; but nowadays, with the growing popularity of summer hotels, we are able to add a brand still lower, the golf you find at places like Marvis Bay.

To Ferdinand Dibble, coming from a club where the standard of play was rather unusually high, Marvis Bay was a revelation, and for some days after his arrival there he went about dazed, like a man who cannot believe it is really true. To go out on the links at this summer resort was like entering a new world. The hotel was full of stout, middle-aged men, who, after a misspent youth devoted to making money, had taken to a game at which real proficiency can only be acquired by those who start playing in their cradles and keep their weight down. Out on the course each morning you could see representatives of every nightmare style that was ever invented. There was the man who seemed to be attempting to deceive his ball and lull it into a false security by looking away from it and then making a lightning slash in the apparent hope of catching it off its guard. There was the man who wielded his mid-iron like one killing snakes. There was the man who addressed his ball as if he were stroking a cat, the man who drove as if he were cracking a whip, the man who brooded over each shot like one whose heart is bowed down by bad news from home, and the man who scooped with his mashie as if he were ladling soup. By the end of the first week Ferdinand Dibble was the acknowledged champion of the place. He had gone through the entire menagerie like a bullet through a cream puff.

First, scarcely daring to consider the possibility of success, he had taken on the man who tried to catch his ball off its guard and had beaten him five up and four to play. Then, with gradually growing confidence, he tackled in turn the Cat-Stroker, the Whip-Cracker, the Heart Bowed Down, and the Soup-Scooper, and walked all over their faces with spiked shoes. And as these were the leading local amateurs, whose prowess the octogenarians and the men who went round in bath-chairs vainly strove to emulate, Ferdinand Dibble was faced on the eighth morning of his visit by the startling fact that he had no more worlds to conquer. He was monarch of all he surveyed, and, what is more, had won his first trophy, the prize in the great medal-play handicap tournament, in which he had nosed in ahead of the field by two strokes, edging out his nearest rival, a venerable old gentleman, by means of a brilliant and unexpected four on the last hole. The prize was a handsome pewter mug, about the size of the old oaken bucket, and Ferdinand used to go to his room immediately after dinner to croon over it like a mother over her child.

You are wondering, no doubt, why, in these circumstances, he did not take advantage of the new spirit of exhilarated pride which had replaced his old humility and instantly propose to Barbara Medway. I will tell you. He did not propose to Barbara because Barbara was not there. At the last moment she had been detained at home to nurse a sick parent and had been compelled to postpone her visit for a couple of weeks. He could, no doubt, have proposed in one of the daily letters which he wrote to her, but somehow, once he started writing, he found that he used up so much space describing his best shots on the links that day that it was difficult to squeeze in a declaration of undying passion. After all, you can hardly cram that sort of thing into a postscript.

He decided, therefore, to wait till she arrived, and meanwhile pursued his conquering course. The longer he waited the better, in one way, for every morning and afternoon that passed was adding new layers to his self-esteem. Day by day in every way he grew chestier and chestier.

Meanwhile, however, dark clouds were gathering. Sullen mutterings were to be heard in corners of the hotel lounge, and the spirit of revolt was abroad. For Ferdinand's chestiness had not escaped the notice of his defeated rivals. There is nobody so chesty as a normally unchesty man who suddenly becomes chesty, and I am sorry to say that the chestiness which had come to Ferdinand was the aggressive type of chestiness which breeds enemies. He had developed a habit of holding the game up in order to give his opponent advice. The Whip-Cracker had not forgiven, and never would forgive, his well-meant but galling criticism of his back-swing. The Scooper, who had always scooped since the day when, at the age of sixty-four, he subscribed to the Correspondence Course which was to teach him golf in twelve lessons by mail, resented being told by a snip of a boy that the mashie-stroke should be a smooth, unhurried swing. The Snake-Killer— But I need not weary you with a detailed recital of these men's grievances; it is enough to say that they all had it in for Ferdinand, and one night, after dinner, they met in the lounge to decide what was to be done about it.

A nasty spirit was displayed by all.

"A mere lad telling me how to use my mashie!" growled the Scooper. "Smooth and unhurried my left eyeball! I get it up, don't I? Well, what more do you want?"

"I keep telling him that mine is the old, full St. Andrew swing," muttered the Whip-Cracker, between set teeth, "but he won't listen to me."

"He ought to be taken down a peg or two," hissed the Snake-Killer. It is not easy to hiss a sentence without a single "s" in it, and the fact that he succeeded in doing so shows to what a pitch of emotion the man had been goaded by Ferdinand's maddening air of superiority.

"Yes, but what can we do?" queried an octogenarian, when this last remark had been passed on to him down his ear-trumpet.

"That's the trouble," sighed the Scooper. "What can we do?" And there was a sorrowful shaking of heads.

"I know!" exclaimed the Cat-Stroker, who had not hitherto spoken. He was a lawyer, and a man of subtle and sinister mind. "I have it! There's a boy in my office—young Parsloe—who could beat this man Dibble hollow. I'll wire him to come down here and we'll spring him on this fellow and knock some of the conceit out of him."

There was a chorus of approval.

"But are you sure he can beat him?" asked the Snake-Killer, anxiously. "It would never do to make a mistake."

"Of course I'm sure," said the Cat-Stroker. "George Parsloe once went round in ninety-four."

"Many changes there have been since ninety-four," said the octogenarian, nodding sagely. "Ah, many, many changes. None of these motor-cars then, tearing about and killing—"

Kindly hands led him off to have an egg-and-milk, and the remaining conspirators returned to the point at issue with bent brows.

"Ninety-four?" said the Scooper, incredulously. "Do you mean counting every stroke?"

"Counting every stroke."

"Not conceding himself any putts?"

"Not one."

"Wire him to come at once," said the meeting with one voice.

That night the Cat-Stroker approached Ferdinand, smooth, subtle, lawyer-like.

"Oh, Dibble," he said, "just the man I wanted to see. Dibble, there's a young friend of mine coming down here who goes in for golf a little. George Parsloe is his name. I was wondering if you could spare time to give him a game. He is just a novice, you know."

"I shall be delighted to play a round with him," said Ferdinand, kindly.

"He might pick up a pointer or two from watching you," said the Cat-Stroker.

"True, true," said Ferdinand.

"Then I'll introduce you when he shows up."

"Delighted," said Ferdinand.

He was in excellent humour that night, for he had had a letter from Barbara saying that she was arriving on the next day but one.

It was Ferdinand's healthy custom of a morning to get up in good time and take a dip in the sea before breakfast. On the morning of the day of Barbara's arrival, he arose, as usual, donned his flannels, took a good look at the cup, and started out. It was a fine, fresh morning, and he glowed both externally and internally. As he crossed the links, for the nearest route to the water was through the fairway of the seventh, he was whistling happily and rehearsing in his mind the opening sentences of his proposal. For it was his firm resolve that night after dinner to ask Barbara to marry him. He was proceeding over the smooth turf without a care in the world, when there was a sudden cry of "Fore!" and the next moment a golf ball, missing him by inches, sailed up the fairway and came to a rest fifty yards from where he stood. He looked round and observed a figure coming towards him from the tee.

The distance from the tee was fully a hundred and thirty yards. Add fifty to that, and you have a hundred and eighty yards. No such drive had

been made on the Marvis Bay links since their foundation, and such is
the generous spirit of the true golfer that Ferdinand's first emotion, after
the not inexcusable spasm of panic caused by the hum of the ball past his
ear, was one of cordial admiration. By some kindly miracle, he supposed,
one of his hotel acquaintances had been permitted for once in his life to
time a drive right. It was only when the other man came up that there
began to steal over him a sickening apprehension. The faces of all those
who hewed divots on the hotel course were familiar to him, and the fact
that this fellow was a stranger seemed to point with dreadful certainty to
his being the man he had agreed to play.

"Sorry," said the man. He was a tall, strikingly handsome youth, with
brown eyes and a dark moustache.

"Oh, that's all right," said Ferdinand. "Er—do you always drive like
that?"

"Well, I generally get a bit longer ball, but I'm off my drive this
morning. It's lucky I came out and got this practice. I'm playing a match
tomorrow with a fellow named Dibble, who's a local champion, or something."

"Me," said Ferdinand, humbly.

"Eh? Oh, you?" Mr. Parsloe eyed him appraisingly. "Well, may the
best man win."

As this was precisely what Ferdinand was afraid was going to happen,
he nodded in a sickly manner and tottered off to his bathe. The magic
had gone out of the morning. The sun still shone, but in a silly, feeble
way; and a cold and depressing wind had sprung up. For Ferdinand's
inferiority complex, which had seemed cured for ever, was back again,
doing business at the old stand.

How sad it is in this life that the moment to which we have looked
forward with the most glowing anticipation so often turns out on arrival,
flat, cold, and disappointing. For ten days Barbara Medway had been
living for that meeting with Ferdinand, when, getting out of the train,
she would see him popping about on the horizon with the love-light
sparkling in his eyes and words of devotion trembling on his lips. The
poor girl never doubted for an instant that he would unleash his pent-up
emotions inside the first five minutes, and her only worry was lest he
should give an embarrassing publicity to the sacred scene by falling on
his knees on the station platform.

"Well, here I am at last," she cried gaily.

"Hullo!" said Ferdinand, with a twisted smile.

The girl looked at him, chilled. How could she know that his peculiar
manner was due entirely to the severe attack of cold feet resultant upon

his meeting with George Parsloe that morning? The interpretation which she placed upon it was that he was not glad to see her. If he had behaved like this before, she would, of course, have put it down to ingrowing goofery, but now she had his written statements to prove that for the last ten days his golf had been one long series of triumphs.

"I got your letters," she said, persevering bravely.

"I thought you would," said Ferdinand, absently.

"You seem to have been doing wonders."

"Yes."

There was a silence.

"Have a nice journey?" said Ferdinand.

"Very," said Barbara.

She spoke coldly, for she was madder than a wet hen. She saw it all now. In the ten days since they had parted, his love, she realised, had waned. Some other girl, met in the romantic surroundings of this picturesque resort, had supplanted her in his affections. She knew how quickly Cupid gets off the mark at a summer hotel, and for an instant she blamed herself for ever having been so ivory-skulled as to let him come to this place alone. Then regret was swallowed up in wrath, and she became so glacial that Ferdinand, who had been on the point of telling her the secret of his gloom, retired into his shell and conversation during the drive to the hotel never soared above a certain level. Ferdinand said the sunshine was nice and Barbara said yes, it was nice, and Ferdinand said it looked pretty on the water, and Barbara said yes, it did look pretty on the water, and Ferdinand said he hoped it was not going to rain, and Barbara said yes, it would be a pity if it rained. And then there was another lengthy silence.

"How is my uncle?" asked Barbara at last.

I omitted to mention that the individual to whom I have referred as the Cat-Stroker was Barbara's mother's brother, and her host at Marvis Bay.

"Your uncle?"

"His name is Tuttle. Have you met him?"

"Oh yes. I've seen a good deal of him. He has got a friend staying with him," said Ferdinand, his mind returning to the matter nearest his heart. "A fellow named Parsloe."

"Oh, is George Parsloe here? How jolly!"

"Do you know him?" barked Ferdinand, hollowly. He would not have supposed that anything could have added to his existing depression, but he was conscious now of having slipped a few rungs farther down the ladder of gloom. There had been a horribly joyful ring in her voice. Ah, well, he reflected morosely, how like life it all was! We never know what the morrow may bring forth. We strike a good patch and are beginning to think pretty well of ourselves, and along comes a George Parsloe.

"Of course I do," said Barbara. "Why, there he is."

The cab had drawn up at the door of the hotel, and on the porch George Parsloe was airing his graceful person. To Ferdinand's fevered eye he looked like a Greek god, and his inferiority complex began to exhibit symptoms of elephantiasis. How could he compete at love or golf with a fellow who looked as if he had stepped out of the movies and considered himself off his drive when he did a hundred and eighty yards?

"Geor-gee!" cried Barbara, blithely. "Hullo, George!"

"Why, hullo, Barbara!"

They fell into pleasant conversation, while Ferdinand hung miserably about in the offing. And presently, feeling that his society was not essential to their happiness, he slunk away.

George Parsloe dined at the Cat-Stroker's table that night, and it was with George Parsloe that Barbara roamed in the moonlight after dinner. Ferdinand, after a profitless hour at the billiard-table, went early to his room. But not even the rays of the moon, glinting on his cup, could soothe the fever in his soul. He practised putting sombrely into his tooth-glass for a while; then, going to bed, fell at last into a troubled sleep.

Barbara slept late the next morning and breakfasted in her room. Coming down towards noon, she found a strange emptiness in the hotel. It was her experience of summer hotels that a really fine day like this one was the cue for half the inhabitants to collect in the lounge, shut all the windows, and talk about conditions in the jute industry. To her surprise, though the sun was streaming down from a cloudless sky, the only occupant of the lounge was the octogenarian with the ear-trumpet. She observed that he was chuckling to himself in a senile manner.

"Good morning," she said, politely, for she had made his acquaintance on the previous evening.

"Hey?" said the octogenarian, suspending his chuckling and getting his trumpet into position.

"I said 'Good morning!' " roared Barbara into the receiver.

"Hey?"

"Good morning!"

"Ah! Yes, it's a very fine morning, a very fine morning. If it wasn't for missing my bun and glass of milk at twelve sharp," said the octogenarian, "I'd be down on the links. That's where I'd be, down on the links. If it wasn't for missing my bun and glass of milk."

This refreshment arriving at this moment he dismantled the radio outfit and began to restore his tissues.

"Watching the match," he explained, pausing for a moment in his bun-mangling.

"What match?"

The octogenarian sipped his milk.

"What match?" repeated Barbara.

"Hey?"

"What match?"

The octogenarian began to chuckle again and nearly swallowed a crumb the wrong way.

"Take some of the conceit out of him," he gurgled.

"Out of who?" asked Barbara, knowing perfectly well that she should have said "whom."

"Yes," said the octogenarian.

"Who is conceited?"

"Ah! This young fellow, Dibble. Very conceited. I saw it in his eye from the first, but nobody would listen to me. Mark my words, I said, that boy needs taking down a peg or two. Well, he's going to be this morning. Your uncle wired to young Parsloe to come down, and he's arranged a match between them. Dibble—" Here the octogenarian choked again and had to rinse himself out with milk, "Dibble doesn't know that Parsloe once went round in ninety-four!"

"What?"

Everything seemed to go black to Barbara. Through a murky mist she appeared to be looking at a negro octogenarian, sipping ink. Then her eyes cleared, and she found herself clutching for support at the back of the chair. She understood now. She realised why Ferdinand had been so distrait, and her whole heart went out to him in a spasm of maternal pity. How she had wronged him!

"Take some of the conceit out of him," the octogenarian was mumbling, and Barbara felt a sudden sharp loathing for the old man. For two pins she could have dropped a beetle in his milk. Then the need for action roused her. What action? She did not know. All she knew was that she must act.

"Oh!" she cried.

"Hey?" said the octogenarian, bringing his trumpet to the ready.

But Barbara had gone.

It was not far to the links, and Barbara covered the distance on flying feet. She reached the clubhouse, but the course was empty except for the Scooper, who was preparing to drive off the first tee. In spite of the fact that something seemed to tell her subconsciously that this was one of the sights she ought not to miss, the girl did not wait to watch. Assuming that the match had started soon after breakfast, it must by now have reached one of the holes on the second nine. She ran down the hill, looking to left and right, and was presently aware of a group of spectators clustered about a green in the distance. As she hurried towards them they moved away, and now she could see Ferdinand advancing to the next tee. With a thrill that shook her whole body she realised that he had the honour. So he must have won one hole, at any rate. Then she saw her uncle.

"How are they?" she gasped.

Mr. Tuttle seemed moody. It was apparent that things were not going altogether to his liking.

"All square at the fifteenth," he replied, gloomily.

"All square!"

"Yes. Young Parsloe," said Mr. Tuttle with a sour look in the direction of that lissom athlete, "doesn't seem to be able to do a thing right on the greens. He has been putting like a sheep with the botts."

From the foregoing remark of Mr. Tuttle you will, no doubt, have gleaned at least a clue to the mystery of how Ferdinand Dibble had managed to hold his long-driving adversary up to the fifteenth green, but for all that you will probably consider that some further explanation of this amazing state of affairs is required. Mere bad putting on the part of George Parsloe is not, you feel, sufficient to cover the matter entirely. You are right. There was another very important factor in the situation—to wit, that by some extraordinary chance Ferdinand Dibble had started right off from the first tee, playing the game of a lifetime. Never had he made such drives, never chipped his chip so shrewdly.

About Ferdinand's driving there was as a general thing a fatal stiffness and over-caution which prevented success. And with his chip-shots he rarely achieved accuracy owing to his habit of rearing his head like the lion of the jungle just before the club struck the ball. But to-day he had been swinging with a careless freedom, and his chips had been true and clean. The thing had puzzled him all the way round. It had not elated him, for, owing to Barbara's aloofness and the way in which she had gambolled about George Parsloe like a young lamb in the springtime, he was in too deep a state of dejection to be elated by anything. And now, suddenly, in a flash of clear vision, he perceived the reason why he had been playing so well to-day. It was just because he was not elated. It was simply because he was so profoundly miserable.

That was what Ferdinand told himself as he stepped off the sixteenth, after hitting a screamer down the centre of the fairway, and I am convinced that he was right. Like so many indifferent golfers, Ferdinand

Dibble had always made the game hard for himself by thinking too much. He was a deep student of the works of the masters, and whenever he prepared to play a stroke he had a complete mental list of all the mistakes which it was possible to make. He would remember how Taylor had warned against dipping the right shoulder, how Vardon had inveighed against any movement of the head; he would recall how Ray had mentioned the tendency to snatch back the club, how Braid had spoken sadly of those who sin against their better selves by stiffening the muscles and heaving.

The consequence was that when, after waggling in a frozen manner till mere shame urged him to take some definite course of action, he eventually swung, he invariably proceeded to dip his right shoulder, stiffen his muscles, heave, and snatch back the club, at the same time raising his head sharply as in the illustrated plate ("Some Frequent Faults of Beginners—No. 3—Lifting the Bean") facing page thirty-four of James Braid's *Golf Without Tears*. To-day he had been so preoccupied with his broken heart that he had made his shots absently, almost carelessly, with the result that at least one in every three had been a lallapaloosa.

Meanwhile, George Parsloe had driven off and the match was progressing. George was feeling a little flustered by now. He had been given to understand that this bird Dibble was a hundred-at-his-best man, and all the way round the fellow had been reeling off fives in great profusion, and had once actually got a four. True, there had been an occasional six, and even a seven, but that did not alter the main fact that the man was making the dickens of a game of it. With the haughty spirit of one who had once done a ninety-four, George Parsloe had anticipated being at least three up at the turn. Instead of which he had been two down, and had to fight strenuously to draw level.

Nevertheless, he drove steadily and well, and would certainly have won the hole had it not been for his weak and sinful putting. The same defect caused him to halve the seventeenth, after being on in two, with Ferdinand wandering in the desert and only reaching the green with his fourth. Then, however, Ferdinand holed out from a distance of seven yards, getting a five; which George's three putts just enabled him to equal.

Barbara had watched the proceedings with a beating heart. At first she had looked on from afar; but now, drawn as by a magnet, she approached the tee. Ferdinand was driving off. She held her breath. Ferdinand held his breath. And all around one could see their respective breaths being held by George Parsloe, Mr. Tuttle, and the enthralled crowd of spectators. It was a moment of the acutest tension, and it was broken by the crack of Ferdinand's driver as it met the ball and sent it hopping along the ground for a mere thirty yards. At this supreme crisis in the match Ferdinand Dibble had topped.

George Parsloe teed up his ball. There was a smile of quiet satisfaction on his face. He snuggled the driver in his hands, and gave it a preliminary swish. This, felt George Parsloe, was where the happy ending came. He could drive as he had never driven before. He would so drive that it would take his opponent at least three shots to catch up with him. He drew back his club with infinite caution, poised it at the top of the swing—

"I always wonder—" said a clear, girlish voice, ripping the silence like the explosion of a bomb.

George Parsloe started. His club wobbled. It descended. The ball trickled into the long grass in front of the tee. There was a grim pause.

"You were saying, Miss Medway—" said George Parsloe, in a small, flat voice.

"Oh, I'm so sorry," said Barbara. "I'm afraid I put you off."

"A little, perhaps. Possibly the merest trifle. But you were saying you wondered about something. Can I be of any assistance?"

"I was only saying," said Barbara, "that I always wonder why tees are called tees."

George Parsloe swallowed once or twice. He also blinked a little feverishly. His eyes had a dazed, staring expression.

"I'm afraid I cannot tell you off-hand," he said, "but I will make a point of consulting some good encyclopædia at the earliest opportunity."

"Thank you so much."

"Not at all. It will be a pleasure. In case you were thinking of inquiring at the moment when I am putting why greens are called greens, may I venture the suggestion now that it is because they are green?"

And, so saying, George Parsloe stalked to his ball and found it nestling in the heart of some shrub of which, not being a botanist, I cannot give you the name. It was a close-knit, adhesive shrub, and it twined its tentacles so loving around George Parsloe's niblick that he missed his first shot altogether. His second made the ball rock, and his third dislodged it. Playing a full swing with his brassie and being by now a mere cauldron of seething emotions he missed his fourth. His fifth came to within a few inches of Ferdinand's drive, and he picked it up and hurled it from him into the rough as if it had been something venomous.

"Your hole and match," said George Parsloe, thinly.

Ferdinand Dibble sat beside the glittering ocean. He had hurried off the course with swift strides the moment George Parsloe had spoken those bitter words. He wanted to be alone with his thoughts.

They were mixed thoughts. For a moment joy at the reflection that he had won a tough match came irresistibly to the surface, only to sink again as he remembered that life, whatever its triumphs, could hold nothing for him now that Barbara Medway loved another.

"Mr. Dibble!"

He looked up. She was standing at his side. He gulped and rose to his feet.

"Yes?"

There was a silence.

"Doesn't the sun look pretty on the water?" said Barbara.

Ferdinand groaned. This was too much.

"Leave me," he said, hollowly. "Go back to your Parsloe, the man with whom you walked in the moonlight beside this same water."

"Well, why shouldn't I walk with Mr. Parsloe in the moonlight beside this same water?" demanded Barbara, with spirit.

"I never said," replied Ferdinand, for he was a fair man at heart, "that you shouldn't walk with Mr. Parsloe beside this same water. I simply said you did walk with Mr. Parsloe beside this same water."

"I've a perfect right to walk with Mr. Parsloe beside this same water," persisted Barbara. "He and I are old friends."

Ferdinand groaned again.

"Exactly! There you are! As I suspected. Old friends. Played together as children, and what not, I shouldn't wonder."

"No, we didn't. I've only known him five years. But he is engaged to be married to my greatest chum, so that draws us together."

Ferdinand uttered a strangled cry.

"Parsloe engaged to be married!"

"Yes. The wedding takes place next month."

"But look here." Ferdinand's forehead was wrinkled. He was thinking tensely. "Look here," said Ferdinand, a close reasoner. "If Parsloe's engaged to your greatest chum, he can't be in love with *you.*"

"No."

"And you aren't in love with him?"

"No."

"Then, by gad," said Ferdinand, "how about it?"

"What do you mean?"

"Will you marry me?" bellowed Ferdinand.

"Yes."

"You will?"

"Of course I will."

"Darling!" cried Ferdinand.

"There is only one thing that bothers me a bit," said Ferdinand, thoughtfully, as they strolled together over the scented meadows, while in the trees above them a thousand birds trilled Mendelssohn's Wedding March.

"What is that?"

"Well, I'll tell you," said Ferdinand. "The fact is, I've just discovered the great secret of golf. You can't play a really hot game unless you're so miserable that you don't worry over your shots. Take the case of a chip-shot, for instance. If you're really wretched, you don't care where the ball is going and so you don't raise your head to see. Grief automatically prevents pressing and over-swinging. Look at the top-notchers. Have you ever seen a happy pro?"

"No. I don't think I have."

"Well, then!"

"But pros are all Scotchmen," argued Barbara.

"It doesn't matter. I'm sure I'm right. And the darned thing is that I'm going to be so infernally happy all the rest of my life that I suppose my handicap will go up to thirty or something."

Barbara squeezed his hand lovingly.

"Don't worry, precious," she said, soothingly. "It will be all right. I am a woman, and, once we are married, I shall be able to think of at least a hundred ways of snootering you to such an extent that you'll be fit to win the Amateur Championship."

"You will?" said Ferdinand, anxiously. "You're sure?"

"Quite, quite sure, dearest," said Barbara.

"My angel!" said Ferdinand.

He folded her in his arms, using the interlocking grip.

JIM BROSNAN

"WHY PITCHERS CAN'T HIT"

*Jim Brosnan, a pitcher with the St. Louis Cardinals, the Chicago White Sox, and the Cincinnati Reds, is one of the very few athletes who has written his books—*The Long Season *and* Pennant Race—*without the aid of a ghostwriter. I once asked him if his editors at Harper Bros. had* *made any suggestions. He replied that, yes, a recommendation had been made that a reference to drinking martinis ought to be removed since the book's appeal was to a juvenile audience.*

"I resisted," Brosnan said with a smile.

I asked how his Cardinal teammates had reacted to The Long Season. *He said that he had been surprised and hurt because his best friends on the Cardinals, Ken Boyer and Larry Jackson, both were critical. Jackson, a fellow pitcher, came up with the odd notion that "Brosnan hasn't pitched well enough to write about the Cardinals." "That was strange coming from him," Brosnan said, "because though it's true I was even on the year, same number of wins and losses, he was only eight and six."*

"What about management?" I asked.

"They were very upset about it," Brosnan replied. "Twenty-seven years after The Long Season *came out, Bing Devine, who was the Cardinals' general manager when it was published, came by and said, 'Hey, there were some funny things in that book!' Twenty-seven* years!"

Management has traditionally been nervous about ballplayers writing firsthand accounts of life on the team. On one occasion, chatting in the Atlanta Braves' clubhouse with Eddie Mathews, the Braves' manager at the time, I happened to mention Jim Bouton's lighthearted memoir about life on the Yankees. Entitled Ball Four, *it described, among other things, Mickey Mantle leading a group of teammates up onto a motel rooftop to spy in on stewardesses getting ready for bed. Mathews had apparently been infuriated by the book. He hopped off the rubbing table as if he had been stung. Somewhat startled, I asked him what in the book had so disturbed him. "What are you talking about?" he asked. "You think I'd* read *that trash??"*

I told Brosnan about my confrontation with Mathews. He laughed and said that Mathews had come up to him once and announced, "If you ever write what you know about me, I'll tear your heart out!" "It was puzzling coming from Eddie," Brosnan said, "because I didn't know *anything about him!"*

March 5, St. Petersburg

Even the most indifferent baseball fan seems to want to know, "Why can't pitchers hit?" Because I've blushed in answering that question too many times in the past ten years, I find myself taking the question seriously. (Actually, no professional in his right mind would think of taking my hitting seriously.) Since it applies to the whole pitching profession the question has insulting overtones that constantly put me on the defensive . . . with a bat in my hands.

Now, *why can't pitchers hit?*

I can answer, as I often have, "We just don't get the necessary practice." Or: "Pitchers bear down harder on other pitchers because it's embarrassing to let an 'out' man get a hit off you." Or: "Who says I can't?"

Serious meditation on the question has led me to the somewhat galling conclusion that the answer lies not within me at all. Nor within the subjective consciousness of any typical nonhitting pitcher. If you don't hit, you can't hit, probably. Good God, it might really be true!

Shaken by this horrible possibility I rushed out to right field seeking the truth. At Lang Field, St. Petersburg, there is a plot of ground seventy-five feet long, fifteen feet wide, completely enclosed by a mesh of three-ply cord. At one end of this cage stands a pitching machine roughly the height of Whitey Ford, with flat tires, guts of iron, and a motor in its rear. This is Iron Mike, and he throws rubber baseballs in the general direction of a plate sixty feet away, much as a flesh-and-blood pitcher does. Some of the pitches go directly over the plate, somewhere in the strike zone. (The Cardinals paid another bundle of money for Iron Mike on the Bonus Baby Theory that someday he would improve his control and become a pitcher.) Many of Mike's pitches are *near-*strikes, close enough for pitchers, at least, to swing at. It is here that pitchers take their batting practice. When a pitcher dares ask Hemus, "Are we gonna hit today?" Solly says, "If you guys want to hit, go get in the cage," his manner suggesting that pitchers just don't belong at home plate with a bat. Unfortunately, taking batting practice from a mechanical apparatus that throws rubber baseballs lends a synthetic, disenchanted feeling to the whole operation.

The only human element in this training procedure is Paul Waner, an ex-wizard at hitting major league pitching, and the object of my search for an authoritative opinion on the question, "Can Pitchers Hit, or Not?"

"Why not?" said Paul. "Let me see you swing a bat."

Waner looks like a gnarled gnome, the figment of a wild Irish imagination. At his best playing weight, 140 pounds, he could have passed for an ex-jockey sidling up to tout a favorite horse. Yet, Fred Fitzsimmons, the pitching coach when I was with the Cubs, said Waner hit the ball through the box harder than any other hitter that Fitz had faced in the major leagues. "He'd stagger up to the plate with that big bat of his and you'd swear you could throw the ball by him. Zip! He'd snap a line drive right by your ear."

"Frankly, Paul," I said, as Waner racked up a dozen balls in the pitching machine, "if you can make a hitter out of me, you're worth more money—both you and Iron Mike."

"Let's see you hit a few first, then I'll see if I can help you. You might

remember that Lew Burdette was one of the worst hitters you ever did
see a couple of years ago. He'd go up to the plate, wave at three pitches,
and laugh all the way back to the bench. We taught him a couple of
things and now he can hurt you if you give him anything too good to
hit." Waner waved me to the other end of the cage and plugged in his
pitcher. For the next few minutes the only sounds to be heard were the
hum of the electric motor, the swish of my bat, and, occasionally, a few
plops and plinks as the ball and bat connected haphazardly.

"You're lounging at the ball," said Paul.

Perhaps he meant "lunging," but then I might just as well have been
lying on a chaise longue, criticizing Iron Mike's control, a subject on
which a pitcher might speak with more authority.

"The first thing you have to try to do," said Paul, "is *belly-button.*
Then, you got to really *block* when you block. You're hitting the bottom
half of the ball, and you should be trying to hit the top half. You got to
wait for the ball to get right up to the plate, and you gotta pop those
wrists when you swing. You're not doing any of those things. That's why
you're lounging at the ball. Now, we'll take up breathing," he added, "as
soon as I fix this thing."

Breathing I was relatively familiar with, so I decided to go along with
the rest, and resumed my position at the plate. Waner worked on Iron
Mike with a pair of pliers. (Some of Mike's pitches were going over my
head as well as over the plate.)

"Now, wait for that ball till it gets right on the plate. Then, *belly-
button!* Get your stomach out front as fast as you can, and that means
you can't step first, then turn. It's all one movement. Snap your hips
around and the bat will follow up naturally."

The crack of the wood sounded so good as I swung that I thought at
first my hip had popped out of place. The batted ball whistled by Iron
Mike, getting no reaction out of the machine but pleasing Paul, who
said, "That's what you call belly-button! After you've pivoted on that
front foot to start your swing you block your hip so it won't turn any
further. The smaller a step you take, the quicker you get your belly
button around and your hip blocked. The longer you wait for the ball to
get to you, the faster you have to block and belly-button, but you cut
down lounging at the ball and you won't have a lazy bat."

"I guess I never could stomach those pitchers before, Paul," I said,
happily. My well-intentioned pun whistled by his ears, and he proceeded. The next pitch was at my head. Iron Mike hasn't much of a
sense of humor either, I suppose. "When you swing at the ball," Waner
went on, "try hitting down on the ball, right through it, like. When you
hit the top half of the ball, she'll rip through the infield like a scared

rabbit. You won't be popping the ball up, or hitting those easy fly balls."

"I thought a hitter was supposed to keep the bat level when he swung, Paul," I said.

"Well, that's what they say, 'cause that's what it looks like, but it's just an optical illusion. What you do is roll your wrists so you can cut into the top of the ball, so you can't have the bat level, really. When you see the ball right there"—he pointed to a spot two feet in front of him, belt-high, just ahead of his front hip—"you move. Block that hip, snap that belly button around, cut down on top of the ball, and watch her go."

The timing was the tough part, waiting for the ball till it got "right there."

"Take a deep breath just before the pitch starts coming," said Waner. "Then, hold your breath till you start to swing. That makes you relax and wait." I had visions of myself turning blue in the face waiting for a slow curve, and collapsing. If any of the batting feats of the great hitters ("All the good ones do like I been telling you") are hereafter described as breathless, I will view them as literally so.

If Waner was right, and he certainly made it sound logical, some of my most cherished, traditional theories about batting were about to be destroyed.

"You really don't hit the ball out in front every time. Only when you're trying to pull it down the line.

"You have to forget about swinging level at the ball.

"Hit down, and through. Hit the top half of the ball."

I can't quite get used to the idea that I should try to hit just part of the ball. It has always been hard enough to see all of the damn thing and to hit *any* part of it. "Paul," I asked, "did you have any trouble when you started wearing glasses and had to play under the lights?"

"No," he said. "I believe I even saw a little better. The ball looked whiter, or something. I could see that top half right out there waiting to be hit."

("Did you ever try clipping individual stitches?" I wondered to myself.)

We gathered the balls from all over the cage, and racked them up for another session. Usually a pitcher is limited to one basket load at a time, but no one was waiting in line. My hands were forming tiny blood blisters as I swung my Wally Moon model at Iron Mike's pitching. But all I could think about was the way the balls sounded when I hit them. A pitcher learns to tell by the sound whether a ball is hit well or not. From the mound you quickly put the three sensations of sight, feel, and hearing together, and you know for sure that the ball is gone, man, gone. You watch your pitch go just where you didn't want to throw it, with not quite as much stuff on it as you wish—and . . . what a vicious sound a line drive makes!

Why can't pitchers hit?

Just call me Tiger, dad.

WILFRID SHEED

"The Old Man and the Tee"

James Thurber once wrote that almost all American males, whatever their age, invariably put themselves to sleep at night striking out the batting order of the New York Yankees, somewhat easier to do these days, it should be said, than back in the days of their various dynasties. In the preface to his delightful collection of sports pieces entitled Baseball and Lesser Sports, *Wilfrid Sheed admits to this sort of thing. He writes that his most reliable pipe dream involved having the longest active career in sports history, presumably baseball, after which he retires into sports writing. Sheed never had the opportunity to live out the first part of his dream: when he was fourteen he became one of the last victims of polio in this country, and today walks with two canes. He writes that he was to remain a fourteen-year-old fan for the next twenty years. But "the urge to play and the joys of reflection are slightly different animals, and it was like a midlife rebirth to find that one could prolong the pleasures of sport indefinitely simply by writing about it and letting the reflections roll." These reflections have been mostly about the sports in which time is not an element, where one can muse on the "spaces between the fun"—baseball, cricket, golf. . .*

There are certain things you never get to see in life because there aren't enough cameras to go round. For instance, the look on a painter's face when he stares at his latest baby and decides that it's finally finished— one more stroke and he could have blown it; or the novelist coming down the home-stretch; or the scientist contemplating his slide and realizing that that unappetizing blob of muck on it spells either glory or twenty years down the tube.

We did, however, get to see Jack Nicklaus play the last four holes at the Masters Tournament this spring (spring for us, that is, autumn for him—non–golf fanciers should be apprised that this was the second oldest man ever to win a major tournament, coming from four strokes down with only four holes to play and passing a menacing herd of young tigers on his way).

To go with his sizzling performance, Nicklaus happened to be wearing the most expressive face I've ever seen on an athlete—because in his own special world he *was* an artist working on a masterpiece that one extra stroke would literally ruin, a scientist with a pack of rivals baying at his heels as he pondered each putt. But above all, he was playing a sport that allows one to show, indeed almost forbids one not to show, one's thoughts.

Consider the alternatives. Football players, bless them, never have to show their faces at all. Baseball hitters' mouths, as photographed, open foolishly at the moment of contact, while pitchers do their best to look like poker players or shell-game operators, which in a sense they are. In track, sprinters' faces tend to burst at the seams, while long-distance guys run as if they were down to their last tank: one animate expression might dislodge something vital in there.

Tennis players have the time to look interesting, but they waste great gobs of it glaring at the linesmen or the umpire or at anything that moves—still, they have their moments. Basketball players seesaw interminably between goofy elation and grim determination all the live night long. With hockey players, who can tell? A man without teeth looks like the Mona Lisa at the best of times, bomb damage at the worst. Jockeys probably look fascinating, but who has time to notice? Golfers for their part do not exactly whiz by: for days they move like snails under glass, until we know every last twitch, with time left over to memorize their wardrobe and decipher its meanings.

However, there was more to Nicklaus's face that day than simple visibility. He is a disciplined man, and there had to be a lot in there for so much to come out. The first item in the Making of the Face was simply that of his age; at forty-six, Nicklaus is at least old enough to *have* a face, as they say in Ireland. But he is also much too old to win a major golf tournament, and this thought must have followed him around the course like a playground pest jumping on his back and trying to pinion his arms, all the while jabbering, "You can't do it because it can't be done, *you can't do* . . ." Scat, said Nicklaus's face. Get that bum out of here. But not until the Face lit up, like Broadway, on the eighteenth green, could we be sure the bum had left.

Then there was the Occasion. The Masters is far and away our classiest tournament—the one the Duchess of Kent would attend if we had a Duchess of Kent. And since Nicklaus's appearances anywhere at this point are on the order of royal visits in themselves, the combination is enough to make even a spectator's knees tremble. The gale-force waves of adulation that crash over the guest of honor on such occasions must make it all the victim can do just to smile and wave weakly like the queen. So imagine her royal self being handed a set of clubs and commanded to play right through the crowd, all the way to the coronation, pitching her ball up the steps and into a little tin cup, before she can claim her crown.

That is more or less what King Jack had to do to get his green jacket, and he admitted that he had to fight tears several times as he strode down those last ringing fairways. Wouldn't it be pleasanter just to relax and enjoy this? It's such a lovely course. . . . No, said the Face.

A third, more mundane factor in the Making of Nicklaus's Face was the simple fact that Nicklaus can't see as well as he used to and no longer has the pleasure of watching those intergalactic drives of his return to Earth. For the Masters, therefore, his son had to double as caddy and long-range Seeing Eye dog, which added for this reporter a curiously Biblical touch to the proceedings. But besides all that, myopia in itself can produce a slightly strained appearance that, as I learned back in school, can pass for thinking if you play it right.

Of course, the fourth factor, or facet, in the Face was that Nicklaus wasn't "playing it" at all. By the fifteenth hole, he probably wasn't even aware that he *had* a face, and he certainly didn't give a damn what it looked like. In fact, if the Devil had popped the question, I daresay old Jack would have willingly put on a fright wig and a bright-red nose in exchange for just one more twenty-five-footer.

Or at least *I* would have. I guess it hardly needs pointing out that all the above was going on in my mind, not his, and that watching a game can be even more nerve-racking than playing one, as I learned from a priest friend who bit clear through his umbrella handle while watching a cricket match. What Nicklaus actually said when this seeming agony in Bobby Jones's garden was over was that he had felt "comfortable" (comfortable!) over the twenty-five-footers and that he hadn't had so much fun in six years.

Well, a champion's idea of fun may not be everybody's. Amounts of tension that would send a normal man screaming into the woods act on him like a tonic, or a wake-up call. Athletes have been known to complain of not feeling enough of it ("Man, I was flat out there"). Basketball's super-cool Bill Russell—and doubtless many others less cool—used to routinely throw up before outings, so that it became almost part of his regimen. John McEnroe favors a level of constant embarrassment to light his phlegm, while Muhammad Ali's weigh-in tantrums used to send his blood pressure into the stratosphere.

But a golfer has no need of such paltry devices. All he has to do is think about putting. The great Sam Snead for one could never resign himself to the idea that this dwarfish stroke, the putt, should count every bit as much as a booming 300-yard drive, and he actually wanted putting declared a separate sport.

It certainly *looks* different. Every other stroke, I am assured, can be played with the same basic swing, variously adjusted—that is, until one approaches the pressure pit, or green, at which point the whole exercise changes its nature from a robust, swinging affair to a pinched little game of skill suitable for saloons. The lords of the fairway are suddenly called upon to hunch over like bank clerks and not move a muscle. The result is almost an anti-swing, a total negation of everything they've been doing. The shoulders remain still, the hips don't swivel, the wrists break not. From behind, the golfer appears to be doing nothing at all, but that's not quite so; what he's doing is growing an ulcer.

That low growl that hangs over the nation's golf courses at all times is mostly about putting. At least in the rough you can hack your way out and mutilate some of the course in revenge, while with water hazards you get to roll up your pants and have a nice paddle. But putting is like drinking tea with your pinkie raised, or more precisely, like threading a needle with a thread that bends at the last moment. (Tournament greens, by the way, are not to be compared with miniature golf; they are more, if you can stand another metaphor, like ice that tilts.)

Testimonials to the human toll exacted by this disgusting practice can be picked up anywhere the strange game is played. The incomparable Ben Hogan had to quit the game because of it. Although Hogan's nerves had won him the name of "Iceman," and although the rest of his game still glittered, he suddenly succumbed to something known as the yips, a degenerative ailment that freezes the hands in terror and renders them incapable of so much as lifting the club head back.

Out of sheer and unprecedented compassion, the unbending masters of golf bent just enough to let Snead use a club shaped like a T square during his later years, with which he could practically putt from between his legs like an aging croquet player (it didn't help). Gene Sarazen, the Grandma Moses of the game, once suggested, but was *not* granted, a six-inch hole. And if the word of an outsider is of any help, Dick Groat, who played shortstop for the Pirates in the hair-raising, seven-game World Series of 1960, said that he didn't know what pressure was until he stepped onto the eighteenth green in a pro-am tournament.

This is the stuff that Nicklaus feels "comfortable" with? Well, saints be praised. One falls back in awe as a champion so simply and casually defines what the word means. He didn't *look* comfortable, but that had nothing to do with it. He looked, among other things, eager, speculative, and about ready to cry. But inside he apparently felt the kind of joy that inhuman pressure brings only to heroes, and you didn't need to be a golf buff to have felt happy to share a species with such a man as the green jacket was finally slipped over his shoulders.

MIKE ROYKO

"A Very Solid Book"

This oddity appeared in the Chicago Tribune *just before the start of the 1987 season. The year before, the New York Mets had won the National League pennant, helped considerably by the efforts of their first baseman, Keith Hernandez. His book about the campaign landed on the desk of Mike Royko, the renowned columnist on the* Tribune *and a fervid Cubs fan, as what follows surely suggests. The enmity for the New York team stems from 1969, when the Mets caught the Cubs in September and defeated them for the National League pennant. Chicagoans have not forgotten.*

A New York publishing house has sent me a copy of a new paperback book it has just brought out.

With it came a note that said: "We take pleasure in presenting you with this review copy and ask that you please send two copies of your notices to our offices."

I seldom review books in my column. The Chicago paper for which I write has a section that takes care of that. But in this case, I'm going to make an exception.

The book is called "If At First . . ." with a subtitle that says "With the exclusive inside story of the 1986 Championship Season."

The author is Keith Hernandez, who is the first baseman on the New York Mets baseball team. Actually, he didn't write it—some professional ghostwriter did. But the words and story originated with Hernandez. I will begin my review by saying that this is a very solid book. The moment I opened the package and saw what it was about, I threw it against my office wall as hard as I could.

Then I slammed it to the floor and jumped up and down on it. I beat on it with a chair for several minutes until I slumped onto my couch, emotionally and physically spent. Although slightly scuffed, the book was still intact.

It is also a book that can cause excitement. I dropped it on the desk of a friend who has had weekend season tickets at Wrigley Field for the past 10 years. It immediately stirred him to emotional heights. He shouted:

"Why are you showing me that piece of (deleted)? I say (deleted) Hernandez and (deleted) the Mets and (deleted) the whole (deleted) city of New York. And (deleted) you, too."

Then he flung it against a wall and gave it a kick. It still remained intact. I told you it was a solid book.

It's a book that can move a sensitive reader to tears, as I discovered when I showed it to a man who has been going to Cub games since 1946, a year that is known as The Beginning of Darkness.

When he looked at the cover, he choked back a sob, a tear trickled down his cheek, and he said: "Why them? Why not us? What was our sin? How can we atone for it? You know, I asked my clergyman that, and he said he wishes he knew, because he lost $50 betting against them."

And it's a powerful book. As reviewers like to say: It can hit you right in the guts. This was proven when I showed it to a confirmed bleacherite who said: "Excuse me. I'm going to throw up."

But enough of generalities. Let us consider the contents of this book.

On the very first page, Hernandez and his ghostwriter say: "ad made the second out on a long the Mets were through for 1986: o out, nobody on, two runs down, ox already leading the World Series en our scoreboard operator at"

And on page 81, Hernandez says: "round during infield practice, I draw a line man and myself and call our manager over avy? I ask. He laughs."

Moving to page 125, we find: "Oh, sweet bird of youth, however, were a different story. It's diff- quietly as I work my way out of a bad me to listen to his judgments. I wrong with my swing. I know hot to th hardheaded. Dand and I have had"

I know, it sounds kind of garbled, incomprehensible. But that's the way a story reads when you rip the pages of a book in half, one by one, as I've been doing.

Don't misunderstand me. I'm not doing that out of spite. I'm a good sport, a cheerful loser. Why, in the last two years, I don't think I've watched my video of the movie "Fail Safe," in which New York City gets nuked, more than 30 or 40 times.

The fact is, I have found this to be a useful book.

I have been tearing out the pages and crumpling them into little wads.

When I have about 30 or 40 of these wads, I put them in my fireplace under the kindling and light them. They're excellent for getting a fire started.

Then I pour myself a drink, lower the lights, sit back, and stare at the crackling flames.

And I pretend that I'm looking at Shea Stadium.

 SUMMER

ROGER ANGELL

"On the Ball"

It weighs just over five ounces and measures between 2.86 and 2.94 inches in diameter. It is made of a composition-cork nucleus encased in two thin layers of rubber, one black and one red, surrounded by 121 yards of tightly wrapped blue-gray wool yarn, 45 yards of white wool yarn, 53 more yards of blue-gray wool yarn, 150 yards of fine cotton yarn, a coat of rubber cement, and a cowhide (formerly horsehide) exterior, which is held together with 216 slightly raised red cotton stitches. Printed certifications, endorsements, and outdoor advertising spherically attest to its authenticity. Like most institutions, it is considered inferior in its present form to its ancient archetypes, and in this case the complaint is probably justified; on occasion in recent years it has actually been known to come apart under the demands of its brief but rigorous active career. Baseballs are assembled and handstitched in Taiwan (before this year the work was done in Haiti, and before 1973 in Chicopee, Massachusetts), and contemporary pitchers claim that there is a tangible variation in the size and feel of the balls that now come into play in a single game; a true peewee is treasured by hurlers, and its departure from the premises, by fair means or foul, is secretly mourned. But never mind: any baseball is beautiful. No other small package comes as close to the ideal in design and utility. It is a perfect object for a man's hand. Pick it up and it instantly suggests its purpose; it is meant to be thrown a considerable distance—thrown hard and with precision. Its feel and heft are the beginning of the sport's critical dimensions; if it were a fraction of an inch larger or smaller, a few centigrams heavier or lighter, the game of baseball would be utterly different. Hold a baseball in your hand. As it happens, this one is not brand-new. Here, just to one side of the curved surgical welt of stitches, there is a pale-green grass smudge, darkening on one edge almost to black—the mark of an old infield play, a tough grounder now lost in memory. Feel the ball, turn it over in your hand; hold it across the seam or the other way, with the seam just to the side of your middle finger. Speculation stirs. You want to go outdoors and throw this spare and sensual object to somebody or, at the very least, watch somebody else throw it. The game has begun.

EARL L. DACHSLAGER

"What Shakespeare Knew about Baseball"

To the Editor:

It's time to settle once and for all the debate over the first references in print to the game of baseball. The earliest references to baseball occur in the plays of William Shakespeare and include the following:

> "And so I shall catch the fly" (*Henry V*, Act V, Scene ii).
> "I'll catch it ere it come to ground" (*Macbeth*, III, v).
> "A hit, a very palpable hit!" (*Hamlet*, V, ii).
> "You may go walk" (*The Taming of the Shrew*, II, i).
> "Strike!" (*Richard III*, I, iv).
> "For this relief much thanks" (*Hamlet*, I, i).
> "You have scarce time to steal" (*Henry VIII*, III, ii).
> "O hateful error" (*Julius Caesar*, V, i).
> "Run, run, O run!" (*King Lear*, V, iii).
> "My arm is sore" (*Antony and Cleopatra*, II, v).
> "I have no joy in this contract" (*Romeo and Juliet*, II, ii).

I trust that the question of who first wrote about baseball is now finally settled.

Earl L. Dachslager
The Woodlands, Texas

THOMAS WOLFE

FROM *OF TIME AND THE RIVER*

The scene is instant, whole and wonderful. In its beauty and design that vision of the soaring stands, the pattern of forty thousand empetalled faces, the velvet and unalterable geometry of the playing field, and the small lean figures of the players, set there, lonely, tense and waiting in their places, bright, desperate solitary atoms encircled by that huge wall of nameless faces, is incredible. And more than anything it is the light, the miracle of light and shade and color—the crisp blue light that swiftly slants out from the soaring stands and, deepening to violet, begins to march across the velvet field and towards the pitcher's box, that gives the thing its single and incomparable beauty.

The batter stands swinging his bat and grimly waiting at the plate, crouched, tense, the catcher, crouched, the umpire, bent, hands clasped behind his back, and peering forward. All of them are set now in the cold blue of that slanting shadow, except the pitcher who stands out there all alone, calm, desperate, and forsaken in his isolation, with the gold-red swiftly fading light upon him, his figure legible with all the resolution, despair and lonely dignity which that slanting, somehow fatal light can give him.

W. P. KINSELLA

"THE THRILL OF THE GRASS"

The idea for "The Thrill of the Grass" came from a line in W. P. Kinsella's first novel, Shoeless Joe. *At one point Joe Jackson says, "I'd wake up in the night with the smell of the ballpark in my nose and the cool of the grass on my feet. The thrill of the grass."*

1981: the summer the baseball players went on strike. The dull weeks drag by, the summer deepens, the strike is nearly a month old. Outside the city the corn rustles and ripens in the sun. Summer without baseball: a disruption to the psyche. An unexplainable aimlessness engulfs me. I stay later and later each evening in the small office at the rear of my shop. Now, driving home after work, the worst of the rush hour traffic over, it is the time of evening I would normally be heading for the stadium.

I enjoy arriving an hour early, parking in a far corner of the lot, walking slowly toward the stadium, rays of sun dropping softly over my shoulders like tangerine ropes, my shadow gliding with me, black as an umbrella. I like to watch young families beside their campers, the mothers in shorts, grilling hamburgers, their men drinking beer. I enjoy seeing little boys dressed in the home team uniform, barely toddling, clutching hotdogs in upraised hands.

I am a failed shortstop. As a young man, I saw myself diving to my left, graceful as a toppling tree, fielding high grounders like a cat leaping for butterflies, bracing my right foot and tossing to first, the throw true as if a steel ribbon connected my hand and the first baseman's glove. I dreamed of leading the American League in hitting—being inducted into the Hall of Fame. I batted .217 in my senior year of high school and averaged 1.3 errors per nine innings.

I know the stadium will be deserted; nevertheless I wheel my car down off the freeway, park, and walk across the silent lot, my footsteps rasping and mournful. Strangle-grass and creeping charlie are already inching up through the gravel, surreptitious, surprised at their own ease. Faded bottle caps, rusted bits of chrome, an occasional paper clip, recede into the earth. I circle a ticket booth, sun-faded, empty, the door closed by an oversized padlock. I walk beside the tall, machinery-green, board fence. A half mile away a few cars hiss along the freeway; overhead a single-engine plane fizzes lazily. The whole place is silent as an empty classroom, like a house suddenly without children.

It is then that I spot the door-shape. I have to check twice to be sure it is there: a door cut in the deep green boards of the fence, more the promise of a door than the real thing, the kind of door, as children, we cut in the sides of cardboard boxes with our mothers' paring knives. As I move closer, a golden circle of lock, like an acrimonious eye, establishes its certainty.

I stand, my nose so close to the door I can smell the faint odor of paint, the golden eye of a lock inches from my own eyes. My desire to be inside the ballpark is so great that for the first time in my life I commit a criminal act. I have been a locksmith for over forty years. I take the small tools from the pocket of my jacket, and in less time than it would take a speedy runner to circle the bases I am inside the stadium. Though the ballpark is open-air, it smells of abandonment; the walkways and seating areas are cold as basements. I breathe the odors of rancid popcorn and wilted cardboard.

The maintenance staff were laid off when the strike began. Synthetic grass does not need to be cut or watered. I stare down at the ball diamond, where just to the right of the pitcher's mound, a single weed, perhaps two inches high, stands defiant in the rain-pocked dirt.

The field sits breathless in the orangy glow of the evening sun. I stare at the potato-colored earth of the infield, that wide, dun arc, surrounded by plastic grass. As I contemplate the prickly turf, which scorches the thighs and buttocks of a sliding player as if he were being seared by hot steel, it stares back in its uniform ugliness. The seams that send routinely hit ground balls veering at tortuous angles are vivid, gray as scars.

I remember the ballfields of my childhood, the outfields full of soft hummocks and brown-eyed gopher holes.

I stride down from the stands and walk out to the middle of the field. I touch the stubble that is called grass, take off my shoes, but find it is like walking on a row of toothbrushes. It was an evil day when they stripped the sod from this ballpark, cut it into yard-wide swathes, rolled it, memories and all, into great green-and-black cinnamonroll shapes, trucked it away. Nature temporarily defeated. But Nature is patient.

Over the next few days an idea forms within me, ripening, swelling, pushing everything else into a corner. It is like knowing a new, wonderful joke and not being able to share. I need an accomplice.

I go to see a man I don't know personally, though I have seen his face peering at me from the financial pages of the local newspaper, and the *Wall Street Journal*, and I have been watching his profile at the baseball stadium, two boxes to the right of me, for several years. He is a fan. Really a fan. When the weather is intemperate, or the game not close, the people around us disappear like flowers closing at sunset, but we are always there until the last pitch. I know he is a man who attends because of the beauty and mystery of the game, a man who can sit during the last of the ninth with the game decided innings ago, and draw joy from watching the first baseman adjust the angle of his glove as the pitcher goes into his windup.

He, like me, is a first-base-side fan. I've always watched baseball from behind first base. The positions fans choose at sporting events are like politics, religion, or philosophy: a view of the world, a way of seeing the universe. They make no sense to anyone, have no basis in anything but stubbornness.

I brought up my daughters to watch baseball from the first-base side. One lives in Japan and sends me box scores from Japanese newspapers, and Japanese baseball magazines with pictures of superstars politely bowing to one another. She has a season ticket in Yokohama; on the first-base side.

"Tell him a baseball fan is here to see him," is all I will say to his secretary. His office is in a skyscraper, from which he can look out over the city to where the prairie rolls green as mountain water to the limits of the eye. I wait all afternoon in the artificially cool, glassy reception area with its yellow and mauve chairs, chrome and glass coffee tables. Finally, in the late afternoon, my message is passed along.

"I've seen you at the baseball stadium," I say, not introducing myself.

"Yes," he says. "I recognize you. Three rows back, about eight seats to my left. You have a red scorebook and you often bring your daughter. . ."

"Granddaughter. Yes, she goes to sleep in my lap in the late innings, but she knows how to calculate an ERA and she's only in Grade 2."

"One of my greatest regrets," says this tall man, whose mustache and carefully styled hair are polar-bear white, "is that my grandchildren all live over a thousand miles away. You're very lucky. Now, what can I do for you?"

"I have an idea," I say. "One that's been creeping toward me like a first baseman when the bunt sign is on. What do you think about artificial turf?"

"Hmmmf," he snorts, "that's what the strike should be about. Baseball is meant to be played on summer evenings and Sunday afternoons, on grass just cut by a horse-drawn mower," and we smile as our eyes meet.

"I've discovered the ballpark is open, to me anyway," I go on. "There's no one there while the strike is on. The wind blows through the high top of the grandstand, whining until the pigeons in the rafters flutter. It's lonely as a ghost town."

"And what is it you do there, alone with the pigeons?"

"I dream."

"And where do I come in?"

"You've always struck me as a man who dreams. I think we have things in common. I think you might like to come with me. I could show you what I dream, paint you pictures, suggest what might happen . . ."

He studies me carefully for a moment, like a pitcher trying to decide if he can trust the sign his catcher has just given him.

"Tonight?" he says. "Would tonight be too soon?"

"Park in the northwest corner of the lot about 1:00 A.M. There is a door about fifty yards to the right of the main gate. I'll open it when I hear you."

He nods.

I turn and leave.

The night is clear and cotton warm when he arrives. "Oh, my," he says, staring at the stadium turned chrome-blue by a full moon. "Oh, my," he says again, breathing in the faint odors of baseball, the reminder of fans and players not long gone.

"Let's go down to the field," I say. I am carrying a cardboard pizza box, holding it on the upturned palms of my hands, like an offering.

When we reach the field, he first stands on the mound, makes an awkward attempt at a windup, then does a little sprint from first to about halfway to second. "I think I know what you've brought," he says, gesturing toward the box, "but let me see anyway."

I open the box in which rests a square foot of sod, the grass smooth and pure, cool as a swatch of satin, fragile as baby's hair.

"Ohhh," the man says, reaching out a finger to test the moistness of it. "Oh, I see."

We walk across the field, the harsh, prickly turf making the bottoms of my feet tingle, to the left-field corner where, in the angle formed by the foul line and the warning track, I lay down the square foot of sod. "That's beautiful," my friend says, kneeling beside me, placing his hand, fingers spread wide, on the verdant square, leaving a print faint as a veronica.

I take from my belt a sickle-shaped blade, the kind used for cutting carpet. I measure along the edge of the sod, dig the point in, and pull carefully toward me. There is a ripping sound, like tearing an old bed sheet. I hold up the square of artificial turf like something freshly killed, while all the time digging the sharp point into the packed earth I have exposed. I replace the sod lovingly, covering the newly bared surface.

"A protest," I say.

"But it could be more," the man replies.

"I hoped you'd say that. It could be. If you'd like to come back. . ."

"Tomorrow night?"

"Tomorrow night would be fine. But there will be an admission charge. . ."

"A square of sod?"

"A square of sod two inches thick. . ."

"Of the same grass?"

"Of the same grass. But there's more."

"I suspected as much."

"You must have a friend. . ."

"Who would join us?"

"Yes."

"I have two. Would that be all right?"

"I trust your judgment."

"My father. He's over eighty," my friend says. "You might have seen him with me once or twice. He lives over fifty miles from here, but if I call him he'll come. And my friend. . ."

"If they pay their admission they'll be welcome. . ."

"And *they* may have friends. . ."

"Indeed they may. But what will we do with this?" I say, holding up the sticky-backed square of turf, which smells of glue and fabric.

"We could mail them anonymously to baseball executives, politicians, clergymen."

"Gentle reminders not to tamper with Nature."

We dance toward the exit, rampant with excitement.

"You will come back? You'll bring others?"

"Count on it," says my friend.

They do come, those trusted friends, and friends of friends, each making a live, green deposit. At first, a tiny row of sod squares begins to inch along toward left-center field. The next night even more people arrive, the following night more again, and the night after there is positively a crowd. Those who come once seem always to return accompanied by friends, occasionally a son or young brother, but mostly men my age or older, for we are the ones who remember the grass.

Night after night the pilgrimage continues. The first night I stand inside the deep green door, listening. I hear a vehicle stop; hear a car door close with a snug thud. I open the door when the sound of soft-soled shoes on gravel tells me it is time. The door swings silent as a snake. We nod curt greetings to each other. Two men pass me, each carrying a grasshopper-legged sprinkler. Later, each sprinkler will sizzle like frying onions as it wheels, a silver sparkler in the moonlight.

During the nights that follow, I stand sentinel-like at the top of the grandstand, watching as my cohorts arrive. Old men walking across a parking lot in a row, in the dark, carrying coiled hoses, looking like the many wheels of a locomotive, old men who have slipped away from their homes, skulked down their sturdy sidewalks, breathing the cool, grassy, after-midnight air. They have left behind their sleeping, gray-haired women, their immaculate bungalows, their manicured lawns. They continue to walk across the parking lot, while occasionally a soft wheeze, a nibbling, breathy sound like an old horse might make, divulges their humanity. They move methodically toward the baseball stadium which hulks against the moon-blue sky like a small mountain. Beneath the tint of starlight, the tall light standards which rise above the fences and grandstand glow purple, necks bent forward, like sunflowers heavy with seed.

My other daughter lives in this city, is married to a fan, but one who watches baseball from behind third base. And like marrying outside the faith, she has been converted to the third-base side. They have their own season tickets, twelve rows up just to the outfield side of third base. I love her, but I don't trust her enough to let her in on my secret.

I could trust my granddaughter, but she is too young. At her age she shouldn't have to face such responsibility. I remember my own daughter, the one who lives in Japan, remember her at nine, all knees, elbows, and missing teeth—remember peering in her room, seeing her asleep, a shower of well-thumbed baseball cards scattered over her chest and pillow.

I haven't been able to tell my wife—it is like my compatriots and I are involved in a ritual for true believers only. Maggie, who knew me when I still dreamed of playing professionally myself—Maggie, after over half a lifetime together, comes and sits in my lap in the comfortable easy chair which has adjusted through the years to my thickening shape, just as she has. I love to hold the lightness of her, her tongue exploring my mouth, gently as a baby's finger.

"Where do you go?" she asks sleepily when I crawl into bed at dawn.

I mumble a reply. I know she doesn't sleep well when I'm gone. I can feel her body rhythms change as I slip out of bed after midnight.

"Aren't you too old to be having a change of life," she says, placing her toast-warm hand on my cold thigh.

I am not the only one with this problem.

"I'm developing a reputation," whispers an affable man at the ballpark. "I imagine any number of private investigators following any number of cars across the city. I imagine them creeping about the parking lot, shining pen-lights on license plates, trying to guess what we're up to. Think of the reports they must prepare. I wonder if our wives are disappointed that we're not out discoing with frizzy-haired teenagers?"

Night after night, virtually no words are spoken. Each man seems to know his assignment. Not all bring sod. Some carry rakes, some hoes, some hoses, which, when joined together, snake across the infield and outfield, dispensing the blessing of water. Others cradle in their arms bags of earth for building up the infield to meet the thick, living sod.

I often remain high in the stadium, looking down on the men moving over the earth, dark as ants, each sodding, cutting, watering, shaping. Occasionally the moon finds a knife blade as it trims the sod or slices away a chunk of artificial turf, and tosses the reflection skyward like a bright ball. My body tingles. There should be symphony music playing. Everyone should be humming "America the Beautiful."

Toward dawn, I watch the men walking away in groups, like small patrols of soldiers, carrying, instead of arms, the tools and utensils which breathe life back into the arid ballfield.

Row by row, night by night, we lay the little squares of sod, moist as chocolate cake with green icing. Where did all the sod come from? I picture many men, in many parts of the city, surreptitiously cutting chunks out of their own lawns in the leafy midnight darkness, listening to the uncomprehending protests of their wives the next day—pretending to know nothing of it—pretending to have called the police to investigate.

When the strike is over I know we will all be here to watch the workouts, to hear the recalcitrant joints crackling like twigs after the forced inactivity. We will sit in our regular seats, scattered like popcorn throughout the stadium, and we'll nod as we pass on the way to the exits, exchange secret smiles, proud as new fathers.

For me, the best part of all will be the surprise. I feel like a magician who has gestured hypnotically and produced an elephant from thin air. I know I am not alone in my wonder. I know that rockets shoot off in half-a-hundred chests; the excitement of birthday mornings, Christmas eves, and hometown doubleheaders boils within each of my conspirators. Our secret rites have been performed with love, like delivering a valentine to a sweetheart's door in that blue-steel span of morning just before dawn.

Players and management are meeting round the clock. A settlement is imminent. I have watched the stadium covered square foot by square foot until it looks like green graph paper. I have stood and felt the cool odors of the grass rise up and touch my face. I have studied the lines between each small square, watched those lines fade until they were visible to my eyes alone, then not even to them.

What will the players think, as they straggle into the stadium and find the miracle we have created? The old-timers will raise their heads like ponies, as far away as the parking lot, when the thrill of the grass reaches their nostrils. And, as they dress, they'll recall sprawling in the lush outfields of childhood, the grass as cool as a mother's hand on a forehead.

"Goodbye, goodbye," we say at the gate, the smell of water, of sod, of sweat, small perfumes in the air. Our secrets are safe with each other. We go our separate ways.

Alone in the stadium in the last chill darkness before dawn, I drop to my hands and knees in the center of the outfield. My palms are sodden. Water touches the skin between my spread fingers. I lower my face to the silvered grass, which, wonder of wonders, already has the ephemeral odors of baseball about it.

IRA BERKOW

"A Snorkeler's Tale"

When the landslide reelection victory for Bill Bradley as United States senator from New Jersey was apparent last Tuesday evening, one of the television commentators discussed the senator's style.

He spoke of the great respect that the tall, dark-haired man with the oddly upturned left eyebrow had earned from both sides of the aisle in the Senate, of how hard he had worked to gain a firm grasp of issues, and of the tremendous popularity he had attained in his state. The commentator also mentioned that Bill Bradley's speaking voice was rather flat, though he had been endeavoring to improve it, and that his sense of humor could be wooden.

Dave DeBusschere and his wife, Gerri, smiled when that last point was made. That's not quite the Bill Bradley they know.

"He's not a joke teller; some people just aren't," said Gerri DeBusschere. "But Dave and I enjoyed his kind of wacko sense of humor, especially when he was with the Knicks."

Dave DeBusschere, now the Knicks' executive vice president and director of basketball operations, was Bill Bradley's roommate on the road when they played together, from 1968 through 1974.

"I remember when a man began writing and calling Bill at hotels," said Gerri, "and Bill would whisper to the guy on the phone, and they'd have meetings in coffee shops. Dave finally asked Bill who the guy was. Bill said, 'He thinks I'm not Bill Bradley. He thinks I'm really an Albanian spy.' And Bill encouraged him."

On the road in basketball, Bradley, the Princeton graduate and Rhodes scholar, also involved himself in such issues as prison reform, the economy, and foreign affairs. Unlike most of the other players, who were dapper, he seemed to have little time for sartorial concerns. He would sometimes forget to bring extra socks and would borrow DeBusschere's, and when a button broke on his shirt he'd replace it with a paper clip. His raincoat was generally wrapped up in a ball and carried under his arm. On seeing it, Dick Barnett would make a sound like a foghorn, an esthetic appraisal of sorts.

After the 1974 playoffs, the DeBusscheres, Bradley and his wife,

Ernestine, and another couple, the Nick Kladdises of Chicago, went to Greece on vacation. Gerri DeBusschere recalls that everyone except Bradley took at least one suitcase—the DeBusscheres had one suitcase just for their scuba-diving equipment. "Bill came with a little gym bag," she said. "He didn't even have a bathing suit. He swam in his Knick practice shorts."

The three couples rented a cabin cruiser and embarked from the port of Piraeus for a two-week trip around the Greek islands. They lay on the deck and watched the islands go by, and Dave and Bill, particularly, would don snorkeling masks and flippers, drop down, and explore the Aegean. From the boat one afternoon, they saw a church on a hill of a tiny, isolated island. They decided to get a closer look.

The island was so small that there was no place to dock the boat, so it remained about a quarter of a mile out to sea. Bradley and DeBusschere swam to shore. DeBusschere came up first, and saw a man sitting on a beach chair, reading a book.

DeBusschere took off his mask, and the man jumped up, his book dropping out of his hands. The man's mouth was agape, and he pointed frantically at DeBusschere.

DeBusschere thought that there might be something wrong with him, or that he was frightened that someone who was 6 feet 6 inches tall was suddenly rising from the sea.

"Then," DeBusschere recalled, "the man stuttered, 'You're, you're you're Dave . . . Dave . . . Dave DeBusschere!' "

DeBusschere was surprised that anyone on this little island could speak English, let alone recognize him.

"Then Bill came out of the water right behind me," DeBusschere recalled. "The guy says, 'Oh, my God! Bill Bradley too! I can't believe this!' "

The man sputtered that he had season tickets under the basket, and that he had been postponing his vacation until after the playoffs, and that he was on this island because he had been so overworked that his wife had said he needed to go to a secluded place for a rest.

"And to see you guys here is—"

"Sure," Bradley said with understanding, "and Willis Reed will be here in a minute."

"The whole team is coming up," said DeBusschere.

The man said, "Wait, wait right here. I've got to get my wife. She'll never believe this. Oh, my God!"

The man flew off down the beach, screaming his wife's name.

Bradley turned to DeBusschere and said with a grin, "Let's leave."

DeBusschere nodded. The pair clamped on their masks and disappeared back into the water.

Gerri DeBusschere happened to be watching this from the deck of the boat. She sees the man now racing back along the beach, dragging his wife by the hand.

He returns to the spot where his chair is, and where his book is lying in the sand. Otherwise, the beach is deserted.

He goes to the water's edge, looking around and pointing. Meanwhile, Bradley and DeBusschere have returned to the boat and are hiding in a cabin below deck. Nick Kladdis revs up the motor, and the boat heads farther out to sea.

On the beach, the man is waving wildly, while his wife is looking at him and then looking at the receding boat.

Bradley and DeBusschere never saw him again. The next season, they looked for him under the baskets at Madison Square Garden, but he wasn't there.

"The guy's wife probably thought he had flipped," said Gerri DeBusschere, "and he never came up to Bill or Dave and said, 'I saw you in Greece.' He was probably too embarrassed. He probably thought he hadn't really seen them, and that he was just suffering from being overworked."

JOHN McPHEE

"Centre Court"

John McPhee's insider's look at Wimbledon is his second extended work on tennis—the first being a book-length description (Levels of the Game) *of a semifinal tennis match between Arthur Ashe and Clark Graebner at Forest Hills. For his research he spent a lot of time with the two, even traveling to Puerto Rico that fall to spend a couple of weeks with the team—which included Ashe and Graebner—training for the Davis Cup match against India. The relationship he developed with the players gave him a special backstage entrée to tournament tennis, specifically Wimbledon. McPhee had a special fondness for Wimbledon, having spent afternoons there while a postgraduate student at Cambridge University. When* Playboy *magazine, whose editors had admired* Levels of the Game, *asked him to do a story on the Wimbledon tournament in 1970, McPhee jumped at the chance.*

The account which follows was McPhee's last about tennis. In fact, he's given up the game itself. "In 1977 something snapped in my arm while I was on the court," he told me. "I couldn't pick up a piece of paper. I needed to train because I was scheduled to go up to Alaska to run around with sled dogs. So I took to the road and ran . . . and discovered that there's not much exercise in tennis. I became a runner."

"And writing about tennis?"

"Well, I think you move on. You become deeply involved, but then you go on and find something else to do."

Hoad on Court 5, weathered and leonine, has come from Spain, where he lives on his tennis ranch in the plains of Andalusia. Technically, he is an old hero trying a comeback, but, win or lose, for this crowd it is enough of a comeback that Hoad is here. There is tempestuous majesty in him, and people have congregated seven deep around his court just to feel the atmosphere there and to see him again. Hoad serves explosively, and the ball hits the fence behind his opponent without first intersecting the ground. His precision is off. The dead always rise slowly. His next serve splits the service line. Hoad is blasting some hapless Swiss into submission. As he tosses the ball up to serve again, all eyes lift above the court and the surrounding hedges, the green canvas fences, the beds of climbing roses, the ivy-covered walls—and at the top of the ball's parabola, it hangs for an instant in the sky against a background of half-timbered houses among plane trees and poplars on suburban hills. Rising from the highest hill is the steeple of St. Mary's Church, Wimbledon, where Hoad was married sixteen years ago. He swings through the ball and hits it very deep. "Fault." Hoad's wife, Jenny, and their several children are at the front of the crowd beside the court, watching with no apparent dismay as Hoad detonates his spectacularly horizontal serves.

Smith, in a remote part of the grounds, is slowly extinguishing Jaime Fillol. Tall, straightforward, All-American, Stan Smith is ranked number one in the United States. He grew up in Pasadena, where his father sold real estate. A fine basketball player, Smith gave it up for tennis. He is a big hitter who thinks with caution. Under the umpire's chair is his wallet. The locker rooms of Wimbledon are only slightly less secure than the vaults of Zurich, but Smith always takes his wallet with him to the court. Fillol, a *Chileno*, supple and blue-eyed, says "Good shot" when Smith drives one by him. Such remarks are rare at Wimbledon, where Alphonse would have a difficult time finding Gaston. The players are not, for the most part, impolite, but they go about their business silently. When they show appreciation of another player's shot, it is genuine. There is no structure to Fillol's game. Now he dominates, now he crumbles. Always he faces the big, controlled, relentless power of the all-but-unwavering Smith. Smith does not like to play on these distant courts close to the walls of the Wimbledon compound. The wind rattles the ivy and the ivy sometimes rattles Smith—but hardly enough to save Fillol.

John Alexander has brown hair that shines from washing. It hangs straight and touches the collar of his shirt in a trimmed horizontal line. The wind gusts, and the hair flows behind him. Not yet twenty, he is tall, good-looking, has bright clear eyes, and could be a Shakespearean page. In his right hand is a Dunlop. He drives a forehand deep crosscourt. There is little time for him to get positioned before the ball comes back—fast, heavy, fizzing with topspin.

In Alexander's mind, there is no doubt that the man on the other side of the net is the best tennis player on earth. He hit with him once, in Sydney, when Laver needed someone to warm him up for a match with Newcombe. But that was all. He has never played against him before, and now, on the Number 1 Court, Alexander feels less the hopeless odds against him than a sense of being honored to be here at all, matched against Laver in the pre-eminent tournament of lawn tennis. The Number 1 Court is one of Wimbledon's two stadiums, and it is a separate closed world, where two players are watched in proximity by seven thousand pairs of eyes. Laver is even quicker and hits harder than Alexander had imagined, and Alexander, in his nervousness, is over-hitting. He lunges, swings hard, and hits wide.

Laver is so far ahead that the match has long since become an exhibition. Nonetheless, he plays every point as if it were vital. He digs for gets. He sends up topspin lobs. He sprints and dives for Alexander's smashes. He punches volleys toward the corners and, when they miss, he winces. He is not playing against Alexander. He is playing against perfection. This year, unlike other years, he does not find himself scratching for form. He feels good in general and he feels good to be here. He would rather play at Wimbledon than anywhere else at all, because, as he explains, "It's what the atmosphere instills here. At Wimbledon things come to a pitch. The best grass. The best crowd. The royalty. You all of a sudden feel the whole thing is important. You play your best tennis."

Laver, playing Alexander in the second round, is in the process of defending the Wimbledon title. In the history of this sport, no player has built a record like Laver's. There have been only three grand slams—one by Budge, two by Laver. Wimbledon is the tournament the players most want to win. It is the annual world championship. Budge won

Wimbledon twice. Perry won it three times. Tilden won it three times. Laver has won Wimbledon four times, and no one at Wimbledon this afternoon has much doubt that he is on his way to his fifth championship. There are one hundred and twenty-eight men in this tournament, and one hundred and twenty-seven of them are crowded into the shadow of this one small Australian. Winning is everything to tennis players, although more than ninety-nine percent of them are certain losers—and they expect to lose to him. Laver, who has a narrow and delicate face, freckles, a hawk's nose, thinning red hair, and the forearm of a Dungeness crab, is known to all of them as Rocket. Alexander, who is also Australian and uses a Dunlop no doubt because Laver does, has just aced the Rocket twice and leads him 40–love. To prepare for this match, Alexander hit with Roger Taylor, who is left-handed, and practiced principally serving to Taylor's backhand. Alexander serves again, to Laver's backhand. When Laver is in trouble, fury comes into his game. He lashes out now and passes Alexander on the right. He passes Alexander on the left. He carries him backward from 40–love to advantage out. Alexander runs to the net under a big serve. A crosscourt backhand goes by him so fast that his racquet does not move. In the press section, Roy McKelvie, dean of English tennis writers, notifies all the other tennis writers that beating Laver would be a feat comparable to the running of the first four-minute mile. The match is over. "Thank you," Laver says to Alexander at the net. "I played well." A person who has won two grand slams and four Wimbledons can say that becomingly. The remark is honest and therefore graceful. Alexander took four games in three sets. "I've improved. I've learned more possibilities," he says afterward. "It should help me. The improvement won't show for a while, but it is there."

Roger Taylor leans against the guardrail on the sun-deck roof of the Players' Tea Room. He is twenty-five feet above the ground—the Players' Tea Room is raised on concrete stilts—and from that high perspective he can see almost all the lawns of Wimbledon. There are sixteen grass courts altogether, and those that are not attended with grandstands are separated by paved walkways ten feet wide. Benches line the edges of the walkways. Wimbledon is well designed. Twenty-five thousand people can move about in its confined spaces without feeling particularly crowded. Each court stands alone and the tennis can be watched at point-blank range. The whole compound is somehow ordered within ten acres and all paths eventually lead to the high front façade of the Centre Court, the name of which, like the name Wimbledon itself, is synecdochical. "Centre Court" refers not only to the *ne plus ultra* tennis lawn but also to the entire stadium that surrounds it. A three-story dodecagon, with a roof that shelters most of its seats, it resembles an Elizabethan theater. Its exterior walls are alive with ivy and in planter boxes on a balcony above its principal doorway are rows of pink and blue hydrangeas. Hydrangeas are the hallmark of Wimbledon. They are not only displayed on high but also appear in flower beds among the outer courts. In their pastel efflorescence, the hydrangeas appear to be geraniums that have escalated socially. When the Wimbledon fortnight begins each year, London newspapers are always full of purple language about the green velvet lawns and the pink and blue hydrangeas. The lawns are tough and hard and frequently somewhat brown. Their color means nothing to the players or to the ground staff, and this is one clue to the superiority of Wimbledon courts over the more lumpy but cosmetic sods of tennis lawns elsewhere. The hydrangeas, on the other hand, are strictly show business. They are purchased for the tournament.

Taylor is watching a festival of tennis from the roof of the tearoom. Szorenyi against Morozova, Roche against Ruffels, Brummer against O'Hara, Drysdale against Spear—he can see fourteen matches going on at the same time, and the cork-popping sound of the tennis balls fills the air. "This is the greatest tournament in the world," he says. "It is a tremendous thrill to play in it. You try to tune yourself up for it all year." Taylor is somewhat unusual among the people milling around him on the sun deck. For the most part, of course, they are aliens and their chatter is polyglot. Hungarians, Japanese, Finns, Colombians, Greeks— they come from forty nations, while home to Taylor is a three-room flat in Putney, just up the road from Wimbledon. Taylor is a heavy-set man with dark hair and a strong, quiet manner. His father is a Sheffield steelworker. His mother taught him his tennis. And now he is seeded sixteenth at Wimbledon. It took him five sets to get out of the first round, but that does not seem to have shaken his composure. His trouble would appear to be in front of him. In the pattern of the draw, the sixteenth seed is the nearest seeded player to the number-one seed, which is tantamount to saying that Taylor's outlook is pale.

On the promenade below, a Rolls-Royce moves slowly through the crowd. It contains Charlie Pasarell, making his appearance to compete in singles. Is Pasarell so staggeringly rich that he can afford to ride to his matches in a Rolls-Royce? Yes—as it happens—but the Rolls in this case is not his. It is Wimbledon's and it has been sent by the tennis club to fetch him. Wimbledon is uniquely considerate toward players, going to great lengths to treat them as if they were plenipotentiaries from their respective nations and not gifted gibbons, which is at times their status elsewhere. Wimbledon has a whole fleet of Rolls-Royces—and Mercedes, Humbers, and Austin Princesses—that deploys to all parts of

London, to wherever the players happen to be staying, to collect them for their matches. Each car flies from its bonnet a small pennon in the colors of Wimbledon—mauve and green. Throughout the afternoons, these limousines enter the gates and murmur through the crowd to deliver to the locker rooms not only the Emersons, the Ashes, the Ralstons, and the Roches but also the Dowdeswelles, the Montrenauds, the Dibleys, and the Phillips-Moores.

In the Players' Tea Room, the players sit on pale-blue wicker chairs at pale-blue wicker tables eating strawberries in Devonshire cream. The tearoom is glassed-in on three sides, overlooking the courts. Hot meals are served there, to players only—a consideration absent in all other places where they play. Wimbledon is, among other things, the business convention of the tennis industry, and the tearoom is the site of a thousand deals—minor endorsements, major endorsements, commitments to tournaments over the coming year. The Players' Tea Room is the meat market of international tennis. Like bullfight impresarios converging on Madrid from all parts of Spain at the *Feria* of San Isidro, tournament directors from all parts of the world come to the Players' Tea Room at Wimbledon to bargain for—as they put it—"the horseflesh." The tearoom also has a first-rate bar, where, frequently enough, one may encounter a first-rate bookie. His name is Jeff Guntrip. He is a trim and modest-appearing man from Kent. His credentials go far deeper than the mere fact that he is everybody's favorite bookie. Years ago, Guntrip was a tennis player. He competed at Wimbledon.

In the Members' Enclosure, on the Members' Lawn, members and their guests are sitting under white parasols, consuming best-end-of-lamb salad and strawberries in Devonshire cream. Around them are pools of goldfish. The goldfish are rented from Harrods. The members are rented from the uppermost upper middle class. Wimbledon is the annual convention of this stratum of English society, starboard out, starboard home. The middle middle class must have its strawberries and cream, too, and—in just the way that hot dogs are sold at American sporting events—strawberries and thick Devonshire cream are sold for five shillings the dish from stalls on the Tea Lawn and in the Court Buffet. County representatives, whoever they are, eat strawberries and cream in the County Representatives' Enclosure. In the Officials' Buttery, officials, between matches, eat strawberries and cream. An occasional strawberry even makes its way into the players' locker rooms, while almost anything else except an authentic player would be squashed en route. The doors are guarded by bobbies eight feet tall with night sticks by Hillerich & Bradsby. The Ladies' Dressing Room at Wimbledon is so secure that only two men have ever entered it in the history of the tournament—a Frenchman and a blind masseur. The Frenchman was the great Jean Borotra, who in 1925 effected his entry into the women's locker room and subsequently lost his Wimbledon crown.

The Gentlemen's Dressing Room is *sui generis* in the sportive world, with five trainer-masseurs in full-time attendance. Around the periphery of the locker areas are half a dozen completely private tub rooms. When players come off the courts of Wimbledon, they take baths. Huge spigots deliver hot waterfalls into pond-size tubs, and on shelves beside the tubs are long-handled scrub brushes and sponges as big as footballs. The exhausted athletes dive in, lie on their backs, stare at the ceiling, and float with victory or marinate in defeat. The tubs are the one place in Wimbledon where they can get away from one another. When they are finally ready to arrange themselves for their return to society, they find on a shelf beneath a mirror a bottle of pomade called Extract of Honey and Flowers.

Smith comes into the locker room, slowly removes his whites, and retreats to the privacy of a tub closet, where, submerged for twenty-five minutes, he contemplates the loss of one set in the course of his match with Fillol. He concludes that his trouble was the rustling ivy. Scott comes in after a 14–12 finish in a straight-set victory over Krog. Scott opens his locker. Golf balls fall out. Scott runs four miles a day through the roughs of the golf course that is just across Church Road from the tennis club—the All-England Lawn Tennis and Croquet Club, Wimbledon. Other players—Graebner, Kalogeropoulos, Diepraam, Tiriac—are dressing for other matches. Upwards of sixty matches a day are played on the lawns of Wimbledon, from two in the afternoon until sundown. The sun in the English summer takes a long time going down. Play usually stops around eight P.M.

Leaving the locker room dressed for action, a tennis player goes in one of two directions. To the right, a wide portal with attending bobbies leads to the outer courts. To the left is a pair of frosted-glass doors that resemble the entry to an operating amphitheater in a teaching hospital. Players going through those doors often enough feel just as they would if they were being wheeled in on rolling tables. Beyond the frosted glass is the Centre Court—with the BBC, the Royal Box, and fourteen thousand live spectators in close propinquity to the hallowed patch of ground on which players have to hit their way through their nerves or fall if they cannot. There is an archway between the locker room and the glass doors, and over this arch the celebrated phrase of Kipling has been painted: "IF YOU CAN MEET WITH TRIUMPH AND DISASTER AND TREAT THOSE TWO IMPOSTORS JUST THE SAME."

Rosewall is on the Number 8 Court, anesthetizing Addison. Rosewall wears on his shirt the monogram BP. What is this for? Has he changed his name? Not precisely. Here in this most august of all the milieus of tennis, here in what was once the bastion of all that was noblest and most amateur in sport, Rosewall is representing British Petroleum. Rosewall represents the oil company so thoroughly, in fact, that on the buff blazer he wears to the grounds each day, the breast pocket is also monogrammed BP. There is nothing unusual in this respect about Rosewall. All the tennis players are walking billboards. They are extensions of the outdoor-advertising industry. Almost everything they drink, wear, and carry is an ad for some company. Laver won his grand slams with a Dunlop. He has used a Dunlop most of his life. His first job after he left his family's farm in Queensland was in a Dunlop factory in Sydney, making racquets. Recently, though, he has agreed to use Donnay racquets in certain parts of the world, and Chemold [gold-colored metal] racquets elsewhere, for an aggregate of about thirty thousand dollars a year. In the United States, he still uses his Dunlops. Donnay has him under contract at Wimbledon; however, the word among the players is that the Rocket is still using his Dunlops but has had them repainted to look like Donnays. Roche and Emerson are under contract to Chemold. They also have golden rackets. All things together. As he makes about one hundred and twenty-five thousand dollars a year through such deals. He gets fifty thousand dollars for using the Head Competition, the racquet that looks like a rug beater. He gets twenty-five thousand dollars from Coca-Cola for personal appearances arranged by the company and for drinking Coke in public as frequently as he can, particularly when photographers happen to be shooting him. Lutz and Smith are under contract to consume Pepsi-Cola—in like volume but for less pay. Ask Pasarell if he likes Adidas shoes. "I do, in Europe," he enthuses. He is paid to wear Adidas in Europe, but in the United States he has a different deal, the same one Lutz, Graebner, Smith, and King have, with Uniroyal Pro Keds.

Players endorse nets, gut, artificial court surfaces, and every item of clothing from the jock on out. Some players lately have begun to drink— under contract—a mysterious brown fluid called Biostrath Elixir. Made in a Swiss laboratory, it comes in small vials and contains honey, malt, orange juice, and the essences of ninety kinds of medicinal herbs. Others have signed contracts to wear copper bracelets that are said to counteract voodoo, rheumatism, and arthritis. Nearly everyone's clothing contract is with one or the other of the two giants of tennis haberdashery—Fred Perry and René Lacoste. When Pilic appears in a Perry shirt and Ashe in a Lacoste shirt, they are not so much wearing these garments as advertising them. Tennis is a closed world. Its wheeler-dealers are bygone players (Kramer, Dell). Its outstanding bookie is a former player. Even its tailors, apparently, must first qualify as Wimbledon champions—Lacoste, 1925, 1928; Perry, 1934, 1935, 1936. Rosewall has somehow escaped these two. He wears neither the alligator emblem of Lacoste nor the triumphal garland of Perry. However, he is hardly in his shirt for nothing. In addition to the BP, Rosewall's shirt displays a springing panther—symbol of Slazenger. All this heraldry makes him rich before he steps onto the court, but it doesn't seem to slow him up. He is the most graceful tennis player now playing the game, and gracefully he sutures Addison, two, four and zero.

The Russians advance in mixed doubles. Keldie and Miss Harris have taken a set from the Russians, but that is all the Russians will yield. Keldie is a devastatingly handsome tall fellow who wears tinted wraparound glasses and has trouble returning serve. Miss Harris has no difficulty with returns. In mixed doubles, the men hit just as hard at the women as they do at each other. Miss Harris is blonde, with her part in the middle and pigtails of the type that suggests windmills and canals. She is quite pretty and her body is lissome all the way to her ankles, at which point she turns masculine in Adidas shoes with three black bands. The Russians show no expressions on their faces, which are young and attractive, dark-eyed. The Soviet Union decided to go in for tennis some years ago. A program was set up. Eight Russians are now at Wimbledon, and these—Metreveli and Miss Morozova—are the outstanding two. Both use Dunlops. They play with balletic grace—remarkable, or so it seems, in people to whose part of the world the sport is so alien. Miss Morozova, a severely beautiful young woman, has high cheekbones and almond eyes that suggest remote places to the east—Novosibirsk, Semipalatinsk. The Russians, like so many players from other odd parts of the earth, are camouflaged in their playing clothes. They are haberdashed by Fred Perry, so they appear more to come from Tennis than from Russia. Think how bad but how distinctive they would look if their clothes had come from GUM. Think what the Indians would look like, the Brazilians, the Peruvians, the Japanese, if they brought their clothes from home. Instead, they all go to Fred Perry's stockroom on Vigo Street in London and load up for the year. The Russians are not permitted to take cash back to Russia, so they take clothing instead and sell it when they get home. Perry has a line of colored garments as well as white ones, and the Russians take all that is red. Not a red shirt remains in stock once the Russians have been to Vigo Street. Miss Morozova fluidly hits a backhand to Keldie's feet. He picks it up with a half volley. Metreveli puts it away. Game, set, and match to Metreveli and Miss Morozova. No expression.

Graebner and Tiriac, on Court 3, is a vaudeville act. The draw has put
it together. Graebner, the paper salesman from Upper Middle Manhattan, has recently changed his image. He has replaced his horn-rimmed
glasses with contact lenses, and he has grown his soft and naturally
undulant dark-brown hair to the point where he is no longer an exact
replica of Clark Kent but is instead a living simulacrum of Prince Valiant. Tiriac hates Wimbledon. Tiriac, who is Rumanian, feels that he
and his doubles partner, Nastase, are the best doubles team in the world.
Wimbledon disagrees. Tiriac and Nastase are not seeded in doubles, and
Tiriac is mad as hell. He hates Wimbledon and by extension he hates
Graebner. So he is killing Graebner. He has taken a set from him, now
leads him in the second, and Graebner is fighting for his life. Tiriac is of
middle height. His legs are unprepossessing. He has a barrel chest. His
body is encased in a rug of hair. Off court, he wears cargo-net shirts. His
head is covered with medusan wires. Above his mouth is a mustache that
somehow suggests that this man has been to places most people do not
imagine exist. By turns, he glowers at the crowd, glares at the officials,
glares at God in the sky. As he waits for Graebner to serve, he leans
forward, swaying. It is the nature of Tiriac's posture that he bends forward all the time, so now he appears to be getting ready to dive into the
ground. Graebner hits one of his big crunch serves, and Tiriac slams it
back, down the line, so fast that Graebner cannot reach it. Graebner
throws his racquet after the ball. Tiriac shrugs. All the merchants of
Mesopotamia could not equal Tiriac's shrug. Graebner serves again.
Tiriac returns, and stays on the base line. Graebner hits a backhand that
lands on the chalk beside Tiriac. "Out!" shouts the linesman. Graebner
drops his racquet, puts his hands on his hips, and examines the linesman
with hatred. The linesman is seventy-two years old and has worked his
way to Wimbledon through a lifetime of similar decisions in Somerset,
Cornwall, and Kent. But if Graebner lives to be ninety, he will never
forget that call, or that face. Tiriac watches, inscrutably. Even in his
Adidas shoes and his Fred Perry shirt, Tiriac does not in any way resemble a tennis player. He appears to be a panatela ad, a triple agent from
Alexandria, a used-car salesman from central Marrakesh. The set intensi-
fies. Eleven all. Twelve all. Graebner begins to chop the turf with his
racket. Rain falls. "Nothing serious," says Mike Gibson, the referee.
"Play on." Nothing is serious with Gibson until the balls float. Wimbledon sometimes has six or eight showers in an afternoon. This storm lasts
one minute and twenty-two seconds. The sun comes out. Tiriac snaps a
backhand past Graebner, down the line. "Goddamn it!" Graebner
shouts at him. "You're so lucky! My God!" Tiriac has the air of a man
who is about to close a deal in a back room behind a back room. But

Graebner, with a Wagnerian forehand, sends him spinning. Graebner, whose power is as great as ever, has continually improved as a competitor in tight places. The forehands now come in chords. The set ends 14–12, Graebner; and Graebner is still alive at Wimbledon.

When the day is over and the Rolls-Royces move off toward central London, Graebner is not in one. Graebner and his attorney waive the privilege of the Wimbledon limousines. They have something of their own—a black Daimler, so long and impressive that it appears to stop for two traffic lights at once. Graebner's attorney is Scott, who is also his doubles partner. They have just polished Nowicki and Rybarczyk off the court, 6–3, 10–12, 6–3, 6–3, and the Daimler's chauffeur takes them the fifteen miles to the Westbury, a hotel in Mayfair that is heavy with tennis players. Emerson is there, and Ashe, Ralston, Pasarell, Smith, Lutz, van Dillen, Dell and Kramer are both there. Dell, lately captain of the American Davis Cup Team, has created a principality within the anarchy of tennis. He is the attorney-manager of Ashe, Lutz, Pasarell, Smith, Kodes, and others. Dell and Kramer sit up until three A.M. every night picking lint off the shoulders of chaos. Their sport has no head any more, no effective organization, and is still in the flux of transition from devious to straightforward professionalism. Kramer, who is, among other things, the most successful impresario the game has ever known, once had all the power in his pocket. Dell, who is only thirty-two, nightly tries to pick the pocket, although he knows the power is no longer there. Every so often they shout at each other. Kramer is an almost infinitely congenial man. He seems to enjoy Dell in the way that a big mother cat might regard the most aggressive of the litter—with nostalgic amusement and, now and again, a paw in the chops.

Ashe goes off to Trader Vic's for dinner dressed in a sunburst dashiki, and he takes with him two dates. Ralston joins them, and raises an eyebrow. "There is no conflict here," Ashe says, calmly spreading his hands toward the two women. Later in the evening, Ashe will have still another date, and she will go with him to a casino, where they will shoot craps and play blackjack until around one A.M., when Ashe will turn into a tennis player and hurry back to the hotel to get his sleep.

In his flat in Dolphin Square, Laver spends the evening, as he does most evenings, watching Western films on television. Many players take flats while they are in England, particularly if they are married. They prefer familial cooking to the tedium of room service. Some stay in boardinghouses. John Alexander and fifteen other Australians are in a boardinghouse in Putney. Dolphin Square is a vast block of flats, made of red brick, on the Embankment overlooking the Thames. Laver sits there in the evening in front of the television set, working the grips of his racquets. He wraps and rewraps the grips, trying for just the right feel in his hand. If the movie finishes and some commentator comes on and talks tennis, Laver turns him off and rotates the selector in quest of additional hoofbeats. He unwraps a new grip for the third or fourth time and begins to shave the handle with a kitchen knife. He wraps the grip again, feels it, moves the racket through the arc of a backhand, then unwraps the grip and shaves off a little more wood.

Gonzales sometimes drills extremely small holes in his racquets to change the weight. Gonzales, who is not always consistent in his approach to things, sometimes puts lead tape on his racquets to increase the weight. Beppe Merlo, the Italian tennis player, strings his own racquets, and if a string breaks while he is playing, he pulls gut out of his cover and repairs the damage right there on the court. Merlo likes to string his racquets at thirty pounds of tension—each string as tight as it would be if it were tied to a rafter and had a thirty-pound weight hanging on it. Since most players like their racquets at sixty pounds minimum, Merlo is extremely eccentric. He might as well be stringing snowshoes. When someone serves to him, the ball disappears into his racquet. Eventually, it comes out and it floats back toward his opponent like a milkweed seed. Merlo's game does not work at all well on grass. He is fantastic on clay.

Many players carry their own sets of gut with them. Professional stringers do the actual work, of course, using machines that measure the tension. Emerson likes his racquets at sixty-three pounds, very tight, and so does Smith. Since the frame weight of "medium" tennis racquets varies from thirteen to thirteen and three-quarters ounces, Smith goes to the Wilson factory whenever he can and weighs and feels racquets until he has selected a stack of them. He kills a racquet in six weeks. The thing doesn't break. It just becomes flaccid and dies. Strings go dead, too. They last anywhere from ten to twenty-eight days. Smith likes a huge grip—four and seven-eighths inches around. Some Americans wrap tape around their handles to build them up, and then they put new leather grips on. Australians generally like them smaller, four and five-eighths, four and a half. As Laver whittles away beside the television, he is progressing toward four and a half. When he is ready to go to bed, he switches off the television and, beside it, leaves a little pile of wood chips and sawdust on the floor.

Dennis Ralston carries his own pharmacy with him wherever he goes—Achromycin, Butazolidin, Oxazepam, Robaxin, Sodium Butabarbital. He is ready for anything, except sleep. The night before a match, he lies with a pillow over his head and fights total awareness. At three A.M., he complains bitterly about the traffic on New Bond Street outside the Westbury. There is no traffic on New Bond Street, outside the Westbury. Mayfair is tranquil in the dead of night, even if the tennis players are not. All over London, tennis players are staring open-eyed at dark ceilings. Some of them get up in the night and walk around talking to themselves—while Laver sleeps in Dolphin Square. Laver can sleep anywhere—in cars, trains, planes. He goes to bed around one A.M., and always sets an alarm clock or he would oversleep, even before a final.

Laver becomes quieter before a match. He and his wife, Mary, ordinarily laugh and joke and kid around a lot together, but he becomes silent as a match draws near. "The faster the pace, the more demands there are upon him, the better," she says. So Laver goes out in the morning and does the shopping. He drops off the laundry. Sometimes he washes clothes in the bathtub. He goes to his favorite butcher and buys a steak. He also buys eggs and greens. Back in the flat, two and a half hours before the match, he cooks his training meal. It is always the same—steak, eggs, and greens. He likes to cook, and prefers to do it himself. It keeps him busy. Then he gets into his car—a hired English Ford—and drives to Wimbledon. He ignores the club limousines. He wants to drive. "If he weren't a tennis player, he'd be a road racer," Mary says. "He has a quick, alert mind. He's fast. He's fast of body, and his mind works that way as well. The faster the pace of things, the faster he moves." He particularly likes driving on the left-hand side of the road. It reminds him of Australia, of which he sees very little any more. His home is in California. Each day, he plots a different route through Greater South London to Wimbledon. This is his private rally. It is a rule of the tournament that if a player is so much as ten minutes late, his opponent wins by a walkover. Laver knows his labyrinth—every route alternative, every mews and byway, between the Embankment and the tennis club, and all the traffic of London has yet to stop him. He turns off Church Road into the parking lot. His mind for many hours has been preoccupied with things other than tennis, with cowboys and sleep and shopping lists and cooking and driving. He never ponders a draw or thinks about an opponent. But now he is ready to concentrate his interest on the game—for example, on Wimbledon's opening day, when the defending champion starts the tournament with a match in the Centre Court.

Laver walks under the Kipling line and through the glass doors, and fourteen thousand people stand up and applaud him, for he is the most emphatic and enduring champion who has ever played on this court. He stacks his extra racquets against the umpire's chair, where the tournament staff has placed bottles of orange squash and of Robinson's Lemon Barley Water should he or his opponent require them during changeovers. There is plain water as well, in a jug called the Bartlett Multipot. Behind the umpire's chair is a green refrigerator, where tennis balls are kept until they are put into play. A ball boy hands him two and Laver takes the court. He swings easily through the knockup. The umpire says, "Play." Laver lifts his right hand, sending the first ball up into the air, and the tournament is under way. He swings, hits. His opponent can barely touch the ball with his racquet. It is a near ace, an unplayable serve, 15–love. Laver's next serve scythes into the backhand court. It is also unplayable. 30–love.

The man across the net is extremely nervous. His name is George Seewagen. He comes from Bayside, New York. This is his first Wimbledon and his friends have told him that if you don't get a game in the first round, you never get invited back. Seewagen would like to get two games. At Forest Hills thirty-four years ago, Seewagen's father played J. Donald Budge in the opening round. The score was 6–0, 6–1, 6–0. When Seewagen, Jr., arrived in London, he was, like nearly everyone else, tense about the luck of the coming draw, and before it was published he told his doubles partner, "Watch me. I'll have to play Laver in the Centre Court in the first round." The odds were one hundred and eleven to one that this would not happen, but Seewagen had read the right tea leaf, as he soon learned.

"It was hard to believe. I sort of felt a little bit upset. Moneywise, London's pretty expensive. First-round losers get a hundred pounds and that's not much. I figured I needed to win at least one match in order to meet my expenses, but now I'd had it. Then I thought of the instant recognition. People would say, 'There's the guy that's opening up Wimbledon with Laver.' At least my name would become known. But then, on the other hand, I thought, What if I don't get a game? Think of it. What if I don't win even one game?"

Seewagen is an extremely slender—in fact, thin—young man with freckles, a toothy grin, tousled short hair. He could be Huckleberry Finn. He looks nineteen and is actually twenty-three. His credentials are that he played for Rice University, that he beat someone named Zan Guerry in the final of the 1969 amateur championship in Rochester, and that he is the varsity tennis coach at Columbia University. There were, in other words, grounds for his gnawing fears. By the eve of Wimbledon, Seewagen's appearance was gaunt.

Everyone goes to Hurlingham on that ultimate Sunday afternoon. All through the previous fortnight, the tennis players of the world have gradually come to London, and by tradition they first convene at Hurlingham. Hurlingham is a Victorian sporting club with floor-to-ceiling windows, sixteen chimney pots, and wide surrounding lawns—bowling lawns, tennis lawns, croquet lawns, putting lawns—under giant copper beeches, beside the Thames. Some players play informal sets of doubles. Others merely sit on the lawns, sip Pimm's Cups under the sun, and watch women in pastel dresses walking by on maroon pathways. In the background are people in their seventies, dressed in pure white, tapping croquet balls with deadly skill across textured grasses smooth as broadloom. A uniformed band, with folding chairs and music stands, plays "Bow, Bow, Ye Lower Middle Classes" while tea is served beneath the trees—a strawberry tart, sandwiches, petits fours, fruitcake, and a not-so-bitter macaroon. Arthur Ashe, eating his tea, drinking the atmosphere, says, "This is my idea of England." On a slope a short distance away, Graham Stillwell, Ashe's first-round opponent, sits with his wife and his five-year-old daughter, Tiffany. This is the second straight year that Ashe has drawn Stillwell in the first round at Wimbledon, and last year Stillwell had Ashe down and almost out—twice Stillwell was serving for the match—before Ashe won the fifth set, 12–10. Reporters from the *Daily Mirror* and the *Daily Sketch* now come up to Ashe and ask him if he has been contacted by certain people who plan to demonstrate against the South African players at Wimbledon. "Why should they contact me?" Ashe says. "I'm not a South African." Mrs. Stillwell rises from the sloping lawn and stretches her arms. "My God! She's pregnant again," Ashe observes. Jean Borotra, now seventy-two, is hitting beautiful ground strokes with Gardnar Mulloy. Borotra wears long white trousers. Two basset hounds walk by, leashed to a man in a shirt of broad pink and white stripes. The band is playing the music of Albéniz. The lady tennis players drift about, dressed, for some reason, in multicolored Victorian gowns. Laver, in dark slacks and a sport shirt of motley dark colors, stands near the clubhouse, watching it all with his arms folded. He seems uncomfortable. He looks incongruous—small, undynamic, unprepossessing, vulnerable—but every eye at Hurlingham, sooner or later in the afternoon, watches him in contemplation. He stands out no more than a single blade of grass, but no one fails to see him, least of all Seewagen, who stands at the edge of the party like a figure emerging from a haunted forest. He wears an old, worn-out pair of light-weight sneakers, of the type that tennis players do not use and sailors do, and a baggy gray sweater with the sleeves shoved far up his thin brown arms. Veins stand out on the backs of his hands and across his forearms. He grins a little, but his eyes are sober. His look is profoundly philosophical. Gene Scott informs him that players scheduled for the Centre Court are entitled to a special fifteen minutes of practice on an outside court beforehand. "Good, I'll take McManus," Seewagen says. McManus, from Berkeley and ranked tenth in the United States, is left-handed. He is also short and red-headed. He has the same build Laver has, much the same nose, and similar freckles as well. Players practicing with McManus easily fantasize that they are hitting with the Rocket himself, and thus they inflate their confidence. McManus is the favorite dummy of everyone who has to play against Laver. Ashe speaks quietly to Seewagen and tells him not to worry. "You'll never play better," Ashe says. "You'll get in there, in the Centre Court, and you'll get inspired, and then when the crowd roars for your first great shot, you'll want to run into the locker room and call it a day."

"I hope it isn't a wood shot," says Seewagen, looking straight ahead.

Game to Laver. He leads, one game to love, first set. Laver and Seewagen change ends of the court. Laver went out to the Pontevecchio last night, on the Old Brompton Road. He ate lasagna and a steak *filet* with tomato sauce. He drank Australian beer. Then he went home and whittled a bit before retiring. At Chesham House, in Victoria, Seewagen fell asleep in his bed reading *Psycho Cybernetics,* by Maxwell Maltz. After one game, Seewagen has decided that Laver is even better than he thought he was. Laver is, for one thing, the fastest of all tennis players. He moves through more square yards per second than anyone else, covering ground like a sonic boom. In his tennis clothes, he is not unprepossessing. His legs are powerfully muscled. His left forearm looks as if it could bring down a tree. He is a great shotmaker, in part because he moves so well. He has every shot from everywhere. He can hurt his opponent from any position. He has extraordinary racquet-handling ability because his wrist is both strong and flexible. He can come over his backhand or slice it. He hits big shots, flick shots, spin shots, and rifle shots on the dead run. He lobs well. He serves well. His forehand is the best in tennis. He has one weakness. According to Gonzales, that is, Laver has one weakness—his bouncing overhead. The bouncing overhead is the shot a tennis player hits when a bad lob bounces at his feet and he cannon-balls his helpless opponent. Gonzales is saying that Laver has no weaknesses at all. Seewagen walks to the base line, visibly nervous, and prepares to serve. He is not pathetic. There is something tingling about a seven-hundred-to-one shot who merely shows up at the gate. In the end, at the net, Laver, shaking hands, will say to him gently, "You looked nervous. It's very difficult playing in here the first time over." Seewagen begins with a double fault. Love–15. Now, however, a deep atavistic athleticism rises in him and defeats his nerves. He serves, rushes, and punches two volleys past Laver, following them with an unplayable serve. 40–15. Serve, rush, volley—game to Mr. Seewagen. Games are one all, first set.

"His topspin is disguised," Seewagen notes, and he prepares, with a touch of unexpected confidence, for Laver's next service assault. Game to Mr. Laver. He leads, two games to one, first set. Seewagen now rises again, all the way to 40–15, from which level he is shoved back to deuce. Tossing up the ball, he cracks a serve past Laver that Laver can barely touch, let alone return. Advantage Seewagen. The source of all this power is not apparent, but it is coming from somewhere. He lifts the ball. He blasts. Service ace. Right through the corner. The crowd roars. It is Seewagen's first great shot. He looks at the scoreboard—two all—and it gives him what he will describe later as a charge. ("At that moment, I should have walked off.") 6–2, 6–0, 6–2.

Hewitt, in anger, hits one into the grandstand and it goes straight toward an elderly lady. She makes a stabbing catch with one hand and flips the ball to a ball boy. There is nothing light-weight about this English crowd. Ted Heath, Margaret, Anne, Charles, Lady Churchill, and the odd duke or baron might turn up—diverting attention to the Royal Box—but withal one gets the impression that there is a high percentage of people here who particularly know where they are and what they are looking at. They queue for hours for standing room in the Centre Court. They miss nothing and they are polite. The crowd at Forest Hills likes dramaturgy and emotion—players thanking God after chalk-line shots or falling to their knees in total despair—and the crowd in the Foro Italico throws cushions. But the British do not actually approve of that sort of thing, and when one of the rogue tennis players exhibits conduct they do not like, they cry, "Shame!"

"You bloody fools!" Hewitt shouts at them.

Hewitt has the temper of a grenade. He hits another ball in anger. This time it goes over the roof and out of sight. "Shame, Hewitt, shame!"

Rain falls. Umbrellas bloom. Mike Gibson's mustache is drooping from the wet, but he says, "It's not much. Play on." All matches continue. The umbrellas are black, red, green, yellow, orange, pink, paisley, and transparent. It is cold at Wimbledon. It often is—shirt sleeves one day, two pullovers and a mack the next. Now the players are leaving water tracks on the courts, and Gibson at last suspends play. Groundsmen take down the nets and cover the lawns with canvas. The standees do not give up their places, in the cold rain. The groundsmen go in under the grandstand to the Groundsmen's Bar, where they drink lager and offer one another cigarettes. "Will you have a smoke, Jack, or would you rather have the money?" The sun comes out for exactly three minutes. Then more rain falls. Half an hour later, play resumes.

Dell is supposed to be on Court 14, playing mixed doubles, but he is still in a phone booth talking to the office of Guntrip, the bookie. Dell bets heavily on his own players—one hundred pounds here, two hundred there—and even more heavily against Laver. Dell is a talented gambler, and he views the odds as attractive. Besides, Dell and Laver are the same age, and Dell can remember beating Laver when they were boys. Shrewd and realistic, Dell reasons that anyone who ever lost to Donald Dell cannot be invincible. In the end, he repeats his name to the clerk at Guntrip's, to be sure the clerk has it right. "Dell," he says. "D as in David, E as in Edward, L as in loser, L as in loser."

The field of women players is so think that even some of the women themselves are complaining. Chubby little girls with orange ribbons in their hair hit parabolic ground strokes back and forth and seem incongruous on courts adjacent to an Emerson, a Lutz, or a Pasarell, whose ground strokes sound like gunfire. Billie Jean King slaps a serve into the net and cries out, "That stinks!" Billie Jean is trimmer, lighter, more feminine than she was in earlier years, and somehow less convincing as a challenger to Margaret Court. Yet everyone else seems far below these two. Miss Goolagong is still some distance away. "Have you seen the abo, Jack?" says Robert Twynam, head groundsman, to his assistant, John Yardley. The interesting new players are the ones the groundsmen find interesting. They go to watch Miss Goolagong and they notice that her forehand has a tendency to go up and then keep going up. When it starts coming down, they predict, she will be ready for anybody, for her general game is smooth and quite strong and unflinchingly Australian. Australians never give up, and this one is an aborigine, a striking figure with orange-brown hair and orange-brown skin, in a Teddy Tinling dress and Adidas shoes, with a Dunlop in her hand. Margaret Court is breaking everything but the cool reserve of Helga Niessen, the Berlin model. Between points, Miss Niessen stands with her feet crossed at the ankles. The ankles are observed by a Chinese medical student who is working the tournament with the ground staff. "Look at those ankles. Look at those legs," he says. "She is a woman." He diverts his attention to Margaret Court, who is five feet eight, has big strong hands and, most notably, the ripple-muscled legs of a runner. "Look at those legs," says the Chinese medical student. "The lady is a man."

Hoad, in the Centre Court, is moving so slowly that a serve bounces toward him and hits him in the chest. The server is El Shafei, the chocolate-eyed Egyptian. Hoad is in here because all Britain wants to see him on television. Stiffened by time and injury, he loses two sets before his cartilage begins to bend. In the third set, his power comes, and he breaks the Egyptian. The Egyptian is a heavy-framed man, like Hoad, and in the fourth set, they pound each other, drive for drive—wild bulls of the tennis court. Hoad thinks he is getting bad calls and enormous anger is rising within him. The score is three all. Shafei is serving, at deuce. He lifts the ball and blows one past Hoad for a service ace. Hoad looks toward the net-cord judge with expanding disbelief. He looks toward Shafei, who has not moved from the position from which he hit the serve—indicating to Hoad that Shafei expected to hit a second one. Slowly, Hoad walks forward, toward the officials, toward Shafei, toward the center of the court. The crowd is silent. Hoad speaks. A microphone in Scotland could pick up what he says. "That goddamned ball was a let!" The net-cord judge is impassive. The umpire says, "May I remind you that play is continuous." Hoad replies, repeats, "That goddamned ball was a let!" He turns to the Egyptian. Unstirring silence is still the response of the crowd, for one does not throw hammers back at Thor. "The serve was a let. You know that. Did you hear it hit the tape?" Hoad asks, and Shafei says, "No." Hoad lifts his right arm, extends it full length, and points steadily at the Egyptian's eyes. "You lie!" he says slowly, delivering each syllable to the roof. A gulf of quiet follows and Hoad does not lower his arm. He draws a breath slowly, then says again, even more slowly, "You lie." Only Garrick, possibly Burton, could have played that one. It must have stirred bones in the Abbey, and deep in the churchyards of Wimbledon, for duels of great moment here have reached levels more serious than sport. This is where Canning fought Castlereagh, where Pitt fought Tierney, where Lord Winchelsea fought the Duke of Wellington. Ceawlin of the West Saxons fought Ethelbert of Kent here, when the terrain was known as Wibbas dune—home of the Saxon, Wibba (Wibbas dune, Wipandune, Wilbaldowne, Wymblyton). Hoad returns to the base line, and when the Egyptian serves again, Hoad breaks him into pieces. Game and fourth set to Hoad. Sets are two all. In his effort, though, Hoad has given up the last of his power. Time has defeated him. Twice the champion, he has failed his comeback. His energy drains away in the fifth set—his last, in all likelihood, at Wimbledon.

Ralston, at the umpire's chair, pries the cap off a vial of Biostrath and sucks out the essences of the ninety medicinal herbs. Dennis has no contract with Biostrath. He is not drinking the stuff for money. He is drinking it for his life. Beside him stands his opponent, John Newcombe, the second-best forehand, the second-best volley, the second-best tennis player in the world. Dennis follows the elixir with a Pepsi-Cola, also without benefit of a contract. The score is 4–5, first set. Ralston and Newcombe return to the base lines, and Ralston tosses up a ball to serve. The crowd is chattering, gurgling like a mountain stream. Prince Charles has just come in and is settling into his seat. "Quiet, please," says the umpire, and the stream subsides. Ralston serves, wins—six all.

Seven all. Eight all. Nine all. Ten all. There is a lot of grinning back and
forth across the net. Newcombe drives a backhand down the line. Ralston leaps, intercepts it, and drops the ball into Newcombe's court for a
winner. Newcombe looks at Ralston. Ralston grins. Newcombe smiles
back. It is an attractive match, between two complete professionals.
Newcombe passes Ralston with a forehand down the line. "Yep," says
Ralston. Ralston finds a winner in a drop shot overhead. "Good shot,"
calls Newcombe. Eleven all. When they shout, it is at themselves. Newcombe moves to the net behind a fragile approach shot, runs back under
a humiliatingly good lob, and drives an off-balance forehand into the net.
"John!" he calls out. "Idiotic!" Ralston tosses a ball up to serve, but
catches it instead of hitting it. He is having a problem with the sun, and
he pauses to apologize to Newcombe for the inconvenience the delay
might be causing him. Small wonder they can't beat each other. Grace
of this kind has not always been a characteristic of Ralston—of Newcombe, yes, but Ralston grew up tightly strung in California, and in his
youth his tantrums were a matter of national report. He is twenty-seven
now and has changed. Quiet, serious, introspective, coach of the United
States Davis Cup Team, he has become a professional beyond the imagination of most people who only knew him long ago. He plans his
matches almost on a drawing board. Last night, he spent hours studying
a chart he has made of every shot Newcombe has hit in this tournament.
13–12. Dennis opens another Biostrath and another Pepsi-Cola. He
knows what the odds have become. The winner of this set, since it has
gone so far, will in all likelihood be the winner of the match. Ralston has
been a finalist at Wimbledon. But he has never won a major international tournament. In such tournaments, curiously enough, he has
played Newcombe ten times and has won seven, but never for the biggest prize. Newcombe has a faculty for going all the way. Ralston, meanwhile, has pointed his life toward doing so at least once, and, who knows,
he tells himself, this could be the time. He toes the line and tosses up the
ball. He catches it, and tosses it up again. The serve is bad. The return is
a winner. Love–15. He has more trouble with the sun. Love–30. Catas-
trophe is falling from nowhere. Love–40. Serve, return, volley. 15–40.
He serves. Fault. He serves again. Double fault. Game and first set to
Newcombe, 14–12. Ralston looks up, over the trigger of a thousand old
explosions, and he forces a smile. 14–12, 9–7, 6–2. When it is over, the
ball boys carry out seven empty bottles of Pepsi-Cola and four empty
vials of the ninety medicinal herbs.

Kramer is in a glassed-in booth at one corner of the court, comment-
ing on the action for the BBC. For an American to be engaged to
broadcast to the English, extraordinary credentials, of one kind or an-

other, are required. Just after the Second World War, Kramer first displayed his. Upwards of fifty American players now come to Wimbledon annually, but Kramer, in 1946, was one of three to cross the ocean. "Now it's a sort of funsy, 'insy' thing to do," he has said. "But in my time, if you didn't think you had a top-notch chance, you didn't come over. To make big money out of tennis, you had to have the Wimbledon title as part of your credits. I sold my car, a 1941 Chevrolet, so I could afford to bring my wife, Gloria with me." That was long before the era of the Perry-Lacoste-Adidas bazaar, and Kramer, at Wimbledon, wore his own clothes—shorts that he bought at Simpson's and T-shirts that had been issued to him during the war, when he was a sailor in the United States Coast Guard. Now, as he watches the players before him and predicts in his expert way how one or the other will come slowly unstuck, he looks past them across the court and up behind the Royal Box into an entire segment of the stadium that was gone when he first played here. At some point between 1939 and 1945, a bomb hit the All-England tennis club, and with just a little more wind drift it would have landed in the center of the Centre Court. Instead, it hit the roof over the North East Entrance Hall. Kramer remembers looking up from the base line, ready to serve, into a background of avalanched rubble and twisted girders against the sky. He slept in the Rembrandt, which he remembers as "an old hotel in South Kensington," and he ate steak that he had brought with him from the United States, thirty pounds or so of whole tenderloins. Needless to say, there was no Rolls-Royce flying Wimbledon colors to pick him up at the Rembrandt. Kramer went to Wimbledon, with nearly everyone else, on the underground—Gloucester Road, Earl's Court, Fulham Broadway, Parsons Green, Putney Bridge, East Putney, Southfields, Wimbledon. He lost the first time over. A year later, he returned with his friend Tom Brown and together they hit their way down opposite sides of the draw and into the Wimbledon final. A few hours before the match, Kramer took what remained of his current supply of *filet mignon,* cut it in half, and shared it with Tom Brown. Kramer was twenty-five and his game had come to full size—the Big Game, as it was called, the serve, the rush, the jugular volley. When Kramer proved what he could do, at Wimbledon, he changed for all foreseeable time the patterns of the game. He destroyed Brown in forty-seven minutes, still the fastest final in Wimbledon's history, and then— slender, crewcut, big in the ears—he was led to the Royal Box for a word or two with the King and Queen. The Queen said to him, "Whatever happened to that redheaded young man?" And Kramer told her that Donald Budge was alive and doing O.K. The King handed Kramer the Wimbledon trophy. "Did the court play well?" the King asked him.

"Yes, it did, sir," Kramer answered. It was a tennis player's question. In 1926, the King himself had competed in this same tournament and had played in the Centre Court. A faraway smile rests on Kramer's face as he remembers all this. "Me in my T shirt," he says, with a slight shake of his head.

Frew McMillan, on Court 2, wears a golfer's billowing white visored cap, and he looks very much like a golfer in his style of play, for he swings with both hands and when he completes a stroke his arms follow the racquet across one shoulder and his eyes seem to be squinting down a fairway. Court 2 has grandstands on either side and they are packed with people. McMillan is a low-handicap tennis player who can dig some incredible ground strokes out of the rough. A ball comes up on his right side and he drives it whistling down the line, with a fading hook on the end. The ball comes back on his left side and, still with both hands, overlapping grip, he hits a crosscourt controlled-slice return for a winner. The gallery applauds voluminously. McMillan volleys with two hands. The only strokes he hits with one hand are the serve and the overhead. He has an excellent chip shot and a lofty topspin wedge. He putts well. He is a lithe, dark, attractive, quiet South African. In the South African Open, he played Laver in the final. Before Laver had quite figured out what sort of a match it was, McMillan had him down one set to nought. Then Laver got out his mashie and that was the end of McMillan in the South African Open. When McMillan arrived in London and saw the Wimbledon draw, he felt, in his words, a cruel blow, because his name and Laver's were in the same pocket of the draw, and almost inevitably they would play in the third round. "But maybe I have a better chance against him earlier than later," he finally decided. "You feel you have a chance. You have to—even if it is a hundred to one." Now the grand-stands are jammed in Court 2 and, high above, the railing is crowded on the Tea Room roof, for McMillan, after losing the first set, has broken Laver and leads him 5–3 in the second.

"I got the feeling during the match that I had more of a chance beating him on the court than thinking about it beforehand. You realize the chap isn't infallible. It's almost as if I detected a chip in his armor."

Laver has netted many shots and has hit countless others wide or deep. He cannot find the lines. He is preoccupied with his serves, which are not under control. He spins one in too close to the center of the service box. McMillan blasts it back. Advantage McMillan. Laver lifts the ball to serve again. Fault. He serves again. Double fault. Game and set to McMillan, 6–3.

When this sort of thing happens, Laver's opponent seldom lives to tell the tale. One consistent pattern in all the compiled scores in his long record is that when someone takes a set from him, the score of the next set is 6–o, Laver, or something very near it. Affronted, he strikes twice as hard. "He has the physical strength to hit his way through nervousness," McMillan says. "That's why I believe he's a great player."

Laver breaks McMillan in the opening game of the third set. He breaks him again in the third game. His volleys hit the corners. His drives hit the lines. McMillan's most powerful blasts come back at him faster than they left his racquet. McMillan hits a perfect drop shot. Laver is on it like the light. He snaps it unreachably down the line. Advantage Laver. McMillan hits one deep to Laver's backhand corner, and Laver, diving as he hits it, falls. McMillan sends the ball to the opposite corner. Laver gets up and sprints down the base line. He not only gets to the ball—with a running forehand rifle shot, he puts it away. It is not long before he is shaking McMillan's hand at the net. "Well played," McMillan says to him (6–2, 3–6, 6–o, 6–2). "Yes, I thought I played pretty well," Laver tells him. And they make their way together through the milling crowd. McMillan will frequently say what a gentle and modest man he finds Laver to be. "It may be why he is what he is," McMillan suggests. "You can see it in his eyes."

B. M. L. de Roy van Zuydewijn is a loser in the Veterans' Event— gentlemen's doubles. So is the seventy-two-year-old Borotra. Riggs and Drobny, on Court 5, persevere. Over the years, Riggs and Drobny have eaten well. Each is twice the shadow of his former self. The Hungarians Bujtor and Stolpa are concentrating on Riggs as the weaker of the two.

Game to Seewagen and Miss Overton, the honey-blonde Miss Overton. They lead Dell and Miss Johnson five games to four, second set. Dell is not exactly crumbling under the strain. These peripheral matches are fairly informal. Players talk to one another or to their friends on the side lines, catching up on the news. Seewagen and Miss Overton appear to be playing more than tennis. Dell is tired—up half the night making deals and arguing with Kramer, up early in the morning to do business over breakfast with bewildered Europeans, who find him in his hotel room in a Turkish-towel robe, stringy-haired and wan, a deceptive glaze in his eyes, offering them contracts written on flypaper.

The Russians enter the Centre Court to play mixed doubles. Princess Anne is in the Royal Box. The Russians hesitate, and look at each other in their ceramic way, and then they grin, they shrug, and they turn toward the Royal Box and bend their heads. The people applaud.

Nastase is Nijinsky—leaping, flying, hitting jump-shot overheads, sweeping forehands down the line. Tiriac is in deep disgrace. Together they have proved their point. They have outlasted most of the seeded pairs in the gentlemen's doubles. But now they are faltering against

Rosewall and Stolle, largely because Tiriac is playing badly. Stolle hits an overhead. Tiriac tries to intercept it near the ground. He smothers it into the court. Nastase, behind him, could have put the ball away after it had bounced. Tiriac covers his face with one hand and rubs his eyes. He slinks back to the base line like someone caught red-handed. But now he redeems himself. The four players close in for a twelve-shot volley, while the ball never touches the ground. It is Tiriac who hits number twelve, picking it off at the hip and firing it back through Stolle.

Lutz crashes and the injury appears to be serious. Playing doubles in the Centre Court with his partner, Smith, he chases an angled overhead and he crashes into the low wall at the front of the grandstands. He makes no effort to get up. He quivers. He is unconscious. "Get a doctor, please," says the umpire. A nurse, in a white cap and a gray uniform that nearly reaches her ankles, hurries across the lawn. The crowd roars with laughter. There is something wondrous in the English sense of humor that surfaces in the presence of accidents, particularly if they appear to be fatal. The laughter revives Lutz. He comes to, gets up, returns to the court, shakes his head a few times, resumes play, and drives a put-away into the corner after an eight-shot ricochet volley. Lutz is tough. He was a high-school football player in California, and he once promised himself that he would quit tennis and concentrate on football unless he should happen to win the national junior championship. He won, and gave up football. Additional medical aid comes from outside the stadium. Another nurse has appeared. She hovers on the edge of play. When she sees an opportunity, she hurries up to Smith and gives him an aspirin.

If Lutz had broken three ribs, he would not have mentioned it as long as he continued to play, and in this respect he is like the Australians. There is an Australian code on the matter of injuries and it is one of the things that gives the Australians a stature that is not widely shared by the hypochondriac Americans and the broken-wing set from mainland Europe. The Australian code is that you do not talk about injuries, you hide them. If you are injured, you stay out, and if you play, you are not injured. The Australians feel contempt for players who put their best injury forward. An Australian will say of such a man, "I have never beaten him when he was healthy." Laver developed a bad wrist a year or so ago, at Wimbledon, and he and his wife together got into a telephone kiosk so that she could tape the wrist in secrecy. If he had taped it himself, no one would ever have known the story. His wife would rather praise him than waltz with the Australian code. His wife is an American.

"Bad luck, Roger." This is what Roger Taylor's friends are saying to him, because he has to play Laver, in the fourth round, in the Centre Court tomorrow. The champion always plays in one of the two stadiums or on the Number 2 Court, the only places that can take in all the people who want to see him. "Don't worry, though, Roger. It's no disgrace if Rocket is the man who puts you out. You've got nothing to lose."

"I've got everything to lose," Taylor tells them. "To lose at Wimbledon is to lose. This is what competition is all about. You've got to think you have a chance. You might hope for twenty-five let cords or something, but you always think there's a chance you'll get through."

"Bad luck, Roger."

Roger takes a deep hot bath, goes home to his two-bedroom flat on Putney Hill, and continues to work himself up, talking to his mother, his father, and his wife, over a glass of beer.

"That's enough beer, Roger."

"I don't live like a monk. I want to loosen up." He eats a slice of fried liver and opens another beer. "All my chances will hinge on how well I serve. I'll have to serve well to him, to keep him a little off balance on his returns. If I can't do that, I'll be in dire trouble. If you hit the ball a million miles an hour, he hits it back harder. You can't beat a player like that with sheer speed—unless he's looking the other way. I plan to float back as many service returns as I can. The idea is not to let it get on top of you that you're going to play these people. There's a tendency to sort of lie down and roll over."

Games are three all, first set. Taylor feels weak from tension. Laver is at ease. "We'd played often enough," Laver will say later. "I knew his game—left-handed, slice serve, better forehand than backhand, a good lob. He's very strong. He moves well for a big man. There was no special excitement. My heart wasn't pounding quite as hard as it sometimes does."

Taylor floats back a service return, according to plan. Laver reaches high, hits a semi-overhead volley, and the ball lands in the exact corner of the court. It bounces into the stadium wall. The crowd roars for him, but he is also hitting bad shots. There is a lack of finish on his game. He wins the first set, 6–4.

"My concentration lapsed continually. I was aware of too many things—the troublesome wind, the court being dry and powdery. I magnified the conditions. I played scratchy in the first set. I felt I'd get better in the next set."

A break point rises against Laver in the first game of the second set. He lifts the ball to serve. He hits it into the net. "Fault." He spins the next one—into the net. "Double fault." "Oh, just throw it up and hit it," he says aloud to himself, thumping his fist into the strings of his racquet.

"When you lose your rhythm, serving, it's because of lack of concentration. I found myself thinking too much where the ball should be going. You don't think about your serve, you think about your first volley. If you think about getting your serve in, you make errors. I didn't know where my volleys were going. I missed easy smashes."

Taylor is floating back his returns. He is keeping Laver off balance. With his ground strokes, he is hitting through the wind. There is an explosion of applause for him when he wins the second set, 6–4. No one imagines that he will do more, but it is enough that Taylor, like McMillan, has won a set from Laver—and more than enough that he is English.

"Roger was playing some good tennis. When I played fairly well, he played better."

First game, third set—love–40—Laver serving. There is chatter in the crowd, the sound of the mountain stream. "Quiet, please!" Laver hits his way back to 30–40. He serves, rushes, and punches a volley down the line—out. Game and another service break to Taylor. Five times, Laver has hit his running rifle-shot forehand into the net. He has repeatedly double-faulted. His dinks fall short. His volleys jump the base line. Taylor, meanwhile, is hitting with touch and power. He is digging for everything. Laver is not covering the court. Both feet off the ground, Laver tries a desperation shot from the hip and he nets it. Advantage Taylor. Taylor serves—a near ace, unplayable. Game and third set to Taylor, 6–2. He leads two sets to one. Unbelievable. Now the time has certainly come for Laver to react, as he so often does, with vengeance.

"When your confidence is drained, you tend to do desperation shots. My desperation shots, a lot of times, turn matches. I felt something was gone. I didn't have strength to get to the net quickly. I can't explain what it was. If you're not confident, you have no weight on the ball. You chase the ball. You look like a cat on a hot tin roof."

Laver serves, moves up, and flips the volley over the base line. "Get it down!" he shouts to himself. His next volley goes over the base line. Now he double-faults. Now he moves under a high, soft return. He punches it into a corner. Taylor moves to the ball and sends it back, crosscourt. Laver, running, hits a rolling topspin backhand—over the base line. Advantage Taylor. Break point. The whispering of the crowd has become the buzz of scandal.

His red hair blowing in the wind, Laver lifts the ball to serve against the break. Suddenly, he looks as fragile as he did at Hurlingham and the incongruity is gone. The spectators on whom this moment is making the deepest impression are the other tennis players—forty or so in the grandstands, dozens more by the television in the Players' Tea Room. Something in them is coming free. The man is believable. He is vulnerable. He has never looked more human. He is not invincible.

"The serve is so much of the game. If you serve well, you play well. If not, you are vulnerable. If you play against someone who is capable of hitting the ball as hard as Roger can, you are looking up the barrel."

Laver serves. "Fault." He serves again. "Double fault." Game and service break to Taylor, fourth set. Laver, without apparent emotion, moves into the corner, and the shadow that until moments ago seemed to reach in a hundred directions now follows him alone. The standard he has set may be all but induplicable, but he himself has returned to earth. He will remain the best, and he will go on beating the others. The epic difference will be that, from now on, they will think that they can beat him.

Taylor lobs. Laver runs back, gets under the bouncing ball, kneels, and drives it into the net. He is now down 1–5. He is serving. He wins three points, but then he volleys into the net, again he volleys into the net, and again he volleys into the net—deuce. He serves. He moves forward. He volleys into the net. Advantage Taylor—match point. The sound of the crowd is cruel. "Quiet, please!" the umpire says. Laver serves, into the net. He appears to be trembling. He serves again. The ball does not touch the ground until it is out of the court beyond the base line.

Photographers swarm around him and around Taylor. "Well done, Roger. Nice," Laver says, shaking Taylor's hand. His eyes are dry. He walks patiently through the photographers, toward the glass doors. In the locker room, he draws a cover over his racquet and gently sets it down. On the cover are the words ROD LAVER—GRAND SLAM.

"I feel a little sad at having lost. I played well early in the tournament. I felt good, but I guess deep down something wasn't driving me hard enough. When I had somewhere to aim my hope, I always played better. Deep down in, you wonder, 'How many times do you have to win it?' "

JOHN UPDIKE

"The Pro"

I never knew John Updike had much interest in golf, until in the process of writing a curious essay on death I happened to ask him how he envisioned his own. He wrote me: "I can't decide if I'd rather go after the thirteenth or the fourteenth line of a sonnet; the thirteenth would give you something to do in the afterlife. By the same reasoning, while the ball is in the air, off the face of a perfectly-swung 5-iron, and yet has not hit the green where it is certain to fall." This lovely vision of contin- uing an act in an afterlife—presumably Updike would step up and sink that five-iron shot for a birdie—has stayed with me since I read it. Then I ran across the piece that follows.

I am on my four-hundred-and-twelfth golf lesson, and my drives still have that pushed little tail, and my irons still take the divot on the wrong side of the ball. My pro is a big gloomy sun-browned man—age about thirty-eight, weight around a hundred and ninety-five. When he holds a club in his gloved hand and swishes it nervously (the nervousness comes over him after the first twenty minutes of our lesson), he makes it look light as a feather, a straw, a baton. Once I sneaked his three wood from his bag, and the head weighed more than a cannonball. "Easy does it, Mr. Wallace," he says to me. My name is not Wallace, but he smooths his clients toward one generic, acceptable name. I call him Dave.

"Easy does it, Mr. Wallace," he says. "That ball is not going any- where by itself, so what's your hurry?"

"I want to clobber the bastard," I say. It took me two hundred lessons to attain this pitch of frankness.

"You dipped again," he tells me, without passion. "That right shoul- der of yours dipped, and your knees locked, you were so anxious. Ride those knees, Mr. Wallace."

"I can't. I keep thinking about my wrists. I'm afraid I won't pronate them."

This is meant to be a joke, but he doesn't smile. "Ride those knees, Mr. Wallace. Forget your wrists. Look." He takes my five iron into his hands, a sight so thrilling it knocks the breath out of me. It is like, in the movies we all saw as children (oh, blessed childhood!), the instant when King Kong, or the gigantic Cyclops, lifts the beautiful blonde, who has blessedly fainted, over his head, and she becomes utterly weightless, a thing of sheer air and vision and pathos. I love it, I feel half sick with pleasure, when he lifts my club, and want to tell him so, but I can't. After four hundred and eleven lessons, I still repress.

"The hands can't *help* but be right," he says, "if the *knees* are right." He twitches the club, so casually I think he is brushing a bee from the ball's surface. There is an innocent click; the ball whizzes into the air and rises along a line as straight as the edge of a steel ruler, hangs at its remote apogee for a moment of meditation, and settles like a snowflake twenty yards beyond the shagging caddie.

"Gorgeous, Dave," I say with an affectation of camaraderie, though my stomach is a sour churning of adoration and dread.

He says, "A little fat, but that's the idea. Did you see me grunt and strain?"

"No, Dave." This is our litany.

"Did you see me jerk my head, or freeze at the top of the backswing, or rock forward on my toes?"

"No, Dave, no."

"Well then, what's the problem? Step up and show me how."

I assume my stance, and take back the club, low, slowly; at the top, my eyes fog over, and my joints dip and swirl like barn swallows. I swing. There is a fruitless commotion of dust and rubber at my feet. "Smothered it," I say promptly. After enough lessons, the terminology becomes second nature. The whole process, as I understand it, is essentially one of self-analysis. The pro is merely a catalyst, a random sample, I have read somewhere, from the grab bag of humanity.

He insists on wearing a droll porkpie hat from which his heavy brown figure somehow downflows; his sloping shoulders, his hanging arms, his faintly pendulous belly, and his bent knees all tend toward his shoes, which are ideally natty—solid as bricks, black and white, with baroque stitching, frilled kilties, and spikes as neat as alligator teeth. He looks at me almost with interest. His grass-green irises are tiny, whittled by years of concentrating on the ball. "Loosen up," he tells me. I love it, I clench with gratitude, when he deigns to be directive. "Take a few practice swings, Mr. Wallace. You looked like a rusty mechanical man on that one. Listen. Golf is an effortless game."

"Maybe I have no aptitude," I say, giggling, blushing, hoping to deflect him with the humility bit.

He is not deflected. Stolidly he says, "Your swing is sweet. When it's there." Thus he uplifts me and crushes me from phrase to phrase. "You're blocking yourself out," he goes on. "You're not open to your own potential. You're not, as we say, *free.*"

"I know, I know. That's why I'm taking all these expensive lessons."

"Swing, Mr. Wallace. Show me your swing."

I swing, and feel the impurities like bubbles and warps in glass: hurried backswing, too much right hand at impact, failure to finish high.

The pro strips off his glove. "Come over to the eighteenth green." I think we are going to practice chipping (a restricted but relaxed pendulum motion) for the fiftieth time, but he says, "Lie down."

The green is firm yet springy. The grounds crew has done a fine job watering this summer, through that long dry spell. Not since childhood have I lain this way, on sweet flat grass, looking up into a tree, branch above branch, each leaf distinct in its generic shape, as when, in elementary school, we used to press them between wax paper. The tree is a sugar maple. For all the times I have tried to hit around it, I never noticed its species before. In the fall, its dried-up leaves have to be brushed from the line of every putt. This spring, when the branches were tracery dusted with a golden budding, I punched a nine iron right through the crown and salvaged a double bogey.

Behind and above me, the pro's voice is mellower than I remember it, with a lulling grittiness, like undissolved sugar in tea. He says, "Mr. Wallace, tell me what you're thinking about when you freeze at the top of your backswing."

"I'm thinking about my shot. I see it sailing dead on the pin, hitting six feet short, taking a bite with lots of backspin, and dribbling into the cup. The crowd goes *ooh* and cheers."

"Who's in the crowd? Anybody you know personally?"

"No . . . wait. There is somebody. My mother. She has one of those cardboard periscope things and shouts out, 'Gorgeous, Billy!' "

"She calls you Billy."

"That's my name, Dave. William. Willy. Billy. Bill. Let's cut out this Mr. Wallace routine. You call me Bill. I'll call you Dave." He is much easier to talk to, the pro, without the sight of his powerful passionless gloom, his hands (one bare, one gloved) making a mockery of the club's weight.

"Anybody else you know? Wife? Kids?"

"No, my wife's had to take the baby-sitter home. Most of the kids are at camp."

"What else do you see up there at the top of the backswing?"

"I see myself quitting lessons." It was out, *whiz,* before I had time to censor. Silence reigns in the leafy dome above me. A sparrow is hopping from branch to branch, like a pencil point going from number to number in those children's puzzles we all used to do.

At last the pro grunts, which, as we said, he never does. "The last time you were out, Mr. Wallace, what did you shoot?"

"You mean the last time I kept count?"

"Mm."

"A hundred eight. But that was with some lucky putts."

"Mm. Better stand up. Any prolonged pressure, the green may get a fungus. This bent grass is hell to maintain." When I stand, he studies me, chuckles, and says to an invisible attendant, "A hundred eight, with a hot putter yet, and he wants to quit lessons."

I beg, "Not quit forever—just for a vacation. Let me play a few different courses. You know, get out into the world. Maybe even try a public course. Hell, or go to a driving range and whack out a bucket of balls. You know, learn to live with the game I've got. Enjoy life."

His noble impassivity is invested with a shimmering, twinkling humorousness; his leathery face softens toward a smile, and the trace of a dimple is discovered in his cheek. "Golf is life," he says softly, and his green eyes expand, "and life is lessons," and the humps of his brown muscles merge with the hillocks and swales of the course, whose red flags prick the farthest horizon, and whose dimmest sand traps are indistinguishable from galaxies. I see that he is right, as always, absolutely; there is no life, no world, beyond the golf course—just an infinite and terrible falling-off. "If I don't give *you* lessons," he is going on, "how will I pay for *my* lessons?"

"You take lessons?"

"Sure. I hook under pressure. Like Palmer. I'm too strong. Any rough on the left, there I am. You don't have that problem, with your nice pushy slice."

"You mean there's a sense," I ask, scarcely daring, "in which *you* need *me?"*

He puts his hand on my shoulder, the hand pale from wearing the glove, and I become a feather at the touch, all air and ease. "Mr. Wallace," he says, "I've learned a lot from your sweet swing. I hate it when, like now, the half hour's up."

"Next Tuesday, eleven-thirty?"

Solemnly my pro nods. "We'll smooth out your chipping. Here in the shade."

RING LARDNER

"ALIBI IKE"

As mentioned briefly in the introduction, Ring Lardner was astonishingly self-deprecatory about his sportswriting. In his preface to an edition of You Know Me, Al *he wrote facetiously that Will Rogers had written an introduction but it had been returned by the publishers be-*

cause *"it was better than the book." Nobody else shared his opinion. Edmund Wilson, the preeminent critic, complained about Lardner's attitude. "He. . .tried to pretend that he has never attempted to write anything good at all. Yet he has qualities which should make it more nearly possible for him than for perhaps any other living American to produce another* Huckleberry Finn.*"*

Virginia Woolf, though one of the more isolated literary figures, certainly from the sports arena, wrote that "he writes the best prose that has come our way." She went on to say: "Mr. Lardner's interest in games has solved one of the most difficult problems of the American writer; it has given him a clue, a centre, a meeting place for the divers activities of people whom a vast continent isolates, whom no tradition controls. Games give him what society gives his English brothers."

One might suppose that Lardner's cynicism about his work might be related to his disaffection with baseball itself. A traveling reporter (nicknamed "Old Hawk Eye") with the Chicago White Sox, he was deeply affected when the team threw the 1919 World Series and became known thereafter as the "Black Sox."

His son, Ring Lardner, Jr., felt that while this obviously was a contributing factor, equally disenchanting was the introduction of the lively (or "crazy") baseball, which made the game a batter's rather than a pitcher's. Lardner always maintained that this was done to suit Babe Ruth's ability to hit the long ball. Very much a traditionalist, he never thought the movies would succeed as a medium. He never had anyone place a telephone call for him, and would refuse to answer anyone using a secretary to reach him. Extremely prudish, he wouldn't listen to a risqué joke or story, and frowned on off-color language, which must have made it awkward for him in the scatology-laced language of the locker rooms. He once had a month's allowance confiscated from his two young children for the following jape delivered at the dinner table.

Q: What was the longest slide in the Bible?

A: When Joshua went from Jericho to Jerusalem on his ass.

The story representing Lardner here ("Alibi Ike") is one of a series originally called "A Busher's Letters Home." The character of Jack Keefe (the Busher), who is the narrator of the stories, was drawn from a player on the 1908 Chicago White Sox who could neither read nor write, but bluffed his way through the day by pretending he could. With great care he would study the menus in hotels and diners and then order steak and baked potatoes, or ham and eggs, or both. Keefe, of course, was able to write, and prolifically, but his view of life was essentially based on that of the player Lardner referred to as "Jake Gibbs" in his reminiscences.

For his "Busher" stories Lardner used the form of a succession of letters from Keefe back to his best friend in rural Indiana. Originally the series (Lardner's first fiction) was planned for the New York Tribune, *but the Sunday editor there thought the prose was too unorthodox for its readers. So the first of the "Busher" letters was offered to the* Saturday Evening Post. *Lardner was paid $250.*

"Alibi Ike" is the most famous of the series. Indeed, one of the anthologies in which it was included simply dispensed with an introduction for the simple heading "The Big One."

His right name was Frank X. Farrell, and I guess the X stood for "Excuse me." Because he never pulled a play, good or bad, on or off the field, without apologizin' for it.

"Alibi Ike" was the name Carey wished on him the first day he reported down South. O' course we all cut out the "Alibi" part of it right away for the fear he would overhear it and bust somebody. But we called him "Ike" right to his face and the rest of it was understood by everybody on the club except Ike himself.

He ast me one time, he says:

"What do you all call me Ike for? I ain't no Yid."

"Carey give you the name," I says. "It's his nickname for everybody he takes a likin' to."

"He mustn't have only a few friends then," says Ike. "I never heard him say 'Ike' to nobody else."

But I was goin' to tell you about Carey namin' him. We'd been workin' out two weeks and the pitchers was showin' somethin' when this bird joined us. His first day out he stood up there so good and took such a reef at the old pill that he had everyone lookin'. Then him and Carey was together in left field, catchin' fungoes, and it was after we was through for the day that Carey told me about him.

"What do you think of Alibi Ike?" ast Carey.

"Who's that?" I says.

"This here Farrell in the outfield," says Carey.

"He looks like he could hit," I says.

"Yes," says Carey, "but he can't hit near as good as he can apologize."

Then Carey went on to tell me what Ike had been pullin' out there. He'd dropped the first fly ball that was hit to him and told Carey his glove wasn't broke in good yet, and Carey says the glove could easy of been Kid Gleason's gran'father. He made a whale of a catch out o' the next one and Carey says "Nice work!" or somethin' like that, but Ike says he could of caught the ball with his back turned only he slipped when he started after it and, besides that, the air currents fooled him.

"I thought you done well to get to the ball," says Carey.

"I ought to been settin' under it," says Ike.

"What did you hit last year?" Carey ast him.

"I had malaria most o' the season," says Ike. "I wound up with .356."

"Where would I have to go to get malaria?" says Carey, but Ike didn't wise up.

I and Carey and him set at the same table together for supper. It took him half an hour longer'n us to eat because he had to excuse himself every time he lifted his fork.

"Doctor told me I needed starch," he'd say, and then toss a shovelful o' potatoes into him. Or, "They ain't much meat on one o' these chops," he'd tell us, and grab another one. Or he'd say: "Nothin' like onions for a cold," and then he'd dip into the perfumery.

"Better try that apple sauce," says Carey. "It'll help your malaria."

"Whose malaria?" says Ike. He'd forgot already why he didn't only hit .356 last year.

I and Carey begin to lead him on.

"Whereabouts did you say your home was?" I ast him.

"I live with my folks," he says. "We live in Kansas City—not right down in the business part—outside a ways."

"How's that come?" says Carey. "I should think you'd get rooms in the post office."

But Ike was too busy curin' his cold to get that one.

"Are you married?" I ast him.

"No," he says. "I never run round much with girls, except to shows onct in a wile and parties and dances and roller skatin'."

"Never take 'em to the prize fights, eh?" says Carey.

"We don't have no real good bouts," says Ike. "Just bush stuff. And I never figured a boxin' match was a place for the ladies."

Well, after supper he pulled a cigar out and lit it. I was just goin' to ask him what he done it for, but he beat me to it.

"Kind o' rests a man to smoke after a good work-out," he says. "Kind o' settles a man's supper, too."

"Looks like a pretty good cigar," says Carey.

"Yes," says Ike. "A friend o' mine give it to me—a fella in Kansas City that runs a billiard room."

"Do you play billiards?" I ast him.

"I used to play a fair game," he says. "I'm all out o' practice now—can't hardly make a shot."

We coaxed him into a four-handed battle, him and Carey against Jack Mack and I. Say, he couldn't play billiards as good as Willie Hoppe; not quite. But to hear him tell it, he didn't make a good shot all evenin'. I'd leave him an awful-lookin' layout and he'd gather 'em up in one try and then run a couple o' hundred, and between every carom he'd say he'd put too much stuff on the ball, or the English didn't take, or the table wasn't true, or his stick was crooked, or somethin'. And all the time he had the balls actin' like they was Dutch soldiers and him Kaiser William. We started out to play fifty points, but we had to make it a thousand so as I and Jack and Carey could try the table.

The four of us set round the lobby a wile after we was through playin', and when it got along toward bedtime Carey whispered to me and says:

"Ike'd like to go to bed, but he can't think up no excuse."

Carey hadn't hardly finished whisperin' when Ike got up and pulled it:

"Well, good night, boys," he says. "I ain't sleepy, but I got some gravel in my shoes and it's killin' my feet."

We knowed he hadn't never left the hotel since we'd came in from the grounds and changed our clo'es. So Carey says:

"I should think they'd take them gravel pits out o' the billiard room."

But Ike was already on his way to the elevator, limpin'.

"He's got the world beat," says Carey to Jack and I. "I've knew lots o' guys that had an alibi for every mistake they made; I've heard pitchers say that the ball slipped when somebody cracked one off'n 'em; I've heard infielders complain of a sore arm after heavin' one into the stand, and I've saw outfielders tooken sick with a dizzy spell when they've misjudged a fly ball. But this baby can't even go to bed without apologizin', and I bet he excuses himself to the razor when he gets ready to shave."

"And at that," says Jack, "he's goin' to make us a good man."

"Yes," says Carey, "unless rheumatism keeps his battin' average down to .400."

Well, sir, Ike kept whalin' away at the ball all through the trip till everybody knowed he'd won a job. Cap had him in there regular the last few exhibition games and told the newspaper boys a week before the season opened that he was goin' to start him in Kane's place.

"You're there, kid," says Carey to Ike, the night Cap made the 'nnouncement. "They ain't many boys that wins a big league berth their third year out."

"I'd of been up here a year ago," says Ike, "only I was bent over all season with lumbago."

It rained down in Cincinnati one day and somebody organized a little game o' cards. They was shy two men to make six and ast I and Carey to play.

"I'm with you if you get Ike and make it seven-handed," says Carey.

So they got a hold of Ike and we went up to Smitty's room.

"I pretty near forgot how many you deal," says Ike. "It's been a long wile since I played."

I and Carey give each other the wink, and sure enough, he was just as ig'orant about poker as billiards. About the second hand, the pot was opened two or three ahead of him, and they was three in when it come his turn. It cost a buck, and he throwed in two.

"It's raised, boys," somebody says.

"Gosh, that's right, I did raise it," says Ike.

"Take out a buck if you didn't mean to tilt her," says Carey.

"No," says Ike, "I'll leave it go."

Well, it was raised back at him and then he made another mistake and raised again. They was only three left in when the draw come. Smitty'd opened with a pair o' kings and he didn't help 'em. Ike stood pat. The guy that'd raised him back was flushin' and he didn't fill. So Smitty checked and Ike bet and didn't get no call. He tossed his hand away, but I grabbed it and give it a look. He had king, queen, jack, and two tens. Alibi Ike he must have seen me peekin', for he leaned over and whispered to me.

"I overlooked my hand," he says. "I thought all the wile it was a straight."

"Yes," I says, "that's why you raised twice by mistake."

They was another pot that he come into with tens and fours. It was tilted a couple o' times and two o' the strong fellas drawed ahead of Ike. They each drawed one. So Ike throwed away his little pair and come out with four tens. And they was four treys against him. Carey'd looked at Ike's discards and then he says:

"This lucky bum busted two pair."

"No, no, I didn't," says Ike.

"Yes, yes, you did," says Carey, and showed us the two fours.

"What do you know about that?" says Ike. "I'd of swore one was a five spot."

Well, we hadn't had no pay day yet, and after a wile everybody except Ike was goin' shy. I could see him gettin' restless and I was wonderin' how he'd make the get-away. He tried two or three times. "I got to buy some collars before supper," he says.

"No hurry," says Smitty. "The stores here keeps open all night in April."

After a minute he opened up again.

"My uncle out in Nebraska ain't expected to live," he says. "I ought to send a telegram."

"Would that save him?" says Carey.

"No, it sure wouldn't," says Ike, "but I ought to leave my old man know where I'm at."

"When did you hear about your uncle?" says Carey.

"Just this mornin'," says Ike.

"Who told you?" ast Carey.

"I got a wire from my old man," says Ike.

"Well," says Carey, "your old man knows you're still here yet this afternoon if you was here this mornin'. Trains leavin' Cincinnati in the middle o' the day don't carry no ball clubs."

"Yes," says Ike, "that's true. But he don't know where I'm goin' to be next week."

"Ain't he got no schedule?" ast Carey.

"I sent him one openin' day," says Ike, "but it takes mail a long time to get to Idaho."

"I thought your old man lived in Kansas City," says Carey.

"He does when he's home," says Ike.

"But now," says Carey, "I s'pose he's went to Idaho so as he can be near your sick uncle in Nebraska."

"He's visitin' my other uncle in Idaho."

"Then how does he keep posted about your sick uncle?" ast Carey.

"He don't," says Ike. "He don't even know my other uncle's sick. That's why I ought to wire and tell him."

"Good night!" says Carey.

"What town in Idaho is your old man at?" I says.

Ike thought it over.

"No town at all," he says. "But he's near a town."

"Near what town?" I says.

"Yuma," says Ike.

Well, by this time he'd lost two or three pots and he was desperate. We was playin' just as fast as we could, because we seen we couldn't hold him much longer. But he was tryin' so hard to frame an escape that he couldn't pay no attention to the cards, and it looked like we'd get his whole pile away from him if we could make him stick.

The telephone saved him. The minute it begun to ring, five of us jumped for it. But Ike was there first.

"Yes," he says, answerin' it. "This is him. I'll come right down."

And he slammed up the receiver and beat it out o' the door without even sayin' good-by.

"Smitty'd ought to locked the door," says Carey.

"What did he win?" ast Carey.

We figured it up—sixty-odd bucks.

"And the next time we ask him to play," says Carey, "his fingers will be so stiff he can't hold the cards."

Well, we set round a wile talkin' it over, and pretty soon the telephone rung again. Smitty answered it. It was a friend of his'n from Hamilton and he wanted to know why Smitty didn't hurry down. He was the one that had called before and Ike had told him he was Smitty.

"Ike'd ought to split with Smitty's friend," says Carey.

"No," I says, "he'll need all he won. It costs money to buy collars and to send telegrams from Cincinnati to your old man in Texas and keep him posted on the health o' your uncle in Cedar Rapids, D.C."

And you ought to heard him out there on that field! They wasn't a day when he didn't pull six or seven, and it didn't make no difference whether he was goin' good or bad. If he popped up in the pinch he should of made a base hit and the reason he didn't was so-and-so. And if he cracked one for three bases he ought to had a home run, only the ball wasn't lively, or the wind brought it back, or he tripped on a lump o' dirt, roundin' first base.

They was one afternoon in New York when he beat all records. Big Marquard was workin' against us and he was good.

In the first innin' Ike hit one clear over that right-field stand, but it was a few feet foul. Then he got another foul and then the count come to two and two. Then Rube slipped one acrost on him and he was called out.

"What do you know about that!" he says afterward on the bench. "I lost count. I thought it was three and one, and I took a strike."

"You took a strike all right," says Carey. "Even the umps knowed it was a strike."

"Yes," says Ike, "but you can bet I wouldn't of took it if I'd knew it was the third one. The score board had it wrong."

"That score board ain't for you to look at," says Cap. "It's for you to hit that old pill against."

"Well," says Ike, "I could of hit that one over the score board if I'd knew it was the third."

"Was it a good ball?" I says.

"Well, no, it wasn't," says Ike. "It was inside."

"How far inside?" says Carey.

"Oh, two or three inches or half a foot," says Ike.

"I guess you wouldn't of threatened the score board with it then," says Cap.

"I'd of pulled it down the right foul line if I hadn't thought he'd call it a ball," says Ike.

Well, in New York's part o' the innin' Doyle cracked one and Ike run

back a mile and a half and caught it with one hand. We was all sayin'
what a whale of a play it was, but he had to apologize just the same as for
gettin' struck out.

"That stand's so high," he says, "that a man don't never see a ball till
it's right on top o' you."

"Didn't you see that one?" ast Cap.

"Not at first," says Ike; "not till it raised up above the roof o' the
stand."

"Then why did you start back as soon as the ball was hit?" says Cap.

"I knowed by the sound that he'd got a good hold of it," says Ike.

"Yes," says Cap, "but how'd you know what direction to run in?"

"Doyle usually hits 'em that way, the way I run," says Ike.

"Why don't you play blindfolded?" says Carey.

"Might as well, with that big high stand to bother a man," says Ike.
"If I could of saw the ball all the time I'd of got it in my hip pocket."

Along in the fifth we was one run to the bad and Ike got on with one
out. On the first ball throwed to Smitty, Ike went down. The ball was
outside and Meyers throwed Ike out by ten feet.

You could see Ike's lips movin' all the way to the bench and when he
got there he had his piece learned.

"Why didn't he swing?" he says.

"Why didn't you wait for his sign?" says Cap.

"He give me his sign," says Ike.

"What is his sign with you?" says Cap.

"Pickin' up some dirt with his right hand," says Ike.

"Well, I didn't see him do it," Cap says.

"He done it all right," says Ike.

Well, Smitty went out and they wasn't no more argument till they
come in for the next innin'. Then Cap opened it up.

"You fellas better get your signs straight," he says.

"Do you mean me?" says Smitty.

"Yes," Cap says. "What's your sign with Ike?"

"Slidin' my left hand up to the end o' the bat and back," says Smitty.

"Do you hear that, Ike?" ast Cap.

"What of it?" says Ike.

"You says his sign was pickin' up dirt and he says it's slidin' his hand.
Which is right?"

"I'm right," says Smitty. "But if you're arguin' about him goin' last
innin', I didn't give him no sign."

"You pulled your cap down with your right hand, didn't you?" ast Ike.

"Well, s'pose I did," says Smitty. "That don't mean nothin'. I never
told you to take that for a sign, did I?"

"I thought maybe you meant to tell me and forgot," says Ike.

They couldn't none of us answer that and they wouldn't of been no more said if Ike had of shut up. But wile we was settin' there Carey got on with two out and stole second clean.

"There!" says Ike. "That's what I was tryin' to do and I'd of got away with it if Smitty'd swang and bothered the Indian."

"Oh!" says Smitty. "You was tryin' to steal then, was you? I thought you claimed I give you the hit and run."

"I didn't claim no such a thing," says Ike. "I thought maybe you might of gave me a sign, but I was goin' anyway because I thought I had a good start."

Cap prob'ly would of hit him with a bat, only just about that time Doyle booted one on Hayes and Carey come acrost with the run that tied.

Well, we go into the ninth finally, one and one, and Marquard walks McDonald with nobody out.

"Lay it down," says Cap to Ike.

And Ike goes up there with orders to bunt and cracks the first ball into that right-field stand! It was fair this time, and we're two ahead, but I didn't think about that at the time. I was too busy watchin' Cap's face. First he turned pale and then he got red as fire and then he got blue and purple, and finally he just laid back and busted out laughin'. So we wasn't afraid to laugh ourselfs when we seen him doin' it, and when Ike come in everybody on the bench was in hysterics.

But instead o' takin' advantage, Ike had to try and excuse himself. His play was to shut up and he didn't know how to make it.

"Well," he says, "if I hadn't hit quite so quick at that one I bet it'd of cleared the center-field fence."

Cap stopped laughin'.

"It'll cost you plain fifty," he says.

"What for?" says Ike.

"When I say 'bunt' I mean 'bunt,' " says Cap.

"You didn't say 'bunt,' " says Ike.

"I says 'Lay it down,' " says Cap. "If that don't mean 'bunt,' what does it mean?"

" 'Lay it down' means 'bunt' all right," says Ike, "but I understood you to say 'Lay on it.' "

"All right," says Cap, "and the little misunderstandin' will cost you fifty."

Ike didn't say nothin' for a few minutes. Then he had another bright idear.

"I was just kiddin' about misunderstandin' you," he says. "I knowed you wanted me to bunt."

"Well, then, why didn't you bunt?" ast Cap.

"I was goin' to on the next ball," says Ike. "But I thought if I took a good wallop I'd have 'em all fooled. So I walloped at the first one to fool 'em, and I didn't have no intention o' hittin' it."

"You tried to miss it, did you?" says Cap.

"Yes," says Ike.

"How'd you happen to hit it?" ast Cap.

"Well," Ike says, "I was lookin' for him to throw me a fast one and I was goin' to swing under it. But he come with a hook and I met it right square where I was swingin' to go under the fast one."

"Great!" says Cap. "Boys," he says, "Ike's learned how to hit Marquard's curve. Pretend a fast one's comin' and then try to miss it. It's a good thing to know and Ike'd ought to be willin' to pay for the lesson. So I'm goin' to make it a hundred instead o' fifty."

The game wound up 3 to 1. The fine didn't go, because Ike hit like a wild man all through that trip and we made pretty near a clean-up. The night we went to Philly I got him cornered in the car and I says to him:

"Forget them alibis for a wile and tell me somethin'. What'd you do that for, swing that time against Marquard when you was told to bunt?"

"I'll tell you," he says. "That ball he throwed me looked just like the one I struck out on in the first innin' and I wanted to show Cap what I could of done to that other one if I'd knew it was the third strike."

"But," I says, "the one you struck out on in the first innin' was a fast ball."

"So was the one I cracked in the ninth," says Ike.

You've saw Cap's wife, o' course. Well, her sister's about twict as good-lookin' as her, and that's goin' some.

Cap took his missus down to St. Louis the second trip and the other one come down from St. Joe to visit her. Her name is Dolly, and some doll is right.

Well, Cap was goin' to take the two sisters to a show and he wanted a beau for Dolly. He left it to her and she picked Ike. He'd hit three on the nose that afternoon—off'n Sallee, too.

They fell for each other that first evenin'. Cap told us how it come off. She begin flatterin' Ike for the star game he'd played and o' course he begin excusin' himself for not doin' better. So she thought he was modest and it went strong with her. And she believed everything he said and that made her solid with him—that and her make-up. They was together every mornin' and evenin' for the five days we was there. In the afternoons Ike played the grandest ball you ever see, hittin' and runnin' the bases like a fool and catchin' everything that stayed in the park.

I told Cap, I says: "You'd ought to keep the doll with us and he'd make Cobb's figures look sick."

But Dolly had to go back to St. Joe and we come home for a long serious.

Well, for the next three weeks Ike had a letter to read every day and he'd set in the clubhouse readin' it till mornin' practice was half over. Cap didn't say nothin' to him, because he was goin' so good. But I and Carey wasted a lot of our time tryin' to get him to own up who the letters was from. Fine chanct!

"What are you readin'?" Carey'd say. "A bill?"

"No," Ike'd say, "not exactly a bill. It's a letter from a fella I used to go to school with."

"High school or college?" I'd ask him.

"College," he'd say.

"What college?" I'd say.

Then he'd stall a wile and then he'd say:

"I didn't go to the college myself, but my friend went there."

"How did it happen you didn't go?" Carey'd ask him.

"Well," he'd say, "they wasn't no colleges near where I lived."

"Didn't you live in Kansas City?" I'd say to him.

One time he'd say he did and another time he didn't. One time he says he lived in Michigan.

"Where at?" says Carey.

"Near Detroit," he says.

"Well," I says, "Detroit's near Ann Arbor and that's where they got the university."

"Yes," says Ike, "they got it there now, but they didn't have it there then."

"I come pretty near goin' to Syracuse," I says, "only they wasn't no railroads runnin' through there in them days."

"Where'd this friend o' yours go to college?" says Carey.

"I forget now," says Ike.

"Was it Carlisle?" ast Carey.

"No," says Ike, "his folks wasn't very well off."

"That's what barred me from Smith," I says.

"I was goin' to tackle Cornell's," says Carey, "but the doctor told me I'd have hay fever if I didn't stay up North."

"Your friend writes long letters," I says.

"Yes," says Ike; "he's tellin' me about a ball player."

"Where does he play?" at Carey.

"Down in the Texas League—Fort Wayne," says Ike.

"It looks like a girl's writin'," Carey says.

"A girl wrote it," says Ike. "That's my friend's sister, writin' for him."

"Didn't they teach writin' at this here college where he went?" says Carey.

"Sure," Ike says, "they taught writin', but he got his hand cut off in a railroad wreck."

"How long ago?" I says.

"Right after he got out o' college," says Ike.

"Well," I says, "I should think he'd of learned to write with his left hand by this time."

"It's his left hand that was cut off," says Ike; "and he was left-handed."

"You get a letter every day," says Carey. "They're all the same writin'. Is he tellin' you about a different ball player every time he writes?"

"No," Ike says. "It's the same ball player. He just tells me what he does every day."

"From the size o' the letters, they don't play nothin' but double-headers down there," says Carey.

We figured that Ike spent most of his evenin's answerin' the letters from his "friend's sister," so we kept tryin' to date him up for shows and parties to see how he'd duck out of 'em. He was bugs over spaghetti, so we told him one day that they was goin' to be a big feed of it over to Joe's that night and he was invited.

"How long'll it last?" he says.

"Well," we says, "we're goin' right over there after the game and stay till they close up."

"I can't go," he says, "unless they leave me come home at eight bells."

"Nothin' doin'," says Carey. "Joe'd get sore."

"I can't go then," says Ike.

"Why not?" I ast him.

"Well," he says, "my landlady locks up the house at eight and I left my key home."

"You can come and stay with me," says Carey.

"No," he says, "I can't sleep in a strange bed."

"How do you get along when we're on the road?" says I.

"I don't never sleep the first night anywheres," he says. "After that I'm all right."

"You'll have time to chase home and get your key right after the game," I told him.

"The key ain't home," says Ike. "I lent it to one o' the other fellas and he's went out o' town and took it with him."

"Couldn't you borry another key off'n the landlady?" Carey ast him.

"No," he says, "that's the only one they is."

Well, the day before we started East again, Ike come into the clubhouse all smiles.

"Your birthday?" I ast him.

"No," he says.

"What do you feel so good about?" I says.

"Got a letter from my old man," he says. "My uncle's goin' to get
well."

"Is that the one in Nebraska?" says I.

"Not right in Nebraska," says Ike. "Near there."

But afterwards we got the right dope from Cap. Dolly'd blew in from
Missouri and was goin' to make the trip with her sister.

Well, I want to alibi Carey and I for what come off in Boston. If we'd of
had any idear what we was doin', we'd never did it. They wasn't nobody
outside o' maybe Ike and the dame that felt worse over it than I and
Carey.

The first two days we didn't see nothin' of Ike and her except out to
the park. The rest o' the time they was sight-seein' over to Cambridge
and down to Revere and out to Brook-a-line and all the other places
where the rubes go.

But when we come into the beanery after the third game Cap's wife
called us over.

"If you want to see somethin' pretty," she says, "look at the third
finger on Sis's left hand."

Well, o' course we knowed before we looked that it wasn't goin' to be
no hangnail. Nobody was su'prised when Dolly blew into the dinin'
room with it—a rock that Ike'd bought off'n Diamond Joe the first trip
to New York. Only o' course it'd been set into a lady's-size ring instead o'
the automobile tire he'd been wearin'.

Cap and his missus and Ike and Dolly ett supper together, only Ike
didn't eat nothin', but just set there blushin' and spillin' things on the
table-cloth. I heard him excusin' himself for not havin' no appetite. He
says he couldn't never eat when he was clost to the ocean. He'd forgot
about them sixty-five oysters he destroyed the first night o' the trip
before.

He was goin' to take her to a show, so after supper he went upstairs to
change his collar. She had to doll up, too, and o' course Ike was through
long before her.

If you remember the hotel in Boston, they's a little parlor where the
piano's at and then they's another little parlor openin' off o' that. Well,
when Ike come down Smitty was playin' a few chords and I and Carey
was harmonizin'. We seen Ike go up to the desk to leave his key and we

called him in. He tried to duck away, but we wouldn't stand for it.

We ast him what he was all duded up for and he says he was goin' to the theayter.

"Goin' alone?" says Carey.

"No," he says, "a friend o' mine's goin' with me."

"What do you say if we go along?" says Carey.

"I ain't only got two tickets," he says.

"Well," says Carey, "we can go down there with you and buy our own seats; maybe we can all get together."

"No," says Ike. "They ain't no more seats. They're all sold out."

"We can buy some off'n the scalpers," says Carey.

"I wouldn't if I was you," says Ike. "They say the show's rotten."

"What are you goin' for, then?" I ast.

"I didn't hear about it bein' rotten till I got the tickets," he says.

"Well," I says, "if you don't want to go I'll buy the tickets from you."

"No," says Ike, "I wouldn't want to cheat you. I'm stung and I'll just have to stand for it."

"What are you goin' to do with the girl, leave her here at the hotel?" I says.

"What girl?" says Ike.

"The girl you ett supper with," I says.

"Oh," he says, "we just happened to go into the dinin' room together, that's all. Cap wanted I should set down with 'em."

"I noticed," says Carey, "that she happened to be wearin' that rock you bought off'n Diamond Joe."

"Yes," says Ike. "I lent it to her for a wile."

"Did you lend her the new ring that goes with it?" I says.

"She had that already," says Ike. "She lost the set out of it."

"I wouldn't trust no strange girl with a rock o' mine," says Carey.

"Oh, I guess she's all right," Ike says. "Besides, I was tired o' the stone. When a girl asks you for somethin', what are you goin' to do?"

He started out toward the desk, but we flagged him.

"Wait a minute!" Carey says. "I got a bet with Sam here, and it's up to you to settle it."

"Well," says Ike, "make it snappy. My friend'll be here any minute."

"I bet," says Carey, "that you and that girl was engaged to be married."

"Nothin' to it," says Ike.

"Now look here," says Carey, "this is goin' to cost me real money if I lose. Cut out the alibi stuff and give it to us straight. Cap's wife just as good as told us you was roped."

Ike blushed like a kid.

"Well, boys," he says, "I may as well own up. You win, Carey."

"Yatta boy!" says Carey. "Congratulations!"

"You got a swell girl, Ike," I says.

"She's a peach," says Smitty.

"Well, I guess she's O. K.," says Ike. "I don't know much about girls."

"Didn't you never run round with 'em?" I says.

"Oh, yes, plenty of 'em," says Ike. "But I never seen none I'd fall for."

"That is, till you seen this one," says Carey.

"Well," says Ike, "this one's O. K., but I wasn't thinkin' about gettin' married yet a wile."

"Who done the askin'—her?" says Carey.

"Oh, no," says Ike, "but sometimes a man don't know what he's gettin' into. Take a good-lookin' girl, and a man gen'ally almost always does about what she wants him to."

"They couldn't no girl lasso me unless I wanted to be lassoed," says Smitty.

"Oh, I don't know," says Ike. "When a fella gets to feelin' sorry for one of 'em it's all off."

Well, we left him go after shakin' hands all round. But he didn't take Dolly to no show that night. Some time wile we was talkin' she'd came into that other parlor and she'd stood there and heard us. I don't know how much she heard. But it was enough. Dolly and Cap's missus took the midnight train for New York. And from there Cap's wife sent her on her way back to Missouri.

She'd left the ring and a note for Ike with the clerk. But we didn't ask Ike if the note was from his friend in Fort Wayne, Texas.

When we'd came to Boston Ike was hittin' plain .397. When we got back home he'd fell off to pretty near nothin'. He hadn't drove one out o' the infield in any o' them other Eastern parks, and he didn't even give no excuse for it.

To show you how bad he was, he struck out three times in Brooklyn one day and never opened his trap when Cap ast him what was the matter. Before, if he'd whiffed oncet in a game he'd of wrote a book tellin' why.

Well, we dropped from first place to fifth in four weeks and we was still goin' down. I and Carey was about the only ones in the club that spoke to each other, and all as we did was remind ourself o' what a boner we'd pulled.

"It's goin' to beat us out o' the big money," says Carey.

"Yes," I says. "I don't want to knock my own ball club, but it looks like a one-man team, and when that one man's dauber's down we couldn't trim our whiskers."

"We ought to knew better," says Carey.

"Yes," I says, "but why should a man pull an alibi for bein' engaged to such a bearcat as she was?"

"He shouldn't," says Carey. "But I and you knowed he would or we'd never started talkin' to him about it. He wasn't no more ashamed o' the girl than I am of a regular base hit. But he just can't come clean on no subjec'."

Cap had the whole story, and I and Carey was as pop'lar with him as an umpire.

"What do you want me to do, Cap?" Carey'd say to him before goin' up to hit.

"Use your own judgment," Cap'd tell him. "We want to lose another game."

But finally, one night in Pittsburgh, Cap had a letter from his missus and he come to us with it.

"You fellas," he says, "is the ones that put us on the bum, and if you're sorry I think they's a chancet for you to make good. The old lady's out to St. Joe and she's been tryin' her hardest to fix things up. She's explained that Ike don't mean nothin' with his talk; I've wrote and explained that to Dolly, too. But the old lady says that Dolly says that she can't believe it. But Dolly's still stuck on this baby, and she's pinin' away just the same as Ike. And the old lady says she thinks if you two fellas would write to the girl and explain how you was always kiddin' with Ike and leadin' him on, and how the ball club was all shot to pieces since Ike quit hittin', and how he acted like he was goin' to kill himself, and this and that, she'd fall for it and maybe soften down. Dolly, the old lady says, would believe you before she'd believe I and the old lady, because she thinks it's her we're sorry for, and not him."

Well, I and Carey was only too glad to try and see what we could do. But it wasn't no snap. We wrote about eight letters before we got one that looked good. Then we give it to the stenographer and had it wrote out on a typewriter and both of us signed it.

It was Carey's idear that made the letter good. He stuck in somethin' about the world's serious money that our wives wasn't goin' to spend unless she took pity on a "boy who was so shy and modest that he was afraid to come right out and say that he had asked such a beautiful and handsome girl to become his bride."

That's prob'ly what got her, or maybe she couldn't of held out much longer anyway. It was four days after we sent the letter that Cap heard from his missus again. We was in Cincinnati.

"We've won," he says to us. "The old lady says that Dolly says she'll give him another chance. But the old lady says it won't do no good for Ike to write a letter. He'll have to go out there."

"Send him to-night," says Carey.

"I'll pay half his fare," I says.

"I'll pay the other half," says Carey.

"No," says Cap, "the club'll pay his expenses. I'll send him scoutin'."

"Are you goin' to send him to-night?"

"Sure," says Cap. "But I'm goin' to break the news to him right now. It's time we win a ball game."

So in the clubhouse, just before the game, Cap told him. And I certainly felt sorry for Rube Benton and Red Ames that afternoon! I and Carey was standin' in front o' the hotel that night when Ike come out with his suitcase.

"Sent home?" I says to him.

"No," he says, "I'm goin' scoutin'."

"Where to?" I says. "Fort Wayne?"

"No, not exactly," he says.

"Well," says Carey, "have a good time."

"I ain't lookin' for no good time," says Ike. "I says I was goin' scoutin'."

"Well, then," says Carey, "I hope you see somebody you like."

"And you better have a drink before you go," I says.

"Well," says Ike, "they claim it helps a cold."

DAVID ALLAN EVANS

"Nineteen Big Ones"

A hot June night, the two of them on a hotel bed naked, on their backs, with the sheet pulled up just above the knees. He is next to the window. There's a fan in the other window, pulling a light cool breeze over them.

"You know what Jack Nicklaus did last weekend after the first round of the British Open?" he says.

"No," she says.

"He shot a 79, seven over par, and then—do you know what par is?"

"No."

"Let's say on a given hole it takes four strokes to get the ball in the hole. They gauge it by how many strokes a very good golfer would need to get the ball into the hole. Let's say the par is four. Then you take every hole of the 18 holes, add up the pars, what a very good golfer would shoot—and that's par for the golf course . . . okay?"

"Yeh."

"You getting a breeze?"

"Yeh."

"You know what Nicklaus did the other day—last Thursday—after he shot a miserable round of 79, seven strokes over?"

"Yeh?"

"Are you listening?"

"Yeh."

"Now you have to realize, Jack Nicklaus is the very greatest golfer of all time. When he retires . . . he's my age, exactly. I know because I've been following him on TV for 20 years . . . we're both 42 . . . his birthday's in March, mine's in April. . . . Anyway, he shoots a 79 in the first round—seven over—and then he goes out that evening by himself and drives balls for two hours in the rain. Two hours in the rain . . . can you believe it?"

"No."

"You know what a driver is?"

"No."

"That's the wooden club you use to drive off the tee. Every hole has a tee and you drive the ball off the tee for your first shot. Nicklaus and a few other pros—only a very few—can actually drive a golfball 300 yards . . . you know how long a football field is?"

"Yeh?"

"A football field is 300 feet long, end zone to end zone. One hundred yards. Right?"

"Yeh?"

"Nicklaus can hit a golfball off the tee the length of three football fields, end to end. Can you imagine that?"

"No."

"So he goes out, after all these years, at the age of 42—and most of the guys on the tour he's playing with are in their late 20s and early 30s—Tom Watson is only 32—and Nicklaus drives golfballs for two hours in the goddamn rain. You know what par is now, don't you?"

"Yeh?"

"So the next day—listen to this—the next day he goes out and shoots a 66. That's six *under* par. Can you believe it?"

"No."

"That breeze feels good . . . you feel it?"

"A little."

"You want to trade sides?"

"No, it's okay."

"But I was thinking today, down in my office . . . what will I ever do in my whole life that'll even be a whisper to what Nicklaus does in just one tournament, one weekend? He's won 19 of the big ones now, and nobody'll ever come within miles of that record . . . you know what I mean by the big tournaments, the big four?"

"No."

"The British Open, the U.S. Open, the PGA, which is the Professional Golfers' Association, and the Masters. These are the big ones . . . he pretty much plays only the big ones anymore . . . he doesn't need the money . . . he's been playing with Spaulding clubs all his life, and then, just this year he bought stock in the company . . . he damn near owns Spaulding now . . . you've heard of Spaulding?"

"No."

"You tired?"

"No."

"It's a huge sporting goods company. He endorses their products, and they pay him millions for endorsing them, and he buys out the company. Almost."

"Yeh?"

"But I was thinking . . . what will I do in my whole life, working 50 years, that will even be a whisper to what he does in one weekend? . . . just one goddamn weekend, one tournament? One time he made an impossible shot from about 20 yards out on a tricky hole in some tournament—this was years ago—and somebody in the gallery . . . you can't imagine the size of the gallery when Nicklaus plays . . . somebody in the crowd yells out:

" 'Hey Jack, you're lucky!'

"So Nicklaus laughed—I read about this, it might've been the Open or the Masters—and he says to the guy:

" 'Yeh,' he says, 'the more I practice the luckier I get.'

". . . I was thinking today, 23 years I've been working, really busting my ass, and what's it all going to mean? . . . what will my kids think of me when I'm gone? . . . maybe the only thing that'll come back to them when they think of me is the sound of my pipe knocking the ashtray in the basement . . . that'll be the one thing of me they'll have . . . you know what I mean?

". . . You know what I mean?"

"Huh?"

"Are you still awake?"

"Yeh."

"You know what Tom Watson said about Nicklaus?"

"No."

"You know who Tom Watson is?"

"No."

"He might be the greatest golfer since Nicklaus. He's already won seven of the big four and he's only 32 . . . you know what he said about Nicklaus . . . he beat Nicklaus by one lucky chipshot this year in the Open, the U.S. Open . . . you know what he said?"

"What?"

"He told the reporter that this was the greatest scene he could imagine—I saw the interview just after he won—'Pebble Beach,' he said, 'Pebble Beach, the U.S. Open, and Jack Nicklaus, the greatest golfer of all time.' . . . are you awake?"

"What?"

"Nicklaus will maybe win two or three more big ones and then when he retires—Sally?"

"Huh?"

"Did you hear me?"

"What?"

"I love you."

"I love you."

"Goodnight."

"Goodnight."

ROGER ANGELL

"Up at the Hall"

In the foreword to his first collection of baseball pieces, The Summer Game, *Roger Angell wrote as follows: "When I began writing sports pieces for the* New Yorker, *it was clear to me that the doings of big-league baseball—the daily happenings on the field, the managerial strategies, the celebration of heroes, the medical and financial bulletins, the clubhouse gossip—were so enormously reported in the newspapers that I would have to find some other aspect of the game to study. I decided to sit in the stands—for a while at least—and watch the baseball*

*from there. I wanted to pick up the feel of the game as it happened to
the people around me."*

*He went on to describe his progression from there to the press box and
eventually to summoning up "the nerve to talk to some ballplayers face-
to-face." Always, he felt that his main job was "to continue to try to give
the feel of things—to explain the baseball as it happened to me, at a
distance and in retrospect. And this was the real luck, for how could I
have guessed then that baseball, of all team sports anywhere, should turn
out to be so complex, so rich and various in structure and aesthetics and
emotion as to convince me, after ten years as a writer and forty years as a
fan, that I have not yet come close to its heart."*

It should be added here what a considerable contribution the New
Yorker *has made to high-quality sports literature. Harold Ross, the
founding editor, and William Shawn, who succeeded him, allotted an
astonishing number of pages to sports reportage considering neither had
any interest in sports at all—horse racing (Audax Minor, the pseudonym
of George T. Rytall, who wrote the column into his nineties, in his later
years handing his manuscript over to a copyboy on the Jamaica station
platform), boxing (A. J. Liebling), fishing (Sparse Grey Hackle, a.k.a.
Alfred W. Miller), football (John Lardner), sailing (Tony Gibbs), golf
and tennis (Herbert Warren Wind), and baseball (Roger Angell). The
present editor, Robert Gottlieb, tells me that, in the tradition, he has no
interest in sports either—that on occasion he is "amused" enough to
watch perhaps ten minutes or so of a baseball game on television. This
does not mean a change in policy. "The magazine has always been
writer-driven," he explained. "Ross hated boxing, but Liebling's stuff
was in the magazine because he wrote so well about it. We would never
set out to find someone to write about a particular sports event. . .here it
works the other way around." Gottlieb went on to say that an article had
just come in on court tennis, the arcane progenitor of lawn tennis, which
he looked forward to publishing for its literary quality despite the fact
that the game is played only by a couple of hundred people around the
world.*

Summer 1987

Here we are, and here it all is for us: already too much to remember.
Here's a meerschaum pipe presented to Cy Young by his Red Sox teammates after his perfect game in 1904. Here are Shoeless Joe Jackson's
shoes. Here's a life-size statue of Ted Williams, beautifully done in
basswood; Ted is just finishing his swing, and his eyes are following the
flight of the ball, into the right-field stands again. Here is John

McGraw's little black mitt, from the days when he played third base for
the old Orioles: a blob of licorice, by the looks of it, or perhaps a small
flattened animal, dead on the highway. Here's a ball signed by seven-
teen-year-old Willie McCovey and his teammates on the 1955 Class D
Sandersville (Georgia) club—Stretch's first address in organized ball—
and over *here* is a ball from a June 14, 1870, game between Cincinnati
and the Brooklyn Atlantics; Brooklyn won, snapping the Red Stockings'
astounding winning streak of two full years. Babe Ruth, in a floor-to-
ceiling photomural, sits behind the wheel of an open touring car, with
his manager, little Miller Huggins, almost hidden beside him. The Babe
is wearing driving gauntlets, a cap, a fur-collared coat, and a sullen,
assured look: Out of the way, world! Let's hum a song or two (from the
sheet music for "Home Run Bill" or "The Marquard Glide" or "That
Baseball Rag") while we think about some intrepid barnstormers of the
game: the Chicago White Sox arrayed in front of the Egyptian Pyramids
in 1889; King George V (in a derby) gravely inspecting a visiting American exhibition squad (in uniforms and spikes) in 1913; and shipboard
high jinks by the members of a 1931 team headed for Japan (Mickey
Cochrane is sporting white-and-tan wingtips). The 1935 Negro League
Pittsburgh Crawfords were travelers, too; their blurry team photograph
has them lined up, in smiles and baggy uniforms, in front of their dusty,
streamlined team bus. Over here are some all-time minor-league records
for us to think about: Ron Necciai pitched a no-hitter for the Appalachian League's Bristol Twins in 1952 and struck out all twenty-seven
batters in the process; and Joe Wilhoit hit safely in sixty-nine consecutive games for the Wichita Wolves in 1919. Wilhoit was on his way
down by then, after four undistinguished wartime seasons with four
different big-league clubs, but Necciai's feat won him an immediate
starting spot with the Pittsburgh Pirates—and a lifetime one-season 1–6
record in the majors, with a 7.08 earned-run average. Hard lines, but
another kid made more of *his* chances after hitting safely in sixty-one
consecutive games with the San Francisco Seals in 1933: Joe DiMaggio.

Enough. Come sit down and take a load off—let's sit here on these old
green ballpark seats and watch this movie tape. I think it's—Yes, it *is:*

COSTELLO: Now, wait. What's the name of the first baseman?

ABBOTT: No, What's the name of the second baseman.

COSTELLO: I don't know.

ABBOTT: He's the third baseman.

COSTELLO: Let's start over.

ABBOTT: O.K. Who's on first.

COSTELLO: I'm asking *you* what's the name of the first baseman.

ABBOTT: What's the name of the second baseman.

COSTELLO: I don't know.
ABBOTT: He's on third . . .

What about bats? Pete Rose had a nearly knobless bat, with six separate strips of tape on the handle—or at least that's what he swung when
he rapped out his four-thousandth hit (he was with the Expos then),
against the Phillies, in 1984. Probably he wouldn't have done so well
with Babe Ruth's thick-waisted model, or with Home Run Baker's
mighty mace. Maybe weight isn't what matters: here's Jim Bottomley's
modest-looking bat lying on its side in a case—the bat he used in a
September 16, 1924, game, when he went six for six against the Dodgers
(Sunny Jim played for the Cardinals, of course) and batted in twelve
runs. I won't forget *that*, I'm sure, but here in the World Series section
(there is a cutout silhouette of Joe Rudi making that beautiful catch up
against the wall in 1974: I was there!) some text tells us that the Tigers
batted .455 against the Padres' starting pitchers in the 1984 Series—and
how in the world could I have forgotten that, now that I know forever
that Cy Young's 1954 Ohio license plate was "C-511-Y" (Cy won five
hundred and eleven games, lifetime) and that Mrs. Lou Gehrig's New
York plate for 1942 (Lou had died the year before) was "1-LG"?

This clotted flow is an inadequate representation of the National Baseball Hall of Fame and Museum in Cooperstown, but it is perhaps a good
tissue sample of one man's brain taken after a couple of hours in the
marvelous place. What has been left out so far is the fans themselves—
dozens and scores and hundreds of them, arrayed throughout the four
floors of the modest Georgian edifice on any summer afternoon, with
wives (or husbands) and kids and grandfathers and toddlers in tow, and
all of them talking baseball a mile a minute: "Pop, look at *this!* Here's
Roger Clemens' cap and his gloves and his shoes he wore on the day he
struck out all those guys last year—you know, that twenty-strikeout
game?" and "Ralph Kiner led the National League in home runs his first
seven years running—how do you like that, honey!" and "Alison! Alison-
n-n! Has anybody seen Alison?" I have done some museum time in my
day—if I had to compare the Hall with any other museum in the world it
would be the Victoria and Albert, in London—but I can't recollect a
more willing and enthusiastic culture-crawl anywhere. It took me a little
while to dope this out, and the answer, it became clear, is geographical.
The Hall of Fame draws a quarter of a million visitors every year—a total
that cannot be fashioned out of drop-in locals from Cooperstown (pop.
2,300), plus a handful of idle music lovers, up for the nearby Glimmerglass Opera summer season, and a few busloads of kids from day camps
scattered along adjoining Otsego Lake. (There are other tourist attrac-

tions in town as well: the Farmers' Museum and Fenimore House, the latter of which displays some furnishings of the eponymous and tireless non–Cleveland Indian publicist James Fenimore Cooper.) Cooperstown is an inviting little village, with flowering window baskets set out in front of its dignified old brickfront stores, but it isn't near anyplace else, unless you count Cobleskill or Cazenovia. From New York City, it's three hours up the New York Thruway and another hour out west of Albany before you hit the winding back-country road that takes you thirty miles to the lake and the town. Folks who come to the Hall are pilgrims, then; they want to be there, and most of the visitors I talked to during a couple of recent stays told me they had planned their trip more than a year before. The place is a shrine.

I had resisted it, all these years, for just that reason. I've been a baseball fan all my life—starting long before the Hall of Fame opened, in 1939—but lately when each summer came along I realized once again that I preferred to stay with the new season, close to the heat and fuss and noise and news of the games, rather than pay my respects to baseball's past. Cooperstown seemed too far away, in any case, and I secretly suspected that I wouldn't like it. I was afraid I'd be bored—a dumb idea for a baseball fan, if you think about it. By mid-June this year, however, up-close baseball had begun to lose its flavor for me. The World Champion Mets—*my* Mets—had lost most of their dashing pitching staff to injuries and other unhappy circumstances, and the team fell victim to bad nerves and bickering as it slipped farther behind in the standings. The Red Sox, who also held my fealty, were even worse off: twelve games behind and already out of the race, it seemed—a terrible letdown after their championship season of 1986. Spoiled and sulky, I suddenly remembered Cooperstown one afternoon in late June, and within an hour had extemporized a northward expedition with Charles, a colleague of mine and a fellow-Soxperson, and his ten-year-old Soxson, Ben—perfect companions, it turned out. We cheated a little by flying up from La Guardia on a Catskill Airways commuter hop to Oneonta, where we rented a car and instantly resumed our colloquy (it was too noisy in the plane to talk about baseball or anything else), which went on uninterrupted through two soggy days and four meals and three bottom-to-top sojourns in the Hall of Fame; an essential trip, we decided, maybe even for Yankee fans.

Like other shrines, perhaps, the Baseball Hall of Fame is founded on a fantasy—the highly dubious possibility that baseball was "invented" in Cooperstown by a local youth, Abner Doubleday, while he was fooling around with some friends in a pasture one day in the summer of 1839. In

1905, a committee of baseball panjandrums and politicos, the Mills Commission, forgathered to determine the origins of the national pastime, and after three years of deliberation it bestowed the garland on Doubleday, who had not done damage to his cause by growing up to become a major general and fight in the Mexican and Civil Wars. (He himself never laid claim to the baseball invention.) The commission, we might note, was convened at a time when organized professional baseball was not quite thirty years old and the modern, two-league era (and the first World Series) was only three years old. Teddy Roosevelt was in office, in a time of glowing national self-assurance, and the Mills Commission reacted with alac-rity to a letter from one Abner Graves, a mining engineer who had grown up in Cooperstown and swore he had been on hand on the day when nineteen-year-old Abner Doubleday scratched out the first diamond in the dust of a Cooperstown pasture, put bases at three angles, and added a pitcher and a catcher for good measure. Subsequent and more cautious baseball historians have agreed that the American game almost surely evolved out of a British boys' amusement called rounders, and that the true father of baseball was Alexander Cartwright, a young engineer and draftsman and volunteer fireman, who first marked off the crucial ninety feet between the bases and formulated the pretty and sensible arrangement of nine innings to a game and nine men to a side; his team, the New York Knickerbockers, came into being in Hoboken in 1845, and their sort of baseball—"The New York Game"— became the sport we know today. The Cooperstown chimera persisted, however, and was wonderfully transfused by the 1934 discovery of a tattered homemade baseball among the effects of the aforementioned Graves, in Fly Creek, New York, three miles west of Cooperstown. The ball—soon ennobled as The Doubleday Baseball—was purchased for five dollars by Stephen C. Clark, a Cooperstown millionaire who had established a fortune with the Singer Sewing Machine Company. The ancient pill became the centerpiece of Clark's small private collection of baseball memorabilia and, very soon thereafter, of the National Baseball Museum—an idea happily seized upon and pushed forward by Ford C. Frick, the president of the National League, and by other gamekeepers of the era, including Commissioner Kenesaw Mountain Landis. The museum opened its doors on June 12, 1939. It is providential, I think, that the Hall has no official connection with organized baseball, although Commissioner Peter Ueberroth and his predecessor, Bowie Kuhn, are both on the Hall's current board of directors, as are the two league presidents and a couple of team owners. The Hall is also financially independent, making do nicely on its gate receipts (admission is five dollars for adults, two for kids), donations, and the revenues derived from an overflowing and popular souvenir shop. The place seems to belong to the fans.

The Doubleday Baseball, the touchstone of the sport, is on view in the Cooperstown Room of the H. of F.: a small dark sphere, stuffed with cloth, which looks a good deal like some artifact—possibly a pair of rolled-up socks—exhumed from a Danish peat bog. Near its niche, on the same wall of the Cooperstown Room, there is an eloquent and un-apologetic establishing text (it was written by Carl Lundquist, a long-term early publicist) that disarms and pleases in equal measure:

> Abner Doubleday, who started baseball in Farmer Phinney's Cooperstown pasture, is not enshrined in the Hall of Fame. However, it is known that as a youth he played in the pasture and that a homemade ball, found in a trunk, belonged to him. Of such facts are legends made. As a Civil War general, Doubleday performed deeds of valor that earned him a place in history; but in the hearts of those who love baseball he is remembered as the lad in the pasture where the game was invented. Only cynics would need to know more.

The journey that even the most distant fan must endure to arrive at the Hall of Fame is but a few steps compared to the passage required of its members—one hundred and ninety-nine retired major-league players, players from the defunct Negro Leagues, old umpires, old managers, baseball pioneers, celebrated bygone executives—whose bronze plaques, each with inscribed name and feats and features, line the wall of the Hall of Fame Gallery and form the centerpiece and raison d'être of the pan-theon. Elections consist of an annual polling of four hundred members of the Baseball Writers' Association of America, and to be selected for the Hall a player must be named on seventy-five percent of the ballots. To be eligible for the ballot, the candidate must have put in at least ten years' service in the majors, plus a five-year waiting period following retirement. A backup system permits election by the Committee on Veterans, an august eighteen-man body (baronial old players, executives, and writers, including Stan Musial, Roy Campanella, Monte Irvin, Gabe Paul, and Shirley Povich) that selects notables of the distant and not so distant past who have somehow been passed over by the B.B.W.A.; a subcommittee picks players from the Negro Leagues, which went out of business in the early fifties. (Eleven Negro League players have been elected to date.) In the early days of the Hall, the Veterans Committee was the more active body, since it had to deal with the claims and statistics of many hundreds of old-timers, dating back into the nine-teenth century, while the writers were voting on players most of them had actually seen on the field. One hundred and twenty-six plaques in the Hall (ninety of them depicting players) are attributable to the Veterans Committee, but a more accurate view of the workings of the present system emerges when one sorts out the fifty-four living players now in the Hall, sixteen of whom ascended by way of the Veterans Committee and thirty-eight by way of the writers' poll.

Election of the immortals began even before the Hall was completed, and by Dedication Day four years' balloting had produced twenty-five members—senior gods, if you will. One of the riveting exhibits at the Hall is a formal photograph of the living inductees (there were eleven of them, and ten are in the picture) who came to Cooperstown that sunny June afternoon in 1939. Connie Mack, spare and erect and fatherly in a dark suit and high collar, sits next to Babe Ruth in the front row; the Babe, moon-faced and gone to beef, has an open collar above his double-breasted suit, and his crossed left leg reveals that his socks have been rolled down to shoe-top level. Tris Speaker, playing short center field as usual, stands directly behind Ruth, and Honus Wagner and Walter Johnson, with their famous country sweetness perfectly visible, occupy the corners. As you study the photograph (never a quick process, no matter how many times you have seen it), your gaze stops at the other men's faces, one by one, as recollection of their deeds and their flair for the game comes flooding back: Eddie Collins, Grover Cleveland Alexander, Nap Lajoie, Cy Young (pipe in hand), and George Sisler—old warriors squinting in the sun, comfortable at last. The one man missing is Ty Cobb. He had car trouble on the road and missed the photo opportunity by ten minutes—late for the first time in his life.

The Hall of Fame Gallery—part Parthenon, part bus terminal—is a long hall, windowed at the far end, with dark columns that set off the raised and illuminated galleries, left and right, in which the plaques are arrayed. You want to resist the place, but you can't—or at least *I* couldn't. I am an old cosmopolitan, and I live in a city where wonders are thrust at you every day, but not many gala openings have produced the skipped heartbeat, the prickle down the neck, the interior lampglow of pleasure that I felt every time I walked into this room. Others there felt the same way—I heard them, every time—and I noticed, too, that the bronze memorials, which are hung in double rows within alcoves, elicit a neighborly flow of baseball talk and baseball recollection among the strangers standing together before them. The familiar plaques—the immortal's likeness, in framed bas-relief, supra, with accompanying decorative bats and laurel spray, and the ennobling text and stats below—start on the right, as you enter, and proceed by years and order of election down that wall and then, doubling back, up the left side of the room.

The early texts tend to be short: Jove needs few encomiums. Ty Cobb's five lines read, "Led American League in batting twelve times and created or equalled more major-league records than any other player. Retired with 4,191 major-league hits." Babe Ruth: "Greatest drawing card in history of baseball. Holder of many home-run and other batting records. Gathered 714 home runs in addition to fifteen in World Series." That "gathered" is felicitous, but all the texts—almost fifty years of them now—have a nice ring to them: a touch of Westminster Abbey, a whiff of the press box. Christy Mathewson (he died young, in 1925) was among the first five players voted into the Hall, and the shining raised lines on his plaque sound the trumpets, all right: "Greatest of all the great pitchers in the 20th century's first quarter, pitched 3 shut-outs in 1905 World Series. First pitcher of the century ever to win 30 games in 3 successive years. Won 37 games in 1908. 'Matty was master of them all.' "

The early likenesses on the plaques (no one seems to know the name of the first sculptor)* show an assurance and zest that lift them above the heroic genre. Different (and sometimes indifferent) talents have worked the portraits in subsequent years, but no matter: fine art isn't quite the point here. Ted Williams, who waltzed into the Hall in 1966 (his first year of eligibility, of course), so disliked the looks of his plaque that he persuaded the Hall to have another one struck off and hung in its place. This one missed him, too, but you overlook that when you notice that his nose and the brim of his cap have been worn to brightness by the affectionate touches of his fans. ("I'm a *saint*, you mean?" he said when I told him about this not long ago, and he gave one of his bearlike huffs of pleasure.) In time, my visits to the Gallery became random cruises from alcove to alcove, until I would be brought to a stop by a likeness, a name, a juxtaposition, or a thunderous line or two of stats. I found Casey Stengel, Burleigh Grimes, Larry MacPhail, Hank Aaron, Rube Waddell. Amos Rusie (the Hoosier Thunderbolt) adjoined Addie Joss, my father's favorite pitcher. Here was Freddie Lindstrom. ("As youngest player [he was eighteen] in World Series history, he tied record with four hits in game in 1924.") And here, all in a cluster, were Yogi Berra, Josh Gibson, Sandy Koufax ("Sanford Koufax . . . Set all-time records with 4 no-hitters in 4 years, capped by 1965 perfect game, and by capturing earned-run title five seasons in a row"), Buck Leonard, and Early Wynn. Hack

*A few weeks after the publication of this story in the *New Yorker*, I received a letter from Benjamin and Philip Bayman, who identified the sculptor of the early plaques (from 1939 through 1959) as their father, the late Leo Bayman, of New York. Leo Bayman's distinctive contribution to the Hall is now part of the archives.

Wilson's plaque showed his determined jaw but stopped just above the place where he became interesting: his mighty shoulders and thick, short body (he was five feet six), which powered fifty-six homers and a record one hundred and ninety R.B.I.s in 1930. I found Roberto Clemente (". . . rifle-armed defensive star set N.L. mark by pacing outfielders in assists five years") and Eppa Rixey (but why did they delete his nickname: Eppa *Jephtha* Rixey?). I looked up Johnny Mize and learned something I had forgotten about the Big Cat, if indeed, I'd ever known it ("Keen-eyed slugger . . . set major-loop records by hitting three homers in a game six times"). The plaques of this year's Hall of Famers—Catfish Hunter, Billy Williams, and Ray Dandridge (another star from the Negro Leagues)—were not yet in place, of course, and after I looked at the bare wall that awaited them I moved along into an empty alcove and thought about the faces that would be hung up there in bronze over the next few summers: Willie Stargell, Johnny Bench, Carl Yastrzemski, Gaylord Perry, Rod Carew, Jim Palmer, Pete Rose . . . I could almost see the plaques already, and I pretty well knew what the lines on them would say, but these longtime favorites of mine would be altered, in quiet, thrilling fashion.

Men embronzed have a certified look to them, as if they had always belonged here, but for many of them the selection process has been far from peaceful. Great stars usually jump into the Hall on their very first year of eligibility—in the past decade, these have included Willie Mays, Bob Gibson, Frank Robinson, Brooks Robinson, and Willie McCovey. But Juan Marichal had to wait three years before garnering the requisite seventy-five percent of the writers' ballots, and Don Drysdale waited out ten. Looking back, we detect other excruciations, some of them (but perhaps not all of them) inexplicable. Charlie Gehringer didn't pass muster until his fifth ballot; Gabby Hartnett waited nine years and Lou Boudreau thirteen. Ralph Kiner made it on his thirteenth try, and Ducky Medwick on his fifteenth, and last, year of eligibility. Candidates who fall shy after fifteen Baseball Writers' ballots must survive three further years in limbo before their names and feats can be taken up by the Veterans Committee—twenty-three years after their retirement from the game. Johnny Mize, whose apotheosis was decreed twenty-eight years after he had hung up his spikes, told me that he was grateful for the honor, but confessed that he had lost interest in the process along the way; he had been particularly unhappy whenever he saw his name slip lower in the writers' estimation because of some arriviste youngster on the ballot. Jack Lang, of the *News,* who, in his capacity as the near-perennial secretary-treasurer of the B.B.W.A., supervises the voting (he himself was voted into the writers' section of the Hall at this year's induction), told me that many newly eligible stars experience an early ground swell of support and then tail off in ensuing ballots. Columnists and owners and fan clubs have been known to campaign intensively for favorites (Joe Sewell, a stubby little shortstop with the Indians in the nineteen-twenties, and Bob Lemon, the big Cleveland right-hander, inspired an inundation of letters before being admitted), but the process can backfire. Phil Rizzuto, the Yankee shortstop, has become the Harold Stassen of the Hall in recent years, and Lang believes that the sort of electioneering for the Scooter conducted by George Steinbrenner and by segments of the New York media helped bring about the defiant selection of another diminutive shortstop from the same town and the same era: Pee Wee Reese. The committees have considerable power, when you come to think about it, and one must assume that the writers are more reliable today than they were at times in the past: twenty-three B.B.W.A. voters left Willie Mays' name off their ballots altogether when he first came up for consideration, in 1979. He survived this knockdown pitch and made it home that first year just the same. Lang is uneasy when asked to speculate for long about such matters, and so is another good gray baseball friend of mine, Seymour Siwoff, the chief flamekeeper at the Elias Sports Bureau. He and I had a telephone conversation about the vagueness of the statistics emanating from the old Negro Leagues, and he said, "The numbers just aren't there, so we have to rely on what the guys who played with him say about a player we're thinking about for the Hall. But I don't worry about it. When a man is in, he's in, and we should be happy for him. We need the Hall, is how I see it. You gotta have that romance."

Museums wear you down, and Ben and Charles and I took time off from the Hall whenever the bats and stats and babies and souvenir Astro key rings and genuine Cubs Christmas-tree balls began to swim and blur in our heads. We visited Doubleday Field, the lovely old brick-grandstand ballpark (it's owned by the village) where an annual exhibition game between two big-league teams is played during Induction Weekend; a local high-school team and a semi-pro club play here, too, but the field was sopping on the morning we got there, and the only players on it were some robins busily working the base paths. Ben took a shot at an adjoining baseball range, and his father and I watched him swing like Yaz, like Wade Boggs, and now perhaps like Mickey Mantle and Tris Speaker and Joe D. as well. Mostly, though, we used our time away from the Hall to talk about the Hall. Ben's favorite feature was the I.B.M. Major League Leaders computer stations, where you could punch in the names of players (nine hundred and twenty-two of them) in more than eleven

hundred categories, and doodle them around on the screen. "I didn't
know all that much about Ty Cobb before this," he said at lunch one
day. "I'd read about him in books, but I didn't pay much attention,
because he was such a rat. But he was great—I have to admit it." Charles
was fond of a second-floor nook given over to the old Boston Beaneater
teams and their near-prehistoric stars, like Jimmy Collins, Kid Nichols,
King Kelly, Hughie Duffy, and Billy Hamilton, who had battled Ned
Hanlon's Orioles for dominance of the National League at the end of
the last century. A splendid photomural of the Beaneater fans shows a
thousand derbies. "I think there was a song way back then called 'Slide,
Kelly, Slide,' " Charles said, "and when I was a kid there was a 'Slide,
Kelly, Slide' ride at Whalom Park, in Fitchburg, Massachusetts. I'll bet
it's still there."

All three of us loved the basement in the Hall, and we kept going back
there. It was a catchall—a *basement*—full of leftovers and old board
games and stuff: Abner Doubleday's campaign trunk; a Hillerich &
Bradsby batmaking lathe; an awesome red iron pitching machine (circa
1942) on rubber wheels—a farm implement, you would guess—which
fired balls plateward with a mighty rubber band, after a black paddle had
flipped up to alert the batter just before the *twangg!* In another sector we
found an assemblage of slotted All-Time Leaders boards—lists of the
individual lifetime standings in hits, doubles, runs batted in, and so
forth; it reminded you of the lobby of a high-school gym. The names
Aaron and Cobb and Musial ran across the offensive boards like bright
threads in a tapestry. The lists were up to the minute, with Reggie
Jackson's five hundred and fifty-five home runs, putting him sixth on the
Home Runs roster, eighteen back of Harmon Killebrew and nineteen up
on Mickey Mantle. Nearby, I lingered over a little exhibit about the
handful of perfect games that the sport has produced in its long history,
from John Richmond's 1–0 victory over Cleveland for the Worcester
Ruby Legs, on June 12, 1880, down to Mike Witt's perfecto on September 30, 1984, when his Angels beat the Rangers by the same score.
(Catfish Hunter had a perfect game to his credit, too: Oakland 4–Twins
zip, in 1968.) These had been quick entertainments. Cy Young whipped
the Athletics in an hour and twenty-five minutes in 1904, and Sandy
Koufax needed only eighteen additional minutes to wrap up his famous
outing (Dodgers 1–Cubs 0) in 1965. There have been only eleven perfect, nobody-on-base-at-all games in big-league play, if you count Don
Larsen's win over the Dodgers in the 1956 World Series, and *don't*
count Harvey Haddix's twelve perfect innings for the Pirates against the
Braves in 1959. (He lost the no-hitter, and the game, in the thirteenth.)
John Montgomery Ward, pitching for the Providence Grays against the

Buffalo Bisons, pulled off the second perfect game in the National League only five days after Richmond's feat, and the *next* perfect game in that league came along eighty-four years later: Jim Bunning and the Phillies over the Mets, 6–0, on June 21, 1964. You can't beat baseball.

Now and then, I sensed a fleeting wish that the Hall were less optimistic and decorous. I think I would have enjoyed a visit to Cliché Corner, in a sector devoted to baseball and the language, and perhaps a downside exhibit—Boot Hall, let's say—of celebrated gaffes of the sport: Merkle's Boner, Snodgrass's Muff, and so forth, right on down to Bill Buckner's through-the-wickets error in Game Six of the Series last year. Sometimes you wonder if the Hall isn't excessively preoccupied with the past, but the charge doesn't quite hold up. The Great Moments display that catches your eye the moment you walk in has Joe DiMaggio's fifty-six-game hitting streak and Johnny Vander Meer's successive no-hitters in 1938 and Babe Ruth's sixty homers (and Roger Maris's sixty-one), and so on, but Roger Clemens is up there, too, striking out those twenty batters (they were Mariners) on April 29th last year. The sport is ongoing and indivisible, and the Hall's Baseball Today room downstairs has every single Topps Bubble Gum card for 1987 *and* the bats wielded by Marvell Wynne, Tony Gwynn, and John Kruk when they led off the Padres' first inning against the Giants on April 13th this year with a first-ever three home runs in succession. "I wouldn't give up my bat if I'd done something like that," Ben said on inspecting this wonder. "I'd sell it. No—I'd *keep* it."

The Hall, in any case, wouldn't have bought Ben's bat; it doesn't buy stuff. Aside from a few objects on loan, all twenty-three or twenty-four thousand artifacts on view or tucked away in Curator William T. Spencer's workroom have been acquired by gift—often a solicited gift, to be sure. The regularly incoming flood of baseball memorabilia and baseball junk is so heavy that a staff committee, which includes Director Howard C. Talbot, Jr., Associate Director William J. Guilfoile, and Registrar Peter Clark, who are the worthies most responsible for the imagination and wit and good sense evident in the present Hall, meets every Friday to decide what to accept and (mostly) what to turn down. Dozens of putative Babe Ruth home-run balls are offered by mail, and so, too, are "authentic" Babe Ruth bats, including innumerable samples of a Louisville Slugger model, once turned out by the hundreds, with the Babe's imprinted signature on the barrel. The committee is slow to reject, however, for slim leads often yield treasures. A hesitant letter about a box full of clothes belonging to "somebody named Bender" that turned up in an attic in Washington, D.C., three years ago eventually produced Chief Bender's dazzling white 1914 Athletics uniform, which is now to be seen in the General History sector on the second floor, next to a dandy photo of the Chippewa fireballer. Players are prime sources, of course, and some—Hank Aaron among them—have almost emptied their lockers for the Hall, possibly on the theory that immortality can always be improved a little.

Bill Guilfoile has spent a lifetime in baseball. (He writes the texts for the current plaques, among other things.) Before he came to Cooperstown, in 1979, he was assistant to the general manager and director of public relations for the Pirates, and I suspect that he may be responsible for the acquisition of the life-size wax statue of Roberto Clemente that now stands just outside his office door. This mysterious-looking effigy used to live in a back room at Three Rivers Stadium, in Pittsburgh, and one day—this was long before Clemente's untimely death in a plane crash—Pirate trainer Tony Bartirome and pitcher Jim Rooker spirited the thing down to the clubhouse and laid it out on the trainer's table, and turned off most of the lights. Then they told team physician Dr. Joe Finegold that Clemente had just fainted on the field, during batting practice. Dr. Finegold—or so the story goes—hurried in, took one appalled look, and felt for a pulse.

If I have slighted Mr. Guilfoile and his colleagues here, the National Baseball Library, which adjoins and is part of the Hall itself, must suffer a similar inadequate dismissal. I did pay a brief visit to the library, where the director, Tom Heitz, shrugged and laughed when I asked him to tell me about the four or five million newspaper documents, the hundred and twenty-five thousand photographs, the fifteen thousand–odd baseball books, the old radio-broadcast tapes, and so forth, that are in his care. The library is the custodian of the famous John Tattersall Collection of early-to-recent box scores, and Heitz told me that game information and biographical material about eighty-five percent of all the men who have ever played the game, at any professional level, were readily at hand. He permitted me to leaf through the files of that day's letters and applications to visit the stacks (ten thousand or so scholars consult the library every year), and I found queries from someone who wanted a photograph of the 1934 World Series; from someone who needed the box scores of games he had attended in 1934, 1961, and 1965 (there's a lot of this, Heitz said); from someone who wanted the name of every pitcher who had ever struck out ten or more batters in a single game (not feasible to sort out, Heitz said); an extensive communication from a Belgian scholar, Léon Vanvière, who is the world's No. 1 expert on baseball references in stamps; a letter from Bill Marshall, a scholar at the University of Kentucky, who is preparing a work on the mid-America, lower-minors Kitty, Bluegrass, Ohio State, and Appalachian Leagues; and two or three letters asking for information about a family member or ancestor who claimed or was said to have played professional ball once. Almost a quarter of such heroes, Heitz told me, turn out to be phantoms. But, like Bill Guilfoile, he is cautious. A woman who called up the library a few months ago was found to be a relative to Ted Welch, who pitched in three games for the St. Louis Terriers, in the old Federal League, in 1914 (Won 0–Lost 0; E.R.A. 6.00). The library knew nothing else about him—not even his birthplace—but a research questionnaire was mailed off, and Heitz expects that Ted Welch will have an extra agate line or two in the next edition of the *Baseball Encyclopedia.*

Before I said goodbye, I asked Heitz if his staff could dredge up the box score of a game played in the spring of 1930, in which Lefty Gomez, pitching his first big-league game, beat the White Sox at Yankee Stadium. I was pretty sure about that much, because I was there that day (I was nine years old), and because I had talked with Gomez about the game a few years back. The box score came to me in the mail two days later, and the first thing I noticed when I looked it over was that there were five future Hall of Famers on the field that day, including both pitchers: Red Faber and Lefty Gomez. Lefty fanned the side in the first inning (there was a little game summary attached to the box score), and the Yankees went on to win, 4–1.

I hadn't planned to go back to Cooperstown at once, but when Induction Weekend came along, late in July, I couldn't stay away. I was a little nervous about too much pomp and oratory, but what I encountered was a jolly family party of baseball. Twenty-five Hall of Fame members came back, to welcome the inductees—Hunter, Williams, and Dandridge—and so did their wives and (in many cases) children and grandchildren, and so did neighbors, brothers and sisters, and old teammates. Mary Rice, the widow of Hall of Fame outfielder Sam Rice, of the old Washington Senators, came back, as usual (Sam died in 1974), and so did her daughter Christine and her granddaughter Kimberly; this was Kimberly's nineteenth reunion at Cooperstown. Hall of Famer Happy Chandler—former commissioner, former Kentucky governor, former Kentucky senator—turned up, still hale and handshaking at eighty-nine, and so did Willie Mays, Ralph Kiner, Bill Dickey, Robin Roberts, the Splendid Splinter (more a tree now), Campy, Cool Papa, Country, Pee Wee, the Big Cat, Stan the Man, and more. The noble, Doric-columned old Otesaga Hotel, whose lawns run down to the glistening Otsego waters, took us all in (my wife and me included), and, hanging out in and around its lobby, bars, deep verandas, and restaurants, you heard baseball and nothing else for three steaming, cheerful summer days and nights. The fans were there, too, though at a distance—eight to ten thousand of them, heavily familied as well. The Hall had set up a long airy tent down

by the lakefront for three extended autograph sessions—all comers on
the first and third days, kids only on the second—and the waiting lines
were so long that they had to be mercifully truncated; the foresighted
early arrivals had camped out all night to hold their places. I sought no
autographs (one small girl in a Mariners T-shirt asked for *my* signature,
somehow under the impression that I was Billy Williams), but I happily
stuck around, and there in Cooperstown, encircled by great souls and
heroes of the pastime, I bathed in a Ganges of baseball:

Johnny Mize *(at seventy-four, he is melon-faced and massively calm—
unchanged):* These batters today are so nervous. You look at Winfield
and he's *duh, duh, dah-duh* at the plate. They're doing a dance up there.
I'd always walk into the box, drop my bat down, get my feet right, and
then I'd be on base or out of there . . . My worst day was when I got
traded to the Giants and I knew I'd have to hit in the Polo Grounds all
year, with that five-hundred-foot center field. It was four hundred and
twenty-two feet to right-center, where I liked to hit the ball. Bill Terry
hit straightaway and he batted .400 in the Polo Grounds before I got
there, and to me that's .500, easy, in any other park.

Ray Dandridge *(square and squatty, with bowed legs and broad, large
hands; he wore a snowy white cap by day and an engaging smile at all
times; seventy-three years old, possibly older):* I played shortstop and
second base, but third base was my real position. I played with the
Detroit Stars in 1933, then in Newark—the Newark Dodgers that
turned into the Newark Eagles. I played all year round, mostly for fifteen
dollars a week. Went to Puerto Rico, and it was fifteen dollars a week;
went to Cuba, fifteen dollars a week; Venezuela and Santo Domingo and
Mexico, fifteen dollars a week. I played seven years in Mexico and made
some money there in the end. We won the championship for Mexico
City . . . I'm a place-hitter—hit the ball to all fields. I'm a Stan Musial
man. I loved to see that man hit. He's my idol, because I hit like him—or
he hit like me.

Monte Irvin *(played in the Negro Leagues and then for seven years
with the Giants and, briefly, the Cubs; he batted .458 in the 1951 World
Series; tall and dignified):* Ray Dandrige played third base with style and
class. He had the quickest hands—I never saw anybody come in and
sweep up the swinging bunt the way he could do it. He's in a class with
Brooks Robinson . . . If the major leagues had integrated ten years
earlier, you'd have seen the great Negro League stars in their prime—
Satchel, Buck Leonard, Josh Gibson. We had some sure Hall of Fame
pitchers you probably never heard of—Roy Partlow, Raymond Brown,
and Leon Day. Leon is here this weekend, you should talk to him . . .
Back then, you had to go easy at the beginning with your team, because

there'd likely be an old-timer holding down your spot. He'd say, "Boy, this position belongs to *me*—go play somewhere else." So you learned to play all over the place.

Ted Williams *(no description needed; he talked about hitting, of all things):* The man who made that statue of me noticed something most people never did: I shortened up on the bat. I knew I was smarter than ninety-nine percent of the other hitters—not mentally but baseballi-cally. I said to myself, "The quicker I am, the longer I can wait. The longer I can wait, the less I'm likely to get fooled. So how can I be quick? Don't get too heavy a bat. Don't swing from the end of the bat. And with two strikes don't try to pull the ball all the time. And *get a good pitch to hit.*" That's all there is to it! When I was first in the Pacific Coast League, I went to see Lefty O'Doul, because I was a student of hitting. I talked to him one afternoon—he was with the Seals—when he was sitting on the grass out in center field, taking some sun. He said, "Kid, don't let anybody ever change you." And that's when I thought, Boy, I must be pretty good!

Ernie Banks *(still narrow as a slat at fifty-six; still talking, here to Ted Williams, in the next chair in the autographing tent):* You should be a Rhodes Scholar, Ted—baseball's never had one. We need a Rhodes Scholar, because this game takes brains. You even *look* smart, so you could have done it. You and me, we're the same kind of players. We like people who focus on the task, not the results. It's not the gold, it's the getting.

Billy Williams *(eavesdropping from the next chair in line):* Oh, no. Not again. I was Ernie's roommate, so I heard this stuff for sixteen years. But I'm all right. I'll survive it.

Joe Sewell *(eighty-eight years old, and probably an inch or two under his listed height of five feet seven back with the Indians in the twenties; struck out only three times in 1930 and again in 1932, and only a hundred and fourteen times lifetime, in more than seven thousand at-bats; wears thick glasses now and carried nine pens and pencils in his shirt pocket):* I have the bat at home that I used for fourteen years. The same bat. It weighs forty ounces. I never cracked it, because I knew how to swing the right way. I took good care of it—worked on it every single day. I rubbed it with a chicken bone and a plug of tobacco, and then I'd roll it up and down with a smooth bottle. The bat was your tool, so you took care of it. They want that bat up here at the Hall, but I'm keeping it.

Catfish Hunter *(at forty-one, he is the second-youngest player—second to Koufax—ever to attain the Hall; he looks even better than he did when he was out there painting the corners):* I don't miss the game, because I'm still in it, coaching my boys. One son, Todd, I coached up from

Little League right on through Legion ball. Now he's graduating, so I'm going back to wait for my son Paul, who'll be ready for Little League in a couple of years. I'm a Little League groundskeeper right now. Some parents think Little League pressure is too much for kids, but you got to get used to pressure sometime if you're going to want to play . . . My wife and my three kids are here. My three sisters will be here tomorrow, and three of my four brothers, and *their* kids. There's two busloads and ten or twenty carloads of folks coming from North Carolina, so my home-town—there's twenty-five hundred inhabitants, same as when I was a kid—will be not at home tomorrow.

Leon Day *(he is not young—he must be in his late seventies—but is broad, low, and still powerful-looking, with long arms; sunny disposition; many believe he will be the next player from the Negro Leagues to attain the Hall):* With the Newark Eagles, we played every day it didn't rain. Played all kinds of teams, in the league and out of the league. One Fourth of July, we played at Bay Ridge Parkway, in Brooklyn, in the morning—I think it was the Bushwicks that game. Then we played a league doubleheader in the afternoon at Ebbets Field—the Dodgers was away on the road. Then we played another game someplace that night. The same pitcher, a fellow named Jackman, started all four games. He got knocked out of the box each time, but he'd say "Gimme the ball, I can beat these guys," so he ended up losing four games on the same day . . . I had the reputation of being the kind of pitcher who'd knock you down if you'd got a hit off of me, but I wouldn't always do it on the first pitch. Maybe I'd throw you a knuckleball instead. Then a curveball. Then a nice change of pace. You'd start to think, Good, he forgot about that hit, and right then—*whap*—down you'd go. *(Laughs delightedly.)*

Each of the Hall of Famers had his own round table at the banquet that night, and the Lefty Gomez party made room for me and my wife. I had brought along my old 1930 box score—I had to read it to Gomez, who had forgotten his reading glasses—and he thanked me and said, "My God, I was six feet two and I weighed a hundred and forty-nine pounds that year. I was a *ghost.*" He looked around the crowded, cheerful room and said, "When I was a kid in the game, the older players would talk about all the famous guys that had once played with them or against them, but I never listened. I just wasn't interested. Now that's all I ever do."

I sat next to a delightful daughter of Lefty's who told me that she was Vernona Lois Gomez (Lefty is Vernon) and that the name had been selected after her parents had held personal consultations with the editor of a "Your Baby's Name" feature in the Boston *Post.* I asked her what the runner-up handle had been. "Juanita," she said.

Then I looked across the table at her slim and radiant mother, and a buried line or two of five-decades-old sports-page chatter came paddling up out of my memory: "The Gay Castilian [Lefty Gomez, in the sports parlance of that day], accompanied by his fiancée, Broadway's beautiful June O'Dea . . ."

"Is your mother the beautiful June O'Dea?" I asked Vernona.

"She certainly is," she said.

A little later, the B.J.O'D. told me that she and Lefty had met in a night club, the Woodmansten Inn, up in the Bronx, and that he had been absolutely tongue-tied that first evening. "We were engaged in two weeks, but we didn't get married for two years," she said. "I was playing in 'Of Thee I Sing' by then. We had a one-night honeymoon in Atlantic City, and the next morning he said, 'So long, sweetheart, I'm going to spring training,' and I didn't lay eyes on him for six weeks. That was fifty-four years ago, so I guess you could say we worked it out."

When the gala party moved over to the Hall for dessert and drinks, there were crowds of fans jammed together on the sidewalk and beside the front steps there, waiting to cheer for the old stars as they came in; it reminded you a little of the mobs at the Oscar awards, in Los Angeles, but without the kitsch and the craziness. The players had the museum to themselves that night; the Catfish Hunters just about wiped out the souvenir shop single-handed.

I chatted with Warren Spahn in the Gallery, and at one point he made a little gesture toward the party and the plaques and said, "There's such a *feeling* to this place. I go to Washington a lot—I was there last week—and I always get a thrill when I see the Capitol or visit the Congress. I feel the same way here. It's awe. I look around and I see all these men who played the game so well—great players, you know—and did it for peanuts, because they loved to play. I'm lucky to be part of something like that. I'll be back next year. I always come back."

When my wife and I left—it was after eleven o'clock—it happened that we walked out of the Hall directly behind Cool Papa Bell, who went carefully down the steps on the arm of his daughter. He is eighty-four now. There were still some fans outside, waiting in the warm summer night, and when they saw who it was they came forward and gave him a terrific round of applause, and Cool Papa shifted his cane to the other hand and waved to them in reply.

The induction ceremonies the next day were more of the same, really: it was as if the party had gone on into the following afternoon. The weather gave us a break at last, and there was a gusty fresh breeze moving in the thick, tall trees in Cooper Park, where the thousands of sitting and standing fans almost engulfed the handsome verdigris-green statue of James Fenimore Cooper. Up on the steps of the library, the

Hall of Famers were introduced, one by one. Ted Williams was wearing
a bright-green blazer. Willie Mays—or maybe Roy Campanella—got
the biggest hand. The sun shone, and the speeches and encomiums were
sweet and boring and almost not too long. The Commissioner reminded
us that Catfish Hunter had played for both Charlie Finley and George
Steinbrenner (they were both there, down front with the V.I.P.s), which
was enough in itself, he said, to put a man into the Hall of Fame. Jack
Lang was teary, and Jack Buck (the voice of the Cardinals, who received
the Ford C. Frick Award for his long career in baseball broadcasting) was
lengthily grateful. Each of the inductees introduced all the members of
his family after he received his plaque, and then delivered an acceptance
address. Hunter told us about his long-ago contract negotiations with the
Yankees; and Billy Williams, who had memorized and also copyrighted
his speech, said it was high time that baseball became fully integrated by
giving blacks and other minorities a chance at jobs in the front office and
as managers. This day, he said, was "the most precious thing in my life."
Ray Dandridge was the best. "The only thing I ever wanted to do was to
put one foot into the major leagues, but they didn't want it," he told us.
"Now I can thank each and every veteran on the committee for allowing
me to smell the roses . . . I love baseball, and today it looks like baseball
loves me."

CLAY FELKER

"Casey Stengel's Secret"

*I was once lucky enough to be invited to the White House on the
occasion of baseball's centennial. Just about everyone involved with
baseball at the time was there—writers as well as the baseball fraternity—and the climax of the two-day celebration was to file through the
East Room to shake hands with Richard Nixon. He stood on a slightly
raised platform so that he was forced to bend down to speak to those he
recognized. A functionary stood alongside to identify in a whisper those
of us far down the scale of immediate recognition. Casey Stengel was
about ten people in front. I happened to be with a small group of writers;
we all wondered aloud to each other what kind of exchange would occur
between Stengel and the president, given Stengel's unique way of put-*

ting things. Indeed, at the instant of their meeting, with Nixon's head slightly turned as Stengel spoke up into his ear, something of a surge took place in the line as some of us tried to get within range to overhear what they were saying. I was only at the perimeter, but afterward I was told what had happened—that Stengel, who at the time had retired and was involved in the banking business in Glendale, California, was curious about the government's position on banking regulations, or at least so my informant thought, and questioned Nixon about this in his curiously tortured phraseology. Nixon was expecting a revelation about baseball, some little anecdote that would amuse him. A glazed look crossed his face (I could see it from where I was standing). He bent slightly and asked Stengel a baseball question—none of us could overhear, perhaps something about the Mets, or if it was true about the sparrow that flew out when he lifted his hat to an umpire, or whatever—and Stengel, expecting an answer about banking practices, couldn't adjust at all. "Both looked dumbfounded," the closest of us observed afterward. "Ships passing in the night."

A mere sports writer should have known he couldn't get anything out of Stengel against his wishes. Even the United States Senate armed with the power of subpoena found itself helpless when faced with a determined Casey, for he put on one of his greatest shows of verbal gymnastics there in July, 1958. Stengel, and several star players including Stan Musial, Mickey Mantle, and Ted Williams were called as witnesses before the Senate Anti-Trust and Monopoly Subcommittee of the Judiciary, chaired by that demon investigator, Senator Estes Kefauver. The committee was seeking information on proposed legislation to exempt baseball and other team sports from the anti-trust laws.

When the inquiring senators attempted a squeeze play to get a direct answer to a direct question, Casey cleverly left them confused but laughing. A headline in *The Sporting News* summed it up succinctly: "Casey Was Eloquent, But What Did He Say?"

A partial transcript of Casey in full flight reveals him in a historic performance:

SENATOR KEFAUVER: "Mr. Stengel, are you prepared to answer particularly why baseball wants this bill passed?"

MR. STENGEL: "Well, I would have to say at the present time, I think that baseball has advanced in this respect for the player help. That is an amazing statement for me to make, because you can retire with an annuity at 50 and what organization in America allows you to retire at 50 and receive money?

"I want to further state that I am not a ball player, that is, put into that pension fund committee. At my age, and I have been in baseball, well, I will say I am possibly the oldest man who is working in baseball. I would say that when they start an annuity for the ball players to better their conditions, it should have been done, and I think it has been done.

"I think it should be the way they have done it, which is a very good thing.

"The reason they possibly did not take the managers in at that time was because radio and television or the income to ball clubs was not large enough that you could have put in a pension plan.

"Now I am not a member of the pension plan. You have young men here who are, who represent the ball clubs.

"They represent the players and since I am not a member and don't receive pension from a fund which you think, my goodness, he ought to be declared in that, too, but I would say that is a great thing for the ball players.

"That is one thing I will say for the ball players they have an advanced pension fund. I should think it was gained by radio and television or you could not have enough money to pay anything of that type.

"Now the second thing about baseball that I think is very interesting to the public or to all of us that it is the owner's own fault if he does not improve his club, along with the officials in the ball club and the players.

"Now what causes that?

"If I am going to go on the road and we are a traveling ball club and you know the cost of transportation now—we travel sometimes with three Pullman coaches, the New York Yankees and remember I am just a salaried man and do not own stock in the New York Yankees. I found out that in traveling with the New York Yankees on the road and all, that it is the best, and we have broken records in Washington this year, we have broken them in every city but New York and we have lost two clubs that have gone out of the city of New York.

"Of course we have had some bad weather, I would say that they are mad at us in Chicago, we fill the parks.

"They have come out to see good material, I will say they are mad at us in Kansas City, but we broke their attendance record.

"Now on the road we only get possibly 27 cents. I am not positive of these figures, as I am not an official.

"If you go back 15 years or if I owned stock in the club I would give them to you."

SENATOR KEFAUVER: "Mr. Stengel, I am not sure that I made my question clear." (Laughter)

MR. STENGEL: "Yes, sir. Well, that is all right. I am not sure I am going to answer yours perfectly either." (Laughter)

SENATOR KEFAUVER: "I was asking you, sir, why is it that baseball wants this bill passed."

MR. STENGEL: "I would say I would not know, but I would say the reason why they want it passed is to keep baseball going as the highest paid ball sport that has gone into baseball and from the baseball angle, I am not going to speak of any other sport.

"I am not in here to argue about other sports, I am in the baseball business. It has been run cleaner than any business that was ever put out in the 100 years at the present time.

"I am not speaking about television or I am not speaking about income that comes into the ball parks. You have to take that off. I don't know too much about it. I say the ball players have a better advancement at the present time. . . ."

SENATOR KEFAUVER: "Very well. Senator Langer?"

SENATOR LANGER: "Mr. Stengel?"

MR. STENGEL: "Yes, sir."

SENATOR LANGER: "What do you think is the future of baseball? Is it going to be expanded to include more clubs than are in existence at the present time?"

MR. STENGEL: "I think every chamber of commerce in the major league cities would not change a franchise, I think they will be delighted because they have a hard time to put in a convention hall or to let people to come to your city and if it is going to be like Milwaukee or Kansas City or Baltimore, I think they would want a major league team."

SENATOR LANGER: "Can the owners of the New York Yankees, for example, sell out to anyone who may want to buy the club at a big price without the consent of the other owners?"

MR. STENGEL: "That is a very good thing that I will have to think about but I will give you an example.

"I think that is why they put in as a commissioner Judge Landis, and he said if there is a cloud on baseball I will take it off, and he took the cloud off and they have only had one scandal or if they had it is just one major league city.

"How can you be a ball player and make 25 ball players framed without it being heard?

"It is bound to leak, and your play will show it.

"I don't think an owner possibly could do something but he can't play the game for you. It is the most honest profession I think that we have, everything today that is going on outside—"

SENATOR LANGER: "Mr. Chairman, my final question. This is the Anti-Monopoly Subcommittee that is sitting here."

MR. STENGEL: "Yes, sir."

SENATOR LANGER: "I want to know whether you intend to keep on monopolizing the world's championship in New York City."

MR. STENGEL: "Well, I will tell you, I got a little concern yesterday in the first three innings when I say the three players I had gotten rid of and I said when I lost nine what am I going to do, and when I had a couple of my players, I thought so great of that did not do so good up to the sixth inning, I was more confused, but I finally had to go and call on a young man in Baltimore that we don't own and the Yankees don't own him, and he is doing pretty good, and I would actually have to tell you that I think we are more the Greta Garbo type now from success."

For forty-five minutes he talked, which, considering the fact that he has talked nothing but baseball for more than fifty years, really wasn't much of a strain, although it left the listening senators stunned. In 7,000 words he avoided saying anything about the legislation. The verbal *coup de grace* was, however, delivered by Mickey Mantle, who followed Stengel. In answer to a question, he told the committee, "My views are about the same as Casey's."

ROBERT WALLACE

"A Snapshot for Miss Bricka Who Lost in the Semi-Final Round of the Pennsylvania Lawn Tennis Tournament at Haverford, July, 1960"

Applause flutters onto the open air
like starlings bursting from a frightened elm,
and swings away across the lawns
in the sun's green continuous calm

of far July. Coming off the court,
you drop your racket by the judge's tower
and towel your face, alone, looking off,
while someone whispers to the giggling winner,

and the crowd rustles, awning'd in tiers
or under umbrellas at court-end tables,
glittering like a carnival
against the mute distance of maples

along their strumming street beyond
the walls of afternoon. Bluely, loss
hurts in your eyes—not loss merely,
but seeing how everything is less

that seemed so much, how life moves on
past either defeat or victory,
how, too old to cry, you shall find steps
to turn away. Now others volley

behind you in the steady glare;
the crowd waits in its lazy revel,

holding whiskey sours, talking, pointing,
whose lives (like yours) will not unravel

to a backhand, a poem, or a sunrise,
though they may wish for it. The sun
brandishes softly his swords of light
on faces, grass, and sky. You'll win

hereafter, other days, when time
is kinder than this worn July
that keeps you like a snapshot: losing,
your eyes, once, made you beautiful.

GORDON FORBES

"Art Larsen"

One of the finest books about tennis is Gordon Forbes's beautifully titled A Handful of Summers. *Ranked around twenty or so during the late fifties and sixties, Forbes was considered (with his countryman Abe Segal as a partner) one of the world's best doubles players. From his earliest years Forbes kept a diary; in* A Handful of Summers *entries from it are used to enhance an account written while on tour in 1968. Cer-*

tainly, Forbes's stature as a writer surpasses his athletic ranking. Indeed, he belongs in the small group of writer-athletes who have written superb books on their own—Jim Brosnan, Peter Gent, Ken Dryden, Bobby Jones. Even the complexities of metaphor seem to come easily to him. Here he is on Ken Rosewall, whom he refers to as a surgeon: "He moves about with a racquet sharpened to a razor's edge, and carves his way through cumbersome opponents, leaving large slices of their games lying about on the grass. He is a precision instrument, a splitter of hairs, a specialist. Watching his backhand, one feels involuntarily that that is the only way that a backhand can be struck."

The section that follows is one of the many portraits in the book—in this case one of Art Larsen, the U.S. men's singles champion in 1950, whose career was cut short a few years later by a serious motorcycle crash in Oakland, California. I interviewed Larsen once in Oakland where he was in charge of some rather shopworn public courts. I remembered one of his stranger ideas was that on the court in his great days he imagined he was being advised by an eagle circling overhead which between points would drop down to perch on his shoulder and whisper advice. The bird was so solidly set in Larsen's imagination that his shoulder would sag slightly under its weight as he would cock his head to listen. Sitting in his small living room, I asked Larsen about the eagle. "What's he doing these days?" His eyes shifted slightly. "Why, he's sitting right there on your shoulder," he said with a slight smile. "Listen."

I can't think of tennis in Paris without remembering Art Larsen. Abe Segal first told me about him. Abe had toured Europe for a season before I arrived on the scene, and gave graphic descriptions of things or people who impressed him.

"This Larsen," he said to me one day, with the inevitable forefinger prodding my chest, "has got to be unreal. A genius at tennis, for a start. Play him and you think you've got yourself mixed up with that Spanish stuff they had."

"Inquisition?" I asked tentatively.

"That's it, Inquisition," said Abie. "He stretches you about so much you think you've invented rubber! You move one way an' he goes the other. Your shoes wear out an' your knees cave in! An' that's only for starters. Go around with Larsen for a while and you've got to see a psychiatrist—and if you go to the psychiatrist too often, *he* has to go to *his* psychiatrist. I went around with Larsen for a month and after a while I stops and says to myself: 'Hold it, buddy. Hold it a shake. One of us is crazy. Only I can't figure out which one!' So I 'phoned Herbie (Flam) and says to him: 'Hey Herbie, do I sound OK to you, or do I sound like I've gone a little soft?' So Herbie says, 'Keep talkin' a while, Abie. How can I tell how you sound if you only say a few words?' So I talk a bit longer, and suddenly Herbie says, 'OK, that's enough. You sound the same to me. That doesn't mean you're not crazy. Just that you haven't changed. So if you figure you weren't crazy before, then you're OK now!' That's Herbie! He's also mad, mind you! Talk about the deaf leadin' the deaf."

Abe went on at some length about the vagaries of Larsen's behaviour, throwing in phrases about "eagles on his shoulder," "gettin' stuck in doors," or "goin' about tappin' people."

"That's why he's called Tappy," he said, "because on certain days at certain times he has to tap certain things, and only he knows when!"

Although I knew that Abie was given to exaggeration, I looked forward to meeting Larsen.

For once, there was something in what Abie had told me. I met Tappy Larsen at last, in Naples, and he was, it turned out, almost everything everyone had said of him. A natural left-handed player of almost uncanny ability, he had that rare gift enjoyed by only a very few tennis players—a perfect touch, a feel for the ball, an inner knowledge of exactly what was going on between the strings of his racket and the melton cloth attached to the rubber inside of the ball.

But Larsen's tennis was not the most extraordinary part of him. Stories about him were legion: that he had survived a desperate situation in the war when all his comrades had been killed or wounded; that he'd been in a plane accident or a burning tank. Others similar. His superstitions were said to have been caused by these events. Whatever the cause, the superstitions were real enough. He did tap all kinds of people and things. He did, constantly, glance upward and backwards over his shoulder, sometimes even during rallies, watching for eagles.

We played together in the doubles of the Paris championships in 1956. Not the French championships, but the Paris ones, the ones that Budge Patty always used to win. Larsen and I were put together in the doubles, and after many adventures found ourselves in the finals against the wily French Davis Cup team, Paul Remy and Marcel Bernard. I was young and eager, and, apart from being excited about the opportunity to play doubles with Larsen, I badly wanted to win the tournament. Although I am sure that he, too, wanted to win, I think that the urgency of the thing escaped him. Besides, he greatly enjoyed devising surprises during the course of matches and seldom missed the opportunity of ending points with extraordinary strokes—like making sliced drop-shots come back over the net, or turning what appeared to be enormous smashes into the softest of pats. The more important the point, the more excited he became when one of his tricks succeeded, sometimes bowing to his partner, tapping the net with his racket, and nibbling at his shirt collar before continuing. I was far too young and nervous to fool about with cheeky style, and ruthlessly bludgeoned even the easiest of sitters, never daring to try clever things. As it was, Larsen's tricks badly scared me on a number of occasions.

"Don't you think, Art," I said to him once, tentatively, "that you should maybe just knock off the easy ones?"

"Don't be crazy, kid," he replied, "we have points to spare. There's no fun going about killing balls like a butcher!"

As far as I was concerned, I *never* had points to spare. With me, even at 5–1, forty love, and my serve, I was still barrelling about, looking for things to kill.

The score in our doubles final crept along, dead even. At one set all and about 8–8, the match was balanced on a knife edge. I held my service from 15–40 down and Larsen muttered something about it "never being in doubt" as we changed ends, although he'd picked up an extraordinary half volley from somewhere between his legs at 40–30. We fought to deuce on Remy's service and eventually got a set point at our ad. Larsen's chipped return developed into a flurry of volleys out of which, to my infinite relief, came a mis-hit lob-volley, straight to Larsen. A sitter to end all sitters. With a typical display of Gallic despair, Remy and Bernard turned their backs, dropped their heads, and walked towards the baseline. Larsen meanwhile, sensing an irresistible opportunity for a queer kill, began stalking the ball, waving his racket in circles like a sword and baring his teeth with a growling sound. Dumbstruck, I watched the ball bounce, watched him close in for a mighty smash, then suddenly check his swing and, with the end of the handle of his racket protruding beyond the heel of his hand, like a billiard cue, he tapped the ball over for a tiny dropshot winner.

The spectators leapt up with a roar of delight and Larsen waved his racket to them and turning to me said: "Scared you badly, eh kid? Thought I was going to foul it up, eh?" and laughed the happy laugh that he used when things were going according to plan.

On the way to the centre court that day, Tappy got stuck in the door—hung up, really, with no visible obstruction. He just stood there, nibbling his shirt collar and saying: "God damn, buddy, get me through this thing." I had to unhook him from nothing—and finally as I lifted his foot over some last invisible obstruction, he burst free and ran onto court calling to me: "Okay, kid, take it away, swing it wide, baby, and play the net on my service; we got beers waiting!"

He never trained, seldom practised, smoked a lot, drank beer, sat in damp clothes and cold winds after his matches, stayed up all night, slept in the dressing-rooms, and had difficulty changing into tennis gear— often getting stuck in his trousers, when halfway up his legs and having to hobble all over the changing-room and chat to people about their matches before the trousers would slide up and fit him. Sometimes his sweater would jam, and he would walk onto the court with only one arm in a sleeve, and the rest of the sweater wound round his neck like a scarf. On the court he would either *have* to step on lines, or *not have* to step on them, and was able to cross over on only one side of the net, usually the umpire's side, where he could give the fellow a tap or two in passing. He had about six cameras, all expensive, including one movie one, and one day each week he would hang all of them around his neck and shoulders and go out taking millions of shots, sometimes peering through the viewfinder of one while pressing the button of another.

"This is for colour, this for black and white slow film, this grainy, this fast, etc.," he would explain proudly. "You want me to take a colour shot of you? Sure. Just stand over there. That's the boy. Over there!"

The players loved him to the point of adoration and never missed watching his matches. In Rome he beat Andy Stern 6–0, 6–0, 5–7, 6–0 because, he said, a set off him was a "good result" for Andy (which it was) but that he shouldn't "spoil him." Larsen verged on greatness and won many large tournaments, including Forest Hills. His accident was a tragedy and deprived tennis prematurely of one of the great individualists of the game.

MAXINE KUMIN

"PROTHALAMION"

The far court opens for us all July.
Your arm, flung up like an easy sail bellying,
comes down on the serve in a blue piece of sky
barely within reach, and you, following,
tip forward on the smash. The sun sits still
on the hard white canvas lip of the net. Five-love.
Salt runs behind my ears at thirty-all.

At game, I see the sweat that you're made of.
We improve each other, quickening so by noon
that the white game moves itself, the universe
contracted to the edge of the dividing line
you toe against—limbering for your service,
arm up, swiping the sun time after time—
and the square I live in, measured out with lime.

GEORGE PLIMPTON
AND WILLIAM CURRY

"Vince Lombardi"

A few years after my participatory stint with the Detroit Lions I went back into the game to make a television special entitled "The Great Quarterback Sneak." This time I joined the Baltimore Colts, which the year before, with John Unitas at quarterback, had won the Super Bowl. I went in as a quarterback for four plays against my old teammates, the Lions, in an exhibition game at Ann Arbor, Michigan, on a hot August afternoon before 106,000 spectators, the largest crowd, I believe, to see a professional game up until then. I improved considerably from my performance with the Lions. There I started the team on the thirty-yard line and in four plays moved it back to the one. With the Colts I moved the team forward eighteen yards in four plays—fifteen of those yards, I must admit, on a roughing-the-passer penalty!

The center on the Colts team was Bill Curry, articulate, thoughtful, observant. I always thought he should go into another line of work—communications, politics. But he chose instead to stick to football as a coach (Georgia Tech, Alabama, Kentucky). What I particularly remember about him at the Colts training camp was that he was one of the few players who moved around the dining room and sat at different tables as if to check out his constituency and his relationship to it. He behaved like an excellent reporter on a long assignment. Blessed with astonishing recall and a born storyteller, he was an splendid collaborator on a book we did together—One More July. The framework of the book was an auto journey from Louisville, Kentucky, up to Green Bay, Wisconsin, where Bill was going back to take one last crack at football—"one more July," as players refer to it—with the Packers, where he had started his football career a decade before. What follows is a portrait of his first professional coach.

As we drove north from Louisville, Lombardi's name began to crop up increasingly—not surprising, since Curry had gone through a near traumatic relationship with him (which was probably true of any Green Bay Packer), and the more I heard about him, the harder I pressed for details. I spent quite a lot of time saying, "What?" or "That's hard to believe," or most often, "Well, I don't see how you went on with someone like that."

Curry was patient. "You see, the key to him was that he believed that games are won not by systems or superstar players but by execution. So a player had to suffer the consequences of being driven to execute. Everything was directed at that. It was brilliantly simple. In fact, the technical part of football was much simpler than I thought it was going to be—the simplest of all the systems I played under. When I first got to Green Bay, Ken Bowman, who was the other center, went through all the plays with me in one afternoon. Then the next day, Lombardi himself sat down with me and on one sheet of a yellow legal pad he drew up every single play that the Green Bay Packers had. I think of all the documents, the awards, all the memorabilia of my career, and I'd give them up for that one sheet of paper, which I lost, or never thought was worth keeping. The famous one on the paper, of course, was the power sweep. Lombardi's theory was that nobody could stop the power sweep without giving away something else. So if they could stop forty-nine, then you ran thirty-seven, which was an off-tackle play, because in order to stop the sweep they had to move the linebacker out. So then you ran inside him. There was no need for any fancy deception or anything of the sort, in his way of thinking. We had a reverse in our play-book. I don't think we ever ran it while I was there.

"So Lombardi's main theory was, 'You don't win games with systems; you win games with execution. Whatever the system is, you do it the same way every time.' So we would run the Green Bay power sweep five, ten, fifteen, twenty times in a row. The same play over and over. In the huddle the call for it was simply forty-nine or forty-eight, depending on which direction we were going to run it. It was the play that made Jerry Kramer and Fuzzy Thurston famous, because they were the pulling guards and they'd come out around, leading Paul Hornung or Jimmy Taylor. If Jimmy was carrying the ball, it was called thirty-eight or thirty-nine.

"Given this theory, everything depended on how you could execute. If you couldn't fit into the way he thought you should execute, well, then, that was the end of you there."

"How did he let his men go?" I asked. I had always been appalled by the methods of dismissing players in the NFL.

"If people went—were cut," Curry said, "there was no explanation. None needed. Lombardi never said, 'Well, we had to cut Joe Smith and John Black today.' They were just gone. The locker next door would be empty, like the guy had disappeared into thin air. Pat Peppler did the cutting for him. He was a big, bald, jovial guy, always with a grin on his face, who could do the painful job and I'm sure make it as painless as anybody. He'd look in after breakfast and he'd say, 'The coach wants to see you, and bring your playbook,' which meant 'So long, Charlie.' On the day of the last cut my rookie year, I was sitting alone in my room. My roommate had been injured; he was in the hospital. I hadn't made the team for sure—there were some other good centers in camp—and I was sitting by myself, just apoplectic . . . waiting. Sure enough, there was a rap at the door. My heart jumped. I opened the door and it was Peppler. I could feel the blood just drain from my face.

"He said, 'Bill, my wife, Lindy, wants Carolyn to go to a luncheon with her tomorrow. Have Carolyn call her, would you?' and he turned and started to walk off.

"I leaned out the door. I said, 'Mr. Peppler, if you ever do anything like this to me again, I'm going to break your neck!' He turned around, bewildered. He didn't realize what he'd done. We laugh about it today. He scared me to death. I could've killed him.

"With that there was a huge letdown. I'd made the Packers . . . what I had aimed for all those years. I was a professional athlete. I had made the team, one of the best teams in the business. Then my good friend Rich Koeper, who had been the other rookie center and who had been moved from center to offensive tackle when I showed up from the All Star game, came to my room and he said, 'Bill, could you help me load my stuff in the car?'

" 'What do you mean?'

" 'I'm leaving,' he said.

"He saw how low I looked. 'Hell, man,' he said, 'you've won the battle; you've defeated someone else. You've taken the job, and *you're* there instead of them.'

"But I felt none of that. I helped him load his things, and then I began to drive him to the motel where he was going to catch a limousine for the airport. I began to *weep.* I cried and cried and I couldn't stop! It was just humiliating . . . finally a big hero, stud athlete, and here I was making an ass of myself. Rich Koeper was crying too. That was a real scene."

"I'll say," I remarked.

By this time we were miles up Route 65, long past the great curve of the expressway above the candy-making factories in the north section of Louisville . . . out in the country with the heat beginning to build up, the air waves beginning to shimmer over the fields.

I asked Curry if there was a way one could distinguish a Green Bay Packers other than their habit of breaking down and weeping occasionally.

Curry grinned and said that one of the earmarks of the Green Bay Packers was their tremendous physical condition . . . that driven by Lombardi, a player had to be in shape, in *great* shape, to survive. "Take Jimmy Taylor, the great fullback," Curry explained. "He was just about the best-conditioned athlete I've ever seen. He knew that I had a background of having worked a little with weights. Not much; I'm not a power guy at all. But Jimmy would get me to lift weights with him between the morning and the afternoon practices. It'd be ninety-nine degrees and like a furnace outside. My locker was next to his. He'd say, 'Come on.' I'd say, 'Well, gee, Mr. Taylor, we've got to go back out and practice this afternoon.' 'Well, we're going to do our bench presses, kid.' And we'd go and do bench presses.

"It was worth it. Lombardi would just *destroy* you physically if you weren't in shape. The calisthenics period before practice was incredible—not fifteen side-straddle hops but a *hundred.* Then at the conclusion of these calisthenics, which were led by a coach, Lombardi would walk up to the front of the group with a sadistic grin on his face and he'd say, 'Okay, let's go.' It was time for the grass drill. We'd start running in place. He wanted you to pick up those knees to your chest, and when he said 'Down,' you'd dive on the ground; he'd say, 'Up,' and you'd jump to your feet, running in place. He would make you do them until you literally could not get off the ground. I've seen our offensive captain, Bob Skoronski, pass out. Guys were vomiting on the field, other guys could not get up off the ground, and he'd go over and say, 'Get up! Get up!' and they couldn't. That kind of thing.

"We'd just keep going. One time we did seventy-eight of them, up and down, which is an *awful* lot. Ken Bowman and I used to count them to keep from going insane with the pain. Willie Wood was famous for not . . . he would just quit! Lombardi'd say, 'Stop the drill!' which thrilled us because we could puff a bit. 'Willie, you're going to do those right! Now get going, you're going to do it for everybody.' Willie still couldn't do them. He'd fall down on the ground and he'd push himself up on one knee and then fall over again. You had to be as good a football player as Willie to be able to get away with that sort of thing. Finally Lombardi'd say, 'Oh, God, that's okay, okay,' and then we'd go on.

"Then, at the end of the grass drills, when everybody was just literally staggering, Lombardi would blow the whistle and we'd sprint around the goal post and back to the far end of the field . . . probably two hundred and fifty yards, and you had to *sprint*. If you were last you were in big trouble. When you'd start to run after those grass drills, your legs wouldn't work! Literally would not function! They'd just wobble, and it took a conscious effort to get one in front of the other. Then you'd recover a bit and you'd get to where you were actually running and you'd get around to the far end of the field, when you'd get about thirty seconds to get a breath of air; everybody'd just drop to a knee and just gasp and pant . . . even losing an occasional breakfast and that sort of thing.

"I always took great pride in being in good shape and doing every grass drill. Some guys would watch Lombardi when he'd walk by them, and when he had his back to them, they'd quit. When he'd come back, then they'd get going again. Well, I always did every single one of them, and when he blew his whistle for the sprint, I ran just as fast as I could. I wasn't fast enough to be first in from running around the goal post, but I always would *try* to be near.

"One day in my second year with the Packers, Jimmy Taylor came up to me and said, 'Now, Bill, you know you're a veteran now.' 'Yeah, that's right,' I said. 'You know you've gotta help set a good example for these young guys, these rookies.'

" 'Right.'

" 'Now, you know when we do our grass drills and run around the goal post?'

"I thought he was about to compliment me on how hard I tried.

" 'Well, when you get back over to the far end of the field . . . when we get to our little break, you know? Don't breathe so hard.'

" 'What?' I said. 'What do you mean, don't breathe so hard? I'm dying!'

" 'Well, you're in good shape,' he said, 'but you shouldn't be breathing so hard. These new guys, these rookies, will think you're tired and that you're not tough. Gotta be a tough guy.'

"I thought he was kidding. I started to laugh.

" 'I mean it,' he said. 'When you get back, blow it out. Then you'll feel all right. You don't have to be huffing and puffing.'

"Well, I thought, this man's crazy! The next morning I watched him. He did every single grass drill. He hit the ground, he picked his knees up higher than anybody else. In fact, Lombardi'd watch him and go crazy: 'Attaboy, Jimmy, attaboy! Look here, everybody, here's somebody in shape. Jimmy Taylor's always in shape!' That kind of thing. And he'd sprint around the goal post and come back. Sure enough! Everybody's dying and Jimmy Taylor was not breathing hard! He was just superbly conditioned. I thought I was in shape and I was just nothing compared to him. And then, to match his physical heft, he had this supreme self-confidence. At meetings, during the film critiques, Lombardi would jump on him, and he'd just sit in the back of the room with his cigar and grin. He'd take a couple of puffs on that big cigar."

I interrupted. "Do you mean with all that emphasis on conditioning he'd let people smoke?"

"Yeah," Curry said. "You could even smoke in the locker room. This was one of the great shocks to me . . . when I'd come in and Hornung would light up at half-time. . . . Well, Lombardi'd jump on Jimmy for making a mistake that showed up in the films, and Jimmy would take a drag off his cigar, a big puff of smoke would drift up, and he'd look around and grin and flick the ash off the cigar like Groucho Marx and he'd say, 'Guess I'm washed up, Coach.' Unbelievable self-confidence.

"In practice he'd sneak off to the field where the kickers were. Lombardi'd yell at him, 'Taylor, get over heah—what you been up to?' and Taylor'd raise his arms up over his face defensively and he'd say, 'Coach, I was working on my field goal block.' He could get away with it because he was such an extraordinary football player. But then, of course, Taylor played out his option and went to play in New Orleans. It destroyed their relationship."

"I remember that," I said. "They never spoke again, did they?"

"Loyalty was such a big thing," Curry said. "Jimmy was a very tough negotiator on contracts, but Lombardi was too. Sometimes he would just tell a guy, 'You get your ass up there and sign that contract.' And they'd do it. Because of this one-on-one relationship with players, Lombardi hated agents. He told the guys, 'Don't send some agent in here to negotiate for you.' This was a long time before the lawyer-agent kind of representative got to be the vogue. Well, Jim Ringo thought he could take the chance. He was a great center for the Packers, and he probably regarded himself as almost indispensable because he called all the blocking—a key figure in the offensive line—and besides, he had this phenomenal reputation around the league. So he sent a lawyer, an agent, into Lombardi's office to negotiate for him. The gentleman walked in and said, 'Mr. Lombardi, I'm here to represent Jim Ringo in his contract negotiations.' Lombardi said, 'You'll excuse me for a moment,' and he got up and left the room. About five minutes later he came back and he said, 'I'm sorry, you're talking to the wrong person.'

" 'I don't understand,' the agent said.

" 'Well, Jim Ringo now plays with the Philadelphia Eagles,' Lombardi said. 'You'll have to talk to them.' "

"And that's what happened with Taylor?" I asked.

"Something like that," Curry said. "Lombardi could not intimidate Jimmy into signing. He played out his option and went to play for New Orleans. I'm told Lombardi never forgave him. He never referred to him again by name. He called him 'the other guy.' They put Paul Hornung's jersey up in the Packer museum showcase, but not Taylor's. Lombardi said, 'We miss Hornung around here, but we could always do without the other guy.' "

I shook my head and remarked that I didn't understand how all that effort Taylor had made in his behalf—all those years of painful effort tearing through the middle of opposing lines—would not balance out just about *anything* that Lombardi could have held against him.

"He just wasn't an easy man," Curry said simply. "At times I couldn't stand the sight of him. Neither could the rest of us. I remember Gale Gillingham, his first week at Green Bay, was sitting in the backseat while somebody was driving us from practice back to the locker room. Gillingham had never said a word. In fact, I don't think I had heard him say a word since he'd arrived. He'd broken his right hand in the All Star game, and he had a big cast on it. We'd had those awful grass drills. Of course, to Lombardi, there was no such thing as an injury. Gilly did every one of those grass drills with one hand. Everybody noticed him and realized: We've got one here; he's going to be all right! The rest of us were struggling to do them with *two*. Well, on the drive back somebody said, 'Lombardi was *so* bad today.' You know the term that's applied when somebody's in an especially bad mood? 'He was on the rag today.' That was usually the comment somebody would make about him on an especially tough day. Well, Gillingham was sitting in the backseat and he suddenly said, unsolicited, the first words any of us had ever heard him say: 'That is the most disgusting man I've ever seen in my life.' I said, 'Boy, that sums it up.' "

"I would have sulked," I said. "I would have hangdogged around just to show him how awful I thought he was."

Curry laughed. "There was no way you could manipulate him. And yet the devastating thing about *him*—which caused the love-hate relationship the players had with him—was the way he used his ability to manipulate *you*, to make you do whatever he wanted you to do. He could ruin your whole day in a matter of seconds. In the morning I'd be starting on my weight program and he'd walk in and scowl. I'd try to speak to him. He'd ignore me, or mumble something, and I hated him even more, and he'd get me thinking: What the hell am I *doing* in this business? And then ten minutes later he'd walk up and put his arm on my shoulder and say, 'I like the way you work. You're doing a good job, and I'm proud of you,' and I'd *die* for him! Do anything for him! Then the realization would come: My God, I'm being manipulated like a piece of Silly Putty. He flattens me out when he wants me flat. He makes me round and bounces me when he wants to bounce me. He *makes* me. . . . It was somehow demeaning, and yet at the same time it was exhilarating to be a part of all this because you knew—and I don't care what anybody says about him—that you were in the presence of greatness. Anybody who can move men like that.

"He completely dominated me for two football seasons, and to this day, anytime I'm in a bind with a difficult problem to overcome, without exception I always think of him. Always! I think of him telling me, 'Son, the only thing you can do is to get off your ass and stop feeling sorry for yourself and overcome the pain and *do it.* Work out your method. Work out your system, and execute it. And don't tell me about a sprained ankle, and don't tell me that somebody's not being fair to you. I don't want to hear *any* of that. Do it!' That *always* rings in my mind."

"Well, was he fair?" I asked. "I mean in the sense of being equitable."

"Not especially," Curry said. "I remember one day in 1966, we were watching a film of a great game we had played the previous Sunday against the Cleveland Browns. It was the year after they had won the title. They just ate us up in the first half. The score was 14–0 when we went into the locker room. . . . Frank Ryan, their quarterback, was having a big day. We came out in the second half and began to peck away. Finally, with about two minutes left, the score was 20–14 in favor of the Browns. Lou Groza had kicked this mammoth forty-nine-yard field goal, which had hit the crossbar and bounced over for three points for them. With a couple of minutes left and six points behind, we started from our own twenty and gradually moved down the field. Finally, on their nine-yard line, it was fourth and goal, and time for a last play. Bart called a pass play. The wide receivers were covered, so he dumped it off to Jimmy Taylor in the flat. There were three tacklers—you've got to see this to believe it—and all they had to do was get him on the ground and the game was over. Well, he went by the first, around the second, and he ran over a third, and got into the end zone. We kicked the extra point and won the game 21–20. You can imagine the satisfaction. It was very hot. When I weighed in after the game I weighed two hundred and eighteen pounds. I had lost fourteen pounds.

"But in the film Lombardi began to notice *my* afternoon. I had been playing against Vince Costello, who was a very good middle linebacker. He was a very cagey guy. The week before, Lombardi had told me the way to work on him when we ran our sweep was not to take a sharp angle to cut him off, because he'd get around behind me to make the play. He wanted me to take an angle more directly at him, which is an unusual way to do it. Well, I did what the coach said. Costello beat me all day long. It was painfully obvious in the film that Tuesday. I'd go flying straight at him. He just ignored me. I'd miss him completely, and he'd make the tackle on Hornung or somebody. Lombardi stopped the projector and ran it back again. He didn't say a word. Ran it back again. Ran it back once more. Finally he stopped the projector, and in the dark I could see those glasses turn toward me. He said, 'Curry, you know that's God-awful.' All my teammates were sitting there. He said, 'How would you describe that?' Well, I was just burning. I was just *dying* to say, 'Coach, you *told* me to do it that way!' But of course I didn't. He went on, 'We're going to look at this again.' He ran it again, and then he went into one of his tirades. 'That's God-awful! You stink! *You* stink! And you know something else? Your snaps for punts have been stinking, too.' It went on for five minutes or so."

"I don't understand why you didn't get up and tell him, 'Well, you told me to, Coach,' " I said.

"Because," Curry replied, "all this time it kept running through my mind that though I kept excusing myself because, really, he *had* told me to use that technique, the point was that the only thing that matters is: Did you accomplish your mission? And if you didn't, there's no such thing as an excuse."

"Did anyone stand up to him?" I asked.

"Just about the only person who could handle these critiques was Fuzzy Thurston. Fuzzy would sit up in front, and when he knew that one of his bad plays was coming up, he'd begin to rant and rave before Lombardi could. It was really a riot. Some behemoth would thrash by Fuzzy, who'd missed his block—someone like Roger Brown of the Detroit Lions, who weighed three hundred pounds, and even before Roger could get into the backfield and crush Bart to the ground, Fuzzy'd be saying, 'Oh, look at that! Isn't that the worst block you've ever seen! That's awful!' Lombardi, in spite of himself, would have to laugh. He'd say, 'Fuzzy, you're right. That's *bad*. Okay, next play.' And Fuzzy could get away with it!

"Really no one was immune. The great veterans, everybody—it didn't make any difference. I remember him saying things to Jerry Kramer, who was an All-Pro guard. 'Did you see that, Jerry? Do you think that you're worth what we're paying you? Do you think for a minute that your football deserves the kind of dollars that you're getting?'

"Jerry'd be sitting there, a huge, powerful guy, literally leaning backward and bending the back of his metal folding chair in anguish. Just a devastating kind of thing! You asked about Lombardi being fair. Henry Jordan's great contribution about playing under Lombardi was: 'Lombardi is very fair: he treats us all alike—like dogs.'

"As he moved around the practice field, it was a presence that you could sense. It motivated people to perform. It wasn't malevolent. It scared. It was unique. Joe Thomas, when he was general manager of the Colts, had a presence when he appeared on the field . . . but it was sort of debilitating; everybody got tense and angry when he came around. When Lombardi came around, everybody got afraid . . . but highly active. The voice, like the personality, had just the most indescribable intensity. Everything he said was for effect. One day while we were practicing, a little dog came out and started prancing around the practice field. Nobody could concentrate because he was running in and out between people's legs. Just a cute little setter dog. Guys were trying to shoo him away—'Go! Go!'—and he'd scamper off and then run back, wagging his tail and having a good time. Lombardi was about sixty yards away at the other end of the field and suddenly this voice came booming from down there: *'Get the hell off the field!'* I swear I saw this happen: the dog tucked his tail between his legs, and the last time we saw him he was rounding a corner two blocks away from the field."

We drove on for a while through the Indiana countryside; the green overhang sign announced that we were coming up on a state road that swung off to a town called Franklin. We started chatting about other matters. Curry began talking about stereo equipment, but abstractedly, his mind still on Lombardi, and suddenly he said, "The difficult thing to articulate is how really forceful his presence was. Jerry Kramer didn't get it in his book, *Instant Replay*. He just didn't capture it. Nobody has. They did a TV show with Ernest Borgnine and it was just pathetic. Borgnine wasn't pathetic—Borgnine was superb. But they decided the Lombardi story was about a man going from New York, where he'd hoped to be a head coach, to an obscure town in Wisconsin that his wife didn't like. Crazy. The real story should have been about this man's ability to shock, to frighten, to overpower other people with whatever means he had to use. On the first day he gathered the team together he always showed the film of the championship game from the year before. He didn't comment on it; he just showed it, whether the Packers were in it or not. And then he'd turn off the projector and he'd say, 'Gentlemen, I have no illusions about what's going to happen to me if I don't win. So don't you have any illusions about what's going to happen to you if you don't produce for me. . . . There are three things that're important in your life: your religion, your family, and the Green Bay Packers—in that order.' And then, as soon as we'd get on the field, he'd get the order mixed up in his own mind. What was paramount was—by whatever means—to build in you that sense that you had to be the best ever. When I first came to pro ball I just wanted to make the team; then when I did I decided I sure would like to be first-string; then after that I made All Pro, and I thought: Now I want to be All Pro every year. The obsession to be best was precisely Lombardi's. Time and time again he'd say things like this: 'When you go on the field, I want you thinking about one thing—that is, for this day I'm going to be the greatest center in football. When those people walk out of the stands, I want that guy to turn to his wife and say, "We just saw the greatest offensive center who ever played.' "

"So he had this uncanny talent for manipulating people to be exactly what he wanted them to be. He would select a role for each player. He wrote the play, he did the choreography, and if you didn't fit the role, he would change your personality so that you could play the part. If you didn't like the role, it didn't make any difference; he manipulated you and made you what he wanted you to be until you could play it better than anybody else in the National Football League. *Or* he would get rid of you. I heard him tell Steve Wright, who was a guy who grinned a lot—he'd miss a block and come back to the huddle with a smile on his face, which would drive Lombardi insane. 'Goddammit, Wright, you think that's funny! You're never gonna be a man! You're never gonna make it! *Yes,* you are! *I'm* gonna make you, I'm gonna create you. I'm gonna make you into something before I'm through with you.'

"I heard him tell another guy, 'I'm gonna make you work. I'm gonna make you hurt before I get rid of you!' And he did get rid of him. That was Rich Marshall. He had this forefinger cut off at the knuckle so that when he took his stance it looked like he'd stuck a finger in the ground. He got a lot of kidding about it. 'Git your finger out of the ground, Marshall!' "

"How Lombardi treated him just seems arbitrarily cruel," I commented. "What do you truly think he thought of all you players?"

Curry thought for a while, and then he said, "This will be argued by some players, but I believe that Lombardi really did love us. I don't think he could've appealed to our better instincts if we didn't feel that he really cared about us. I've seen him cry when we lost a game. Here we go again—those weeping Packers. It wasn't for appearance's sake. I mean, I've just seen the tears in his eyes. Of course, it was foremost because *he* had lost. But he also had genuine affection for . . . he liked to be around 'the guys.' He wanted to be accepted. When he was admonishing us about our behavior, he used to say things to us like: 'Don't you think that I'd like to go get drunk downtown too? Don't you think I'd like to go out and do that? Don't you think I'd like you guys to like me? I know you don't like me. But I don't give a crap about that. We're here to do a job. Your liking me is not near as important as winning football games. So I don't *care* if you like me.' That kind of thing. Every now and then it would surface, but it was very rare. He was such an odd contradiction. He was very profane, yet he went to church every day; he was a daily celebrant, Catholic, very devout. He considered the priesthood at one point. Bart Starr said, 'When I heard about this man taking over the team in 1959, I could hardly wait to meet a man that went to church every day.' Then he went on to say, 'I worked for him for two weeks and then I realized this man *needs* to go to church every day.' "

Curry shifted slightly in his seat behind the steering wheel. "You were asking me a while back if anyone stood up to him. I remember Starr one time. We were in Cleveland playing an exhibition game. Lombardi was into one of his tirades up and down the sidelines. Our offense was driving—Bowman was the center—and they got to Cleveland's four-yard line with a first down when Bart took too long in the huddle and they marched off a delay-of-game penalty against him. Lombardi went insane. He started *screaming:* 'What the hell's going on out there?' This terrible voice that everyone in that huge stadium—there were eighty-one thousand people there—could hear. I saw Bart slip back out of the huddle to glare at Lombardi; then he called the play and threw a touchdown pass to Boyd Dowler.

"At this point I started out on the field, trotting past Lombardi, to snap the ball for the extra point. That was my job. But to my surprise I saw Starr coming toward us, which was odd because he was supposed to be the holder for the extra-point play. So I stopped . . . baffled. I thought perhaps he was hurt. As he got alongside me, about fifteen feet from Lombardi, he yelled out at the top of his lungs and just *laced* him with the most incredible verbal barrage.

"I almost went to my knees. Bart Starr! This kind and decent churchman, one of the gentlest people, never a word of profanity or anything of the sort, and here he was yelling these things at Lombardi in a big, booming, resonant voice. I turned around and Lombardi was standing there, just agape; he couldn't believe it, either. Well, we ran on the field, kicked the extra point, and nothing was said about it. Lombardi didn't say another word the rest of that game—truly stunned, probably—and he was nice to us for about two weeks after that. Then he began to get mean again.

"We had a sort of war council, in which there were about six guys—Bob Skoronski, who was the offensive captain, and Tom Moore and Bart and Paul Hornung, guys like that—and every now and then when things got really bad, about once a year, they'd go to Lombardi and say, 'Coach, you're going to have to let up. You're driving us all crazy! We can't function under this withering kind of abuse.' Maybe he'd let up for a day or two. Maybe we'd have a good game, and he'd be nice for a few days. But then we'd have a bad game, and he'd stomp back in on Tuesday morning and everybody'd just be sitting there aquiver. He'd say, 'I tried it your way. I'm sick and tired of being father confessor for a bunch of yellow, no-good punks. The whip! That's the only thing you understand. And I'm going to whip you again, and drive you, make you! Why do I always have to make you? Don't you think I get tired of being this way?' Once again everybody would squirm and feel that somehow they'd made the wrong choice for a profession: What am I doing with this person here? Why? But invariably he would come back in the next breath and win everybody over again . . . although sometimes you couldn't imagine how he could do it.

"Once in 1965 we had been to Los Angeles and had lost a game to the Rams that we *had* to win. Los Angeles was the last-place team in the league and they just *stomped* us. On the way back, Lionel Aldridge—the big defensive end—began to sing. A couple of beers and he was singing! Lombardi heard about it. Well, on Tuesday morning he came into the meeting and he began to question Lionel's ancestry. He got into such an emotional shouting binge that it was like one of those tirades you'd see in films of Hitler going through a frenzy—though I don't mean to draw any parallel. I'm talking about awesome, forceful personalities, not the quality of what they did or the kind of people they were. Finally Lombardi said, 'I want all the assistant coaches out of this room and all the doors shut. I want to be here with these football players . . . if that's what you can call them.' So everybody cleared out. Scurried out."

"The assistant coaches?" I asked.

"Oh, yes. The assistant coaches were terrified of him too. Absolutely. You could hear him in the next room dressing *them* down the same way he did us, though of course he never did it in front of us.

"When the coaches were out and the doors were shut, Lombardi really went at it. The meeting seemed to go on for an hour and a half, with Lombardi screaming, shouting: 'Goddammit, you guys don't care if you win or lose. I'm the only one that cares. I'm the only one that puts his blood and his guts and his heart into the game! You guys show up, you listen a little bit, you concentrate . . . you've got the concentration of three-year-olds. You're nothing! I'm the only guy that gives a damn if we win or lose.'

"Suddenly there was a stirring in the back of the room, a rustle of chairs. I turned around and there was Forrest Gregg, on his feet, bright red, with a player on either side, holding him back by each arm, and he was straining forward. Gregg was another real gentlemanly kind of guy, very quiet. Great football player. Lombardi looked at him and stopped. Forrest said, 'Goddam-mit, Coach . . . excuse me for the profanity.' Even at his moment of rage he was still both respectful enough and intimidated enough that he stopped and apologized. Then he went on: ' 'Scuse the language, Coach, but it makes me sick to hear you say something like that. We lay it on the line for you every Sunday. We live and die the same way you do, and it hurts.' Then he began straining forward again, trying to get up there to punch Lombardi out. Players were holding him back. Then Bob Skoronski stood up, very articulate. He was the captain of the team. 'That's right,' he said. 'Dammit, don't you tell us that we don't care about winning. That makes me sick. Makes me want to puke. We care about it every bit as much as you do. It's our knees and our bodies out there that we're throwing around.'

"So there it was. The coach had been confronted, the captain of a ship facing a mutinous crew, with the first mate standing and staring him down face-to-face, and it truly looked as though he had lost control of the situation.

"But then damned if the master didn't triumph again. After just a moment's hesitation he said, 'All right. Now *that's* the kind of attitude I want to see. Who else feels that way?'

"Well, at this very moment Willie Davis was nervously rocking back and forth on his metal folding chair. Willie was known as Dr. Feelgood on the team because every day at practice, with everybody limping around and tired and moaning and complaining, somebody always looked over, and asked, 'Willie, how you feel?' He always said the same thing: 'Feel *good*, man!' So there was Dr. Feelgood rocking back and forth and you know how those chairs are. He lost his balance and he fell forward! He fell right out into the middle of the room . . . onto his feet; it looked as if he had leapt from his chair just as Lombardi asked, 'Who else feels that way?' And Willie sort of grinned sheepishly and he said, 'Yeah, me, too! I feel that way, man!' Lombardi said, 'All right, Willie, that's great.' And it swept through the room; everybody said, 'Yeah, hell—me too!' and suddenly you had forty guys that could lick the world. That's what Lombardi created out of that situation. He went around to each player in that room with the exception of the rookies—he skipped the four of us rookies—and as he looked in each man's face he said, 'Do you want to win football games for me?' And the answer was 'Yes, sir'—forty times. He wended his way through that mass of people sitting around in that disarray of chairs and looked each guy nose to nose two inches from his face and he said that thing: 'Do you want to win football games?' and every man said, 'Yes, sir,' and we did not lose another game that year."

CARL SANDBURG

"Hits and Runs"

I remember the Chillicothe ball players grappling the
   Rock Island ball players in a sixteen-inning
   game ended by darkness.

And the shoulders of the Chillicothe players were a
   red smoke against the sundown and the shoulders of the Rock Island players were a yellow
   smoke against the sundown.

And the umpire's voice was hoarse calling balls and
   strikes and outs, and the umpire's throat fought
   in the dust for a song.

SIR BERNARD DARWIN

"The Best-Known Figure in England"

Rather than representing Bernard Darwin with a selection on golf (which would be logical since he is by all odds the best golf writer so far), I have picked his 1934 portrait of W. G. Grace, the legendary cricket player, so famous himself that he was commonly referred to by the initials of his given names.

A word about Darwin. The grandson of the great naturalist, he was educated at Cambridge University. He covered athletic events for a London paper until he was sacked for "gross partiality." After his graduation he practiced law for a while, but then in 1907 he sold his wig and gown, as they say, and began writing columns which appeared every Saturday in the Times. *Blessed with many of the attributes any sports journalist would wish to possess, he was equipped with an extraordinary memory. On one occasion he recited the names of the entire Welsh rugby team that had beaten New Zealand thirty years before. His special gift was a style that was fluent, polished, and humorous. He was critical of those of his profession who ingratiated themselves with great players, the backslappers, referring to them as "fulsome beasts." This particular piece is unique, it seems to me, in that it is unflaggingly honest, without the slightest intention on Darwin's part to make of W. G. Grace someone that he was not.*

If one had to choose a single epithet to describe him, it would, I think, be simple. He did not think very deeply or very subtly about anybody or anything; perhaps not even about cricket, although his knowledge of it was intuitively profound, his judgment of a cricketer unique. His interests were all of the open air. If people wanted to read books, no doubt they got pleasure from it, but it was a pleasure that he could not really understand. Wisden, yes, perhaps, to confirm a memory or refute an argument, or in winter as an earnest of the summer to come; but in a general way books were bad for cricket. "How can you expect to make runs," he said to one of the Gloucestershire side, "when you are always reading?"; and added, almost gratuitously, "You don't catch me that way." I have searched in vain for anyone who ever saw him take the risk, except in the case of a newspaper or a medical book in which he wanted to look up a point.

W. G. was not an intellectual man, and even as regards his own subject his was not an analytical brain, but by instinct or genius—call it what you will—he could form a judgment of a cricketer to which all others bowed. A schoolboy who had made innumerable runs for his school, and was generally regarded as an extraordinary cricketer, played in his first first-class match with W. G., and made a respectable score. Everybody crowded round the oracle to hear the verdict and expected a favourable one. "He'll never make a first-class cricketer"—that was all, and it turned out to be entirely true. Here is a converse example. When Mr. Jessop first appeared for Gloucestershire, those who now realise that they ought to have known better were struck only by the more rough-hewn and bucolic aspects of his batting. "What have you got here, old man?" they asked W. G. rather disparagingly. "Ah, you wait and see what I've got here," he answered with a touch of truculence, and went on to say that in a year or so this would be the finest hitter that had ever been seen. That this verdict also turned out true is hardly worth saying.

He had that sort of quickness of apprehension that may, without disrespect, perhaps be called cunning, and is often to be found, a little surprisingly, in those who seem at first sight simple-minded and almost rustic. He had plenty of shrewdness too in judging the qualities of men, so far as they interested him and came within his sphere. He might occasionally do ill-judged things in the excitement of the moment, but at the bottom of everything there was a good hard kernel of common-sense.

We are told that when W. G. first appeared in first-class cricket he was shy, and we can picture him a tall, gawky, uneasy boy. He had not been to a public school; he came from a small country doctor's family; he had met few people except in his own country neighbourhood, and he suddenly found himself among those who had had a different sort of upbringing. It is no wonder that he was silent and uncomfortable; but fame and popularity are wonderful softeners of that agony of shyness, and if he perhaps kept a little of it deep down inside him, there was no external trace of it. He was perfectly natural with all whom he met, and if he liked them he was soon friendly and hearty with them. He was helped by a wonderful unselfconsciousness. He seemed to take himself for granted, at once a supreme player of his game, and, off the field, as an ordinary person, and did not bother his head about what impression he made. He was far better known by sight than any man in England. Long after his cricketing days were over, he had only to pass through a village street in a motorcar for windows to be thrown up and fingers to be pointed, but he seemed, and really was, as nearly as possible unaware of it, unless perhaps his admirer was a small child, to whom he liked to wave his hand. This unselfconsciousness pervaded his whole existence. He had come, as has been said, from a home comparatively countrified and uncultivated; he kept, to some extent at least, its manners and its way of speech all his life. He mixed constantly with those who were, in a snob-bish sense, his superiors and had other ways and other manners, and I do not believe that he ever gave such things a thought. He recognised different standards in the houses he stayed at, to the extent that there were some to which he ought to take his "dancing-pumps," and that was all. He liked friendliness and cheerfulness wherever he met it; he was ready to give it himself, and never thought of anything else that could be demanded of him.

A whole bottle of champagne was a mere nothing to him; having consumed it he would go down on all fours, and balance the bottle on the top of his head and rise to his feet again. Nothing could disturb that magnificent constitution, and those who hoped by a long and late sitting to shorten his innings next day often found themselves disappointed. His regular habit while cricketing was to drink one large whisky and soda, with a touch of angostura bitters, at lunch, and another when the day's play had ended; this allowance he never varied or exceeded till the evening came, and, despite his huge frame, though he never dieted, he ate sparingly.

He carried his practical joking into the realms of cricket, as when, according to a well-known story, he caused the batsman to look up at the sky to see some imaginary birds, with the result that the poor innocent was blinded by the sun and promptly bowled. With this we come to one of the most difficult questions about W. G.—did he at all, and, if so, how far, overstep the line which, in a game, divides fair play from sharp practice? There is one preliminary thing to say, namely that there is no absolute standard in these matters, and that standards differ with times and societies. The sportsmen of the early nineteenth century did, naturally and unblushingly, things that would be considered very unsportsmanlike nowadays. In those days everything was a "match": each party must look after himself; it was play or pay, and the devil take the hindermost. He would never have dreamed of purposely getting in the way of a fieldsman who might otherwise have caught him, but to shout cheerfully to that fieldsman, "Miss it," was—at any rate in a certain class of cricket—not merely within the law, but rather a good joke.

The law was the law, though in his intense keenness he could not wholly rid himself of the idea that it was sometimes unjustly enforced against him; what the law allowed was allowable. It was always worth appealing; if the umpire thought a man was out l.b.w., it did not matter what the bowler thought. "You weren't out, you know," he was sometimes heard to say to a retiring batsman against whom he had appealed, and thought no shame to do so: everything was open and above board; if the umpire decided you were out—and he sometimes decided wrong— that was all about it. He wanted desperately to get the other side out, and any fair way of doing so was justifiable; he never stooped to what he thought was a mean way. No man knew the law better, and it could seldom be said against him that he was wrong, but rather that he was too desperately right.

His early cricket had been played with a father and three elder brothers who were going to stand no nonsense from the younger ones. The boy was taught to behave himself, and this meant, amongst other things, to stick to the rules. It was natural enough that when he grew older he expected other players to behave themselves too. It may be said that he did not sufficiently distinguish between big points and small ones, but the answer is that, where cricket was concerned, there was for W. G. no such thing as a small point. It might seem trivial to more easy-going or more flexibly minded persons; never to him; and if things were not, as he thought, just right, he came out bluntly and impetuously with his opinion.

JAMES JOYCE

"GAME OLD MERRIMYNN"

Cricket has attracted a number of distinguished authors but rarely to the degree that they mention the sport in their work. The Nobel Prize-winner Samuel Beckett was a great sports enthusiast, every morning turning directly to the sports pages and examining them in detail, including school cricket-match results. And yet in his work scholars have been able to find only one sports reference—a mention of croquet in Molloy. *He shared his love of cricket with his one-time employer, James Joyce, who limited his enthusiasm in his work to a single racy passage in* Finnegans Wake *in which he includes the names of thirty or so famous cricket players. It follows.*

Kickakick. She had to kick a laugh. At her old stick-in-the-block. The way he was slogging his paunch about, elbiduubled, meet oft mate on, like hale King Willow, the robberer. Cainmaker's mace and waxened capapee. But the tarrant's brand on his hottoweyt brow. At half past quick in the morning. And her lamp was all askew and a trumbly wick-in-her, ringeysingey. She had to spofforth, she had to kicker, too thick of the wick of her pixy's loomph, wide lickering jessup the smoky shimiminey. And her duffed coverpoint of a wickedy batter, whenever she druv gehind her stumps for a tyddlesly wink through his tunnil-clefft bagslops after the rising bounder's yorkers, as he studd and stoddard and trutted and trumpered, to see had lordherry's blackham's red bobby abbels, it tickled her innings to consort pitch at kicksolock in the morm. Tipatonguing him on in her pigeony linguish, with a flick at the bails for lubrication, to scorch her faster, faster. Ye hek, ye hok, ye hucky hire-monger! Magrath he's my pegger, he is, for bricking up all my old kent road. He'll win your toss, flog your old tom's bowling and I darr ye, barrackybuller, to break his duck! He's posh. I lob him. We're parring all Oogster till the empsyseas run googlie. Declare to ashes and teste his metch! Three for two will do for me and he for thee and she for you. Goeasyosey, for the grace of the fields, or hooley pooley, cuppy, we'll both be bye and by caught in the slips for fear he'd tyre and burst his dunlops and waken her bornybarnies making his booby-babies. The game old merrimynn, square to leg, with his lolleywide towelhat and his hobbsy socks and his wisden's bosse and his norsery pinafore and his gentleman's grip and his playaboy's plunge and his flannelly feelyfooling, treading her hump and hambledown like a maiden wellheld, ovalled over, with her crease where the pads of her punishments ought to be by womanish rights when, keek, the hen in the doran's shantyqueer began in a kikkery key to laugh it off, yeigh, yeigh, neigh, neigh, the way she was wuck to doodledoo by her gallows bird (how's that? Noball, he carries his bat!) nine hundred and dirty too not out, at all times long past conquering cock of the morgans.

The following cricketing names seem to appear in this extract:
S.A. Block, Charles Stewart Caine, F.A. Tarrant (or George Tarrant), A.B. Quick, Hugh Trumble, K.S. Ranjitsinhji, F.R. Spofforth, G.L. Jessop, R.A. Duff, J.T. Tyldesley, J. Tunnicliffe, C.T. Studd (or Sir Kynaston or G.B. Studd), A.E. Stoddart, A.E. Trott (or G.H.S. Trott), Victor Trumper, Lord Harris, J.M. Blackham, Robert Abel, J. Iremonger (or Albert Iremonger), Tom Richardson, A.G. Daer, C.F. Buller, George Parr, W.G. Grace, Ted Pooley, Alfred Mynn, James Lillywhite (or some member of this family), Sir Jack Hobbs, John Wisden, Dave Nourse (or Dudley Nourse), and J.T. Morgan.

DON MARQUIS

"Why Professor Waddems Never Broke a Hundred"

Don Marquis, the famous humorist of the twenties and thirties, best known for his material supposedly written by a cockroach named Archy ("the insect Voltaire," Christopher Morley called him), usually about his traveling companion, Mehitabel, an incorrigible cat ("toujours gai" her favorite expression). Archy wrote by butting his head against the typewriter keys. Thus, the text was always in lowercase because Archy (or "archy" as he signed his copy) could not depress the shift key to make capitals.

The sportswriter Grantland Rice introduced Marquis to golf, outfitting him with clubs and outsized knickers. Marquis told Rice that what he liked best about the game was that it gave him something to write about in his column, "The Lantern," in the New York Tribune. *On one occasion he took a line from an instruction manual, "Imagine yourself to be a grandfather clock and the club the pendulum," and expanded it into a fantasy in which the golfer cannot get the grandfather-clock image out of his mind and eventually begins ticking loudly throughout the night.*

The best of the Marquis golf material is in the collection The Rivercliff Golf Killings—*which uses a court transcript form to tell of terrible deeds on the golf course. In every case, the judge and jury are wildly biased toward the defendants; the proceedings are hastened along so all in the courtroom can repair to golf courses to get in a few holes before nightfall.*

I am telling this story to the public just as I told it in the grand jury room; the district attorney having given me a carbon copy of my sworn testimony.

THE CASE OF DOC GREEN

QUESTION: Professor Waddems, when did you first notice that Dr. Green seemed to harbor animosity towards you?

ANSWER: It was when we got to the second hole.

QUESTION: Professor, you may go ahead and tell the jury about it in your own words.

ANSWER: Yes, sir. The situation was this: My third shot lay in the sand in the shallow bunker—an easy pitch with a niblick to within a foot or two of the pin, for anyone who understands the theory of niblick play as well as I do. I had the hole in five, practically.

"Professor," said Doc Green, with whom I was playing—

QUESTION: This was Dr. James T. Green, the eminent surgeon, was it not?

ANSWER: Yes, sir. Dr. Green, with whom I was playing, remarked, "You are all wrong about Freud. Psychoanalysis is the greatest discovery of the age."

"Nonsense! Nonsense! Nonsense!" I replied. "Don't be a fool, Doc! I'll show you where Freud is all wrong, in a minute."

And I lifted the ball with an explosion shot to a spot eighteen inches from the pin, and holed out with an easy putt.

"Five," I said and marked it on my card.

"You mean eight," said Doc Green.

"Three into the bunker, four onto the green, and one putt—five," I said.

"You took four strokes in the bunker, Professor," he said. "Every time you said 'Nonsense' you made a swipe at the ball with your niblick."

"Great Godfrey," I said, "you don't mean to say you are going to count those gestures I made to illustrate my argument as *golf strokes?* Just mere gestures! And you know very well I have never delivered a lecture in twenty-five years without gestures like that!"

"You moved your ball an inch or two with your club at every gesture," he said.

QUESTION: Had you really done so, Professor? Remember, you are on oath.

ANSWER: I do not remember. In any case, the point is immaterial. They were merely gestures.

QUESTION: Did you take an eight, or insist on a five?

ANSWER: I took an eight. I gave in. Gentlemen, I am a good-natured person. Too good-natured. Calm and philosophical; unruffled and patient. My philosophy never leaves me. I took an eight.

(Sensation in the grand jury room.)

QUESTION: Will you tell something of your past life, Professor Waddems—who you are and what your lifework has been, and how you acquired the calmness you speak of?

ANSWER: For nearly twenty-five years I lectured on philosophy and psychology in various universities. Since I retired and took up golf it has been my habit to look at all the events and tendencies in the world's news from the standpoint of the philosopher.

QUESTION: Has this helped you in your golf?

ANSWER: Yes, sir. My philosophical and logical training and my specialization in psychology, combined with my natural calmness and patience, have made me the great golfer that I really am.

QUESTION: Have you ever received a square deal, Professor, throughout any eighteen holes of golf?

ANSWER: No, sir. Not once! Not once during the five years since I took the game up at the Rivercliff Country Club.

QUESTION: Have you ever broken a hundred, Professor Waddems?

ANSWER: No, sir. I would have, again and again, except that my opponents, and other persons playing matches on the course, and the very forces of nature themselves are always against me at critical moments. Even the bullfrogs at the three water holes treat me impertinently.

QUESTION: Bullfrogs? You said the bullfrogs, Professor?

ANSWER: Yes, sir. They have been trained by the caddies to treat me impertinently.

QUESTION: What sort of treatment have you received in the locker room?

ANSWER: The worst possible. In the case under consideration, I may say that I took an eight on the second hole, instead of insisting on a five, because I knew the sort of thing Dr. Green would say in the locker room after the match—I knew the scene he would make, and what the comments of my so-called friends would be. Whenever I do get down to a hundred an attempt is made to discredit me in the locker room.

QUESTION: Well, you took an eight on the second hole. What happened at the third hole?

ANSWER: Well, sir, I teed up for my drive, and just as I did so, Doc Green made a slighting remark about the League of Nations. "I think it is a good thing we kept out of it," he said.

QUESTION: What were your reactions?

ANSWER: A person of intelligence could only have one kind of reaction, sir. The remark was silly, narrow-minded, provincial, boneheaded, crass, and ignorant. It was all the more criminal because Dr. Green knew quite well what I think of the League of Nations. The League of Nations was my idea. I thought about it even before the late President Wilson did, and talked about it and wrote about it and lectured about it in the university.

QUESTION: So that you consider Dr. Green's motives in mentioning it when you were about to drive—

ANSWER: The worst possible, sir. They could only come from a black heart at such a time.

QUESTION: Did you lose your temper, Professor?

ANSWER: No, sir! No, sir! No, sir! I *never* lose my temper! Not on any provocation. I said to myself, Be calm! Be philosophical! He's trying to get me excited! Remember what he'll say in the locker room afterwards! Be calm! Show him, show him, show him! Show him he can't get my goat.

QUESTION: Then you drove?

ANSWER: I addressed the ball the second time, sir. And I as about to drive when he said, with a sneer, "You must excuse me, Professor. I forgot that you invented the League of Nations."

QUESTION: Did you become violent, then, Professor?

ANSWER: No, sir! No, sir! I never become violent! I never—

QUESTION: Can you moderate your voice somewhat, Professor?

ANSWER: Yes, sir. I was explaining that I never become violent. I had every right to become violent. Any person less calm and philosophical would have become violent. Doc Green to criticize the League of Nations! The ass! Absurd! Preposterous! Silly! Abhorrent! Criminal! What the world wants is peace! Philosophic calm! The fool! Couldn't he understand that!

QUESTION: Aren't you departing, Professor, from the events of the 29th of last September at the Rivercliff golf course? What did you do next?

ANSWER: I drove.

QUESTION: Successfully?

ANSWER: It was a good drive, but the wind caught it, and it went out of bounds.

QUESTION: What did Dr. Green do then?

ANSWER: He grinned. A crass bonehead capable of sneering at the progress of the human race would sneer at a time like that.

QUESTION: But you kept your temper?

ANSWER: All my years of training as a philosopher came to my aid.

QUESTION: Go on, Professor.

ANSWER: I took my midiron from my bag and looked at it.

QUESTION: Well, go on, Professor. What did you think when you looked at it?

ANSWER: I do not remember, sir.

QUESTION: Come, come, Professor! You are under oath, you know. Did you think what a dent it would make in his skull?

ANSWER: Yes, sir. I remember now. I remember wondering if it would not do his brain good to be shaken up a little.

QUESTION: Did you strike him, then?

ANSWER: No, sir. I knew what they'd say in the locker room. They'd say that I lost my temper over a mere game. They would not understand that I had been jarring up his brain for his own good, in the hope of making him understand about the League of Nations. They'd say I was irritated. I know the things people always say.

QUESTION: Was there no other motive for not hitting him?

ANSWER: I don't remember.

QUESTION: Professor Waddems, again I call your attention to the fact that you are under oath. What was your other motive?

ANSWER: Oh yes, now I recall it. I reflected that if I hit him they might make me add another stroke to my score. People are always getting up the flimsiest excuses to make me add another stroke. And then accusing me of impatience if I do not acquiesce in their unfairness. I am never impatient or irritable!

QUESTION: Did you ever break a club on the course, Professor?

ANSWER: I don't remember.

QUESTION: Did you not break a mashie on the Rivercliff course last week, Professor Waddems? Reflect before you answer.

ANSWER: I either gave it away or broke it, I don't remember which.

QUESTION: Come, come, don't you remember that you broke it against a tree?

ANSWER: Oh, I think I know what you mean. But it was not through temper or irritation.

QUESTION: Tell the jury about it.

ANSWER: Well, gentlemen, I had a mashie that had a loose head on it, and I don't know how it got into my bag. My ball lay behind a sapling, and I tried to play it out from behind the tree and missed it entirely. And then I noticed I had this old mashie, which should have been gotten rid of long ago. The club had never been any good. The blade was laid back at the wrong angle. I decided that the time had come to get rid of it once and for all. So I hit it a little tap against the tree, and the head fell off. I threw the pieces over into the bushes.

QUESTION: Did you swear, Professor?

ANSWER: I don't remember. But the injustice of this incident was that my opponent insisted on counting it as a stroke and adding it to my score—my judicial, deliberate destruction of this old mashie. I never get a square deal.

QUESTION: Return to Dr. James T. Green, Professor. You are now at the third hole, and the wind has just carried your ball out of bounds.

ANSWER: Well, I didn't hit him when he sneered. I carried the ball within bounds.

"Shooting three," I said calmly. I topped the ball. Gentlemen, I have seen Walter Hagen top the ball the same way.

"Too bad, Professor," said Doc Green. He said it hypocritically. I knew it was hypocrisy. He was secretly gratified that I had topped the ball. He knew I knew it.

QUESTION: What were your emotions at this further insult, Professor?

ANSWER: I pitied him. I thought how inferior he was to me intellectually, and I pitied him. I addressed the ball again. "I pity him," I murmured. "Pity, pity, pity, pity, pity!"

He overheard me. "Your pity has cost you five more strokes," he said.

"I was merely gesticulating," I said.

QUESTION: Did the ball move? Remember, you are under oath, and you have waived immunity.

ANSWER: If the ball moved, it was because a strong breeze had sprung up.

QUESTION: Go on.

ANSWER: I laid the ball upon the green and again holed out with one putt. "I'm taking a five," I said, marking it on my card.

"I'm giving you a ten," he said, marking it on his card. "Five gesticulations on account of your pity."

QUESTION: Describe your reactions to this terrible injustice, Professor. Was there a red mist before your eyes? Did you turn giddy and wake up to find him lying lifeless at your feet? Just what happened?

ANSWER: Nothing, sir.

(Sensation in the grand jury room.)

QUESTION: Think again, Professor. Nothing?

ANSWER: I merely reflected that, in spite of his standing scientifically, Dr. James T. Green was a moron and utterly devoid of morality and that I should take this into account. I did not lose my temper.

QUESTION: Did you snatch the card from his hands?

ANSWER: I took it, sir. I did not snatch it.

QUESTION: And then did you cram it down his throat?

ANSWER: I suggested that he eat it, sir, as it contained a falsehood in black and white, and Dr. Green complied with my request.

QUESTION: Did you lay hands upon him, Professor? Remember, now, we are still talking about the third hole.

ANSWER: I think I did steady him a little by holding him about the neck and throat while he masticated and swallowed the card.

QUESTION: And then what?

ANSWER: Well, gentlemen, after that there is very little more to tell until we reached the sixteenth hole. Dr. Green for some time made no further attempt to treat me unjustly and played in silence, acquiescing in the scores I had marked on my card. We were even as to holes, and it was a certainty that I was about to break a hundred. But I knew what was beneath this silence on Doc Green's part, and I did not trust it.

QUESTION: What do you mean? That you knew what he was thinking, although he did not speak?

ANSWER: Yes, sir. I knew just what kind of remarks he would have made if he had made any remarks.

QUESTION: Were these remarks which he suppressed derogatory remarks?

ANSWER: Yes, sir. Almost unbelievably so. They were deliberately intended to destroy my poise.

QUESTION: Did they do so, Professor?

ANSWER: I don't think so.

QUESTION: Go on, Professor.

ANSWER: At the sixteenth tee, as I drove off, this form of insult reached its climax. He accentuated his silence with a peculiar look, just as my club head was about to meet the ball. I knew what he meant. He knew that I knew it, and that I knew. I sliced into a bunker. He stood and watched me, as I stepped into the sand with my niblick—watched me with that look upon his face. I made three strokes at the ball and, as will sometimes happen even to the best of players, did not move it a foot. The fourth stroke drove it out of sight into the sand. The sixth stroke brought it to light again. Gentlemen, I did not lose my temper. I never do. But I admit that I did increase my tempo. I struck rapidly three more times at the ball. And all the time Doc Green was regarding me with that look, to which he now added a smile. Still I kept my temper, and he might be alive today if he had not spoken.

QUESTION: *(by the foreman of the jury):* What did the man say at this trying time?

ANSWER: I know that you will not believe it is within the human heart to make the black remark that he made. And I hesitate to repeat it. But I have sworn to tell everything. What he said was, "Well, Professor, the club puts these bunkers here, and I suppose they have got to be used."

QUESTION: *(by the foreman of the jury):* Was there something especially trying in the way he said it?

ANSWER: There was. He said it with an affectation of joviality.

QUESTION: You mean as if he thought he were making a joke, Professor?

ANSWER: Yes, sir.

QUESTION: What were your emotions at this point?

ANSWER: Well, sir, it came to me suddenly that I owed a duty to society; and for the sake of civilization I struck him with the niblick. It was an effort to reform him, gentlemen.

QUESTION: Why did you cover him with sand afterwards?

ANSWER: Well, I knew that if the crowd around the locker room discovered that I had hit him, they would insist on counting it as another stroke. And that is exactly what happened when the body was discovered—once again I was prevented from breaking a hundred.

THE DISTRICT ATTORNEY: Gentlemen of the jury, you have heard Professor Waddems' frank and open testimony in the case of Dr. James T. Green. My own recommendation is that he be not only released, but complimented, as far as this count is returned. If ever a homicide was justifiable, this one was. And I suggest that you report no indictment against the Professor, without leaving your seats. Many of you will wish to get in at least nine holes before dinner.

JAMES THURBER

"You Could Look It Up"

This story of James Thurber's almost surely inspired Bill Veeck, the general manager of the St. Louis Browns, to sign Ed Gaedel, the famous midget that Zack Taylor, the Browns' manager, sent up to bat against a Detroit pitcher named Bob Cain in the first inning of the second game of a doubleheader played in St. Louis in August 1951. Cain didn't come close to Gaedel's strike zone (about five or six inches), and after four balls had sailed over his head, the midget trotted down to first where an outfielder named Jim Delsing was sent in to run for him. It wasn't Gaedel's last appearance in a baseball game. After his major-league contract was disapproved on the basis that his participation was not in the best interests of baseball, he turned up in a sandlot game in Syracuse, New York. The pitcher wasn't bothered by the tiny strike zone and proceeded to strike out Gaedel on three called strikes. Whereupon the midget wheeled around to the umpire and cried at him shrilly: "You're the worst umpire I ever hope to see!"

It all begun when we dropped down to C'lumbus, Ohio, from Pittsburgh to play an exhibition game on our way out to St. Louis. It was gettin' on into September, and though we'd been leadin' the league by six, seven

games most of the season, we was now in first place by a margin you
could 'a' got it into the eye of a thimble, bein' only a half a game ahead of
St. Louis. Our slump had given the boys the leapin' jumps, and they was
like a bunch a old ladies at a lawn fete with a thunderstorm comin' up,
runnin' around snarlin' at each other, eatin' bad and sleepin' worse, and
battin' for a team average of maybe .186. Half the time nobody'd speak
to nobody else, without it was to bawl 'em out.

Squawks Magrew was managin' the boys at the time, and he was darn
near crazy. They called him "Squawks" 'cause when things was goin' bad
he lost his voice, or perty near lost it, and squealed at you like a little girl
you stepped on her doll or somethin'. He yelled at everybody and
wouldn't listen to nobody, without maybe it was me. I'd been trainin'
the boys for ten year, and he'd take more lip from me than from anybody
else. He knowed I was smarter'n him, anyways, like you're goin' to hear.

This was thirty, thirty-one year ago; you could look it up, 'cause it was
the same year C'lumbus decided to call itself the Arch City, on account
of a lot of iron arches with electric-light bulbs into 'em which stretched
acrost High Street. Thomas Albert Edison sent 'em a telegram, and they
was speeches and maybe even President Taft opened the celebration by
pushin' a button. It was a great week for the Buckeye capital, which was
why they got us out there for this exhibition game.

Well, we just lose a double-header to Pittsburgh, 11 to 5 and 7 to 3, so
we snarled all the way to C'lumbus, where we put up at the Chittaden
Hotel, still snarlin'. Everybody was tetchy, and when Billy Klinger took a
sock at Whitey Cott at breakfast, Whitey throwed marmalade all over
his face.

"Blind each other, whatta I care?" says Magrew. "You can't see
nothin' anyways."

C'lumbus win the exhibition game, 3 to 2, whilst Magrew set in the
dugout, mutterin' and cursin' like a fourteen-year-old Scotty. He bad-
mouthed everybody on the ball club and he bad-mouthed everybody offa
the ball club, includin' the Wright brothers, who, he claimed, had yet to
build a airship big enough for any of our boys to hit it with a ball bat.

"I wisht I was dead," he says to me. "I wisht I was in heaven with the
angels."

I told him to pull hisself together, 'cause he was drivin' the boys crazy,
the way he was goin' on, sulkin' and bad-mouthin' and whinin'. I was
older'n he was and smarter'n he was, and he knowed it. I was ten times
smarter'n he was about this Pearl du Monville, first time I ever laid eyes
on the little guy, which was one of the saddest days of my life.

Now, most people name of Pearl is girls, but this Pearl du Monville
was a man, if you could call a fella a man who was only thirty-four,
thirty-five inches high. Pearl du Monville was a midget. He was part

French and part Hungarian, and maybe even part Bulgarian or some-thin'. I can see him now, a sneer on his little pushed-in pan, swingin' a bamboo cane and smokin' a big cigar. He had a gray suit with a big black check into it, and he had a gray felt hat with one of them rainbow-colored hatbands onto it, like the young fellas wore in them days. He talked like he was talkin' into a tin can, but he didn't have no foreign accent. He might a been fifteen or he might a been a hundred, you couldn't tell. Pearl du Monville.

After the game with C'lumbus, Magrew headed straight for the Chit-taden bar—the train for St. Louis wasn't goin' for three, four hours—and there he set, drinkin' rye and talkin' to this bartender.

"How I pity me, brother," Magrew was tellin' this bartender. "How I pity me." That was alwuz his favorite tune. So he was settin' there, tellin' this bartender how heartbreakin' it was to be manager of a bunch a blindfolded circus clowns, when up pops this Pearl du Monville outa nowheres.

It give Magrew the leapin' jumps. He thought at first maybe the D.T.'s had come back on him; he claimed he'd had 'em once, and little guys had popped up all around him, wearin' red, white, and blue hats.

"Go on, now!" Magrew yells. "Get away from me!"

But the midget clumb up on a chair acrost the table from Magrew and says, "I seen that game today, Junior, and you ain't got no ball club. What you got there, Junior," he says, "is a side show."

"Whatta ya mean, 'Junior'?" says Magrew, touchin' the little guy to satisfy hisself he was real.

"Don't pay him no attention, mister," says the bartender. "Pearl calls everybody 'Junior,' 'cause it alwuz turns out he's a year older'n anybody else."

"Yeh?" says Magrew. "How old is he?"

"How old are you, Junior?" says the midget.

"Who, me? I'm fifty-three," says Magrew.

"Well, I'm fifty-four," says the midget.

Magrew grins and asts him what he'll have, and that was the beginnin' of their beautiful friendship, if you don't care what you say.

Pearl du Monville stood up on his chair and waved his cane around and pretended like he was ballyhooin' for a circus. "Right this way, folks!" he yells. "Come on in and see the greatest collection of freaks in the world! See the armless pitchers, see the eyeless batters, see the in-fielders with five thumbs!" and on and on like that, feedin' Magrew gall and handin' him a laugh at the same time, you might say.

You could hear him and Pearl du Monville hootin' and hollerin' and singin' way up to the fourth floor of the Chittaden, where the boys was packin' up. When it come time to go to the station, you can imagine how disgusted we was when we crowded into the doorway of that bar and seen them two singin' and goin' on.

"Well, well, well," says Magrew, lookin' up and spottin' us. "Look who's here. . . . Clowns, this is Pearl du Monville, a monseer of the old, old school. . . . Don't shake hands with 'em, Pearl, 'cause their fingers is made of chalk and would bust right off in your paws," he says, and he starts guffawin' and Pearl starts titterin' and we stand there givin' 'em the iron eye, it bein' the lowest ebb a ball-club manager'd got hisself down to since the national pastime was started.

Then the midget begun givin' us the ballyhoo. "Come on in!" he says, wavin' his cane. "See the legless base runners, see the outfielders with the butter fingers, see the southpaw with the arm of a little chee-ild!"

Then him and Magrew begun to hoop and holler and nudge each other till you'd of thought this little guy was the funniest guy than even Charlie Chaplin. The fellas filed outa the bar without a word and went on up to the Union Depot, leavin' me to handle Magrew and his new-found crony.

Well, I got 'em outa there finely. I had to take the little guy along, 'cause Magrew had a holt onto him like a vise and I couldn't pry him loose.

"He's comin' along as masket," says Magrew, holdin' the midget in the crouch of his arm like a football. And come along he did, hollerin' and protestin' and beatin' at Magrew with his little fists.

"Cut it out, will ya, Junior?" the little guy kept whinin'. "Come on, leave a man loose, will ya, Junior?"

But Junior kept a holt onto him and begun yellin', "See the guys with the glass arm, see the guys with the cast-iron brains, see the fielders with the feet on their wrists!"

So it goes, right through the whole Union Depot, with people starin' and catcallin', and he don't put the midget down till he gets him through the gates.

"How'm I goin' to go along without no toothbrush?" the midget asts. "What'm I goin' to do without no other suit?" he says.

"Doc here," says Magrew, meanin' me—"doc here will look after you like you was his own son, won't you, doc?"

I give him the iron eye, and he finely got on the train and prob'ly went to sleep with his clothes on.

This left me alone with the midget. "Lookit," I says to him. "Why don't you go on home now? Come mornin', Magrew'll forget all about you. He'll prob'ly think you was somethin' he seen in a nightmare maybe. And he ain't goin' to laugh so easy in the mornin', neither," I says. "So why don't you go on home?"

"Nix," he says to me. "Skiddoo," he says, "twenty-three for you," and he tosses his cane up into the vestibule of the coach and clam'ers on up after it like a cat. So that's the way Pearl du Monville come to go to St. Louis with the ball club.

I seen 'em first at breakfast the next day, settin' opposite each other; the midget playin' "Turkey in the Straw" on a harmonium and Magrew starin' at his eggs and bacon like they was a uncooked bird with its feathers still on.

"Remember where you found this?" I says, jerkin' my thumb at the midget. "Or maybe you think they come with breakfast on these trains," I says, bein' a good hand at turnin' a sharp remark in them days.

The midget puts down the harmonium and turns on me. "Sneeze," he says; "your brains is dusty." Then he snaps a couple drops of water at me from a tumbler. "Drown," he says, tryin' to make his voice deep.

Now, both them cracks is Civil War cracks, but you'd of thought they was brand new and the funniest than any crack Magrew'd ever heard in his whole life. He started hoopin' and hollerin', and the midget started hoopin' and hollerin', so I walked on away and set down with Bugs Courtney and Hank Metters, payin' no attention to this weak-minded Damon and Phidias acrost the aisle.

Well, sir, the first game with St. Louis was rained out, and there we was facin' a double-header next day. Like maybe I told you, we lose the last three double-headers we play, makin' maybe twenty-five errors in the six games, which is all right for the intimates of a school for the blind, but is disgraceful for the world's champions. It was too wet to go to the zoo, and Magrew wouldn't let us go to the movies, 'cause they flickered so bad in them days. So we just set around, stewin' and frettin'.

One of the newspaper boys come over to take a pitture of Billy Klinger and Whitey Cott shakin' hands—this reporter'd heard about the fight—and whilst they was standin' there, toe to toe, shakin' hands, Billy give a back lunge and a jerk, and throwed Whitey over his shoulder into a corner of the room, like a sack a salt. Whitey come back at him with a chair, and Bethlehem broke loose in that there room. The camera was tromped to pieces like a berry basket. When we finely got 'em pulled apart, I heard a laugh, and there was Magrew and the midget standin' in the door and givin' us the iron eye.

"Wrasslers," says Magrew, cold-like, "that's what I got for a ball club, Mr. Du Monville, wrasslers—and not very good wrasslers at that, you ast me."

"A man can't be good at everythin'," says Pearl, "but he oughta be good at somethin'."

This sets Magrew guffawin' again, and away they go, the midget taggin' along by his side like a hound dog and handin' him a fast line of so-called comic cracks.

When we went out to face that battlin' St. Louis club in a double-header the next afternoon, the boys was jumpy as tin toys with keys in their back. We lose the first game, 7 to 2, and are trailin', 4 to 0, when the second game ain't but ten minutes old. Magrew set there like a stone statue, speakin' to nobody. Then, in their half a the fourth, somebody singled to center and knocked in two more runs for St. Louis.

That made Magrew squawk. "I wisht one thing," he says. "I wisht I was manager of a old ladies' sewin' circus 'stead of a ball club."

"You are, Junior, you are," says a familyer and disagreeable voice.

It was that Pearl du Monville again, poppin' up outa nowheres, swingin' his bamboo cane and smokin' a cigar that's three sizes too big for his face. By this time we'd finely got the other side out, and Hank Metters slithered a bat acrost the ground, and the midget had to jump to keep both his ankles from bein' broke.

I thought Magrew'd bust a blood vessel. "You hurt Pearl and I'll break your neck!" he yelled.

Hank muttered somethin' and went on up to the plate and struck out.

We managed to get a couple runs acrost in our half a the sixth, but they come back with three more in their half a the seventh, and this was too much for Magrew.

"Come on, Pearl," he says. "We're gettin' outa here."

"Where you think you're goin'?" I ast him.

"To the lawyer's again," he says cryptly.

"I didn't know you'd been to the lawyer's once, yet," I says.

"Which that goes to show how much you don't know," he says.

With that, they was gone, and I didn't see 'em the rest of the day, nor know what they was up to, which was a God's blessin'. We lose the nightcap, 9 to 3, and that puts us into second place plenty, and as low in our mind as a ball club can get.

The next day was a horrible day, like anybody that lived through it can tell you. Practice was just over and the St. Louis club was takin' the field, when I hears this strange sound from the stands. It sounds like the nervous whickerin' a horse gives when he smells somethin' funny on the wind. It was the fans ketchin' sight of Pearl du Monville, like you have prob'ly guessed. The midget had popped up onto the field all dressed up in a minacher club uniform, sox, cap, little letters sewed onto his chest, and all. He was swingin' a kid's bat and the only thing kept him from lookin' like a real ballplayer seen through the wrong end of a microscope was this cigar he was smokin'.

Bugs Courtney reached over and jerked it outa his mouth and throwed it away. "You're wearin' that suit on the playin' field," he says to him, severe as a judge. "You go insultin' it and I'll take you out to the zoo and feed you to the bears."

Pearl just blowed some smoke at him which he still has in his mouth.

Whilst Whitey was foulin' off four or five prior to strikin' out, I went on over to Magrew. "If I was as comic as you," I says, "I'd laugh myself to death," I says. "Is that any way to treat the uniform, makin' a mockery out of it?"

"It might surprise you to know I ain't makin' no mockery outa the uniform," says Magrew. "Pearl du Monville here has been made a bone-of-fida member of this so-called ball club. I fixed it up with the front office by long-distance phone."

"Yeh?" I says. "I can just hear Mr. Dillworth or Bart Jenkins agreein' to hire a midget for the ball club. I can just hear 'em." Mr. Dillworth was the owner of the club and Bart Jenkins was the secretary, and they never stood for no monkey business. "May I be so bold as to inquire," I says, "just what you told 'em?"

"I told 'em," he says, "I wanted to sign up a guy they ain't no pitcher in the league can strike him out."

"Uh-huh," I says, "and did you tell 'em what size of a man he is?"

"Never mind about that," he says. "I got papers on me, made out legal and proper, constitutin' one Pearl du Monville a bone-of-fida member of this former ball club. Maybe that'll shame them big babies into gettin' in there and swingin', knowin' I can replace any one of 'em with a midget, if I have a mind to. A St. Louis lawyer I seen twice tells me it's all legal and proper."

"A St. Louis lawyer would," I says, "seein' nothin' could make him happier than havin' you makin' a mockery outa this one-time baseball outfit," I says.

Well, sir, it'll all be there in the papers of thirty, thirty-one year ago, and you could look it up. The game went along without no scorin' for seven innings, and since they ain't nothin' much to watch but guys poppin' up or strikin' out, the fans pay most of their attention to the goin's-on of Pearl du Monville. He's out there in front a the dugout, turnin' handsprings, balancin' his bat on his chin, walkin' a imaginary line, and so on. The fans clapped and laughed at him, and he ate it up.

So it went up to the last a the eighth, nothin' to nothin', not more'n seven, eight hits all told, and no errors on neither side. Our pitcher gets the first two men out easy in the eighth. Then up come a fella name of Porter or Billings, or some such name, and he lammed one up against the tobacco sign for three bases. The next guy up slapped the first ball out into left for a base hit, and in come the fella from third for the only run

of the ball game so far. The crowd yelled, the look a death come onto
Magrew's face again, and even the midget quit his tom-foolin'. Their
next man fouled out back a third, and we come up for our last bats like a
bunch a schoolgirls steppin' into a pool of cold water. I was lower in my
mind than I'd been since the day in Nineteen-four when Chesbro
throwed the wild pitch in the ninth inning with a man on third and lost
the pennant for the Highlanders. I knowed something just as bad was
goin' to happen, which shows I'm a clairvoyun, or was then.

When Gordy Mills hit out to second, I just closed my eyes. I opened
'em up again to see Dutch Muller standin' on second, dustin' off his
pants, him havin' got his first hit in maybe twenty times to the plate.
Next up was Harry Loesing, battin' for our pitcher, and he got a base on
balls, walkin' on a fourth one you could a combed your hair with.

Then up come Whitey Cott, our lead-off man. He crotches down in
what was prob'ly the most fearsome stanch in organized ball, but all he
can do is pop out to short. That brung up Billy Klinger, with two down
and a man on first and second. Billy took a cut at one you could a
knocked a plug hat offa this here Carnera with it, but then he gets sense
enough to wait 'em out, and finely he walks, too, fillin' the bases.

Yes, sir, there you are; the tyin' run on third and the winnin' run on
second, first a the ninth, two men down, and Hank Metters comin' to
the bat. Hank was built like a Pope-Hartford and he couldn't run no
faster'n President Taft, but he had five home runs to his credit for the
season, and that wasn't bad in them days. Hank was still hittin' better'n
anybody else on the ball club, and it was mighty heartenin', seein' him
stridin' up towards the plate. But he never got there.

"Wait a minute!" yells Magrew, jumpin' to his feet. "I'm sendin' in a
pinch hitter!" he yells.

You could a heard a bomb drop. When a ball-club manager says he's
sendin' in a pinch hitter for the best batter on the club, you know and I
know and everybody knows he's lost his holt.

"They're goin' to be sendin' the funny wagon for you, if you don't
watch out," I says, grabbin' a holt of his arm.

But he pulled away and run out towards the plate, yellin', "Du Monville battin' for Metters!"

All the fellas begun squawlin' at once, except Hank, and he just stood
there starin' at Magrew like he'd gone crazy and was claimin' to be Ty
Cobb's grandma or somethin'. Their pitcher stood out there with his
hands on his hips and a disagreeable look on his face, and the plate
umpire told Magrew to go on and get a batter up. Magrew told him
again Du Monville was battin' for Metters, and the St. Louis manager
finely got the idea. It brung him outa his dugout, howlin' and bawlin'
like he'd lost a female dog and her seven pups.

Magrew pushed the midget towards the plate and he says to him, he says, "Just stand up there and hold that bat on your shoulder. They ain't a man in the world can throw three strikes in there 'fore he throws four balls!" he says.

"I get it, Junior!" says the midget. "He'll walk me and force in the tyin' run!" And he starts on up to the plate as cocky as if he was Willie Keeler.

I don't need to tell you Bethlehem broke loose on that there ball field. The fans got onto their hind legs, yellin' and whistlin', and everybody on the field begun wavin' their arms and hollerin' and shovin'. The plate umpire stalked over to Magrew like a traffic cop, waggin' his jaw and pointin' his finger, and the St. Louis manager kept yellin' like his house was on fire. When Pearl got up to the plate and stood there, the pitcher slammed his glove down onto the ground and started stompin' on it, and they ain't nobody can blame him. He's just walked two normal-sized human bein's, and now here's a guy up to the plate they ain't more'n twenty inches between his knees and his shoulders.

The plate umpire called in the field umpire, and they talked a while, like a couple doctors seein' the bucolic plague or somethin' for the first time. Then the plate umpire come over to Magrew with his arms folded acrost his chest, and he told him to go on and get a batter up, or he'd forfeit the game to St. Louis. He pulled out his watch, but somebody batted it outa his hand in the scufflin', and I thought there'd be a free-for-all, with everybody yellin' and shovin' except Pearl du Monville, who stood up at the plate with his little bat on his shoulder, not movin' a muscle.

Then Magrew played his ace. I seen him pull some papers outa his pocket and show 'em to the plate umpire. The umpire begun lookin' at 'em like they was bills for somethin' he not only never bought it, he never even heard of it. The other umpire studied 'em like they was a death warren, and all this time the St. Louis manager and the fans and the players is yellin' and hollerin'.

Well, sir, they fought about him bein' a midget, and they fought about him usin' a kid's bat, and they fought about where'd he been all season. They was eight or nine rule books brung out and everybody was thumbin' through 'em, tryin' to find out what it says about midgets, but it don't say nothin' about midgets, 'cause this was somethin' never'd come up in the history of the game before, and nobody'd ever dreamed about it, even when they has nightmares. Maybe you can't send no midgets in to bat nowadays, 'cause the old game's changed a lot, mostly for the worst, but you could then, it turned out.

The plate umpire finely decided the contrack papers was all legal and proper, like Magrew said, so he waved the St. Louis players back to their places and he pointed his finger at their manager and told him to quit hollerin' and get on back in the dugout. The manager says the game is percedin' under protest, and the umpire bawls, "Play ball!" over 'n' above the yellin' and booin', him havin' a voice like a hog-caller.

The St. Louis pitcher picked up his glove and beat at it with his fist six or eight times, and then got set on the mound and studied the situation. The fans realized he was really goin' to pitch to the midget, and they went crazy, hoopin' and hollerin' louder'n ever, and throwin' pop bottles and hats and cushions down onto the field. It took five, ten minutes to get the fans quieted down again, whilst our fellas that was on base set down on the bags and waited. And Pearl du Monville kept standin' up there with the bat on his shoulder, like he'd been told to.

So the pitcher starts studyin' the setup again, and you got to admit it was the strangest set up in a ball game since the players cut off their beards and begun wearin' gloves. I wisht I could call the pitcher's name—it wasn't old Barney Pelty nor Nig Jack Powell nor Harry Howell. He was a big right-hander, but I can't call his name. You could look it up. Even in a crotchin' position, the ketcher towers over the midget like the Washington Monument.

The plate umpire tries standin' on his tiptoes, then he tries crotchin' down, and he finely gets hisself into a stanch nobody'd ever seen on a ball field before, kinda squattin' down on his hanches.

Well, the pitcher is sore as a old buggy horse in fly time. He slams in the first pitch, hard and wild, and maybe two foot higher'n the midget's head.

"Ball one!" hollers the umpire over 'n' above the racket, 'cause everybody is yellin' worsten ever.

The ketcher goes on out towards the mound and talks to the pitcher and hands him the ball. This time the big right-hander tried a undershoot, and it comes in a little closer, maybe no higher'n a foot, foot and a half above Pearl's head. It would a been a strike with a human bein' in there, but the umpire's got to call it, and he does.

"Ball two!" he bellers.

The ketcher walks on out to the mound again, and the whole infield comes over and gives advice to the pitcher about what they'd do in a case like this, with two balls and no strikes on a batter that oughta be in a bottle of alcohol 'stead of up there at the plate in a big-league game between the teams that is fightin' for first place.

For the third pitch, the pitcher stands there flat-footed and tosses up the ball like he's playin' ketch with a little girl.

Pearl stands there motionless as a hitchin' post, and the ball comes in big and slow and high—high for Pearl, that is, it bein' about on a level with his eyes, or a little higher'n a grown man's knees.

They ain't nothin' else for the umpire to do, so he calls, "Ball three!"

Everybody is onto their feet, hoopin' and hollerin', as the pitcher sets to throw ball four. The St. Louis manager is makin' signs and faces like he was a contorturer, and the infield is givin' the pitcher some more advice about what to do this time. Our boys who was on base stick right onto the bag, runnin' no risk of bein' nipped for the last out.

Well, the pitcher decides to give him a toss again, seein' he come closer with that than with a fast ball. They ain't nobody ever seen a slower ball throwed. It come in big as a balloon and slower'n any ball ever throwed before in the major leagues. It come right in over the plate in front of Pearl's chest, lookin' prob'ly big as a full moon to Pearl. They ain't never been a minute like the minute that followed since the United States was founded by the Pilgrim grandfathers.

Pearl du Monville took a cut at that ball, and he hit it! Magrew give a groan like a poleaxed steer as the ball rolls out in front a the plate into fair territory.

"Fair ball!" yells the umpire, and the midget starts runnin' for first, still carryin' that little bat, and makin' maybe ninety foot an hour. Bethlehem breaks loose on that ball field and in them stands. They ain't never been nothin' like it since creation was begun.

The ball's rollin' slow, on down towards third, goin' maybe eight, ten foot. The infield comes in fast and our boys break from their bases like hares in a brush fire. Everybody is standin' up, yellin' and hollerin', and Magrew is tearin' his hair outa his head, and the midget is scamperin' for first with all the speed of one of them little dashhounds carryin' a satchel in his mouth.

The ketcher gets to the ball first, but he boots it on out past the pitcher's box, the pitcher fallin' on his face tryin' to stop it, the shortstop sprawlin' after it full length and zaggin' it on over towards the second baseman, whilst Muller is scorin' with the tyin' run and Loesing is roundin' third with the winnin' run. Ty Cobb could a made a three-bagger outa that bunt, with everybody fallin' over theirself tryin' to pick the ball up. But Pearl is still maybe fifteen, twenty feet from the bag, toddlin' like a baby and yeepin' like a trapped rabbit, when the second baseman finely gets a holt of that ball and slams it over to first. The first baseman ketches it and stomps on the bag, the base umpire waves Pearl out, and there goes your old ball game, the craziest ball game ever played in the history of the organized world.

Their players start runnin' in, and then I see Magrew. He starts after Pearl, runnin' faster'n any man ever run before. Pearl sees him comin' and runs behind the base umpire's legs and gets a holt onto 'em. Magrew

comes up, pantin' and roarin', and him and the midget plays ring-
around-a-rosy with the umpire, who keeps shovin' at Magrew with one
hand and tryin' to slap the midget loose from his legs with the other.

Finely Magrew ketches the midget, who is still yeepin' like a stuck
sheep. He gets holt of that little guy by both his ankles and starts whirlin'
him round and round his head like Magrew was a hammer thrower and
Pearl was the hammer. Nobody can stop him without gettin' their head
knocked off, so everybody just stands there and yells. Then Magrew lets
the midget fly. He flies on out towards second, high and fast, like a
human home run, headed for the soap sign in center field.

Their shortstop tries to get to him, but he can't make it, and I knowed
the little fella was goin' to bust to pieces like a dollar watch on a asphalt
street when he hit the ground. But it so happens their center fielder is
just crossin' second, and he starts runnin' back, tryin' to get under the
midget, who had took to spiralin' like a football 'stead of turnin' head
over foot, which give him more speed and more distance.

I know you never seen a midget ketched, and you prob'ly never even
seen one throwed. To ketch a midget that's been throwed by a heavy-
muscled man and is flyin' through the air, you got to run under him and
with him and pull your hands and arms back and down when you ketch
him, to break the compact of his body, or you'll bust him in two like a
matchstick. I seen Bill Lange and Willie Keeler and Tris Speaker make
some wonderful ketches in my day, but I never seen nothin' like that
center fielder. He goes back and back and still further back and he pulls
that midget down outa the air like he was liftin' a sleepin' baby from a
cradle. They wasn't a bruise onto him, only his face was the color of cat's
meat and he ain't got no air in his chest. In his excitement, the base
umpire, who was runnin' back with the center fielder when he ketched
Pearl, yells, "Out!" and that give hysteries to the Bethlehem which was
ragin' like Niagry on that ball field.

Everybody was hoopin' and hollerin' and yellin' and runnin', with the
fans swarmin' onto the field, and the cops tryin' to keep order, and some
guys laughin' and some of the women fans cryin', and six or eight of us
holdin' onto Magrew to keep him from gettin' at that midget and fini-
shin' him off. Some of the fans picks up the St. Louis pitcher and the
center fielder, and starts carryin' 'em around on their shoulders, and they
was the craziest goin's-on knowed to the history of organized ball on this
side of the 'Lantic Ocean.

I seen Pearl du Monville strugglin' in the arms of a lady fan with a
ample bosom, who was laughin' and cryin' at the same time, and him
beatin' at her with his little fists and bawlin' and yellin'. He clawed his
way loose finely and disappeared in the forest of legs which made that

ball field look like it was Coney Island on a hot summer's day.

That was the last I ever seen of Pearl du Monville. I never seen hide nor hair of him from that day to this, and neither did nobody else. He just vanished into the thin of the air, as the fella says. He was ketched for the final out of the ball game and that was the end of him, just like it was the end of the ball game, you might say, and also the end of our losin' streak, like I'm goin' to tell you.

That night we piled onto a train for Chicago, but we wasn't snarlin' and snappin' any more. No, sir, the ice was finely broke and a new spirit come into that ball club. The old zip come back with the disappearance of Pearl du Monville out back a second base. We got to laughin' and talkin' and kiddin' together, and 'fore long Magrew was laughin' with us. He got a human look onto his pan again, and he quit whinin' and complainin' and wishtin' he was in heaven with the angels.

Well, sir, we wiped up that Chicago series, winnin' all four games, and makin' seventeen hits in one of 'em. Funny thing was, St. Louis was so shook up by that last game with us, they never did hit their stride again. Their center fielder took to misjudgin' everything that come his way, and the rest a the fellas followed suit, the way a club'll do when one guy blows up.

'Fore we left Chicago, I and some of the fellas went out and bought a pair of them little baby shoes, which we had 'em golded over and give 'em to Magrew for a souvenir, and he took it all in good spirit. Whitey Cott and Billy Klinger made up and was fast friends again, and we hit our home lot like a ton of dynamite and they was nothin' could stop us from then on.

I don't recollect things as clear as I did thirty, forty year ago. I can't read no fine print no more, and the only person I got to check with on the golden days of the national pastime, as the fella says, is my friend, old Milt Kline, over in Springfield, and his mind ain't as strong as it once was.

He gets Rube Waddell mixed up with Rube Marquard, for one thing, and anybody does that oughta be put away where he won't bother nobody. So I can't tell you the exact margin we win the pennant by. Maybe it was two and a half games, or maybe it was three and a half. But it'll all be there in the newspapers and record books of thirty, thirty-one year ago and, like I was sayin', you could look it up.

TOM CLARK

"Son of Interesting Losers"

Eddie Gaedel came from Chicago

In 1951 he was 26 years old and stood 3 feet 7 inches tall

Bill Veeck signed Eddie Gaedel to a St. Louis Browns contract on Saturday night July 18, 1951, the night before a big doubleheader in Sportsmans Park against the Detroit Tigers, a Sunday doubleheader celebrating the Golden Anniversary of the American League

Veeck's promise of a holiday promotion brought out better than eighteen thousand people

Nobody was disappointed or surprised when the Browns lost the first game to the Tigers

Between games, members of the ground crew wheeled a huge birthday cake out onto the field, the cake had 50 candles, one for each American League season

The midget Eddie Gaedel stood at his full height inside the birthday cake, wearing his white St. Louis Browns home uniform, with the number "⅛" on the back in brown

Eddie was nervous it was dark inside the cake

When they got to home plate the bearers put the cake down and knocked on the side to let Eddie Gaedel know it was time to come out

He came out

The crowd cheered

Bill Veeck, the one-legged war vet, wearing his famous open-neck sports shirt, grinned from the press box

The second game started

While the Tigers batted in the first inning, Browns manager Zack Taylor helped Eddie Gaedel tie his shoelaces in the dugout

Eddie's hands were shaking

The Tigers finished batting and came off the field

Carrying a tiny kid's bat, Eddie climbed out of the dugout and approached the plate

He informed umpire Ed Hurley that he would be a pinch-hitter for the Browns' lead-off man, Frank Saucier

Hurley stood apart from his mind for a moment and took a second look

Gunfighter-fashion, his strike hand shot back to his pants pocket Where it got a good grip on the rule book

Zack Taylor loped out of the dugout to show Hurley Eddie Gaedel's official contract with the St. Louis Browns

The mists of time cleared from the umpire's eyes

Eddie Gaedel stepped into the batter's box

Bob Cain, the Detroit pitcher, wound up and fired

The ball exploded into the catcher's mitt a foot above Eddie's head for ball one

The next two pitches blasted in high and wide of Eddie's tiny strike zone

Bob Cain swore softly and spat into the grass in front of the mound

"Shit," he thought, and then he threw the softest pitch he could throw; Eddie never saw it: he had his eyes squeezed shut

"Ball Four," said Hurley

Eddie Gaedel trotted off to first base

Immediately Zack Taylor replaced him with a pinch runner

The next day the American League banished midgets from its playing fields for all time

League President Will Harridge ordered that Eddie Gaedel's statistics be erased from the record books for all time, and it was done

Bill Veeck paid Eddie Gaedel a hundred bucks

The Browns went on losing, Zack Taylor's hair kept falling out, Bill
   Veeck split, the Browns went off to Baltimore and became winners,
   and Eddie Gaedel got bookings on the after dinner circuit

Over meat and potato leavings he told the fathers of high school letter
   winners about his day in the big leagues

Years passed

In the late 50s Bill Veeck got back into baseball with the Chicago White
   Sox

One day he called Eddie Gaedel and asked him to drop by with a couple
   of his pals

Veeck dressed the four midgets up in plastic outfits to look like Men
   from Mars

Then he hired a helicopter and had it circle over the infield at Comiskey
   Park

Eddie Gaedel and his fellow Martians came down the sky ladder and
   landed at second base, where they captured two White Sox infielders at raygun-point

It was like a St. Louis Browns Reunion!

GARRISON KEILLOR

"ATTITUDE"

Long ago I passed the point in life when major-league ballplayers begin
to be younger than yourself. Now all of them are, except for a few aging
trigenarians and a couple of quadros who don't get around on the fastball

as well as they used to and who sit out the second games of doubleheaders. However, despite my age (thirty-nine), I am still active and have a lot of interests. One of them is slow-pitch softball, a game that lets me go through the motions of baseball without getting beaned or having to run too hard. I play on a pretty casual team, one that drinks beer on the bench and substitutes freely. If a player's wife or girlfriend wants to play, we give her a glove and send her out to right field, no questions asked, and if she lets a pop fly drop six feet in front of her, nobody agonizes over it.

Except me. This year. For the first time in my life, just as I am entering the dark twilight of my slow-pitch career, I find myself taking the game seriously. It isn't the bonehead play that bothers me especially—the pop fly that drops untouched, the slow roller juggled and the ball then heaved ten feet over the first baseman's head and into the next diamond, the routine singles that go through outfielders' legs for doubles and triples with gloves flung after them. No, it isn't our stone-glove fielding or pussyfoot base-running or limp-wristed hitting that gives me fits, though these have put us on the short end of some mighty ridiculous scores this summer. It's our attitude.

Bottom of the ninth, down 18–3, two outs, a man on first and a woman on third, and our third baseman strikes out. *Strikes out!* In slow-pitch, not even your grandmother strikes out, but this guy does, and after his third strike—a wild swing at a ball that bounces on the plate—he topples over in the dirt and lies flat on his back, laughing. *Laughing!*

Same game, earlier. They have the bases loaded. A weak grounder is hit toward our second baseperson. The runners are running. She picks up the ball, and she looks at them. She looks at first, at second, at home. We yell, "Throw it! Throw it!" and she throws it, underhand, at the pitcher, who has turned and run to back up the catcher. The ball rolls across the third-base line and under the bench. Three runs score. The batter, a fatso, chugs into second. The other team hoots and hollers, and what does she do? She shrugs and smiles ("Oh, silly me"); after all, it's only a game. Like the aforementioned strikeout artist, she treats her error as a joke. They have forgiven themselves instantly, which is unforgivable. It is *we* who should forgive them, who can say, "It's all right, it's only a game." They are supposed to throw up their hands and kick the dirt and hang their heads, as if this boner, even if it is their sixteenth of the afternoon—*this* is the one that really and truly breaks their hearts.

That attitude sweetens the game for everyone. The sinner feels sweet remorse. The fatso feels some sense of accomplishment; this is no bunch of rumdums he forced into an error but a team with some class. We, the sinner's teammates, feel momentary anger at her—dumb! dumb play!—

but then, seeing her grief, we sympathize with her in our hearts (any one of us might have made that mistake or one worse), and we yell encouragement, including the shortstop, who, moments before, dropped an easy throw for a force at second. "That's all right! Come on! We got 'em!" we yell. "Shake it off! These turkeys can't hit!" This makes us all feel good, even though the turkeys now lead us by ten runs. We're getting clobbered, but we have a winning attitude.

Let me say this about attitude: Each player is responsible for his or her own attitude, and to a considerable degree you can *create* a good attitude by doing certain little things on the field. These are certain little things that ballplayers do in the Bigs, and we ought to be doing them in the Slows.

1. When going up to bat, don't step right into the batter's box as if it were an elevator. The box is your turf, your stage. Take possession of it slowly and deliberately, starting with a lot of back-bending, knee-stretching, and torso-revolving in the on-deck circle. Then, approaching the box, stop outside it and tap the dirt off your spikes with your bat. You don't have spikes, you have sneakers, of course, but the significance of the tapping is the same. Then, upon entering the box, spit on the ground. It's a way of saying, "This here is mine. This is where I get my hits."

2. Spit frequently. Spit at all crucial moments. Spit correctly. Spit should be *blown,* not ptuied weakly with the lips, which often results in dribble. Spitting should convey forcefulness of purpose, concentration, pride. Spit down, not in the direction of others. Spit in the glove and on the fingers, especially after making a real knucklehead play; it's a way of saying, "I dropped the ball because my glove was dry."

3. At bat and in the field, pick up dirt. Rub dirt in the fingers (especially after spitting on them). Toss dirt, as if testing the wind for velocity and direction. Smooth the dirt. Be involved with dirt. If no dirt is available (e.g., in the outfield), pluck tufts of grass. Fielders should be grooming their areas constantly between plays, flicking away tiny sticks and bits of gravel.

4. Take your time. Tie your laces. Confer with your teammates about possible situations that may arise and conceivable options in dealing with them. Extend the game. Three errors on three consecutive plays can be humiliating if the plays occur within the space of a couple of minutes, but if each error is separated from the next by extensive conferences on the mound, lace-tying, glove adjustments, and arguing close calls (if any), the effect on morale is minimized.

5. Talk. Not just an occasional "Let's get a hit now" but continuous

rhythmic chatter, a flow of syllables: "Hey babe hey babe c'mon babe good stick now hey babe long tater take him downtown babe . . . hey good eye good eye."

Infield chatter is harder to maintain. Since the slow-pitch pitch is required to be a soft underhand lob, infielders hesitate to say, "Smoke him babe hey low heat hey throw it on the black babe chuck it in there back him up babe no hit no hit." Say it anyway.

6. One final rule, perhaps the most important of all: When your team is up and has made the third out, the batter and the players who were left on base do not come back to the bench for their gloves. *They remain on the field, and their teammates bring their gloves out to them.* This requires some organization and discipline, but it pays off big in morale. It says, "Although we're getting our pants knocked off, still we must conserve our energy."

Imagine that you have bobbled two fly balls in this rout and now you have just tried to stretch a single into a double and have been easily thrown out sliding into second base, where the base runner ahead of you had stopped. It was the third out and a dumb play, and your opponents smirk at you as they run off the field. You are the goat, a lonely and tragic figure sitting in the dirt. You curse yourself, jerking your head sharply forward. You stand up and kick the base. How miserable! How degrading! Your utter shame, though brief, bears silent testimony to the worthiness of your teammates, whom you have let down, and they appreciate it. They call out to you now as they take the field, and as the second baseman runs to his position he says, "Let's get 'em now," and tosses you your glove. Lowering your head, you trot slowly out to right. There you do some deep knee bends. You pick grass. You find a pebble and fling it into foul territory. As the first batter comes to the plate, you check the sun. You get set in your stance, poised to fly. Feet spread, hands on hips, you bend slightly at the waist and spit the expert spit of a veteran ballplayer—a player who has known the agony of defeat but who always bounces back, a player who has lost a stride on the base paths but can still make the big play.

This is *ball*, ladies and gentlemen. This is what it's all about.

Autumn

JAMES WRIGHT

"Autumn Begins in Martins Ferry, Ohio"

In the Shreve High football stadium,
I think of Polacks nursing long beers in Tiltonsville,
And gray faces of Negroes in the blast furnace at Benwood,
And the ruptured night watchman of Wheeling Steel,
Dreaming of heroes.

All the proud fathers are ashamed to go home.
Their women cluck like starved pullets,
Dying for love.

Therefore,
Their sons grow suicidally beautiful
At the beginning of October,
And gallop terribly against each other's bodies.

ERNEST LAWRENCE THAYER

"Casey at the Bat"

Ernest Thayer's "Casey at the Bat" is, of course, the best-known baseball, if not sports, poem ever written. It first appeared on June 3, 1888, in
the San Francisco Examiner in a humor column Thayer wrote for the
paper's Sunday supplement. Thayer, a Harvard product and editor of the
Harvard Lampoon, was astonished at the enormous popularity of the
poem. Indeed, in answer to a publisher who wanted to discuss payment
for a reprinting, Thayer replied: "All I ask is never to be reminded of it
again. Make it anything you wish."

Certainly a contributor to the ballad's popularity was de Wolfe Hopper, a young actor and comedian. In 1889 he was performing in the

comic opera Prince Methusalem. *Hearing one afternoon that members of the New York Giants and Chicago White Stockings baseball teams would be in attendance that night, he hoped to do something specifically for them. A friend of his recommended the Thayer ballad—a frayed clipping of which he was carrying around in his wallet. Hopper memorized it and in the middle of the second act stopped the performance and dedicated the poem to the ballplayers to their astonishment and delight, as well as the audience's. Hopper added the piece to his repertoire and estimated at the end of his career that he had performed it over 10,000 times.*

Literally dozens of sequels, imitations, and parodies exist—many of them by writers unable to bear the cruel twist of Casey's striking out and who have him hit a homer to win the game. The most familiar of these is Grantland Rice's "Casey's Revenge." The various takeoffs would comprise a hefty volume. Even Casey's relatives get into the act: "Mrs. Casey," "Casey's Son," "Casey's Sister at the Bat," each of whom, incidentally, strikes out. The last stanza of "Casey's Daughter at the Bat" (she is playing in a softball game for the Mudvillettes) goes as follows:

> Oh! somewhere in this favored land the moon is
>   shining bright;
> And somewhere there are softball honeys winning
>   games tonight
> And somewhere there are softball fans who scream
>   and yell and shout;
> But there's no joy in Mudville—Casey's daughter
>   has struck out.

The outlook wasn't brilliant for the Mudville nine that day;
The score stood four to two with but one inning more to play.
And then, when Cooney died at first, and Barrows did the same,
A sickly silence fell upon the patrons of the game.

A straggling few got up to go in deep despair. The rest
Clung to that hope which springs eternal in the human breast;
They thought, If only Casey could but get a whack at that
We'd put up even money now, with Casey at the bat.

But Flynn preceded Casey, as did also Jimmy Blake,
And the former was a lulu and the latter was a cake;

So upon that stricken multitude grim melancholy sat,
For there seemed but little chance of Casey's getting to the bat.

But Flynn let drive a single, to the wonderment of all,
And Blake, the much despiséd, tore the cover off the ball;
And when the dust had lifted, and men saw what had occurred,
There was Jimmy safe at second, and Flynn a-hugging third.

Then from five thousand throats and more there rose a lusty yell;
It rumbled through the valley, it rattled in the dell;
It knocked upon the mountain and recoiled upon the flat,
For Casey, mighty Casey, was advancing to the bat.

There was ease in Casey's manner as he stepped into his place;
There was pride in Casey's bearing and a smile on Casey's face.
And when, responding to the cheers, he lightly doffed his hat,
No stranger in the crowd could doubt 'twas Casey at the bat.

Ten thousand eyes were on him as he rubbed his hands with dirt,
Five thousand tongues applauded when he wiped them on his
    shirt;
Then while the writhing pitcher ground the ball into his hip,
Defiance gleamed from Casey's eye, a sneer curled Casey's lip.

And now the leather-covered sphere came hurtling through the air,
And Casey stood a-watching it in haughty grandeur there.
Close by the sturdy batsman the ball unheeded sped;
"That ain't my style," said Casey. "Strike one," the umpire said.

From the benches, black with people, there went up a muffled
    roar,
Like the beating of the storm waves on a stern and distant shore.
"Kill him! Kill the umpire!" shouted someone on the stand;
And it's likely they'd have killed him had not Casey raised his
    hand.

With a smile of Christian charity great Casey's visage shone;
He stilled the rising tumult, he bade the game go on;
He signaled to the pitcher, and once more the spheroid flew;
But Casey still ignored it, and the umpire said, "Strike two."

"Fraud!" cried the maddened thousands, and echo answered
    "Fraud!"

But one scornful look from Casey and the audience was awed;
They saw his face grow stern and cold, they saw his muscles strain,
And they knew that Casey wouldn't let that ball go by again.

The sneer is gone from Casey's lip, his teeth are clenched in hate,
He pounds with cruel violence his bat upon the plate;
And now the pitcher holds the ball, and now he lets it go,
And now the air is shattered by the force of Casey's blow.

Oh, somewhere in this favored land the sun is shining bright,
The band is playing somewhere, and somewhere hearts are light;
And somewhere men are laughing, and somewhere children shout,
But there is no joy in Mudville—mighty Casey has struck out.

ART BUCHWALD

"Casey Has Struck Out"

NEWS ITEM—Judge rules that women reporters must be permitted in baseball locker rooms.

It seemed extremely rocky for the Mudville Nine that day;
They blew the game in Springfield on a stupid double play.
So when a girl reporter walked in their locker room
They decided to play ball with her to take away the gloom.

Cooney made the first pass, and he fell upon his face;
Burrows tried to sacrifice, but couldn't get to base.
Flynn was left in right field, and never got her name;
It looked as though poor Mudville would lose another game.

Then from the locker players went up a joyous yell;
It rumbled in the showers, it rattled in the dell.
It struck upon the saunas, and rebounded on the flat;
For Casey, Mighty Casey, was advancing to the bat.

There was ease in Casey's manner, a smile on Casey's face,
As he whispered to the lady, "Would you like to see my place?"
"Pas ce soir," the lady said, "and please take off your hat."
"That's no way to talk," Flynn said, "when Casey's up to bat."

She frowned in great displeasure, a hand upon her hip.
She stuck a mike in Casey's face and almost cut his lip.
"Strike One," the shortstop called out, as he doubled up and roared.
"Casey's swinging wildly and he hasn't even scored."

Casey dug his feet in as he made another pitch:
"Let's have a drink at your place and take away this itch."
"I have a date," the lady said, "so knock off all the chatter;
Tell me why you blew the game as Mudville's greatest batter."

"Strike Two," the catcher shouted as he rolled upon the floor.
Casey blushed with anger for he could not take much more.
"I have a brand-new Caddy sitting in the parking lot."
The news hen shrugged her shoulders, "I guess that's all you've got."

"Fraud!" cried Casey's teammates and the echo answered, "Fraud!"
But a scornful look from Casey and the locker room was awed.
They saw his face grow stern and cold, they saw his muscles strain,
And they knew that Mighty Casey would not foul out again.

"Look, honey," he said plaintively, "I'll talk about my pain.
Let's do it over pizzas and a bottle of champagne."
"I haven't time to mess around," the lovely girl cried out.
"I've got to meet a deadline; that's what news is all about."

The sneer was gone from Casey's lips, his teeth were clenched in fear.
He put his arm around the girl—she socked him in the ear.
She took her mike and hit his hand, and kicked him in the shin.
"Now tell me, when you get your breath, just why you didn't win!"

Oh, somewhere in this favored land, the moon is shining bright,
And girls are doing disco in pants that are too tight;
And somewhere men are laughing and drinking Guinness stout,
But there's no joy in mudville—Mighty Casey just struck out.

T. CORAGHESSAN BOYLE

"The Hector Quesadilla Story"

He was no Joltin' Joe, no Sultan of Swat, no Iron man. For one thing, his feet hurt. And God knows no legendary immortal ever suffered so prosaic a complaint. He had shinsplints too, and corns and ingrown toenails and hemorrhoids. Demons drove burning spikes into his tailbone each time he bent to loosen his shoelaces, his limbs were skewed so awkwardly his elbows and knees might have been transposed, and the once-proud knot of his frijole-fed belly had fallen like an avalanche. Worse: he was old. Old, old, old, the graybeard hobbling down the rough-hewn steps of the Senate building, the Ancient Mariner chewing on his whiskers and stumbling in his socks. Though they listed his birthdate as 1942 in the program, there were those who knew better: it was way back in '54, during his rookie year for San Buitre, that he had taken Asunción to the altar, and even in those distant days, even in Mexico, twelve-year-olds didn't marry.

When he was younger—really young, nineteen, twenty, tearing up the Mexican League like a saint of the stick—his ears were so sensitive he could hear the soft rasping friction of the pitcher's fingers as he massaged the ball and dug in for a slider, fastball, or changeup. Now he could barely hear the umpire bawling the count in his ear. And his legs. How they ached, how they groaned and creaked and chattered, how they'd gone to fat! He ate too much, that was the problem. Ate prodigiously, ate mightily, ate as if there were a hidden thing inside him, a creature all of jaws with an infinite trailing ribbon of gut. Huevos con chorizo with beans, tortillas, camarones in red sauce, and a twelve-ounce steak for breakfast, the chicken in mole to steady him before afternoon games, a sea of beer to wash away the tension of the game and prepare his digestive machinery for the flaming machaca and pepper salad Asunción prepared for him in the blessed evenings of the home stand.

Five foot seven, one hundred eighty-nine and three-quarters pounds. Hector Hernán Jesus y María Quesadilla. Little Cheese, they called him. Cheese, Cheese, Cheesus, went up the cry as he stepped in to pinch-hit in some late inning crisis, Cheese, Cheese, Cheesus, building to a roar until Chavez Ravine resounded as if with the holy name of the Savior Himself when he stroked one of the clean line-drive singles that were his signature or laid down a bunt that stuck like a finger in jelly. When he fanned, when the bat went loose in the fat brown hands and he went down on one knee for support, they hissed and called him *Viejo.*

One more season, he tells himself, though he hasn't played regularly for nearly ten years and can barely trot to first after drawing a walk, One more. He tells Asunción too: One more, One more, as they sit in the gleaming kitchen of their house in Boyle Heights, he with his Carta Blanca, she with her mortar and pestle for grinding the golden petrified kernels of maize into flour for the tortillas he eats like peanuts. *Una más,* she mocks. What do you want, the Hall of Fame? Hang up your spikes Hector.

He stares off into space, his mother's Indian features flattening his own as if the legend were true, as if she really had taken a spatula to him in the cradle, and then, dropping his thick lids as he takes a long slow swallow from the neck of the bottle, he says: Just the other day driving home from the park I saw a car on the freeway, a Mercedes with only two seats, a girl in it, her hair out back like a cloud, and you know what the license plate said? His eyes are open now, black as pitted olives. Do you? She doesn't. Cheese, he says. It said Cheese.

Then she reminds him that Hector Jr. will be twenty-nine next month and that Reina has four children of her own and another on the way. You're a grandfather, Hector—almost a great-grandfather if your son ever settled down. A moment slides by, filled with the light of the sad waning sun and the harsh Yucatano dialect of the radio announcer. *Hombres* on first and third, one down. *Abuelo,* she hisses, grinding stone against stone until it makes his teeth ache. Hang up your spikes, *abuelo.*

But he doesn't. He can't. He won't. He's no grandpa with hair the color of cigarette stains and a blanket over his knees, he's no toothless old gasser sunning himself in the park—he's a big leaguer, proud wearer of the Dodger blue, wielder of strick and glove. How can he get old? The grass is always green, the lights always shining, no clocks or periods or halves or quarters, no punch-in and punch-out: This is the game that never ends. When the heavy hitters have fanned and the pitchers' arms gone sore, when there's no joy in Mudville, taxes are killing everybody, and the Russians are raising hell in Guatemala, when the manager paces the dugout like an attack dog, mind racing, searching high and low for the canny veteran to go in and do single combat, there he'll be—always, always, eternal as a monument—Hector Quesadilla, utility infielder, with the .296 lifetime batting average and service with the Reds, Phils, Cubs, Royals, and L.A. Dodgers.

So he waits. Hangs on. Trots his aching legs round the outfield grass before the game, touches his toes ten agonizing times each morning, takes extra batting practice with the rookies and slumping millionaires. Sits. Watches. Massages his feet. Waits through the scourging road trips in the Midwest and along the East Coast, down to muggy Atlanta, across to stormy Wrigley and up to frigid Candlestick, his gut clenched round an indigestible cud of meatloaf and instant potatoes and wax beans, through the terrible nightgames with the alien lights in his eyes, waits at the end of the bench for a word from the manager, for a pat on the ass, a roar, a hiss, a chorus of cheers and catcalls, the marimba pulse of bat striking ball and the sweet looping arc of the clean base hit.

And then comes a day, late in the season, the homeboys battling for the pennant with the big-stick Braves and the sneaking Jints, when he wakes from honeyed dreams in his own bed that's like an old friend with the sheets that smell of starch and soap and flowers, and feels the pain stripped from his body as if at the touch of a healer's fingertips. Usually he dreams nothing, the night a blank, an erasure, and opens his eyes on the agonies of the martyr strapped to a bed of nails. Then he limps to the toilet, makes a poor discolored water, rinses the dead taste from his mouth, and staggers to the kitchen table where food, only food, can revive in him the interest in drawing another breath. He butters tortillas and folds them into his mouth, spoons up egg and melted jack cheese and frijoles refritos with the green salsa, lashes into his steak as if it were cut from the thigh of Kerensky, the Atlanta relief ace who'd twice that season caught him looking at a full-count fastball with men in scoring position. But not today. Today is different, a sainted day, a day on which sunshine sits in the windows like a gift of the Magi and the chatter of the starlings in the crapped-over palms across the street is a thing that approaches the divine music of the spheres. What can it be?

In the kitchen it hits him: pozole in a pot on the stove, carnitas in the saucepan, the table spread with sweetcakes, buñuelos, and the little marzipan *dulces* he could kill for. *Feliz cumpleaños,* Asunción pipes as he steps through the doorway. Her face is lit with the smile of her mother, her mother's mother, the line of gift-givers descendant to the happy conquistadors and joyous Aztecs. A kiss, a *dulce,* and then a knock at the door and Reina, fat with life, throwing her arms around him while her children gobble up the table, the room, their grandfather, with eyes that swallow their faces. Happy birthday, Daddy, Reina says, and Franklin, her youngest, is handing him the gift.

And Hector Jr.?

But he doesn't have to fret about Hector Jr., his firstborn, the boy with these same great sad eyes who'd sat in the dugout in his Reds uniform when they lived in Cincy and worshiped the pudgy icon of his father until the parish priest had to straighten him out on his hagiography, Hector Jr. who studies English at USC and day and night writes his thesis on a poet his father has never heard of, because here he is, walking in the front door with his mother's smile and a store-wrapped gift—a book, of course. Then Reina's children line up to kiss the *abuelo*— they'll be sitting in the box seats this afternoon—and suddenly he knows so much: He will play today, he will hit, oh yes, can there be a doubt? He sees it already. Kerensky, the son of a whore. Extra innings. Koerner or Manfredonia or Brooksie on third. The ball like an orange, a mango, a muskmelon, the clean swipe of the bat, the delirium of the crowd, and the gimpy *abuelo*, a big leaguer still, doffing his cap and taking a tour of the bases in a stately trot, Sultan for a day.

Could things ever be so simple?

In the bottom of the ninth, with the score tied at five and Reina's kids full of Coke, hotdogs, peanuts, and ice cream and getting restless, with Asunción clutching her rosary as if she were drowning and Hector Jr.'s nose stuck in some book, Dupuy taps him to hit for the pitcher with two down and Fast Freddie Phelan on second. The eighth man in the lineup, Spider Martinez from Muchas Vacas, D.R., has just whiffed on three straight pitches and Corcoran, the Braves' left-handed relief man, is all of a sudden pouring it on. Throughout the stadium a hush has fallen over the crowd, the torpor of suppertime, the game poised at apogee. Shadows are lengthening in the outfield, swallows flitting across the face of the scoreboard, here a fan drops into his beer, there a big mama gathers up her purse, her knitting, her shopping bags and parasol and thinks of dinner. Hector sees it all. This is the moment of catharsis, the moment to take it out.

As Martinez slumps toward the dugout, Dupuy, a laconic, embittered man who keeps his suffering inside and drinks Gelusil like water, takes hold of Hector's arm. His eyes are red-rimmed and paunchy, doleful as a basset hound's. Bring the runner in, Champ, he rasps. First pitch fake a bunt, then hit away. Watch Booger at third. Uh-huh, Hector mumbles, snapping his gum. Then he slides his bat from the rack—white ash, tape-wrapped grip, personally blessed by the Archbishop of Guadalajara and his twenty-seven acolytes—and starts for the dugout steps, knowing the course of the next three minutes as surely as his blood knows the course of his veins. The familiar cry will go up—Cheese, Cheese, Cheesus—and he'll amble up to the batter's box, knocking imaginary dirt

from his spikes, adjusting the straps of his golf gloves, tugging at his
underwear and fiddling with his batting helmet. His face will be impene-
trable. Corcoran will work the ball in his glove, maybe tip back his cap
for a little hair grease and then give him a look of psychopathic hatred.
Hector has seen it before. Me against you. My record, my career, my
house, my family, my life, my mutual funds and beer distributorship
against yours. He's been hit in the elbow, the knee, the groin, the head.
Nothing fazes him. Nothing. Murmuring a prayer to Santa Griselda,
patroness of the sun-blasted Sonoran village where he was born like a
heat blister on his mother's womb, Hector Hernán Jesus y María Quesadilla will step into the batter's box, ready for anything.

But it's a game of infinite surprises.

Before Hector can set foot on the playing field, Corcoran suddenly
doubles up in pain, Phelan goes slack at second, and the catcher and
shortstop are hustling out to the mound, tailed an instant later by trainer
and pitching coach. First thing Hector thinks is a groin pull, then appen-
dicitis, and finally, as Corcoran goes down on one knee, poison. He'd
once seen a man shot in the gut at Obregon City, but the report had
been loud as a thunderclap and he hears nothing now but the enveloping
hum of the crowd. Corcoran is rising shakily, the trainer and pitching
coach supporting him while the catcher kicks meditatively in the dirt,
and now Mueller, the Atlanta *cabeza*, is striding big-bellied out of the
dugout, head down as if to be sure his feet are following orders. Halfway
to the mound, Mueller flicks his right hand across his ear quick as a horse
flicking its tail, and it's all she wrote for Corcoran.

Poised on the dugout steps like a bird dog, Hector waits, his eyes
riveted on the bullpen. Please, he whispers, praying for the intercession
of the Niño and pledging a hundred votary candles—at least, at least.
Can it be? Yes, milk of my Mother, yes—Kerensky himself strutting out
onto the field like a fighting cock. Kerensky!

Come to the birthday boy, Kerensky, he murmurs, so certain he's
going to put it in the stands he could point like the immeasurable Bambino. His tired old legs shuffle with impatience as Kerensky stalks across
the field, and then he's turning to pick Asunción out of the crowd. She's
on her feet now, Reina too, the kids come alive beside her. And Hector
Jr., the book forgotten, his face transfigured with the look of rapture he
used to get when he was a boy sitting on the steps of the dugout. Hector
can't help himself: He grins and gives them the thumbs-up sign.

Then, aas Kerensky fires his warm-up smoke, the loudspeaker crackles
and Hector emerges from the shadow of the dugout into the tapering
golden shafts of the late-afternoon sun. That pitch, I want that one, he
mutters, carrying his bat like a javelin and shooting a glare at Kerensky,

but something's wrong here, the announcer's got it screwed up: BAT-TING FOR RARITAN, NUMBER THIRTY-NINE, DAVE TOOL. What the—? And now somebody's tugging at his sleeve and he's turning to gape with incomprehension at the freckle-faced batboy, Dave Tool striding out of the dugout with his big forty-two-ounce stick, Dupuy's face locked up like a vault, and the crowd, on its feet, chanting Tool, Tool, Tool! For a moment he just stands there, frozen with disbelief. Then Tool is brushing by him and the idiot of a batboy is leading him toward the dugout as if he were an old blind fisherman poised on the edge of the dock.

He feels as if his legs have been cut from under him. Tool! Dupuy is yanking him for Tool? For what? So he can play the lefty-righty percentages like some chess head or something? Tool, of all people. Tool, with his thirty-five home runs a season and lifetime B.A. of .234, Tool who's worn so many uniforms they had to expand the league to make room for him, what's he going to do? Raging, Hector flings down his bat and comes at Dupuy like a cat tossed in a bag. You crazy, you jerk, he sputters. I woulda hit him, I woulda won the game. I dreamed it. And then, his voice breaking: It's my birthday for Christ's sake!

But Dupuy can't answer him, because on the first pitch Tool slams a real worm burner to short and the game is going into extra innings.

By seven o'clock, half the fans have given up and gone home. In the top of the fourteenth, when the visitors came up with a pair of runs on a two-out pinch-hit home run, there was a real exodus, but then the Dodgers struck back for two to knot it up again. Then it was three up and three down, regular as clockwork. Now, at the end of the nineteenth, with the score deadlocked at seven all and the players dragging themselves around the field like gutshot horses, Hector is beginning to think he may get a second chance after all. Especially the way Dupuy's been using up players like some crazy general on the western front, yanking pitchers, juggling his defense, throwing in pinch runners and pinch hitters until he's just about gone through the entire roster. Asunción is still there among the faithful, the foolish, and the self-deluded, fumbling with her rosary and mouthing prayers for Jesus Christ Our Lord, the Madonna, Hector, the hometeam, and her departed mother, in that order. Reina too, looking like the survivor of some disaster, Franklin and Alfredo asleep in their seats, the niñitas gone off somewhere—for Coke and dogs, maybe. And Hector Jr. looks like he's going to stick it out too, though he should be back in his closet writing about the mystical so-and-so and the way he illustrates his poems with gods and mean and serpents. Watching him, Hector can feel his heart turn over.

In the bottom of the twentieth, with one down and Gilley on first—
he's a starting pitcher but Dupuy sent him in to run for Manfredonia
after Manfredonia jammed his ankle like a turkey and had to be helped
off the field—Hector pushes himself up from the bench and ambles
down to where Dupuy sits in the corner, contemplatively spitting a gout
of tobacco juice and saliva into the drain at his feet. Let me hit, Bernard,
come on, Hector says, easing down beside him.

Can't, comes the reply, and Dupuy never even raises his head. Can't
risk it, Champ. Look around you—and here the manager's voice quavers
with uncertainty, with fear and despair and the dull edge of hopeless-
ness—I got nobody left. I hit you, I got to play you.

No, No, you don't understand—I'm going to win it, I swear.

And then the two of them, like old bankrupts on a bench in Miami
Beach, look up to watch Phelan hit into a double play.

A buzz runs through the crowd when the Dodgers take the field for the
top of the twenty-second. Though Phelan is limping, Thorkelsson's
asleep on his feet, and Dorfman, fresh on the mound, is the only pitcher
left on the roster, the moment is electric. One more inning and they tie
the record set by the Mets and Giants back in '64, and then they're
making history. Drunk, sober, and then drunk again, saturated with fats
and nitrates and sugar, the crowd begins to come to life. Go Dodgers!
Eat shit! Yo Mama! Phelan's a bum!

Hector can feel it too. The rage and frustration that had consumed
him back in the ninth are gone, replaced by a dawning sense of wonder—he could have won it then, yes, and against his nemesis Kerensky
too—but the Niño and Santa Griselda have been saving him for something greater. He sees it now, knows it in his bones: He's going to be the
hero of the longest game in history.

As if to bear him out, Dorfman, the kid from Albuquerque, puts in a
good inning, cutting the bushed Braves down in order. In the dugout,
Doc Pusser, the team physician, is handing out the little green pills that
keep your eyes open and Dupuy is blowing into a cup of coffee and
staring morosely out at the playing field. Hector watches as Tool, who'd
stayed in the game at first base, fans on three straight pitches, then he
shoves in beside Dorfman and tells the kid he's looking good out there.
With his big cornhusker's ears and nose like a tweezer, Dorfman could
be a caricature of the green rookie. He says nothing. Hey, don't let it get
to you, kid—I'm going to win this one for you. Next inning or maybe the
inning after. Then he tells him how he saw it in a vision and how it's his
birthday and the kid's going to get the victory, one of the biggest of all
time. Twenty-four, twenty-five innings maybe.

Hector had heard of a game once in the Mexican League that took three days to play and went seventy-three innings, did Dorfman know that? It was down in Culiacán. Chito Martí, the converted bullfighter, had finally ended it by dropping down dead of exhaustion in centerfield, allowing Sexto Silvestro, who'd broken his leg rounding third, to crawl home with the winning run. But Hector doesn't think this game will go that long. Dorfman sighs and extracts a bit of wax from his ear as Pantaleo, the third string catcher, hits back to the pitcher to end the inning. I hope not, he says, uncoiling himself from the bench, my arm'd fall off.

Ten o'clock comes and goes. Dorfman's still in there, throwing breaking stuff and a little smoke at the Braves, who look as if they just stepped out of *Night of the Living Dead.* The hometeam isn't doing much better. Dupuy's run through the whole team but for Hector, and three or four of the guys have been in there since two in the afternoon; the rest are a bunch of ginks and gimps who can barely stand up. Out in the stands, the fans look grim. The vendors ran out of beer an hour back, and they haven't had dogs or kraut or Coke or anything since eight-thirty.

In the bottom of the twenty-seventh Phelan goes berserk in the dugout and Dupuy has to pin him to the floor while Doc Pusser shoves something up his nose to calm him. Next inning the balls-and-strikes ump passes out cold and Dorfman, who's beginning to look a little fagged, walks the first two batters but manages to weasel his way out of the inning without giving up the go-ahead run. Meanwhile, Thorkelsson has been dropping ice cubes down his trousers to keep awake, Martinez is smoking something suspicious in the can, and Ferenc Fortnoi, the third baseman, has begun talking to himself in a tortured Slovene dialect. For his part, Hector feels stronger and more alert as the game goes on. Though he hasn't had a bite since breakfast he feels impervious to the pangs of hunger, as if he were preparing himself, mortifying his flesh like a saint in the desert.

And then, in the top of the thirty-first, with half the fans asleep and the other half staring into nothingness like the inmates of the asylum of Our Lady of Guadeloupe where Hector had once visited his halfwit uncle when he was a boy, Pluto Morales cracks one down the first-base line and Tool flubs it. Right away it looks like trouble, because Chester Bubo is running around right field looking up at the sky like a bird-watcher while the ball snakes through the grass, caroms off his left foot, and coasts like silk to the edge of the warning track. Morales meanwhile is rounding second and coming on for third, running in slow motion, flat-footed and hump-backed, his face drained of color, arms flapping like the undersized wings of some big flightless bird. It's not even close. By the time Bubo can locate the ball, Morales is ten feet from the plate,

pitching into a face-first slide that's at least three parts collapse and
that's it, the Braves are up by one. It looks black for the hometeam. But
Dorfman, though his arm has begun to swell like a sausage, shows some
grit, bears down and retires the side to end the historic top of the unprecedented thirty-first inning.

Now, at long last, the hour has come. It'll be Bubo, Dorfman, and
Tool for the Dodgers in their half of the inning, which means that
Hector will hit for Dorfman. I been saving you, Champ, Dupuy rasps,
the empty Gelusil bottle clenched in his fist like a hand grenade. Go on
in there, he murmurs and his voice fades away to nothing as Bubo pops
the first pitch up in back of the plate. Go on in there and do your stuff.

Sucking in his gut, Hector strides out onto the brightly lit field like a
nineteen-year-old, the familiar cry in his ears, the haggard fans on their
feet, a sickle moon sketched in overhead as if in some cartoon strip
featuring drunken husbands and the milkman. Asunción looks as if she's
been nailed to the cross, Reina wakes with a start and shakes the little
ones into consciousness, and Hector Jr. staggers to his feet like a battered
middleweight coming out for the fifteenth round. They're all watching
him. The fans whose lives are like empty sacks, the wife who wants him
home in front of the TV, his divorced daughter with the four kids and
another on the way, his son, pride of his life, who reads for the doctor of
philosophy while his crazy *padrecito* puts on a pair of long stockings and
chases around after a little white ball like a case of arrested development.
He'll show them. He'll show them some *cojones*, some true grit and
desire: The game's not over yet.

On the mound for the Braves is Bo Brannerman, a big mustachioed
machine of a man, normally a starter but pressed into desperate relief
service tonight. A fine pitcher—Hector would be the first to admit it—
but he just pitched two nights ago and he's worn thin as wire. Hector
steps up to the plate, feeling legendary. He glances over at Tool in the
on-deck circle, and then down at Booger, the third-base coach. All systems go. He cuts at the air twice and then watches Brannerman rear
back and release the ball: Strike one. Hector smiles. Why rush things?
Give them a thrill. He watches a low outside slider that just about
bounces to even the count, and then stands there like a statue as Brannerman slices the corner of the plate for strike two. From the stands, a
chant of *Viejo, Viejo,* and Asunción's piercing soprano, Hit him, Hector!

Hector has no worries, the moment eternal, replayed through games
uncountable, with pitchers who were over the hill when he was a rookie
with San Buitre, with pups like Brannerman, with big leaguers and Hall
of Famers. Here it comes, Hector, ninety-two m.p.h., the big *gringo*

trying to throw it by you, the matchless wrists, the flawless swing, one terrific moment of suspended animation—and all of a sudden you're starring in your own movie.

How does it go? The ball cutting through the night sky like a comet, arching high over the centerfielder's hapless scrambling form to slam off the wall while your legs churn up the base paths, rounding first in a gallop, taking second, and heading for third . . . but wait, you spill hot coffee on your hand and you can't feel it, the demons apply the live wire to your tailbone, the legs give out and they cut you down at third while the stadium erupts in howls of execration and abuse and the *niñitos* break down, faces flooded with tears of humiliation, Hector Jr. turning his back in disgust, and Asunción raging like a harpie, *Abuelo! Abuelo! Abuelo!*

Stunned, shrunken, humiliated, you stagger back to the dugout in a maelstrom of abuse, paper cups, flying spittle, your life a waste, the game a cheat, and then, crowning irony, that bum Tool, worthless all the way back to his washerwoman grandmother and the drunken muttering whey-faced tribe that gave him suck, stands tall like a giant and sends the first pitch out of the park to tie it. Oh, the pain. Flat feet, fire in your legs, your poor tired old heart skipping a beat in mortification. And now Dupuy, red in the face, shouting: The game could be over but for you, you crazy gimpy old beaner washout! You want to hide in your locker, bury yourself under the shower room floor, but you have to watch as the next two men reach base and you pray with fervor that they'll score and put an end to your debasement. But no, Thorkelsson whiffs and the new inning dawns as inevitably as the new minute, the new hour, the new day, endless, implacable, world without end.

But wait, wait: Who's going to pitch? Dorfman's out, there's nobody left, the astonishing thirty-second inning is marching across the scoreboard like an invading army and suddenly Dupuy is standing over you— no, no, he's down on one knee, begging. Hector, he's saying, didn't you use to pitch down in Mexico when you were a kid, didn't I hear that someplace? Yes, you're saying, yes, but that was—

And then you're out on the mound, in command once again, elevated like some half-mad old king in a play, and throwing smoke. The first two batters go down on strikes and the fans are rabid with excitement, Asunción will raise a shrine, Hector Jr. worships you more than all the poets that ever lived, but can it be? You walk the next three and then give up the grand slam to little Tommy Oshimisi! Mother of God, will it never cease? But wait, wait, wait: Here comes the bottom of the thirty-second and Brannerman's wild. He walks a couple, gets a couple out, somebody reaches on an infield single, and the bases are loaded for you, Hector

Quesadilla, stepping up to the plate now like the Iron Man himself. The wind up, the delivery, the ball hanging there like a *piñata,* like a birthday gift, and then the stick flashes in your hands like an archangel's sword, and the game goes on forever.

ANONYMOUS

"MOTHER" (CIRCA 1886)

Mother, may I slay the umpire,
May I slay him right away?
So he cannot be here, Mother,
When the clubs begin to play.
Let me clasp his throat, dear Mother,
In a dear, delightful grip
With one hand and with the other
Bat him several in the lip.
Let me climb his frame, dear Mother
While the happy people shout.
I'll not kill him, dearest Mother,
I will only knock him out.
Let me mop the ground up, Mother,
With his person, dearest, do.
If the ground can stand it, Mother,
I don't see why you can't too.

TOM WOLFE

"The Last American Hero"

When Tom Wolfe went down to North Carolina to research his article on Junior Johnson, the stock-car racer, he thought he ought to dress for the occasion. Putting aside the elegant, tailored white ensembles for which he is known, he picked a green tweed suit, a blue button-down shirt, a black tie, brown suede shoes, and a brown Borsolini hat which he described as "fuzzy."

"Junior Johnson," he told me, "turned out to be a very courtly gentleman, but after a while he remarked that he didn't mean to say anything out of place but . . . and I had the sudden feeling a number of people had asked him: 'Who's that little green man following you around?' It dawned on me that I was the only person within sixty square miles wearing a tie."

Wolfe went on to say that it was actually a liberating moment—that his job was easier because he was so obviously an outsider, "as if I'd arrived in North Carolina from Mars. It makes it easier to ask about overhead cams. They're always talking about overhead cams and if you're dressed the way they are, you're supposed to know about overhead cams. Never again will I try to blend in. People like to have an outsider around so they can explain things like overhead cams."

I asked: "So if you'd gone down to North Carolina in coveralls, crossed suspenders, a red bandana in your hip pocket, cowboy boots, and an Atlanta Braves baseball cap, you probably wouldn't have come away with this great story."

"Quite likely."

Ten o'clock Sunday morning in the hills of North Carolina. Cars, miles of cars, in every direction, millions of cars, pastel cars, aqua green, aqua blue, aqua beige, aqua buff, aqua dawn, aqua dusk, aqua Malacca, Malacca lacquer, Cloud lavender, Assassin pink, Rake-a-Cheek raspberry, Nude Strand coral, Honest Thrill orange, and Baby Fawn Lust cream-colored cars are all going to the stock-car races, and that old mothering North Carolina sun keeps exploding off the windshields.

Seventeen thousand people, me included, all of us driving out Route 421, out to the stock-car races at the North Wilkesboro Speedway, seventeen thousand going out to a five-eighths-mile stock-car track with a Coca-Cola sign out front. This is not to say there is no preaching and shouting in the South this morning. There is preaching and shouting. Any of us can turn on the old automobile transistor radio and get all we want:

"They are greedy dogs. Yeah! They ride around in big cars. Unnh-hunh! And chase women. Yeah! And drink liquor. Unnh-hunh! And smoke cigars. Oh yes! And they are greedy dogs. Yeah! Unh-hunh! Oh yes! Amen!"

There are also some commercials on the radio for Aunt Jemima grits, which cost ten cents a pound. There are also the Gospel Harmonettes, singing: "If you dig a ditch, you better dig two. . . ."

There are also three fools in a panel discussion on the New South, which they seem to conceive of as General Lee running the new Dulci-dreme Labial Cream factory down at Griffin, Georgia.

And suddenly my car is stopped still on Sunday morning in the middle of the biggest traffic jam in the history of the world. It goes for ten miles in every direction from the North Wilkesboro Speedway. And right there it dawns on me that as far as this situation is concerned, anyway, all the conventional notions about the South are confined to . . . the Sunday radio. The South has preaching and shouting, the South has grits, the South has country songs, old mimosa traditions, clay dust, Old Bigots, New Liberals—and all of it, all of that old mental cholesterol, is confined to the Sunday radio. What I was in the middle of—well, it wasn't anything one hears about in panels about the South today. Miles and miles of eye-busting pastel cars on the expressway, which roar right up into the hills, going to the stock-car races. Fifteen years of stock-car racing, and baseball—and the state of North Carolina alone used to have forty-four professional baseball teams—baseball is all over with in the South. We were all in the middle of a wild new thing, the southern car world, and heading down the road on my way to see a breed such as sports never saw before, southern stock-car drivers, all lined up in these two-ton mothers that go over 175 mph, Fireball Roberts, Freddie Lorenzen, Ned Jarrett, Richard Petty, and—the hardest of all the hard chargers, one of the fastest automobile racing drivers in history—yes! Junior Johnson.

The legend of Junior Johnson! In this legend, here is a country boy, Junior Johnson, who learns to drive by running whiskey for his father, Johnson Senior, one of the biggest copper-still operators of all time, up in Ingle Hollow, near North Wilkesboro, in northwestern North Carolina, and grows up to be a famous stock-car racing driver, rich, grossing $100,000 in 1963, for example, respected, solid, idolized in his hometown and throughout the rural South. There is all this about how good old boys would wake up in the middle of the night in the apple shacks and hear a supercharged Oldsmobile engine roaring over Brushy Mountain and say, "Listen at him—there he goes!" although that part is doubtful, since some nights there were so many good old boys taking off down the road in supercharged automobiles out of Wilkes County, and running loads to Charlotte, Salisbury, Greensboro, Winston-Salem, High Point, or wherever, it would be pretty hard to pick one out. It was Junior Johnson specifically, however, who was famous for the "bootleg turn" or "about-face," in which, if the Alcohol Tax agents had a roadblock up for you or were too close behind, you threw the car up into second gear, cocked the wheel, stepped on the accelerator and made the car's rear end skid around in a complete 180-degree arc, a complete about-face, and tore on back up the road exactly the way you came from. God! The Alcohol Tax agents used to burn over Junior Johnson. Practically every good old boy in town in Wilkesboro, the county seat, got to know the agents by sight in a very short time. They would rag them practically to their faces on the subject of Junior Johnson, so that it got to be an obsession. Finally, one night they had Junior trapped on the road up toward the bridge around Millersville, there's no way out of there, they had the barricades up and they could hear this souped-up car roaring around the bend, and here it comes—but suddenly they can hear a siren and see a red light flashing in the grille, so they think it's another agent, and boy, they run out like ants and pull those barrels and boards and sawhorses out of the way, and then—Ggghhzzzzzzzhhhhhhggggg-zzzzzzzeeeeeong!—gawdam! there he goes again, it was him, Junior Johnson! with a gawdam agent's si-reen and a red light in his grille!

I wasn't in the South five minutes before people started making oaths, having visions, telling these hulking great stories, all on the subject of Junior Johnson. At the Greensboro, North Carolina, airport there was one good old boy who vowed he would have eaten "a bucket of it" if that would have kept Junior Johnson from switching from a Dodge racer to a Ford. Hell yes, and after that—God-almighty, remember that 1963 Chevrolet of Junior's? Whatever happened to that car? A couple of more good old boys join in. A good old boy, I ought to explain, is a generic term in the rural South referring to a man, of any age, but more often young than not, who fits in with the status system of the region. It usually means he has a good sense of humor and enjoys ironic jokes, is tolerant and easygoing enough to get along in long conversations at places like on the corner, and has a reasonable amount of physical courage. The term is usually heard in some such form as: "Lud? He's a good old boy from over at Crozet." These good old boys in the airport, by the way, were in their twenties, except for one fellow who was a cabdriver and was about forty-five, I would say. Except for the cabdriver, they all wore neo-Brummellian clothes such as Lacoste tennis shirts, Slim Jim pants, windbreakers with the collars turned up, "fast" shoes of the winkle-picker genre, and so on. I mention these details just by way of pointing out that very few grits, Iron Boy overalls, clodhoppers, or hats with ventilation holes up near the crown enter into this story. Anyway, these good old boys are talking about Junior Johnson and how he has switched to Ford. This they unanimously regard as some kind of betrayal on Johnson's part. Ford, it seems, they regard as the car symbolizing the established power structure. Dodge is kind of a middle ground. Dodge is at least a challenger, not a ruler. But the Junior Johnson they like to remember is the Junior Johnson of 1963, who took on the whole field of NASCAR (National Association for Stock Car Auto Racing) Grand National racing with a Chevrolet. All the other drivers, the drivers driving Fords, Mercurys, Plymouths, Dodges, had millions, literally millions when it is all added up, millions of dollars in backing from the Ford and Chrysler Corporations. Junior Johnson took them all on in a Chevrolet without one cent of backing from Detroit. Chevrolet had pulled out of stock-car racing. Yet every race it was the same. It was never a question of whether anybody was going to *outrun* Junior Johnson. It was just a question of whether he was going to win or his car was going to break down, since, for one thing, half the time he had to make his own racing parts. God! Junior Johnson was like Robin Hood or Jesse James or Little David or something. Every time that Chevrolet, No. 3, appeared on the track, wild curdled yells, "Rebel" yells, they still have those, would rise up. At Daytona, at Atlanta, at Charlotte, at Darlington, South Carolina; Bristol, Tennessee; Martinsville, Virginia—Junior Johnson!

And then the good old boys get to talking about whatever happened to that Chevrolet of Junior's, and the cabdriver says he knows. He says Junior Johnson is using that car to run liquor out of Wilkes County. What does he mean? For Junior Johnson ever to go near another load of bootleg whiskey again—he would have to be insane. He has this huge racing income. He has two other businesses, a whole automated chicken farm with forty-two thousand chickens, a road-grading business—but the cabdriver says he has this dream Junior is still roaring down from Wilkes County, down through the clay cuts, with the Atlas Arc Lip jars full in the back of that Chevrolet. It is in Junior's blood—and then at this point he puts his right hand up in front of him as if he is groping through fog, and his eyeballs glaze over and he looks out in the distance and he describes Junior Johnson roaring over the ridges of Wilkes County as if it is the ghost of Zapata he is describing, bounding over the Sierras on a white horse to rouse the peasants.

A stubborn notion! A crazy notion! Yet Junior Johnson has followers who need to keep him, symbolically, riding through nighttime like a demon. Madness! But Junior Johnson is one of the last of those sports stars who is not just an ace at the game itself, but a hero a whole people or class of people can identify with. Other, older examples are the way Jack Dempsey stirred up the Irish or the way Joe Louis stirred up the Negroes. Junior Johnson is a modern figure. He is only thirty-three years old and still racing. He should be compared to two other sports heroes whose cultural impact is not too well known. One is Antonino Rocca, the professional wrestler, whose triumphs mean so much to New York City's Puerto Ricans that he can fill Madison Square Garden, despite the fact that everybody, the Puerto Ricans included, knows that wrestling is nothing but a crude form of folk theater. The other is Ingemar Johanssen, who had a tremendous meaning to the Swedish masses— they were tired of that old king who played tennis all the time and all his friends who keep on drinking Cointreau behind the screen of socialism. Junior Johnson is a modern hero, all involved with car culture and car symbolism in the South. A wild new thing—

Wild—gone wild, Fireball Roberts's Ford spins out on the first turn at the North Wilkesboro Speedway, spinning, spinning, the spin seems almost like slow motion—and then it smashes into the wooden guardrail. It lies up there with the frame bent. Roberts is all right. There is a new layer of asphalt on the track, it is like glass, the cars keep spinning off the first turn. Ned Jarrett spins, smashes through the wood. "Now, boys, this ice ain't gonna get one goddamn bit better, so you can either line up and qualify or pack up and go home—"

I had driven from the Greensboro airport up to Wilkes County to see Junior Johnson on the occasion of one of the two yearly NASCAR Grand National stock-car races at the North Wilkesboro Speedway.

It is a long, very gradual climb from Greensboro to Wilkes County. Wilkes County is all hills, ridges, woods and underbrush, full of pin oaks, sweet-gum maples, ash, birch, apple trees, rhododendron, rocks, vines, tin roofs, little clapboard places like the Mount Olive Baptist Church, signs for things like Double Cola, Sherrill's Ice Cream, Eckard's Grocery, Dr. Pepper, Diel's Apples, Google's Place, Suddith's Place, and— yes!—cars. Up onto the highway, out of a side road from a hollow, here comes a 1947 Hudson. To almost anybody it would look like just some old piece of junk left over from God knows when, rolling down a country road ... the 1947 Hudson was one of the first real "hot" cars made after the war. Some of the others were the 1946 Chrysler, which had a "kick-down" gear for sudden bursts of speed, the 1955 Pontiac, and a lot of the Fords. To a great many good old boys a hot car was a symbol of heating up life itself. The war! Money even for country boys! And the money bought cars. In California they suddenly found kids of all sorts involved in vast drag-racing orgies and couldn't figure out what was going on. But in the South the mania for cars was even more intense, although much less publicized. To millions of good old boys, and girls, the automobile represented not only liberation from what was still pretty much a land-bound form of social organization but also a great leap forward into twentieth-century glamour, an idea that was being dinned in on the South like everywhere else. It got so that one of the typical rural sights, in addition to the red rooster, the gray split-rail fence, the Edgeworth Tobacco sign, and the rusted-out harrow, one of the typical rural sights would be ... you would be driving along the dirt roads and there beside the house would be an automobile up on blocks or something, with a rope over the tree for hoisting up the motor or some other heavy part, and a couple of good old boys would be practically disappearing into its innards, from below and from above, draped over the side under the hood. It got so that on Sundays there wouldn't be a safe straight stretch of road in the county, because so many wild country boys would be out racing or just raising hell on the roads. A lot of other kids, who weren't basically wild, would be driving like hell every morning and every night, driving to jobs perhaps thirty or forty miles away, jobs that were available only because of automobiles. In the morning they would be driving through the dapple shadows like madmen. In the hollows, sometimes one would come upon the most incredible tar-paper hovels, down near the stream, and out front would be an incredible automobile creation, a late-model car with aerials, Continental kit overhangs in the back, mud-guards studded with reflectors, fender skirts, spotlights, God knows what all, with a girl and perhaps a couple of good old boys communing over it and giving you rotten looks as you drove by. On Saturday night every-body would drive into town and park under the lights on the main street and neck. Yes! There was something about being right in there in town underneath the lights and having them reflecting off the baked enamel on the hood. Then if a good old boy insinuated his hands here and there on the front seat with a girl and began ... necking ... somehow it was all more *complete*. After the war there was a great deal of stout-burgher talk about people who lived in hovels and bought big-yacht cars to park out front. This was one of the symbols of a new, spendthrift age. But there was a great deal of unconscious resentment buried in the talk. It was resentment against (a) the fact that the good old boy had his money at all and (b) the fact that the car symbolized freedom, a slightly wild, careening emancipation from the old social order. Stock-car racing got started about this time, right after the war, and it was immediately regarded as some kind of manifestation of the animal irresponsibility of the lower orders. It had a truly terrible reputation. It was—well, it looked *rowdy* or something. The cars were likely to be used cars, the tracks were dirt, the stands were rickety wood, the drivers were country boys, and they had regular feuds out there, putting each other "up against the wall" and "cutting tires" and everything else. Those country boys would drive into the curves full tilt, then slide maniacally, sometimes coming around the curve sideways, with red dirt showering up. Sometimes they would race at night, under those weak-eyed yellow-ocher lights they have at small tracks and baseball fields, and the clay dust would start showering up in the air, where the evening dew would catch it, and all evening long you would be sitting in the stands or standing out in the infield with a fine clay-mud drizzle coming down on you, not that anybody gave a damn— except for the southern upper and middle classes, who never attended in those days, but spoke of the "rowdiness."

But mainly it was the fact that stock-car racing was something that was welling up out of the lower orders. From somewhere these country boys and urban proles were getting the money and starting this hellish sport.

Stock-car racing was beginning all over the country, at places like Allentown, Langhorne, and Lancaster, Pennsylvania, and out in California and even out on Long Island, but wherever it cropped up, the Establishment tried to wish it away, largely, and stock-car racing went on in a kind of underground world of tracks built on cheap stretches of land well out from the town or the city, a world of diners, drive-ins, motels, gasoline stations, and the good burghers might drive by from time to time, happen by on a Sunday or something, and see the crowd gathered from out of nowhere, the cars coming in, crowding up the highway a little, but Monday morning they would be all gone, and all would be as it was.

Stock-car racing was building up a terrific following in the South during the early fifties. Here was a sport not using any abstract devices, any *bat* and *ball*, but the same automobile that was changing a man's own life, his own symbol of liberation, and it didn't require size, strength, and all that, all it required was a taste for speed, and the guts. The newspapers in the South didn't seem to catch on to what was happening until late in the game. Of course, newspapers all over the country have looked backward over the tremendous rise in automobile sports, now the second-biggest type of sports in the country in terms of attendance. The sports pages generally have an inexorable lower-middle-class outlook. The sportswriter's "zest for life" usually amounts, in the end, to some sort of gruff Mom's Pie sentimentality at a hideously cozy bar somewhere. The sportswriters caught on to Grand Prix racing first because it had "tone," a touch of defrocked European nobility about it, what with a few counts racing here and there, although, in fact, it is the least popular form of racing in the United States. What finally put stock-car racing onto the sports pages in the South was the intervention of the Detroit automobile firms. Detroit began putting so much money into the sport that it took on a kind of massive economic respectability and thereby, in the lower-middle-class brain, status.

What Detroit discovered was that thousands of good old boys in the South were starting to form allegiances to brands of automobiles, according to which were hottest on the stock-car circuits, the way they used to have them for the hometown baseball team. The South was one of the hottest car-buying areas in the country. Cars like Hudsons, Oldsmobiles, and Lincolns, not the cheapest automobiles by any means, were selling in disproportionate numbers in the South, and a lot of young good old boys were buying them. In 1955, Pontiac started easing into stock-car racing, and suddenly the big surge was on. Everybody jumped into the sport to grab for themselves The Speed Image. Suddenly, where a good old boy used to have to bring his gasoline to the track in old filling-station pails and pour it into the tank through a funnel when he made a pit stop, and change his tires with a hand wrench, suddenly, now, he had these "gravity" tanks of gasoline that you just jam into the gas pipe, and air wrenches to take the wheels off, and whole crews of men in white coveralls to leap all over a car when it came rolling into the pit, just like they do at Indianapolis, as if they are mechanical apparati *merging* with the machine as it rolls in, forcing water into the radiator, jacking up the car, taking off wheels, wiping off the windshield, handing the driver a cup of orange juice, all in one synchronized operation. And now, today, the *big money* starts descending on this little place, the North Wilkesboro, North Carolina, Speedway, a little five-eights-of-a-mile stock-car track with a Coca-Cola sign out by the highway where the road in starts.

The private planes start landing out at the Wilkesboro Airport. Freddie Lorenzen, the driver, the biggest money winner last year in stock-car racing, comes sailing in out of the sky in a twin-engine Aero Commander, and there are a few good old boys out there in the tall grass by the runway already with their heads sticking up watching this hero of the modern age come in and taxi up and get out of that twin-engine airplane with his blond hair swept back as if by the mother internal combustion engine of them all. And then Paul Goldsmith, the driver, comes in in a

310 Cessna, and *he* gets out, all these tall, lanky, hard-boned Americans in their thirties with these great profiles like a comic-strip hero or something, and then Glenn (Fireball) Roberts—Fireball Roberts!—Fireball is *hard*—he comes in in a Comanche 250, like a flying yacht, and then Ray Nichels and Ray Fox, the chief mechanics, who run big racing crews for the Chrysler Corporation, this being Fox's last race for Junior as his mechanic, before Junior switches over to Ford, they come in in two-engine planes. And even old Buck Baker—hell, Buck Baker is a middling driver for Dodge, but even he comes rolling down the landing strip at two hundred miles an hour with his southern-hero face at the window of the cockpit of a twin-engine Apache, traveling first class in the big status boat that has replaced the yacht in America, the private plane.

And then the Firestone and Goodyear vans pull in, huge mothers, bringing in huge stacks of racing tires for the race, big wide ones, 8.20s, with special treads, which are like a lot of bumps on the tire instead of grooves. They even have special tires for qualifying, soft tires, called "gumballs," they wouldn't last more than ten times around the track in a race, but for qualifying, which is generally three laps, one to pick up speed and two to race against the clock, they are great, because they hold tight on the corners. And on a hot day, when somebody like Junior Johnson, one of the fastest qualifying runners in the history of the sport, 170.777 mph in a 100-mile qualifying race at Daytona in 1964, when somebody like Junior Johnson really pushes it on a qualifying run, there will be a ring of blue smoke up over the whole goddamned track, a ring like an oval halo over the whole thing from the gumballs burning, and some good old boy will say, "Great smokin' blue gumballs God-almighty dog! There goes Junior Johnson!"

The thing is, each one of these tires costs fifty-five to sixty dollars, and on a track that is fast and hard on tires, like Atlanta, one car might go through ten complete tire changes, easily, forty tires, or almost twenty-five hundred dollars' worth of tires just for one race. And he may even be out of the money. And then the Ford van and the Dodge van and the Mercury van and the Plymouth van roll in with new motors, a whole new motor every few races, a 427-cubic-inch stock-car racing motor, 600 horsepower, the largest and most powerful allowed on the track, that probably costs the company a thousand dollars or more, when you consider that they are not mass-produced. And still the advertising appeal. You can buy the very same car that these fabulous wild men drive every week at these fabulous wild speeds, and some of their power and charisma is yours. After every NASCAR Grand National stock-car race, whichever company has the car that wins, this company will put big ads in the southern papers, and papers all over the country if it is a very big race, like the Daytona 500, the Daytona Firecracker 400, or the Atlanta and Charlotte races. They sell a certain number of these 427-cubic-inch cars to the general public, a couple of hundred a year, perhaps, at eight or nine thousand dollars apiece, but it is no secret that these motors are specially reworked just for stock-car racing. Down at Charlotte there is a company called Holman & Moody that is supposed to be the "garage" or "automotive-engineering" concern that prepares automobiles for Freddie Lorenzen and some of the other Ford drivers. But if you go by Holman & Moody out by the airport and Charlotte, suddenly you come upon a huge place that is a *factory,* for godsake, a big long thing, devoted mainly to the business of turning out stock-car racers. A whole lot of other parts in stock-car racers are heavier than the same parts on a street automobile, although they are made to the same scale. The shock absorbers are bigger, the wheels are wider and bulkier, the swaybars and steering mechanisms are heavier, the axles are much heavier, they have double sets of wheel bearings, and so forth and so on. The bodies of the cars are pretty much the same, except that they use lighter sheet metal, practically tinfoil. Inside, there is only the driver's seat and a heavy set of roll bars and diagonal struts that turn the inside of the car into a rigid cage, actually. That is why the drivers can walk away unhurt—most of the time—from the most spectacular crackups. The gearshift is the floor kind, although it doesn't make much difference, as there is almost no shifting gears in stock-car racing. You just get into high gear and go. The dashboard has no speedometer, the main thing being the dial for engine revolutions per minute. So, anyway, it costs about fifteen thousand dollars to prepare a stock-car racer in the first place and another three or four thousand for each new race, and this does not even count the costs of mechanics' work and transportation. All in all, Detroit will throw around a quarter of a million dollars into it every week while the season is on, and the season runs, roughly, from February to October, with a few big races after that. And all this turns up even out at the North Wilkesboro Speedway in the up-country of Wilkes County, North Carolina.

Sunday! Racing day! There is the Coca-Cola sign out where the road leads in from the highway, and hills and trees, but here are long concrete grandstands for about seventeen thousand and a paved five-eights-mile oval. Practically all the drivers are out there with their cars and their crews, a lot of guys in white coveralls. The cars look huge . . . and curiously nude and blind. All the chrome is stripped off, except for the grilles. The headlights are blanked out. Most of the cars are in the pits. The so-called pit is a paved cutoff on the edge of the infield. It cuts off from the track itself like a service road off an expressway at the shopping center. Every now and then a car splutters, hacks, coughs, hocks a lunga, rumbles out onto the track itself for a practice run. There is a lot of esoteric conversation going on, speculation, worries, memoirs:

"What happened?"

"Mother—— condensed on me. Al brought it up here with him. Water in the line."

"Better keep Al away from a stable, he'll fill you up with horse manure."

". . . they told me to give him one, a creampuff, so I give him one, a creampuff. One goddam race and the son of a bitch, he *melted* it. . . ."

". . . he's down there right now pettin' and rubbin' and huggin' that car just like those guys do a horse at the Kentucky Derby. . . ."

". . . They'll blow you right out of the tub. . . ."

". . . No, the quarter inch, and go on over and see if you can get Ned's blowtorch. . . ."

". . . Rear end's loose. . . ."

". . . I don't reckon this right here's got nothing to do with it, do you? . . ."

". . . Aw, I don't know, about yea big. . . ."

". . . Who the hell stacked them gumballs on the bottom? . . ."

". . . th'owing rocks. . . ."

". . . won't turn seven thousand. . . ."

". . . strokin' it. . . ."

". . . blistered. . . ."

". . . spun out. . . ."

". . . muvva. . . ."

Then, finally, here comes Junior Johnson. How he does come on. He comes tooling across the infield in a big white dreamboat, a brand-new white Pontiac Catalina four-door hard-top sedan. He pulls up and as he gets out he seems to get more and more huge. First his crew-cut head and then a big jaw and then a bigger neck and then a huge torso, like a wrestler's, all done up rather modish and California modern, with a red-and-white candy-striped sport shirt, white ducks, and loafers.

"How are you doing?" says Junior Johnson, shaking hands, and then he says, "Hot enough for ye'uns?"

Junior is in an amiable mood. Like most up-hollow people, it turns out, Junior is reserved. His face seldom shows an emotion. He has three basic looks: amiable, amiable and a little shy, and dead serious. To a lot of people, apparently, Junior's dead-serious look seems menacing. There are no cowards left in stock-car racing, but a couple of drivers tell me that one of the things that can shake you up is to look into your rearview mirror going around a curve and see Junior Johnson's car on your tail trying to "root you out of the groove," and then get a glimpse of Junior's dead-serious look. I think some of the sportswriters are afraid of him. One of them tells me Junior is strong, silent—and explosive. Junior will only give you three answers, "Uh-huh," "Uh-unh," and "I don't know," and so forth and so on. Actually, I found he handles questions easily. He has a great technical knowledge of automobiles and the physics of speed, including things he never fools with, such as Offenhauser engines. What he never does offer, however, is small talk. This gives him a built-in poise, since it deprives him of the chance to say anything asinine. "Ye'uns," "we'uns," "h'it" for "it," "growed" for "grew," and a lot of other unusual past participles—Junior uses certain older forms of English, not exactly "Elizabethan," as they are sometimes called, but older forms of English preserved up-country in his territory, Ingle Hollow.

Kids keep coming up for Junior's autograph and others are just hanging around and one little boy comes up, he is about thirteen, and Junior says: "This boy here goes coon hunting with me."

One of the sportswriters is standing around, saying: "What do you shoot a coon with?"

"Don't shoot 'em. The dogs tree 'em and then you flush 'em out and the dogs fight 'em."

"Flush 'em out?"

"Yeah. This boy right here can flush 'em out better than anybody you ever did see. You go out at night with the dogs, and soon as they get the scent, they start barking. They go on out ahead of you and when they tree a coon, you can tell it, by the way they sound. They all start baying up at that coon—h'it sounds like, I don't know, you hear it once and you not likely to forget it. Then you send a little old boy up to flush him out and he jumps down and the dogs fight him."

"How does a boy flush him out?"

"Aw, he just climbs up there to the limb he's on and starts shaking h'it and the coon'll jump."

"What happens if the coon decides he'd rather come back after the boy instead of jumping down to a bunch of dogs?"

"He won't do that. A coon's afraid of a person, but he can kill a dog. A coon can take any dog you set against him if they's just the two of them fighting. The coon jumps down on the ground and he rolls right over on his back with his feet up, and he's got claws about like this. All he has to do is get a dog once in the throat or in the belly, and he can kill him, cut him wide open just like you took a knife and did it. Won't any dog even fight a coon except a coon dog."

"What kind of dogs are they?"

"*Coon* dogs, I guess. Black and tans, they call 'em sometimes. They's bred for it. If his mammy and pappy wasn't coon dogs, he ain't likely to be one either. After you got once, you got to train him. You trap a coon, live, and then you put him in a pen and tie him to a post with a rope on him and then you put your dog in there and he has to fight him. Sometimes you get a dog just don't have any fight in him and he ain't no good to you."

Junior is in the pit area, standing around with his brother Fred, who is part of his crew, and Ray Fox and some other good old boys, in a general atmosphere of big stock-car money, a big ramp truck for his car, a white Dodge, Number 3, a big crew in white coveralls, huge stacks of racing tires, a Dodge PR man, big portable cans of gasoline, compressed air hoses, compressed water hoses, the whole business. Herb Nab, Freddie Lorenzen's chief mechanic, comes over and sits down on his haunches and Junior sits down on his haunches and Nab says:

"So Junior Johnson's going to drive a Ford."

Junior is switching from Dodge to Ford mainly because he hasn't been winning with the Dodge. Lorenzen drives a Ford, too, and the last year, when Junior was driving the Chevrolet, their duels were the biggest excitement in stock-car racing.

"Well," says Nab, "I'll tell you, Junior. My ambition is going to be to outrun your ass every goddamned time we go out."

"That was your ambition last year," says Junior.

"I know it was," says Nab, "and you took all the money, didn't you? You know what my strategy was. I was going to outrun everybody else and outlast Junior, that was my strategy."

Setting off his California modern sport shirt and white ducks Junior has on a pair of twenty-dollar rimless sunglasses and a big gold Timex watch, and Flossie, his fiancée, is out there in the infield somewhere with the white Pontiac, and the white Dodge that Dodge gave Junior is parked up near the pit area—and then a little thing happens that brings the whole thing right back there to Wilkes County, North Carolina, to Ingle Hollow and to hard muscle in the clay gulches. A couple of good old boys come down to the front of the stands with the screen and the width of the track between them and Junior, and one of the good old boys comes down and yells out in the age-old baritone raw-curdle yell of the southern hills:

"Hey! Hog jaw!"

Everybody gets quiet. They know he's yelling at Junior, but nobody says a thing. Junior doesn't even turn around.

"Hey, hog jaw! . . ."

Junior, he does nothing.

"Hey, hog jaw, I'm gonna get me one of them fastback roosters, too, and come down there and get you!"

Fastback rooster refers to the Ford—it has a "fastback" design—
Junior is switching to.

"Hey, hog jaw, I'm gonna get me one of them fastback roosters and
run you right out of here, you hear me, hog jaw!"

One of the good old boys alongside Junior says, "Junior, go on up
there and clear out those stands."

Then everybody stares at Junior to see what he's gonna do. Junior, he
doesn't even look around. He just looks a bit dead serious.

"Hey, hog jaw, you got six cases of whiskey in the back of that car you
want to let me have?

"What you hauling in that car, hog jaw!"

"Tell him you're out of that business, Junior," one of the good old
boys says.

"Go on up there and clean house, Junior," says another good old boy.

Then Junior looks up, without looking at the stands, and smiles a little
and says, "You flush him down here out of that tree—and I'll take keer
of him."

Such a howl goes up from the good old boys! It is almost a blood
curdle—

"Goddamn, he *will,* too!"

"Lord, he better know how to do an *about-face* hissef if he comes
down here!"

"Goddamn, get him, Junior!"

"Whooeeee!"

"Mother dog!"

—a kind of orgy of reminiscence of the old Junior before the Detroit
money started flowing, wild *combats d'honneur* up-hollow—and, suddenly, when he heard that unearthly baying coming up from the good
old boys in the pits, the good old boy retreated from the edge of the
stands and never came back.

Later on Junior told me, sort of apologetically, "H'it used to be, if a
fellow crowded me just a little bit, I was ready to crawl him. I reckon that
was one good thing about Chillicothe.

"I don't want to pull any more time," Junior tells me, "but I wouldn't
take anything in the world for the experience I had in prison. If a man
needed to change, that was the place to change. H'it's not a waste of
time there, h'it's good experience.

"H'it's that they's so many people in the world that feel that nobody is
going to tell them what to do. I had quite a temper, I reckon. I always
had the idea that I had as much sense as the other person and I didn't
want them to tell me what to do. In the penitentiary there I found out
that I could listen to another fellow and be told what to do and h'it
wouldn't kill me."

Starting time! Linda Vaughn, with the big blond hair and blossomy breasts, puts down her Coca-Cola and the potato chips and slips off her red stretch pants and her white blouse and walks out of the officials' booth in her Rake-a-Cheek red showgirl's costume with her long honey-dew legs in net stockings and climbs up on the red Firebird float. The Life Symbol of stock-car racing! Yes! Linda, every luscious morsel of Linda, is a good old girl from Atlanta who was made Miss Atlanta International Raceway one year and was paraded around the track on a float and she liked it so much and all the good old boys liked it so much, Linda's flowing hair and blossomy breasts and honeydew legs, that she became the permanent glamour symbol of stock-car racing, and never mind this other modeling she was doing . . . this, she liked it. Right before practically every race on the Grand National circuit Linda Vaughn puts down her Coca-Cola and potato chips. Her momma is there, she generally comes around to see Linda go around the track on the float, it's such a nice spectacle seeing Linda looking so lovely, and the applause and all. "Linda, I'm thirstin', would you bring me a Coca-Cola?" "A lot of them think I'm Freddie Lorenzen's girlfriend, but I'm not any of 'em's girlfriend, I'm real good friends with 'em all, even Wendell," he being Wendell Scott, the only Negro in big-league stock-car racing. Linda gets up on the Firebird float. This is an extraordinary object, made of wood, about twenty feet tall, in the shape of a huge bird, an eagle or something, blazing red, and Linda, with her red showgirl's suit on, gets up on the seat, which is up between the wings, like a saddle, high enough so her long honeydew legs stretch down, and a new car pulls her—Miss Firebird!—slowly once around the track just before the race. It is more of a ceremony by now than the national anthem. Miss Firebird sails slowly in front of the stands and the good old boys let out some real curdle Rebel yells: "Yaaaaaaaaaaaaaghhhhoooooo! Let me at that car!" "Honey, you sure do start my motor, I swear to God!" "Great God and Poonadingdong, I mean!"

And suddenly there's a big roar from behind, down in the infield, and then I see one of the great sights in stock-car racing. That infield! The cars have been piling into the infield by the hundreds, parking in there on the clay and the grass, every which way, angled down and angled up, this way and that, where the ground is uneven, these beautiful blazing brand-new cars with the sun exploding off the windshields and the baked enamel and the glassy lacquer, hundreds, thousands of cars stacked this way and that in the infield with the sun bolting down and no shade, none at all, just a couple of Coca-Cola stands out there. And already the good old boys and girls are out beside the cars, with all these beautiful little buds in short shorts already spread-eagled out on top of the car roofs, pressing down on good hard slick automobile sheet metal, their little cupcake bottoms aimed up at the sun. The good old boys are lollygagging around with their shirts off and straw hats on that have miniature beer cans on the brims and buttons that read, Girls Wanted—No Experience Required. And everybody, good old boys and girls of all ages, is out there with portable charcoal barbecue ovens set up, and folding tubular steel terrace furniture, deck chairs and things, and thermos jugs and coolers full of beer—and suddenly it is not the up-country South at all but a concentration of the modern suburbs, all jammed into that one space, from all over America, with blazing cars and instant goodies, all cooking under the bare blaze—inside a strange bowl. The infield is like the bottom of a bowl. The track around it is banked so steeply at the corners and even on the straightaways, it is like the steep sides of a bowl. The wall around the track, and the stands and the bleachers are like the rim of a bowl. And from the infield, in this great incredible press of blazing new cars, there is no horizon but the bowl, up above only that cobalt-blue North Carolina sky. And then suddenly, on a signal, thirty stock-car engines start up where they are lined up in front of the stands. The roar of these engines is impossible to describe. They have a simultaneous rasp, thunder, and rumble that goes right through a body and fills the whole bowl with a noise of internal combustion. Then they start around on two buildup runs, just to build up speed, and then they come around the fourth turn and onto the straightaway in front of the stands at—here, 130 miles an hour; in Atlanta, 160 miles an hour; at Daytona, 180 miles an hour—and the flag goes down and everybody in the infield and in the stands is up on their feet going mad, and suddenly here is a bowl that is one great orgy of everything in the way of excitement and liberation the automobile has meant to Americans. An orgy!

The first lap of a stock-car race is a horrendous, a wildly horrendous spectacle such as no other sport approaches. Twenty, thirty, forty automobiles, each of them weighing almost two tons, 3,700 pounds, with 427-cubic-inch engines, 600 horsepower, are practically locked together, side to side and tail to nose, on a narrow band of asphalt at 130, 160, 180 miles an hour, hitting the curves so hard the rubber burns off the tires in front of your eyes. To the driver, it is like being inside a car going down the West Side Highway in New York City at rush hour, only with everybody going literally three to four times as fast, at speeds a man who has gone 85 miles an hour down a highway cannot conceive of, and with every other driver an enemy who is willing to cut inside of you, around you, or in front of you, or ricochet off your side in the battle to get into a curve first.

The speeds are faster than those in the Indianapolis 500 race, the cars are more powerful and much heavier. The prize money in southern stock-car racing is far greater than that in Indianapolis-style or European Grand Prix racing, but few Indianapolis or Grand Prix drivers have the raw nerve required to succeed at it.

Although they will deny it, it is still true that stock-car drivers will put each other "up against the wall"—cut inside on the left of another car and ram it into a spin—if they get mad enough. Crashes are not the only danger, however. The cars are now literally too fast for their own parts, especially the tires. Firestone and Goodyear have poured millions into stock-car racing, but neither they nor anybody so far has been able to come up with a tire for this kind of racing at the current speeds. Three well-known stock-car drivers were killed last year, two of them champion drivers, Joe Weatherly and Fireball Roberts, and another, one of the best new drivers, Jimmy Pardue, from Junior Johnson's own home territory, Wilkes County, North Carolina. Roberts was the only one killed in a crash. Junior Johnson was in the crash but was not injured. Weatherly and Pardue both lost control on curves. Pardue's death came during a tire test. In a tire test, engineers from Firestone or Goodyear try out various tires on a car, and the driver, always one of the top competitors, tests them at top speed, usually on the Atlanta track. The drivers are paid three dollars a mile and may drive as much as five or six hundred miles in a single day. At 145 miles an hour average that does not take very long. Anyway, these drivers are going at speeds that, on curves, can tear tires off their casings or break axles. They practically run off from over their own wheels.

Junior Johnson was over in the garden by the house some years ago, plowing the garden barefooted, behind a mule, just wearing an old pair of overalls, when a couple of good old boys drove up and told him to come on up to the speedway and get in a stock-car race. They wanted some local boys to race, as a preliminary to the main race, "as a kind of side show," as Junior remembers it.

"So I just put the reins down," Junior is telling me, "and rode on over 'ere with them. They didn't give us seat belts or nothing, they just roped us in. H'it was a dirt track then. I come in second."

Junior was a sensation in dirt-track racing right from the start. Instead of going into the curves and just sliding and holding on for dear life like the other drivers, Junior developed the technique of throwing himself into a slide about seventy-five feet before the curve by cocking the wheel to the left slightly and gunning it, using the slide, not the brake, to slow down, so that he could pick up speed again halfway through the curve and come out of it like a shot. This was known as his "power slide," and—yes! of course!—every good old boy in North Carolina started saying Junior Johnson had learned that stunt doing those goddamned *about-faces* running away from the Alcohol Tax agents. Junior put on such a show one night on a dirt track in Charlotte that he broke two axles, and he thought he was out of the race because he didn't have any more axles, when a good old boy came running up out of the infield and said, "Goddamn it, Junior Johnson, you take the axle off my car here, I got a Pontiac just like yours," and Junior took it off and put it on his and went out and broke *it* too. Mother dog! To this day Junior Johnson loves dirt-track racing like nothing else in this world, even though there is not much money in it. Every year he sets new dirt-track speed records, such as at Hickory, North Carolina, one of the most popular dirt tracks, last spring. As far as Junior is concerned, dirt-track racing is not so much of a mechanical test for the car as those long five- and six-hundred-mile races on asphalt are. Gasoline, tire, and engine wear aren't so much of a problem. It is all the driver, his skill, his courage—his willingness to mix it up with the other cars, smash and carom off of them at a hundred miles an hour or so to get into the curves first. Junior has a lot of fond recollections of mixing it up at places like Bowman Gray Stadium in Winston-Salem, one of the minor-league tracks, a very narrow track, hardly wide enough for two cars. "You could always figure Bowman Gray was gonna cost you two fenders, two doors, and two quarter panels," Junior tells me with nostalgia.

Anyway, at Hickory, which was a Saturday-night race, all the good old boys started pouring into the stands before sundown, so they wouldn't miss anything, the practice runs or the qualifying or anything. And pretty soon, the dew hasn't even started falling before Junior Johnson and David Pearson, one of Dodge's best drivers, are out there on practice runs, just warming up, and they happen to come up alongside each other on the second curve, and—the thing is, here are two men, each of them driving fifteen-thousand-dollar automobiles, each of them standing to make fifty thousand to a hundred thousand dollars for the season if they don't get themselves killed, and they meet on a curve on a goddamned practice run on a dirt track, and neither of them can resist it. Coming out of the turn they go into a wild-ass race down the backstretch, both of them trying to get into the third turn first, and all the way across the infield you can hear them ricocheting off each other and bouncing at a hundred miles an hour on loose dirt, and then they go into ferocious power slides, red dust all over the goddamned place, and then out of this goddamned red-dust cloud, out of the fourth turn, here comes Junior Johnson first, like a shot, with Pearson right on his tail, and the good old boys in the stands going wild, and the *qualifying* runs haven't started yet, let alone the race.

Junior worked his way up through the minor leagues, the Sportsman and Modified classifications, as they are called, winning championships in both, and won his first Grand National race, the big leagues, in 1955 at Hickory, on dirt. He was becoming known as "the hardest of the hard-chargers," power sliding, rooting them out of the groove, raising hell, and already the Junior Johnson legend was beginning.

He kept hard-charging, power sliding, going after other drivers as though there wasn't room on the track but for one, and became the most popular driver in stock-car racing by 1959. The presence of Detroit and Detroit's big money had begun to calm the drivers down a little. Detroit was concerned about Image. The last great duel of the dying dog-cat-dog era of stock-car racing came in 1959, when Junior and Lee Petty, who was then leading the league in points, had it out on the Charlotte raceway. Junior was in the lead, and Petty was right on his tail, but couldn't get by Junior. Junior kept coming out of the curves faster. So every chance he got, Petty would get up right on Junior's rear bumper and start banging it, gradually forcing the fender in to where the metal would cut Junior's rear tire. With only a few laps to go, Junior had a blowout and spun out up against the guardrail. That is Junior's version. Petty claimed Junior hit a pop bottle and spun out. The fans in Charlotte were always throwing pop bottles and other stuff onto the track late in the race, looking for blood. In any case, Junior eased back into the pits, had the tire changed, and charged out after Petty. He caught him on a curve and—well, whatever really happened, Petty was suddenly "up against the wall" and out of the race, and Junior won.

What a howl went up. The Charlotte chief of police charged out onto the track after the race, according to Petty, and offered to have Junior arrested for "assault with a dangerous weapon," the hassling went on for weeks—

"Back then," Junior tells me, "when you got into a guy and racked him up, you might as well get ready, because he's coming back for you. H'it was dog eat dog. That straightened Lee Petty out right smart. They don't do stuff like that anymore, though, because the guys don't stand for it."

Anyway, the Junior Johnson legend kept building up and building up, and in 1960 it got hotter than ever when Junior won the biggest race of the year, the Daytona 500, by discovering a new technique called "drafting." That year stock-car racing was full of big powerful Pontiacs manned by top drivers, and they would go like nothing else anybody ever saw. Junior went down to Daytona with a Chevrolet.

"My car was about ten miles an hour slower than the rest of the cars, the Pontiacs," Junior tells me. "In the preliminary races, the warm-ups and stuff like that, they was smoking me off the track. Then I remember once I went out for a practice run, and Fireball Roberts was out there in

a Pontiac and I got in right behind him on a curve, right on his bumper.
I knew I couldn't stay with him on the straightaway, but I came out of
the curve fast, right in behind him, running flat out, and then I noticed a
funny thing. As long as I stayed right in behind him, I noticed I picked
up speed and stayed right with him and my car was going faster than it
had ever gone before. I could tell on the tachometer. My car wasn't
turning no more than six thousand before, but when I got into this
drafting position, I was turning sixty-eight hundred to seven thousand.
H'it felt like the car was plumb off the ground, floating along."

"Drafting," it was discovered at Daytona, created a vacuum behind
the lead car and both cars would go faster than they normally would.
Junior "hitched rides" on the Pontiacs most of the afternoon, but was
still second to Bobby Johns, the lead Pontiac. Then, late in the race,
Johns got into a drafting position with a fellow Pontiac that was actually
one lap behind him and the vacuum got so intense that the rear window
blew out of Johns's car and he spun out and crashed and Junior won.

This made Junior the Lion-Killer, the Little David of stock-car racing,
and his performance in the 1963 season made him even more so.

Junior raced for Chevrolet at Daytona in February 1963, and set the
all-time stock-car speed record in a hundred-mile qualifying race, 164.-
083 miles an hour, 21 miles an hour faster than Parnelli Jones's winning
time at Indianapolis that year. Junior topped that at Daytona in July of
1963, qualifying at 166.005 miles per hour in a five-mile run, the fastest
that anyone had ever averaged that distance in a racing car of any type.
Junior Johnson's Chevrolet lasted only twenty-six laps in the Daytona
500 in 1963, however. He went out with a broken push rod. Although
Chevrolet announced they were pulling out of racing at this time, Junior
took his car and started out on the wildest performance in the history of
stock-car racing. Chevrolet wouldn't give him a cent of backing. They
wouldn't even speak to him on the telephone. Half the time he had to
have his own parts made. Plymouth, Mercury, Dodge, and Ford, meantime, were pouring more money than ever into stock-car racing. Yet
Junior won seven Grand National races out of the thirty-three he entered and led most others before mechanical trouble forced him out.

All the while, Junior was making record qualifying runs, year after
year. In the usual type of qualifying run, a driver has the track to himself
and makes two circuits, with the driver with the fastest average time
getting the "pole" position for the start of the race. In a way this presents stock-car danger in its purest form. Driving a stock car does not
require much handling ability, at least not as compared to Grand Prix
racing, because the tracks are simple banked ovals and there is almost no
shifting of gears. So qualifying becomes a test of raw nerve—of how fast
a man is willing to take a curve. Many of the top drivers in competition

are poor at qualifying. In effect, they are willing to calculate their risks only against the risks the other drivers are taking. Junior takes the pure risk as no other driver has ever taken it.

"Pure" risk or total risk, whichever, Indianapolis and Grand Prix drivers have seldom been willing to face the challenge of southern stock-car drivers. A. J. Foyt, last year's winner at Indianapolis, is one exception. He has raced against the southerners and beaten them. Parnelli Jones has tried and fared badly. Driving "southern style" has a quality that shakes a man up. The southerners went on a tour of northern tracks last fall. They raced at Bridgehampton, New York, and went into the corners so hard the marshals stationed at each corner kept radioing frantically to the control booth: "They're going off the track. They're all going off the track."

But this, Junior Johnson's last race in a Dodge, was not his day, either for qualifying or for racing. Lorenzen took the lead early and won the 250-mile race a lap ahead of the field. Junior finished third, but was never in contention for the lead.

"Come on, Junior, do my hand—"

Two or three hundred people come out of the stands and up out of the infield and onto the track to be around Junior Johnson. Junior is signing autographs in a neat left-handed script he has. It looks like it came right out of the Locker book. The girls! Levi's, stretch pants, sneaky shorts, stretch jeans, they press into the crowd with lively narbs and try to get their hands up in front of Junior and say:

"Come on, Junior, do my hand!"

In order to do a hand, Junior has to hold the girl's hand in his right hand and then sign his name with a ball-point pen on the back of her hand.

"Junior, you got to do mine, too!"

"Put it on up here."

All the girls break into . . . smiles. Junior Johnson does a hand. Ah, sweet little cigarette-ad blond! She says:

"Junior, why don't you ever call me up?"

"I 'spect you got plenty of calls 'thout me."

"Oh, Junior! You call me up, you hear now?"

But also a great many older people crowd in, and they say:

"Junior, you're doing a real good job out there, you're driving real good."

"Junior, when you get in that Ford, I want to see you pass that Freddie Lorenzen, you hear now?"

"Junior, you like that Ford better than that Dodge?"

And:

"Junior, here's a young man that's been waiting some time and wanting to see you—" and the man lifts up his little boy in the middle of the crowd and says: "I told you you'd see Junior Johnson. This here's Junior Johnson!"

The boy has a souvenir racing helmet on his head. He stares at Junior through a buttery face. Junior signs the program he has in his hand, and then the boy's mother says:

"Junior, I tell you right now, he's beside you all the way. He can't be moved."

And then:

"Junior, I want you to meet the meanest little girl in Wilkes County."

"She don't look mean to me."

Junior keeps signing autographs and over by the pits the other kids are all over his car, the Dodge. They start pulling off the decals, the ones saying Holly Farms Poultry and Autolite and God knows what-all. They fight over the strips, the shreds of decal, as if they were totems.

All this homage to Junior Johnson lasts about forty minutes. He must be signing about two hundred fifty autographs, but he is not a happy man. By and by the crowd is thinning out, the sun is going down, wind is blowing the Coca-Cola cups around, all one can hear, mostly, is a stock-car engine starting up every now and then as somebody drives it up onto a truck or something, and Junior looks around and says:

"I'd rather lead one lap and fall out of the race than stroke it and finish in the money."

"Stroking it" is driving carefully in hopes of outlasting faster and more reckless cars. The opposite of stroking it is "hard-charging." Then Junior says:

"I hate to get whipped up here in Wilkes County, North Carolina."

Wilkes County, North Carolina! Who was it tried to pin the name on Wilkes County, "The bootleg capital of America"? This fellow Vance Packard. But just a minute . . .

The night after the race Junior and his fiancée, Flossie Clark, and myself went into North Wilkesboro to have dinner. Junior and Flossie came by Lowes Motel and picked us up in the dreamboat white Pontiac. Flossie is a bright, attractive woman, *zaftig*, well-organized. She and Junior have been going together since they were in high school. They are going to get married as soon as Junior gets his new house built. Flossie has been doing the decor. Junior Johnson, in the second-highest income bracket in the United States for the past five years, is moving out of his father's white frame house in Ingle Hollow at last. About three hundred yards down the road. Overlooking a lot of good green land and Anderson's grocery. Junior shows me through the house, it is almost finished, and when we get to the front door, I ask him, "How much of this land is yours?"

Junior looks around for a minute, and then back up the hill, up past his three automated chicken houses, and then down into the hollow over the pasture where his $3,100 Santa Gertrudis bull is grazing, and then he says:

"Everything that's green is mine."

Junior Johnson's house is going to be one of the handsomest homes in Wilkes County. Yes. And—such complicated problems of class and status. Junior is not only a legendary figure as a backwoods boy with guts who made good, he is also popular personally, he is still a good old boy, rich as he is. He is also respected for the sound and sober way he has invested his money. He also has one of the best business connections in town, Holly Farms Poultry. What complicates it is that half the county, anyway, reveres him as the greatest, most fabled night-road driver in the history of southern bootlegging. There is hardly a living soul in the hollows who can conjure up two seconds' honest moral indignation over "the whiskey business." That is what they call it, "the whiskey business." The fact is, it has some positive political overtones, sort of like the IRA in Ireland. The other half of the county—well, North Wilkesboro itself is a prosperous, good-looking town of five thousand, where a lot of hearty modern business burghers are making money the modern way, like everywhere else in the U.S.A., in things like banking, poultry processing, furniture, mirror, and carpet manufacture, apple growing, and so forth and so on. And one thing these men are tired of is Wilkes County's reputation as a center of moonshining. The U.S. Alcohol and Tobacco Tax agents sit over there in Wilkesboro, right next to North Wilkesboro, year in and year out, and they have been there since God knows when, like an Institution in the land, and every day that they are there, it is like a sign saying, Moonshine County. And even that is not so *bad*—it has nothing to do with it being immoral and only a little to do with it being illegal. The real thing is, it is—raw and hillbilly. And one thing thriving modern Industry is not is hillbilly. And one thing the burghers of North Wilkesboro are not about to be is hillbilly. They have split-level homes that would knock your eyes out. Also swimming pools, white Buick Snatchwagons, flagstone *terrasse-*porches enclosed with louvered glass that opens wide in the summertime, and built-in brick barbecue pits and they give parties where they wear Bermuda shorts and Jax stretch pants and serve rum collins and play twist and bossa nova records on the hi-fi and tell Shaggy Dog jokes about strange people ordering martinis. Moonshining . . . just a minute—the truth is, North Wilkesboro . . .

So we are all having dinner at one of the fine new restaurants in North
Wilkesboro, a place of surburban plate-glass elegance. The manager
knows Junior and gives us the best table in the place and comes over and
talks to Junior awhile about the race. A couple of men get up and come
over and get Junior's autograph to take home to their sons and so forth.
Then toward the end of the meal a couple of North Wilkesboro busi-
nessmen come over ("Junior, how are you, Junior. You think you're
going to like that fast-backed Ford?") and Junior introduces them to me.

"You're not going to do like that fellow Vance Packard did, are you?"

"Vance Packard?"

"Yeah, I think it was Vance Packard wrote it. He wrote an article and
called Wilkes County the bootleg capital of America. Don't pull any of
that stuff. I think it was in *American* magazine. The bootleg capital of
America. Don't pull any of that stuff on us."

I looked over at Junior and Flossie. Neither one of them said anything.
They didn't even change their expressions.

The next morning I met Junior down in Ingle Hollow at Anderson's
Store. That's about fifteen miles out of North Wilkesboro on County
Road No. 2400. Junior is known in a lot of southern newspapers as "the
wild man from Ronda" or "the lead-footed chicken farmer from
Ronda," but Ronda is only his post-office-box address. His telephone
exchange, with the Wilkes Telephone Membership Corporation, is
Clingman, North Carolina, and that isn't really where he lives either.
Where he lives is just Ingle Hollow, and one of the communal centers of
Ingle Hollow is Anderson's Store. Anderson's is not exactly a grocery
store. Out front there are two gasoline pumps under an overhanging
roof. Inside there are a lot of things like a soda-pop cooler filled with ice,
Coca-Colas, Nehi drinks, Dr. Pepper, Double Cola, and a gumball machine, a lot of racks of Red Man chewing tobacco, Price's potato chips,
OKay peanuts, cloth hats for working outdoors in, dried sausages, cigarettes, canned goods, a little bit of meal and flour, fly swatters, and I
don't know what-all. Inside and outside of Anderson's there are good old
boys. The young ones tend to be inside, talking, and the old ones tend to
be outside, sitting under the roof by the gasoline pumps, talking. And on
both sides, cars; most of them new and pastel.

Junior drives up and gets out and looks up over the door where there is
a row of twelve coon tails. Junior says:

"Two of them gone, ain't they?"

One of the good old boys says, "Yeah," and sighs.

A pause, and the other one says, "Somebody stole 'em."

Then the first one says, "Junior, that dog of yours ever come back?"

Junior says, "Not yet."

The second good old boy says, "You looking for her to come back?"

Junior says, "I reckon she'll come back."

The good old boy says, "I had a coon dog went off like that. They don't ever come back. I went out 'ere one day, back over yonder, and there he was, cut right from here to here. I swear if it don't look like a coon got him. Something. H'it must of turned him every way but loose."

Junior goes inside and gets a Coca-Cola and rings up the till himself, like everybody who goes into Anderson's does, it seems like. It is dead quiet in the hollow except for every now and then a car grinds over the dirt road and down the way. One coon dog missing. But he still has a lot of the black and tans, named Rock. . . .

. . . Rock, Whitey, Red, Buster are in the pen out back of the Johnson house, the old frame house. They have scars all over their faces from fighting coons. Gypsy has one huge gash in her back from fighting something. A red rooster crosses the lawn. That's a big rooster. Shirley, one of Junior's two younger sisters, pretty girls, is out by the fence in shorts, pulling weeds. Annie May is inside the house with Mrs. Johnson. Shirley has the radio outside on the porch aimed at her, the Four Seasons! "Dawn!—ahhhh, ahhhhh, ahhhhhh!" Then a lot of electronic wheeps and lulus and a screaming disc jockey, yessss! WTOB, the Vibrant Mothering Voice of Winston-Salem, North Carolina. It sounds like WABC in New York. Junior's mother, Mrs. Johnson, is a big, good-natured woman. She comes out and says, "Did you ever see anything like that in your life? Pullin' weeds listenin' to the radio." Junior's father, Robert Glenn Johnson, Sr.—he built this frame house about thirty-five years ago, up here where the gravel road ends and the wood starts. The road just peters out into the woods up a hill. The house has a living room, four bedrooms, and a big kitchen. The living room is full of Junior's racing trophies, and so is the piano in Shirley's room. Junior was born and raised here with his older brothers, L. P., the oldest, and Fred, and his older sister, Ruth. Over yonder, up by that house, there's a man with a mule and a little plow. That's L. P. The Johnsons still keep that old mule around to plow the vegetable gardens. And all around, on all sides, like a rim, are the ridges and the woods. Well, what about those woods, where Vance Packard said the agents come stealing over the ridges and good old boys go crashing through the underbrush to get away from the still and the women start "calling the cows" up and down the hollows as the signal *they were coming.* . . .

Junior motions his hand out toward the hills and says, "I'd say nearly everybody in a fifty-mile radius of here was in the whiskey business at one time or another. When we growed up here, everybody seemed to be more or less messing with whiskey, and myself and my two brothers did quite a bit of transporting. H'it was just a business, like any other business, far as we was concerned. H'it was a matter of survival. During the Depression here, people either had to do that or starve to death. H'it wasn't no gangster type of business or nothing. They's nobody that ever messed with it here that was ever out to hurt anybody. Even if they got caught, they never tried to shoot anybody or anything like that. Getting caught and pulling time, that was just part of it. H'it was just a business, like any other business. Me and my brothers, when we went out on the road at night, h'it was just like a milk run, far as we was concerned. They was certain deliveries to be made and. . . ."

A milk run—yes! Well, it was a business, all right. In fact, it was a regional industry, all up and down the Appalachian slopes. But never mind the Depression. It goes back a long way before that. The Scotch-Irish settled the mountains from Pennsylvania down to Alabama, and they have been making whiskey out there as long as anybody can remember. At first it was a simple matter of economics. The land had a low crop yield, compared to the lowlands, and even after a man struggled to grow his corn, or whatever, the cost of transporting it to the markets from down out of the hills was so great, it wasn't worth it. It was much more profitable to convert the corn into whiskey and sell that. The trouble started with the federal government on that score almost the moment the Republic was founded. Alexander Hamilton put a high excise tax on whiskey in 1791, almost as soon as the Constitution was ratified. The "Whiskey Rebellion" broke out in the mountains of Western Pennsylvania in 1794. The farmers were mad as hell over the tax. Fifteen thousand federal troops marched out to the mountains and suppressed them. Almost at once, however, the trouble over the whiskey tax became a symbol of something bigger. This was a general enmity between the western and eastern sections of practically every seaboard state. Part of it was political. The eastern sections tended to control the legislatures, the economy, and the law courts, and the western sections felt short changed. Part of it was cultural. Life in the western sections was rougher. Religions, codes and styles of life were sterner. Life in the eastern capitals seemed to give off the odor of Europe and decadence. Shays's Rebellion broke out in the Berkshire hills of western Massachusetts in 1786 in an attempt to shake off the yoke of Boston, which seemed as bad as George III's. To this day people in western Massachusetts make proposals, earnestly or with down-in-the-mouth humor, that they all ought to split off from "Boston." Whiskey—the mountain people went right on making it. Whole sections of the Appalachians were a whiskey belt, just as sections of Georgia, Alabama, and Mississippi were a cotton belt. Nobody on either side ever had any moral delusions about why the federal government was against it. It was always the tax, pure and simple. Today the price of liquor is 60 percent tax. Today, of course, with everybody gone wild over the subject of science and health, it has been much easier for the federals to persuade people that they crack down on moonshine whiskey because it is dangerous, it poisons, kills, and blinds people. The statistics are usually specious.

Moonshining was *illegal*, however; that was also the unvarnished truth. And that had a side effect in the whiskey belt. The people there were already isolated, geographically, by the mountains and had strong clan ties because they were all from the same stock, Scotch-Irish. Moonshining isolated them even more. They always had to be careful who came up there. There are plenty of hollows to this day where if you drive in and ask some good old boy where so-and-so is, he'll tell you he never heard of the fellow. Then the next minute, if you identify yourself and give some idea of why you want to see him, and he believes you, he'll suddenly say, "Aw, you're talking about *so-and-so.* I thought you said—" With all this isolation, the mountain people began to take on certain characteristics normally associated, by the diffident civilizations of today, with tribes. There was a strong sense of family, clan, and honor. People would cut and shoot each other up over honor. And physical courage! They were almost like Turks that way.

In the Korean War, there were seventy-eight Medal of Honor winners. Thirty-two of them were from the South, and practically all of the thirty-two were from small towns in or near the Appalachians. The New York metropolitan area, which has more people than all these towns put together, had three Medal of Honor winners, and one of them had just moved to New York from the Appalachian region of West Virginia. Three of the Medal of Honor winners came from within fifty miles of Junior Johnson's side porch.

Detroit had discovered these pockets of courage, almost like a natural resource, in the form of Junior Johnson and about twenty other drivers. There is something exquisitely ironic about it. Detroit is now engaged in the highly sophisticated business of offering the illusion of Speed for Everyman—making their cars go 175 miles an hour on racetracks—by discovering and putting behind the wheel a breed of mountain men who are living vestiges of a degree of physical courage that became extinct in most other sections of the country by 1900. Of course, very few stock-car drivers have ever had anything to do with the whiskey business. A great many always lead quiet lives off the track. But it is the same strong

people among whom the whiskey business developed who produced the
kind of men who could drive the stock cars. There are a few exceptions,
Freddie Lorenzen, from Elmhurst, Illinois, being the most notable. But,
by and large, it is the rural southern code of honor and courage that has
produced these, the most daring men in sports.

Cars and bravery! The mountain-still operators had been running white
liquor with hopped-up automobiles all during the thirties. But it was
during the war that the business was so hot out of Wilkes County, down
to Charlotte, High Point, Greensboro, Winston-Salem, Salisbury, places
like that; a night's run, by one car, would bring anywhere from five
hundred to a thousand dollars. People had money all of a sudden. One
car could carry twenty-two to twenty-five cases of white liquor. There
were twelve half-gallon fruit jars full per case, so each load would have
132 gallons or more. It would sell to the distributor in the city for about
ten dollars a gallon, when the market was good, of which the driver
would get two dollars, as much as three hundred dollars for the night's
work.

The usual arrangement in the white liquor industry was for the elders
to design the distillery, supervise the formulas and the whole distilling
process, and take care of the business end of the operation. The young
men did the heavy work, carrying the copper and other heavy goods out
into the woods, building the still, hauling in fuel—and driving. Junior
and his older brothers, L.P. and Fred, worked that way with their father,
Robert Glenn Johnson, Sr.

Johnson Senior was one of the biggest individual copper-still operators
in the area. The fourth time he was arrested, the agents found a small
fortune in working corn mash bubbling in the vats.

"My daddy was always a hard worker," Junior is telling me. "He
always wanted something a little bit better. A lot of people resented that
and held that against him, but what he got, he always got h'it by hard
work. There ain't no harder work in the world than making whiskey. I
don't know of any other business that compels you to get up at all times
of night and go outdoors in the snow and everything else and work. H'it's
the hardest way in the world to make a living, and I don't think anybody'd do it unless they had to."

Working mash wouldn't wait for a man. It started coming to a head
when it got ready to and a man had to be there to take it off, out there in
the woods, in the brush, in the brambles, in the muck, in the snow.
Wouldn't it have been something if you could have just set it all up
inside a good old shed with a corrugated metal roof and order those parts
like you want them and not have to smuggle all that copper and all that

sugar and all that everything out here in the woods and be a coppersmith and a plumber and a copper and a carpenter and a pack horse and every other goddamned thing God ever saw in this world, all at once.

And live decent hours—Junior and his brothers, about two o'clock in the morning they'd head out to the stash, the place where the liquor was hidden after it was made. Sometimes it would be somebody's house or an old shed or someplace just out in the woods, and they'd make their arrangements out there, what the route was and who was getting how much liquor. There wasn't anything ever written down. Everything was cash on the spot. Different drivers lived to make the run at different times, but Junior and his brother always liked to start out from 3:00 to 4:00 A.M. But it got so no matter when you started out you didn't have those roads to yourself.

"Some guys liked one time and some guys liked another time," Junior is saying, "but starting about midnight they'd be coming out of the woods from every direction. Some nights the whole road was full of bootleggers. It got so some nights they'd be somebody following you going just as fast as you were and you didn't know who h'it was, the law or somebody else hauling whiskey."

And it was just a business, like any other business, just like a milk route—but this funny thing was happening. In those wild-ass times, with the money flush and good old boys from all over the country running that white liquor down the road ninety miles an hour and more than that if you try to crowd them a little bit—well, the funny thing was, it got to be competitive in an almost aesthetic, a pure sporting way. The way the good old boys got to hopping up their automobiles—it got to be a science practically. Everybody was looking to build a car faster than anybody ever had before. They practically got into industrial espionage over it. They'd come up behind one another on those wild-ass nights on the highway, roaring through the black gulches between the clay cuts and the trees, pretending like they were officers, just to challenge them, test them out, race . . . *pour le sport,* you mothers, careening through the darkness, old Carolina moon. All these cars were registered in phony names. If a man had to abandon one, they would find license plates that traced back to . . . nobody at all. It wasn't anything, particularly, to go down to the motor vehicle bureau and get some license plates, as long as you paid your money. Of course, it's rougher now, with compulsory insurance. You have to have your insurance before you can get your license plates, and that leads to a lot of complications. Junior doesn't know what they do about that now. Anyway, all these cars with the magnificent engines were plain on the outside, so they wouldn't attract attention, but they couldn't disguise them altogether. They were jacked up a little in the back and had 8.00 or 8.20 tires, for the heavy loads, and the sound—

"They wasn't no way you could make it sound like an ordinary car," says Junior.

God-almighty, that sound in the middle of the night, groaning, roaring, humming down into the hollows, through the clay gulches—yes! And all over the rural South, hell, all over the South, the legends of wild-driving whiskey running got started. And it wasn't just the plain excitement of it. It was something deeper, the symbolism. It brought into a modern focus the whole business, one and a half centuries old, of the country people's rebellion against the federals, against the seaboard establishment, their independence, their defiance of the outside world. And it was like a mythology for that and for something else that was happening, the whole wild thing of the car as the symbol of liberation in the postwar South.

"They was out about every night, patrolling, the agents and the state police was," Junior is saying, "but they seldom caught anybody. H'it was like the dogs chasing the fox. The dogs can't catch a fox, he'll just take 'em around in a circle all night long. I was never caught for transporting. We never lost but one car and the axle broke on h'it."

The fox and the dogs! Whiskey running certainly had a crazy game-like quality about it, considering that a boy might be sent up for two years or more if he were caught transporting. But these boys were just wild enough for that. There got to be a code about the chase. In Wilkes County nobody, neither the good old boys nor the agents, ever did anything that was going to hurt the other side physically. There was supposed to be some parts of the South where the boys used smoke screens and tack buckets. They had attachments in the rear of the cars, and if the agents got too close they would let loose a smoke screen to blind them or a slew of tacks to make them blow a tire. But nobody in Wilkes County ever did that because that was a good way for somebody to get killed. Part of it was that whenever an agent did get killed in the South, whole hordes of agents would come in from Washington and pretty soon they would be tramping along the ridges practically inch by inch, smoking out the stills. But mainly it was—well, the code. If you got caught, you went along peaceably, and the agents never used their guns. There were some tense times. Once was when the agents started using tack belts in Iredell County. This was a long strip of leather studded with nails that the agents would lay across the road in the dark. A man couldn't see it until it was too late and he stood a good chance of getting killed if it got his tires and spun him out. The other was the time the state police put a roadblock down there at that damned bridge at Millersville to catch a couple of escaped convicts. Well, a couple of good old boys rode up with a load, and there was the roadblock and they were already on the bridge, so they jumped out and dove into the water. The police saw two men jump out of their car and dive in the water, so they opened fire and they shot one good old boy in the backside. As they pulled him out, he kept saying:

"What did you have to shoot at me for? What did you have to shoot at me for?"

It wasn't pain, it wasn't anguish, it wasn't anger. It was consternation. The bastards had broken the code.

Then the federals started getting radio cars.

"The radios didn't do them any good," Junior says. "As soon as the officers got radios, then *they* got radios. They'd go out and get the same radio. H'it was an awful hard thing for them to radio them down. They'd just listen in on the radio and see where they're setting up the roadblocks and go a different way."

And such different ways. The good old boys knew back roads, dirt roads, up people's back lanes and every which way, and an agent would have to live in the North Carolina hills a lifetime to get to know them. There wasn't hardly a stretch of road on any of the routes where a good old boy couldn't duck off the road and into the backcountry if he had to. They had wild detours around practically every town and every intersection in the region. And for tight spots—the legendary devices, the "bootleg slide," the siren and the red light. . . .

It was just a matter of keeping up with the competition. You always have to have the latest equipment. It was a business thing, like any other business, you have to stay on top—"They was some guys who was more dependable, they done a better job"—and it may have been business to Junior, but it wasn't business to a generation of good old boys growing up all over the South. The Wilkes County bootleg cars started picking up popular names in a kind of folk hero worship—"The Black Ghost," "The Grey Ghost," which were two of Junior's, "Old Mother Goose," "The Midnight Traveler," "Old Faithful."

And then one day in 1955 some agents snuck over the ridges and caught Junior Johnson at his daddy's still. Junior Johnson, the man couldn't *any*body catch!

The arrest caught Junior just as he was ready to really take off in his career as a stock-car driver. Junior says he hadn't been in the whiskey business in any shape or form, hadn't run a load of whiskey for two or three years, when he was arrested. He says he didn't need to fool around with running whiskey after he got into stock-car racing, he was making enough money at that. He was just out there at the still helping his daddy with some of the heavy labor, there wasn't a good old boy in Ingle Hollow who wouldn't help his daddy lug those big old cords of ash wood, it doesn't give off much smoke, out in the woods. Junior was sentenced to two years in the federal reformatory in Chillicothe, Ohio.

"If the law felt I should have gone to jail, that's fine and dandy," Junior tells me. "But I don't think the true facts of the case justified the sentence I got. I never had been arrested in my life. I think they was punishing me for the past. People get a kick out of it because the officers can't catch somebody, and this angers them. Soon as I started getting publicity for racing, they started making it real hot for my family. I was out of the whiskey business, and they knew that, but they was just waiting to catch me on something. I got out after serving ten months and three days of the sentence, but h'it was two or three years I was set back, about half of fifty-six and every bit of fifty-seven. H'it takes a year to really get back into h'it after something like that. I think I lost the prime of my racing career. I feel that if I had been given the chance I feel I was due, rather than the sentence I got, my life would have got a real boost."

But, if anything, the arrest only made the Junior Johnson legend hotter.

And all the while Detroit kept edging the speeds up, from 150 mph in 1960 to 155 to 165 to 175 to 180 flat out on the longest straightaway, and the good old boys of southern stock-car racing stuck right with it. Any speed Detroit would give them they would take right with them into the curve, hard-charging even though they began to feel strange things such as the rubber starting to pull right off the tire casing. And God! Good old boys from all over the South roared together after the Stanchion—Speed! Guts!—pouring into Birmingham, Daytona Beach, Randleman, North Carolina; Spartanburg, South Carolina; Weaverville, Hillsboro, North Carolina; Atlanta, Hickory, Bristol, Tennessee; Augusta, Georgia; Richmond, Virginia; Asheville, North Carolina; Charlotte, Myrtle Beach—tens of thousands of them. And still upper- and middle-class America, even in the South, keeps its eyes averted. Who cares! They kept on heading out where we all live, after all, out amongst the drive-ins, white-enameled filling stations, concrete aprons, shopping-plaza apothecaries, show-window steak houses, Burger-Ramas, Bar-B-Cubicles, and Miami aqua-swimming-pool motor inns, on out the highway . . . even outside a town like Darlington, a town of ten thousand souls, God, here they come, down Route 52, up 401, on 340, 151, and 34, on through the South Carolina lespedeza fields. By Friday night already the good old boys are pulling the infield of the Darlington race-way with those blazing pastel dreamboats stacked this way and that on the clay flat and the tubular terrace furniture and the sleeping bags and the thermos jugs and the brown whiskey bottles coming on out. By Sunday—the race!—there are sixty-five thousand piled into the race-track at Darlington. The sheriff, as always, sets up the jail right there in the infield. No use trying to haul them out of there. And now—the *sound* rises up inside the raceway, and a good ole boy named Ralph goes mad and starts selling chances on his Dodge. Twenty-five cents and you can take the sledge he has and smash his car anywhere you want. How they roar when the windshield breaks! The police could interfere, you know, but they are busy chasing a good old girl who is playing Lady Godiva on a hogbacked motorcycle, naked as sin, hauling around and in and out of the clay ruts.

Eyes averted, happy burghers. On Monday the ads start appearing— for Ford, for Plymouth, for Dodge—announcing that we gave it to you, speed such as you never saw. There it was! At Darlington, Daytona, Atlanta—and not merely in the southern papers but in the albino pages of the suburban women's magazines, such as the *New Yorker,* in color— the Ford winners, such as Fireball Roberts, grinning with a cigar in his mouth in the *New Yorker* magazine. And somewhere, some Monday morning, Jim Pascal of High Point, Ned Jarrett of Boykin, Cale Yarborough of Timmonsville and Curtis Crider from Charlotte, Bobby Isaac of Catawba, E. J. Trivette of Deep Gap, Richard Petty of Randleman, Tiny Lund of Cross, South Carolina; Stick Elliott of Shelby—and from out of Ingle Hollow—

And all the while, standing by in full Shy, in alumicron suits—there is Detroit, hardly able to believe itself what it has discovered, a breed of good old boys from the fastnesses of the Appalachian hills and flats—a handful from this rare breed—who have given Detroit . . . speed . . . and the industry can present it to a whole generation as . . . yours. And the Detroit PR men themselves come to the tracks like folk worshipers and the millions go giddy with the thrill of speed. Only Junior Johnson goes about it as if it were . . . the usual. Junior goes on down to Atlanta for the Dixie 400 and drops by the federal penitentiary to see his daddy. His daddy is in on his fifth illegal distillery conviction; in the whiskey business that's just part of it; an able craftsman, an able businessman, and the law kept hounding him, that was all. So Junior drops by and then goes on out to the track and gets in his new Ford and sets the qualifying speed record for Atlanta Dixie 400, 146.301 mph; later on he tools on back up the road to Ingle Hollow to tend to the automatic chicken houses and the road-grading operation. Yes.

Yet how can you tell that to . . . anybody . . . out on the bottom of that bowl as the motor thunder begins to lift up through him like a sigh and his eyeballs glaze over and his hands reach up and there, riding the rim of the bowl, soaring over the ridges, is Junior's yellow Ford . . . which is his white Chevrolet . . . which is a White Ghost, forever rousing the good old boys . . . hard-charging! . . . up with the automobile into their America, and the hell with arteriosclerotic old boys trying to hold on to the whole pot with arms of cotton seersucker. Junior!

PAUL WEST

"PELÉ"

I do not look where I am going, not so long as others do it for me. I am that holy rubber eel, the missing link who shoots to kill and cries out *Love, Love, Love.* To read my mind you have to catch my body first. I make full use of the void between chin and kneecap, and you do not. I live off it, even when I am upside down.

My fame, they say, is the trigonometry of feint, then a ball struck curving by the first and only Brazilian atomic foot cannon. I do comets without tails. I am a black fluid with a volcanic alias. You cannot find me with anything in my possession. I loll at the horizon, *belo horizonte,* waiting to head the ball into play. I am Brazil's whispered S, and when I uncoil I am no longer human or Brazilian. I am the wind, the wave, the crown prince of skywriting. Gather up my dust.

Pay-lay, they cry, a hundred thousand at each adoration. *Pay-lay,* Pelé cries back with tears of trembling awe. Now pass the sun to me, between their legs, behind their backs, without seeming to do anything at all, and watch me cage it in the net.

RICHMOND LATTIMORE

"Sky Diving"

They step from the high plane and begin to tumble
down. Below is the painted ground, above
is bare sky. They do not fumble
with the catch, but only fall; drop sheer; begin to move

in the breakless void; stretch and turn, freed
from pressure; stand in weightless air
and softly walk across their own speed;
gather and group, these dropping bundles, where

the neighbor in the sky stands, reach touch
and clasp hands, separate and swim
back to station (did swimmer ever shear such
thin water?) falling still. Now at last pull the slim

cord. Parasols bloom in the air, slow
the swift sky fall. Collapsed tents cover
the ground. They rise up, plain people now.
Their little sky-time is over.

LAWRENCE RITTER

"Fred Snodgrass"

*One of the more taxing things about the baseball profession is that it
never forgives or forgets its major sinners. Their reputations are stamped
irrevocably with their misfortunes—as if a debt to society had been
incurred which could never be absolved: Bill Buckner of the Red Sox*

who let a ball go through his legs, Mickey Owen who dropped a third strike, Ralph Branca who served up Bobby Thomson's home run . . . the list is long. I once talked to Branca about the effect his error had on him. He was rather encouraging. "If I walked down the street with Bobby Thomson," he said, "I think more people would recognize me. They look at me and wonder if I'm all right. I went through that terrible thing. What did it do to me? It's not that they appreciate a loser. But they're curious about how a man's difficulties affect him—it's awfully close to their own lives, and it makes them feel better to see that someone can go through that and walk around and smile and function. They want reassurances."

Perhaps the most extraordinary example of being branded seemingly forever is the case of Fred Snodgrass of the New York Giants. His dropped fly ball in the 1912 World Series supposedly cost the Giants the Series. His indiscretion didn't bother him any more than Branca was bothered by his. After he retired from baseball, he became a successful banker and rancher, and eventually the mayor of Oxnard, California. But when he died fifty-nine years after his error, the headline in the New York Times *read "FRED SNODGRASS DIES: BALLPLAYER MUFFED 1912 FLY." The article began "Fred Carlisle Snodgrass, who muffed an easy fly ball that helped cost the New York Giants in the 1912 World Series, died Friday at the age of 86." The obituary writer did relate Snodgrass's post-baseball triumphs in California, but kept being drawn back to dwell on the indiscretion committed during the course of a second or so on a fall day nearly sixty years before. "Mr. Snodgrass made a two-base muff of pinch hitter Clyde Engle's pop fly [note that Snodgrass is not let off the hook with an unmodified "fly"—it is an "easy" chance] to set up the tying run. One man walked and another singled, driving in Mr. Engle to tie the game and put the winning run on third. A long outfield fly scored the winning run. He is survived by his widow, Josephine; two daughters," etc.*

What follows is Lawrence Ritter's edited interview with Snodgrass which appears in his book The Glory of Their Times.

Often I have been asked to tell what I did to Fred Snodgrass
after he dropped that fly ball in the World Series of 1912,
eleven years ago. Well, I will tell you exactly what I did: I
raised his salary $1,000.

     —JOHN J. McGRAW, *My Thirty Years in Baseball*

I look back at my years in baseball with a tremendous amount of pleasure. Yes, I'd love to do it all over again, and that in spite of the fact that I had what might be called a rather stormy career in baseball.

For over half a century I've had to live with the fact that I dropped a ball in a World Series—"Oh yes, you're the guy that dropped that fly ball, aren't you?"—and for years and years, whenever I'd be introduced to somebody, they'd start to say something and then stop, you know, afraid of hurting my feelings. But nevertheless, those were wonderful years, and if I had the chance I'd gladly do it all over again, every bit of it.

Of course, playing baseball was more than just fun. For a youngster, it was quite an education, too. Especially it was an education to play under John J. McGraw. He was a great man, really a wonderful fellow, and a great manager to play for.

Naturally, McGraw and I didn't always see things alike. I was a headstrong, quick-tempered, twenty-year-old kid when I joined the Giants in 1908. And sometimes Mr. McGraw would bawl the dickens out of me, as he did everybody else. Any mental error, any failure to think, and McGraw would be all over you. And I do believe he had the most vicious tongue of any man who ever lived. Absolutely! Sometimes that wasn't very easy to take, you know.

However, he'd never get on you for a mechanical mistake, a fielding error or failure to get a hit. He was a very fair man, and it was only when you really had it coming to you that you got it. And once he'd bawled you out good and proper, and I do mean proper, then he'd forget it. He wouldn't ever mention it again, and in public he would always stand up for his players. It was really a lot of fun to play for McGraw.

As a matter of fact, it was because Mr. McGraw's favorite form of relaxation was watching the ponies that I became a professional ballplayer in the first place. He loved to follow the horses, you know, and in February of 1908 he came out here to Los Angeles to attend the races. He didn't bring his team, he was out here by himself. While he was here, he'd put on a uniform and work out to get himself in shape before spring training began, so he could sort of get the jump on all those old-timers who were on the Giants then.

At the time, the only contact I had with baseball was playing Sundays on a semipro team called the Hoegee Flags. (We were sponsored by a sporting-goods house, and on our backs we had flags of all nations.) We played teams all over southern California, and I still remember the one that was toughest. It was a team down by Santa Ana, for which Walter Johnson pitched. If people think Walter was fast later on, they should have seen him then. Whew! Most of the time you couldn't even see the ball!

Anyway, one of my friends was helping Mr. McGraw work out at the ball park, shagging flies for him and things like that. McGraw asked a question about me, remembering I guess that the year before the Giants had played three exhibition games against St. Vincent's College in Los Angeles and that as a student there I had caught for St. Vincent's. Mr. McGraw had been the umpire, and we had argued and quarreled constantly all through those three games.

"Oh, Snodgrass is the best catcher in semipro around here," my friend said.

"Well," McGraw said, "if you see him, tell him I would like to talk to him."

Word got to me, and I discussed it with my parents. There didn't seem to be any harm in talking to him, so I called him up at his hotel. He asked me to meet him in the lobby the next day, which I did.

"Are you thinking about playing baseball?" McGraw asked me.

"A little bit," I said, "but not too seriously. Although I did have an offer from Peoria in the Three-I League."

He reached into his pocket and said, "Here's a contract. Take it home and talk it over with your father and mother. If they think you ought to try baseball, our train leaves for spring training in four days. Let me know what you decide, will you?"

Well, as you can well imagine, I was on that train four days later, going to Marlin, Texas. That's the way I got started in baseball. Of course, my contract only called for $150 a month. And, to tell the truth, at the time I couldn't even name all the clubs in the two Big Leagues. But suddenly there I was, at spring training with the New York Giants.

You see, in those days they didn't have an army of coaches and scouts and things of that kind. The way they got young players was by direct observation themselves. Or some friend of the club would tip off John McGraw, or other managers, that here was a likely kid, and they would bring him up and look him over.

The Giants had bought a piece of property in Marlin, Texas, a town of about 4,000 or 5,000 people, and had constructed a ball park there for spring-training purposes. They thought that in a little town like that they could keep the fellows under control better. The ball park was about two miles from our hotel, and every day twice a day, morning and afternoon, we walked from the hotel to the ball park along some railroad tracks that ran close by. We trained there every spring I was with the Giants, which was until 1915.

Of course, spring training was very different in those days, compared to today. It was simpler, and it was tougher. Today you have specialized teachers and coaches and schools and blackboards, and all that sort of thing. You have mass calisthenics and mechanical pitchers and moving pictures to look at to see what you're doing wrong, and a host of other things. Maybe it's helpful and maybe it isn't. I guess it must be.

But we didn't have any of those things. We didn't have ten coaches, each a professional teacher in some aspect of baseball. We had one old-timer, Arlie Latham, who had been a first-rate ballplayer and who was a fine fellow, but who was probably the worst third-base coach who ever lived. They didn't make a specialty of such things then. In those days, you see, it was strictly up to the individual to improve himself and to get himself into condition. If he was intelligent, and if he was a man who wanted to make that team and become a first-class baseball player, he himself had to have it in his heart to work at it. He wasn't made to do things. In fact, he wasn't even encouraged very much.

Of course, we trotted to and from the park every day, and McGraw insisted that we run so many times around the park, and naturally we'd have batting and fielding practice. However, it was practically impossible for a youngster, a rookie, to get up to the plate in batting practice. A youngster was an outsider, and those old veterans weren't about to make it easy for him to take away one of their jobs. The Giants then had mostly rough and tough old characters, men who had been around quite a while—men like Mike Donlin, Joe McGinnity, Cy Seymour, Spike Shannon, and a lot of others. When I came up in 1908 it was mostly a team of veterans, a lot of them nearing the end of their baseball careers. But that didn't mean they accepted that fact.

And yet, when I look back, I realize that I owe a great deal to one of those veterans. I was assigned to room with Spike Shannon. He was about thirty years old and had been an outfielder in the Big Leagues for about five years. He took me under his wing, helped me, encouraged me, and told me what to do and what not to do. I doubt if I'd have made the club that year if it hadn't been for Shannon.

But I did make it. I was the third-string catcher in 1908, behind Roger Bresnahan and Tom Needham. I sat on the bench all through that season. That was the year of the famous Merkle incident, when we should have won the pennant but didn't. In 1909 I was still the third-string catcher until the last month of the season, when McGraw put me in the outfield for about 20 games. In 1910 I was a catcher again in spring training, and when the season opened I was once more spending most of my time sitting on the bench. By then Bresnahan had left and Chief Meyers was doing most of the catching.

Then on the first road trip of the 1910 season McGraw came to me in the hotel in Cincinnati.

"Snow," he said, "how would you like to play center field?"

Well, I had been very unhappy sitting on the bench, and I immediately thought he was going to send me out to some minor league club. So I said, "With what club?"

"Why, *this* club, of course."

"You mean you're going to take Cy Seymour out of center field?"

"Yes," he said, "would you like to try it?"

So from then on I was the regular center fielder for the Giants. I never went back to catching. I was also the substitute first baseman for Fred Merkle whenever something happened and Merkle couldn't play. As a matter of fact, I preferred playing first base. I didn't particularly like the outfield. You can be out there all day without a chance, or maybe just backing up some play. I like to be in the middle of things and fight a little bit.

That was quite a team we had in those days, you know. We won the pennant in '11, '12, and '13. Fred Merkle was at first base, Larry Doyle at second, Al Bridwell and then Art Fletcher at short, and Art Devlin or Buck Herzog at third. In the outfield Red Murray was on one side of me, and Josh Devore or George Burns on the other. The battery was Chief Meyers behind the plate and Mathewson, Rube Marquard, Jeff Tesreau, Leon Ames, Hooks Wiltse, Otis Crandall, or Bugs Raymond pitching. What a club that was!

Marquard! What a great record Rube had. In 1912 he won 19 straight games, almost every one a complete game. And I still remember that wonderful 21-inning game he pitched against Pittsburgh—I think it was in 1914. We won that game, 3–1, in 21 innings, and Rube pitched the whole game. As a matter of fact, I think Babe Adams pitched all 21 innings for Pittsburgh, too. You know, in those days pitchers were *expected* to pitch the whole game. Today it's entirely different. Five or six pitchers a game isn't at all unusual now. But then it was a disgrace if a pitcher didn't finish what he started.

And Mathewson! The great pitcher that he was! He pitched a complete game almost every time he went out there. Matty was the greatest pitcher who ever lived, in my opinion. He was a wonderful, wonderful man, too, a reserved sort of fellow, a little hard to get close to. But once you got to know him, he was a truly good friend.

Matty could do *everything* well. He was checker champion of half a dozen states—he'd play several opponents simultaneously and beat them all—a good billiard player, a pretty fair golfer, and a terrific poker player. He made a good part of his expenses every year playing poker. He was a good bridge player, too.

And did you know that he never pitched on Sunday, or even dressed in uniform? Of course, in those days we never played Sunday ball in the East—in New York, Philadelphia, Boston, or Pittsburgh—although we did in Chicago, St. Louis, and Cincinnati. But Matty never would. I'm not saying that he was a very religious man, but he got started that way, I guess because of some belief he had, and he continued it throughout his career.

For contrast, we also had Bugs Raymond. Bugs drank too much and came to an early tragic end, but when he was sober, and sometimes when he wasn't, he was one of the greatest spitball pitchers who ever lived. McGraw tried to help him, but he didn't succeed. He tried fining him when he'd break training, but fining Bugs didn't have any effect. Bugs would go into any bar, pull a baseball out of his pocket and autograph it, and he'd get all the free drinks he wanted. Actually, McGraw didn't keep the fines; he would send the money to Bugs' wife, although he never let Bugs know this.

Even when he wasn't drinking, Bugs did the strangest things. I remember once, in spring training, we all went to a fish fry on the final day before leaving camp. Somebody brought along a couple of target guns, and we were all shooting at targets. Bugs said, "Here, hit this." And he took out his pocket watch, a very good watch that had been given to him in the minor leagues. I remember Al Bridwell was shooting at the time. Bugs threw the watch up in the air, and Al put a bullet right through the middle of it!

On the way back to New York that same spring, we stopped for three days at the Belvedere Hotel in Baltimore. The Belvedere was one of the finest hotels in the East, and they just about tripled our eating allowance there, because it was so expensive. Bugs was never seen by anybody all three days we were there. On the morning we were to leave for New York we were all down in the lobby, reading the newspapers and waiting to go, when somebody saw two waiters and two busboys going into the elevators, all with loaded trays. It turned out to be Bugs Raymond's breakfast. Bugs hadn't eaten at the hotel for the three days, and sure enough he had taken the menu and figured out exactly the amount that he could spend, item by item. He spent the whole three days' meal allowance for that breakfast. And, of course, he was too much under the weather to eat any part of it!

Bugs had a good sense of humor and was a lot of fun. But he couldn't stay away from drinking, and as a result you never could be sure he'd show up. McGraw tried bringing his wife and children along with the team, both at home and on the road, so they could be with him all the time. It worked pretty well for a while, but then that flew all to pieces, too. Bugs and McGraw finally had it out one night on the train, and Bugs was told that the next time he didn't show up would mean the end of his career.

The next day we were playing in St. Louis. We were supposed to be at the park at noon, and by two o'clock Bugs still hadn't shown up. Finally, we saw Bugs, in civilian clothes, walking across the field toward the clubhouse out beyond center field. McGraw met him at the door.

"Bugs," he said, "you're through in baseball. Here's your uniform [that was the year we had to buy our own uniforms]. See Mr. Foster, and he'll give you a ticket back to New York. You're through with the Giants."

When we finally got back to New York ourselves, hanging in the window of the nearest saloon to the Polo Grounds was Bugs Raymond's uniform, with a sign on it that said "Bugs Raymond Tending Bar Here." That was in 1911, and Bugs never pitched another game in professional baseball. He was an outcast, and the next year, at the age of thirty, he died.

But when I think of my teammates on the Giants, other than Bugs Raymond, I can't name a single player that I ever saw under the influence of liquor. A lot of those boys were rough and tough, but they weren't heavy drinkers. A few beers now and then, that was about it.

I will tell you something about those players, though, that I think is usually overlooked. They were rough and tough, all right, but they were good thinkers, too. Players in my day played baseball with their brains as much as their brawn. They were intelligent, smart ballplayers. Why, you *had* to be! You didn't stay in the Big Leagues very long in those days unless you used your head every second of every game.

You see, it was a different game then compared to today. Now they're all trying to hit the ball over the fence. It's mostly brute strength. They're always trying to get a flock of runs at once. But in my day a home run was a rarity. You *couldn't* hit balls over the fence in most parks in those days, because the ball was too dead! So we were always playing for small scores, for one run or two.

As a result, there was a premium on intelligence in those days, on the ability to outwit and outthink the other team. And on speed and strategy. We used heavier, thicker bats and choked up on them so we could bunt more effectively and place our hits. Very few held the bat all the way down at the end, the way they do today. The only one I can remember was Frank Schulte, with the Cubs in the famous days of Tinker to Evers to Chance. Schulte held the bat down at the end. But most of us were choke hitters who punched at the ball trying to get singles and doubles, not home runs.

For example, take a simple thing like the art of getting hit with the ball when you're at bat. To get up there and deliberately *attempt* to get hit by a pitched ball. It's a lost art today; just not done anymore. I used to lead the league in that. I had baggy uniforms, a baggy shirt, baggy pants—any ball thrown close inside, why I turned with it and half the time I wasn't really hit, just my uniform was nicked. Or the ball might hit your bat close to your hands and you'd fall down on your belly, and while you were down you'd try to make a red spot by squeezing your hand or something. If you had a good red spot there, the umpire might believe it hit you rather than the bat. And off you'd go to first base.

Of course, in those days baseball was a pitcher's game much more than it is today. Not only did we have a dead ball, but pitchers were allowed to use such deliveries as the spitball, the emery ball, and what have you. And we hardly ever saw a new baseball, a clean one. If the ball went into the stands and the ushers couldn't get it back from the spectators, only then would the umpire throw out a new one.

He'd throw the ball out to the pitcher, who would promptly sidestep it. It would go around the infield once or twice and come back to the pitcher as black as the ace of spades. All the infielders were chewing tobacco or licorice, and spitting into their gloves, and they'd give that ball a good going over before it ever got to the pitcher. Believe me, that dark ball was hard to see coming out of the shadows of the stands.

Also, there were a lot of pitchers in those days who were quick-delivery artists. You didn't dare step into the batter's box without being ready, because somebody with a quick delivery would have that ball by you before you knew what happened. That was part of the game. The instant you stepped into that batter's box you had to be ready. If you were looking at your feet or something, the way they do today to get just the right position and all, well, by that time the ball would already be in the catcher's mitt. Particularly I remember Pat Flaherty, of the Boston Braves, and Joe McGinnity of the Giants was another—both quick-return artists. The catcher would throw them the ball and bang, right back it would come!

But to get back to this matter of intelligence and thinking in baseball. You know, a lot of what I read in newspapers and books about baseball in the old days is absolutely 100 percent wrong. For instance, they seem to think that John McGraw directed every move we made on the field, that he was an absolute dictator who told us when to do this and when to do that, down to the last detail. Well, that's just not so, and it wasn't so for most other managers, either.

The fact of the matter is that thinking and alertness were crucial aspects of baseball then. Most of the time we were on our own. We used our own judgment. Nowadays they look at the manager or the coach for directions on almost everything. They aren't permitted to use their own judgment. They are told what to do on every darn pitch. But in our time we were supposed to *know* how to play baseball, and were expected to do the right thing at the right time.

McGraw allowed initiative to his men. We stole when we thought we had the jump and when the situation demanded it. We played hit-and-run when we felt that was what was called for. We bunted when we thought it was appropriate. Every player on the team was expected to know how to play baseball, and that was the kind of a game baseball was in those days. How many games do you see lost today just because they don't know how to bunt? That's a lost art, too. There was a lot of strategy in baseball then, and there isn't very much today. We played a game in which the two key words were "think" and "anticipate."

Of course, McGraw took charge sometimes. At certain points in a game he'd give instructions. But most of the time, as I say, the initiative was ours. The player of my day was allowed to think for himself, instead of having somebody do his thinking for him.

Why, do you know that we hardly ever had a pregame meeting on the Giants the whole eight years I was there? Hardly ever! Today they always have a meeting before the game to discuss what they're going to do. We didn't *need* any meetings. Most of us spent all our waking hours talking baseball anyway, so it would have been silly to have a meeting. Just about the only meetings we ever had on the Giants while I was there were to divide up the World Series money.

And signs! McGraw hardly ever used signs. The belief that he signaled what was to be done on every play is ridiculous. We were supposed to do things on our own. For instance, we had a base-running club. In 1911, '12, and '13 we had six or seven men who would each average 40 or so stolen bases a season. In 1911 we stole 347 bases. Just the New York Giants—347 stolen bases in one season! Look it up, if you don't believe it. And most of the time we ran on our own. We had signs among ourselves, so we could tell each other what we were planning to do. Signs between the batter and a man on base, for instance. But those were *our* signs, not McGraw's.

On rare occasions, McGraw would indeed tell us to steal. Do you know how he'd do it? On his fingers, with the deaf-and-dumb sign language. A deaf mute, Dummy Taylor, was a pitcher on the club, so all of us knew the sign language. McGraw would sit there on the bench and spell out S-T-E-A-L so plain that anyone in the park who could read deaf-and-dumb language would know what was happening. We had no complicated signals. A nod of the head, or something in sign language; he might just as well have said "go on," like that, and off you'd go.

We could all read and speak the deaf-and-dumb sign language, because Dummy Taylor took it as an affront if you didn't learn to converse with him. He wanted to be one of us, to be a full-fledged member of the team. If we went to the vaudeville show, he wanted to know what the joke was, and somebody had to tell him. So we all learned. We practiced all the time. We'd go by elevated train from the hotel to the Polo

Grounds, and all during the ride we'd be spelling out the advertising signs. Not talking to one another, but sitting there spelling out the advertising messages. Even today, when I pass a billboard I find myself doing it.

Intelligent as they were, most ballplayers were also superstitious in those days. Just as they are today, for that matter. There's an interesting true story about that. Hard to believe, but true. Early in the 1911 season we were playing in St. Louis, and in those days neither team had a dugout in that park. We had a bench under an awning, about halfway between the grandstand and the foul line. We—the Giants—were having batting practice, when out of the grandstand walked a tall, lanky individual in a dark suit, wearing a black derby hat. He walked across the grass from the grandstand to the bench, and said he wanted to talk to Mr. McGraw. So some of us pointed McGraw out, and he went over to him.

"Mr. McGraw," he said, "my name is Charles Victory Faust. I live over in Kansas, and a few weeks ago I went to a fortune-teller who told me that if I would join the New York Giants and pitch for them that they would win the pennant."

McGraw looked at him, being superstitious, as most ballplayers were—and are. "Well, that's interesting," he said. "Take off your hat and coat, and here's a glove. I'll get a catcher's mitt and warm you up, and we'll see what you have."

They got up in front of the bench and tossed a few balls back and forth. "I'd better give you my signals," Charles Victory Faust said. So they got their heads together, and he gave McGraw five or six signals. Mr. McGraw would give him a signal, and he would proceed to wind up. His windup was like a windmill. Both arms went around in circles for quite a little while, before Charlie finally let go of the ball. Well, regardless of the sign that McGraw would give, the ball would come up just the same. There was no difference in his pitches whatsoever. And there was no speed—probably enough to break a pane of glass, but that was about all. So McGraw finally threw his glove away and caught him bare-handed, thinking to himself that this guy must be a nut and he'd have a little fun with him.

"How's your hitting?" McGraw asked him.

"Oh," he said, "pretty good."

"Well," McGraw said, "we're having batting practice now, so get a bat and go up there. I want to see you run, too, so run it out and see if you can score."

Word was quickly passed around to the fellows who were shagging balls in the infield. Charlie Faust dribbled one down to the shortstop, who juggled it a minute as Charlie was turning first, and then they deliberately slid him into second, slid him into third, and slid him into home, all in his best Sunday suit—to the obvious enjoyment of everyone.

Well, that night we left for Chicago, and when we got down to the train and into our private Pullman car, who was there but Charles Victory Faust. Everybody looked at him in amazement.

"We're taking Charlie along to help us win the pennant," the superstitious Mr. McGraw announced.

So, believe it or not, every day from that day on, Charles Victory Faust was in uniform and he warmed up sincerely to pitch that game. He thought he was going to pitch that *particular* game. Every day this happened. To make a long story shorter, this was 1911, and although Charlie Faust warmed up every day to pitch, he never pitched a game.

He wasn't signed to a contract, but John J. McGraw gave him all the money that was necessary. He went to the barbershop almost every day for a massage and a haircut, he had plenty of money to tip the waiters— in the small amounts that we tipped in those days—and we *did* win the pennant.

Spring came around the next year and Charles Victory Faust appeared in the training camp. He warmed up every day in 1912, and *again* we won the pennant.

In 1913 he was again in the spring-training camp, and during the season he continued to warm up every day to pitch. By that time he had become a tremendous drawing card with the fans, who would clamor for McGraw to actually put him in to pitch. Finally, one day against Cincinnati they clamored so hard and so loud for McGraw to put him in to pitch that in a late inning McGraw *did* send him to the mound. He pitched one full inning, without being under contract to the Giants, and he didn't have enough stuff to hit. They didn't score on him. One of those nothing-ball pitchers, you know.

Well, it was Charlie Faust's turn to come to bat when three outs were made, but the Cincinnati team stayed in the field for the *fourth* out to let Charlie come to bat. And the same thing happened then that happened the very first time that Charlie ever came on the field in St. Louis in his Sunday clothes: they slid him into second, third, and home.

He was such a drawing card at this point that a theatrical firm gave him a contract on Broadway in one of those six-a-day shows, starting in the afternoon and running through the evening, and he got four hundred dollars a week for it. He dressed in a baseball uniform and imitated Ty Cobb, Christy Mathewson, and Honus Wagner. In a very ridiculous way, of course, but *seriously* as far as Charlie was concerned. And the fans loved it and went to see Charlie on the stage. He was gone four days, and we lost four ball games!

The fifth day Charlie showed up in the dressing room at the Polo Grounds, and we all said to him, "Charlie, what are you doing here? What about your theatrical contract?"

"Oh," he said, "I've got to pitch today. You fellows need me."

So he went out there and warmed up, with that windmill warm-up he had that just tickled the fans so, and we won the game. And in 1913 we won the pennant *again*.

That fall I joined a group of Big Leaguers and we made a barnstorming trip, starting in Chicago and going through the Northwest and down the Coast and over to Honolulu. In Seattle, who came down to the hotel to see me but Charlie Faust.

"Snow," he said to me, "I'm not very well. But I think if you could prevail on Mr. McGraw to send me to Hot Springs a month before spring training, I could get into shape and help the Giants win another pennant."

But, unfortunately, that never came to pass. Because Charlie Faust died that winter, and we did not win the pennant the next year. Believe it or not, that's the way it happened. It's a true story, from beginning to end.

Which reminds me of that other pennant we did not win, which as I said before we should have won. That was in 1908, the year of the famous Merkle incident. For almost 60 years poor Fred Merkle had been unfairly blamed for losing the pennant for us in 1908. What actually happened was quite understandable, and anyone who puts all the blame on Merkle has to be blind to a lot of other things that happened that season, things which contributed just as much, if not more, to our losing the pennant.

Fred Merkle had joined the Giants in the fall of 1907, at the age of eighteen, before I joined the following spring. So in 1908, when I met him, and when the so-called Merkle "bonehead" occurred, he was a kid only nineteen years old. As a result of what happened he took more abuse and vituperation than any other nineteen-year-old I've ever heard of.

There were six of us youngsters who made the club that year: Fred Merkle, Larry Doyle, Art Fletcher, Buck Herzog, Otis Crandall, and me. Mostly we were bench warmers. I was a substitute catcher behind the great Roger Bresnahan, so you know I didn't play much. And Fred Merkle was the substitute first baseman behind Fred Tenney. He was nineteen and I was twenty, and we were both amazed that we were even on the Giants. I doubt if either of us got to play in as many as 25 games that season.

Anyway, as soon as a game was over at the Polo Grounds, any game, all of us fellows who were sitting on the bench were in the habit, when the last out was made, of jumping up and running like the dickens for our clubhouse, which was out beyond right center field. We wanted to get there before the crowd could get on the field.

In those days, as soon as a game ended at the Polo Grounds the ushers would open the gates from the stands to the field, and the people would all pour out and rush at you. Of course, all they wanted to do was touch you, or congratulate you, or maybe cuss you out a bit. But, because of that, as soon as a game was over we bench warmers all made it a practice to sprint from the bench to the clubhouse as fast as we could. And that was precisely the reason why Fred Merkle got into that awful jam. He was so used to sitting on the bench all during the game, and then at the end of the game jumping up with the rest of us and taking off as fast as he could for the clubhouse, that on this particular day he did it by force of habit and never gave it a second thought.

The famous game in which it all happened took place in New York in late September of 1908. The Giants were playing the Chicago Cubs and we were both about tied for the league lead, with only a week or two of the season remaining. Merkle was playing first base for us. I think Fred Tenney, the regular first baseman, was injured or something, and that this was the very first game Merkle had been put in the starting lineup all season.

Mathewson was pitching for us, against Jack Pfiester for the Cubs. The game went down to the last half of the ninth inning, with the score tied 1–1. And then, in the last of the ninth, with two out and Moose McCormick on first, Merkle hit a long single to right and McCormick went to third. Men were on first and third, with two out. The next man up was Al Bridwell, our shortstop. Al hit a line single into center field. McCormick, of course, scored easily from third—he could have walked in—with what appeared to be the winning run.

Merkle started for second base, naturally. But the minute he saw the ball was a safe hit, rolling toward the fence out in right center, with McCormick across the plate and the game presumably over and won, he turned and lit out for the clubhouse, exactly as he had been doing all season long. And that was Merkle's downfall. Because technically the rules of baseball are that to formally complete the play he had to touch second base, since Bridwell now occupied first.

As soon as McCormick crossed the plate, *everyone* thought the game was over. Everyone except Johnny Evers, anyway. The crowd began to come on the field, we bench sitters sprinted out through right center field for our clubhouse, as usual, along with Merkle and everybody else, and the two umpires walked toward their dressing room, which was behind the press box in back of home plate. So neither of the umpires saw what happened after that, because they were both going directly opposite from where the ball went.

Well, of course, what happened was that the great infield of Stein-feldt, Tinker, Evers, and Chance were playing for Chicago, and Johnny Evers, an old-timer at the game, saw that Merkle hadn't touched second base. Evers began to call to the Cubs' center fielder, Artie Hofman, to go and get the ball. Hofman hadn't even chased it, because the game was over as far as he was concerned. But Evers made so much noise about getting the ball and throwing it into second base, that Hofman finally retrieved it and threw it in.

However, Joe McGinnity, another old-timer, was coaching at third base for us, and he sensed what was going on. He ran out, intercepted the ball, and threw it up into the left field bleachers. He threw it clear out of the park. They say Evers got another ball from somewhere else and touched second with it, but I don't think so. I never saw that.

By this time, of course, there were thousands of people milling around on the infield, absolute bedlam around there. Frank Chance, the Chicago manager, went into the umpires' dressing room and insisted that the two umpires—Hank O'Day and Bob Emslie—come out and see what was going on. Chance claimed Evers had gotten the ball and touched second base with it, so that Merkle was out and the game should continue, still a 1–1 tie. And since the field was now total chaos, that the game should be forfeited to Chicago both because of McGinnity's inter-ference and because the Giants couldn't clear their own field. So Chance dragged the umpires out there and said, "Look at this." They saw these thousands of fans on the field, arguing, milling around, not knowing what was going on, complete pandemonium. Everything was in an up-roar.

Finally, Hank O'Day, who was the senior umpire, ruled that Merkle was indeed out, the third out, that therefore McCormick's run didn't count, and that the game had ended in a tie, 1–1. It was appealed to the highest league levels, but after three days of deliberations they finally upheld the umpires and ruled that it was a tie game and would have to be replayed as a play-off game after the season, if necessary. Well, it was necessary. We ended the season tied for first place with the Cubs, and the game had to be played over to decide the pennant race. As you know, the Cubs beat us in that play-off game, so we didn't win the pennant in 1908.

In that famous play-off game, by the way, we tried to get Frank Chance thrown out of the game, but didn't succeed. Before the game we talked over in the clubhouse how in the world we could get Chance out of there. Matty was to pitch for us, and Frank always hit Matty pretty well. We felt if we could get him out, in some way, that we had a better chance of winning the play-off game and the pennant. Besides, we thought the pennant was ours by right, anyway. We thought the call on Merkle was a raw deal, and any means of redressing the grievance was legitimate.

So it was cooked up that Joe McGinnity was to pick a fight with Chance early in the game. They were to have a knockdown, drag-out fight, Chance and McGinnity, and both would get thrown out of the game. Of course, we didn't need McGinnity, but they needed Chance. McGinnity did just as he was supposed to. He called Chance names on some pretext or other, stepped on his toes, pushed him, actually spit on him. But Frank wouldn't fight. He was too smart. And they beat us, with Chance getting a key hit and Three-Fingered Brown beating Christy Mathewson. I believe that was the year Brown won 29 games and Matty won 37.

It is very unfair to put all the blame on Merkle for our losing the pennant in 1908. McGraw never did, and neither did the rest of us. It was mostly the newspapers. They were the ones who invented the term "bonehead."

How could you blame Merkle, when we lost the play-off game, and besides that we lost five other games *after* the Merkle incident? If we had won any one of those five games we would have won the pennant in the regular season, and we wouldn't even have had to play a play-off game. We lost a double-header to Cincinnati, and then we played the Philadelphia Phillies and Harry Coveleski pitched against us three times in one week. He pitched against us on Tuesday, Thursday, and Saturday, and beat us all three times. That's when he acquired the nickname "Giant Killer." Coveleski beating us three times in one week surely wasn't Merkle's fault.

And do you know that we ran Harry Coveleski clear out of the league the next season. It was the craziest, most foolish thing that ever happened. McGraw was told by a friend of his who had managed Coveleski in the minor leagues, before he came up to Philadelphia, that Coveleski always carried some bologna in his back pocket and chewed on that bologna throughout the game—and that he did this more or less secretly, maybe somewhat ashamed of his habit. It was sort of an obsession with him.

So this manager told McGraw, and McGraw saw to it that some of us players would always meet Coveleski as he was going to and from the pitcher's box whenever he pitched against us. We'd stop him and say, "Hey, give us a chew of that bologna, will you?" Well, this so upset this fellow that he couldn't pitch against us to save his life. He never beat us again, word got around the league and the other clubs started doing the same thing, and it chased him right back to the minors—or at least that's what we Giants always claimed.

Often when the Merkle "bonehead" is recalled, in the next breath they talk about Snodgrass's "$30,000 muff." I've had to live with it for years—"Oh yes, you're the guy that dropped the fly ball in the World Series, aren't you?"

I never lost that World Series. I never took the blame for losing any World Series. I was terribly incensed a few years ago when a book on baseball facts and history came out. A friend of mine said to me, "Have you seen the book?" I said that I hadn't.

"Well," he said, "you'd better get a copy. They have a section in there on World Series Heroes and Goats, and you're listed as the Goat in the 1912 World Series."

So I got hold of a copy and read it. It said that in the 1912 World Series, the Red Sox versus the Giants, in the 10th inning of the last game Fred Snodgrass, the center fielder for the Giants, dropped an easy fly ball and let the tying and winning runs score. And thereby lost the Series for the Giants.

I did drop a fly ball. There's no doubt about that. But I didn't let the tying and winning runs score; I couldn't very well, because it happened with the *first* man up in the bottom of the 10th inning. It was the eighth and last game of the Series (one game had ended in a tie) and the score was tied, 1–1, at the end of the regulation 9 innings. In the top of the 10th we scored a run—on a hit by Fred Merkle, by the way—and went into the bottom of the 10th with Matty pitching and a one-run lead. If we could have held that one-run lead, we would have won the World Series.

The first man up for Boston in the bottom of the 10th was Clyde Engle, who was pinch-hitting for Smoky Joe Wood. He hit a great big, lazy, high, fly ball halfway between Red Murray in left field and me. Murray called for it first, but as center fielder I had preference over left and right, so there'd never be a collision. I yelled that I'd take it and waved Murray off, and—well—I dropped the darn thing. It was so high that Engle was sitting on second base before I could get it back to the infield.

Well, Harry Hooper was the next batter. And in the 10th inning of a tie game, the last game of a World Series, we were just certain that he would bunt to move the man over to third. So my position in center field was fairly close in behind second. Matty was holding Engle close to second, so that we could get him at third on the bunt, and I was in pretty close, figuring that if Matty threw to second and the ball got by second in any way I could still keep Engle from going to third.

But instead of bunting, Hooper cracked a drive way over my head. I made one of the greatest plays of my life on it, catching the ball over my shoulder while on the dead run out in deep left center. They always forget about that play when they write about that inning. In fact, I almost doubled up Engle at second base. He was turning third when I caught the ball. He thought it was gone, you know, and the play at second was very close.

So that's one out. Then Matty walked Steve Yerkes, unfortunately, with what proved to be the winning run. Two men on and only one out. And up comes Tris Speaker, one of the greatest hitters in the game. The crowd was making so much noise it was deafening.

What does Speaker do but take a swing at the ball and hit a nice easy pop-up, a foul ball, over near first base. Suddenly the crowd was so quiet you could have heard a pin drop. And that ball was never touched. Merkle didn't have to go thirty feet to get it, it was almost in the first-base coaching box. Chief Meyers, our catcher, tried to catch it, but couldn't quite get there. It was too far from home plate. Matty could have put it in his hind pocket himself. But no one ever touched it.

Well, given that reprieve, Speaker hit a clean line drive over the first baseman's head that scored the man I put on and put Yerkes on third base. Another long fly to right by Larry Gardner and Yerkes scored after the catch. The game is over and, according to the newspapers, Fred Snodgrass lost the World Series. I did drop that fly ball, and that did put what turned out to be the tying run on base, but that's a long way from "losing a World Series." However, the facts don't seem to matter.

Oh, those were stormy days. I always seemed to be getting involved in hassles of one sort or another. Like the time when they claimed I spiked Home Run Baker. That was in the 1911 World Series, when we were playing Connie Mack's Philadelphia Athletics. In fact, that was the Series in which Frank Baker acquired his famous nickname of Home Run Baker. He hit two home runs against us in that World Series, and in those days that was an extraordinary performance.

Before the Series began, we had been told by friends that Baker was spike-shy, that he'd get out of your way at third base if the occasion arose. But to start at the beginning: in the 1905 World Series, six years before, the Giants had beaten the Athletics four games to one. That was the Series in which Matty had shut out the A's three times and Joe McGinnity had shut them out once. In that Series the Giants had been dressed in black broadcloth uniforms.

So superstitious McGraw, and he *was* superstitious, he ordered new black broadcloth uniforms for the 1911 Series. We went out on the field first, all dressed in black, and as we sat on the bench waiting for the Athletics to walk past us to get to the visiting team's bench, we all had a shoe off in one hand and a file in the other, and we were all busily sharpening our spikes. We figured that might have some effect on them, because we were a base-running club and we wanted them to get the idea that they'd better get out of our way. As I said, we stole 347 bases that season.

Well, I happened to be the first man in the game to get to second base who had occasion to try to go to third. Chief Bender was pitching for the A's, and throwing his beautiful curve in the dirt, and the catcher was having trouble digging it out. One pitch got away from the catcher and I lit out for third base.

But Baker knew that we had been told that he was spike-shy, and he just had guts enough to try to block me off that base. So he was down on one knee in front of the bag, with the ball, waiting for me to slide. Well, I couldn't hook the bag, in or out, because he'd ride me right off, so all I could do was go hard into him and try to upset him, which I did, and I was safe. In doing so I cut his pants, from his knee clear to his hip. They went and got another pair of pants and a blanket, put the new pants on him right at third base, and the game proceeded.

This same play happened again a few days later. I'm on second, a passed ball, and I take off for third. This time I was out, but I ripped his pants again, plus a little abrasion on his leg. Not a cut, no blood, nothing like that. Oh, I was the dirtiest player in baseball! Newspaper stories told how I'd jumped at Baker waist high, which wasn't true at all, and how I'd deliberately spiked him. Was I ever roasted! They built it up until Baker's bone showed from the knee to the hip.

In fact, a news report went out that some fanatic had shot Snodgrass in the hotel, and it was reported that I had been taken to the hospital in critical condition. They didn't have radio then, and that story went out over the wires. My parents out here in California heard that I had been killed, and it was several hours before a retraction came out and they found out I was all right.

And then there was that crazy incident in Boston, when Mayor Curley tried to have me thrown out of a game. That was in 1914, the year of the Boston Braves "Miracle Team," which came from last place on July 4th to beat us out for the pennant. We had been leading the league all season. But the Braves made this wonderful climb up the ladder from last place until by Labor Day, playing against the Giants, they had a chance to pass us and go into first place.

The crowd that wanted to get into the ball park in Boston that day

was far greater than the seating capacity, so they started putting spectators in the outfield. In fact, the Boston Braves borrowed Fenway Park
from the Red Sox that day, because the Braves' own park was too small
to hold the crowd. They put ropes up in the outfield and thousands of
people were sitting and standing behind the ropes, right on the playing
field. They were standing right behind my back in center field.

We had a big inning in about the sixth or seventh inning and scored
four runs to go well ahead of Boston. I came up to bat after we'd scored
all those runs, with nobody on base and two men out. George Tyler, who
was pitching for the Braves, was pretty disgusted by then, and he took it
out on me by aiming four shots straight at my head. I hit the dirt four
times, and the fourth one hit the button on my cap. So on my way to first
base I went by way of the pitcher's box. I stood in front of that guy and
called him everything I could think of. He never said a word. Finally,
when I ran out of adjectives, I went over to first base. Meanwhile, that
huge crowd was hooting and hissing and booing me, and making a terrific din. They knew they weren't going to get into first place that day,
and they were pretty sore about it.

When I got to first base, Tyler looked over at me and tossed the ball
into the air and dropped it, a pantomime of the fact that two years
before I'd dropped that fly ball in the World Series. Well, the crowd just
loved that, and the hooting and booing got even louder, if that was
possible. The next man made the third out, and I started out for my
position in center field. And as I approached the crowd behind the ropes
out there, booing and yelling at me, I just thumbed my nose at the whole
bunch of them. Just an old-fashioned nose-thumbing, to let them know
what I thought of them.

Well, that *really* set them off. It was the signal for all the pop bottles
and trash of any kind that people had to come flying out on the field, in
my general direction. The place was in an uproar.

And just then a fellow jumped out of his box seat near the home
dugout, and marched onto the field, accompanied by a couple of high-
helmeted policemen. He had on a long-tailed coat, spats, and a top hat,
and he paraded over to the umpires. It was the Honorable James M.
Curley, the Mayor of Boston. He said I had insulted the good citizens of
Boston and demanded that I be removed from the field immediately. It
was just before election time, and he was making what you might call a
grandstand play for votes.

After a big argument, Bill Klem, who was umpiring, chased him off
the field, and the game was finally finished without further trouble. But
you can bet I didn't play a very deep center field the rest of that game,
and they tell me that after the last out was made in the ninth inning I ran

in from center field so fast that I was easily the first one into our dugout.

Well, life has been good to me since I left baseball. My lovely wife, Josephine, and I have enjoyed success and things have gone well, very well, through these many years. In contrast, my years in baseball had their ups and downs, their strife and their torment. But the years I look back at most fondly, and those I'd like most to live over, are the years when I was playing center field for the New York Giants.

ROGER KAHN

"The Crucial Role Fear Plays in Sports"

A theory that fear is something experienced only by the intelligent has spread almost as fast as strontium-90 during the past ten years. I suspect that the theory was devised by a smart coward in search of prestige, but its precise origin remains unknown and somehow people accept it as tradition and even apply it to such innocent fields as sports.

Do you know why Ralph Branca is now selling insurance near New York City instead of pitching every fourth day for the Los Angeles Dodgers? "It's because he's bright and went to NYU," one NYU man suggests, modestly. "If Ralph were dumber, Bobby Thomson's homer wouldn't have preyed on his mind, because he wouldn't have had the sense to worry. Hell, a dumb Branca would win twenty games every year."

Do you know why Joe Louis was a great champion? "Because he was too slow-witted to be afraid," insists a quick-witted club fighter, who quit just in time to preserve his brain pan. "Joe wasn't sharp enough to know how much he could be hurt. A smarter Louis would have dropped that second fight to Schmeling."

Perhaps two dozen other examples come to mind, but by now I imagine the concept has come clear. Sports is the one area in which stupidity counts. Smart guys finish last. The good rockhead always beats the good egghead. The trouble with each of these statements is also the trouble with the theory that lies behind them. They withstand everything except analysis.

A few hours after the Dodgers had turned the harvest moon blue by winning the 1955 World Series from the New York Yankees, Pee Wee Reese was idling at the bar in an aged Brooklyn hotel which was the site of the official victory party. Reese had thrown out the final batter on a routine ground ball to shortstop.

"Hey, Pee Wee," said a nearby semi-drunk, "what was you thinking with two outs in the ninth?"

Reese smiled benignly. "I was just hoping the next man wouldn't hit the ball to me," he said.

"Shmerf?" said the drunk, in surprise, as his beer asserted itself.

Well, there it was. Honest, intelligent Pee Wee Reese had given an honest, intelligent answer, and anyone within hearing distance could now report that a great professional had known the cold hand of fear in the clutch. But had the drunk asked the same question of a duller ball-player, had he picked on a triumphant rockhead, things might well have been reversed. Pinned against a stein of beer, the rockhead probably would have been the man to say, *"Shmerf?"*

The quick conclusion, which is that the dull athlete was not touched by fright, is careless and probably incorrect. A dull athlete might have felt far more fear than Reese did, but he could not have put the feeling into intelligible English. Emotion, not words, is the issue, and it's ridiculous to assert that you have to be smart to be afraid. I know a six-year-old shortstop, not especially precocious, who feels exactly as Reese did, every time he sees his pitcher throw the ball.

One day last spring, I was driving down a flat, narrow Florida highway to cover a sports car race at Sebring. It had been raining and water lay in dull, black puddles near the palmettos along the side of the road. The car jerked and hissed through the water as I kept it at 60 miles an hour and I remember thinking that the men who were trying to do 120 at Sebring must be having a difficult time.

It was night when I reached the race course, and Phil Hill, a slim Californian who is accepted as the best American driver, was pacing near the pits, his driving done, his team's victory all but assured. Hill is a sensitive-looking man, just over thirty, who reads a great deal and whose musical taste runs to Beethoven.

"How was it out there?" I said.

"What kind of a question is that?" Hill said, intensely. "Can't you imagine what it was like?"

I had to admit I'd never driven a Ferrari.

"A bloody nightmare," Hill said, his face going pale. "Some courses drain. This one doesn't. Trying to control the car out there for me was like it would be for you trying to drive on ice. I was moving. There must have been five, six, a dozen times, when I thought I was dead. I'd hit a puddle and the car would start to go and I'd be skidding toward somebody and I'd figure this was it. It wasn't, but don't ask me how. Lord, don't ask me how I'm still alive." Hill's hands were shaking. They continued to shake and for a time he was so wound up in tension that he was unable to stop talking.

Two years ago, before the start of an equally dangerous auto race, a reporter asked Juan Manuel Fangio, the former world champion driver, if he was thinking about death.

"Death?" Fangio said. "I only give it a quick, glancing thought."

Fangio is a phlegmatic man who once drove a bus in Argentina and who seems far less imaginative than Hill. Again the outward signs indicate that the egghead, Hill, was frightened, and the duller man, Fangio, was not. But last year, still in his prime and still a champion, Fangio quietly retired from Grand Prix racing. Despite his stolid disposition, he was afraid that matters might turn around, that Death might now give quick, glancing thoughts to Juan Manuel Fangio.

Fear strikes athletes without regard to race, creed, or intelligence. It also strikes them without regard to the actual peril in their work. For the fear athletes feel is composed of two distinct things. First, there is the fear of physical pain. Here we have auto racers afraid of auto wrecks, jockeys afraid of horses' hooves, halfbacks afraid of linebackers, batters afraid of beanballs, and swimmers afraid of the water. Then there is the fear, psychological but still real, of performing badly in front of an audience. Thus we have pitchers afraid to throw changeups, quarterbacks afraid to call their own plays, golfers afraid of the first tee, and girl tennis players afraid that their gold panties won't catch the summer sunlight.

Sometimes an athlete feels such physical fear that he cannot so much as move his head out of the way of an inside pitch. Sometimes he feels such psychological fear he cannot pick up the sort of grounder he has handled ten thousand times before. Sometimes an athlete's fear is a combination of the physical and psychological. But at different times and in different ways, all athletes learn what it is to be afraid.

During the 1952 Olympics, Ingemar Johansson, the Swedish Tiger, was matched against the late Ed Sanders in a heavyweight bout. After a few moments of preliminary sparring, Johansson sized up his opponent and ran. He didn't actually run out of the ring, because the ropes were in the way, but he fled as best he could inside the ring, obviously terrified, until kindly Olympic officials intervened and awarded the fight to Sanders.

"INGEMAR, FOR SHAME!" one Swedish newspaper headlined, unkindly. "He's worse than the British heavies," an American sportswriter said. "They always get knocked out, but at least they take a couple of punches first."

Johansson himself had no comment. Sanders outweighed him by more than twenty pounds and possessed a fierce scowl, but no losing fighter ever pleads fright. The difference between Johansson then and Johansson now is partly craft, but it is also that he has learned to control the fear all fighters feel. When Johansson is frightened these days, he punches or back-pedals or clinches or covers up. He no longer does what comes naturally, which is to run.

A jockey, to be successful, must be willing to urge his horse into potentially fatal positions. He must move up between a rival horse and the rail even though the outside horse may lug in at any time, closing the gap. He must move between two other horses, although either may veer and cause an accident.

Some years ago, in spots of this sort, Eddie Arcaro had four spills in ten days. Each time, as he lay in the dirt, horses thundered past, their hooves knifing up clods of dirt and drumming like a charge of cavalry. "For around two weeks," Arcaro said, "I couldn't get to sleep without seeing those hooves around my head." Gradually, the fear waned. "I wouldn't say I'm ever afraid of a horse now," Arcaro insisted recently. "I'm nervous about some, sure, but if I was actually afraid of one, what the hell, I just wouldn't ride him, and that hasn't happened."

Some riders become so involved with fear that they stop taking chances. In the tack room, their colleagues say simply, "He's riding like a married jock." There is no quicker way for a jockey to go out of business. He must either find a way to live with his fear or quit.

Ten days before the Army-Navy football game last fall, Red Blaik, the cool, analytical man who coached Army football for almost two decades, was holding forth on halfbacks he had known. Traditionally, Army halfbacks run with a difference: knees high, head up, driving over, around, or through the opposition. "Speed," Blaik was saying, "and feinting and intelligence." He was walking across a practice field where Pete Dawkins and Bob Anderson were running against a scrub line. "Watch them," Blaik said.

The backs ran hard, and after they were hit, they sprang up instantly, as if unwilling to give their tacklers any more than the bare minimum of satisfaction. Another Army back was hit and limped slightly.

"All right," Blaik said, "no limping. If you have to limp, don't scrimmage. If you want to scrimmage, don't limp."

The limp disappeared in a hurry.

"Over here," Blaik said, indicating another part of the field, "is a boy with as much physically as Anderson or Dawkins. Maybe he even has more."

A jayvee halfback was plunging, but not in the accepted Army style. He ran well, but just before he was hit, there was a slight but noticeable change in frame. The body tightened, stiffened, tensed, and it was clear that the back was bracing for a fall even before the lineman touched him. When a tackler missed, the back, ready to be tackled, lost a step before regaining full speed.

"Something you have to understand," Blaik said, "is that this isn't a question of courage, pure and simple. The boy could turn out to be a war hero. It's just that he doesn't like body contact. I've seen this hundreds of times and you can nearly always tell from the beginning. Some of them do and some of them don't. A boy who doesn't like contact shouldn't play football, because he isn't going to change."

If fighters change and jockeys change and learn to live with fear, why not college halfbacks? The answer ultimately comes down to time. Johannson was young enough to be a college student when he ran and Arcaro, in his sleepless days, was only slightly older. A college halfback is through at twenty-two.

Dealing with physical fear is a question of gradually accepting hazards, day after day, week after week, until suddenly they no longer seem dangerous. Humans are adaptable, but the adaptations require patience. One simply does not march into a battle area the first time as calmly as one does the second or third. A fighter of twenty-two is likely to be more frightened than he will be three years, or thirty bouts, later.

But there is a point where things turn around, where too many years of living with fear break down human drive. Fangio reached that point before he quit. Jersey Joe Walcott fought superbly against Rocky Marciano once, but the second time he sat down promptly after a punch of indeterminate power. Walcott knew Marciano could hit. He took his second purse without a review lesson.

The path of physical fear varies with the athlete, of course, but a general pattern does exist. First, the athlete encounters fear. This may come when he is a child, or when he is older, or only after he has been hurt. Then, for a time, he is at war with himself. Is the fun of the game and the pleasure of victory worth the risk of pain? The good athlete always answers yes, and sets about controlling his fear. Finally, after enough years in sports, it all gets to be too much trouble and he quits. He either sits down in the ring or he retires.

The other fear in sports, fear of failure, is less predictable, more common, less understood, more discussed, and runs into the science of psychiatry. To me it has seemed clearest in terms of poker.

Consider the frightened poker player who is dealt three kings. He blinks, his stomach talks, and he raises like a man who has been dealt a pair of deuces. It isn't purely money, for he plays with the same outrageous caution, regardless of stakes. It's chiefly that fear drives common sense out of his head.

He looks at his three kings and he considers. The man at his right is due for a straight. (No one is ever due for anything in cards. Each deal is independent of the others.) The next man seems confident. Maybe he has a full house. The dealer is smiling. He probably loaded the deck. So it goes and eventually the man with three kings gets about half of what he would have won if he had kept his head.

The non-frightened poker player knows that three kings will probably be good enough. He bids accordingly and if he loses, he goes ahead and the next time he has three kings he plays exactly the same way. At its worst, fear paralyzes, but rarely in sports does fright assume such proportions. What psychological fear does most frequently is block the normal reasoning process.

When Early Wynn pitches against the Yankees, he glares and knocks hitters down precisely as he would against any other team. But it is not quite the same operation. "Sometimes," he says, "when I get behind to a hitter, I figure I got to do something because here is Mantle coming up and maybe Berra and Skowron. I get behind and I figure I can't walk this guy and I can just feel that fear."

Wynn's solution, arrived at over the years, is to inhale mightily. "After I take that deep breath," he says, "I feel okay." The deep breath doesn't throw strikes, but it enables Wynn to forget what might happen and concentrate on the business at hand.

The best clutch ballplayer I remember was a man who suffered a nervous collapse during World War II, who jumped a team because he was homesick and who absolutely refused to travel by airplane. His name is Billy Cox, and although there have been many better ballplayers, I can't think of anyone whose game improved so much under pressure.

Cox was a third baseman, a small, wiry man with big bony wrists, who subdued ground balls with a little scooping motion and was one of the finest fielders of his time. Before ordinary games, Cox often busied himself thinking up excuses for not playing, but whenever the Brooklyn Dodgers were faced with an important series, he was almost eager to go to work.

In the big ones, he was everywhere. He guarded the line, cut in front of the shortstop, and charged topped balls with such agility that Casey Stengel once complained during a World Series, "He ain't a third baseman. He's an unprintable acrobat." Cox was never a great hitter, but he was far better swinging in a clutch than he was when it didn't matter.

"I can't explain it," Cox once said. "My wife says I have 'fearless nerves.' Anyway, before the big ones, I feel my nerves all tightening up, sort of getting ready. You know what I mean?"

"But what about the homesickness?"

Cox's lean face was grim. He did not usually have much to say. "I believe that everybody has some kind of problem," he said. "No matter how good a ballplayer is, there's something that bothers him. My problem was that I got lonesome on the road. It takes nerve to lick your problem, but you got to have it."

"Well, doesn't it take nerve to play in clutch games?"

"They never bothered me," Cox said. "I never got scared. The thing that bothered me was that I wanted to go home."

Stan Musial insists that no one can be afraid and play baseball well. "If you're worried about what happens when you go bad," Musial says, "you shouldn't even get in the business." Musial is calling this as he sees it, but he forgets his own outlook when he left Donora, Pennsylvania, for the great world of baseball, with his wife, whose father owned a grocery.

"I'm not scared," he told a friend, "because if the baseball doesn't work out, I can always get a job in the store."

In the theater, stagefright, a single word, sums up all fear of failure. But in sports, which cover so large an area and employ so varied a jargon, there are a dozen words for what is roughly the same thing. "Choke" is currently most popular.

"When I get out on the field before the opening kickoff I feel it," Randy Duncan, Iowa's great quarterback last season, has remarked. "I can't eat breakfast that day, and when I see the crowd, I guess you could say I'm choked up. Then, on the kickoff, I have to belt someone. As soon as I block a guy hard, the fear disappears. Just body contact once, and I stop choking."

Tennis player Gussie Moran, in her greatest days, found a less taxing solution. "On the pro tour," she says, "I'd get so worried I wouldn't make a good showing, I started taking a slug of Canadian Club before each match. I got so I couldn't play at all without the slug."

The only tie between Phil Hill, trembling after an auto race, and Gussie, downing a shot before the first serve, is the fact of fear, and this drives to the root of the crucial role fear plays in sports. It doesn't matter what there is to be afraid of, whether it's death, or failure, or disgrace, or a double fault. The point is that there is something to cause fear in every avenue of sport, and whatever exists is sufficient. To the athlete, fear is a condition of the job.

Sometimes, after much research, a man announces that fighters or bull fighters or pitchers who have learned to beat the Yankees are the bravest men in sports. But no one knows the fear someone else feels and so no one can prepare a valid yardstick of athletes' bravery. Only this much is sure: They are all afraid of different things in different ways at different times. It is never possible to conquer fear, but it can be subdued

for a time. Watch the great athlete work at his craft and you see someone who has known fear before and who will know fear again but who
goes about his job fearlessly. This is the courage of an athlete and it is
towering to behold.

GAY TALESE

"THE LOSER"

*An important turning point in Gay Talese's writing career can be linked
to the strikes against the* New York Times *in 1955 and 1962. "I love
strikes," he said. "I'm not one to cross picket lines, so what happens is
that you don't have to go to the office. You can sit at home and write
about a subject in depth rather than just skimming off the top. It's a
great departure, because in those days if you took time off your job at the*
Times *you lost your job. In fact, I enjoyed the strikes so much that I
finally left the paper."*

"And why Floyd Patterson?"

"I'd written about thirty short pieces on him for the Times *and other
publications. I'd followed him around. People must have thought I was
part of his entourage. So I had all that background material and because
of the strikes the time to put it together in a single essay for* Esquire."

I asked how Patterson reacted to being branded a loser.

*"I don't think anyone can be so casual about life as to not understand
losing," Talese explained. "You learn early. I was a hopeless failure in
parochial school. The only reason I got through was that my father was
the second major financial contributor to the school (after the Ford
dealer) and did the nuns' laundry for free. I think Patterson accepted my
piece on him. I see him from time to time at dinners. He's one of the few
fighters who's moved into middle age and still maintained his pride
outside the ring. He hasn't lost that."*

At the foot of a mountain in upstate New York, about sixty miles from
Manhattan, there is an abandoned country clubhouse with a dusty dance

floor, upturned barstools, and an untuned piano; and the only sounds heard around the place at night come from the big white house behind it—the clanging sounds of garbage cans being toppled by raccoons, skunks, and stray cats making their nocturnal raids down from the mountain.

The white house seems deserted, too; but occasionally, when the animals become too clamorous, a light will flash on, a window will open, and a Coke bottle will come flying through the darkness and smash against the cans. But mostly the animals are undisturbed until daybreak, when the rear door of the white house swings open and a broad-shouldered Negro appears in gray sweat clothes with a white towel around his neck.

He runs down the steps, quickly passes the garbage cans, and proceeds at a trot down the dirt road beyond the country club toward the highway. Sometimes he stops along the road and throws a flurry of punches at imaginary foes, each jab punctuated by hard gasps of his breathing— *"hegh-hegh-hegh"*—and then, reaching the highway, he turns and soon disappears up the mountain.

At this time of morning farm trucks are on the road, and the other drivers wave at the runner. And later in the morning other motorists see him, and a few stop suddenly at the curb and ask:

"Say, aren't *you* Floyd Patterson?"

"No," says Floyd Patterson. "I'm his brother, Raymond."

The motorists move on, but recently a man on foot, a disheveled man who seemed to have spent the night outdoors, staggered behind the runner along the road and yelled, "Hey, Floyd Patterson!"

"No, I'm his brother, Raymond."

"Don't tell *me* you're not Floyd Patterson. I know what Floyd Patterson looks like."

"Okay," Patterson said, shrugging, "if you want me to be Floyd Patterson, I'll be Floyd Patterson."

"So let me have your autograph," said the man, handing him a rumpled piece of paper and a pencil.

He signed it—"Raymond Patterson."

One hour later Floyd Patterson was jogging his way back down the dirt path toward the white house, the towel over his head absorbing the sweat from his brow. He lives alone in a two-room apartment in the rear of the house, and has remained there in almost complete seclusion since getting knocked out a second time by Sonny Liston.

In the smaller room is a large bed he makes up himself, several record albums he rarely plays, a telephone that seldom rings. The larger room has a kitchen on one side and, on the other, adjacent to a sofa, is a

fireplace from which are hung boxing trunks and T-shirts to dry, and a
photograph of him when he was the champion, and also a television set.
The set is usually on except when Patterson is sleeping, or when he is
sparring across the road inside the clubhouse (the ring is rigged over
what was once the dance floor), or when, in a rare moment of painful
honesty, he reveals to a visitor what it is like to be the loser.

"Oh, I would give up anything to just be able to work with Liston, to
box with him somewhere where nobody would see us, and to see if I
could get past three minutes with him," Patterson was saying, wiping his
face with the towel, pacing slowly around the room near the sofa. "I
know I can do better. . . . Oh, I'm not talking about a rematch. Who
would pay a nickel for another Patterson-Liston fight? I know *I*
wouldn't. . . . But all I want to do is get past the first round."

Then he said, "You have no idea how it is in the first round. You're
out there with all those people around you, and those cameras, and the
whole world looking in, and all that movement, that excitement, and
'The Star Spangled Banner,' and the whole nation hoping you'll win,
including the president. And do you know what all this does? It blinds
you, just blinds you. And then the bell rings, and you go at Liston and
he's coming at you, and you're not even aware that there's a referee in
the ring with you. . . .

"Then you can't remember much of the rest, because you don't want
to. . . . All you recall is, all of a sudden you're getting up, and the referee
is saying, 'You all right?' and you say, 'Of *course* I'm all right,' and he
says, 'What's your name?' and you say, 'Patterson.'

"And then, suddenly, with all this screaming around you, you're down
again, and you know you have to get up, but you're extremely groggy,
and the referee is pushing you back, and your trainer is in there with a
towel, and the people are all standing up, and your eyes focus directly at
no one person—you're sort of floating.

"It is not a *bad* feeling when you're knocked out," he said. "It's a *good*
feeling, actually. It's not painful, just a sharp grogginess. You don't see
angels or stars; you're on a pleasant cloud. After Liston hit me in Nevada,
I felt, for about four or five seconds, that everybody in the arena was
actually in the ring with me, circled around me like a family, and you feel
warmth toward all the people in the arena after you're knocked out. You
feel lovable to all the people. And you want to reach out and kiss everybody—men and women—and after the Liston fight somebody told me I
actually blew a kiss to the crowd from the ring. I don't remember that.
But I guess it's true because that's the way you feel during the four or five
seconds after a knockout. . . .

"But then," Patterson went on, still pacing, "this good feeling leaves you. You realize where you are, and what you're doing there, and what has just happened to you. And what follows is a hurt, a confused hurt— not a physical hurt—it's a hurt combined with anger; it's a what-will-people-think hurt; it's an ashamed-of-my-own-ability hurt . . . and all you want then is a hatch door in the middle of the ring—a hatch door that will open and let you fall through and land in your dressing room instead of having to get out of the ring and face those people. The worst thing about losing is having to walk out of the ring and face those people. . . ."

Then Patterson walked over to the stove and put on the kettle for tea. He remained silent for a few moments. Through the walls could be heard the footsteps and voices of the sparring partners and the trainer who live in the front of the house. Soon they would be in the clubhouse getting things ready should Patterson wish to spar. In two days he was scheduled to fly to Stockholm and fight an Italian named Amonti, Patterson's first appearance in the ring since the last Liston fight.

Next he hoped to get a fight in London against Henry Cooper. Then, if his confidence was restored, his reflexes reacting, Patterson hoped to start back up the ladder in this country, fighting all the leading contenders, fighting often, and not waiting so long between each fight as he had done when he was a champion in the 90 percent tax bracket.

His wife, whom he finds little time to see, and most of his friends think he should quit. They point out that he does not need the money. Even he admits that, from investments alone on his $8 million gross earnings, he should have an annual income of about thirty-five thousand dollars for the next twenty-five years. But Patterson, who is only twenty-nine years old and barely scratched, cannot believe that he is finished. He cannot help but think that it was something more than Liston that destroyed him—a strange, psychological force was also involved, and unless he can fully understand what it was, and learn to deal with it in the boxing ring, he may never be able to live peacefully anywhere but under this mountain. Nor will he ever be able to discard the false whiskers and mustache that, ever since Johansson beat him in 1959, he has carried with him in a small attaché case into each fight so he can slip out of the stadium unrecognized should he lose.

"I often wonder what other fighters feel, and what goes through their minds when they lose," Patterson said, placing the cups of tea on the table. "I've wanted so much to talk to another fighter about all this, to compare thoughts, to see if he feels some of the same things I've felt. But who can you talk to? Most fighters don't talk much anyway. And I can't even look another fighter in the eye at a weigh-in, for some reason.

"At the Liston weigh-in, the sportswriters noticed this, and said it showed I was afraid. But that's not it. I can never look *any* fighter in the eye because . . . well, because we're going to fight, which isn't a nice thing, and because . . . well, once I actually did look a fighter in the eye. It was a long, long time ago. I must have been in the amateurs then. And when I looked at this fighter, I saw he had such a nice face . . . and then he looked at *me* . . . and *smiled* at me . . . and *I* smiled back! It was strange, very strange. When a guy can look at another guy and smile like that, I don't think they have any business fighting.

"I don't remember what happened in that fight, and I don't remember what the guy's name was. I only remember that, ever since, I have never looked another fighter in the eye."

The telephone rang in the bedroom. Patterson got up to answer it. It was his wife, Sandra. So he excused himself, shutting the bedroom door behind him.

Sandra Patterson and their four children live in a $100,000 home in an upper-middle-class white neighborhood in Scarsdale, New York. Floyd Patterson feels uncomfortable in this home surrounded by a manicured lawn and stuffed with furniture, and since losing his title to Liston, he has preferred living full time at his camp, which his children have come to know as "daddy's house." The children, the eldest of whom is a daughter named Jeannie now seven years old, do not know exactly what their father does for a living. But Jeannie, who watched the last Liston-Patterson fight on closed-circuit television, accepted the explanation that her father performs in a kind of game where the men take turns pushing one another down; he had his turn pushing them down, and now it is their turn.

The bedroom door opened again, and Floyd Patterson, shaking his head, was very angry and nervous.

"I'm not going to work out today," he said. "I'm going to fly down to Scarsdale. Those boys are picking on Jeannie again. She's the only Negro in this school, and the older kids give her a rough time, and some of the older boys tease her and lift up her dress all the time. Yesterday she went home crying, and so today I'm going down there and plan to wait outside the school for those boys to come out, and. . . ."

"How old are they?" he was asked.

"Teenagers," he said. "Old enough for a left hook."

Patterson telephoned his pilot friend, Ted Hanson, who stays at the camp and does public-relations work for him, and has helped teach Patterson to fly. Five minutes later Hanson, a lean white man with a crew cut and glasses, was knocking on the door; and ten minutes later both were in the car that Patterson was driving almost recklessly over the narrow, winding country roads toward the airport, about six miles from the camp.

"Sandra is afraid I'll cause trouble; she's worried about what I'll do to those boys; she doesn't want trouble!" Patterson snapped, swerving around a hill and giving his car more gas. "She's just not firm enough! She's afraid . . . she was afraid to tell me about that groceryman who's been making passes at her. It took her a long time before she told me about that dishwasher repairman who comes over and calls her 'baby.' They all know I'm away so much. And that dishwasher repairman's been to my home about four, five times this month already. That machine breaks down every week. I guess he fixes it so it breaks down every week. Last time, I laid a trap. I waited forty-five minutes for him to come, but then he didn't show up. I was going to grab him and say, 'How would you like it if I called *your* wife *baby?* You'd feel like punching me in the nose, wouldn't you? Well, that's what I'm going to do—if you ever call her *baby* again. You call her Mrs. Patterson; or Sandra, if you know her. But you don't know her, so call her Mrs. Patterson.' And then I told Sandra that these men, this type of white man, he just wants to have some fun with colored women. He'll never marry a colored woman, just wants to have some fun. . . ."

Now he was driving into the airport's parking lot. Directly ahead, roped to the grass airstrip, was the single-engine green Cessna that Patterson bought and learned to fly before the second Liston fight. Flying was a thing Patterson had always feared—a fear shared by, maybe inherited from, his manager, Cus D'Amato, who still will not fly.

D'Amato, who took over training Patterson when the fighter was seventeen or eighteen years old and exerted a tremendous influence over his psyche, is a strange but fascinating man of fifty-six who is addicted to Spartanism and self-denial and is possessed by suspicion and fear: He avoids subways because he fears someone might push him onto the tracks; never has married, never reveals his home address.

"I must keep my enemies confused," D'Amato once explained. "When they are confused, then I can do a job for my fighters. What I do not want in life, however, is a sense of security; the moment a person knows security, his senses are dulled—and he begins to die. I also do not want many pleasures in life; I believe the more pleasures you get out of living, the more fear you have of dying."

Until a few years ago, D'Amato did most of Patterson's talking, and ran things like an Italian *padrone.* But later Patterson, the maturing son, rebelled against the Father Image. After losing to Sonny Liston the first time—a fight D'Amato had urged Patterson to resist—Patterson took flying lessons. And before the second Liston fight, Patterson had conquered his fear of height, was master at the controls, was filled with renewed confidence—and knew, too, that even if he lost, he at least possessed a vehicle that could get him out of town, fast.

But it didn't. After the fight, the little Cessna, weighed down by too much luggage, became overheated ninety miles outside of Las Vegas. Patterson and his pilot companion, having no choice but to turn back, radioed the airfield and arranged for the rental of a larger plane. When they landed, the Vegas air terminal was filled with people leaving town after the fight. Patterson hid in the shadows behind a hangar. His beard was packed in the trunk. But nobody saw him.

Later the pilot flew Patterson's Cessna back to New York alone. And Patterson flew in the larger, rented plane. He was accompanied on this flight by Hanson, a friendly, forty-two-year-old, thrice-divorced Nevadan who once was a crop duster, a bartender, and a cabaret hoofer; later he became a pilot instructor in Las Vegas, and it was there that he met Patterson. The two became good friends. And when Patterson asked Hanson to help fly the rented plane back to New York, Hanson did not hesitate, even though he had a slight hangover that night—partly due to being depressed by Liston's victory, partly due to being slugged in a bar by a drunk after objecting to some unflattering things the drunk had said about the fight.

Once in the airplane, however, Ted Hanson became very alert. He had to, because after the plane had cruised awhile at ten thousand feet, Floyd Patterson's mind seemed to wander back to the ring, and the plane would drift off course, and Hanson would say, "Floyd, Floyd, how's about getting back on course?", and then Patterson's head would snap up and his eyes would flash toward the dials. And everything would be all right for a while. But then he was back in the arena, reliving the fight, hardly believing that it had really happened. . . .

". . . And I kept thinking, as I flew out of Vegas that night, of all those months of training before the fight, all the roadwork, all the sparring, all the months away from Sandra . . . thinking of the time in camp when I wanted to stay up until eleven-fifteen P.M. to watch a certain movie on* The Late Show. *But I didn't because I had roadwork the next morning. . . .*

". . . And I was thinking about how good I'd felt before the fight, as I lay on the table in the dressing room. I remember thinking, 'You're in excellent physical condition, you're in good mental condition—but are you vicious?' But you tell yourself, 'Viciousness is not important now, don't think about it now; a championship fight's at stake, and that's important enough and, who knows? maybe you'll get vicious once the bell rings.'

". . . And so you lay there trying to get a little sleep . . . but you're only in a twilight zone, half asleep, and you're interrupted every once in a while by voices out in the hall, some guy's yelling 'Hey, Jack,' or 'Hey, Al,' or 'Hey, get those four-rounders into the ring.' And when you hear that, you think, 'They're not ready for you yet.' So you lay there . . . and wonder, 'Where

*will I be tomorrow? Where will I be three hours from now?' Oh, you think
all kinds of thoughts, some thoughts completely unrelated to the fight
. . . you wonder whether you ever paid your mother-in-law back for all
those stamps she bought a year ago . . . and you remember that time at two
A.M. when Sandra tripped on the steps while bringing a bottle up to the
baby . . . and then you get mad and ask: 'What am I thinking about these
things for?' . . . and you try to sleep . . . but then the door opens and
somebody says to somebody else, 'Hey, is somebody gonna go to Liston's
dressing room to watch 'em bandage up?'*

*". . . And so then you know it's about time to get ready. . . . You open
your eyes. You get off the table. You glove up, you loosen up. Then
Liston's trainer walks in. He looks at you, he smiles. He feels the bandages and later he says, 'Good luck, Floyd,' and you think, 'He didn't have
to say that; he must be a nice guy.'*

*". . . And then you go out, and it's the long walk, always a long walk,
and you think, 'What am I gonna be when I come back this way?' Then
you climb into the ring. You notice Billy Eckstine at ringside leaning over
to talk to somebody, and you see the reporters—some you like, some you
don't like—and then it's 'The Star Spangled Banner,' and the cameras are
rolling, and the bell rings. . . .*

*". . . How could the same thing happen twice? How? That's all I kept
thinking after the knockout. . . . Was I fooling these people all these
years? . . . Was I ever the champion? . . . And then they lead you out of the
ring . . . and up the aisle you go, past those people, and all you want is to
get to your dressing room, fast . . . but the trouble was in Las Vegas they
made a wrong turn along the aisle, and when we got to the end there was
no dressing room there . . . and we had to walk all the way back down the
aisle, past the same people, and they must have been thinking, 'Patterson's not only knocked out, but he can't even find his dressing room. . . .'*

*". . . In the dressing room I had a headache. Liston didn't hurt me
physically—a few days later I only felt a twitching nerve in my teeth—it
was nothing like some fights I've had: like that Dick Wagner fight in
fifty-three when he beat my body so bad I was urinating blood for days.
After the Liston fight, I just went into the bathroom, shut the door behind
me, and looked at myself in the mirror. I just looked at myself, and asked,
'What happened?' and then they started pounding on the door, and saying, 'Com'on out, Floyd, com'on out; the press is here, Cus is here,
com'on out, Floyd. . . .'*

*". . . And so I went out, and they asked questions, but what can you say?
What you're thinking about is all those months of training, all the conditioning, all the depriving; and you think, 'I didn't have to run that extra
mile, didn't have to spar that day, I could have stayed up that night in*

camp and watched The Late Show. . . . *I could have fought this fight
tonight in no condition. . . .' "*

"Floyd, Floyd," Hanson had said, "let's get back on course. . . ."

Again Patterson would snap out of his reverie, and refocus on the
omniscope, and get his flying under control. After landing in New Mexico, and then in Ohio, Floyd Patterson and Ted Hanson brought the
little plane into the New York airstrip near the fight camp. The green
Cessna that had been flown back by the other pilot was already there,
roped to the grass at precisely the same spot it was on this day five
months later when Floyd Patterson was planning to fly it toward perhaps
another fight—this time a fight with some schoolboys in Scarsdale who
had been lifting up his little daughter's dress.

Patterson and Ted Hanson untied the plane, and Patterson got a rag
and wiped from the windshield the splotches of insects. Then he walked
around behind the plane, inspected the tail, checked under the fuselage,
then peered down between the wing and the flaps to make sure all the
screws were tight. He seemed suspicious of something. D'Amato would
have been pleased.

"If a guy wants to get rid of you," Patterson explained, "all he has to
do is remove these little screws here. Then, when you try to come in for a
landing, the flaps fall off, and you crash."

Then Patterson got into the cockpit and started the engine. A few
moments later, with Hanson beside him, Patterson was racing the little
plane over the grassy field, then soaring over the weeds, then flying high
above the gentle hills and trees. It was a nice takeoff.

Since it was only a forty-minute flight to the Westchester airport,
where Sandra Patterson would be waiting with a car, Floyd Patterson did
all the flying. The trip was uneventful until, suddenly behind a cloud, he
flew into heavy smoke that hovered above a forest fire. His visibility
gone, he was forced to the instruments. And at this precise moment, a fly
that had been buzzing in the back of the cockpit flew up front and
landed on the instrument panel in front of Patterson. He glared at the
fly, watched it crawl slowly up the windshield, then shot a quick smash
with his palm against the glass. He missed. The fly buzzed safely past
Patterson's ear, bounced off the back of the cockpit, circled around.

"This smoke won't keep up," Hanson assured. "You can level off."

Patterson leveled off.

He flew easily for a few moments. Then the fly buzzed to the front
again, zigzagging before Patterson's face, landed on the panel, and proceeded to crawl across it. Patterson watched it, squinted. Then he
slammed down at it with a quick right hand. Missed.

Ten minutes later, his nerves still on edge, Patterson began the descent. He picked up the radio microphone—"Westchester tower . . . Cessna 2729 uniform . . . three miles northwest . . . land in one-six on final . . ."—and then, after an easy landing, he climbed quickly out of the cockpit and strode toward his wife's station wagon outside the terminal.

But along the way a small man smoking a cigar turned toward Patterson, waved at him, and said, "Say, excuse me, but aren't you . . . aren't you . . . Sonny Liston?"

Patterson stopped. He glared at the man, bewildered. He wasn't sure whether it was a joke or an insult, and he really did not know what to do.

"Aren't you Sonny Liston?" the man repeated, quite serious.

"No," Patterson said, quickly passing by the man, "I'm his brother."

When he reached Mrs. Patterson's car, he asked, "How much time till school lets out?"

"About fifteen minutes," she said, starting up the engine. Then she said, "Oh, Floyd, I just should have told Sister, I shouldn't have. . . ."

"You tell Sister; *I'll* tell the boys. . . ."

Mrs. Patterson drove as quickly as she could into Scarsdale, with Patterson shaking his head and telling Ted Hanson in the back, "Really can't understand these school kids. This is a religious school, and they want twenty thousand dollars for a glass window—and yet, some of them carry these racial prejudices, and it's mostly the Jews who are shoulder to shoulder with us, and. . . ."

"Oh, Floyd," cried his wife, "Floyd, I have to get along here . . . you're not here, you don't live here, I . . ."

She arrived at the school just as the bell began to ring. It was a modern building at the top of a hill, and on the lawn was the statue of a saint, and behind it a large white cross. "There's Jeannie," said Mrs. Patterson.

"Hurry, call her over here," Patterson said.

"Jeannie! Come over here, honey."

The little girl, wearing a blue school uniform and cap, and clasping books in front of her, came running down the path toward the station wagon.

"Jeannie," Floyd Patterson said, rolling down his window, "point out the boys who lifted your dress."

Jeannie turned and watched as several students came down the path; then she pointed to a tall, thin curly-haired boy walking with four other boys, all about twelve to fourteen years of age.

"Hey," Patterson called to him, "can I see you for a minute?"

All five boys came to the side of the car. They looked Patterson directly in the eye. They seemed not at all intimidated by him.

"You the one that's been lifting up my daughter's dress?" Patterson asked the boy who had been singled out.

"Nope," the boy said casually.

"Nope?" Patterson said, caught off guard by the reply.

"Wasn't him, mister," said another boy. "Probably was his little brother."

Patterson looked at Jeannie. But she was speechless, uncertain. The five boys remained there, waiting for Patterson to do something.

"Well, er, where's your little brother?" Patterson asked.

"Hey, kid!" one of the boys yelled. "Come over here."

A boy walked toward them. He resembled his older brother; he had freckles on his small, upturned nose, had blue eyes, dark curly hair, and, as he approached the station wagon, he seemed equally unintimidated by Patterson.

"You been lifting up my daughter's dress?"

"Nope," the boy said.

"Nope!" Patterson repeated, frustrated.

"Nope, I wasn't lifting it. I was just touching it a little . . ."

The other boys stood around the car looking down at Patterson, and other students crowded behind them, and nearby Patterson saw several white parents standing next to their parked cars; he became self-conscious, began to tap nervously with his fingers against the dashboard. He could not raise his voice without creating an unpleasant scene, yet could not retreat gracefully; so his voice went soft, and he said, finally:

"Look, boy, I want you to stop it. I won't tell your mother—that might get you in trouble—but don't do it again, okay?"

"Okay."

The boys calmly turned and walked, in a group, up the street.

Sandra Patterson said nothing. Jeannie opened the door, sat in the front seat next to her father, and took out a small blue piece of paper that a nun had given her and handed it across to Mrs. Patterson. But Floyd Patterson snatched it. He read it. Then he paused, put the paper down, and quietly announced, dragging out the words, *"She didn't do her religion. . . ."*

Patterson now wanted to get out of Scarsdale. He wanted to return to camp. After stopping at the Patterson home in Scarsdale and picking up Floyd Patterson, Jr., who is three, Mrs. Patterson drove them all back to the airport. Jeannie and Floyd, Jr., were seated in the back of the plane, and then Mrs. Patterson drove the station wagon alone up to camp, planning to return to Scarsdale that evening with the children.

It was four P.M. when Floyd Patterson got back to the camp, and the shadows were falling on the clubhouse, and on the tennis court routed by weeds, and on the big white house in front of which not a single automobile was parked. All was deserted and quiet; it was a loser's camp.

The children ran to play inside the clubhouse; Patterson walked slowly toward his apartment to dress for the workout.

"What could I do with those schoolboys?" he asked. "What can you do to kids of that age?"

It still seemed to bother him—the effrontery of the boys, the realization that he had somehow failed, the probability that, had those same boys heckled someone in Liston's family, the school yard would have been littered with limbs.

While Patterson and Liston both are products of the slum, and while both began as thieves, Patterson had been tamed in a special school with help from a gentle Negro spinster; later he became a Catholic convert, and learned not to hate. Still later he bought a dictionary, adding to his vocabulary such words as "vicissitude" and "enigma." And when he regained his championship from Johansson, he became the Great Black Hope of the Urban League.

He proved that it is not only possible to rise out of a a Negro slum and succeed as a sportsman, but also to develop into an intelligent, sensitive, law-abiding citizen. In proving this, however, and in taking pride in it, Patterson seemed to lose part of himself. He lost part of his hunger, his anger—and as he walked up the steps into his apartment, he was saying, "I became the good guy. . . . After Liston won the title, I kept hoping that he would change into a good guy, too. That would have relieved me of the responsibility, and maybe I could have been more of the bad guy. But he didn't. . . . It's okay to be the good guy when you're winning. But when you're losing, it is no good being the good guy."

Patterson took off his shirt and trousers and, moving some books on the bureau to one side, put down his watch, his cuff links, and a clip of bills.

"Do you do much reading?" he was asked.

"No," he said. "In fact, you know I've never finished reading a book in my whole life? I don't know why. I just feel that no writer today has anything for me; I mean, none of them has felt any more deeply than I have, and I have nothing to learn from them. Although Baldwin to me seems different from the rest. What's Baldwin doing these days?"

"He's writing a play. Anthony Quinn is supposed to have a part in it."

"Quinn doesn't like me."

"Why?"

"I read or heard it somewhere; Quinn had been quoted as saying that my fight was disgraceful against Liston, and Quinn said something to the effect that he could have done better. People often say that—*they* could have done better! Well I think that if *they* had to fight, *they* couldn't even go through the experience of waiting for the fight to begin. They'd be up the whole night before, and would be drinking, or taking drugs. They'd probably get a heart attack. I'm sure that, if I was in the ring with Anthony Quinn, I could wear him out without even touching him. I would do nothing but pressure him, I'd stalk him, I'd stand close to him. I wouldn't touch him, but I'd wear him out and he'd collapse. But Anthony Quinn's an old man, isn't he?"

"In his forties."

"Well, anyway," Patterson said, "getting back to Baldwin, he seems like a wonderful guy. I've seen him on television and, before the Liston fight in Chicago, he came by my camp. You meet Baldwin on the street and you say, 'Who's this poor slob?'—he seems just like another guy; and this is the same impression *I* give people when they don't know me. But I think Baldwin and me, we have much in common, and someday I'd just like to sit somewhere for a long time and talk to him. . . ."

Patterson, his trunks and sweat pants on, bent over to tie his shoe-laces, and then, from a bureau drawer, took out a T-shirt across which was printed *Deauville*. He has several T-shirts bearing the same name. He takes good care of them. They are souvenirs from the high point of his life. They are from the Deauville Hotel in Miami Beach, which is where he trained for the third Ingemar Johansson match in March of 1961.

Never was Floyd Patterson more popular, more admired than during that winter. He had visited President Kennedy; he had been given a thirty-five-thousand-dollar jeweled crown by his manager; his greatness was conceded by sportswriters—and nobody had any idea that Patterson, secretly, was in possession of a false mustache and dark glasses that he intended to wear out of Miami Beach should he lose the third fight to Johansson.

It was after being knocked out by Johansson in their first fight that Patterson, deep in depression, hiding in humiliation for months in a remote Connecticut lodge, decided he could not face the public again if he lost. So he bought false whiskers and a mustache, and planned to wear them out of his dressing room after a defeat. He had also planned, in leaving his dressing room, to linger momentarily within the crowd and perhaps complain out loud about the fight. Then he would slip undiscovered through the night and into a waiting automobile.

Although there proved to be no need for bringing disguise into the second or third Johansson fights, or into a subsequent bout in Toronto against an obscure heavyweight named Tom McNeeley, Patterson brought it anyway; and, after the first Liston fight, he not only wore it during his thirty-hour automobile ride from Chicago to New York, but he also wore it while in an airliner bound for Spain.

"As I got onto this plane, you'd never have recognized me," he said. "I had on this beard, mustache, glasses, and hat—and I also limped, to make myself look older. I was alone. I didn't care what plane I boarded; I just looked up and saw this sign at the terminal reading 'Madrid,' and so I got on that flight after buying a ticket.

"When I got to Madrid I registered at a hotel under the name Aaron Watson. I stayed in Madrid about four or five days. In the daytime I wandered around to the poorer sections of the city, limping, looking at the people, and the people stared back at me and must have thought I was crazy because I was moving so slow and looked the way I did. I ate food in my hotel room. Although once I went to a restaurant and ordered soup. I hate soup. But I thought it was what old people would order. So I ate it. And after a week of this, I began to actually think I was somebody else. I began to believe it. And it is nice, every once in a while, being somebody else."

Patterson would not elaborate on how he managed to register under a name that did not correspond to his passport; he merely explained, "With money, you can do anything."

Now, walking slowly around the room, his black silk robe over his sweat clothes, Patterson said, "You must wonder what makes a man do things like this. Well, I wonder too. And the answer is, I don't know . . . but I think that within me, within every human being, there is a certain weakness. It is a weakness that exposes itself more when you're alone. And I have figured out that part of the reason I do the things I do, and cannot seem to conquer that one word—*myself*—is because . . . is because . . . I am a coward. . . ."

He stopped. He stood very still in the middle of the room, thinking about what he had just said, probably wondering whether he should have said it.

"I am a coward," he then repeated softly. "My fighting has little to do with that fact, though. I mean you can be a fighter—and a *winning* fighter—and still be a coward. I was probably a coward on the night I won the championship back from Ingemar. And I remember another night, long ago, back when I was in the amateurs, fighting this big tremendous man named Julius Griffin. I was only a hundred fifty-three pounds. I was petrified. It was all I could do to cross the ring. And then he came at me, and moved close to me . . . and from then on I don't know anything. I have no idea what happened. Only thing I know is, I saw him on the floor. And later somebody said, 'Man, I never saw anything like it. You just jumped up in the air, and threw thirty different punches. . . .' "

"When did you first think you were a coward?" he was asked.

"It was after the first Ingemar fight."

"How does one see this cowardice you speak of?"

"You see it when a fighter loses. Ingemar, for instance, is not a coward. When he lost the third fight in Miami, he was at a party later in the Fountainebleau. Had I lost, I couldn't have gone to that party. And I don't see how he did. . . ."

"Could Liston be a coward?"

"That remains to be seen." Patterson said. "We'll find out what he's like after somebody beats him, how he takes it. It's easy to do anything in victory. It's in defeat that a man reveals himself. In defeat I can't face people. I haven't the strength to say to people, 'I did my best, I'm sorry, and whatnot."

"Have you no hate left?"

"I have hated only one fighter," Patterson said. "And that was Ingemar in the second fight. I had been hating him for a whole year before that—not because he beat me in the first fight, but because of what he did after. It was all that boasting in public, and his showing off his right-hand punch on television, his thundering right, his 'toonder and lightning.' And I'd be home watching him on television, and *hating* him. It is a miserable feeling, hate. When a man hates, he can't have any peace of mind. And for one solid year I hated him because, after he took everything away from me, deprived me of everything I was, he *rubbed it in.* On the night of the second fight, in the dressing room, I couldn't wait until I got into the ring. When he was a little late getting into the ring, I thought, 'He's holding me up; he's trying to unsettle me—well, I'll get him!' "

"Why couldn't you hate Liston in the second match?"

Patterson thought for a moment, then said, "Look, if Sonny Liston walked into this room now and slapped me in the face, then you'd see a fight. You'd see the fight of your life because, then, a principle would be involved. I'd forget he was a human being. I'd forget I was a human being. And I'd fight accordingly."

"Could it be, Floyd, that you made a mistake in becoming a prize-fighter?"

"What do you mean?"

"Well, you say you're a coward; you say you have little capacity for hate; and you seemed to lose your nerve against those schoolboys in Scarsdale this afternoon. Don't you think you might have been better suited for some other kind of work? Perhaps a social worker, or. . . ."

"Are you asking why I continue to fight?"

"Yes."

"Well," he said, not irritated by the question, "first of all, I love boxing. Boxing has been good to me. And I might just as well ask you the question: 'Why do you write?' Or, 'Do you retire from writing everytime you write a bad story?' And as to whether I should have become a fighter in the first place, well, let's see how I can explain it. . . . Look, let's say you're a man who has been in an empty room for days and days without food . . . and then they take you out of that room and put you into another room where there's food hanging all over the place . . . and the first thing you reach for, you eat. When you're hungry, you're not choosy, and so I chose the thing that was closest to me. That was boxing. One day I just wandered into a gymnasium and boxed a boy. And I beat him. Then I boxed another boy. I beat him, too. Then I kept boxing. And winning. And I said, 'Here, finally, is something I can do!'

"Now I wasn't a sadist," he quickly added. "But I liked beating people because it was the only thing I could do. And whether boxing was a sport or not, I wanted to make it a sport because it was a thing I could succeed at. And what were the requirements? Sacrifice. That's all. To anybody who comes from the Bedford-Stuyvesant section of Brooklyn, sacrifice comes easy. And so I kept fighting, and one day I became heavyweight champion, and I got to know people like you. And you wonder how I can sacrifice, how I can deprive myself so much. You just don't realize where I've come from. You don't understand where I was when it began for me.

"In those days, when I was about eight years old, everything I got—I stole. I stole to survive, and I did survive, but I seemed to hate myself. My mother told me I used to point to a photograph of myself hanging in the bedroom and say, 'I don't like that boy!' One day my mother found three large X's scratched with a nail or something over that photograph of me. I don't remember doing it. But I do remember feeling like a parasite at home. I remember how awful I used to feel at night when my father, a longshoreman, would come home so tired that, as my mother fixed food before him, he would fall asleep at the table because he was that tired. I would always take his shoes off and clean his feet. That was my job. And I felt so bad because here I was, not going to school, doing nothing, just watching my father come home; and on Friday nights it was even worse. He would come home with his pay, and he'd put every nickel of it on the table so my mother could buy food for all the children. I never wanted to be around to see that. I'd run and hide. And then I decided to leave home and start stealing—and I did. And I would never come home unless I brought something that I had stolen. Once I remember I broke into a dress store and stole a whole mound of dresses, at two A.M., and here I was, this little kid, carrying all those dresses over the wall, thinking they were all the same size, my mother's size, and thinking the cops would never notice me walking down the street with all those dresses piled over my head. They did, of course. . . . I went to the Youth House. . . ."

Floyd Patterson's children, who had been playing outside all this time around the country club, now became restless and began to call him, and Jeannie started to pound on his door. So Patterson picked up his leather bag, which contained his gloves, his mouthpiece, and adhesive tape, and walked with the children across the path toward the clubhouse.

He flicked on the light switches behind the stage near the piano. Beams of amber streaked through the dimly lit room and flashed onto the ring. Then he walked to one side of the room, outside the ring. He took off his robe, shuffled his feet in the rosin, skipped rope, and then began to shadowbox in front of the spit-stained mirror, throwing out quick combinations of lefts, rights, lefts, rights, each jab followed by a *"hegh-hegh-hegh-hegh."* Then, his gloves on, he moved to the punching bag in the far corner, and soon the room reverberated to his rhythmic beat against the bobbing bag—rat-tat-tat-*tetteta,* rat-tat-tat-*tetteta,* rat-tat-tat-*tetteta,* rat-tat-tat-*tetteta!*

The children, sitting on pink leather chairs moved from the bar to the fringe of the ring, watched him in awe, sometimes flinching at the force of his pounding against the leather bag.

And this is how they would probably remember him years from now: a dark, solitary, glistening figure punching in the corner of a forlorn spot at the bottom of a mountain where people once came to have fun—until the clubhouse became unfashionable, the paint began to peel, and Negroes were allowed in.

As Floyd Patterson continued to bang away with lefts and rights, his gloves a brown blur against the bag, his daughter slipped quietly off her chair and wandered past the ring into the other room. There, on the other side of the bar and beyond a dozen round tables, was the stage. She climbed onto the stage and stood behind a microphone, long dead, and cried out imitating a ring announcer, "Ladieeees and gentlemen . . . tonight we present. . . ."

She looked around, puzzled. Then seeing that her little brother had followed her, she waved him up to the stage and began again: "Ladiees and gentlemen . . . tonight we present . . . *Floydie Patterson.* . . ."

Suddenly, the pounding against the bag in the other room stopped. There was silence for a moment. Then Jeannie, still behind the microphone and looking down at her brother, said, "Floydie, come up here!"

"No," he said.

"Oh, come up here!"

"No," he cried.

Then Floyd Patterson's voice, from the other room, called: "Cut it out. . . . I'll take you both for a walk in a minute."

He resumed punching—rat-tat-tat-*tetteta*—and they returned to his side. But Jeannie interrupted, asking, "Daddy, how come you sweating?"

"Water fell on me," he said, still pounding.

"Daddy," asked Floyd, Jr., "how come you spit water on the floor before?"

"To get it out of my mouth."

He was about to move over to the heavier punching bag when the sound of Mrs. Patterson's station wagon could be heard moving up the road.

Soon she was in Patterson's apartment cleaning up a bit, patting the pillows, washing the teacups that had been left in the sink. One hour later the family was having dinner together. They were together for two more hours; then, at ten P.M., Mrs. Patterson washed and dried all of the dishes, and put the garbage out in the can—where it would remain until the raccoons and skunks got to it.

And then, after helping the children with their coats and walking out to the station wagon and kissing her husband good-bye, Mrs. Patterson began to drive down the dirt road toward the highway. Patterson waved once, and stood for a moment watching the taillights go, and then he turned and walked slowly back toward the house.

JOHN CIARDI

"POLO MATCH"

Helmeted, booted, numbered, horsed, and always at
          a distance,
the polo players mill, fumble, jostle, and one at last
          clicks
the white ball far on its high arc while six knot up
          behind
and one in an epic lunge chases the white curve to hit
          or miss

the nothing between two uprights. He is, of course,
    pursued
by the giant that is always there to oppose giants, and
    who means
to deflect the diagram his way, spinning the arc back
    through
the pack, and beyond, and to click it home to his own
    nothing
between the uprights at the other end of the world.
                                              So
from pole to pole they go, Greeks and Trojans,
    identical
to the end and great in their distances, their seven-
    and-a-half
minutes at a time and six times over till the last
    diagram
has been risked, the falls taken, the horses lathered,
    replaced,
and lathered again, and the crowd, forever small in
    its distance,
has applauded again and again like wind rattling the
    dry trees
of a hill beyond.
                    Then, breathing hard, they walk their
                    horses
to the grooms, station wagons, and trailers that wait
to pack distances close and take them expensively to
    rest
between glories; and the players, dismounted, with
    towels
around their necks and their hair sweat-curled, light
    cigarettes
and are no longer giants in the dusty world the cars
    leave
for their home beyond heroes; till only the field is left,
like an emptied world, its grasses charged by great
    shadows.

JOHN UPDIKE

"Hub Fans Bid Kid Adieu"

John Updike wrote me a note about his much-anthologized piece. "I wasn't sure I wanted to go to Williams's last game, but another engagement fell through and I went, and the events there were so stirring I was moved to write my only extended sports piece. I wrote it in five days, with very little research material on hand. But, though I was not a great student of baseball, I was a keen student of Williams, and twenty years of doting Williams-watching came back to me. I loved Ted, in the way that adolescents can love an unattainable celebrity-object, and the love comes through, as Boston's love for the Splendid Splinter came through that day."

Fenway Park, in Boston, is a lyric little bandbox of a ball park. Everything is painted green and seems in curiously sharp focus, like the inside of an old-fashioned peeping-type Easter egg. It was built in 1912 and rebuilt in 1934, and offers, as do most Boston artifacts, a compromise between Man's Euclidean determinations and Nature's beguiling irregularities. Its right field is one of the deepest in the American League, while its left field is the shortest; the high left-field wall, three hundred and fifteen feet from home plate along the foul line, virtually thrusts its surface at right-handed hitters. On the afternoon of Wednesday, September 28, as I took a seat behind third base, a uniformed groundskeeper was treading the top of this wall, picking batting-practice home runs out of the screen, like a mushroom gatherer seen in Wordsworthian perspective on the verge of a cliff. The day was overcast, chill, and uninspirational. The Boston team was the worst in twenty-seven seasons. A jangling medley of incompetent youth and aging competence, the Red Sox were finishing in seventh place only because the Kansas City Athletics had locked them out of the cellar. They were scheduled to play the Baltimore Orioles, a much nimbler blend of May and December, who had been dumped from pennant contention a week before by the insatiable Yankees. I, and 10,453 others, had shown up primarily because this was the Red Sox's last home game of the season, and therefore the last time in all eternity that their regular left fielder, known to the headlines as TED, KID, SPLINTER, THUMPER, TW, and, most cloyingly, MISTER WONDERFUL, would play in Boston. "WHAT WILL WE DO WITHOUT TED? HUB FANS ASK" ran the headline on a newspaper being read by a bulb-nosed cigar smoker a few rows away. Williams's retirement had been announced, doubted (he had been threatening retirement for years), confirmed by Tom Yawkey, the Red Sox owner, and at least widely accepted as the sad but probable truth. He was forty-two and had redeemed his abysmal season of 1959 with a—considering his advanced age—fine one. He had been giving away his gloves and bats and had grudgingly consented to a sentimental ceremony today. This was not necessarily his last game; the Red Sox were scheduled to travel to New York and wind up the season with three games there.

I arrived early. The Orioles were hitting fungos on the field. The day before, they had spitefully smothered the Red Sox, 17–4, and neither their faces nor their drab gray visiting-team uniforms seemed very gracious. I wondered who had invited them to the party. Between our heads and the lowering clouds a frenzied organ was thundering through, with an appositeness perhaps accidental, "You *maaaade* me love you, I didn't wanna do it, I didn't wanna do it . . ."

The affair between Boston and Ted Williams has been no mere summer romance; it has been a marriage, composed of spats, mutual disappointments, and, toward the end, a mellowing hoard of shared memories. It falls into three stages, which may be termed Youth, Maturity, and Age; or Thesis, Antithesis, and Synthesis; or Jason, Achilles, and Nestor.

First, there was the by now legendary epoch when the young bridegroom came out of the West and announced "All I want out of life is that when I walk down the street folks will say 'There goes the greatest hitter who ever lived.' " The dowagers of local journalism attempted to give elementary deportment lessons to this child who spake as a god, and to their horror were themselves rebuked. Thus began the long exchange of backbiting, hat-flipping, booing, and spitting that has distinguished Williams's public relations. The spitting incidents of 1957 and 1958 and the similar dockside courtesies that Williams has now and then extended to the grandstand should be judged against this background: The left-field stands at Fenway for twenty years have held a large number of customers who have bought their way in primarily for the privilege of showering abuse on Williams. Greatness necessarily attracts debunkers, but in Williams's case the hostility has been systematic and unappeasable. His basic offense against the fans has been to wish that they weren't there. Seeking a perfectionist's vacuum, he has quixotically desired to sever the game from the ground of paid spectatorship and publicity that supports it. Hence his refusal to tip his cap to the crowd or turn the other cheek to newsmen. It has been a costly theory—it has probably cost him, among other evidences of goodwill, two Most Valuable Player awards, which are voted by reporters—but he has held to it from his rookie year on. While his critics, oral and literary, remained beyond the reach of his discipline, the opposing pitchers were accessible, and he spanked them to the tune of .406 in 1941. He slumped to .356 in 1942 and went off to war.

In 1946, Williams returned from three years as a marine pilot to the second of his baseball avatars, that of Achilles, the hero of incomparable prowess and beauty who nevertheless was to be found sulking in his tent while the Trojans (mostly Yankees) fought through to the ships. Yawkey, a timber and mining maharajah, had surrounded his central jewel with many gems of slightly lesser water, such as Bobby Doerr, Dom DiMaggio, Rudy York, Birdie Tebbetts, and Johnny Pesky. Throughout the late forties, the Red Sox were the best paper team in baseball, yet they had little three-dimensional to show for it, and if this was a tragedy, Williams was Hamlet. A succinct review of the indictment—and a fair sample of appreciative sports-page prose—appeared the very day of Williams's valedictory, in a column by Huck Finnegan in the *Boston American* (no sentimentalist, Huck):

> Williams's career, in contrast [to Babe Ruth's], has been a series of failures except for his averages. He flopped in the only World Series he ever played in (1946) when he batted only .200. He flopped in the playoff game with Cleveland in 1948. He flopped in the final game of the 1949 season with the pennant hinging on the outcome (Yanks 5, Sox 3). He flopped in 1950 when he returned to the lineup after a two-month absence and ruined the morale of a club that seemed pennant-bound under Steve O'Neill. It has always been Williams's records first, the team second, and the Sox non-winning record is proof enough of that.

There are answers to all this, of course. The fatal weakness of the great Sox slugging teams was not-quite-good-enough pitching rather than Williams's failure to hit a home run every time he came to bat. Again, Williams's depressing effect on his teammates has never been proved. Despite ample coaching to the contrary, most insisted that they *liked* him. He has been generous with advice to any player who asked for it. In an increasingly combative baseball atmosphere, he continued to duck beanballs docilely. With umpires he was gracious to a fault. This courtesy itself annoyed his critics, whom there was no pleasing. And against the ten crucial games (the seven World Series games with the St. Louis Cardinals, the 1948 play-off with the Cleveland Indians, and the two-game series with the Yankees at the end of the 1949 season, winning either one of which would have given the Red Sox the pennant) that make up the Achilles' heel of Williams's record, a mass of statistics can be set showing that day in and day out he was no slouch in the clutch. The correspondence columns of the Boston papers now and then suffer a sharp flurry of arithmetic on this score; indeed, for Williams to have distributed all his hits so they did nobody else any good would constitute a feat of placement unparalleled in the annals of selfishness.

Whatever residue of truth remains of the Finnegan charge those of us who love Williams must transmute as best we can, in our own personal crucibles. My personal memories of Williams begin when I was a boy in Pennsylvania, with two last-place teams in Philadelphia to keep me company. For me, "W'ms, lf" was a figment of the box scores who always seemed to be going 3-for-5. He radiated, from afar, the hard blue glow of high purpose. I remember listening over the radio to the All-Star Game of 1946, in which Williams hit two singles and two home runs, the second one off a Rip Sewell "blooper" pitch; it was like hitting a balloon out of the park. I remember watching one of his home runs from the bleachers of Shibe Park; it went over the first baseman's head and rose meticulously along a straight line and was still rising when it cleared the fence. The trajectory seemed qualitatively different from anything anyone else might hit. For me, Williams is the classic ballplayer of the game on a hot August weekday, before a small crowd, when the only thing at stake is the tissue-thin difference between a thing done well and a thing done ill. Baseball is a game of the long season, of relentless and gradual averaging-out. Irrelevance—since the reference point of most individual games is remote and statistical—always threatens its interest, which can be maintained not by the occasional heroics that sportswriters feed upon but by players who always *care;* who care, that is to say, about themselves and their art. Insofar as the clutch hitter is not a sportswriter's myth, he is a vulgarity, like a writer who writes only for money. It may be that, compared to managers' dreams such as Joe DiMaggio and the always helpful Stan Musial, Williams is an icy star. But of all team sports, baseball, with its graceful intermittences of action, its immense and tranquil field sparsely settled with poised men in white, its dispassionate mathematics, seems to me best suited to accommodate, and be ornamented by, a loner. It is an essentially lonely game. No other player visible to my generation has concentrated within himself so much of the sport's poignance, has so assiduously refined his natural skills, has so constantly brought to the plate that intensity of competence that crowds the throat with joy.

By the time I went to college, near Boston, the lesser stars Yawkey had assembled around Williams had faded, and his craftsmanship, his rigorous pride, had become itself a kind of heroism. This brittle and tempermental player developed an unexpected quality of persistence. He was always coming back—back from Korea, back from a broken collarbone, a shattered elbow, a bruised heel, back from drastic bouts of flu and ptomaine poisoning. Hardly a season went by without some enfeebling mishap, yet he always came back, and always looked like himself. The delicate mechanism of timing and power seemed locked, shockproof, in some case outside his body. In addition to injuries, there were a heavily publicized divorce, and the usual storms with the press, and the Williams Shift—the maneuver, custom-built by Lou Boudreau, of the Cleveland Indians, whereby three infielders were concentrated on the right side of the infield, where a left-handed pull hitter like Williams generally hits the ball. Williams could easily have learned to punch singles through the vacancy on his left and fattened his average hugely. This was what Ty Cobb, the Einstein of average, told him to do. But the game had changed since Cobb; Williams believed that his value to the club and to the game was as a slugger, so he went on pulling the ball, trying to blast it through three men, and paid the price of perhaps fifteen points of lifetime average. Like Ruth before him, he bought the occasional home run at the cost of many directed singles—a calculated sacrifice certainly not, in the case of a hitter as average-minded as Williams, entirely selfish.

After a prime so harassed and hobbled, Williams was granted by the relenting fates a golden twilight. He became at the end of his career perhaps the best *old* hitter of the century. The dividing line came between the 1956 and the 1957 seasons. In September of the first year, he and Mickey Mantle were contending for the batting championship. Both were hitting around .350, and there was no one else near them. The season ended with a three-game series between the Yankees and the Sox, and living in New York then, I went up to the Stadium. Williams was slightly shy of the four hundred at-bats needed to qualify; the fear was expressed that the Yankee pitchers would walk him to protect Mantle. Instead, they pitched to him—a wise decision. He looked terrible at the plate, tired and discouraged and unconvincing. He never looked very good to me in the Stadium. (Last week, in *Life*, Williams, a sportswriter himself now, wrote gloomily of the Stadium, "There's the bigness of it. There are those high stands and all those people smoking—and, of course, the shadows. . . . It takes at least one series to get accustomed to the Stadium and even then you're not sure.") The final outcome in 1956 was Mantle .353, Williams .345.

The next year, I moved from New York to New England, and it made all the difference. For in September of 1957, in the same situation, the story was reversed. Mantle finally hit .365; it was the best season of his career. But Williams, though sick and old, had run away from him. A bout of flu had laid him low in September. He emerged from his cave in the Hotel Somerset haggard but irresistible; he hit four successive pinch-hit home runs. "I feel terrible," he confessed, "but every time I take a swing at the ball it goes out of the park." He ended the season with thirty-eight home runs and an average of .388, the highest in either league since his own .406, and, coming from a decrepit man of thirty-nine, an even more supernal figure. With eight or so of the "leg hits" that a younger man would have beaten out, it would have been .400. And the next year, Williams, who in 1949 and 1953 had lost batting championships by decimal whiskers to George Kell and Mickey Vernon, sneaked in behind his teammate Pete Runnels and filched his sixth title, a bargain at .328.

In 1959, it seemed all over. The dinosaur thrashed around in the .200 swamp for the first half of the season, and was even benched ("rested," Manager Mike Higgins tactfully said). Old foes like the late Bill Cunningham began to offer batting tips. Cunningham thought Williams was jiggling his elbows; in truth, Williams's neck was so stiff he could hardly turn his head to look at the pitcher. When he swung, it looked like a Calder mobile with one thread cut; it reminded you that since 1953 Williams's shoulders had been wired together. A solicitous pall settled over the sports pages. In the two decades since Williams had come to Boston, his status had imperceptibly shifted from that of a naughty prodigy to that of a municipal monument. As his shadow in the record books lengthened, the Red Sox teams around him declined, and the entire American League seemed to be losing life and color to the National. The inconsistency of the new superstars—Mantle, Colavito, and Kaline—served to make Williams appear all the more singular. And off the field, his private philanthropy—in particular, his zealous chairmanship of the Jimmy Fund, a charity for children with cancer—gave him a civic presence somewhat like that of Richard Cardinal Cushing. In religion, Williams appears to be a humanist, and a selective one at that, but he and the cardinal, when their good works intersect and they appear in the public eye together, make a handsome and heartening pair.

Humiliated by his 1959 season, Williams determined, once more, to come back. I, as a specimen Williams partisan, was both glad and fear-

ful. All baseball fans believe in miracles; the question is, how *many* do
you believe in? He looked like a ghost in spring training. Manager Jurges
warned us ahead of time that if Williams didn't come through he would
be benched, just like anybody else. As it turned out, it was Jurges who
was benched. Williams entered the 1960 season needing eight home
runs to have a lifetime total of 500; after one time at bat in Washington,
he needed seven. For a stretch, he was hitting a home run every second
game that he played. He passed Lou Gehrig's lifetime total, then the
number 500, then Mel Ott's total, and finished with 521, thirteen behind Jimmy Foxx, who alone stands between Williams and Babe Ruth's
unapproachable 714. The summer was a statistician's picnic. His two-
thousandth walk came and went, his eighteen-hundredth run batted in,
his sixteenth All-Star Game. At one point, he hit a home run off a
pitcher, Don Lee, off whose father, Thornton Lee, he had hit a home
run a generation before. The only comparable season for a forty-two-
year-old man was Ty Cobb's in 1928. Cobb batted .323 and hit one
homer. Williams batted .316 but hit twenty-nine homers.

In sum, though generally conceded to be the greatest hitter of his era,
he did not establish himself as "the greatest hitter who ever lived."
Cobb, for average, and Ruth, for power, remain supreme. Cobb, Rogers
Hornsby, Joe Jackson, and Lefty O'Doul, among players since 1900,
have higher lifetime averages than Williams's .344. Unlike Foxx, Gehrig, Hack Wilson, Hank Greenberg, and Ralph Kiner, Williams never
came close to matching Babe Ruth's season home-run total of sixty. In
the list of major league batting records, not one is held by Williams. He
is second in walks drawn, third in home runs, fifth in lifetime averages,
sixth in runs batted in, eighth in runs scored and in total bases, fourteenth in doubles, and thirtieth in hits. But if we allow him merely
average seasons for the four-plus seasons he lost to two wars, and add
another season for the months he lost to injuries, we get a man who in all
the power totals would be second, and not a very distant second, to
Ruth. And if we further allow that these years would have been not
merely average but prime years, if we allow for all the months when
Williams was playing in sub-par condition, if we permit his early and
later years in baseball to be some sort of index of what the middle years
could have been, if we give him a right-field fence that is not, like
Fenway's, one of the most distant in the league, and if—the least excus-
able "if"—we imagine him condescending to outsmart the Williams
Shift, we can defensibly assemble, like a colossus induced from the siz-
able fragments that do remain, a statistical figure not incommensurate
with his grandiose ambition. From the statistics that are on the books, a
good case can be made that in the *combination* of power and average

Williams is first; nobody else ranks so high in both categories. Finally, there is the witness of the eyes; men whose memories go back to Shoeless Joe Jackson—another unlucky natural—rank him and Williams together as the best-looking hitters they have seen. It was for our last look that ten thousand of us had come.

Two girls, one of them with pert buckteeth and eyes as black as vest buttons, the other with white skin and flesh-colored hair, like an underdeveloped photograph of a redhead, came and sat on my right. On my other side was one of those frowning, chestless young-old men who can frequently be seen, often wearing sailor hats, attending ball games alone. He did not once open his program but instead tapped it, rolled up, on his knee as he gave the game his disconsolate attention. A young lady, with freckles and a depressed, dainty nose that by an optical illusion seemed to thrust her lips forward for a kiss, sauntered down into the box seats and with striking aplomb took a seat right behind the roof of the Oriole dugout. She wore a blue coat with a Northeastern University emblem sewed to it. The girls beside me took it into their heads that this was Williams's daughter. She looked too old to me, and why would she be sitting behind the visitors' dugout? On the other hand, from the way she sat there, staring at the sky and French-inhaling, she clearly was *some-body*. Other fans came and eclipsed her from view. The crowd looked less like a weekday ball park crowd than like the folks you might find in Yellowstone National Park, or emerging from automobiles at the top of scenic Mount Mansfield. There were a lot of competitively well-dressed couples of tourist age, and not a few babes in arms. A row of five seats in front of me was abruptly filled with a woman and four children, the youngest of them two years old, if that. Someday, presumably, he could tell his grandchildren that he saw Williams play. Along with these tots and second-honeymooners, there were Harvard freshmen, giving off that peculiar nervous glow created when a quantity of insouciance is saturated with insecurity; thick-necked army officers with brass on their shoulders and lead in their voices; pepperings of priests; perfumed bouquets of Roxbury Fabian fans; shiny salesmen from Albany and Fall River; and those gray, hoarse men—taxidrivers, slaughterers, and bartenders—who will continue to click through the turnstiles long after everyone else has deserted to television and tramporamas. Behind me, two young male voices blossomed, cracking a joke about God's five proofs that Thomas Aquinas exists—typical Boston College levity.

The batting cage was trundled away. The Orioles fluttered to the side-lines. Diagonally across the field, by the Red Sox dugout, a cluster of men in overcoats were festering like maggots. I could see a splinter of white uniform, and Williams's head, held at a self-deprecating and eva-sive tilt. Williams's conversational stance is that of a six-foot-three-inch man under a six-foot ceiling. He moved away to the patter of flash bulbs, and began playing catch with a young Negro outfielder named Willie Tasby. His arm, never very powerful, had grown lax with the years, and his throwing motion was a kind of muscular drawl. To catch the ball, he flicked his glove hand onto his left shoulder (he batted left but threw right, as every schoolboy ought to know) and let the ball plop into it comically. This catch session with Tasby was the only time all afternoon I saw him grin.

A tight little flock of human sparrows who, from the lambent and pampered pink of their faces, could only have been Boston politicians moved toward the plate. The loudspeakers mammothly coughed as someone huffed on the microphone. The ceremonies began. Curt Gowdy, the Red Sox radio and television announcer, who sounds like everybody's brother-in-law, delivered a brief sermon, taking the two words "pride" and "champion" as his text. It began, "Twenty-one years ago, a skinny kid from San Diego, California . . ." and ended, "I don't think we'll ever see another like him." Robert Tibolt, chairman of the board of the Greater Boston Chamber of Commerce, presented Wil-liams with a big Paul Revere silver bowl. Harry Carlson, a member of the sports committee of the Boston Chamber, gave him a plaque, whose inscription he did not read in its entirety, out of deference to Williams's distaste for this sort of fuss. Mayor Collins presented the Jimmy Fund with a thousand-dollar check.

Then the occasion himself stooped to the microphone, and his voice sounded, after the others, very Californian; it seemed to be coming, excellently amplified, from a great distance, adolescently young and as smooth as a butternut. His thanks for the gifts had not died from our ears before he glided, as if helplessly, into "In spite of all the terrible things that have been said about me by the maestros of the keyboard up there . . ." He glanced up at the press rows suspended above home plate. (All the Boston reporters, incidentally, reported the phrase as "knights of the keyboard," but I heard it as "maestros" and prefer it that way.) The crowd tittered, appalled. A frightful vision flashed upon me, of the press gallery pelting Williams with erasers, of Williams clambering up the foul screen to slug journalists, of a riot, of Mayor Collins being crushed. ". . . And they *were* terrible things," Williams insisted, with level melancholy, into the mike. "I'd like to forget them, but I can't." He paused, swallowing his memories, and went on. "I want to say that my years in Boston have been the greatest thing in my life." The crowd, like an immense sail going limp in a change of wind, sighed with relief.

Taking all the parts himself, Williams then acted out a vivacious little morality drama in which an imaginary tempter came to him at the beginning of his career and said, "Ted, you can play anywhere you like." Leaping nimbly into the role of his younger self (who in biographical actuality had yearned to be a Yankee), Williams gallantly chose Boston over all the other cities, and told us that Tom Yawkey was the greatest owner in baseball and we were the greatest fans. We applauded ourselves heartily. The umpire came out and dusted the plate. The voice of doom announced over the loudspeakers that after Williams's retirement his uniform number, 9, would be permanently retired—the first time the Red Sox had so honored a player. We cheered. The national anthem was played. We cheered. The game began.

Williams was third in the batting order, so he came up in the bottom of the first inning, and Steve Barber, a young pitcher who was not yet born when Williams began playing for the Red Sox, offered him four pitches, at all of which he disdained to swing, since none of them were within the strike zone. This demonstrated simultaneously that Williams's eyes were razor-sharp and that Barber's control wasn't. Shortly, the bases were full, with Williams on second. "Oh, I hope he gets held up at third! That would be wonderful," the girl beside me moaned, and, sure enough, the man at bat walked and Williams was delivered into our foreground. He struck the pose of Donatello's David, the third-base bag being Goliath's head. Fiddling with his cap, swapping small talk with the Oriole third baseman (who seemed delighted to have him drop in), swinging his arms with a sort of prancing nervousness, he looked fine—flexible, hard, and not unbecomingly substantial through the middle. The long neck, the small head, the knickers whose cuffs were worn down near his ankles— all these points, often observed by caricaturists, were visible in the flesh.

One of the collegiate voices behind me said, "He looks old, doesn't he, old; big deep wrinkles in his face . . ."

"Yeah," the other voice said, "but he looks like an old hawk, doesn't he?"

With each pitch, Williams danced down the baseline, waving his arms and stirring dust, ponderous but menacing, like an attacking goose. It occurred to about a dozen humorists at once to shout "Steal home! Go, go!" Williams's speed afoot was never legendary. Lou Clinton, a young Sox outfielder, hit a fairly deep fly to center field. Williams tagged up and ran home. As he slid across the plate, the ball, thrown with unusual heft by Jackie Brandt, the Oriole center fielder, hit him on the back.

"Boy, he was really loafing, wasn't he?" one of the boys behind me said.

"It's cold," the other explained. "He doesn't play well when it's cold. He likes heat. He's a hedonist."

The run that Williams scored was the second and last of the inning. Gus Triandos, of the Orioles, quickly evened the score by plunking a home run over the handy left-field wall. Williams, who had had this wall at his back for twenty years, played the ball flawlessly. He didn't budge. He just stood there, in the center of the little patch of grass that his patient footsteps had worn brown, and, limp with lack of interest, watched the ball pass overhead. It was not a very interesting game. Mike Higgins, the Red Sox manager, with nothing to lose, had restricted his major league players to the left-field line—along with Williams, Frank Malzone, a first-rate third baseman, played the game—and had peopled the rest of the terrain with unpredictable youngsters fresh, or not so fresh, off the farms. Other than Williams's recurrent appearances at the plate, the *maladresse* of the Sox infield was the sole focus of suspense; the second baseman turned every grounder into a juggling act, while the shortstop did a breathtaking impersonation of an open window. With this sort of assistance, the Orioles wheedled their way into a 4–2 lead. They had early replaced Barber with another young pitcher, Jack Fisher. Fortunately (as it turned out), Fisher is no cutie; he is willing to burn the ball through the strike zone, and inning after inning this tactic punctured Higgins's string of test balloons.

Whenever Williams appeared at the plate—pounding the dirt from his cleats, gouging a pit in the batter's box with his left foot, wringing resin out of the bat handle with his vehement grip, switching the stick at the pitcher with an electric ferocity—it was like having a familiar Leonardo appear in a shuffle of *Saturday Evening Post* covers. This man, you realized—and here, perhaps, was the difference, greater than the difference in gifts—really intended to hit the ball. In the third inning, he hoisted a high fly to deep center. In the fifth, we thought he had it; he smacked the ball hard and high into the heart of his power zone, but the deep right field in Fenway and the heavy air and a casual east wind defeated him. The ball died. Al Pilarcik leaned his back against the big "380" painted on the right-field wall and caught it. On another day, in another park, it would have been gone. (After the game, Williams said, "I didn't think I could hit one any harder than that. The conditions weren't good.")

The afternoon grew so glowering that in the sixth inning the arc lights were turned on—always a wan sight in the daytime, like the burning headlights of a funeral procession. Aided by the gloom, Fisher was slicing through the Sox rookies, and Williams did not come to bat in the seventh. He was second up in the eighth. This was almost certainly his last time to come to the plate in Fenway Park, and instead of merely cheering, as we had at his three previous appearances, we stood, all of us—stood and applauded. Have you ever heard applause in a ball park? Just applause—no calling, no whistling, just an ocean of handclaps, minute after minute, burst after burst, crowding and running together in continuous succession like the pushes of surf at the edge of the sand. It was a somber and considered tumult. There was not a boo in it. It seemed to renew itself out of a shifting set of memories as the kid, the marine, the veteran of feuds and failures and injuries, the friend of children, and the enduring old pro evolved down the bright tunnel of twenty-one summers toward this moment. At last, the umpire signaled for Fisher to pitch; with the other players, he had been frozen in position. Only Williams had moved during the ovation, switching his bat impatiently, ignoring everything except his cherished task. Fisher wound up, and the applause sank into a hush.

Understand that we were a crowd of rational people. We knew that a home run cannot be produced at will; the right pitch must be perfectly met and luck must ride with the ball. Three innings before, we had seen a brave effort fail. The air was soggy; the season was exhausted. Nevertheless, there will always lurk, around a corner in a pocket of our knowledge of the odds, an indefensible hope, and this was one of the times, which you now and then find in sports, when a density of expectation hangs in the air and plucks an event out of the future.

Fisher, after his unsettling wait, was wide with the first pitch. He put the second one over, and Williams swung mightily and missed. The crowd grunted, seeing that classic swing, so long and smooth and quick, exposed. Fisher threw the third time, Williams swung again, and there it was. The ball climbed on a diagonal line into the vast volume of air over center field. From my angle, behind third base, the ball seemed less an object in flight than the tip of a towering, motionless construct, like the Eiffel Tower or the Tappan Zee Bridge. It was in the books while it was still in the sky. Brandt ran back to the deepest corner of the outfield grass; the ball descended beyond his reach and struck in the crotch where the bullpen met the wall, bounced chunkily, and, as far as I could see, vanished.

Like a feather caught in a vortex, Williams ran around the square of bases at the center of our beseeching screaming. He ran as he always ran out home runs—hurriedly, unsmiling, head down, as if our praise were a storm of rain to get out of. He didn't tip his cap. Though we thumped, wept, and chanted "We want Ted" for minutes after he hid in the dugout, he did not come back. Our noise for some seconds passed beyond excitement into a kind of immense open anguish, a wailing, a cry to be saved. But immortality is nontransferable. The papers said that the other players, and even the umpires on the field, begged him to come out and acknowledge us in some way, but he refused. Gods do not answer letters.

Every true story has an anticlimax. The men on the field refused to disappear, as would have seemed decent, in the smoke of Williams's miracle. Fisher continued to pitch, and escaped further harm. At the end of the inning, Higgins sent Williams out to his left-field position, then instantly replaced him with Carrol Hardy, so we had a long last look at Williams as he ran out there and then back, his uniform jogging, his eyes steadfast on the ground. It was nice, and we were grateful, but it left a funny taste.

One of the scholasticists behind me said, "Let's go. We've seen everything. I don't want to spoil it." This seemed a sound aesthetic decision. Williams's last word had been so exquisitely chosen, such a perfect fusion of expectation, intention, and execution, that already it felt a little unreal in my head, and I wanted to get out before the castle collapsed. But the game, though played by clumsy midgets under the feeble glow of the arc lights, began to tug at my attention, and I loitered in the runway until it was over. Williams's homer had, quite incidentally, made the score 4–3. In the bottom of the ninth inning, with one out, Marlin Coughtry, the second-base juggler, singled. Vic Wertz, pinch-hitting, doubled off the left-field wall, Coughtry advancing to third. Pumpsie Green walked, to load the bases. Willie Tasby hit a double-play ball to the third baseman, but in making the pivot throw Billy Klaus, an ex–Red Sox infielder, reverted to form and threw the ball past the first baseman and into the Red Sox dugout. The Sox won, 5–4. On the car radio as I drove home I heard that Williams had decided not to accompany the team to New York. He had met the little death that awaits athletes. He had quit.

RED SMITH

"1951: NEW YORK GIANTS 5, BROOKLYN DODGERS 4"

When the Herald-Tribune *folded in the late 1960s, Red Smith's distraught New York readers could only find his column locally in* Women's Wear Daily. *Eventually he was hired by the* New York Times.

His column appeared six days weekly until the age of sixty-five when he throttled back to five. Almost perversely self-deprecatory, he once described himself as a "seedy amateur with watery eyes behind glittering glasses, a retiring chin, a hole in his frowzy haircut." He often joked about his preparation for sports reporting—an elevator boy in Green Bay's Northland Hotel, a soda jerk, a grocer's delivery boy, worker in a truck garden, among other part-time jobs, who never played golf and at tennis was invariably beaten by girls younger than himself. Whatever his background, he became known as the best sports reporter in the business—"the Master."

Now it is done. Now the story ends. And there is no way to tell it. The art of fiction is dead. Reality has strangled invention. Only the utterly impossible, the inexpressibly fantastic, can ever be plausible again.

Down on the green and white and earth-brown geometry of the playing field, a drunk tries to break through the ranks of ushers marshaled along the foul lines to keep profane feet off the diamond. The ushers thrust him back and he lunges at them, struggling in the clutch of two or three men. He breaks free, and four or five tackle him. He shakes them off, bursts through the line, runs head-on into a special park cop, who brings him down with a flying tackle.

Here comes a whole platoon of ushers. They lift the man and haul him, twisting and kicking, back across the first-base line. Again he shakes loose and crashes the line. He is through. He is away, weaving out toward center field, where cheering thousands are jammed beneath the windows of the Giants' clubhouse.

At heart, our man is a Giant, too. He never gave up.

From center field comes burst upon burst of cheering. Pennants are waving, uplifted fists are brandished, hats are flying. Again and again the dark clubhouse windows blaze with the light of photographers' flash bulbs. Here comes that same drunk out of the mob, back across the green turf to the infield. Coattails flying, he runs the bases, slides into third. Nobody bothers him now.

And the story remains to be told, the story of how the Giants won the 1951 pennant in the National League. The tale of their barreling run through August and September and into October.... Of the final day of the season, when they won the championship and started home with it from Boston, to hear on the train how the dead, defeated Dodgers had risen from the ashes in the Philadelphia twilight.... Of the three-game play-off in which they won, and lost, and were losing again with one out in the ninth inning yesterday when—Oh, why bother?

Maybe this is the way to tell it: Bobby Thomson, a young Scot from Staten Island, delivered a timely hit yesterday in the ninth inning of an enjoyable game of baseball before 34,320 witnesses in the Polo Grounds. . . . Or perhaps this is better:

"Well!" said Whitey Lockman, standing on second base in the second inning of yesterday's play-off game between the Giants and Dodgers.

"Ah, there," said Bobby Thomson, pulling into the same station after hitting a ball to left field. "How've you been?"

"Fancy," Lockman said, "meeting you here!"

"Ooops!" Thomson said. "Sorry."

And the Giants' first chance for a big inning against Don Newcombe disappeared as they tagged Thomson out. Up in the press section, the voice of Willie Goodrich came over the amplifiers announcing a macabre statistic: "Thomson has now hit safely in fifteen consecutive games." Just then the floodlights were turned on, enabling the Giants to see and count their runners on each base.

It wasn't funny, though, because it seemed for so long that the Giants weren't going to get another chance like the one Thomson squandered by trying to take second base with a playmate already there. They couldn't hit Newcombe, and the Dodgers couldn't do anything wrong. Sal Maglie's most splendrous pitching would avail nothing unless New York could match the run Brooklyn had scored in the first inning.

The story was winding up, and it wasn't the happy ending that such a tale demands. Poetic justice was a phrase without meaning.

Now it was the seventh inning and Thomson was up, with runners on first and third base, none out. Pitching a shutout in Philadelphia last Saturday night, pitching again in Philadelphia on Sunday, holding the Giants scoreless this far, Newcombe had now gone twenty-one innings without allowing a run.

He threw four strikes to Thomson. Two were fouled off out of play. Then he threw a fifth. Thomson's fly scored Monte Irvin. The score was tied. It was a new ball game.

Wait a minute, though. Here's Pee Wee Reese hitting safely in the eighth. Here's Duke Snider singling Reese to third. Here's Maglie wild-pitching a run home. Here's Andy Pafko slashing a hit through Thomson for another score. Here's Billy Cox batting still another home. Where does his hit go? Where else? Through Thomson at third.

So it was the Dodgers' ball game, 4 to 1, and the Dodgers' pennant. So all right. Better get started and beat the crowd home. That stuff in the ninth inning? That didn't mean anything.

A single by Al Dark. A single by Don Mueller. Irvin's pop-up, Lockman's one-run double. Now the corniest possible sort of Hollywood schmaltz—stretcher-bearers plodding away with an injured Mueller between them, symbolic of the Giants themselves.

There went Newcombe and here came Ralph Branca. Who's at bat? Thomson again? He beat Branca with a home run the other day. Would Charley Dressen order him walked, putting the winning run on base, to pitch to the dead-end kids at the bottom of the batting order? No, Branca's first pitch was a called strike.

The second pitch—well, when Thomson reached first base he turned and looked toward the left-field stands. Then he started jumping straight up in the air, again and again. Then he trotted around the bases, taking his time.

Ralph Branca turned and started for the clubhouse. The number on his uniform looked huge. Thirteen.

ROBERT W. CREAMER

"Kaleidoscope: Personality of the Babe"

One day in 1930, before the first of a routine series of games in St. Louis between the Yankees and the Browns, Ruth was behind the batting cage talking with Bill Killefer, the Browns' manager, Tony Lazzeri, and a reporter.

"Your face is getting fatter and fatter," Killefer said.

"Yeah?" said Ruth. He spat some tobacco juice. "Well, I don't hit with my face."

"Is the wife on the trip with you?"

"Sure."

"Having a hard time dodging the old phone calls?" Killefer said, grinning.

"Oh, go to hell."

"Who do you like in the Derby?" the reporter asked.

"I'm not playing the ponies."

"What books are you reading?"

"Books?" Ruth looked at him. "Reading isn't good for a ballplayer.

Not good for his eyes. If my eyes went bad even a little bit I couldn't hit home runs. So I gave up reading."

"You must do some reading. Who are your favorite authors?" The reporter pronounced it in the midwestern way, alien to Ruth's semi-southern ear.

"My favorite Arthurs? Nehf and Fletcher."

"Not Arthurs," the reporter said patiently. "Authors, writers."

"Oh, writers. My favorite writer is Christy Walsh."

"Seriously, what President of the United States do you admire most?"

"Well, I liked Harding a lot, and I liked Wilson a lot. Coolidge was all right. Hoover is okay with me, but Al Smith was my favorite for the job."

"What is the psychology of home runs?"

"Say, are you kidding me?"

"No, of course not. I just want an explanation of why you get so many home runs."

Ruth spat again. "Just swinging," he said.

"Have you ever had an idol, someone you thought more of than anyone else?"

"Sure he has," Lazzeri said. "Babe Ruth."

"Go to hell," Ruth said, and to the reporter, "Excuse me, it's my turn to hit."

When he finished he ducked under the stands for a few minutes and came back with a hot dog. He sat on the Browns' bench next to Killefer and the reporter.

"What was the biggest thrill you ever got out of a ballgame?" the reporter asked.

"Biggest thrill?" Ruth said. He bit off half the hot dog and gulped it down. "That's easy. It happened right here in St. Louis when I got three home runs in one World Series game and made that running catch off Frankie Frisch. Picked the ball right out of the stands. And I got a thrill out of little Sherdel trying to sneak that strike over on me when I wasn't looking and then hitting one out."

"How much did you earn last year? I mean, from everything—baseball, exhibitions, testimonials, everything."

"A hundred and ten thousand dollars."

"Are you saving any money?"

"Lots of it," Ruth replied. He finished the hot dog. "I started a trust fund three years ago and I've got $120,000 in it right now. I got an older one with $50,000 in it. Right now I'm good for $500 a month for as long as I live."

"What are you going to do when your baseball days are over?"

"Take life easy," Ruth said. "Excuse me, I've got to hit again."

Later the Yankee batboy and mascot, Eddie Bennett, a hunchback, came down to the runway into the Browns' dugout. He was carrying a cup of some sort of whitish liquid.

"What have you got there?" Killefer asked.

"Some bicarbonate of soda for the Babe."

"How many hot dogs did he have?" Killefer asked.

"Three."

"How often does he do that?" asked the reporter.

"Every day," Bennett said, shaking his head. "Every day."

Ruth drank bicarbonate of soda every day in the dugout. He called it his milk. He began the habit one day after he gobbled down a couple of hot dogs too quickly and felt bloated just before game time. The trainer recommended bicarbonate. It made him feel good and he decided that was the ideal diet before a game: a couple of hot dogs and a glass of bicarb. He chewed tobacco and gum, smoked cigars and occasionally cigarettes or a pipe, took snuff in such vast amounts that some of the dust became impacted in his nasal passages. A doctor ordered him to quit taking it after that.

Before the game that day in St. Louis a photographer asked Ruth to pose for pictures and he willingly complied. He always went along. A photographer asked him one day to have his picture taken with "another champion, the greatest egglayer in Nebraska." He was handed a chicken and an egg. He posed amiably with the chicken cuddled in one hand, the egg in the other, a huge grin on his face and his eyes all crinkled up from laughing. He was relaxed with reporters, and would go out of his way to be cooperative with them, although he was often subjected to bizarre questions. "What do you think of the Chinese situation?" he was asked. "The hell with it," he replied. But when Will Grimsley of the Associated Press was a young reporter, Ruth patiently answered all his questions one day even though his teammates were yelling at him to hurry up.

On the road he always had a suite, sometimes in a different hotel from the one the team was staying at. He liked to lounge around in red slippers and a red robe, smoking a cigar. Dozens of people streamed in and out of the suite day and night. He always carried a wind-up portable phonograph with him on road trips. He loved to sing. Occasionally he would strum a ukulele. He was always shaved by a barber. ("That's what they're for, aren't they?") In St. Louis he liked to eat at a German restaurant that made barbecued spare ribs. Often, on the day the Yankees were leaving town, he'd go from the ballpark to the restaurant and order a mess of ribs and home brew and take it to the train. He would set up shop in a washroom and sell the ribs to the players for fifty cents a portion. He insisted on being paid too, but he also provided beer, and the players could have all the beer they wanted for their fifty cents.

He was apolitical, although he called himself a Democrat until Franklin D. Roosevelt ran for a third term, and apparently he never cast a vote in a national election until 1944. Yet he created a mild political furor in September 1928, when Herbert Hoover was running for President. Hoover appeared at the ballpark and a publicity man ran down to the Yankee clubhouse to get Ruth to come and pose with the Republican candidate.

"No, sir," said Ruth, "nothing doing on politics." He had been burned a few days earlier by a story saying he was supporting Hoover. He denied it, saying he was for Al Smith, and now he declined to appear with Smith's rival. But, graciously, he said, "Tell him I'll be glad to talk to him if he wants to meet me under the stands." No doubt here as to which was king.

Reporters with Hoover heard about all this, and it became a headline story: "RUTH REFUSES TO POSE WITH HOOVER." Christy Walsh almost died. Republican newspapers were threatening to drop Ruth's syndicated column. Walsh got in touch with Babe and hurriedly prepared a statement, ostensibly by Ruth, saying he regretted that because of a misunderstanding he had been unable to pose with the Republican candidate. He would be happy to, he declared, and a photo was duly taken of Ruth and Hoover together.

Despite the earlier publicity, Hoover's camp was happy to have the photograph, because Ruth's personality was pervasive. The crudity, the vulgarity, the indifference, the physical humor that bordered on brutality, the preoccupation with his own needs that ignored Hoover and hurt Helen—none of it mattered when Ruth smiled or laughed or moved or did almost anything. "He was one of those exciting people who make life fun, and who give more to life than they take from it," said Arthur Robinson, a New York sportswriter who was another of the Babe's ghosts. "God, we liked that big son of a bitch," said Hoyt. "He was a constant source of joy." When Roger Maris was chasing Ruth's home run record in 1961, Jimmy Dykes said, "Maris is a fine ballplayer, but I can't imagine him driving down Broadway in a low-slung convertible, wearing a coonskin coat." Dugan said, "What a fantastic ballplayer he was, the things he could do. But he wasn't human. He dropped out of a tree."

He was so alive, so attractive, like an animal or a child: ingenuous, unselfconscious, appealing. Frank Graham said, "He was a very simple man, in some ways a primitive man. He had little education, and little need for what he had." Tom Meany said he had the supreme self-confidence of the naïve. On a stifling hot day at the Washington ball-park he said to President Harding, "Hot as hell, ain't it, Prez?" He met Marshal Foch when that renowned French hero of World War I was making a tour of the United States early in the 1920s and said politely, "I suppose you were in the war?"

Introduced before a game to a man he had never seen before, Ruth said, "You sound like you have a cold." The man admitted he did. Ruth reached into the hip pocket of his uniform and pulled out a big onion. "Here, gnaw on this," he said. "Raw onions are cold-killers." During a blistering heat wave Ruth brought a cabbage into the dugout and put it in the team's old-fashioned water cooler, and each inning before he went on the field he took a fresh cabbage leaf and put it under his cap to keep himself cool.

Famous for not remembering names (when Waite Hoyt was leaving the Yankees in 1930 after eleven seasons as Babe's teammate in Boston and New York, Ruth shook hands and said solemnly, "Goodbye, Walter"), he had nicknames for other players, not necessarily complimentary nicknames. His teammates were Chicken Neck, Flop Ears, Duck Eye, Horse Nose, Rubber Belly. People he did not know or remember he called Doc or Kid, which he usually pronounced Keed, in the flashy slang pronunciation of the time. He called older men Pop, older women Mom. Younger women he needed no special name for. He usually called Claire [his second wife], Clara. He himself was called Jidge by the Yankees, a corruption of George that was apparently first used by Dugan.

His appetite was enormous, although accounts of it were often exaggerated. A report of one dinner says he had an entire capon, potatoes, spinach, corn, peas, beans, bread, butter, pie, ice cream, and three or four cups of coffee. He was known to have eaten a huge omelet made of eighteen eggs and three big slices of ham, plus half a dozen slices of buttered toast and several cups of coffee. Ty Cobb, no stickler for accuracy in his memoirs of baseball life, said, "I've seen him at midnight, propped up in bed, order six club sandwiches, a platter of pigs' knuckles, and a pitcher of beer. He'd down all that while smoking a big black cigar. Next day, if he hit a homer, he'd trot around the bases complaining about gas pains and a bellyache." He belched magnificently and, I was told, could fart at will.

He was, as noted, a sexual athlete. In a St. Louis whorehouse he announced he was going to go to bed with every girl in the house during the night, and did, and after finishing his rounds sat down and had a huge breakfast. In the early 1930s the Yankees signed a superior pitcher named Charlie Devens out of Harvard, who abandoned a promising major league career a year or two later to join his family's banking business in Boston. Devens joined the team in St. Louis, reporting in at the hotel. He was given the key to his room and went up and unpacked. His roommate, some secondary figure on the team, was not around. Just as he finished unpacking, the phone rang and a voice asked, "Devens?"

"Yes."

"Bring your room key with you and come down to the lobby."

Obediently Devens took his key and went downstairs. When the elevator doors opened at the lobby floor, there was Babe Ruth, a girl on each arm.

"You Devens?" Ruth asked.

Devens nodded. Ruth put out his hand. Devens looked at him dumbly.

"The key," Ruth snapped. Devens gave him the key and Babe and his friends swept into the elevator. Later Devens learned that when Mrs. Ruth was with Babe on road trips he occasionally preempted teammates' rooms for extracurricular activities.

There were inevitable stories that Ruth was exceptionally well equipped sexually, and a male nurse who took care of him in his terminal illness was impressed by the size of Ruth's genitals. But apparently any abnormality in size then was a product of illness. One teammate, asked if Ruth had an exceptionally big penis, frowned a little as he searched his memory and shook his head. "No," he said. "It was normal size, judging from locker room observation. Nothing extraordinary. Del Pratt's was. And Home Run Baker's. My God, you wouldn't believe Home Run Baker's. It looked like it belonged to a horse. But Babe's wasn't noticeably big. What was extraordinary was his ability to keep doing it all the time. He was continually with women, morning and night. I don't know how he kept going." He was very noisy in bed, visceral grunts and gasps and whoops accompanying his erotic exertions. "He was the noisiest fucker in North America," a whimsical friend recalled.

There is a story, probably apocryphal, about a time he and Meusel were barnstorming together. They shared a hotel suite. Meusel was half asleep when Ruth came in with a girl, went into his room, and made love to her in his usual noisy fashion. Afterwards he came out to the living room of the suite, lit a cigar, and sat in a chair by the window, smoking it contemplatively. When he finished the cigar he went back into the bedroom and made love again. And then came out and smoked another cigar. In the morning Meusel asked, "How many times did you lay that girl last night?" Ruth glanced at the ashtray, and so did Meusel. There were seven butts in the tray. "Count the cigars," said Ruth.

On the other side of the coin there is another story, about a barnstorming trip with Gehrig. Ruth came back to the suite boisterously drunk with two girls and went into the bedroom with both of them. During the night one of the girls came out to Gehrig and said, "You better come and see if you can straighten out your friend." Lou went into the bedroom and found Ruth sitting naked on the side of the bed, sobs racking his shoulders, tears running down his face. In bits, from Ruth and the girls, Gehrig discovered what was wrong. However successful he had been earlier in the night with his friends, Ruth was crying because he was unable now to service both girls.

Everything about him reflected sexuality—the restless, roving energy; the aggressive skills; fastball pitching; home run hitting; the speed with which he drove cars; the loud, rich voice; the insatiable appetite; the constant need to placate his mouth with food, drink, a cigar, chewing gum, anything. When he played poker, he liked to raise even when his cards did not justify a raise, and when he lucked into a pot he chortled happily. He was a fairly skillful bridge player, but he wanted to play every hand himself and often outbid his partner as well as their opponents. In retirement his favorite sports were golf and bowling; he liked to hit a golf ball a long way, and in bowling to keep track of the total number of pins he knocked down rather than his average score. He loved to win in whatever he did. He received absolute physical joy from cards, baseball, golf, bowling, punching the bag, sex.

He liked to fish and would go with Gehrig before their friendship became strained, but he was a better hunter than a fisherman. His physical stamina, superb eyesight, and quick reflexes helped his hunting, and he also had a quality seldom in evidence anywhere else: extraordinary patience. Once in Georgia he stalked a wild turkey for seven hours before getting close enough to shoot. Then he picked it off the top of a tree with one shot.

Physically he was a paradox. He was big, strong, muscular, exceptionally well coordinated, yet he was often injured and he suffered from a surprising number of colds and infections. This would indicate a low resistance to disease, yet he had an amazing ability to recover quickly. He dramatized injuries; no player in big league history was carried off the field on his shield as often as the massive Bambino. But he could ignore both illness and injury and play superlatively well despite them.

In his later years Ruth was often babied by the Yankees. He and Jimmy Reese, a rookie second baseman who weighed seventy-five pounds less than the Babe, crashed into each other running for a fly ball. They staggered apart and fell to the ground, both apparently hurt. The trainer and others ran from the bench, past Reese's prostrate form, and gathered around Babe. When Lefty Gomez was a rookie, he was pitching batting practice in spring training. Hoyt came past the mound just as

Ruth was stepping in to hit. "Nothing but fastballs right down the pipe," Hoyt told Gomez. "Don't get cute, kid. And for God's sake, don't hit him or you're gone."

In the summer of 1931, going after a fly ball, Babe smashed into a chicken-wire screen that was serving as a temporary outfield fence during renovations. A strand of loose wire ripped into his finger, cutting it badly and tearing the nail off. The trainer ran out, took one look, and said Ruth would have to come out of the game. Holding the damaged hand with the other, his face screwed up in pain, Ruth limped all the way in from right field, even though his legs had not been hurt. In the trainer's room he was told the damaged nail would have to be cut away. "Not without gas," he declared. "Nobody's going to cut me unless I have gas." He made a great fuss before the nail was removed and the finger bandaged, and everybody laughed about the limp and the gas. But the next day he played, torn finger and all, and stole a base. His second wife reacted to the well-publicized stories about Mickey Mantle having to have his legs bandaged each day during his career because of his osteomyelitis by saying, "No one ever mentions that my husband played with bandaged legs practically every day of his career." Old teammates verified this. When Ruth slid into base he slid with abandon, and because he would not wear sliding pads under his uniform his thighs and hips were scraped raw by the rough pebbly soil of the old infields. His legs were richly decorated with raw "strawberry" wounds which persisted all season. He would have them doused with alcohol and wrapped in bandages and go on playing.

"He was very brave at the plate," Casey Stengel said. "You rarely saw him fall away from a pitch. He stayed right in there. No one drove him out."

His weight fluctuated throughout his career. When he signed with the Orioles he weighed about 185 and with the Red Sox he went up to 198 and then to 212 in a couple of seasons. He got down below 200 again, but not for long, and after 1919 his weight was seldom below 220. It soared to 240 in Cuba late in 1920 and stayed around 230 in 1921 and 1922. In the spring of 1923, after his first reformation, he was down briefly to 215, but a year later he was up to 230 again. In January 1925 he weighed 256 and was probably more than 260 at the time of his collapse in Asheville. Determined work at McGovern's gymnasium the following winter got him down to 212; thereafter his weight as a player varied from about 225 to 240, depending on the time of the year. But he continued to work with McGovern every winter, and he was in much better shape at that weight than he used to be. When he first went to McGovern during the winter of 1925–26 his chest measured 43 inches normal and

45 inches expanded; both his waist (49¾ inches) and his hips (47 inches) were larger than his chest. But in the winter of 1931–32, approaching his thirty-eighth birthday and weighing 235½, his waist was 38 and his hips 40, and his chest was 41 normal and 48 expanded.

Because of Ruth's bulk, Ruppert decided to dress the Yankees in their now-traditional pinstripe uniform and dark blue stockings. The natty, clothes-conscious Ruppert felt the new uniform would make Ruth look trimmer. The Yankees also introduced uniform numbers to the major leagues in 1929. Ruth's number was number 3 because he batted third, Gehrig's 4 because he batted fourth, and so on.

When Ruth left the ballpark or the hotel, usually to meet a girl, he would say, "I'm going to see a party." He seldom if ever went to popular night clubs or famous restaurants. He much preferred out-of-the-way places where he knew the owner and could relax in relative peace and quiet. One of his favorites was a spot in northern New Jersey called Donahue's. The owner fixed up a private room for him where he could eat and drink and talk with his guests without being bothered by strangers. He seldom had many people with him, usually four or five at the most.

His voice was rich and warm, his accent very slightly southern. "Less go out to the *bowl* game," he would say, pronouncing "ball" that way and stressing it heavily. His speech was splattered with vulgarities. "Piss pass the butter," he would say childishly if he was dining with a teammate. Or, asked how he was feeling, he'd reply, "Pussy good, pussy good." In the early 1920s he saw a teammate on the street with a pretty girl. Next day he asked, "Who was that cunt you were with?" The teammate said, "For God's sake, Babe, that was my wife."

"Oh," Ruth said, "I'm sorry. I *knew* she wasn't no whore."

He was sitting around a table with several players and their wives in Hot Springs in 1923. "Excuse me," he said, getting up. "I've got to take a piss."

Herb Pennock, very much a gentleman and also very much a friend of Ruth's, followed Babe out to the men's room. "Babe," he said, "you shouldn't say that in front of the ladies."

"Say what?"

"Say piss like that. You just don't say that in front of women. You should say, 'Excuse me, I have to go to the bathroom,' or something like that."

"I'm sorry, Herb."

"Okay."

They went back to the table and sat down, and Ruth said to the women, "I'm sorry I said piss."

After Ruth came back from a trip to the Far East in the 1930s, a friend who had just been married came to visit, bringing along his new wife. Babe told them stories about the trip, including a long anecdote about a game in Manila.

"Then these Hawaiians tried to tell us—" he began.

"Not Hawaiians, Babe," said Mrs. Ruth, "Filipinos."

"Yeah, Filipinos." He went on and after another couple of sentences said, "Then this little Hawaiian—"

"Filipino," said Mrs. Ruth.

"Filipino. This little guy came over. . ." He went on to the end of the story, laughed uproariously, and said, "Those Hawaiians thought they were pulling a fast one on us."

"Filipinos."

"Oh, Christ, call them Eskimos. Who gives a goddamn?"

He told another story about sitting next to Lefty Gomez's wife at dinner one evening on the trip. "They brought out this great caviar, and they started it around the table from one side of me. Lefty's wife was sitting on the other side. It goes all the way around the table, and there's only a little left when it gets to her, and she takes it all. 'Oh, I love this stuff,' she said. So I asked the waiter to bring some more, and they bring it and it goes around the table again, and damn if she didn't take the last bit again. She was sitting there eating it on bits of toast. My God, she ate so much of that stuff she looked like a seagull eating shit."

The friend was wondering uneasily how his lovely new wife was taking this, and he got Ruth to talking instead about his trophies. Babe gave them a quick guided tour. He pointed to one silver cup and said, "Look at this one. You know what I got it for?"

"No, what?"

"I won first place in a farting contest. Honest. Read the writing on it. Boy, I had to down a lot of beer and limburger to win that one."

The friend left the apartment a bit shaken. In the elevator he looked nervously at his wife. But she seemed exhilarated.

"What a fascinating man," she said.

"Ruth's language *was* pretty bad," Frick said, "but, you know, it's a remarkable thing. My wife is a very genteel lady, *very* genteel, yet she always enjoyed seeing Ruth, and we were with him a great deal in those years. In all the time I knew him, I cannot recall one instance when he ever said anything crude or obscene in front of her." Meany said he was with Ruth at a party on Long Island when Babe decided to tell a joke, something he rarely did. Before he began, he insisted that all the women leave the room. And the anecdote turned out to be fairly innocuous.

Many stories about Ruth were turned into legend by the encrustations of time. Here are three of them, with a factual basis for each. The story of Johnny Sylvester is one of the most famous in Ruth lore. The simplest version says that Johnny, a young boy, lay dying in a hospital. Ruth came to visit him and promised him he would hit a home run for him that afternoon. And he did, which so filled Johnny with the will to live that he miraculously recovered. The facts are parallel, if not so melodramatic. In 1926 eleven-year-old Johnny Sylvester was badly hurt in a fall from a horse and was hospitalized. To cheer him up, a friend of Johnny's father brought him baseballs autographed by players on the Yankees and the Cardinals just before the World Series that year, as well as a promise from Ruth that he would hit a home run for him. Ruth hit four homers in the Series, and after it was over paid a visit to Johnny in the hospital, which thrilled the boy. The visit was given the tears-and-lump-in-the-throat treatment in the press, and the legend was born. After that, few writers reviewing Ruth's career failed to mention a dying boy and the home run that saved his life.

The following spring Ruth was sitting with a couple of baseball writers when a man came up to him and said, "Mr. Ruth, I'm Johnny Sylvester's uncle. I just want to thank you again for what you did for him."

"That's all right," Ruth said, "glad to do it. How is Johnny?"

"He's fine. He's home, and everything looks okay."

"That's good," said Ruth. "Give him my regards."

The man left. Ruth watched him walk away and said, "Now who the hell is Johnny Sylvester?"

There is a legend that Ruth once hit a ball so hard that it went between the pitcher's legs and over the center fielder's head for a home run. In 1927 the Yankees played the Senators when Hod Lisenbee was pitching for Washington and Tris Speaker was playing center field. Lisenbee was in his first year in the majors and Speaker in his next to last. There was a runner on second taking a big lead, although he was keeping his eyes on both the shortstop and the second baseman. Speaker began a favorite maneuver of his: sneaking in from center field toward second base in the hopes of getting a quick throw from the pitcher and picking the runner off second. Lisenbee ignored Speaker's move and threw to the plate. Ruth hit a low line drive directly back at the pitcher, who leaped and lifted his right leg frantically to avoid being hit by it. The ball ticked the underside of his thigh as it went past. It hit the ground a few feet past second, took a huge bounce, and went over Speaker's head. One of the other outfielders retrieved it, but Ruth got an extra-base hit out of it—not a home run.

And there is a legend, seldom printed but often talked about in baseball circles, that says Leo Durocher stole Babe Ruth's watch, which is not true. What is true is that Ruth did not like Durocher. When he saw Leo, a rookie, wearing a tuxedo in the lobby of a spring-training hotel, Ruth asked with considerable distaste, "Who's the little gink in the monkey suit?" He resented Leo's cockiness, and the two never got along, although Leo tried to—at first.

Durocher was in a hotel elevator late one night with a couple of other players when Ruth got on. "Oh, am I drunk," said the Babe. "Somebody's got to undress me and put me to bed. You guys have to help me."

The other players backed away rapidly, but Leo said, "I'll help you, pal."

"Thank you, pal," Ruth said. Leo helped him off the elevator and down the hall to Babe's room. The next morning Ruth decided that he was missing something—money in one version of the story, his watch in another. Although he was drunk on the town the night before and had been in the Lord knows what places, he blamed Durocher. As Leo said, in a half-angry, half-mocking tone, "Jesus Christ, if I was going to steal anything from him I'd steal his goddamned Packard."

Ruth continued to harass Durocher. One night on the train as he was getting undressed by his berth, he called to Durocher.

"Hey, Leo, you want to see something?" He held up a glittering bit of jewelry. "See that, Leo? Isn't that beautiful? That cost me seventy-five hundred bucks, Leo. I'm going to give it to Claire when we get to New York. Tonight I'm putting it under my pillow. And, Leo, I want it to be there when I wake up in the morning."

After that, Durocher disliked Ruth as much as Babe disliked him, although in a year or so their paths parted. After the 1929 season Durocher was sold out of the American League to Cincinnati. Explaining the sale, which was made when he was manager, Shawkey said, "You'll never see a better fielding shortstop than Leo, but he couldn't hit. And he was a little too much of an individual."

Ruth did not like Ty Cobb much either, primarily because of Cobb's bench jockeying, which was cruel and humorless. When the story about Ruth never changing his underwear got around the league during his early years with the Red Sox, Cobb would say the same thing whenever he saw Ruth: "You fellows smell something around here? Oh, hello, Babe." Ruth's usual reply to Cobb's gibes was a stream of obscenity. Cobb and some of the other Tigers were riding Ruth about the 1922 Series, and Cobb said, "We hear that little Johnny Rawlings ran you out of the Giant clubhouse. Is that true?" Ruth said, "It ain't a goddamned bit true, and you sons of bitches can go fuck yourselves." Cobb said that when Ruth extended himself he had a vocabulary that stood alone, even in the purple atmosphere of dugout and clubhouse. Ruth and Cobb had a fight of sorts on the field in 1924 when a free-for-all broke out between the Yankees and Tigers, but they were separated before anything much happened. Ruth was not much of a brawler. His quick temper got him into a lot of mixups, but, according to Meany, he never won a fight. He never really lost one either. He had a lot of No Decisions. He seldom stayed angry very long.

Ruth's tendency to get into trouble, particularly during his first decade in the majors, gave rise to a fairly widespread opinion that he was subnormal mentally (Ban Johnson said he had the mind of a fifteen-year-old) or else was so primitive that he could not accept a moral code. "He was an animal," Dugan said. "He ate a hat once. He did. A straw hat. Took a bite out of it and ate it."

But Ernie Shore said, "You have to remember, he had grown up in that Catholic reformatory. When they let him out it was like turning a wild animal out of a cage. He wanted to *go* every place and *see* everything and *do* everything."

"Ruth recognized the difference between right and wrong," Frick said. "What he did not recognize, or could not accept, was the right of society to tell him what he should do, or not do."

He had a perceptive understanding of things in certain areas and, in his own way, a refreshing sense of taste. When he met Red Grange after the Illinois football hero turned professional in the mid-1920s, Ruth said to him, "Kid, don't ever forget two things I'm going to tell you. One, don't believe everything that's written about you. Two, don't pick up too many checks." Someone introduced him to Max Schmeling when he and the then heavyweight champion of the world happened to be riding on the same train. After Schmeling returned to his own compartment, a friend said to Ruth, "You should have asked him for his autograph." Ruth said, "Who the hell wants to collect that crap?" Frick said, "He drank a great deal and he was a ladies' man, but he never led a young ballplayer astray and he never took advantage of an innocent girl."

He understood clearly what he was doing when he batted, despite his habit of saying, "I just keep swinging," when people asked him the secret of hitting home runs. Once, seriously discussing his batting, he said, "I swing as hard as I can, and I try to swing right through the ball. In boxing, your fist usually stops when you hit a man, but it's possible to hit so hard that your fist doesn't stop. I try to follow through the same way. The harder you grip the bat, the more you can swing it through the ball, and the farther the ball will go. I swing big, with everything I've got. I hit big or I miss big. I like to live as big as I can." He held his bat at the very end, with his right hand curled over the knob. He had a big callus in the palm of his right hand as a result, along with the usual calluses that all batters have on their fingers and thumbs.

"He liked anything connected with playing baseball," Frick said, "but he liked home runs best. Whenever he hit one, he laughed. Sometimes before a game he'd say, 'I feel hitterish today. I'm due to hit one.' And if he did hit one, he'd talk about it long after the game."

He could be thoughtlessly cruel at times. Bud Mulvey, whose family used to own a substantial part of the Brooklyn Dodgers and still retains an interest in the Los Angeles Dodgers, remembered a baseball writers' dinner he was taken to as a boy. Ruth, retired by then, was there, and before the dinner he began to fool with Jackie Farrell, a tiny man literally half Ruth's weight, who later worked in the Yankee publicity department. Mulvey watched in distaste as Ruth playfully twisted Farrell's arm. "Jackie was really in pain," Mulvey said, "and Ruth was roaring with laughter. I never could like him after that."

Bob Condon, whose father knew Charlie McManus, the Yankee Stadium supervisor, was sometimes a backstage guest at the Stadium when he was a boy, which was relatively late in the Babe's career. Once, while a game was going on outside on the field, Condon was playing by himself in an open area under the stands behind the Yankee dugout. Ruth left the game for some reason, possibly a minor injury, and came angrily up the runway from the dugout. As he did, the ball Condon was playing with took a freak bounce directly into Ruth's path. The boy dove for it and fell flat in front of the Babe, who irritably shoved him out of the way with his foot. Kick may be too strong a word for the action, but substantially that is what Ruth did. "Stay out of the Babe's way," someone warned the tearful boy.

Alice Doubleday Rhodes recalled a time when Ruth played an exhibition in her small town when she was about ten. For some reason she accepted a dare to get Ruth's autograph, and well before the game she sneaked onto the field and walked to the Yankee bench. She had to ask, "Which one is Babe Ruth?" and this, to her confusion, made everyone laugh. He was pointed out and when she walked over to him he said, pleasantly enough, "You want to see me, sister?" She handed him her school notebook and a pen, a brand-new pen that had just been given to her for her birthday. "Here," she said. He signed his name, in "a beautiful, even hand" and gave her back her schoolbook and pen. "There you are, sister," he said. "Now don't go home and sell it." But she had promised to get autographs for her schoolmates too. She handed book and pen back to him and said, "Write some more. Write on all the lines." The other players broke up laughing. Ruth shrugged and slowly wrote his name on line after line until the page was filled. "That okay now?" he said, not smiling. He handed her the book and, looking out at the field, absentmindedly put the pen in his own pocket. Her marvelous birthday pen. She did not know what to do. Ruth looked at her coldly.

"Something else on your mind, little girl?" he asked. She shook her head and said, "No, sir," and left. Chagrined and not a little afraid, it took her some time to get up the courage to tell her father what had happened, and she was totally unable to understand his hilarity when she did tell him. "Babe Ruth swiped your pen?" he howled.

Yet his affection for children was genuine, and it remained with him all his life. In 1943 he played a round of golf in the rain at the Commonwealth Country Club near Boston. As he was teeing up on the first hole he noticed two boys staring through a chain-link fence.

"Hey," he called to them. "You want to follow me around? It won't be any drier but it'll be more fun. You want to?"

The kids nodded. "Show them how to get into this joint," Ruth said to Russ Hale, the club pro. He waited until the boys reached the tee before he hit his drive, and he walked down the fairway with one arm around each, talking. He played nine holes in the rain, most of the time laughing and joking with the other men in his foursome but always returning to the kids to make sure they were enjoying themselves.

A decade earlier Jack Redding, who was to become librarian of the National Baseball Library at Cooperstown, caddied for him at Wheatley Hills on Long Island. "He'd give us a two-dollar tip if he won, a dollar and a half if he lost," Redding said. Was that a good tip? "Hell, yes," Redding said. "The usual tip was a quarter, or at best a half dollar. And on the thirteenth hole, where the refreshment stand was, that's where you tested your man. Some golfers would buy you a soft drink, some wouldn't buy you anything. Ruth always said, 'Get whatever you want.' "

He was a frequent and interested visitor to hospitals, orphanages, children's wards, and the like. He could create a holiday spirit in a ward merely by being himself. Many of his visits were well publicized—Walsh saw to that—but they were not done for publicity. Ruth always, or almost always, made himself available to the press, but the publicity was coincidental. After someone made fun of all the newspaper copy he received from such visits, he avoided mention of them, and for every one that got public notice several more did not.

Stories about the time and trouble he took to call on the sick and distressed are innumerable. Even when he was ill himself, he continued the practice. A year or so before he died, racked with pain from the cancer that was to kill him, he went with Paul Carey to visit a man who had gone blind. After they left, Ruth said of the blind man, "Some guys get all the bad breaks, don't they?"

He liked seeing children the best. He enjoyed them. He was comfortable with them. "He's just a big kid" was a common description of him, and perhaps the only time he was truly at ease was when he was with children. With them there were no rules, no authority, no need to apologize, to explain, to explode, to drink, to fuck, to prove himself over and over. Without thinking about it, he knew who they were and they knew who he was. They got along. Like a child, he did not like to wait or plan for the right moment. He did not like to wait for anything. "It might rain tomorrow," he would say.

He did things impulsively, the way a child does. Children are emotionally neutral to things that deeply affect adults. Without malice, they casually hurt the feelings of a close friend. Without love, they do an act of exceptional thoughtfulness for a casual acquaintance. In his novel *Stop-Time* Frank Conroy wrote, "Like all children, I was unsentimental." Hoyt said of Ruth, "Babe was not a sentimentalist and generally made no outward demonstration of affection either by word or action."

This may explain a curious thing that Paul Carey, his great friend, said when he was asked about Ruth's feelings toward Claire. "I don't think the Babe really loved Claire," Carey said. "I don't think he really loved anybody."

GARRISON KEILLOR

"The Babe"

The Babe had retired in 1935 and was dying of cancer, but even a dying man has bills to pay, and so he took to the road for Sorbasol, and Lake Wobegon was the twenty-fourth stop on the trip, a day game on November 12. The All-Star train of two sleepers and a private car for the Babe backed up the sixteen-mile spur into Lake Wobegon, arriving at 10:00 A.M. with a blast of whistle and a burst of steam, but hundreds already were on hand to watch it arrive.

The Babe was a legend then, much like God is today. He didn't give interviews, in other words. He rode around on his train and appeared only when necessary. It was said that he drank Canadian rye whiskey, ate hot dogs, won thousands at poker, and kept beautiful women in his private car, *Excelsior*, but that was only talk.

The sleepers were ordinary deluxe Pullmans; the *Excelsior* was royal

green with gold-and-silver trim and crimson velvet curtains tied shut—
not that anyone tried to look in; these were proud country people, not a
bunch of gawkers. Men stood by the train, their backs to it, talking
purposefully about various things, looking out across the lake, and when
other men straggled across the field in twos and threes, stared at the
train, and asked, "Is he really in there?" the firstcomers said, "Who? Oh!
You mean the Babe? Oh, yes, I reckon he's here all right—this is his
train, you know. I doubt that his train would go running around without
the Babe in it, now, would it?" and resumed their job of standing by the
train, gazing out across the lake. A proud moment for them.

At noon the Babe came out in white linen knickers. He looked lost. A
tiny black man held his left arm. Babe tried to smile at the people and
the look on his face made them glance away. He stumbled on a loose
plank on the platform and men reached to steady him and noticed he
was hot to the touch. He signed an autograph. It was illegible. A young
woman was carried to him who'd been mysteriously ill for months, and
he laid his big hand on her forehead and she said she felt something.
(Next day she was a little better. Not recovered but improved.)

However, the Babe looked shaky, like a man who ate a bushel of
peaches whole and now was worried about the pits. He's drunk, some
said, and a man did dump a basket of empty beer bottles off the train,
and boys dove in to get one for a souvenir—but others who came close to
his breath said no, he wasn't drunk, only dying. So it was that an immense crowd turned out at the Wally (Old Hard Hands) Bunsen Memo-
rial Ballpark: twenty cents per seat, two bits to stand along the foul line,
and a dollar to be behind a rope by the dugout, where the Babe would
shake hands with each person in that section.

He and the All-Stars changed into their red Sorbasol uniforms in the
dugout, there being no place else, and people looked away as they did it
(nowadays people would look, but then they didn't), and the Babe and
his teammates tossed the ball around, then sat down, and out came the
Schroeders. They ran around and warmed up and you could see by their
nonchalance how nervous they were. E.J. batted grounders to them and
hit one grounder zinging into the visitors' dugout, missing the Babe by
six inches. He was too sick to move. The All-Stars ran out and griped to
the ump but the Babe sat like he didn't know where he was. The ump
was scared. The Babe hobbled out to home plate for the ceremonial
handshakes and photographs, and E.J. put his arm around him as the
crowd stood cheering and grinned and whispered, "We're going to kill
ya, ya big mutt. First pitch goes in your ear. This is your last game. Bye,
Babe." And the game got under way.

It was a good game, it's been said, though nobody remembers much about it specifically, such as the score, for example. The All-Stars were nobodies, only the Babe mattered to the crowd, and the big question was Would he play? He looked too shaky to take the field, so some said, "Suspend the rules! Why not let him just go up and bat! He can bat for the pitcher! Why not? It wouldn't hurt anything!" And nowadays they might do it, but back then you didn't pick up the bat unless you picked up your glove and played a position, and others said that maybe it wouldn't hurt anything but once you start changing the rules of the game for convenience, then what happens to our principles? Or do we change those, too?

So the game went along, a good game except that the Babe sat sprawled in the dugout, the little black man dipping cloths in a bucket of ice and laying them on the great man's head—a cool fall day but he was hot—and between innings he climbed out and waved to the fans and they stood and cheered and wondered would he come to bat. E.J. said to Bernie, "He'll bat all right, and when he comes, remember the first pitch: hard and high and inside."

"He looks too weak to get the bat off his shoulder, Dad. He looks like a breeze would blow him over. I can't throw at Babe Ruth."

"He's not sick, he's pretending so he don't have to play like the rest of us. Look at him: big fat rich New York son of a bitch, I bet he's getting five hundred dollars just to sit there and have a pickaninny put ice on him. Boy, I'd put some ice on him you-know-where, boy, he'd get up quick then, he'd be ready to play then. He comes up, I want you to give him something to think about so he knows we're not all a bunch of dumb hicks out here happy just to have him show up. I want him to know that some of us *mean it.* You do what I say. I'm serious."

It was a good game and people enjoyed it, the day cool and bright, delicious, smelling of apples and leather and woodsmoke and horses, blazed with majestic colors as if in a country where kings and queens ride through the cornfields into the triumphant reds and oranges of the woods, and men in November playing the last game of summer, waiting for the Babe, everyone waiting for the Babe as runs scored, hours passed, the sky turned red and hazy. It was about time to quit and go home, and then he marched out, bat in hand, and three thousand people threw back their heads and yelled as loud as they could. They yelled for one solid minute and then it was still.

The Babe stood looking toward the woods until everything was silent, then stepped to the plate and waved the bat, and Bernie looked at him. It was so quiet you could hear coughing in the crowd. Way to the rear a man said, "Merle, you get your hands off her and shut up now," and hundreds turned and shushed *him.* Then Bernie wound up. He bent way down and reached way back and kicked up high and the world turned and the ball flew and the umpire said, "BALL ONE!" and the catcher turned and said, "Be quiet, this doesn't concern you," and the umpire blushed. He knew immediately that he was in the wrong. Babe Ruth was not going to walk, he would sooner strike out and would do it himself, with no help from an umpire. So the umpire turned and walked away.

The Babe turned and spat and picked up a little dirty and rubbed his hands with it (people thought, Look, that's our dirt and he's putting it on his hands, as if the Babe might bring his own) and then stood in and waved the bat and Bernie bent way down and reached way back and kicked high and the world turned and the ball flew and the Babe swung and missed; he said *huhhhnnnn* and staggered. And the next pitch. He swung and cried in pain and the big slow curve slapped into the catcher's mitt.

It was so still, they heard the Babe clear his throat, like a board sliding across dirt. They heard Bernie breathing hard through his nose.

The people were quiet, wanting to see, hear, and smell everything and remember it forever: the wet fall dirt, the pale-white bat, the pink cotton candy and the gentlemen's hats, the smell of wool and the glimmer of a star in the twilight, the touch of your dad's big hand and your little hand in it. Even E.J. was quiet, chewing, watching his son. The sun had set beyond right field, darkness was settling, you had to look close to see— Bernie took three steps toward home and pointed at the high outside corner of the plate, calling his pitch, and the Babe threw back his head and laughed four laughs. (People were glad to hear he was feeling better, but it was scary to hear a man laugh at home plate; everyone knew it was bad luck.) He touched the corner with his bat. Bernie climbed back on the mound, he paused, he bent down low and reached way back and kicked real high and the world turned and the ball flew and the Babe swung and it cracked and the ball became a tiny white star in the sky. It hung there as the Babe went around the bases in his famous Babe Ruth stride, the big graceful man trotting on slim little feet, his head down until the roar of the crowd rose like an ocean wave on the prairie and he looked up as he turned at third, he smiled, lifted his cap, strode sound-lessly across home plate looking like the greatest ballplayer in the history of the world. The star was still in the sky, straight out due northwest of the centerfield fence, where he hit it. The ball was never found, though they searched for it for years.

DON DeLILLO

FROM *END ZONE*

*The following extract describes the moments just before a football game
between two West Texas Division Two colleges, Logos and West Centrex Biotechnical Institute. DeLillo describes the game through the eyes
of a Logos running back, Gary Harkness, the book's protagonist. Each
play in the game is described in detail, starting with the quarterback's
signal in the huddle—"blue turk right, double slot, zero snag delay," and
so forth. Logos, a considerable underdog, loses in the fourth quarter. The
game takes up a number of chapters in the middle of the novel and
would be too lengthy to include here. What follows after the break is
part of a chapter describing an event in the winter of that same season.*

In the morning we went out to the stadium, suited up without pads or
headgear and had an extra mild workout, just getting loose, tossing the
ball around, awakening our bodies to the feel of pigskin and turf. The
place seemed fairly new. It was shaped like a horseshoe and probably
seated about 22,000. Our workout progressed in virtual silence. It was a
cool morning with no breeze to speak of. We went back in and listened
to the coaches for a while. Then we rode back to the motels. At four
o'clock we had our pregame meal—beef consommé, steak and eggs. At
five-thirty we went back out to the stadium and slowly, very slowly, got
suited up in fresh uniforms. Nobody said much until we went through
the runway and took the field for our warmup. In the runway a few
people made their private sounds, fierce alien noises having nothing to
do with speech or communication of any kind. It was a kind of frantic
breathing with elements of chant, each man's sound unique and yet
mated to the other sounds, a mass rhythmic breathing that became more
widespread as we emerged from the runway and trotted onto the field.
We did light calisthenics and ran through some basic plays. Then the
receivers and backs ran simple pass patterns as the quarterbacks took
turns throwing. Off to the side the linemen exploded from their stances,
each one making his private noise, the chant or urgent breathing of men

in preparation for ritual danger. We returned to the locker room in silence and listened to our respective coaches issue final instructions. Then I put on my helmet and went looking for Buddy Shock. He and the other linebackers were still being lectured by Vern Feck. I waited until the coach was finished and then I grabbed Buddy by the shoulder, spun him around and hit him with a forearm across the chest, hard. He answered with three open-hand blows against the side of my helmet.

"Right," I said. "Right, right, right."

"Awright. Aw-*right,* Gary boy."

"Right, right, right."

"Awright, aw-*right.* "

"Get it up, get it in."

"Work, work, work."

"Awright."

"Awright. Aw-riiiight."

I walked slowly around the room, swinging my arms over my head. Some of the players were sitting or lying on the floor. I saw Jerry Fallon and approached him. He was standing against a wall, fists clenched at his sides, his helmet on the floor between his feet.

"Awright, Jerry boy."

"Awright, Gary."

"We move them out."

"Huh huh huh."

"How to go, big Jerry."

"Huh huh huh."

"Awright, awright, awright."

"We hit, we hit."

"Jerry boy, big Jerry."

Somebody called for quiet. I turned and saw Emmett Creed standing in front of a blackboard at the head of the room. His arms were crossed over his chest and he held his baseball cap in his right hand. It took only a few seconds before the room was absolutely still. The cap dangled from his fingers.

"I want the maximal effort," he said.

Then we were going down the runway, the sounds louder now, many new noises, some grunts and barks, everyone with his private noise, hard fast rhythmic sounds. We came out of the mouth of the tunnel and I saw the faces looking down from both sides, the true, real, and honest faces, Americans on a Saturday night, even the more well-to-do among them bearing the look of sharecroppers, a vestigial line of poverty wearing thin but still present on every face, the teen-agers looking like prewar kids, 1940, poorly cut short hair and a belligerent cleanliness. After the introductions I butted pads with Bobby Hopper and then bounced up and down on the sideline as we won the coin toss. The captains returned and we all gathered together around Creed, all of us making noises, a few prayers said, some obscenities exchanged, men jumping, men slapping each other's helmets. Creed said something into all the noise and then the kick-return team moved onto the field. I glanced across at Centrex. They looked big and happy. They were wearing red jerseys with silver pants and silver helmets. We wore white jerseys with green pants and green and white helmets. My stomach was tight; it seemed to be up near my chest somewhere. I was having trouble breathing and an awful sound was filling my helmet, a sound that seemed to be coming from inside my head. I could see people getting up all over the stadium and the cheer-leaders jumping and a couple of stadium cops standing near an exit. I could see the band playing, the movements of the band members as they played, but I couldn't hear the music. I looked down to my right. Bobby Iselin and Taft Robinson were the deep men. Speed and superspeed. About sixty-eight yards upfield the kicker raised his right arm, gave a little hop, and began to move toward the ball.

Jim Deering brought a football out to the parade grounds and we played for several hours in the fresh snow. It began as a game of touch, five on a side, no contact except for brush blocks and tagging the ballcarrier. The snow was ankle-high. We let the large men do all the throwing. Some of us cut classes in order to keep playing. It was very cold at first but we didn't notice so much after a while. Nobody cared how many passes were dropped or badly thrown and it didn't matter how slowly we ran or if we fell trying to cut or stop short. The idea was to keep playing, keep moving, get it going again. Some students and teachers, walking to and from classes, stood and watched for a few minutes and then went away. Two more players entered the game, making it six to a side. They left their books on top of the pile of heavy coats in the snow. Most of us wore regular shoes and nothing heavier than a sweater. George Dole, his first chance to play quarterback, wore a checkered cowboy shirt with the sleeves rolled way up. Nobody wore gloves after John Jessup said gloves were outlawed. Toward the end of the first hour it began getting windy. The wind blew loose snow into our faces, making it hard to keep track of the ball's flight. Between plays I crossed my arms over my chest, keeping my hands wedged in my armpits for warmth. We blocked a little more emphatically now, partly to keep warm, to increase movement, and also to compensate for the wind, the poor playing conditions; more hitting helped us forget the sting of cold snow blowing in our faces. Each team had just one deep back to do all the throwing and running; there were three linemen blocking and two receivers. Defense was a 3–3 most of the time. It was getting harder to complete a pass or turn the corner on a

running play. I noticed that Buddy Shock's nose was bleeding. It started
to snow now, lightly at first, then more heavily, and in time it was almost
impossible to see beyond the limits of the parade grounds. It was lovely
to be hemmed in that way, everything white except for the clothes we
wore and the football and the bundle of coats and books in the snow
nearby. We were part of the weather, right inside it, isolated from objects on the land, from land, from perspective itself. There were no
spectators now; we were totally alone. I was beginning to enjoy skidding
and falling. I didn't even try to retain my balance when I felt myself
slipping. Certain reflexes were kept slack; it seemed fitting to let the
conditions determine how our bodies behaved. We were adrift within
this time and place and what I experienced then, speaking just for myself, was some variety of environmental bliss. Jessup outlawed the placing of hands under armpits between plays. I found merit in this regulation; even the smallest warmth compromised immersion in the
elements. Then he outlawed huddles and the making of plays in the
usual way. Each play, he decreed, would be announced aloud by the
team with the ball. There would be no surprise at all, not the slightest
deception; the defense would know exactly what was coming. Again I
found it easy to agree. We were getting extremely basic, moving into
elemental realms, seeking harmony with the weather and the earth. The
snowfall was very heavy now, reducing visibility to about fifteen yards.
Suddenly Tim Flanders and Larry Nix were standing near the coats.
Someone had told them about the game and they had come down hoping to get in. That made it seven men on each team, four blockers, an
unbalanced line, a 4–3 defense. I was playing center now, stooped way
over, my body warped and about to buckle, hands positioned on the cold
wet ball, eyes on huge George Dole awaiting the snap four yards behind
me and upside-down, calling out the play and number, his face that of an
outlandishly large Navaho infant, dull muddy red in color, his feet lost in
snow, sniffling now as he shouted out the cadence, white haired in the
biting wind, abominable and looming. The blocking became more spirited and since we wore no equipment it was inevitable that tempers
would flare. Randall and Nix butted each other a few times, throwing no
punches because of the severe cold. Then Jessup outlawed passing plays.
It became strictly a ground game. After two plays it was decided, by
unanimous consent, to replace tagging with tackling. Naturally the
amount of hitting increased. Somebody tore my sweater and left me
buried in snow. I got up and kept going. With passing outlawed the
game changed completely. Its range was now limited to a very small area
and its degree of specialization diminished. There were no receivers and
defenders to scatter the action. We were all blockers, all tacklers. Only
the ballcarrier, one man, could attempt to use evasion and finesse in

avoiding the primal impact. After a clumsy double-reverse I stood alone watching Ron Steeples, way over at the far rim of vision, whirl in a rotary cloud of snow and take a swing at Jim Deering, whose back was turned. Steeples lost his balance as he swung; the punch missed completely and he fell. Deering, unaware of any of this, trotted over to his side of the line. Steeples got up and walked slowly toward the defense, wiping his hands on his stiff wet trousers. At this point Jessup banned reverses of any kind. The ball had to be handled by one man and one man alone. Even fake reverses were outlawed. No offensive player could pass in front of or behind the ballcarrier while the ballcarrier was still behind the line of scrimmage. Jessup shouted these regulations into the wind. I asked about laterals. Absolutely forbidden, Jessup said. My hands were numb. I looked at them. They were purplish red. Snow on my lashes blurred everything. Lines of sight shortened. My shoes weighed me down. We kept playing, we kept hitting, and we were comforted by the noise and brunt of our bodies in contact, by the simple physical warmth generated through violent action, by the sight of each other, the torn clothing, the bruises and scratches, the wildness of all fourteen, numb, purple, coughing, white heads solemn in the healing snow. Jessup banned end runs. It became a straight-ahead game, tackle to tackle. We hand-fought and butted. Linemen fired out and the ballcarrier just lowered his head and went pounding into the tense rhythmic mass. Blocking did not necessarily cease when the ballcarrier went down. Private battles continued until one man gave ground or was buried in snow. These individual contests raged on every play, each man grunting and panting, trying to maintain traction, to move the other man, to chop him down, to overwhelm him. Randall grabbed me by the shoulders and tried to toss me off to the side. I slipped out of his grip, getting hit on the back of the neck with a stray elbow, and then I rammed a shoulder into his gut and kept on moving, kept driving, making him give way; but he tightened up, hardening considerably now, too strong for me, coming back with a slap to my left ear which turned me half-around and then moving straight in with everything, head, shoulders, hands, until he buried me. He dug me out and slapped me on the rump. On the next play I cross-blocked, going after Deering, more my size, standing him up with two shoulder-blows to the chest, getting shoved from behind and going down with three or four others. The cold was painful now; it hurt more than the blocking and tackling. I got up, one shoe missing. I saw it a few yards away. I went over and picked it up. It felt like a dead animal. I forced it over my foot. The laces were stiff and my hands too frozen to make a knot. I looked up. Oscar Veech was standing directly in front of me, wearing a padded ski jacket and a pair of snow goggles.

"Coach wants to see you," he said.

Everybody stood around watching. I went over and found my coat. I put it over my head and followed Veech into the dimness and silence. We went over to Staley Hall. Veech didn't say anything. We went downstairs and he simply nodded toward the closed door at the end of the isometrics room. I left my coat bundled on a scale. Then I blew my nose, walked to the door and knocked. The room was small and barely furnished, just an army cot, a small folding table, two folding chairs. There were no windows. On the wall was a page torn from a book, a black-and-white plate of a girl praying in a medieval cell, an upper corner of the page loose and casting a limp shadow. Near the door, at my shoulder, a whistle hung from a string looped over a bent nail. Emmett Creed was in a wheelchair. His legs were covered with a heavy blanket, gray and white, not quite the school colors. Ten or twelve loose-leaf binders were stacked neatly on the floor.

"Sit down, Gary."

"Yes sir."

"I'm told it's a near blizzard out there."

"We were going at it," I said. "We were playing. We were ignoring the weather and going right at it."

"So I'm told."

"How are you feeling, Coach? A lot of the guys have tried to get in to see you. I'm sure they'd appreciate it if I brought back word."

"Everything is progressing as anticipated."

"Yes sir. Very good. I know they'd appreciate hearing that."

"A near blizzard is what they tell me."

"It's really snowing," I said. "It's coming down thick and steady. Visibility must be zero feet."

"Maybe that's the kind of weather we needed over at Centrex."

"None of us can forget that game, Coach."

"We learned a lot of humility on that field."

"It was hard to accept. We had worked too hard to lose, going all the way back to last summer, scrimmaging in that heat. We had worked too hard. It was impossible to believe that anybody had worked harder than we had. We had sacrificed. We had put ourselves through a series of really strenuous ordeals. And then to step out on that field and be overwhelmed the way we were."

"It takes character to win," he said. "It's not just the amount of mileage you put in. The insults to the body. The humiliation and fear. It's dedication, it's character, it's pride. We've got a ways to go yet before we develop these qualities on a team basis."

"Yes sir."

"I've never seen a good football player who didn't know the value of self-sacrifice."

"Yes sir."

"I've never seen a good football player who wanted to learn a foreign language."

"Yes."

"I've been married three times but I was never blessed with children. A son. So maybe I don't know as much about young men as I think I do. But I've managed to get some good results through the years. I've tried to extract the maximal effort from every body I've ever coached. Or near as possible. Football is a complex of systems. It's like no other sport. When the game is played properly, it's an interlocking of a number of systems. The individual. The small cluster he's part of. The larger unit, the eleven. People stress the violence. That's the smallest part of it. Football is brutal only from a distance. In the middle of it there's a calm, a tranquillity. The players accept pain. There's a sense of order even at the end of a running play with bodies strewn everywhere. When the systems interlock, there's a satisfaction to the game that can't be duplicated. There's a harmony."

"Absolutely," I said.

"But I didn't intend getting into that. You know all that. A boy of your intelligence doesn't have to be told what this game is all about."

"Thank you," I said.

"No boy of mine has ever broken the same rule twice."

"Yes sir."

"No boy in all my years of coaching has ever placed his personal welfare above the welfare of the aggregate unit."

"Yes sir."

"Our inner life is falling apart. We're losing control of things. We need more self-sacrifice, more discipline. Our inner life is crumbling. We need to renounce everything that turns us from the knowledge of ourselves. We're getting too far away from our own beginnings. We're roaming all over the landscape. We need to build ourselves up mentally and spiritually. Do that and the body takes care of itself. I learned this as a small boy. I was very sickly, a very sickly child. I had this and that disease. I was badly nourished. My legs were no thicker than the legs of that chair. But I built myself up by determination and sacrifice. The mind first and then the body. It was a lonely life for a boy. I had no friends. I lived in an inner world of determination and silence. Mental resolve. It made me strong; it prepared me. Things return to their beginnings. It's been a long circle from there to here. But all the lessons hold true. The inner life must be disciplined just as the hand or eye. Loneliness is strength. The Sioux purified themselves by fasting and solitude. Four days without food in a sweat lodge. Before you went out to lament for your nation, you had to purify yourself. Fasting and solitude. If you can survive loneliness, you've got an inner strength that can take you anywhere. Four days. You wore just a bison robe. I don't think there's anything makes more sense than self-denial. It's the only way to attain moral perfection. I've wandered here and there. I've made this and that mistake. But now I'm back and I'm back for good. A brave nation needs discipline. Purify the will. Learn humility. Restrict the sense life. Pain is part of the harmony of the nervous system."

I said nothing.

"What I called you in here for," Creed said. . . . "Kimbrough graduates in the spring. You're offensive captain."

"I never expected anything like this," I said. "I'm not a senior. Doesn't it go to seniors?"

"Never mind that."

"Frankly I thought I was here to be disciplined."

"Maybe that's what it all amounts to. I'll be demanding extra. I'll be after you every minute. As team leader you'll be setting an example for the rest of them. You'll have to give it everything you've got and then some."

"I'll be ready," I said.

"I know you will, son. You'll find Oscar Veech in the training room. Send him in here."

"One thing I've been meaning to ask since the minute I walked in. What's that picture taped to the wall? Who is that in the picture? Is it anybody in particular?"

"Somebody sent that picture to me many years ago. Looks like it came from some kind of religious book for kids. People were always sending me things. Good luck things or prayers or all kinds of advice. Not so much now. They've been keeping pretty quiet of late. But that's a Catholic saint. I've kept that picture with me for many years now. Teresa of Avila. She was a remarkable woman. A saint of the church. Do you know what she used to do in order to remind herself of final things?"

"Something to do with a skull, I think."

"She used to eat food out of a human skull."

"I'll go find Veech," I said.

In my room later I became depressed. No American accepts the deputy's badge without misgivings; centuries of heroic lawlessness have captured our blood. I felt responsible for a vague betrayal of some local code or lore. I was now part of the apparatus. No longer did I circle and watch, content enough to be outside the center and even sufficiently cunning to plan a minor raid or two. Now I was the law's small tin glitter. Suck in that gut, I thought.

WINTER

ROBERT BLY

"The Hockey Poem"

for Bill Duffy

1. THE GOALIE

The Boston College team has gold helmets, under which the long
black hair of the Roman centurion curls out. . . . And they begin. How
weird the goalies look with their African masks! The goalie is so lonely
anyway, guarding a basket with nothing in it, his wide lower legs wide
as ducks'. . . . No matter what gift he is given, he always rejects it. . . .
He has a number like 1, a name like Mrazek, sometimes wobbling his
legs waiting for the puck, or curling up like a baby in the womb to hold
it, staying a second too long on the ice.

The goalie has gone out to mid-ice, and now he sails sadly back to his
own box, slowly; he looks prehistoric with his rhinoceros legs; he looks
as if he's going to become extinct, and he's just taking his time. . . .

When the players are at the other end, he begins sadly sweeping the
ice in front of his house; he is the old witch in the woods, waiting for
the children to come home.

2. THE ATTACK

They all come hurrying back toward us, suddenly, knees dipping like
oil wells; they rush toward us wildly, fins waving, they are pike
swimming toward us, their gill fins expanding like the breasts of opera
singers; no, they are twelve hands practicing penmanship on the same
piece of paper. . . . They flee down the court toward us like birds,
swirling two and two, hawks hurrying for the mouse, hurrying down
wind valleys, swirling back and forth like amoebae on the pale slide, as
they sail in the absolute freedom of water and the body, untroubled
by the troubled mind, only the body, with wings as if there were no
grave, no gravity, only the birds sailing over the cottage far in the deep
woods. . . .

Now the goalie is desperate . . . he looks wildly over his left shoulder,
rushing toward the other side of his cave, like a mother hawk whose

chicks are being taken by two snakes . . . suddenly he flops on the ice
like a man trying to cover a whole double bed. He has the puck. He
stands up, turns to his right, and drops it on the ice at the right
moment; he saves it for one of his children, a mother hen picking up a
seed and then dropping it . . .

But the men are all too clumsy, they can't keep track of the puck . . .
no, it is the *puck*, the puck is too fast, too fast for human beings, it
humiliates them. The players are like country boys at the fair watching
the con man—the puck always turns up under the wrong walnut shell. . . .

They come down ice again, one man guiding the puck this time . . .
and Ledingham comes down beautifully, like the canoe through white
water, or the lover going upstream, every stroke right, like the stallion
galloping up the valley surrounded by his mares and colts, how
beautiful, like the body and soul crossing in a poem. . . .

3. TROUBLE

The player in position pauses, aims, pauses, cracks his stick on the
ice, and a cry as the puck goes in! The goalie stands up disgusted, and
throws the puck out. . . .

The player with a broken stick hovers near the cage. When the play
shifts, he skates over to his locked-in teammates, who look like a nest of
bristling owls, owl babies, and they hold out a stick to him. . . .

Then the players crash together, their hockey sticks raised like
lobster claws. They fight with slow motions, as if undersea . . . they are
fighting over some tribal insult or a god, but like lobsters they forget
what they're battling for; the clack of the armor plate distracts them,
and they feel a pure rage.

Or a fighter sails over to the penalty box, where ten-year-old boys
wait, to sit with the criminal, who is their hero. . . . They know society
is wrong, the wardens are wrong, the judges hate individuality. . . .

4. THE GOALIE

And this man with his peaked mask, with slits, how fantastic he is,
like a white insect, who has given up on evolution in this life; his family
hopes to evolve after death, in the grave. He is ominous as a Dark Ages
knight . . . the Black Prince. His enemies defeated him in the day, but
every one of them died in their beds that night. . . . At his father's
funeral, he carried his own head under his arm.

He is the old woman in the shoe, whose house is never clean, no
matter what she does. Perhaps this goalie is not a man at all, but a

woman, all women; in her cage everything disappears in the end; we all long for it. All these movements on the ice will end, the advertisements come down, the stadium walls bare. . . . This goalie with his mask is a woman weeping over the children of men, that are cut down like grass, gulls that stand with cold feet on the ice. . . . And at the end, she is still waiting, brushing away the leaves, waiting for the new children developed by speed, by war. . . .

PAUL GALLICO

"A LARGE NUMBER OF PERSONS"

Crowd: A large number of persons congregated or collected into a close body without order; a great number of persons; especially, the great body of people; the populace; the masses; the multitude. . . .
— Webster's New International Dictionary

The fight crowd is a beast that lurks in the darkness behind the fringe of white light shed over the first six rows by the incandescents atop the ring, and is not to be trusted with pop bottles or other hardware. The tennis crowd is the pansy of all the great sports mobs and is always preening and shushing itself. The golf crowd is the most unwieldy and most sympathetic, and is the only horde given to mass production of that absurd noise written generally as "tsk tsk tsk tsk," and made between tongue and teeth with head-waggings to denote extreme commiseration. The baseball crowd is the most hysterical, the football crowd the best-natured, and the polo crowd the most aristocratic. Racing crowds are the most restless, wrestling crowds the most tolerant, and soccer crowds the most easily incitable to riot and disorder. Every sports crowd takes on the characteristics of the individuals who compose it. Each has its particular note of hysteria, its own little cruelties, mannerisms, and bad mannerisms, its own code of sportsmanship, and its own method of expressing its emotions.

For instance, people who go to horse races want to win money. People who follow golf matches are bad golfers. People who go to tennis matches are pleased with rhythm and beauty. People who go to baseball games are all grandstand experts and thoroughly familiar with the game. People who attend the polo matches are either somebody or trying to be. The spectators at big college football games are the most wholesome people in the world but they know nothing about the game and care less.

People who go to prize fights are sadistic.

When two prominent pugilists are scheduled to pummel one another in public on a summer's evening, men and women file into the stadium in the guise of human beings, and thereafter become a part of a gray thing that squats in the dark until, at the conclusion of the blood-letting, they may be seen leaving the arena in the same guise they wore when they entered.

The only time I ever knew a fight crowd to do the proper thing was the night that Jack Sharkey fought Max Schmeling for the heavyweight championship of the world, at the Yankee Stadium, and came running down the aisles and into the ring with an American flag draped around his shoulders. There were eighty thousand people sitting in the darkness waiting to acclaim the American champion. Shocked by the display of inexcusable vulgarity on the part of the fighter's handlers, they loosed upon him instead a sirocco of boos and jeers that all but swept him from the platform.

But, as a rule, the mob that gathers to see men fight is unjust, vindictive, swept by intense, unreasoning hatreds, vain of its swift recognition of what it believes to be sportsmanship. It is quick to greet the purely phony move of the boxer who extends his gloves to his rival, who has slipped or been pushed to the floor, and to reward this stimulating but still baloney *beau geste* with a pattering of hands which indicates the following: "You are a good sport. We recognize that you are a good sport, and we know a sporting gesture when we see one. Therefore we are all good sports, too. Hurrah for us!"

The same crowd doesn't see the same boxer stick his thumb in his opponent's eye or try to cut him with the laces of his glove, butt him or dig him a low one when the referee isn't in a position to see. It roots consistently for the smaller man, and never for a moment considers the desperate psychological dilemma of the larger of the two. It howls with glee at a good finisher making his kill. The Roman hordes were more civilized. Their gladiators asked them whether the *coup de grâce* should be administered or not. The *pièce de résistance* at the modern prize fight is the spectacle of a man clubbing a helpless and vanquished opponent into complete insensibility. The referee who stops a bout to save a slugged and punch-drunken man from the final ignominy is hissed by the assembled sportsmen. The crowd in Cleveland was apathetic and voiceless until Schmeling suddenly battered Stribling to the floor and swayed forward, tiger-like, to finish his work of destruction, as somehow the stricken boy arose. Then the spectators were up out of their seats, swaying towards the ring, the white-crested wave again rolled out of their throats, and as I stood up and dictated the finish of the battle, I could see their hot, angry eyes reflecting the ring-lights and their inhuman, distorted, cry-torn mouths.

The golf gallery is the Punchinello of the great sports mob, the clown crowd, an uncontrollable, galloping, galumphing horde, that wanders hysterically over manicured pasture acreage of an afternoon, clucking to itself, trying to keep quiet, making funny noises, sweating, thundering over hills ten thousand strong, and gathering, mousey-still, around a little hole in the ground to see a man push a little ball into the bottom of it, with a crooked iron stick. If the ball goes in they raise a great shout and clap their hands and sometimes slap one another on the back, crying "Oh, boy!" and "Beautiful, beautiful, magnificent!" And when the white pellet just sneaks past the rim of the orifice or twists out of it, or goes up and looks in and sticks on the edge, a great mass-murmur of pity runs through the group and they sound their "Oh's" like a green chorus greeting the arrival of a new set of catastrophes. Then it is that they make their absurd clucking noises and shake their heads, some in unison, some in anti-unison, like mechanical dolls all set off at once.

The golf gallery is closest of any to the game that is being played. Every individual in the stampede is familiar with the implements used and the problems that arise from tee to green. They are really vicarious players, and the crass outsider who rattles a toy movie camera at one of the artists just as he is about to apply a delicate brush of his poker against the side of the quiescent ball is given the hissing and glaring-at of his life. The Jones' galleries were something to see, up and away over the hills before the master had completed the poem of his follow-through, running, crowding, tearing, galloping, hustling—men, women, and children, in sunshine or in cloudburst, their tongues hanging out, their faces red, their sports clothing disheveled, elbowing one another in the wild route over the lea to secure a momentary vantage point from which to bear witness to the next miracle.

The tennis audiences were always my favorites, preening themselves, bestowing refined approval in well-bred and well-repressed little outbursts, beaming upon the contestants and on one another, glaring at someone rustling a piece of paper, expressing righteous indignation at the unwelcome intrusion of an ordinary spectator who vulgarly screams, "Come on, you Johnny, sock it again!"

They are experts at registering shocked and delighted approval when an erring player cries "Nuts," or "God damn," to let them know that they feel he has been a muggins, but withal a virile and manly one. They, too, hum with smug sympathy when a player pouts or makes a move at a missed ball, pat-a-caking their hands to indicate recognition of the fine points of the game, and rooting for the player with the most slickum on his hair.

Baseball and football crowds are happiest when they feel that they have become a part of the game that is being played for them. The solidly packed football stands begin to chant, "We want a touchdown," or "Hold that line!" And when the touchdown is scored or the line holds, the crowd takes part credit. In baseball, sections of the rooters set out deliberately to rattle a pitcher with rhythmic or anti-rhythmic hand-clappings, whichever they think will annoy him the most, or by setting up a bedlam of sound, or by waving somewhat cloudy pocket-handker-chiefs at him. Most rooting, as a matter of fact, grows out of the individual spectator's desire to identify himself with the proceedings on the field, to shake himself free of the anonymity of the crowd and become an active participant in a sport for which nature happens not to have fitted him.

The loveliest girls in the world sit in the football crowds, their fresh faces framed in fur. The toughest babies in town seem to collect at the ball games, idle sisters sitting in pairs chewing gum, fanning themselves with their score cards, and adding their harsh screams to the hullabaloo that accompanies a sharply hit ball or the race between ball and man for the base. The baseball crowd is cosmopolitan. It contains representatives from every walk in life and from every profession. It is the most expert gathering in the world, and the most appreciative of skill. The crowd of sixty thousand that sits in the Yankee Stadium on a Sunday afternoon in midsummer, and the World Series crowd of the same number that watches the interleague play-off in the fall, are as different as black and white, although both are looking at the same game. World Series spectators aren't regular baseball fans. Most of them have never seen a game before. They are drawn by the ballyhoo, the publicity and the higher prices. They sit on their hands and refuse to warm up to the rising and falling tides of battle. The bleacher crowd gets a better view of the game than the snootier patrons in the stands and boxes. They see the game the way the players see it.

Horse-racing crowds are nervous, greedy, fortune-hunting, always milling and moving about, whispering, circulating, muttering until the wheeling ponies suddenly freeze them into a temporary immobility, feverish in its intensity, the same pregnant calm that falls upon the onlookers when the little pill is hippity-skipping on the whirling wheel, between *rouge et noir.*

WILLIAM HAZLITT

"The Fight"

Bernard Darwin, then well into his eighties, was once asked whom he considered the finest writer he had read. Darwin replied, "Oh, that's easy. Hazlitt. I thought so as a young man, and I think so now."

Reader, have you ever seen a fight? If not, you have a pleasure to come, at least if it is a fight like that between the Gas-man and Bill Neate. The crowd was very great when we arrived on the spot; open carriages were coming up, with streamers flying and music playing, and the country-people were pouring in over hedge and ditch in all directions, to see their hero beat or be beaten. The odds were still on Gas, but only about five to four. Gully had been down to try Neate, and had backed him considerably, which was a damper to the sanguine confidence of the adverse party. About two hundred thousand pounds were pending. The Gas says, he has lost £3000, which were promised him by different gentlemen if he had won. He had presumed too much on himself, which had made others presume on him. This spirited and formidable young fellow seems to have taken for his motto the old maxim, that "there are three things necessary to success in life—*Impudence! Impudence! Impudence!*" It is so in matters of opinion, but not in the *Fancy,* which is the most practical of all things, though even here confidence is half the battle, but only half. Our friend had vapoured and swaggered too much, as if he wanted to grin and bully his adversary out of the fight. The difference of weight between the two combatants (14 stone to 12) was nothing to the sporting men. Great, heavy, clumsy, long-armed Bill Neate kicked the beam in the scale of the Gas-man's vanity. The amateurs were frightened at his big words, and thought that they would make up for the difference of six feet and five feet nine. Truly, the *Fancy* are not men of imagination. They judge of what has been, and cannot conceive of anything that is to be. The Gas-man had won hitherto; therefore he must beat a man half as big again as himself—that to a certainty. Besides, there are as many feuds, factions, prejudices, pedantic notions in the *Fancy* as in the state or in the schools. Mr. Cully is almost the only cool, sensible man among them, who exercises an unbiased discretion, and is not a slave to his passions in these matters. But enough of reflections, and to our tale.

The day, as I have said, was fine for a December morning. The grass was wet, and the ground miry, and ploughed up with multitudinous feet, except that, within the ring itself, there was a spot of virgin-green closed in and unprofaned by vulgar tread, that shone with dazzling brightness in the mid-day sun. For it was now noon, and we had an hour to wait. This is the trying time. It is then the heart sickens, as you think what the two champions are about, and how short a time will determine their fate. After the first blow is struck, there is no opportunity for nervous apprehensions; you are swallowed up in the immediate interest of the scene— but

> "Between the acting of a dreadful thing
> And the first motion, all the interim is
> Like a phantasma, or a hideous dream."

I found it so as I felt the sun's rays clinging to my back, and saw the white wintry clouds sink below the verge of the horizon. "So," I thought, "my fairest hopes have faded from my sight!—so will the Gas-man's glory, or that of his adversary, vanish in an hour."

The *swells* were parading in their white box-coats, the outer ring was cleared with some bruises on the heads and shins of the rustic assembly (for the *cockneys* had been distanced by the sixty-six miles); the time drew near, I had got a good stand; a bustle, a buzz ran through the crowd, and from the opposite side entered Neate, between his second and bottle-holder. He rolled along swathed in his loose great coat, his knock-knees bending under his hugh bulk; and, with a modest cheerful air, threw his hat into the ring. He then just looked round, and began quietly to undress; when from the other side there was a similar rush and an opening made, and the Gas-man came forward with a conscious air of anticipated triumph, too much like the cock-of-the-walk. He strutted about more than became a hero, sucked oranges with a supercilious air, and threw away the skin with a toss of his head, and went up and looked at Neate, which was an act of supererogation. The only sensible thing he did was, as he strode away from the modern Ajax, to fling out his arms, as if he wanted to try whether they would do their work that day.

By this time they had stripped, and presented a strong contrast in appearance. If Neate was like Ajax, "with Atlantean shoulders, fit to bear" the pugilistic reputation of all Bristol, Hickman might be compared to Diomed, light, vigorous, elastic, and his back glistened in the sun, as he moved about, like a panther's hide. There was now a dead pause—attention was awe-struck. Who at that moment, big with a great event, did not draw his breath short—did not feel his heart throb? All was ready. They tossed up for the sun, and the Gas-man won. They were led up to the *scratch*—shook hands, and went at it.

In the first round everyone thought it was all over. After making play a short time, the Gas-man flew at his adversary like a tiger, struck five blows in as many seconds, three first, and then following him as he staggered back, two more, right and left, and down he fell, a mighty ruin. There was a shout, and I said, "There is no standing this." Neate seemed like a lifeless lump of flesh and bone, round which the Gas-man's blows played with the rapidity of electricity or lightning, and you imagined he would only be lifted up to be knocked down again. It was as if Hickman held a sword or a fire in that right hand of his, and directed it against an unarmed body. They met again, and Neate seemed, not cowed, but particularly cautious. I saw his teeth clenched together and his brows knit close against the sun. He held out both his arms at full length straight before him, like two sledgehammers, and raised his left an inch or two higher. The Gas-man could not get over this guard—they struck mutually and fell, but without advantage on either side.

It was the same in the next round; but the balance of power was thus restored—the fate of the battle was suspended. No one could tell how it would end. This was the only moment in which opinion was divided; for, in the next, the Gas-man aiming a mortal blow at his adversary's neck, with his right hand, and failing from the length he had to reach, the other returned it with his left at full swing, planted a tremendous blow on his cheek-bone and eyebrow, and made a red ruin of that side of his face. The Gas-man went down, and there was another shout—a roar of triumph as the waves of fortune rolled tumultuously from side to side. This was a settler. Hickman got up, and "grinned horrible a ghastly smile," yet he was evidently dashed in his opinion of himself; it was the first time he had ever been so punished; all one side of his face was perfect scarlet, and his right eye was closed in dingy blackness, as he advanced to the fight, less confident, but still determined.

After one or two more rounds, not receiving another such remembrancer, he rallied and went at it with his former impetuosity. But in vain. His strength had been weakened,—his blows could not tell at such a distance,—he was obliged to fling himself at his adversary, and could not strike from his feet; and almost as regularly as he flew at him with his right hand, Neate warded the blow, or drew back out of its reach, and felled with the return of his left. There was little cautious sparring—no half-hits—no tapping and trifling, none of the *petit-maîtreship* of the art—they were almost all knock-down blows:—the fight was a good stand-up fight. The wonder was the half-minute time. If there had been a minute or more allowed between each round, it would have been intelligible how they should by degrees recover strength and resolution; but to see two men smashed to the ground, smeared with gore, stunned, senseless, the breath beaten out of their bodies; and then, before you recover from the shock, to see them rise up with new strength and courage, stand ready to inflict or receive mortal offence, and rush upon each other "like two clouds over the Caspian"—this is the most astonishing thing of all:—this is the high and heroic state of man! From this time forward the event became more certain every round; and about the twelfth it seemed as if it must have been over.

Hickman generally stood with his back to me; but in the scuffle, he had changed positions, and Neate just then made a tremendous lunge at him, and hit him full in the face. It was doubtful whether he would fall backwards or forwards; he hung suspended for a second or two, and then fell back, throwing his hands in the air, and with his face lifted up to the sky. I never saw any thing more terrific than his aspect just before he fell. All traces of life, of natural expression, were gone from him. His face was like a human skull, a death's head, spouting blood. The eyes were filled with blood, the nose streamed with blood, the mouth gaped blood. He was not like an actual man, but like a preternatural, spectral appearance, or like one of the figures in Dante's *Inferno*.

Yet he fought on after this for several rounds, still striking the first desperate blow, and Neate standing on the defensive, and using the same cautious guard to the last, as if he had still all his work to do; and it was not till the Gas-man was so stunned in the seventeenth or eighteenth round, that his senses forsook him, and he could not come to time, that the battle was declared over.

Ye who despise the *Fancy*, do something to shew as much *pluck*, or as much self-possession as this, before you assume a superiority which you have never given a single proof of by any one action in the whole course of your lives!—When the Gas-man came to himself, the first words he uttered were, "Where am I? What is the matter, Tom,—you have lost the battle, but you are the bravest man alive." And Jackson whispered to him, "I am collecting a purse for you, Tom."—Vain sounds, and unheard at that moment! Neate instantly went up and shook him cordially by the hand, and seeing some old acquaintance, began to flourish with his fists, calling out, "Ah, you always said I couldn't fight—What do you think now?" But all in good humour, and without any appearance of arrogance; only it was evident Bill Neate was pleased that he had won the fight.

When it was over, I asked Cribb if he did not think it was a good one?

He said, *"Pretty well!"* The carrier-pigeons now mounted into the air, and one of them flew with the news of her husband's victory to the bosom of Mrs. Neate. Alas, for Mrs. Hickman!

BILL RUSSELL

"Sports"

This selection is from Bill Russell's book entitled Second Wind—*a rarity among sports autobiographies in that less than half the book is about basketball although its author was one of the great players of the game. His athletic career was remarkable: twice all-American on the University of San Francisco basketball team which went undefeated for fifty-five games and won the NCAA championship two years in a row; member of the gold-medal-winning 1956 Olympic team; center on the Boston Celtics NBA team which won eleven championships in thirteen years, largely because of Russell's defensive play; player-coach of that same team, 1966–69; five times voted most valuable player in the NBA.*

I spent some time with him during the 1969 season. He was an impressive and imposing figure—not only as an athlete but as an intellect. He was in turn outspoken, funny, cantankerous, reflective, extremely principled. It always struck me that he refused to sign autographs—indeed, it was awkward to walk with him through the parking lots after a game and look at the puzzled looks of kids being turned down. Bill rationalized this on the grounds that a signature was a private talisman which had a value as such, and therefore it should not be cheapened by being given away indiscriminately to people one didn't know.

Somewhere in his book he writes, "Most of us today are like cows; we will quietly stand in any line or fill out any form if there's a sign telling us that's what we should do. As a result, the country is filled with those who either paint signs or stand in line. I don't like doing either one."

Small wonder that the subtitle of Bill's book is "The Memoirs of an Opinionated Man."

I used to have fits of worry every now and then about the usefulness of basketball. In fact, I doubted the worth of *any* sport. "It's only a game,"

I kept saying to myself, and there were a lot of people who felt the same. How can anything as playful and childish as a game be important? When I was a basketball star, a carpenter or a doctor would fawn all over me, and I'd be embarrassed because I thought what *they* were doing was real. But then I read a book by an English writer who said that war is only a game. Some people think love is only a game. On Wall Street they have a game called the Stock Exchange. Almost anything looks like a game from a certain angle, so maybe sports aren't so frivolous after all. If Shakespeare can compare all of life to a stage, maybe it's not odd to believe that part of the play can take place on a basketball court.

Some athletes try to figure out what role sports fulfill in the world, where they fit, and how we should think about them. I used to talk with Bob Cousy on the subject and compare thoughts with football players like Jim Brown and Bernie Casey. If we're professional athletes, we'd say to ourselves, just what is our "profession" all about? It's not an easy question. If a kid goes into any other field, from fireman to statesman, he'll learn why it is necessary and find a lot of literature on the subject, but he won't find much clear thinking about sports or athletes. There is no philosophy of sports worth mentioning.

It's natural for people to be curious about their work, especially those of us who stumbled on sports on our way to an ordinary career. Think of it: you're rolling along through life, heading for the office or the shipyard, and all of a sudden you wake up and find yourself about to run out on the floor of the Boston Garden for a championship game on national television. You've already vomited in the dressing room, and your teammates have a dazed look in their eyes, as if they realize they're about to be run over by a car but can't do anything about it. Even Red Auerbach is quiet; that's how tense it is. While you're waiting there, shivering in your own sweat, you can literally feel the energy being released by the fans in the stands. Perfectly respectable people are yelling and screaming, behaving as they never would anywhere else. I used to joke that if you could bottle all the emotion let loose in a basketball game, you'd have enough hate to fight a war and enough joy to prevent one. As a player, you're about to run your guts out in five or six miles of short, frantic springs. The President of the United States has expressed interest in the outcome of the game, and bookmakers have covered their margins on millions of dollars' worth of bets. And while you're trying to rest there in your own private cocoon before the action starts, there's generally a moment when you find yourself wondering how it all came together.

As I see it, the world of sports is in very fine company, with a fine heritage. It is one of the Big Four. Only four kinds of events—politics, religion, the arts, and sports—have been able to draw consistently large crowds of paying customers throughout history. That must mean something. From the early Greek Olympics, the gladiators in the Roman Coliseum, and the tribal games of Africa, sports have appealed to something deep in people. Sports may have been neglected by historians, but they have been popular for as long as there have been players and spectators around, and unlike the other three fields they draw people to their events mostly on the basis of enthusiasm. At any concert, church service, or political event, you'll find a lot of people showing up out of duty.

In all Big Four events, rules are crucial. In politics we have criminal rules, tax rules, international rules, and the rules of war. In religion there is everything from rules on food and sex to rules of worship. In art there are prevailing conventions of poetry, music, literature, or film-making. These rules serve vastly different purposes in each field. In politics rules are what you fight over, and a new government is elected to change or defend them. A revolution produces a whole new rulebook that even changes the *way* you fight over rules. In religion the rules are what you fail to live up to. In art, rules can be what you ignore or break to create something fresh and unique.

In sports the rules make everything fair. Everyone accepts the goals of the game as defined by the rules, and the way the game is played. Only when all questions of ends and means are answered do you really have a game. Sports *must be* fair; justice is always swift and exact, according to the rules, which answer all necessary questions and not a single extra one. At least that's what the referees say.

There are occasional disputes, however. That's why we get pictures of baseball managers kicking umpires in the shins, and that's why I spent years watching Red Auerbach yell at referees with the veins on his neck standing out as thick as ropes. Kids will become so angry and indignant that they can't have a game; one of them will pick up his ball and go home, or one player will have a fight with another. In sports there is a fine line between order and anarchy. Arguments about justice, while vehement, tend to be simple, with a lot of cussing and name-calling. They may lead to a rhubarb, but they are soon over. Even with millions of dollars of prize money at stake, disputes over an interpretation of the rules almost never threaten a sport itself. Fans may yell, "We wuz robbed!" but eventually everyone accepts the outcome of the game as it was declared.

Rules open doors in the sports world. They are boundaries, starting points, frames of reference. They solve several of the most difficult problems of ordinary life by determining what's fair and real. Everything that is out of bounds is not real, and you don't have to pay any attention to it. The rules control all space and motion within the game, and in many sports the time as well. You can call time-out and stop the clock, but when time-out is over, you step into the real world where the rules apply and everything else vanishes. You lose yourself in the spirit of the game, whether you are playing or watching. If it is a rhythmical sport like basketball, Ping-Pong, or tennis, you soon absorb the rhythm of the game. Back and forth across the net or up and down off the floor bounces the ball. Sometimes it's slow and lazy enough to hypnotize you. Then all of a sudden the rhythm changes to blinding speed and there's a long instant of tension. Will he make it? Then the answer, and the rhythm changes again.

Whatever the game, each one has its own personality. The rules make its character. You can see how sports fit into the grand scheme of things by comparing their unique approach to rules with those of politics, religion, and art. Sports may have the time-out, but war has the truce and art has the intermission. The basic difference between the four is how big a chunk of time each one tries to handle. Religion bites off the biggest bite you can imagine—eternity—and claims it. Time is endemic to all religions; they're always considering the long run. Art is similar in its approach; the artist may not speak of it, but he is searching for immortality and "eternal truths." Even in politics one is dealing with lengthy periods. How long will the principles of the Constitution last? A long time.

Sports have the shortest view. Nothing lasts much longer than a season, and the basic unit of time is the moment. Sports fans and players appreciate each instant; a relic from sports is a "great moment." The only sports people who indulge in long-range thinking are statisticians and record freaks; they try to make each moment in sports bigger by comparing it with every other moment in as many ways as possible. Thus we hear about "The Most Rebounds in One Quarter of a Championship Series Game in the NBA—19, by Bill Russell, Boston Celtics vs. Los Angeles Lakers, April 19, 1962," or about the "Most Consecutive Strike-Outs by a Left-Handed Batter in World Series Play." Such records give a little immortality to nearly every contest, where time is diced up into thousands of tiny pieces, so that almost every moment can have a record attached to it. But whenever a record is broken you can expect it to be followed by the next broken record. Records march on, pretty much like time itself.

Sports not only claim smaller bits of time, they smaller bits of truth. Artists or professors of literature say quite seriously that "Art is truth." They don't mean a fleeting bit of the truth: they mean *The* truth. Religious leaders say the same thing, and so do politicians ("We hold these truths to be self-evident . . ."). Sports have a humble approach; the only truth they claim is the score, which changes all the time. The "final" score lasts only until the next game. Such humility has a liberating effect. Because sports don't assert any overarching truth, people can say just about anything they want. Sport is the land of exaggeration, and the bigger the yarn the better people like it. You can have "The Game of the Century" every week or so, and you can say, "There is no tomorrow" in the heat of the finals, and all that happens is that spectators become a little more nervous about the outcome. Think of the reaction if the Pope or the President of the United States announced that there was no tomorrow.

In sports, exaggerations that would otherwise be threatening or enraging seem humorous. "I am the greatest!" shouts Muhammad Ali. People may agree or disagree, but there is a chuckle running underneath it all. Or Babe Ruth can point to the right-field wall before a pitch and then hit a home run there, and the gesture will become part of baseball's mythology. "The King of Swat" could hit the ball "a country mile." On the field, sports figures can swagger and act like children. They can even be a little crazy; in fact, they probably *must* be a little crazy. All of which is fine, because it threatens no one. And the reason it doesn't is because it all takes place in the sports world, where no rigid truth has to be respected.

The athlete or fan can make up any nickname, trademark, or eccentricity; the sky's the limit. Sports are so fundamentally unpretentious that the craziest of pretensions appear funny. All sports have an element of humor, perhaps because it's so patently ridiculous to be out there knocking another man down, jumping over a hurdle, or trying to knock a little white ball in a hole with a stick. Even some of the players' nicknames seem to jump out and tickle: Earl "The Pearl" Monroe, "Dizzy" Dean, "Too Tall" Jones, "Sugar Ray" Robinson, "Minnesota Fats," "Big Daddy" Lipscomb. You can go on forever. (Only in the Republican sports like golf is there a run of pedestrian names.) Every outlandish name is insurance against pomposity.

I think of all sports as a mixture of art and war. The mixture changes with different sports, but it's always there. The art jumps out at you in a sport like women's gymnastics, a sport of dance and body sculpture, but I can tell you from having seen several Olympiads that those young girls are as competitive as any boxer. They're out there to win, and they'd sharpen their teeth on the balance beam if it would help.

Looking at all sports on a scale between art and war, I've always thought of basketball as being on the artistic side, more of a ballet than a brawl. But of course every athlete tends to emphasize the artistic qualities of his own sport. Still, when we see Julius ("Doctor J.") Erving fly through the air and under the basket, his back arched, his arms stretched, holding the ball like an orange, and see him make an impossible twist at the last instant to stuff the ball backwards through the basket, we say that was a beautiful move. And everybody means that adjective literally. Doctor J.'s moves *are* beautiful in the same way that an ice skater's leap is beautiful—or even in the same way that a painting is beautiful. The form inspires wonder, and the motion has something to say. Among other things it says that Doctor J. is a great basketball player. (The flamboyant moves are pretty, but I feel that the more difficult and artistic move is whatever Dr. J. had to do to get the defensive men out of the way.)

In any sport a spectacular star will be known as an "artist" of the game. Pelé was one in soccer. When he played, photographers focused on him to get shots of him in the air, his feet, his moves. Jim Brown had the same sort of grace in football. I've observed people, who don't like football, watching slow-motion films of him running with the ball, spellbound by the way he did it. If there's an ideal way for the mind to control the body, Brown had it.

On a fast break in basketball, the ball flies between three offensive players running at full speed—zip! zip! zip! zip!—and lastly to the unexpected man cutting under the basket at a rakish angle, who goes up and banks the ball off the glass in a lay-up, while the fully extended body of the defensive player climbs the glass after it within a quarter of an inch of touching it before the ball plops through the net. All this within two seconds. By their speed, eyes, minds, and coordination, the three offensive players controlled the ball so that it approaches the net from just one of millions of possible angles and heights; at the same time the defensive player figures all this out instantly and inserts his hand at the only point in all that space where he might intercept the ball if his timing was perfect. The whole play has a collective beauty to it. (My own opinion is that the play would have been even more beautiful if the defensive man had blocked the shot, but I'm prejudiced.)

There is individual and collective beauty in all sports, but much of it is hidden from the unsophisticated viewer. You can't really appreciate the art of a hit-and-run in baseball unless you can recognize one. Many of the most difficult moves in basketball take place away from the ball, where no one sees or understands them. There is even some art to all that growling, gouging, and earth-moving that huge linemen do in football, I suppose, though their mothers may be the only people who really appreciate it.

It is possible to change the mixture of art and war in any sport by changing its sacred rules. Let's imagine that in another time and another world, Florence Nightingale suddenly became Commissioner of the NBA. To eliminate all violence from basketball and to reward artistry, she threw out the automatic two-point basket and installed a panel of judges to award points based on the beauty of each particular basket scored. Doctor J. might get ten points for one of his flying whirlygigs, but only a point or two for a "garbage" shot off a rebound. But there was still too much hostility in the game, so Commissioner Nightingale eliminated the scoreboard. All beautiful plays in basketball should be appreciated on their own merits, she decreed, without regard to which team made them. As a result, basketball games became exhibitions of jumping, weaving through people, dribbling, leaping, and marksmanship; players were motivated only by their love of the art. With all its warlike elements removed, the sport soon became a form of dance for elongated players with certain peculiar moves. Wilt Chamberlain and I came out of retirement to resume our careers and did a splendid *pas de deux* together. My *arabesque* came together with his *pirouette* in what looked like a hook shot from the old brand of competitive basketball.

Curious fans turned out in droves to see the first few games of Commissioner Nightingale's reformed basketball, featuring the bizarre but serene partnership of Chamberlain and Russell. But after a few performances the crowds began dwindling; attendance was soon way down. It fell even further when Wilt and I quit. He walked out because he wasn't getting paid enough, and I because I didn't like having him step all over my feet. Commissioner Nightingale didn't last long; her basketball had ceased to be a sport at all.

This doesn't mean that basketball should never be modified, only that each sport has its own balance and that it can't be tampered with too much. The competitive aspects of basketball aren't important only because they pack fans into the seats; they are vital because once they are in effect the art will take care of itself. If the players are turned loose within the rules, the game will work automatically; they will keep inventing newer and more glorious moves to counter the inventions of the other players. All that is required to choreograph the action is the ball; just throw it out there and the moves will gather around the ball wherever it goes. This is true of many major sports: the ball provokes the art all by itself. A baseball player like Willie Mays can stand all night out in some deserted pasture called center field, but if nothing is hit near him, he doesn't really deserve watching. Once there's a fly to center field, however, the picture changes instantly. He runs in that pigeon-toed sprint, all concentration, with a hundred thousand eyes in the stadium glued to every step. Those eyes belong to people whose entire days are improved by the sight of what Willie does when he gets to the ball. What a catch!

NORMAN MAILER

"Death [of Paret]"

The selection that follows is from Norman Mailer's The Presidential
Papers—*the eleventh paper to be exact, which is entitled "Death." Its
main subject is the Sonny Liston–Floyd Patterson fight in Chicago in
1962—a fiasco, at least for Patterson who was knocked out in 2.06 of the
first round. The complete article is just over twenty thousand words in
length. A subtitle reads "Ten Thousand Words a Minute"— indicating
that Norman devoted ten thousand words for each minute of the fracas.
The description of the Benny Kid Paret–Emile Griffith fight that follows
is a flashback incorporated in the main body of the text. The article
eventually appeared in* Esquire.

*Mailer's enthusiasm for boxing was such that he has sparred with a
number of fighters, starting with an early father-in-law whose record in
the professional ranks was 2 won and 2 lost. His most exalted competition was José Torres, the world's light-heavyweight champion in the
mid-sixties. They often sparred one summer at Norman's property in
Vermont. Mailer remembered: "Torres occasionally gave me a hole to
hit through so I wouldn't get demoralized, but he didn't like it. He said it
made him feel wrong. So he made me work very hard . . . it was like
boxing a puma." On one occasion Mailer hit Torres with a right, which
so excited Torres, the proud instructor, that he ran around the lawn
shouting, "He hit me with a right, a* right!"

*The two actually appeared on television—on Dick Cavett's show.
Torres, influenced by the public's being on hand in the studio audience,
hit Mailer in the stomach much harder than he intended, grimacing as
he did so, much as one would dropping a vase, as if he expected Norman
to disintegrate on the floor. Torres was so relieved that Mailer survived
the punch that later he called up Cus D'Amato, the distinguished fight
manager, and cried out, "Cus, I hit him hard in the stomach and he
didn't go down. Not* hard, *but* hard."

On the afternoon of the night Emile Griffith and Benny Paret were to
fight a third time for the welterweight championship, there was murder

in both camps. "I hate that kind of guy," Paret had said earlier to Pete Hamill about Griffith. "A fighter's got to look and talk and act like a man." One of the Broadway gossip columnists had run an item about Griffith a few days before. His girl friend saw it and said to Griffith, "Emile, I didn't know about you being that way." So Griffith hit her. So he said. Now at the weigh-in that morning, Paret had insulted Griffith irrevocably, touching him on the buttocks, while making a few more remarks about his manhood. They almost had their fight on the scales.

The accusation of homosexuality arouses a major passion in many men; they spend their lives resisting it with a biological force. There is a kind of man who spends every night of his life getting drunk in a bar, he rants, he brawls, he ends in a small rumble on the street; women say, "For God's sakes, he's homosexual. Why doesn't he just turn queer and get his suffering over with." Yet men protect him. It is because he is choosing not to become homosexual. It was put best by Sartre who said that a homosexual is a man who practices homosexuality. A man who does not, is not homosexual—he is entitled to the dignity of his choice. He is entitled to the fact that he chose not to become homosexual, and is paying presumably his price.

The rage in Emile Griffith was extreme. I was at the fight that night, I had never seen a fight like it. It was scheduled for fifteen rounds, but they fought without stopping from the bell which began the round to the bell which ended it, and then they fought after the bell, sometimes for as much as fifteen seconds before the referee could force them apart.

Paret was a Cuban, a proud club fighter who had become welterweight champion because of his unusual ability to take a punch. His style of fighting was to take three punches to the head in order to give back two. At the end of ten rounds, he would still be bouncing, his opponent would have a headache. But in the last two years, over the fifteen-round fights, he had started to take some bad maulings.

This fight had its turns. Griffith won most of the early rounds, but Paret knocked Griffith down in the sixth. Griffith had trouble getting up, but made it, came alive and was dominating Paret again before the round was over. Then Paret began to wilt. In the middle of the eighth round, after a clubbing punch had turned his back to Griffith, Paret walked three disgusted steps away, showing his hindquarters. For a champion, he took much too long to turn back around. It was the first hint of weakness Paret had ever shown, and it must have inspired a particular shame, because he fought the rest of the fight as if he were seeking to demonstrate that he could take more punishment than any man alive. In the twelfth, Griffith caught him. Paret got trapped in a corner. Trying to duck away, his left arm and his head became tangled on the wrong side of the top rope. Griffith was in like a cat ready to rip the life out of a huge boxed rat. He hit him eighteen right hands in a row, an act which took perhaps three or four seconds, Griffith making a pent-up whimpering sound all the while he attacked, the right hand whipping like a piston rod which has broken through the crankcase, or like a baseball bat demolishing a pumpkin. I was sitting in the second row of that corner—they were not ten feet away from me, and like everybody else, I was hypnotized. I had never seen one man hit another so hard and so many times. Over the referee's face came a look of woe as if some spasm had passed its way through him, and then he leaped on Griffith to pull him away. It was the act of a brave man. Griffith was uncontrollable. His trainer leaped into the ring, his manager, his cut man, there were four people holding Griffith, but he was off on an orgy, he had left the Garden, he was back on a hoodlum's street. If he had been able to break loose from his handlers and the referee, he would have jumped Paret to the floor and whaled on him there.

And Paret? Paret died on his feet. As he took those eighteen punches something happened to everyone who was in psychic range of the event. Some part of his death reached out to us. One felt it hover in the air. He was still standing in the ropes, trapped as he had been before, he gave some little half-smile of regret, as if he were saying, "I didn't know I was going to die just yet," and then, his head leaning back but still erect, his death came to breathe about him. He began to pass away. As he passed, so his limbs descended beneath him, and he sank slowly to the floor. He went down more slowly than any fighter had ever gone down, he went down like a large ship which turns on end and slides second by second into its grave. As he went down, the sound of Griffith's punches echoed in the mind like a heavy ax in the distance chopping into a wet log.

Paret lay on the ground, quivering gently, a small froth on his mouth. The house doctor jumped into the ring. He knelt. He pried Paret's eyelid open. He looked at the eyeball staring out. He let the lid snap shut. He reached into his satchel, took out a needle, jabbed Paret with a stimulant. Paret's back rose in a high arch. He writhed in real agony. They were calling him back from death. One wanted to cry out, "Leave the man alone. Let him die." But they saved Paret long enough to take him to a hospital where he lingered for days. He was in coma. He never came out of it. If he lived, he would have been a vegetable. His brain was smashed. But they held him in life for a week, they fed him chemicals, and made exploratory operations into his skull, and fed details of his condition to The Goat. And The Goat kicked clods of mud all over the place, and spoke harshly of prohibiting boxing. There was shock in the land. Children had seen the fight on television. There were editorials, gloomy forecasts that the Game was dead. The managers and the prize-fighters got together. Gently, in thick, depressed hypocrisies, they tried to defend their sport. They did not find it easy to explain that they shared an unstated view of life which was religious.

It was of course not that religion which is called Judeo-Christian. It was an older religion, a more primitive one—a religion of blood, a murderous and sensitive religion which mocks the effort of the understanding to approach it, and scores the lungs of men like D. H. Lawrence, and burns the brain of men like Ernest Hemingway when they explore out into the mystery, searching to discover some part of the secret. It is the view of life which looks upon death as a condition which is more alive than life or unspeakably more deadening. As such it is not a very attractive notion to the Establishment. But then the Establishment has nothing very much of even the Judeo-Christian tradition. It has a respect for legal and administrative aspects of justice, and it is devoted to the idea of compassion for the poor. But the Establishment has no idea of death, no tolerance for Heaven or Hell, no comprehension of bloodshed. It sees no logic in pain. To the Establishment these notions are a detritus from the past.

Like a patient submerged beneath the plastic cover of an oxygen tent, boxing lives on beneath the cool, bored eyes of the doctors in the Establishment. It would not take too much to finish boxing off. Shut down the oxygen, which is to say, turn that switch in the mass media which still gives sanction to organized pugilism, and the fight game would be dead.

But the patient is permitted to linger for fear the private detectives of the Establishment, the psychiatrists and psychoanalysts, might not be able to neutralize the problem of gang violence. Not so well as the Game. Of course, the moment some piece of diseased turnip capable of being synthesized cheaply might prove to have the property of tranquilizing a violent young man for a year, the Establishment would wipe out boxing. Every time a punk was arrested, the police would prescribe a pill, and violence would walk the street sheathed and numb. Of course the Mob would lose revenue, but then the Mob is also part of the Establishment, it, and the labor unions and the colleges and the newspapers and the corporations are all part of the Establishment. The Establishment is never simple. It needs the Mob to grease the chassis on its chariot. Therefore, the Mob would be placated. In a society with strong central government, it is not so difficult to turn up a new source of revenue. What is more difficult is to enter the plea that violence may be an indispensable element of life. This is not the place to have the argument: it is enough to say that if the liberal Establishment is right in its unstated credo that death is a void, and man leads out his life suspended momentarily above that void, why then there is no argument at all. Whatever shortens life is monstrous. We have not the right to shorten life, since life is the only possession of the psyche, and in death we have only nothingness. What then can there be said in defense of sports-car racing, war, or six-ounce gloves?

But if we go from life into a death which is larger than our life has been, or into a death which is small, if death comes to nothing for one man because he swallowed his death in his life, and if for another death is alive with dimension, then the certitudes of the Establishment lose power. A drug which offers peace to a pain may dull the nerve which could have taught the mind how to carry that pain into the death which comes on the next day or on the decades that follow. A tranquilizer gives coma to an anxiety which may later smell of the dungeon, beneath the ground. If we are born into life as some living line of intent from an eternity which may have tortured us or nurtured us in death, then we may be obliged to go back to death with more courage and art than we left it. Or face the dim end of going back with less.

That is the existential venture, the unstated religious view of boxers trying to beat each other into unconsciousness or, ultimately, into death. It is the culture of the killer who sickens the air about him if he does not find some half-human way to kill a little in order not to deaden all. It is a defense against the plague, against that plague which comes from violence converted into the nausea of all that nonviolence which is void of peace. Paret's death was with horror, but not all the horror was in the beating, much was in the way his death was cheated. Which is to say that his death was twice a nightmare. I knew that something in boxing was spoiled forever for me, that there would be a fear in watching a fight now which was like the fear one felt for any *novillero* when he was having an unhappy day, the bull was dangerous, and the crowd was ugly. You knew he would get hurt. There is fascination in seeing that the first time, but it is not as enjoyable as one expects. It is like watching a novelist who has written a decent book get run over by a car.

Something in boxing was spoiled. But not the principle, not the right for one man to try to knock another out in the ring. That was perhaps not a civilized activity, but it belonged to the tradition of the humanist, it was a human activity, it showed a part of what man was like, it belonged to his ability to create art and artful movement on the edge of death or pain or danger or attack, and it had much to say about the subtleties of human style. For there are boxers whose bodies move like a fine brain, and there are others who pound the opposition down with the force of a trade-union leader, there are fools and wits and patient craftsmen among boxers, wild men full of a sense of outrage, and steady oppressive peasants, clever spoilers, dogged infantrymen who walk forward all night, hypnotists (like Liston), dancers, lovers, mothers giving a scolding, horsemen high on their legs. There is knowledge to be found about our nature, and the nature of animals, of big cats, lions, tigers, gorillas, bears, walruses (Archie Moore), birds, elephants, jackals, bulls. No, I was not down on boxing, but I loved it with freedom no longer. It was more like somebody in your family was fighting now. And the feeling one had for a big fight was no longer clear of terror in its excitement. There was awe in the suspense.

DIANE ACKERMAN

"Patrick Ewing Takes a Foul Shot"

Ewing sweating,
molding the ball
with spidery hands,
packing it, packing it,
into a snowball's
chance of a goal,
rolling his shoulders
through a silent earthquake,
rocking from one foot
to the other, sweating,
bouncing it, oh, sweet
honey, molding it,
packing it tight,
he fires:

floats it up on one palm
as if surfacing
from the clear green Caribbean
with a shell
whose roar wraps around him,
whose surf breaks
deep into his arena
where light and time
and pupils jump
because he jumps

ROCH CARRIER

"The Hockey Sweater"
(translated by Sheila Fischman)

*This little unpretentious story about the influence of the Montreal
Canadiens hockey team is probably the best-known and most beloved
piece of writing throughout the Canadian provinces, especially Quebec,
short of the national anthem.*

The winters of my childhood were long, long seasons. We lived in three
places—the school, the church, and the skating-rink—but our real life
was on the skating-rink. Real battles were won on the skating-rink. Real
strength appeared on the skating-rink. The real leaders showed themselves on the skating-rink. School was a sort of punishment. Parents
always want to punish children and school is their most natural way of
punishing us. However, school was also a quiet place where we could
prepare for the next hockey game, lay out our next strategies. As for
church, we found there the tranquillity of God: there we forgot school
and dreamed about the next hockey game. Through our daydreams it
might happen that we would recite a prayer: we would ask God to help
us play as well as Maurice Richard.

We all wore the same uniform as he, the red, white, and blue uniform
of the Montreal Canadiens, the best hockey team in the world; we all
combed our hair in the same style as Maurice Richard, and to keep it in
place we used a sort of glue—a great deal of glue. We laced our skates
like Maurice Richard, we taped our sticks like Maurice Richard. We cut
all his pictures out of the papers. Truly, we knew everything about him.

On the ice, when the referee blew his whistle the two teams would
rush at the puck; we were five Maurice Richards taking it away from five
other Maurice Richards; we were ten players, all of us wearing with the
same blazing enthusiasm the uniform of the Montreal Canadiens. On
our backs, we all wore the famous number 9.

One day, my Montreal Canadiens sweater had become too small;
then it got torn and had holes in it. My mother said: "If you wear that
old sweater people are going to think we're poor!" Then she did what she

did whenever we needed new clothes. She started to leaf through the catalog the Eaton company sent us in the mail every year. My mother was proud. She didn't want to buy our clothes at the general store; the only things that were good enough for us were the latest styles from Eaton's catalog. My mother didn't like the order forms included with the catalog; they were written in English and she didn't understand a word of it. To order my hockey sweater, she did as she usually did; she took out her writing paper and wrote in her gentle schoolteacher's hand: "Cher Monsieur Eaton, Would you be kind enough to send me a Canadiens' sweater for my son who is ten years old and a little too tall for his age and Docteur Robitaille thinks he's a little too thin? I'm sending you three dollars and please send me what's left if there's anything left. I hope your wrapping will be better than last time."

Monsieur Eaton was quick to answer my mother's letter. Two weeks later we received the sweater. That day I had one of the greatest disappointments of my life! I would even say that on that day I experienced a very great sorrow. Instead of the red, white, and blue Montreal Canadiens sweater, Monsieur Eaton had sent us a blue and white sweater with a maple leaf on the front—the sweater of the Toronto Maple Leafs. I'd always worn the red, white, and blue Montreal Canadiens sweater; all my friends wore the red, white, and blue sweater; never had anyone in my village ever worn the Toronto sweater, never had we even seen a Toronto Maple Leafs sweater. Besides, the Toronto team was regularly trounced by the triumphant Canadiens. With tears in my eyes, I found the strength to say:

"I'll never wear that uniform."

"My boy, first you're going to try it on! If you make up your mind about things before you try, my boy, you won't go very far in this life."

My mother had pulled the blue and white Toronto Maple Leafs sweater over my shoulders and already my arms were inside the sleeves. She pulled the sweater down and carefully smoothed all the creases in the abominable maple leaf on which, right in the middle of my chest, were written the words "Toronto Maple Leafs." I wept.

"I'll never wear it."

"Why not? This sweater fits you . . . like a glove."

"Maurice Richard would never put it on his back."

"You aren't Maurice Richard. Anyway, it isn't what's on your back that counts, it's what you've got inside your head."

"You'll never put it in my head to wear a Toronto Maple Leafs sweater."

My mother sighed in despair and explained to me:

"If you don't keep this sweater which fits you perfectly I'll have to write to Monsieur Eaton and explain that you don't want to wear the

Toronto sweater. Monsieur Eaton's an *Anglais;* he'll be insulted because he likes the Maple Leafs. And if he's insulted do you think he'll be in a hurry to answer us? Spring will be here and you won't have played a single game, just because you didn't want to wear that perfectly nice blue sweater."

So I was obliged to wear the Maple Leafs sweater. When I arrived on the rink, all the Maurice Richards in red, white, and blue came up, one by one, to take a look. When the referee blew his whistle I went to take my usual position. The captain came and warned me I'd be better to stay off the forward line. A few minutes later the second line was called; I jumped onto the ice. The Maple Leafs sweater weighed on my shoulders like a mountain. The captain came and told me to wait; he'd need me later, on defense. By the third period I still hadn't played; one of the defensemen was hit in the nose with a stick and it was bleeding. I jumped on the ice: my moment had come! The referee blew his whistle; he gave me a penalty. He claimed I'd jumped on the ice when there were already five players. That was too much! It was unfair! It was persecution! It was because of my blue sweater! I struck my stick against the ice so hard it broke. Relieved, I bent down to pick up the debris. As I straightened up I saw the young vicar, on skates, before me.

"My child," he said, "just because you're wearing a new Toronto Maple Leafs sweater unlike the others, it doesn't mean you're going to make the laws around here. A proper young man doesn't lose his temper. Now take off your skates and go to the church and ask God to forgive you."

Wearing my Maple Leafs sweater I went to the church, where I prayed to God; I asked him to send, as quickly as possible, moths that would eat up my Toronto Maple Leafs sweater.

KEN DRYDEN

"Guy Lafleur"

The Forum is disturbingly empty: just a few players sit quietly cocooned away in a dressing room; twenty-five or thirty staff work in distant upstairs offices; throughout the rest of its vast insides a few dozen men are busy washing, painting, fixing, tidying things up. There is one other person. Entering the corridor to the dressing room, I hear muffled, reverberating sounds from the ice, and before I can see who it is, I know it's Lafleur. Like a kid on a backyard rink, he skates by himself many minutes before anyone joins him, shooting pucks easily off the boards, watching them rebound, moving skates and gloved hands wherever his inventive instincts direct them to go. Here, far from the expedience of a game, away from defenders and linemates who shackle him to their banal predictability, alone with his virtuoso skills, it is his time to create.

The Italians have a phrase, *inventa la partita.* Translated, it means to "invent the game." A phrase often used by soccer coaches and journalists, it is now, more often than not, used as a lament. For in watching modern players with polished but plastic skills, they wonder at the passing of soccer *genius*—Pelé, di Stefano, Puskas—players whose minds and bodies in not so rare moments created something unfound in coaching manuals, a new and continuously changing game for others to aspire to.

It is a loss they explain many ways. In the name of team play, there is no time or place for individual virtuosity, they say; it is a game now taken over by coaches, by technocrats and autocrats who empty players' minds to control their bodies, reprogramming them with X's and O's, driving them to greater *efficiency* and *work rate,* to move *systems* faster, to move games faster, until achieving mindless pace. Others fix blame more on the other side: on smothering defenses played with the same technical sophistication, efficiency, and work rate, but in the nature of defense, easier to play. Still others argue it is the professional sports culture itself which says that games are not won on good plays, but by others' mistakes, where the safe and sure survive, and the creative and not-so-sure may not.

But a few link it to a different kind of cultural change, the loss of what they call "street soccer": the mindless hours spent with a ball next to your feet, walking with it as if with a family pet, to school, to a store, or anywhere, playing with it, learning new things about it and about yourself, in time, as with any good companion, developing an *understanding.* In a much less busy time undivided by TV, rock music, or the clutter of modern lessons, it was a child's diversion from having nothing else to do. And, appearances to the contrary, it was creative diversion. But now, with more to do, and with a sophisticated, competitive society pressing on the younger and younger the need for training and skills, its time has run out. Soccer has moved away from the streets and playgrounds to soccer fields, from impromptu games to uniforms and referees, from any time to specific, scheduled time; it has become an *activity* like anything else, organized and maximized, done right or not at all. It has become something to be taught and learned, then tested in games; the answer at the back of the book, the one and only answer. So other time, time not spent with teams in practices or games, deemed wasteful and inefficient, has become time not spent at soccer.

Recently, in Hungary, a survey was conducted asking soccer players from 1910 to the present how much each practiced a day. The answer, on a gradually shrinking scale, was three hours early in the century to eight minutes a day today. Though long memories can forget, and inflate what they don't forget, if the absolute figures are doubtful, the point is nonetheless valid. Today, except in the barrios of Latin America, in parts of Africa and Asia, "street soccer" is dead, and many would argue that with it has gone much of soccer's creative opportunity.

When Guy Lafleur was five years old, his father built a small rink in the backyard of their home in Thurso, Quebec. After school and on weekends, the rink was crowded with Lafleur and his friends, but on weekdays, rushing through lunch before returning to school, it was his alone for half an hour or more. A few years later, anxious for more ice time, on Saturday and Sunday mornings he would sneak in the back door of the local arena, finding his way unseen through the engine room, under the seats, and onto the ice. There, from 7:30 until just before the manager awakened about 11, he played alone; then quickly left. Though he was soon discovered, as the manager was also coach of his team Lafleur was allowed to continue, by himself, and then a few years later with some of his friends.

There is nothing unique to this story; only its details differ from many others like it. But because it's about Lafleur it is notable. At the time, there were thousands like him across Canada on other noon-hour rinks, in other local arenas, doing the same. It was when he got older and nothing changed that his story became special. For as others in the whirl of more games, more practices, more off-ice diversions, more travel and everything else gave up solitary time as boring and unnecessary, Lafleur did not. When he moved to Quebec City at fourteen to play for the Remparts, the ice at the big Colisée was unavailable at other times, so he began arriving early for the team's 6 P.M. practices, going on the ice at 5, more than thirty minutes before any of his teammates joined him. Now, many years later, the story unchanged, it seems more and more remarkable to us. In clichéd observation some would say it is a case of the great and dedicated superstar who is first on the ice, last off. But he is not. When practice ends, Lafleur leaves, and ten or twelve others remain behind, skating and shooting with Ruel. But every day we're in Montreal, at 11 A.M., an hour before Bowman steps from the dressing room as signal for practice to begin, Lafleur goes onto the ice with a bucket of pucks to be alone.

Not long ago, thinking of the generations of Canadians who learned hockey on rivers and ponds, I collected my skates and with two friends drove up the Gatineau River north of Ottawa. We didn't know it at the time, but the ice conditions we found were rare, duplicated only a few times the previous decade. The combination of a sudden thaw and freezing rain in the days before had melted winter-high snow, and with temperatures dropping rapidly overnight, the river was left with miles of smooth glare ice. Growing up in the suburbs of a large city, I had played on a river only once before, and then as a goalie. On this day, I came to the Gatineau to find what a river of ice and a solitary feeling might mean to a game.

We spread ourselves rinks apart, breaking into river-wide openings for passes that sometimes connected, and other times sent us hundreds of feet after what we had missed. Against the wind or with it, the sun glaring in our eyes or at our backs, we skated for more than three hours, periodically tired, continuously renewed. The next day I went back again, this time alone. Before I got bored with myself an hour or two later, with no one watching and nothing to distract me, loose and daring, joyously free, I tried things I had never tried before, my hands and feet discovering new patterns and directions, and came away feeling as if something was finally clear.

The Canadian game of hockey was weaned on long northern winters uncluttered by things to do. It grew up on ponds and rivers, in big open spaces, unorganized, often solitary, only occasionally moved into arenas for practices or games. In recent generations, that has changed. Canadians have moved from farms and towns to cities and suburbs; they've discovered skis, snowmobiles, and southern vacations; they've civilized winter and moved it indoors. A game we once played on rivers and ponds, later on streets and driveways and in backyards, we now play in arenas, in full team uniform, with coaches and referees, or to an ever-increasing extent we don't play at all. For, once a game is organized, unorganized games seem a wasteful use of time; and once a game moves in doors, it won't move outdoors again. Hockey has become suburbanized, and as part of our suburban middle-class culture, it has changed.

Put in uniform at six or seven, by the time a boy reaches the NHL, he is a veteran of close to 1,000 games—30-minute games, later 32-, then 45-, finally 60-minute games, played more than twice a week, more than seventy times a year between late September and late March. It is more games from a younger age, over a longer season than ever before. But it is less hockey than ever before. For, every time a twelve-year-old boy plays a 30-minute game, sharing the ice with teammates, he plays only about ten minutes. And ten minutes a game, anticipated and prepared for all day, traveled to and from, dressed and undressed for, means ten minutes of hockey a day, more than two days a week, more than seventy days a hockey season. And every day that a twelve-year-old plays only ten minutes, he doesn't play two hours on a backyard rink, or longer on school or playground rinks during weekends and holidays.

It all has to do with the way we look at free time. Constantly preoccupied with time and keeping ourselves busy (we have come to answer the ritual question "How are you?" with what we apparently equate with good health, "Busy"), we treat non-school, non-sleeping, or non-eating time, unbudgeted free time, with suspicion and no little fear. For, while it may offer opportunity to learn and do new things, we worry that the time we once spent reading, kicking a ball, or mindlessly coddling a puck might be used destructively, in front of TV, or "getting into trouble" in endless ways. So we organize free time, scheduling it into lessons—ballet, piano, French—into organizations, teams, and clubs, fragmenting it into impossible-to-be-boring segments, creating in ourselves a mental metabolism geared to moving on, making free time distinctly unfree.

It is in free time that the special player develops, not in the competitive experience of games, in hour-long practices once a week, in mechanical devotion to packaged, processed, coaching-manual, hockey-school skills. For while skills are necessary, setting out as they do the limits of anything, more is needed to transform those skills into something special. Mostly it is time—unencumbered, unhurried, time of a different quality, more time, time to find wrong answers to find a few that are right; time to find your own right answers; time for skills to be practiced to set higher limits, to settle and assimilate and become fully and completely yours, to organize and combine with other skills comfortably and easily in some uniquely personal way, then to be set loose, trusted, to find new instinctive directions to take, to create.

But without such time a player is like a student cramming for exams. His skills are like answers memorized by his body, specific, limited to what is expected, random and separate, with no overviews to organize and bring them together. And for those times when more is demanded, when new unexpected circumstances come up, when answers are asked for things you've never learned, when you must intuit and piece together what you already know to find new answers, memorizing isn't enough. It's the difference between knowledge and understanding, between a super-achiever and a wise old man. And it's the difference between a modern suburban player and a player like Lafleur.

For a special player has spent time with his game. On backyard rinks, in local arenas, in time alone and with others, time without short-cuts, he has seen many things, he has done many things, he has *experienced* the game. He understands it. There is *scope* and *culture* in his game. He is not a born player. What he has is not a gift, random and otherworldly, and unearned. There is surely something in his genetic makeup that allows him to be great, but just as surely there are others like him who fall short. He is, instead, *a natural.*

"Muscle memory" is a phrase physiologists sometimes use. It means that for many movements we make, our muscles move with no message from the brain telling them to move, that stored in the muscles is a learned capacity to move a certain way, and, given stimulus from the spinal cord, they move that way. We see a note on a sheet of music, our fingers move; no thought, no direction, and because one step of the transaction is eliminated—the information-message loop through the brain—we move faster as well.

When first learning a game, a player thinks through every step of what he's doing, needing to direct his body the way he wants it to go. With practice, with repetition, movements get memorized, speeding up, growing surer, gradually becoming part of the muscle's memory. The great player, having seen and done more things, more different and personal things, has in his muscles the memory of more notes, more combinations and patterns of notes, played in more different ways. Faced with a situation, his body responds. Faced with something more, something new, it finds an answer he didn't know was there. He *invents the game.*

Listen to a great player describe what he does. Ask Lafleur or Orr, ask Reggie Jackson, O. J. Simpson, or Julius Erving what makes them special, and you will get back something frustratingly unrewarding. They are inarticulate jocks, we decide, but in fact they can know no better than we do. For ask yourself how you walk, how your fingers move on a piano keyboard, how you do any number of things you have made routine, and you will know why. Stepping outside yourself you can think about it and decide what *must* happen, but you possess no inside story, no great insight unavailable to those who watch. Such movement comes literally from your body, bypassing your brain, leaving few subjective hints behind. Your legs, your fingers move, that's all you know. So if you want to know what makes Orr or Lafleur special, watch their bodies, fluent and articulate, let them explain. They know.

When I watch a modern suburban player, I feel the same as I do when I hear Donnie Osmond or René Simard sing a love song. I hear a skillful voice, I see closed eyes and pleading outstretched fingers, but I hear and see only fourteen-year-old boys who can't tell me anything.

Hockey has left the river and will never return. But like the "street," like an "ivory tower," the river is less a physical place than an *attitude,* a metaphor for unstructured, unorganized time alone. And if the game no longer needs the place, it needs the attitude. It is the rare player like Lafleur who reminds us.

ROBERT PENN WARREN

"Skiers"

With the motion of angels, out of
Snow-spume and swirl of gold mist, they
Emerge to the positive sun. At
That great height, small on that whiteness,
With the color of birds or of angels,
They swoop, sway, descend, and descending,
Cry their bright bird-cries, pure
In the sweet desolation of distance.
They slowly enlarge to our eyes. Now

On the flat where the whiteness is
Trodden and mud-streaked, not birds now,
Nor angels even, they stand. They

Are awkward, not yet well adjusted
To this world, new and strange, of Time and
Contingency, who now are only
Human. They smile. The human

Face has its own beauty.

JOE H. PALMER

"Stymie—Common Folks"

Red Smith described Joe H. Palmer as not only America's best-known racing writer but "in the opinion of many the best writer of sports anywhere." He joined the New York Herald-Tribune in 1946 and wrote for the paper until 1952. This selection about the people's racehorse Stymie is from a book of Palmer's collected pieces entitled This Was Racing, *which Red Smith, who was a neighbor and a close friend, put together after Palmer's death as a labor of love. Herbert Warren Wind, who wrote about golf and tennis for the* New Yorker, *has praised this particular piece as "almost flawless . . . and will probably live as long as Hazlitt's essay on Cavanagh which it resembles in its coalescence of spontaneity of phrase and reflectiveness of mood."*

On the cold blustery afternoon of January 28, 1921, several hundred persons huddled in the wind-swept stands of the old Kentucky Association track at Lexington to see one horse gallop past them. Down he came, a great red chestnut with a copper mane and a high head, flying the black and yellow silks of Samuel D. Riddle. This was Man o' War, leaving the race tracks forever.

Fourteen years passed before Lexington considered another horse worth a turnout. Then, on March 11, 1935, some five hundred citizens assembled, on a foul, wet afternoon, to see Equipoise take his last public gallop. This was at the private track of the C. V. Whitney farm, because it was in that unbelievable two-year period when Lexington had no public race track.

The next performance, and as far as I know the last one, came on August 8, 1943, when Calumet Farm celebrated "Whirlaway Day." By this time the Chamber of Commerce had got into the act, and there was a remarkable spate of Congressmen, Southern oratory, news cameras, and radio announcers. This is not a complete list.

It is unlikely (though you can never tell about a chamber of commerce) that there will be any such doings over Stymie, when he arrives to enter the stud at Dr. Charles Hagyard's Green Ridge Farm. It isn't that the other three were Kentuckians coming home, and that Stymie's an outlander from Texas. It was thoroughly appropriate that Stymie should have his final public appearance at Jamaica, because he's a Jamaica kind of horse. Though I have no doubt he will do well in the stud, his kinship is with the race track, not the breeding farm.

Man o' War, Equipoise, and Whirlaway all were equine royalty from the day they were foaled. Stymie was common folks. It is true that he carries the blood of both Equipoise and Man o' War, but all pedigrees are purple if you go back a little. He was the son of a horse that had won two common races, out of a mare that couldn't win any. Nobody ever thought the first three were anything but good. Stymie began as a fifteen hundred dollar plater that couldn't get out of his own way.

Stymie wasn't, of course, as good as any of the three. But he was immeasurably tougher. Could he have got to the races one more time, he would have started as many times as all three of the others together. If you want to clutter your mind with a perfectly useless bit of information, Man o' War made his reputation by blazing nineteen miles and five furlongs; Equipoise, stopping now and then to grow a new hoof, ran just a trifle over fifty miles in competition. Whirlaway lasted a little longer, and lacked half a furlong of running sixty-six miles. But Stymie's journey to leadership among the world's money winners took him 142 miles, plus half a furlong and sixty yards. That's more than the other three together.

Man o' War and Equipoise and Whirlaway each won the first time out, at short odds, as they were expected to do. Stymie was 31 to 1 in a $2,500 claiming race and he ran as he was expected to do, too, finishing seventh. He was out fourteen times before he could win, and that was a $3,300 claimer.

You are not to imagine that Stymie was accidentally and mistakenly dropped into a claiming race before any one appreciated his quality. He ran twelve times in claiming races and got beat in eleven of them. He was, until the fall of his two-year-old season, right where he belonged. Then, from this beginning, he went on to win $918,485.

This is, you will see, basically the story of the ugly duckling, of Cinderella among the ashes, of Dick Whittington and his cat, and of all the world's stories none has ever been preferred to that which leads to the public and very glorious triumph of the oppressed and the downtrodden. Jamaica's horseplayers are to some extent oppressed and downtrodden, and perhaps in Stymie they find a vicarious success.

The horse envisioned by a breeder, in Kentucky or elsewhere, is the son of a Derby winner out of an Oaks mare, which can sweep the futurities at two and the classics at three, and then come back to the stud to send other great racers to the wars. These are, roughly, the specifications which fit such horses as Citation and Count Fleet and War Admiral, and the like.

But the race-trackers, I think, save most of their affection for the Exterminators and the Stymies and the Seabiscuits, who do it the hard way in the handicaps, pounding out mile after bitter mile, giving weight and taking their tracks wet or dry, running for any jockey, and trying with what they've got, even when they haven't got enough. That's why Stymie fitted a farewell at Jamaica better than a welcome in Kentucky.

He's a curious horse, this obscurely bred Texas product. This tourist leaned on Jack Skinner's back fence at Middleburg one December for maybe a half hour, just studying Stymie, which did not return the compliment, but went on picking at the scanty winter grass. Except for the crooked blaze which gives him a devil-may-care expression, he's the most average horse you ever saw. Not tall, not short, not long, not close-coupled. Good bone, good muscle, good chest—nothing outstanding, nothing poor. As a result, of course, he is almost perfectly balanced, and maybe this is what makes him tick.

However, there is another matter. When Stymie comes to the peak of condition, he exudes vitality so you expect to hear it crackle. He comes to a hard, lean fitness that you seldom see in domestic animals, unless in a hunting dog that has been working steadily, or perhaps a hunter that has been having his ten miles a day over the fields. This is when, as Hirsch Jacobs says, he gets "rough." It isn't temper or meanness. He just gets so full of himself that he wants things to happen.

The faster he goes the higher he carries his head, which is all wrong according to the book, but is a characteristic of the tribe of Man o' War, to which he is inbred. This tourist, who doesn't scare easily in print, will long remember the way Stymie came around the turn in the Pimlico Cup Handicap with his chopper mane flying in the wind, making pretty good horses look as if they had just remembered a pressing engagement with the quarter pole.

He is not a great horse, in the sense that Man o' War and Equipoise were great. He isn't versatile. There are dozens of horses around that can beat him at a mile, and even at a mile and a quarter he would have trouble with Armed or Lucky Draw, just as he had trouble with Devil Diver. He can't make his own pace and he can't win slow races. He needs something up ahead to draw the speed from the field, to soften it up for his long, sweeping rush at the end.

But give him a field with speed in it, at a mile and a half or more, and horses had better get out of his way, even Whirlaway.

Anyway, another fine and ardent and satisfactory story of the turf was brought to a close at Jamaica. And it was happy to note that, for all the long campaign, it was no battered and limping warrior which left us. Stymie never looked better with his bronze coat in great bloom, and the high head carried as proudly as ever.

As he stood for the last time before the stands, people around the winner's enclosure were shouting to his groom, "Bring him in here, for just one more time."

The groom didn't obey, and probably he was right. Stymie never got in a winner's circle without working for it. It was no time to begin.

GEORGE PLIMPTON

FROM *Open Net*

The account which follows is a description of what it is like for an amateur to find himself in the exalted world of the professional—in this case playing in the goal for the Boston Bruins in an exhibition game in Philadelphia's Spectrum against the Flyers. Ice hockey was one game I never thought I would attempt as a participatory journalist. I am very poor on skates. I have weak ankles. Friends joke that I am the same height on the ice as I am off. I trained with the Bruins for a month. They were in a constant state of merriment about my troubles on the ice— especially my inability to stop sharply. Often I would crash into the boards to stop. The Bruins joked that I was the only hockey player in the National Hockey League who would check himself *into the boards. My stay with the Bruins is recounted in a book entitled* Open Net, *from which this extract is taken. The scene is the Bruins' locker room just prior to the game with the Flyers.*

We had just a few minutes left. Bridgework was removed: when the teeth came out and were put in the paper cups, the face took on a slightly different aspect, collapsing slightly, like the first twinge of an umbrella being closed. Cheevers leaned across from his stool. He looked very serious. He had one last thing he wanted me to remember. "Stand up!

Stand up!" he said, meaning, of course, to remind me to keep myself aloft on the ice, that I was useless if I fell down. Under the stress of the moment I misunderstood him. I thought he was telling me, for some odd reason, to stand up there in the locker room. I shot up from my bench abruptly, towering over him on my skates, and looked down at him questioningly.

"Not in here, for God's sake," Cheevers said. "Out on the ice." He shook his head. "A basket case."

[Don] Cherry read out the lines: Mike Forbes and Al Sims at defense, and the McNab line, with Dave Forbes and Terry O'Reilly at the wings, would start. He read out my name as the goaltender somewhat perfunctorily, I thought, making nothing of it in any jocular way, as if it were a perfectly natural choice to make, and then he looked over at me and said: "It's time. Lead them out."

I put on my mask and clumped to the locker room door. I had forgotten my stick. Someone handed it to me. I was the first Bruin in the tunnel. I could hear the Bruins beginning to yell behind me as we started out.

The tunnel to the rink is dark, with the ice right there at its lip, so that one flies out of it, like a bat emerging from a cast-iron pipe, into the brightest sort of light—the ice a giant opaque glass. The great banks of spectators rose up from it in a bordering mass out of which cascaded a thunderous assault of boos and catcalls. Cherry was right. The Bruins were not at all popular in Philadelphia.

We wheeled around in our half of the ice . . . the Flyers in theirs. There was no communication between the two teams; indeed, the players seemed to put their heads down as they approached the center line, sailing by within feet of each other without so much as a glance. Seaweed [Pettie, my training-camp roommate] had told me: "In hockey you don't talk to the guys from the other team at all, ever. You don't pick him up when he falls down, like in football." He told me about a pre-game warm-up in the Soviet-Canada series in which Wayne Cashman had spotted a Russian player coming across the center line to chase down a puck that had escaped their zone; Cashman had skated over to intercept him and checked him violently into the boards. "Well, the guy was in the wrong place," Seaweed said when I expressed my astonishment. "He should have known better."

I skated over to the boards, working at the clasp at my chin to adjust my mask. The fans leaned forward and peered in at me through the bars of the mask—as if looking into a menagerie cage at some strange inmate within. "Hey, lemme see." A face came into view, just inches away, the mouth ajar, and then it withdrew to be replaced by another, craning to see. I could hear the voice on the public address system announcing me as the goaltender for a special five-minute game. The Bruins were motioning me to get in the goal. We were a minute or so away. I pushed off the boards and reached the goal in a slow glide, stopping, and turning myself around slowly and carefully.

The three officials came out onto the ice. The organist was playing a bouncy waltzlike tune that one's feet tapped to almost automatically, but I noticed the officials pointedly tried not to skate to its rhythm as they whirled around the rink to warm up, perhaps because they would seem to demean their standings as keepers of order and decorum if they got into the swing of the music. They too came up and inspected me briefly, glancing through the bars of my mask without a word and with the same look of vague wonder that I had noticed from the fans.

The Bruins began skating by, cuffing at my pads with their sticks as they passed. Tapping the goaltender's pads is perhaps the most universal procedure just before the game—in most cases, of course, a simple gesture of encouragement, like a pat on the back, but in other instances a most distinctive act of superstition. The Buffalo Sabres had a player, Ric Seiling, their rightwing, who had it fixed in his head that things would go badly if he were not the last of the starters on the ice to top the goaltender's pads. The trouble was that the Sabres had another player, a big defenseman, Jerry Korab, of exactly the same inclination. On one odd occasion Bill Inglis, the Sabres' coach, put both men on the ice to start the game; the two of them, as the other players got set, began wheeling around the net, tapping the goaltender's pads, one after the other, to be sure to be the last before the puck was dropped—a sight so worrisome that Inglis made a quick substitution and got one of them out of there.

For me, even as I wobbled slightly in the crease from the impact of some of the stronger blows from my Bruin teammates as they skated by, I felt a surge of appreciation and warmth towards them for doing it. Two of the Bruins stopped and helped me rough up the ice in front of the cage—this a procedure so the goalie gets a decent purchase with his skate blades. Invariably, it is done by the goalie himself—long, scraping side thrusts with skates to remove the sheen from the new ice. It occurred to me later that to be helped with this ritual was comparable to a pair of baseball players coming out to help a teammate get set in the batter's box, kneeling down and scuffing out toe-holds for him, smoothing out the dirt, dusting his bat handle, and generally preparing things for him, as if the batter were as unable to shift for himself as a store-front mannequin. However odd this may have appeared from the stands—the three of us toiling away in front of the net—it added to my sense of common endeavor. "Thank you, thank you," I murmured.

Other Bruins stopped by while this was going on, and peering into my mask they offered last-minute advice. "Chop 'em down! Chop 'em down!" I looked out at Bobby Schmautz and nodded. His jaw was moving furiously on some substance. "Chop 'em down!" he repeated as he skated off. Slowly the other Bruins withdrew, skating up the ice toward the bench or their positions to stand for the national anthem.

I spent the anthem (which was a Kate Smith recording rather than the real article) wondering vaguely whether my face mask constituted a hat, and if I should remove it. My worry was that if I tampered with any of the equipment I might not have it in proper working order at the opening face-off. The puck would be dropped . . . and the Flyers would sail down the ice towards a goaltender who would be standing bareheaded, face down, fiddling with the chin strap of his mask, his big mitt tucked under his arm to free his fingers for picking at the clasp, his stick lying across the top of the net . . . no, it was not worth contemplating. I sang loudly inside my mask to compensate for any irreverence.

A roar went up at the anthem's conclusion—something grim and anticipatory about that welter of sound, as if, Oh my! we're really going to see something good now, and I saw the players at the center of the rink slide their skates apart, legs spread and stiff, their sticks down, the upper parts of their bodies now horizontal to the ice—a frieze of tension—and I knew the referee in his striped shirt, himself poised at the circle and ready for flight once he had dropped the puck, was about to trigger things off. I remember thinking, "Please, Lord, don't let them score more than five"—feeling that a goal a minute was a dismaying enough fate to plead against to a Higher Authority—and then I heard the sharp cracking of sticks against the puck.

For the first two minutes the Bruins kept the play in the Flyers end. Perhaps they realized that a torrid offense was the only hope of staving off an awkward-sounding score. They played as if the net behind them were empty . . . as if their goalie had been pulled in the last minute of a game they had hoped to tie with the use of an extra forward. I saw the leg-pad of the Flyers' goaltender fly up to deflect a shot.

Well, this isn't bad at all, I thought.

There can be nothing easier in sport than being a hockey goalie when the puck is at the opposite end. Nonchalance is the proper attitude. One can do a little housekeeping, sliding the ice shavings off to one side with the big stick. Humming a short tune is possible. Tretiak, the Russian goaltender, had a number of relaxing exercises he would put himself through when the puck was at the opposite end of the rink. He would hunch his shoulder muscles, relaxing them, and he'd make a conscious effort to get the wrinkles out of his brow. "To relax, pay attention to your face. Make it smooth," he would add, the sort of advice a fashion model might tend to.

It is a time for reflection and observation. During a static spell, Ken Dryden from the Montreal goal noticed that the great game clock that hung above the Boston Garden was slightly askew.

With the puck at the other end, it was not unlike (it occurred to me) standing at the edge of a mill pond, looking out across a quiet expanse at some vague activity at the opposite end almost too far to be discernible—could they be bass fishing out there?—but then suddenly the distant, aimless, waterbug scurrying becomes an oncoming surge of movement as everything—players, sticks, the puck—starts coming on a direct line, almost as if a *tsunami*, that awesome tidal wave of the South Pacific, had suddenly materialized at the far end of the mill pond and was beginning to sweep down toward one.

"A tsunami?" a friend of mine had asked.

"Well, it *is* like that," I said. "A great encroaching wave full of things being borne along toward you full tilt—hockey sticks, helmets, faces with no teeth in them, those black, barrel-like hockey pants, the skates, and somewhere in there that awful puck. And then, of course, the noise."

"The noise?"

"Well, the crowd roars as the wings come down the ice, and so the noise seems as if it were being generated by the wave itself. And then there's the racket of the skates against the ice, and the thump of bodies against the boards, and the crack of the puck against the sticks. And then you're inclined to do a little yelling yourself inside your face mask—the kind of sounds cartoon characters make when they're agonized."

"Arrrgh?"

"Exactly. The fact is it's very noisy all of a sudden, and not only that, but it's very crowded. You're joined by an awful lot of people," I said, "and very quickly. There's so much movement and scuffling at the top of the crease that you feel almost smothered."

What one was trained to do in this situation (I told my friend) was to keep one's eye on the puck at all costs. I only had fleeting glimpses of it—it sailed elusively between the skates and sticks as shifty as a rat in a hedgerow: it seemed impossible to forecast its whereabouts . . . my body jumped and swayed in a series of false starts. Cheevers had explained to me that at such moments he instinctively understood what was going on, acutely aware of the patterns developing, to whose stick the puck had gone, and what the player was likely to do with it. The motion of the puck was as significant to him as the movement of a knight on a chess board. His mind busied itself with possibilities and solutions. For me, it was enough to remember the simplest of Cheever's instructions: "Stand up! Keep your stick on the ice!"

The first shot the Flyers took went in. I had only the briefest peek at the puck . . . speeding in from the point off to my right, a zinger, and catching the net at the far post, tipped in on the fly, as it turned out, by a Philadelphia player named Kindrachuk, who was standing just off the crease. The assists were credited to Rick Lapointe and Barry Dean. I heard this melancholy news over the public address system, just barely distinguishing the names over the uproar of a Philadelphia crowd pleased as punch that a Bruins team had been scored on, however circumspect and porous their goaltender.

Seaweed had given me some additional last minute tips at training camp on what to do if scored upon. His theory was that the goaltender should never suggest by his actions on the ice that he was in any way responsible for what had happened. The goalie should continue staring out at the rink in a poised crouch (even if he was aware that the puck had smacked into the nets behind) as if he had been thoroughly screened and did not know the shot had been taken. In cases where being screened from the shot was obviously not a contributing cause of the score, Seaweed suggested making a violent, abusive gesture at a defenseman, as if that unfortunate had made the responsible error.

When the Flyer goal was scored, I had not the presence or the inclination to do any of the things Seaweed had recommended. I yelled loudly in dismay and beat the side of my face mask with my catching glove. I must have seemed a portrait of guilt and ineptitude. "I didn't see the damn thing!" I called out. As I reached back to remove the puck, the thought pressed in on my mind that the Flyers had scored on their very first attempt—their shooting average was perfect.

What small sense of confidence I might have had was further eroded when soon after the face-off following the Philadelphia goal, one of the Bruins went to the penalty box for tripping; the Flyers were able to employ their power play, and for the remainder of the action, the puck stayed in the Bruins zone.

I have seen a film taken of those minutes—in slow motion so that my delayed reactions to the puck's whereabouts are emphasized. The big catching mitt rises and flaps slowly long after the puck has passed. There seems to be a near-studied attempt to keep my back to the puck. The puck hits my pads and turns me around, so that then my posture is as if I wished to see if anything interesting happened to be going on in the nets behind me. While the players struggle over the puck, enticingly in front of the crease, the camera catches me staring into the depths of the goal, apparently oblivious of the melee immediately behind me.

The film also shows that I spent a great deal of the time flat on the ice, alas, just where Cheevers and Seaweed had warned me not to be. Not much had to happen to put me there—a nudge, the blow of the puck. Once, a hard shot missed the far post, and in reaching for it, down I went, as if blown over by the passage of the puck going by. The film shows me for an instant grasping one of my defensemen's legs, his stick and skates locked in my grasp, as I try to haul myself back upright, using him like a drunk enveloping a lamppost.

Actually, my most spectacular save was made when I was prostrate on the ice . . . the puck appearing under my nose, quite inexplicably, and I was able to clap my glove over it. I could hear the Bruins breathing and chortling as they clustered over me to protect the puck from being probed out by a Flyer stick.

What was astonishing about those hectic moments was that the Flyers did not score. Five of their shots were actually on goal . . . but by chance my body, in its whirlygig fashion, completely independent of what was going on, happened to be in the right place when the puck appeared.

A friend, who was observing from the seats, said the highest moment of comic relief during all this was when one of the Flyers' shots came in over my shoulder and hit the top bar of the cage and ricocheted away.

"What was funny," my friend said, "was that at first there was absolutely no reaction from you at all—there you were in the prescribed position, slightly crouched, facing out towards the action, stick properly down on the ice and all, and then the puck went by you, head-high, and went off that cross-bar like a golf ball cracking off a branch; it wasn't until four or five seconds, it seemed, before your head slowly turned and sneaked a look at where the puck had . . . well . . . *clanged.* It was the ultimate in the slow double-take."

"I don't remember," I said. "I don't recall any clanging."

"Hilarious," my friend said. "Our whole section was in stitches."

Then, just a few seconds before my five-minute stint was up, Mike Milbury, one of the Bruins defensemen out in front of me, threw his stick across the path of a Flyers wing coming down the ice with the puck. I never asked him why. Perhaps I had fallen down and slid off somewhere, leaving the mouth of the net ajar, and he felt some sort of desperate measure was called for. More likely, he had been put up to it by his teammates and Don Cherry. Actually, I was told a *number* of sticks had been thrown. The Bruins wanted to be sure that my experience would include the most nightmarish challenge a goaltender can suffer . . . alone on the ice and defending against a shooter coming down on him one-on-one. The penalty shot!

At first, I did not know what was happening. I heard the whistles going. I got back into the nets. I assumed a face-off was going to be called. But the Bruins started coming by the goal mouth, tapping me on the pads with their hockey sticks as they had at the start of things, faint smiles, and then they headed for the bench, leaving the rink enormous and stretching out bare from where I stood. I noticed a huddle of players over by the Philadelphia bench.

Up in Fitchburg I had been coached on what the goaltender is supposed to do against the penalty shot . . . which is, in fact, how he maneuvers against the breakaway: as the shooter comes across the blue line with the puck, the goaltender must emerge from the goal mouth and skate out toward him—this in order to cut down the angle on the goal behind him. The shooter at this point has two choices: he can shoot, if he thinks he can whip the puck past the oncoming, hustling bulk of the goaltender, slapping it by on either side, or he can keep the puck on his stick and try to come *around* the goalie; in this case, of course, the goalie must brake sharply, and then scuttle backwards swiftly, always maneuvering to keep himself between the shooter and the goal mouth. I would always tell Seaweed or Cheevers, whomever I was chatting with about the penalty shot, that I had to hope the shooter, if this situation ever came up, did not know that I was not able to stop. All the shooter had to do was come to a stop himself, stand aside, and I would go sailing by him, headed for the boards at the opposite end of the rink.

Penalty shots do not come up that often. Gump Worsley in his twenty-one-year career had only faced two, both of which he was unsuccessful against—not surprising perhaps because the goals came off the sticks of Gordie Howe and Boom-Boom Geoffrion. But Seaweed had told me—despite the Gump Worsley statistics—that he thought the chances favored the goaltender . . . that by skating out and controlling the angle the goalie could force the shooter to commit himself. Also, he pointed out that since the shooter was the only other player on the ice, the goaltender always had a bead on the puck, whereas in the flurry of a game he had often lost sight of it in a melee, or had it tipped in by another player, or passed across the ice to a position requiring a quick shift in the goal. Others agreed with him. Emile Francis believed that the goaltender should come up with a save three times out of five. He pointed out while the goaltender is under considerable pressure, so is the other fellow—the humiliation of missing increased because the shooter *seems* to have the advantage . . . the predator, swift and rapacious, swooping in on a comparatively immobile defender. The compiled statistics seem to bear him out. Up until the time I joined the Bruins, only one penalty shot out of the ten taken in Stanley Cup play has resulted in a score—Wayne Connelly's of the Minnesota North Stars in 1968 off Terry Sawchuck.

The confidence that might have been instilled by knowing such statistics was by no means evident in my own case. I stood in the cage, staring out at the empty rink, feeling lonely and put upon, the vast focus of the crowd narrowing on me as it was announced over the public address system that Reggie Leach would take the penalty shot. Leach? Leach? The name meant little to me. I had heard only one thing that I could remember about him from my résumé of Flyers players, which was that he had scored five goals in a play-off game, a record. I dimly recalled that he was an Indian by birth. Also a slap shot specialist . . . just enough information to make me prickle with sweat under my mask.

I gave one final instruction to myself—murmuring audibly inside the cage of my face mask that I was not to remain rooted helplessly in the goal mouth, mesmerized, but to launch myself out toward Leach . . . and just then I spotted him, moving out from the boards, just beyond the blue line, picking up speed, and I saw the puck cradled in the curve of his stick blade.

As he came over the blue line, I pushed off and skated briskly out to meet him, windmilling my arms in my haste, and as we converged I committed myself utterly to the hope that he would shoot rather than try to come around me. I flung myself sideways to the ice (someone said later that it looked like the collapse of an ancient sofa), and sure enough he *did* shoot. Somewhat perfunctorily, he lifted the puck and it hit the edge of one of my skates and skidded away, wide of the goal behind me.

A very decent roar of surprise and pleasure exploded from the stands. By this time, I think, the Philadelphia fans thought of me less as a despised Bruin than a surrogate member of their own kind. The team identification was unimportant. For an instant, I represented a manifestation of their own curiosity if they happened to find themselves down there on the ice. As for the Bruins, they came quickly off the bench, scrambling over the boards to skate out in a wave of black and gold. It occurred to me that they were coming out simply to get me back up on my skates—after all, I was flat out on the ice—but they wore big grins: they pulled me up and began cuffing me around in delight, the big gloves smothering my mask so I could barely see as in a thick joyous clump we moved slowly to the bench. Halfway there, my skates went out from under me—tripped up perhaps or knocked askew by the congratulatory pummels—and once again I found myself down at ice level; they hauled me up like a sack of potatoes and got me to the bench. I sat down. It was a very heady time. I beamed at them. Someone stuck the tube of a plastic bottle in my mouth. The water squirted in and I choked briefly. A towel was spread around my shoulders.

"How many saves?"

"Oh, twenty or thirty. At least."

"What about that penalty shot?"

"Leach is finished. He may not play again. To miss a penalty shot against you? The Flyers may not recover."

I luxuriated in what they were saying.

"Is that right?"

But their attention began to shift back to the ice. The game was starting up again. The sound of the crowd was different: full and violent. I looked up and down the bench for more recognition. I wanted to hear more. I wanted to tell them what it had been like. Their faces were turned away now.

KENT CARTWRIGHT

"SCORING"

The pass zaps
from behind a back like a mad electron
blasting free,
crackles to his hand, then,
jabs away at the court,
high bounding and hard.
Possessed, pounding,
he fuses in circuit
to the weird ganglion of
bobbling rubber,
stutter-dribbles, hesi-
tates, head fakes,

and breaks,
slicing the stunned circle,
a dazzled filament,
a shard of crystal
splintering clean.
Driving the hoop, he launches,
leaping like energy sizzling
between hot, copper points.

Arched for the lay-up,
sculptured in the detonation

of desire, a glazed arm above
into the stillness,
a touch as soft as fur,
he shoots,
sweeping the volt away,
breaching Zeno's paradox,
crashes to the floor:
forgotten.

Saucy and coy, the ball
jolts a smudgy kiss
on the cold, clear glass,
hangs away on the lip,
moody, weighing the balance,
sighs through the net
like the whisper—
of love.

SCOTT OSTLER

"They Also Serve Who Only Sit and Sit and Sit"

Marty Byrnes, a reserve forward for the Lakers, played for the New
Orleans Jazz last season. He also sat a lot. He remembers a game at
Detroit when he was sitting, as usual, and the Jazz was losing, as usual.
Every Jazz player except Byrnes had been in the game.

"Hey, Byrnes!" yelled a fan behind the Jazz bench. "You gotta be
better than *somebody!*"

Not exactly the type of quote you'd want inscribed on your tomb-
stone, but when you sit on the bench in the NBA, you learn to cope with
the insecurity, inactivity, and cute little remarks from the customers.

The loneliness of a long-distance sitter. It's the hardest easy job in the
world.

The Lakers' non-starters, who refer to themselves collectively as the
Pine Brothers, were discussing the subject recently in an airport as they
sat (what else?) and waited for a team flight.

"Sitting on the bench is tough to deal with," said Laker rookie Brad Holland, who is averaging 46 minutes a game on the bench. "So you try to make it as fun as possible. It's not that we're goofing off or not taking the game seriously. We're kidding around, but it's not really funny."

We'll be the judge of that, Brad.

But first, a little historical background.

The team seating area in basketball used to be called the bench, until about 15 years ago when a frustrated second-string NBA center named Reggie Harding (who is now dead) declared: "I ain't ridin' the pines any more."

Pines. Technically incorrect. Courtside seats in the NBA are not constructed of pine, or any other wood. But backboards in the NBA aren't made from boards, either. And Harding, who had a feel for the language, if not the game, knew it would sound silly to say, "I ain't gonna sit on no metal folding chairs any more."

So the bench became known as the pines (or pine), and ridin' the pines became the accepted term for exile on the bench.

The Lakers' non-starters adopted the name Pine Brothers this season. It's not original. The name was used by subs on rookie Ollie Mack's high school team.

The Pine Brothers: Don Ford (5th season, USCB), Mike Cooper (2nd season, U. of New Mexico), Byrnes (2nd season, Syracuse), Mack (rookie, E. Carolina), and Holland (rookie, UCLA).

The interview went something like this:

Question: Is there a leader of the Pine Brothers?

Cooper: Prez [Don Ford] is our leader. He's my hero. He's President Pine.

Ford: I even use Pine Sol deodorant.

Q: Do you have assigned seats on the bench?

Ford: No, but if the team's going good, no one will change up. That's protocol. If the team's going bad, we'll switch seats around. Sometimes the starters are perturbed when they come out of the game. They like to sit at the end of the bench, so we move. You don't want them to sweat on you, so you give up your seat. Especially if it's a long road trip. You don't want to get your uniform wet and dirty.

Q: Which is the best seat?

Ford: You like to go to the end, away from the coach.

Keith Erickson (Laker broadcaster, eavesdropping on the interview): When I played, some guys would fight to get next to the coach.

Holland: It's the opposite here.

Q: Who usually gets the end seat?

Cooper: Marty or Prez, usually. They leave the huddles early.

Q: Why is the end seat the best?

Byrnes: You don't have to ask for water or Gatorade, you can just reach it for yourself. There are disadvantages. At the Forum there's one cheerleader I've never seen because she sits in the same spot every game and you can't see her from the end of the bench.

Ford: When you sit at the end, you can make comments without being censored. In fact, if the bench is long enough you can barely hear the coach when he calls you into the game.

Holland: The end seat in San Diego is the best because it's angled toward the court so you can see real well.

Ford: That seat is usually taken by Brad or the chicken [San Diego's mascot].

Q: Prez, when interim coach Paul Westhead first took over, he asked you to sit next to him for a few games. Was that a tough adjustment?

Ford: I told him I didn't know if I could enjoy the game from there. It's a completely different angle, you're sitting near midcourt instead of the end line, and everything looks different.

Q: Sort of like switching from shortstop to second base?

Ford: Exactly.

Q: During the game, do you try to notice things about strategy and plays?

Ford: If we knew anything about strategy and plays, we'd be starting. We just try to give a little encouragement, like "Way to go."

Q: How are the fans who sit behind the benches?

Ford: You can establish a relationship with the fans. In Portland they talk to me a lot. Well, actually they yell at me a lot. It's kind of fun really, as long as they don't throw anything. I've been hit with beer, ice, things like that.

Q: What kind of comments do they make?

Ford: They'll say things like, "You'll get in—eventually," or, "What are you this year, Ford? Fourth string or fifth string?"

Byrnes: Last year Rich Kelley [New Orleans center] was having a bad game and he sat down on the bench. A fan handed him a box of popcorn and said, "Here, eat this. You ain't going back in."

Q: Marty, how does this team's bench compare to New Orleans'?

Byrnes: This is a mild bench. At New Orleans they liked to play jokes. I was sitting on the end of the bench and a guy three seats up said (cupping his hands over his mouth to disguise his voice), "Byrnes! Byrnes!" I ran up to the coach, but of course he hadn't called me. That was my initiation.

Q: How are the actual seating accommodations?

Ford: Houston has excellent seats, real thick padding, but there's not enough seats, so you can't spread out. That's especially important on the road, when everyone's got smelly uniforms. Last night [Detroit] was poor. The seats are nice, they're well padded, but the floor is elevated, so you sit with your knees in your chin.

Byrnes: The worst thing is when you're up by 12 points with a minute and a half left and the other team's got three timeouts left. You have to keep getting up and down.

Ford: You can get cramps in your legs.

Q: Speaking of timeouts, where do the Pine Brothers stand during timeouts?

Byrnes: That depends on where the [TV] camera is. If you can, you lean down and try to get on TV.

Ford: We see the red light, that's when we pep up.

Byrnes: If at all possible, you try to show a bandaged hand or a knee brace, so they know why you're not playing. And you have to act like you're into the huddle. You do that for about 15 seconds, then you figure they're into the commercial.

Holland: Ollie keeps his head down like he's paying attention, but his eyes are up, looking in the stands.

Q: You mean looking at girls?

Ford: I noticed Brad stretching like this [bending at the waist, looking back through his legs] the other night. The coach thinks he's dedicated and getting ready to play, but he's really sneaking a look, even if it's upside down.

Q: Do you spend a lot of time looking at girls?

Ford: The starters do when they're on the bench, because they don't have time to do that while they're playing. We have more time, so we can pick our spots.

Q: A few last questions—what do you drink on the bench?

Ford: At Atlanta it's just water. That's horrible. Detroit and Washington are the best, you get something like a Tiki Punch. You have to be careful though. You can drink too much and get a little bloated and you're not hungry later.

Q: Do you get your uniforms cleaned even if you don't play?

Ford: Jack [trainer Jack Curran] will tell us we can get our uniforms washed, then he'll kind of giggle, like it's really necessary to wash 'em.

Q: Is there a Pine Brothers Hall of Fame?

Byrnes: My all-time great Pine Brother is Aaron James [at New Orleans]. He knew what was going on at all times, in the game, on the bench, and in the stands. He was on every player and both officials simultaneously. He could be screaming at the ref and pointing out girls in the stands at the same time.

Ford: I used to idolize Pat [Riley, Lakers assistant coach and a former player—and nonplayer]. He had a lot of style on the end of the bench.

Riley (eavesdropping): I remember after one game, Gail [Goodrich] was really upset. He said to me, "Can you believe I only played 42 minutes?" And here I hadn't played in 10 games. Wilt [Chamberlain] used to tell the coach, "I think you should put Pat in, he hasn't played in 30 games."

Q: When you're introduced in pregame ceremonies, is there anything special you try to do?

Ford: The main concern is not to trip over your warmups.

ROBERT FRANCIS

"Skier"

He swings down like the flourish of a pen
Signing a signature in white on white.

The silence of his skis reciprocates
The silence of the world around him.

Wind is his one competitor
In the cool winding and unwinding down.

On incandescent feet he falls
Unfalling, trailing white foam, white fire.

THOMAS BOSWELL

"99 Reasons Why Baseball Is Better than Football"

In January 1987, Tom Boswell, the sports columnist for the Washington Post, *wrote a now-famous article entitled "99 Reasons Why Baseball Is*

Better than Football." Perhaps one of the reasons for its popularity was that with the Super Bowl about to be played, the football season would finally end; surfeited with the game, one's attention could now turn (especially in the sloughs of winter) to news from the baseball training camps in warmer climes, bringing once again the sense of rebirth that comes with the changing of the seasons. Some of Boswell's 99 reasons were pertinent to that particular time and thus slightly dated; the following is an edited selection.

January 1987—Some people say football's the best game in America. Others say baseball.

Some people are really dumb.

Some people say all this is just a matter of taste. Others know better.

Some people can't wait for next Sunday's Super Bowl. Others wonder why.

Pro football is a great game. Compared with hockey. After all, you've gotta do something when the wind chill is zero and your curveball won't break. But let's not be silly. Compare the games? It's a one-sided laughter. Here are . . . reasons why baseball is better than football. (More after lunch.)

Baseball has fans in Wrigley Field singing "Take Me Out to the Ball Game" at the seventh-inning stretch.

Baseball has Blue Moon, Catfish, Spaceman, and the Sugar Bear. Football has Lester the Molester, Too Mean, and the Assassin.

Baseball has a bullpen coach blowing bubble gum with his cap turned around backward while leaning on a fungo bat; football has a defensive coordinator in a satin jacket with a headset and a clipboard.

Football players and coaches don't know how to bait a ref, much less jump up and down and scream in his face. Baseball players know how to argue with umps; baseball managers even kick dirt on them. Earl Weaver steals third base and won't give it back; Tom Landry folds his arms.

Football coaches talk about character, gut checks, intensity, and reckless abandon. Tommy Lasorda said, "Managing is like holding a dove in your hand. Squeeze too hard and you kill it; not hard enough and it flies away."

Before a baseball game, there are two hours of batting practice. Before a football game, there's a two-hour traffic jam.

A crowd of 30,000 in a stadium built for 55,501 has a lot more fun than a crowd of 55,501 in the same stadium.

No one has ever actually reached the end of the rest room line at an NFL game.

Nine innings means eighteen chances at the hot dog line. Two halves means B.Y.O. or go hungry.

Pro football players have breasts. Many NFLers are so freakishly over-developed, owing to steroids, that they look like circus geeks. Baseball players seem like normal fit folks. Fans should be thankful they don't have to look at NFL teams in bathing suits.

Eighty degrees, a cold beer, and a short-sleeve shirt are better than thirty degrees, a hip flask, and six layers of clothes under a lap blanket. Take your pick: suntan or frostbite.

Having 162 games a year is 10.125 times as good as having 16.

If you miss your favorite NFL team's game, you have to wait a week. In baseball, you wait a day.

Everything George Carlin said in his famous monologue is right on. In football you blitz, bomb, spear, shiver, march, and score. In baseball, you wait for a walk, take your stretch, toe the rubber, tap your spikes, play ball, and run home.

Marianne Moore loved Christy Mathewson. No woman of quality has ever preferred football to baseball.

More good baseball books appear in a single year than have been written about football in the past fifty years. The best football writers, like Dan Jenkins, have the good sense to write about something else most of the time.

The best football announcer ever was Howard Cosell.

The worst baseball announcer ever was Howard Cosell.

All gridirons are identical; football coaches never have to meet to go over the ground rules. But the best baseball parks are unique.

Baseball has one designated hitter. In football, everybody is a desig-nated something. No one plays the whole game anymore. Football wor-ships the specialists. Baseball worships the generalists.

The tense closing seconds of crucial baseball games are decided by distinctive relief pitchers like Bruce Sutter, Rollie Fingers, or Goose Gossage. Vital NFL games are decided by helmeted gentlemen who come on for ten seconds, kick sideways, spend the rest of the game keeping their precious foot warm on the sidelines, and aren't aware of the subtleties of the game. Half of them, in Alex Karras's words, run off the field chirping, "I kick a touchdown."

Nobody on earth really knows what pass interference is. Part judg-ment, part acting, mostly accident.

Baseball has no penalties at all. A home run is a home run. You cheer. In football, on a score, you look for flags. If there's one, who's it on?

When can we cheer? Football acts can all be repealed. Baseball acts stand forever.

Beneath the NFL's infinite sameness lies infinite variety. But we aren't privy to it. So what if football is totally explicable and fascinating to Dan Marino as he tries to decide whether to audible to a quick trap? From the stands, we don't know one-thousandth of what's required to grasp a pro football game. If an NFL coach has to say, "I won't know until I see the films," then how out-in-the-cold does that leave the fan?

While football is the most closed of games, baseball is the most open. A fan with a score card, a modest knowledge of the teams, and a knack for paying attention has all he needs to watch a game with sophistication.

Football has the Refrigerator. Baseball has Puff the Magic Dragon, the Wizard of Oz, Tom Terrific, Doggie, Kitty Kat, and Oil Can.

Football is impossible to watch. Admit it: the human head is at least two eyes shy for watching the forward pass. Do you watch the five eligible receivers? Or the quarterback and the pass rush? If you keep your eye on the ball, you never know who got open or how. If you watch the receivers . . . well, nobody watches the receivers. On TV you don't even know how many receivers have gone out for a pass.

In the NFL, you can't tell the players without an Intensive Care Unit report. Players get broken apart so fast we have no time to build up allegiances to stars. Three-quarters of the NFL's starting quarterbacks are in their first four years in the league. Is it because the new breed is better? Or because the old breed is already lame? A top baseball player lasts fifteen to twenty years. We know him like an old friend.

The baseball Hall of Fame is in Cooperstown, New York, beside James Fenimore Cooper's Lake Glimmerglass; the football Hall of Fame is in Canton, Ohio, beside the freeway.

Baseball means Spring's Here. Football means Winter's Coming.

Best book for a lifetime on a desert island: *The Baseball Encyclopedia.*

Baseball enriches language and imagination at almost every point of contact. As John Lardner put it, "Babe Herman did not triple into a triple play, but he did double into a double play, which is the next best thing."

Who's on first?

Without baseball, there'd have been no Fenway Park. Without football, there'd have been no artificial turf.

A typical baseball game has 9 runs, more than 250 pitches, and about 80 completed plays—hits, walks, outs—in 2½ hours. A typical football game has about 5 touchdowns, a couple of field goals, and fewer than 150 plays spread over 3 hours. Of those plays, perhaps 20 or 25 result in a gain or loss of more than 10 yards. Baseball has more scoring plays, more serious scoring threats, and more meaningful action plays.

Baseball has no clock. Yes, you were waiting for that. The comeback, from three or more scores behind, is far more common in baseball than football.

The majority of players on a football field in any game are lost and unaccountable in the middle of pileups. Confusion hides a multitude of sins. Every baseball player's performance and contribution are measured and recorded in every game.

In baseball, fans catch foul balls. In football, they raise a net so you can't even catch an extra point.

Football coaches walk across the field after the game and pretend to congratulate the opposing coach. Baseball managers head right for the beer.

Quarterbacks have to ask the crowd to quiet down. Pitchers never do.

Football, because of its self-importance, minimizes a sense of humor. Baseball cultivates one. Knowing you'll lose at least sixty games every season makes self-depreciation a survival tool. As Casey Stengel said to his barber, "Don't cut my throat. I may want to do that myself later."

Football is played best full of adrenaline and anger. Moderation seldom finds a place. Almost every act of baseball is a blending of effort and control; too much of either is fatal.

Football's real problem is not that it glorifies violence, though it does, but that it offers no successful alternative to violence. In baseball, there is a choice of methods: the change-up or the knuckleball, the bunt or the hit-and-run.

Baseball is vastly better in person than on TV. Only when you're in the ballpark can the eye grasp and interconnect the game's great distances. Will the wind blow that long fly just over the fence? Will the relay throw nail the runner trying to score from first on a double in the alley? Who's warming up in the bullpen? Where is the defense shading this hitter? Did the base stealer get a good jump? The eye flicks back and forth and captures everything that is necessary. As for replays, most parks have them. Football is better on TV. At least you don't need binoculars. And you've got your replays.

Turning the car radio dial on a summer night.

You'll never see a woman in a fur coat at a baseball game.

You'll never see a man in a fur coat at a baseball game.

A six-month pennant race. Football has nothing like it.

When a baseball player gets knocked out, he goes to the showers. When a football player gets knocked out, he goes to get X-rayed.

Most of all, baseball is better than football because spring training is less than a month away.

LEE GREEN; GEORGE PLIMPTON

"Classics"; "Semi-Classics"

Many compilers have put together collections of witticisms, observations, quotes, one-liners, and so forth from the world of sports. Indeed, an astonishing wealth of them exists although an athlete, especially an unworldly rookie, would not be thought of as a likely source. Once, in his early years, Joe DiMaggio was asked by a reporter for a "quote." The young center fielder had no idea what a quote was. "I thought it was some kind of soft drink." Nonetheless, more memorable quotes are forthcoming from sports than from any other profession that comes to mind—the reason very likely being that sports celebrities are so assiduously pursued to say what they have on their minds. A twenty-year-old who has run for a game-winning touchdown will find himself sitting on a stool in his locker facing a phalanx of writers, notebooks open, tape-machine microphones thrust toward him at the ready. At first, he learns the platitudes ("We had to put the points up on the board"), but then eventually, though not necessarily, moves to a higher plane or freer forms of expression—some unintentionally wise (Yogi Berra), others legitimately insightful.

Lee Green has put together one of the better collections, which is entitled Sportswit. *One section features "Classics"—a department appropriate to include here. It is followed by some of the more sprightly items from his book, to which I have added a number of my own choices from over the years.*

"classics"

Bob Fitzsimmons
heavyweight boxer:

"The bigger they are, the harder they fall."

Sometimes quoted, "The bigger they come, the harder they fall." Fitzsimmons, who had surrendered his heavyweight crown to Jim Jeffries in an 1899 bout, made this taunting remark prior to a rematch in San Francisco on July 25, 1902. But Jeffries didn't fall. Outweighing Fitzsimmons by 39 pounds, the champion knocked out the challenger in the eighth round.

RED SANDERS
Vanderbilt football coach:

"Winning isn't everything, it's the only thing."

One of the best-known quotations ever to emerge from the sporting world. But the line belongs to Sanders, not, as is widely believed, to former NFL coach Vince Lombardi. Sanders's era was earlier than Lombardi's. Moreover, Lombardi himself repeatedly denied ever having made the statement. In his 1973 book *Vince Lombardi on Football,* Vol. 1, Lombardi asserts, "What I said is that 'Winning is not everything—but making the effort to win is.' "

LEO DUROCHER
Brooklyn Dodgers manager:

"Nice guys finish last."

Quoted by sportswriter Frank Graham in a 1948 article in the New York *Journal-American.* By Durocher's own account, he was in the Dodger dugout at the Polo Grounds chatting with several baseball writers prior to a game with the last-place New York Giants. Graham asked him why he was so high on Eddie Stanky, a fiercely competitive player of marginal ability. Durocher, in a lengthy response, said he liked Stanky's temperament. To punctuate his explanation, he nodded in the direction of the Giants as they emerged from their dugout to take their warm-ups. "Take a look at them," the Dodger manager said. "All nice guys. They'll finish last. Nice guys. Finish last."

Graham, a meticulous journalist, reported the remark accurately in his newspaper account the next day. But, according to Durocher, other writers who had been present "ran two sentences together to make it sound as if I were saying that you couldn't be a decent person and succeed."

JACK NORWORTH
lyricist:

"Take me out to the ball game."

The first line of the song that has become baseball's unofficial anthem. "Take Me Out to the Ball Game" was introduced in vaudeville in 1908. Albert von Tilzer composed the music some twenty years before he saw his first baseball game. The song was sung by Ann Sheridan and Dennis Morgan in the 1944 motion picture *Shine On Harvest Moon,* and a 1949 movie starring Gene Kelly, Esther Williams, and Frank Sinatra took the song's title for its name.

At Wrigley Field, Chicago, Harry Carey, the broadcastor, traditionally leads the crowd in this song, leaning out of the press box and waving
his arms like a conductor.

The complete lyrics:

Take Me Out to the Ball Game

Take me out to the ball game,
Take me out to the park—
Buy me some peanuts and cracker jack,
I don't care if I never come back.
Let me root, root, root for the home team,
If they don't win it's a shame.
For it's one, two, three strikes, "You're out!"
At the old ball game.

GRANTLAND RICE
sportswriter:

For when the One Great Scorer comes to mark against your name,
He writes—not that you won or lost—but how you played the Game.

The final lines of Rice's poem "Alumnus Football." This verse
spawned the popular credo, "It's not whether you win or lose, but how
you play the game."

WEE WILLIE KEELER
Brooklyn Dodgers diminutive (5-foot, 4 1/2-inch) outfielder, on the art of
hitting:

"Keep your eye on the ball and hit 'em where they ain't."

Keeler rode this technique into baseball's Hall of Fame with a .345
lifetime batting average. The line is sometimes quoted, "Keep your eye
clear and hit 'em where they ain't." Most current references are ab-
breviated to, simply, "Hit 'em where they ain't."

TONY GALENTO
heavyweight boxer, before his 1939 title bout in New York with champion
Joe Louis:

"I'll moider de bum."

He didn't. Louis knocked him out in the fourth round, but the remark
has inexplicably enjoyed lasting renown. One version of the remark was
that it was in reply to being asked what he thought of William Shakespeare.

CHARLIE DRESSEN
Brooklyn Dodgers manager:

"The Giants is dead."

This pronouncement has lived in infamy since its utterance in 1951 when Dressen's Dodgers were in first place and the Giants were 13½ games back. The remark would have been quickly forgotten but for its inaccuracy. The Giants staged a magnificent stretch drive to tie the Dodgers for first in the regular season, and then beat Brooklyn for the National League pennant on Bobby Thomson's dramatic ninth-inning home run in the third game of the play-offs, often called "the shot heard round the world."

HARRY STEVENS
ballpark concessionaire:

"You can't tell the players without a scorecard."

BILL TERRY
New York Giants manager:

"Is Brooklyn still in the league?"

A facetious question posed by the Giants manager at a press conference in New York prior to the 1934 season. Terry was responding to a journalist's inquiry as to how the Dodgers would fare under new manager Casey Stengel. The previous year, the Dodgers had finished sixth, 26½ games behind the world champion Giants.

As the 1934 season entered its final days, Terry and his Giants found themselves tied for the National League lead with the St. Louis Cardinals. The Giants' final two games were against the Dodgers, who were again floundering in sixth place. Remembering Terry's smug remark, Brooklyn beat the Giants twice, 5–1 and 8–5, preventing their rivals from winning a second straight pennant. Dodger fans in attendance at the Polo Grounds flaunted banners that read, "Yes, We're Still in the League."

JOE JACOBS
fight manager:

"I shoulda stood in bed."

Another unremarkable utterance that not only has survived nearly half a century but has transcended sports, landed in *Bartlett's,* and gained currency in our everyday language. Jacobs made the remark after leaving his sickbed to attend a 1935 World Series game and betting on the loser.

ANONYMOUS YOUNG BOY
to Shoeless Joe Jackson when the Chicago White Sox left fielder emerged from a courtroom after testifying in the grand jury investigation of the 1919 Black Sox scandal:

"Say it ain't so, Joe."
Both the accuracy and the authenticity of this quote remain widely disputed. The remark appeared in papers throughout the country, though some believe it was either the product of hearsay or an intentional fabrication by reporters. It was reported as "It isn't true, is it, Joe?" in the New York *Herald-Tribune;* "It ain't true, is it, Joe?" in the Chicago *Herald;* "Say it ain't so, Joe, say it ain't so" in the Chicago *Daily News;* "It ain't so, Joe, is it?" in the New York *Evening World;* and elsewhere, "You coulda made us proud, Joe."
Jackson consistently denied that any such remark was ever addressed to him. "There weren't any words passed between anybody except me and a deputy sheriff," he once said. "He asked me for a ride, and we got in the car together and left. There was a big crowd hanging around in front of the building, but nobody else said anything to me."
Ultimately, then, Shoeless Joe Jackson did indeed say it wasn't so.

FRANKLIN P. ADAMS
journalist/humorist:

These are the saddest of possible words, "Tinker to Evers to Chance."
Trio of bear cubs, and fleeter than birds, "Tinker to Evers to Chance."
Ruthlessly pricking our gonfalon bubble,
Making a Giant hit into a double—
Words that are heavy with nothing but trouble: "Tinker to Evers to Chance."

Joe Tinker, Johnny Evers, and Frank Chance made up the Chicago Cubs' prolific double-play combination in the early 1900s. The three infielders were voted into baseball's Hall of Fame as a unit.
The poem, entitled "Baseball's Sad Lexicon," first appeared in the New York *Mail* in July 1910.

JOHN L. SULLIVAN
heavyweight boxing champion:

"I can lick any man in the house."
Also quoted, "I can beat any son-of-a-bitch in the house." This boast was a favorite of Sullivan's, often uttered in crowded saloons. Sullivan

won the last bareknuckle title, defeating Jake Kilrain in Richburg, Mississippi, in July 1889.

JOE JACOBS
fight manager:

"We wuz robbed!"

Another unwitting passport to *Bartlett's Familiar Quotations* for Jacobs, who was outraged when his fighter, Max Schmeling, was stripped of his heavyweight championship by Jack Sharkey in a 15-round decision in New York in June 1932.

KNUTE ROCKNE
Notre Dame football coach:

"Win one for the Gipper."

If this is, as has been suggested by *Sports Illustrated,* "One of the hoariest of sporting clichés," it is also one of the most debated. It is reasonably clear that Rockne did indeed, in so many words, exhort his team to win a 1928 game against Army in honor of George Gipp, which the Irish did in a stunning 12–6 upset. Gipp was a Notre Dame football star who fell ill and died quite suddenly following the 1920 season.

What is less clear is whether Gipp actually made a deathbed request of Rockne, imploring the coach to someday, "when the going isn't so easy, when the odds are against us, ask a Notre Dame team to win a game for me—for the Gipper. I don't know where I'll be then, Rock, but I'll know about it and I'll be happy."

It is widely believed that this poignant scene actually occurred; it is also widely believed that it didn't—that Rockne invented the scenario to motivate a downtrodden team.

Sportswriter Grantland Rice claimed Rockne personally told him the deathbed story in intimate detail on the eve of the now-famous Army game. Perhaps the coach was rehearsing. Sportswriter Paul Gallico wrote, "Actually, the real deathbed story was quite different. Rockne, holding the boy's hand, said, 'It must be tough to go, George.' To which Gipp replied unequivocally, 'What's tough about it?' "

With neither Gipp nor Rockne available for comment, presumably the truth will never be known.

Postscript: Just prior to a game against Notre Dame in the mid-fifties, Michigan State coach Duffy Daugherty approached one of his players, Clarence Peaks, and asked, "Clarence, you going to let the Gipper beat you this afternoon?"

"If he shows up," Peaks replied, "Exit 15 is mine."

CASEY STENGEL
major-league manager:

"You could look it up."

Achieved "classic" status through sheer repetition by Stengel. The garrulous manager loved to punctuate his declarative sentences with this simple assertion. You could look it up.

SATCHEL PAIGE
Hall of Fame pitcher:

"Don't look back. Something might be gaining on you."

The sixth and last of Paige's Rules for Staying Young, which were first published in the old *Collier's* magazine. The rules were embroidered by writer Richard Donovan, who pieced them together from the pitcher's colorful conversation. The other rules:

Avoid fried meats, which angry up the blood.

If your stomach disputes you, lie down and pacify it with cool thoughts.

Keep the juices flowing by jangling around gently as you move.

Go very light on the vices, such as carrying on in society. The social ramble ain't restful.

Avoid running at all times.

JOE LOUIS
heavyweight boxing champion:

"He can run, but he can't hide."

Louis's response to those who kept reminding him of challenger Billy Conn's speed and hit-and-run tactics prior to the June 1946 title match between the two fighters. Conn managed to run for seven rounds before the champion caught him in the eighth and knocked him out.

GRANTLAND RICE
sportswriter:

"Outlined against a blue-gray October sky, the Four Horsemen rode again. In dramatic lore they are known as Famine, Pestilence, Destruction, and Death. These are only aliases. Their real names are Stuhldreher, Miller, Crowley, and Layden."

Appeared in the New York *Herald-Tribune* on October 19, 1924, as the lead for Rice's report on the Notre Dame–Army football game, won by the Irish, 13–7. The "Four Horsemen" appellation immortalized the Notre Dame backfield of quarterback Harry Stuhldreher, halfbacks Don Miller and Jim Crowley, and fullback Elmer Layden.

Thirty years later, Miller reminisced with Rice. "Let's face it," Miller said. "We were good, sure. But we'd have been just as dead two years after graduation as any other backfield if you hadn't painted that tag line on us."

To be sure, Miller and the other Horsemen may owe their lasting fame to George Strickler, a student publicist for the Irish in 1924. Three days before the Army game, Strickler had seen the film version of Blasco Ibáñez's novel *Four Horsemen of the Apocalypse,* starring Rudolph Valentino. Seated near Rice in the press box on Saturday, Strickler watched the Notre Dame backfield attack Army. "Just like the Four Horsemen," he observed innocently.

Rice probably heard the remark, but in his recollection of the famous lead, set forth in his book *The Tumult and the Shouting,* he makes no mention of Strickler. In fact, he claims to have had the seed of the idea for the Four Horsemen nickname a year before he actually committed it to print. He had seen the 1923 Army–Notre Dame game at Ebbets Field; and, impressed with the Irish backfield, remarked to a companion, "It's worse than a cavalry charge. They're like a wild horse stampede."

Regardless of how the tag was conceived, its lasting celebrity was guaranteed the day after it was published by a classic photograph of the uniform-clad Four Horsemen on horseback. The picture—Strickler's idea—appeared in newspapers throughout the country.

It's worth mentioning the size of this famous backfield: the quarterback, Stuhldreher, weighed 152 pounds; Crowley and Miller, the halfbacks, 156 pounds; and Layden, the fullback, 162 pounds. Nonetheless, in the three seasons they played, Notre Dame won 29 games, tying one and losing two, both to Nebraska. In 1924 the team went undefeated and beat Stanford 27–10 in the Rose Bowl.

As for the story itself, Rice was on occasion twitted for the curious "worm's-eye" view he uses in the opening paragraph. Whatever, the level of inspiration certainly dropped off markedly in the balance of his account . . . with such hyperbolic lines as "When a tank tears in with the speed of a motorcycle, what chance has flesh and blood to hold," or "Layden went ten yards across the line as if he had just been fired from the black mouth of a howitzer." Mercifully, the complete account is rarely republished.

JACK ROPER
heavyweight boxer:

"I zigged when I should have zagged."

Roper's explanation after champion Joe Louis knocked him out in the first round of their 1939 title bout in Los Angeles.

Muhammad Ali
heavyweight boxing champion:

"I am the greatest."

Ali's trademark boast, backed up by an illustrious ring career that saw him gain the world heavyweight championship an unprecedented three times.

"I just *said* I was the greatest," Ali admitted to a reporter from the Miami *News* late in his career. "I never thought I was."

"Float like a butterfly, sting like a bee"—a line often quoted by Ali to describe his boxing style—was actually made up by Bundini Brown, his trainer.

"I ain't got no argument with them Viet Cong." Said upon refusing to be inducted into the army in April 1967.

Bud Abbott and Lou Costello
comedians:

"Who's on first, What's on second, I Don't Know is on third."

The most memorable line from Abbott and Costello's famous baseball routine, "Who's on First?" The comedians performed the now classic dialogue in burlesque shows in the thirties. They popularized it on CBS radio's *The Kate Smith Hour,* and immortalized it on Broadway in 1939.

In 1945, Abbott and Costello performed "Who's on First?" in their film *The Naughty Nineties* using one of endless variations on the routine. A typical version (it helps to read it aloud):

Who's on First?

Bud: You know, strange as it may seem, they give ballplayers peculiar names nowadays. On the St. Louis team Who's on first, What's on second, I Don't Know is on third.
Lou: That's what I want to find out. I want you to tell me the names of the fellows on the St. Louis team.
Bud: I'm telling you. Who's on first, What's on second, I Don't Know is on third.
Lou: You know the fellows' names?
Bud: Yes.
Lou: Well, then, who's playin' first?
Bud: Yes.
Lou: I mean the fellow's name on first base.
Bud: Who.
Lou: The fellow's name on first base for St. Louis.
Bud: Who.

Lou: The guy on first base.

Bud: Who is on first base.

Lou: Well, what are you askin' me for?

Bud: I'm not asking you, I'm telling you. Who is on first.

Lou: I'm askin' you, Who is on first?

Bud: That's the man's name.

Lou: That's whose name?

Bud: Yes.

Lou: Well, go ahead, tell me.

Bud: Who.

Lou: The guy on first.

Bud: Who.

Lou: The first baseman.

Bud: Who is on first.

Lou: [A NEW APPROACH]: Have you got a first baseman on first?

Bud: Certainly.

Lou: Well, all I'm tryin' to find out is what's the guy's name on first base.

Bud: Oh, no, no. What is on second base.

Lou: I'm not askin' you who's on second.

Bud: Who's on first.

Lou: That's what I'm tryin' to find out.

Bud: Well, don't change the players around.

Lou: [TENSION MOUNTING]: I'm not changin' anybody.

Bud: Now take it easy.

Lou: What's the guy's name on first base?

Bud: What's the guy's name on *second* base.

Lou: I'm not askin' you who's on second.

Bud: Who's on first.

Lou: I don't know.

Bud: He's on third. We're not talking about him.

Lou: [IMPLORINGLY]: How could I get on third base?

Bud: You mentioned his name.

Lou: If I mentioned the third baseman's name, who did I say is playing third?

Bud [INSISTENTLY]: No, Who's playing first.

Lou: Stay offa first, will ya?

Bud: Please, now what is it you'd like to know?

Lou: What is the fellow's name on third base?

Bud: What is the fellow's name on *second* base.

Lou: I'm not askin' ya who's on second.

Bud: Who's on first.

Lou: I don't know.

Bud and Lou in unison: Third base!

Lou [trying a new tack]: You got an outfield?

Bud: Certainly.

Lou: St. Louis got a good outfield?

Bud: Oh, absolutely.

Lou: The left fielder's name?

Bud: Why.

Lou: I don't know. I just thought I'd ask.

Bud: Well, I just thought I'd tell you.

Lou: Then tell me who's playing left field.

Bud: Who's playing first.

Lou: Stay outa the infield!

Bud: Don't mention any names out here.

Lou [firmly]: I wanta know what's the fellow's name in left field.

Bud: What is on second.

Lou: I'm not askin' you who's on second.

Bud: Who is on first.

Lou: I don't know!

Bud and Lou: Third base!

[Lou begins making noises.]

Bud: Now take it easy, man.

Lou: And the left fielder's name?

Bud: Why.

Lou: Because.

Bud: Oh, he's center field.

Lou: Wait a minute. You got a pitcher on the team?

Bud: Wouldn't this be a fine team without a pitcher?

Lou: I dunno. Tell me the pitcher's name.

Bud: Tomorrow.

Lou: You don't want to tell me today?

Bud: I'm telling you, man.

Lou: Then go ahead.

Bud: Tomorrow.

Lou: What time?

Bud: What time what?

Lou: What time tomorrow are you gonna tell me who's pitching?

Bud: Now listen, who is not pitching. Who is on—

Lou [excitedly]: I'll break your arm if you say who is on first!

Bud: Then why come up here and ask?

Lou: I want to know what's the pitcher's name!

Bud: What's on second.

LOU [RESIGNED]: I don't know.

BUD AND LOU: Third base.

LOU: You gotta catcher?

BUD: Yes.

LOU: The catcher's name.

BUD: Today.

LOU: Today. And Tomorrow's pitching.

BUD: Now you've got it.

LOU: That's all. St. Louis got a couple of days on their team. That's all.

BUD: Well, I can't help that. What do you want me to do?

LOU: Gotta catcher?

BUD: Yes.

LOU: I'm a good catcher, too, you know.

BUD: I know that.

LOU: I would like to play for St. Louis.

BUD: Well, I might arrange that.

LOU: I would like to catch. Now Tomorrow's pitching on the team and I'm catching.

BUD: Yes.

LOU: Tomorrow throws the ball and the guy up and bunts the ball.

BUD: Yes.

LOU: So when he bunts the ball, me, bein' a good catcher, I want to throw the guy out at first base. So I pick up the ball and throw it to who?

BUD: Now that's the first thing you've said right!

LOU: *I don't even know what I'm talking about!*

BUD: Well, that's all you have to do.

LOU: I throw it to first base.

BUD: Yes.

LOU: Now who's got it?

BUD: Naturally.

LOU: Who has it?

BUD: Naturally.

LOU: Naturally.

BUD: Naturally.

LOU: I throw the ball to Naturally.

BUD: You throw it to Who.

LOU: Naturally.

BUD: Naturally, well, say it that way.

LOU: That's what I'm saying!

BUD: Now don't get excited, don't get excited.

LOU: I throw the ball to first base.

BUD: Then Who gets it.

LOU: He'd better get it!

BUD: That's it. All right now, don't get excited. Take it easy.

LOU [FRENZIED]: Now I throw the ball to first base, whoever it is grabs the ball, so the guy runs to second.

BUD: Uh-huh.

LOU: Who picks up the ball and throws it to What, What throws it to I Don't Know. I Don't Know throws it back to Tomorrow. A triple play!

BUD: Yeah, it could be.

LOU: Another guy gets up and it's a long fly ball to center. Why? I don't know. And I don't care.

BUD: What was that?

LOU: I said, I don't care.

BUD: Oh, that's our shortstop.

"SEMI-CLASSICS"

ART BUCHWALD
author:

"Although I never played football, I made many contributions. I went to the University of Southern California in the late 1940s and took the English exams for all the Trojan linemen."

ARNOLD (RED) AUERBACH
Boston Celtics coach:

"When people are used to winning, they put out a little more."

JACKIE STEWART
Grand Prix champion:

"In my sport, the quick are too often listed among the dead."

PETER GENT
author, professional football player

"Baseball players are the weirdest of all. I think it's all that organ music."

RED SMITH
sportswriter:

"Ninety feet between bases is the nearest to perfection that man has yet achieved."

JOE MCCARTHY
N.Y. Yankees manager:

"Give a boy a bat and a ball and a place to play and you'll have a good citizen."

CASEY STENGEL
Major-league manager:

"Now, there's three things you can do in a baseball game. You can win, or you can lose, or it can rain."

ROBERT LIPSYTE
sportswriter:

"Well-meaning people often ask sportswriters, even middle-aged sportswriters, what they are going to do when they grow up."

ALBERT CAMUS
author:

"Sport was the main occupation of all of us, and continued to be mine for a long time. That is where I had my only lesson in ethics."

ROY HARRIS
heavyweight boxer:

"It's a funny business, isn't it?—hitting people in the head."

GEORGE CROSS
University of Oklahoma president:

"I want a school my football team can be proud of."

JACQUES PLANTE
Montreal goalie, on goaltending

"How would you like it if you were out on your job or in your office and you made a little mistake? And suddenly a bright red light flashed behind you and then 18,000 people started screaming 'Pig!'; 'Stupid!'; 'Get the bum out of there!' "

BOBBY CLARKE
hockey forward on his team's (the Philadelphia Flyers) hard-hitting style:

"We take the shortest route to the puck and arrive in ill-humor."

ANONYMOUS:

"All great horses are fast but not all fast horses are great."

PELÉ
soccer champion:

"Enthusiasm is everything. It must be as taut and vibrating as a guitar string."

JIMMY CONNORS
tennis champion:

"I hate losing more than I love winning."

FAN TO NBA REFEREE DICK BAVETTA:

"Bavetta, if you had another eye, you'd be a cyclops."

DAVE DEBUSSCHERE
N.Y. Knicks forward:

"When you're through playing, when you're older, you go back to your friends."

MICHAEL NOVAK
author, from The Joy of Sport:

"Basketball is jazz: improvisatory, free, individualistic, corporate, sweaty, fast, exulting, screeching, torrid, explosive, exquisitely designed for letting first the trumpet, then the sax, then the drummer, then the trombonist soar away in virtuoso excellence."

JACK DEMPSEY
heavyweight boxing champion:

"A champion is one who gets up when he can't see."

JACKIE STEWART
Grand Prix champion:

"I don't get my kicks from flirting with death. I flirt with life. It's not that I enjoy the risks, the dangers, and the challenge of the race. I enjoy the life it gives me. When I finish a race, the sky looks bluer, the grass looks greener, the air feels fresher. It's so much better to be alive."

STIRLING MOSS,
Grand Prix champion

"It's necessary to relax your muscles when you can. Relaxing your brain can be fatal."

TED WILLIAMS
Boston Red Sox left fielder:

"Baseball is the only kind of endeavor when a man can succeed three times out of ten and be considered a good performer."

RON LAIRD
U.S. race walker, after going off course in the Pan American Games 20,000-meter walk:

"I knew something was wrong when I came to a locked gate."

DON MARQUIS
author:

"Fishing is a delusion entirely surrounded by liars with clothes."

VINCE LOMBARDI
Green Bay Packers football coach:

"This is a game for madmen."

GEORGE WILL
columnist, New York Times, *on football:*

"It is committee meetings, called huddles, separated by outbursts of violence."

BERNARD DARWIN
author:

"Golf is not a funeral, though both can be very sad affairs."

WOODROW WILSON
28th president of the United States, on golf:

"A game [golf] in which one endeavors to control a ball with instruments ill adapted to the purpose."

FRANK DEFORD
sportswriter, editor:

"Hockey's the only place where a guy can go nowadays and watch two white guys fight."

MAX BAER
heavyweight boxing champion:

"If you get belted and see three fighters through a haze, go after the one in the middle. That's what ruined me—I went after the two guys on the end."

JIM MURRAY
columnist, Los Angeles Times:

"The early rounds of a[n] [Archie] Moore fight always reminded me of a guy opening the hood of an engine and exploring around inside for weaker spots. Only, when he finds this, he doesn't repair them. He makes them worse. It's a trick a lot of mechanics have, but with Mr. Moore it's high art. A loose bolt here, a slick valve here, and by the time Arch has got through tinkering, the transmission falls out."

"When you get in the hole, and mark your score, you say, I had a 5 there. Then you look around, and if no one is looking at you funny you frown and start to erase saying, 'No, that's not right, it was only a 4.' This is known in golf as improving your life. In other words, the first score was a lie, but the second was a better one."

BILL RUSSELL
Boston Celtics:

"I have never seen an athlete, including myself, who I think should be lionized. There are very few athletes I know whom I would want my kids to be like. The only kids I try to set an example for are mine."

BARON PIERRE DE CONBERTIN
founder of the modern Olympic Games:

"The important thing in the Olympic Games is not to win but to take part; the important thing in life is not the triumph but the struggle. The essential thing is not to have conquered but to have fought well. To spread these precepts is to build up a stronger and more valiant and, above all, more scrupulous and more gracious humanity."

EARL WARREN
Chief Justice of the Supreme Court:

"I always turn to the sports pages first. The sports pages record people's accomplishments, the front page nothing but man's failures."

LEFTY GOMEZ
N.Y. Yankees pitcher:

"The secret of my success was clean living and a fast-moving outfield."

ELVIN HAYES
Baltimore Bullets center, on being asked in an airport if he was a basketball player:

"No, I clean giraffe's ears."

ANONYMOUS:

"Horses is smarter than people. You don't see no horses standing in line to bet on no peoples."

ANONYMOUS:

"Golf is like a love affair. If you don't take it seriously it's no fun; if you do take it seriously it breaks your heart."

MAX MCGEE
tight end, Green Bay Packers, on Vince Lombardi:

"When he says sit down, I don't even bother to look for a chair."

DUFFY DAUGHERTY
Michigan State football coach:

"Football is not a contact sport. Football is a collision sport. Dancing is a contact sport."

BRANCH RICKEY
co-owner of the Brooklyn Dodgers:

"Ty Cobb lived off the field as though he wished to live forever. He lived on the field as though it was his last day."

PING BODIE
Chicago White Sox outfielder in the dugout after being struck out by Walter Johnson, Hall of Fame pitcher for the Washington Senators:

"You can't hit what you can't see."

RING LARDNER
author:

"I am still undecided as to which of these two is the hardest shot in golf—any unconceded putt, or the explosion shot off the first tee. Both have caused more strokes than I care to write about."

JIM MURRAY
columnist, Los Angeles Times

"This team has a chance to go all the way. So did the *Titanic.*"

BLAINE NYE
Dallas Cowboys lineman:

"It's not whether you win or lose but who gets the blame."

CHUCK WEPNER
heavyweight contender known as "the Bayonne Bleeder":

"I was 6 feet 1 inch when I started boxing, but with all the uppercuts I'm up to 6 feet 5 inches."

DAMON RUNYON
author:

"One of these days in your travels, a guy is going to come up to you and show you a nice brand-new deck of cards on which the seal is not broken, and this guy is going to offer to bet you that he can make the jack of spades jump out of the deck and squirt cider in your ear. But, son, do not bet this man, for as sure as you stand there, you are going to end up with an earful of cider."

YOGI BERRA
New York Yankees catcher and major-league coach:

"If people don't want to come out to the ballpark, nobody's going to stop them."

P. G. WODEHOUSE
author, from The Clicking of Cuthbert:

"He misses short putts because of the uproar of the butterflies in the adjoining meadows."

CALIFORNIA INSTITUTE OF TECHNOLOGY *BEAVERS* CHEER:

> Secant, cosine, tangent, sine
> Logarithm, logarithm,
> Hyperbolic sine
> 3 point 1 4 1 5 9
> Slipstick, sliderule
> TECH TECH TECH

BILLIE JEAN KING
tennis champion:

"Champions keep playing until they get it right."

CONVERSATION ON A PLANE:

STEWARDESS: Mr. Ali, please fasten your seat belt.
MUHAMMAD ALI: Superman don't need no seat belt.
STEWARDESS: Superman don't need no plane either.

TOM STOPPARD
playwright/cricket enthusiast, on baseball:

"I don't think I can be expected to take seriously any game which takes less than three days to reach its conclusion."

LEE TREVINO
golf champion:

"There are two things not long for this world—dogs that chase cars and pro golfers who chip for pars."

JOHN MCENROE
tennis champion, to an umpire at the French Open:

"Can't you speak English?"

RED SMITH
sportswriter:

"Dying is no big deal. The least of us will manage that. Living is the trick."

LEE TREVINO
golf champion, once struck by lightning and suggesting how others could avoid that fate:

"Hold up a one-iron and walk. Even God can't hit a one-iron."

ALEX KARRAS
Detroit Lions defensive tackle:

"I never graduated from Iowa. I was only there for two terms—Truman's and Eisenhower's."

FRITZIE ZIVIC
Welterweight champion after losing a fight:

"I finished second."

JOE E. LEWIS
comedian:

"I play in the low 80s. If it's any hotter than that, I won't play."

VINCE LOMBARDI
Green Bay Packers football coach:

"No one is ever hurt. Hurt is in the mind."

JAMES MICHENER
author:

"It suddenly occurred to me that these superlative men [star athletes] . . . had been forced to retire from their athletic careers at a time when I, in my profession, had yet to write word one. Their public lives had ended before mine began. In their middle thirties these gifted men had reached the climax of their fame; they had scintillated for a decade, then been required to find another occupation; I had stumbled into a career at which I would work until eighty, if I lived that long."

NOTES ON
CONTRIBUTORS

DIANE ACKERMAN ("Patrick Ewing Takes a Foul Shot," from *Jaguar of Sweet Laughter*) is a longtime contributor to the *New Yorker*. She is the author of *Twilight of the Tenderfoot, Wife of Light,* and *A Natural History of the Senses*.

WOODY ALLEN ("A Fan's Notes on Earl Monroe") has written three collections of short pieces, many of which first appeared in the *New Yorker: Getting Even, Without Feathers,* and *Side Effects.* A renowned director, his many films include *Alice, Manhattan,* and *Annie Hall.*

ROGER ANGELL ("On the Ball," from *Five Seasons*; "Up at the Hall," from *Season Ticket*) is an editor and writer at the *New Yorker.* He is the author of a number of books about baseball: *The Summer Game, Five Seasons, Late Innings, Season Ticket,* and *Once More Around the Park.*

IRA BERKOW ("A Snorkeler's Tale") is a columnist for the *New York Times.* His books include the best-selling *Red: A Biography of Red Smith* and *The Man Who Robbed the Pierre,* which was nominated for the Edgar Award for Best True Crime Book.

ROBERT BLY'S ("The Hockey Poem") most recent books are *Loving a Woman in Two Worlds* (poems), *Selected Poems,* and *Iron John: A Book about Men.*

THOMAS BOSWELL ("99 Reasons Why Baseball Is Better than Football") is a sports columnist for the *Washington Post.* His books include *Game Day, The Heart of the Order,* and *How Life Imitates the World Series.*

T. CORAGHESSAN BOYLE ("The Hector Quesadilla Story") is the author of three collections of stories: *Descent of Man, Greasy Lake,* and *If the River Was Whiskey.* His four novels are *Water Music, Budding Prospects, World's End,* and *East Is East.*

JIM BROSNAN ("Why Pitchers Can't Hit," from *The Long Season*) has written over two hundred sports stories, which have appeared in magazines from *Boy's Life* to *Playboy.* He is the author of seven books, including *Pennant Race* and

The Long Season, which won the Secondary Education Annual Book Award for 1961.

ART BUCHWALD ("Casey Has Struck Out") is a syndicated columnist for the *Los Angeles Times.* In 1982 he won the Pulitzer Prize for Distinguished Commentary and in 1986 was elected to the American Academy and Institute of Arts and Letters. His most recent book, *Whose Rose Garden Is It Anyways?,* was published in 1989.

ROCH CARRIER ("The Hockey Sweater") is the author of many stories, novels, and plays and is equally popular in French- and English-speaking Canada. SHEILA FISCHMAN, his translator, has translated over forty works of Quebec literature, including ten by Roch Carrier. Her awards include the Felix-Antoine Savard Prize from Columbia University, which she has received twice.

KENT CARTWRIGHT ("Scoring") is an associate professor of English at the University of Maryland where he teaches Renaissance literature.

JOHN CIARDI (1916–1985) ("Polo Match") was poetry editor for the *Saturday Review* from 1956 to 1972 and from 1955 to 1972 was director of the Bread Loaf Writers' Conference. His critical works include *How Does a Poem Mean?;* his works of poetry, *I Marry You* and *For Instance.* He also produced a widely read English translation of Dante's *Inferno.*

TOM CLARK ("Son of Interesting Losers") is well known as a baseball poet from his books of the 1970s, including *When Things Get Tough on Easy Street.* He is also a biographer, having written on the lives of sporting and literary figures including Damon Runyon, Charles O. Finley, "Shufflin' Phil" Douglas, Mark "the Bird" Fidrych, Louis-Ferdinand Celine, Ted Berrigan, Jack Kerouac, and Charles Olson. His collections of poetry include *Disordered Ideas, Easter Sunday,* and the forthcoming *Fractured Karma.* Other works include *Champagne and Baloney: The Rise and Fall of Finley's A's.* Mr. Clark teaches poetics at New College of California.

ROBERT W. CREAMER ("Kaleidoscope: Personality of the Babe," from *Babe: The Legend Comes to Life*) was an editor and writer at *Sports Illustrated* for thirty years. He has written several baseball books, including *Stengel* and *Baseball in '41.*

WILLIAM A. CURRY ("Vince Lombardi," from *One More July,* with George Plimpton) is head coach of the University of Kentucky football team. An ex-NFL center for Green Bay, Baltimore, Houston, and Los Angeles, Curry was named to the All-Pro team in 1971 and served as president of the Players' Association in 1974.

EARL L. DACHSLAGER (letter to the editor of the *New York Times:* "What Shakespeare Knew about Baseball") teaches English at the University of Houston.

SIR BERNARD DARWIN (1876–1961) ("The Best-Known Figure in England"), the grandson of Charles Darwin, was an English author and golfer. His latter career was launched when he covered, as sportswriter, the first Walker Cup match between the United States and Great Britain at the National Golf Links in 1922; he ended up substituting for a member of the British team and winning his match.

DON DELILLO (from *End Zone*) is the author of ten novels, including *White Noise*, which received the American Book Award in 1985, and *Libra*, which was winner of the International Fiction Prize. He is a member of the American Academy and Institute of Arts and Letters.

BABETTE DEUTSCH (1895–1982) ("Morning Workout"), poet and critic, was author of *This Modern Poetry*. She was a member of the American Academy and Institute of Arts and Letters.

KEN DRYDEN ("Guy Lafleur," from *The Game*) played for the Montreal Canadiens from 1971 to 1979, and is a member of the Hockey Hall of Fame and the Canadian Sports Hall of Fame. *The Game* was a finalist for the Governor-General's Award for Non-Fiction. He practices law in Montreal.

DAVID ALLAN EVANS ("Nineteen Big Ones") has written three books of poems, *Carnival, Train Windows*, and *Real and False Alarms*, and a book of essays, *Remembering the Soos*. He is a professor of English at South Dakota State University in Brookings. In 1990 he won the Bush Artist Fellowship.

CLAY FELKER ("Casey Stengel's Secret") started his writing career as a writer for the *Sporting News*. A former editor of *New York*, he is now editor-at-large of *M Inc*.

GORDON FORBES ("Art Larsen," from *A Handful of Summers*) won a total of ten national tennis titles in South Africa. With his doubles partner Abe Segal, he won the British Hard Courts twice, and made it to the finals of the French Championships and the semifinals of Wimbledon. He has published tennis stories in *World Tennis* and many newspapers.

ROBERT FRANCIS (1901–1987) ("Skier") lived in Amherst, Massachusetts, from 1926 until his death. His *Collected Poems (1936–1976)* is composed of seven previous volumes of poetry. He won the Academy of American Poets Fellowship in 1984.

PAUL GALLICO (1897–1976) ("A Large Number of Persons"; "The Feel," from *Farewell to Sport*) wrote twenty-six books after his famous *Farewell to Sport*. These later books include *The Snow Goose* and *The Poseidon Adventure*.

LEE GREEN ("Classics," from *Sportswit*) is a California writer whose nonfiction has appeared in *Audubon, Playboy, Sports Illustrated, Esquire* and the *Los Angeles Times Magazine*. Three of his magazine pieces have been included in the annual *Best Sports Stories* anthology. A former columnist and contributing editor for *Outside*, Mr. Green is also the author of *Sportswit*, originally published in 1984 by Harper and Row.

DONALD HALL ("Old Timers' Day," from *Old and New Poems*), poet and essayist, was poetry editor of the *Paris Review* from 1953 until 1961. His nonfiction works include *Dock Ellis in the Country of Baseball* and *Fathers Playing Catch with Sons: Essays on Sport (Mostly Baseball)*.

WILLIAM HAZLITT (1778–1830) ("The Fight"), the literary critic and political essayist, also wrote columns for the *Edinburgh Review* and the *Examiner*.

SIR EDMUND HILLARY ("Adventure's End," from *High Adventure*) was, with his guide Tenzing, the first to reach the summit of Mount Everest, for which he was knighted by Queen Elizabeth II. A native New Zealander, he has served as their ambassador to India.

JAMES JOYCE'S (1882–1941) ("Game Old Merrimynn," from *Finnegans Wake*) *Finnegans Wake* was originally titled *Work in Progress*, and took seventeen years to complete. It was published in 1939.

ROGER KAHN ("The Crucial Role Fear Plays in Sports") has worked for *Esquire*, *Newsweek*, the *Saturday Evening Post*, and the New York *Herald-Tribune*. He is the author of the best-selling *The Boys of Summer*.

GARRISON KEILLOR ("The Babe," from *We Are Still Married;* "Attitude," from *Happy to Be Here*) is the author of four books, the preceding as well as *Lake Wobegon Days* and *Leaving Home*. He is a longtime contributor to the *New Yorker*.

W. P. KINSELLA ("The Thrill of the Grass") wrote the multi–award-winning *Shoeless Joe*, which was turned into the movie *Field of Dreams* in 1989. His other books include *The Fencepost Chronicles*, which won the Leacock Medal for Humor in 1987, and, most recently, *The Miss Hobbema Pageant* and *The Rainbow Warehouse*, co-authored with his wife.

FREDERICK C. KLEIN ("Sports Talk with a Non-Fan") writes the "On Sports" column for the *Wall Street Journal*. He has written five books, including a collection of columns titled *On Sports*.

MAXINE KUMIN ("Prothalamion") was consultant in poetry to the Library of Congress for 1981. In 1973 her book *Up Country* received the Pulitzer Prize for Poetry. Her most recent books include *Nurture* (poetry) and the upcoming *Looking for Luck*.

RING LARDNER (1885–1933) ("Alibi Ike") was well known for his sketches of American life in the early twentieth century, often told from the perspective of athletes. He is the author of *Gullible's Travels* and *The Love Nest and Other Stories*.

RICHMOND LATTIMORE (1906–1984) ("Sky Diving"), poet and translator, received the National Institute of Arts and Letters Award in 1954 and, in 1962, the Bollingen Award for his translation of Aristophanes' *The Frogs*. His books of poetry include *Sestina for a Far-off Summer* and his translations include *The Iliad* and *The Odyssey*.

A. J. LIEBLING (1904–1963) ("Boxing with the Naked Eye," from *The Sweet Science*) wrote for the *New Yorker* from 1935 until his death. He wrote more than a dozen books, including *A Neutral Corner*, *The Honest Rainmaker*, and *The Telephone Booth Indian.*

JAMES LIPTON (from *An Exaltation of Larks*) is an author of both fiction *(Mirrors)* and nonfiction *(An Exaltation of Larks)*, a Broadway playwright and lyricist, and a prolific writer and producer of motion pictures and television. The January 1991 publication of the expanded Ultimate Edition of *An Exaltation of Larks* marks a twenty-two-year career in which the book has never been out of print.

NORMAN MAILER ("Death [of Paret]," from *The Presidential Papers*) has published over thirty works. His *The Executioner's Song* won a Pulitzer Prize in 1979. A co-founder of the *Village Voice*, in 1960 he ran for mayor of New York City. In 1991, his novel, *Harlot's Ghost* was published.

PETER MANSO (excerpt from *Faster*, with Jackie Stewart) is currently completing his long term cultural biography of Marlon Brando which follows on the heels of *Mailer, His Life and Times*. He is a regular contributor to *Vanity Fair* and *Playboy*, among other national magazines.

DON MARQUIS (1878–1937) ("Why Professor Waddems Never Broke a Hundred," from *The Rivercliff Golf Killings*) wrote for the New York *Sun* and the New York *Tribune*. He is remembered above all for his collection of stories and verses *The Lives and Times of Archy and Mehitabel.*

THOMAS MCGUANE ("The Longest Silence," from *An Outside Chance*) is the author of nine books, including *92 in the Shade*, *Nobody's Angel*, and *Keep the Change.*

JOHN MCPHEE ("Centre Court," from *Pieces of the Frame*) is the author of *Wimbledon: A Celebration*. The Ferris Professor of Journalism at Princeton University, his most recent books are *The Control of Nature* and *Looking for a Ship*

SCOTT OSTLER ("They Also Serve Who Only Sit and Sit and Sit") has been a columnist for the *Los Angeles Times* and the now-defunct *The National.*

JOE H. PALMER (1904–1952) ("Stymie—Common Folks," from *This Was Racing*) was a writer for the New York *Herald-Tribune* and, until his death, was the best-known racing writer in America. *This Was Racing* is a compilation of his writings, edited by Red Smith.

GEORGE PLIMPTON ("Vince Lombardi," from *One More July*, with William Curry; from *Open Net*) has written a number of books with a sports background: *Out of My League*, *Paper Lion*, *The Bogey Man*, *The Curious Case of Sidd Finch*, *Open Net*, among them. He has been the editor of the literary quarterly *The Paris Review* since 1953. A columnist for *Esquire*, he is also a special contributor to *Sports Illustrated.*

LAWRENCE RITTER (interview with Fred Snodgrass, from *The Glory of Their Times*) is a professor of finance at New York University. Since writing *The Glory of Their Times* in 1966, he has authored four other baseball books, including a biography of Babe Ruth.

MIKE ROYKO ("A Very Solid Book") is a columnist for the *Chicago Tribune*. He won the Pulitzer Prize in 1972 for Distinguished Commentary. His books include *Boss: Richard T. Daly of Chicago*.

BILL RUSSELL ("Sports," from *Second Wind*), during his thirteen-year career with the Boston Celtics, led them to eleven world championships. He was named the NBA's Most Valuable Player five times and later served as the Celtics' head coach.

CARL SANDBURG (1878–1967) ("Hits and Runs") was part of the Chicago literary renaissance and established his reputation with *Chicago Poems* and *Cornhuskers*. He received two Pulitzer prizes, one for his biography, *Abraham Lincoln: The War Years*, the other for his *Complete Poems*.

WILFRID SHEED ("The Old Man and the Tee," from *Baseball and Lesser Sports*) is also the author of *The Boys of Winter*. His latest book, *The Face of Baseball*, came out in 1990.

RED SMITH (1905–1982) ("1951: New York Giants 5, Brooklyn Dodgers 4"), certainly the best-known sportswriter of his time, was author of the daily column *Views of Sport*. Two books of his collected columns, *The Red Smith Reader* and *Strawberries in the Wintertime*, are considered classics.

JACKIE STEWART (from *Faster*, with Peter Manso), the former Grand Prix champion, is a TV commentator on racing.

GAY TALESE'S ("The Loser") books include *Thy Neighbor's Wife, Honor Thy Father, The Kingdom and the Power*, and *Fame and Obscurity* from which "The Loser" was drawn.

ERNEST LAWRENCE THAYER (1863–1940) ("Casey at the Bat") was editor-in-chief of the *Harvard Lampoon* until 1885 and worked as a journalist with the *Hearst Newspaper* from 1886 to 1888. He was also the author of a number of ballads for the *San Francisco Examiner*.

JAMES THURBER (1894–1961) ("You Could Look It Up," from *My World—And Welcome to It*) was a primary contributor to the *New Yorker* during its early years (1927–1933). His books include *The Seal in the Bedroom and Other Predicaments, My Life and Hard Times*, and *Let Your Mind Alone*.

MARK TWAIN'S (1835–1910) "The Celebrated Jumping Frog of Calaveras County" (included here) was first published in 1865 and in 1867 appeared in his first book, *The Celebrated Jumping Frog*, a collection of stories.

JOHN UPDIKE ("The Pro," from *Museums and Women and Other Stories;* "Hub Fans Bid Kid Adieu") is author of the acclaimed *Rabbit* series and is a contributor to the *New Yorker*. In 1983 he won a Pulitzer Prize for *Rabbit Is Rich*.

ROBERT WALLACE'S ("A Snapshot for Miss Bricka Who Lost in the Semi-Final Round of the Pennsylvania Lawn Tennis Tournament at Haverford, July, 1960") recent publications include *The Common Summer: New and Selected Poems* and *Writing Poems*.

ROBERT PENN WARREN (1905–1989) ("Skiers," from *In the Mountains*) was the author of many novels, including *All the King's Men*, which won the Pulitzer Prize in 1947, as well as several volumes of poetry, two of which, *Promises* and *Now and Then: Poems 1976–1977*, won him Pulitzer prizes; he is the only person to have won Pulitzers in both fiction and poetry. In 1985 he was named the first Poet Laureate of the United States.

PAUL WEST ("Pelé," from *Portable People*) has written thirteen works of fiction, including *Rat Man of Paris* and *Lord Byron's Doctor*. *Portable People* is a collection of biographical sketches of figures from the worlds of science, the arts, politics, and sports.

P. G. WODEHOUSE (1881–1975) ("The Heart of a Goof," from *Divots*), British humorist and author of the acclaimed Jeeves series, also wrote *Leave It to Psmith* and *The Pilot that Thickened*. Collections of his early stories, *The Uncollected Wodehouse* and *The Scoop*, were published posthumously. He became a U.S. citizen in 1955 and was knighted shortly before his death.

THOMAS WOLFE'S (1900–1938) *Of Time and the River* (an excerpt included here) continues the story of Gant from *Look Homeward, Angel*. His other books include *The Web and the Rock* and *You Can't Go Home Again*.

TOM WOLFE'S ("The Last American Hero," from *The Kandy-Kolored Tangerine-Flake Streamline Baby*) magazine pieces have appeared in *New York* magazine, *Esquire*, and *Harper's*. *The Right Stuff*, his book about the early astronauts, won the American Book Award for general nonfiction. His first novel, *The Bonfire of the Vanities*, was serialized in *Rolling Stone* and later made into a movie of the same title.

JAMES WRIGHT (1927–1980) ("Autumn Begins in Martins Ferry, Ohio") was born in Martins Ferry, Ohio. His *Collected Poems* won the 1972 Pulitzer Prize for Poetry. *Above the River: The Complete Poems* was published in 1990.

ACKNOWLEDGMENTS

BUD ABBOTT and LOU COSTELLO: "Who's on First?" Used by permission of Abbott & Costello Enterprises under license authorized by Curtis Management Group, Indianapolis, Indiana, U.S.A.

DIANE ACKERMAN: "Patrick Ewing Takes a Foul Shot," from *Jaguar of Sweet Laughter: New and Selected Poems* by Diane Ackerman. Copyright © 1991 by Diane Ackerman. Reprinted by permission of Random House, Inc.

WOODY ALLEN: "A Fan's Notes on Earl Monroe." Copyright © 1977 Woody Allen, all rights reserved. Reprinted by permission of the author.

ROGER ANGELL: "On the Ball," from *Five Seasons* by Roger Angell. Copyright © 1972, 1973, 1974, 1975, 1976, 1977 by Roger Angell. Used by permission of Simon & Schuster. "Up at the Hall," from *Season Ticket* by Roger Angell. Copyright © 1988 by Roger Angell. Reprinted by permission of Houghton Mifflin Company. All rights reserved.

IRA BERKOW: "A Snorkeler's Tale." Reprinted with the permission of Atheneum Publishers, an imprint of Macmillan Publishing Company, from *Pitchers Do Get Lonely and Other Sports Stories* by Ira Berkow. Copyright © 1988 by Ira Berkow.

ROBERT BLY: "The Hockey Poem" from *The Morning Glory* by Robert Bly, Harper & Row, 1975. Copyright © 1975 by Robert Bly. Reprinted by permission of the author.

THOMAS BOSWELL: "99 Reasons Why Baseball Is Better than Football," from *The Heart of the Order* by Thomas Boswell. Copyright © by Thomas Boswell. Used by permission of Doubleday, a division of Bantam Doubleday Dell Publishing Group, Inc.

T. CORAGHESSAN BOYLE: "The Hector Quesadilla Story," from *Greasy Lake and Other Stories* by T. Coraghessan Boyle. Copyright © 1985 by T. Coraghessan Boyle. Used by permission of Viking Penguin, a division of Penguin Books USA Inc.

JIM BROSNAN: "Why Pitchers Can't Hit," from *The Long Season*. Copyright © 1960 by Jim Brosnan. Used by permission of HarperCollins Publishers.

ART BUCHWALD: "Casey Has Struck Out" reprinted by permission of the author.

ROCH CARRIER: "The Hockey Sweater," from *The Hockey Sweater and Other Stories* by Roch Carrier. Copyright © 1979 by Roch Carrier. Used by permission of Stoddart Publishing Co. Limited, 34 Lesmill Rd., Don Mills, Ontario, Canada. English translation copyright © by SHEILA FISCHMAN. Used by permission of the translator.

KENT CARTWRIGHT: "Scoring," originally published in *Arete: The Journal of Sports Literature*, Spring 1984. Reprinted by permission of the author.

JOHN CIARDI: "Polo Match," from *Person to Person* by John Ciardi. Copyright © 1964 by John Ciardi. Reprinted by permission of Judith H. Ciardi.

TOM CLARK: "Son of Interesting Losers." Copyright © 1974 Tom Clark. Reprinted by permission of the author.

ROBERT W. CREAMER: "Kaleidoscope: Personality of the Babe," from *Babe: The Legend Comes to Life* by Robert W. Creamer. Copyright © 1974 by Robert W. Creamer. Reprinted by permission of Simon & Schuster.

EARL L. DACHSLAGER: "What Shakespeare Knew about Baseball." Copyright © 1990 by the New York Times Company. Reprinted by permission of the New York Times Company and the author.

SIR BERNARD DARWIN: "The Best-Known Figure in England" by Sir Bernard Darwin. Reprinted by permission of A P Watt Limited on behalf of Lady Darwin, Ursula Mommens, and Dr. Paul Ashton.

DON DELILLO: From *End Zone* by Don DeLillo. Copyright © 1972 by Don DeLillo. Used by permission of Viking Penguin, a division of Penguin Books USA.

BABETTE DEUTSCH: "Morning Workout" reprinted by permission of Adam Yarmolinsky.

KEN DRYDEN: "Guy Lafleur," from *The Game* by Ken Dryden. Copyright © 1983 by Ken Dryden. Reprinted by permission of Macmillan Canada.

DAVID ALLAN EVANS: "Nineteen Big Ones" by David Allan Evans. Reprinted by permission of the author. First published in *Arete: The Journal of Sports Literature*, 1983.

CLAY FELKER: "Casey Stengel's Secret" reprinted by permission of the author.

GORDON FORBES: "Art Larsen," from *A Handful of Summers* by Gordon Forbes. Copyright © by Gordon Forbes. Reprinted by permission of the author.

ROBERT FRANCIS: "Skier," from *Robert Francis: Collected Poems, 1936–1976* (Amherst: University of Massachusetts Press, 1976). Copyright © 1959 by Robert Francis. Reprinted by permission of the University of Massachusetts Press and the estate of the author.

PAUL GALLICO: "The Feel," from *Farewell to Sport*, Copyright © 1937, 1938, 1964, 1966, and "A Large Number of Persons," from *Vanity Fair*, September 1931, reprinted by permission of Harold Ober Associates Incorporated.

LEE GREEN: Excerpts from *Sportswit*, researched and compiled by Lee Green. Copyright © 1984 by Lee Green. Reprinted by permission of Harper & Row and the author.

DONALD HALL: "Old Timers' Day," from *Old and New Poems* by Donald Hall. Copyright © 1990 by Donald Hall. Reprinted by permission of Ticknor & Fields, a Houghton Mifflin Company.

SIR EDMUND HILLARY: Excerpt from *High Adventure*. Copyright © 1955 by Sir Edmund Hillary. Copyright renewed © 1983. Reprinted by permission of John Farquharson Ltd.

JAMES JOYCE: From *Finnegans Wake* by James Joyce. Copyright © 1939 by James Joyce. Copyright renewed © 1967 by George Joyce and Lucia Joyce. Used by permission of Viking Penguin, a division of Penguin Books USA Inc.

ROGER KAHN: "The Crucial Role Fear Plays in Sports." Copyright © 1959 by Roger Kahn. Reprinted by permission of the author.

GARRISON KEILLOR: "Attitude" reprinted with the permission of Atheneum Publishers, an imprint of Macmillan Publishing Company, from *Happy to Be Here* by Garrison Keillor. Copyright © 1979 by Garrison Keillor. "The Babe," from *We Are Still Married: Stories and Letters* by Garrison Keillor. Copyright © 1982, 1983, 1984, 1985, 1986, 1987, 1988, 1989 by Garrison Keillor. Used by permission of Viking Penguin, a division of Penguin Books USA Inc., and Penguin Books Canada Limited.

W. P. KINSELLA: "The Thrill of the Grass," from *The Thrill of the Grass* by W. P. Kinsella. Copyright © 1984 by W. P. Kinsella. Used by permission of Viking Penguin, a division of Penguin Books USA Inc., and Penguin Books Canada Limited.

FREDERICK C. KLEIN: "Sports Talk with a Non-Fan" reprinted by permission of the *Wall Street Journal*.

MAXINE KUMIN: "Prothalamion," copyright © 1962 Maxine Kumin. From *Our Ground Time Here Will Be Brief* by Maxine Kumin. Used by permission of Viking Penguin, a division of Penguin Books USA Inc.

RING LARDNER: "Alibi Ike." Copyright © 1924 Charles Scribner's Sons. Copyright renewed © 1952 Ellis A. Lardner. Reprinted by permission of Ring Lardner Jr.

RICHMOND LATTIMORE: "Sky Diving" reprinted with permission of the Trustees Under Will of Richmond Lattimore, Dec'd.

A. J. LIEBLING: "Boxing with the Naked Eye." from *The Sweet Science* by A. J. Liebling. Copyright © 1951, 1952, 1953, 1954, 1955, 1956 by A. J. Liebling. Copyright renewed © 1981, 1982, 1983, 1984 by Norma Stonehill. Used by permission of Viking Penguin, a division of Penguin Books USA Inc.

JAMES LIPTON: From *An Exaltation of Larks* by James Lipton. Copyright © 1968, 1977, 1991 by James Lipton. Used by permission of Viking Penguin, a division of Penguin Books USA.

NORMAN MAILER: "Death [of Paret]," from "Ten Thousand Words a Minute" in *The Presidential Papers* by Norman Mailer. Copyright © 1963 by Norman Mailer. Published by Putnam, New York. Reprinted by permission of the author.

DON MARQUIS: "Why Professor Waddems Never Broke a Hundred," from *The Rivercliff Golf Killings,* copyright © 1921, 1928, 1930, 1934, 1935, 1936 by Don Marquis, from *The Best of Don Marquis* by Don Marquis. Used by permission of Doubleday, a division of Bantam Doubleday Dell Publishing Group, Inc.

THOMAS MCGUANE: "The Longest Silence" reprinted by permission of the author.

JOHN MCPHEE: "Centre Court," from *Pieces of the Frame* by John McPhee. Copyright © 1972, 1975 by John McPhee. Reprinted by permission of Farrar, Straus and Giroux, Inc.

SCOTT OSTLER: "They Also Serve Who Only Sit and Sit and Sit." Copyright © 1980, *Los Angeles Times.* Reprinted by permission.

JOE H. PALMER: "Stymie—Common Folks," from *This Was Racing* by Joe H. Palmer, published by Henry Clay Press, 1973. Reprinted in *Press Box: Red Smith's Favorite Sports Stories,* copyright © 1976 by Rex Taylor & Company, Inc.

LAWRENCE RITTER: "Fred Snodgrass," from *The Glory of Their Times* by Lawrence Ritter. New Preface and Chapters 5, 15, and 25 copyright © 1984 by Lawrence S. Ritter. Remainder copyright © 1966 by Lawrence S. Ritter. Reprinted by permission of the author.

MIKE ROYKO: "A Very Solid Book" reprinted by permission of the author.

BILL RUSSELL: "Sports," from *Second Wind* by Bill Russell. Copyright © 1979 by William F. Russell. Reprinted by permission of the author.

CARL SANDBURG: "Hits and Runs," from *Cornhuskers* by Carl Sandburg, copyright © 1918 by Holt, Rinehart and Winston, Inc. and renewed 1946 by Carl Sandburg, reprinted by permission of Harcourt Brace Jovanovich, Inc.

WILFRID SHEED: "The Old Man and the Tee," from *Baseball and Lesser Sports.* Copyright © 1991 by Wilfrid Sheed. Reprinted by permission of HarperCollins Publishers.

RED SMITH: "1951: New York Giants 5, Brooklyn Dodgers 4" reprinted by permission of Phyllis W. Smith.

JACKIE STEWART and PETER MANSO: "March 8, 1970," "March 9, 1970," and "March 12, 1970" from *Faster,* reprinted by permission of Jackie Stewart and Peter Manso.

GAY TALESE: "The Loser." Copyright © 1970 by Gay Talese. Reprinted by permission of the author.

JAMES THURBER: "You Could Look It Up," from *My World—And Welcome to It,* by James Thurber, published by Harcourt Brace Jovanovich, Inc. Copyright © 1942 James Thurber. Copyright © 1970 Helen Thurber and Rosemary A. Thurber. Reprinted by permission of Rosemary Thurber.

JOHN UPDIKE: "The Pro," from *Museums and Women and Other Stories* by John Updike. Copyright © 1966 by John Updike. Reprinted by permission of Alfred A. Knopf. "Hub Fans Bid Kid Adieu." Copyright © 1960 by John Updike. Reprinted from *Assorted Prose* by John Updike, by permission of Alfred A. Knopf, Inc. Originally appeared in *The New Yorker.*

ROBERT WALLACE: "A Snapshot for Miss Bricka Who Lost in the Semi-Final Round of the Pennsylvania Lawn Tennis Tournament at Haverford, July, 1960," copyright © 1961 by Robert Wallace. Reprinted by permission of the author.

ROBERT PENN WARREN: "Skiers," from *In the Mountains* by Robert Penn Warren. Copyright © 1968 by Robert Penn Warren. Reprinted by permission of the William Morris Agency, Inc., on behalf of the author's estate.

PAUL WEST: "Pelé," from *Portable People* by Paul West. Copyright © 1990 by Paul West. Reprinted by permission of Paris Review Editions.

P. G. WODEHOUSE: "The Heart of a Goof," from *Divots* by P. G. Wodehouse. Reprinted by permission of the author's estate and the agents for the Estate, Scott Meredith Literary Agency, Inc., 845 Third Avenue, New York, New York 10022.

THOMAS WOLFE: From *Of Time and the River* by Thomas Wolfe. Reprinted with permission of Charles Scribner's Sons, an imprint of Macmillan Publishing Company, from *Of Time and the River* by Thomas Wolfe. Copyright © 1935 Charles Scribner's Sons, renewed © 1963 by Paul Gitlin, Administrator C.T.A.

TOM WOLFE: "The Last American Hero," from *The Kandy-Kolored Tangerine-Flake Streamline Baby* by Tom Wolfe. Copyright © 1965 by Tom Wolfe. Reprinted by permission of Farrar, Straus and Giroux, Inc.

JAMES WRIGHT: "Autumn Begins in Martins Ferry, Ohio." Reprinted from *Above the River: The Complete Poems.* Copyright © 1990 by Anne Wright. Introduction © 1990 by Donald Hall. A Wesleyan University Press Edition. By permission of University Press of New England.

INDEX